Foundations of Learning and Memory

Foundations of Learning and Memory

Roger M. Tarpy
Bucknell University

Richard E. Mayer
University of California at Santa Barbara

Scott, Foresman and Company Glenview, Illinois
Dallas, TX   Oakland, NJ   Palo Alto, CA
Tucker, GA   London, England

Library of Congress Cataloging in Publication Data

Tarpy, Roger M.
    Foundations of learning and memory.

    Bibliography: p. 403
    Includes index.
    1. Learning, Psychology of. 2. Memory. I. Mayer,
Richard E., 1947—   , jt. author. II. Title.
BF318.T37   153.1   77 – 16296
ISBN 0 – 673 – 15074 – 7

Acknowledgments

(1-1; 1-2) Courtesy of Ralph Gerbrands Company, Inc.

(2-3) From Hammond, L. J. A traditional demonstration of the active properties of Pavlovian inhibition using differential CER. *Psychonomic Science*, 1967, *9*, 65–66. Reprinted by permission. **(2-4)** From Burdick, C. K., & James, J. P. Spontaneous recovery of conditioned suppression of licking by rats. *Journal of Comparative and Physiological Psychology*, 1970, *72*, 467–70. Copyright © 1970 by the American Psychological Association. Reprinted by permission. **(2-5)** From Riess, D., & Farrar, C. H. UCS duration and conditioned suppression: Acquisition and extinction between-groups and terminal performance within-subjects. *Learning and Motivation*, 1973, *4*, 366–73. Reprinted by permission of Academic Press, Inc., and the authors. **(2-6)** From Kamin, L. J. Temporal and intensity characteristics of the conditioned stimulus. In W. F. Prokasy (Ed.), *Classical conditioning: A symposium*. New York: Irvington Publishers, Inc., 1965. Reprinted by permission. **(2-7)** From Rescorla, R. A. Probability of shock in the presence and absence of CS in fear conditioning. *Journal of Comparative and Physiological Psychology*, 1968, *66*, 1–5. Copyright © 1968 by the American Psychological Association. Reprinted by permission. **(2-8)** From Holland, P. C., & Rescorla, R. A. Second-order conditioning with food unconditioned stimulus. *Journal of Comparative and Physiological Psychology*, 1975, *88*, 459–67. Copyright © 1975 by the American Psychological Association. Reprinted by permission. **(2-11)** From Lubow, R. E. Latent inhibition: Effects of frequency of nonreinforced preexposure of the CS. *Journal of Comparative and Physiological Psychology*, 1965, *60*, 454–57. Copyright © 1965 by the American Psychological Association. Reprinted by permission. **(2-12)** Reprinted with permission of author and publisher from: Lynch, J. J. Pavlovian inhibition of delay in cardiac and somatic responses in dogs: Schizokinesis. *Psychological Reports*, 1973, *32*, 1339–46. **(2-13)** From Jenkins, H. M., & Moore, B. A. The form of the auto-shaped response with food or water reinforcers. *Journal of the Experimental Analysis of Behavior*, 1973, *20*, 163–81. Copyright © 1973 by the Society for the Experimental Analysis of Behavior, Inc. Reprinted by permission of the author and the publisher.

(3-3) From Fox, S. S. Self-maintained sensory input and sensory deprivation in monkeys. *Journal of Comparative and Physiological Psychology*, 1962, *55*, 438–44. Copyright ʻ 1962 by the American Psychological Association. Reprinted by permission. **(3-4)** From Premack, D. Predictions of the comparative reinforcement values of running and drinking. *Science*, March, 1963, *139*, 1062–63. Copyright ʻ 1963 by the American Association for the Advancement of Science. Reprinted by permission of author and publisher. **(3-5)** From Carlson, J. G., & Wielkiewicz, R. M. Delay of reinforcement in instrumental discrimination learning in rats. *Journal of Comparative and Physiological Psychology*, 1972, *81*, 365–70. Copyright ʻ 1972 by the American Psychological Association. Reprinted by permission. **(3-6)** From Capaldi, E. D., & Hovancik, J. R. Effects of previous body weight level on rats' straight-alley performance. *Journal of Experimental Psychology*, 1973, *97*, 93–97. Copyright © 1973 by the American Psychological Association. Reprinted by permission. **(3-7)** From Marx, M. H., & Murphy, W. W. Resistance to extinction as a function of the presentation of a motivating cue in the start box. *Journal of Comparative and Physiological Psychology*, 1961, *54*, 207–10. Copyright ʻ 1961 by the American Psychological Association. Reprinted by permission. **(3-10)** From Flaherty, C. F., & Largen, J. Within-subjects positive and negative contrast effects in rats. *Journal of Comparative and Physiological Psychology*, 1975, *88*, 653–64. Copyright ʻ 1975 by the American Psychological Association. Reprinted by permission. **(3-11)** From Crider, A., Shapiro, D., & Tursky, P. Reinforcement of spontaneous electrodermal activity. *Journal of Comparative and Physiological Psychology*, 1966, *61*, 20–27. Copyright ʻ 1966 by the American Psychological Association. Reprinted by permission.

(continued on page 436)

Preface

This book has been written for anyone who is interested in the psychology of learning and memory. It introduces the basic findings and the major theories that have emerged in the almost one hundred years of scientific study of how animals and human beings learn. As we have assumed no special background knowledge on the part of the reader, the text is appropriate for undergraduate introductory courses in learning, learning and memory, and for experimental psychology courses that include human and animal learning.

We have organized the text with the beginning student of learning in mind. First, we open each chapter with a brief preview—a statement of the scope and purpose of the chapter. Second, we include at the beginning of each chapter a representative example, taken from the real world, that illustrates the major topic to be discussed. Third, we close each chapter with a summary of the major points just covered. This plan is designed to help students to appreciate the broad picture of the subject matter. Finally, we have been generous in our citations of original literature because we hope this book will serve as a resource for students who wish to continue their work in the field of learning and memory. The large number of citations should give a balanced and extensive focus for further study.

We believe that the study of learning and memory is in a state of transition. Many of the topics discussed in our book—such as biological factors in learning and cognitive and information processing approaches to learning—did not appear in the textbooks of a decade ago. We have also emphasized the traditional contexts of classical conditioning and verbal learning from which these new trends have emerged. The result, we believe, highlights the intellectual excitement and stimulation of a field of science that is still in the process of maturing and blending old concepts into new formulations.

It is important to keep in mind that the field of learning and memory is no longer dominated by the giant theoretical systems of the 1940s and 1950s. Research today is aimed at smaller segments of behavior; circumscribed theories are designed to account for rather specific phenomena. However, our knowledge of learning and memory is more than a compendium of unrelated facts, and wherever possible we have stressed the various themes that tie the diverse elements in the field together.

As we planned our book, we had to decide to what extent we should integrate human and animal learning research. For obvious reasons, human and animal research often developed along different lines and the studies and conclusions therefore must be treated somewhat independently. Nevertheless, there are hopeful signs of a growing commonality between the research fields, and we have been careful to point out the relationships.

We also chose to avoid building the text around a single theoretical framework such as behaviorism or cognitivism, because developments within the field have not been confined to strict dogma.

A third decision related to our use of real-world situations to illustrate current thinking in research. Certainly, research in learning and memory has never been more than a few steps removed from real-life applications, and wherever we could draw parallels between the lab and the real world, we did so to make it more meaningful for the student.

We hope that you enjoy reading this book as much as we enjoyed writing it. If you are pleased or fascinated by the issues in learning and memory research, if you appreciate the insightful and often subtle resolutions that have been achieved, or if your curiosity about future resolutions in theory is stimulated, then our efforts will have been more than repaid. In short, we hope that your experience will be similar to ours—in reviewing the latest trends in learning research, we discovered the wisdom and relevance of Ebbinghaus who wrote in 1885: "From the oldest subject we will make the newest science."

Acknowledgments
We wish to thank the many colleagues and students who have contributed, directly or indirectly, to the writing of this volume. Jim Romig and Isobel Hoffman at Scott, Foresman deserve most of the credit for helping to make the book cogent and readable. Kay Ocher, Ruth Robenault, Marlin Bailey, and Cris Clark helped in the typing and preparation of the manuscript. Without their generous assistance, the task would have been nearly impossible. We also want to thank the many authors and publishers who kindly granted us permission to use their materials. We hope that we have not distorted their contributions beyond recognition. Finally, we want to pay special tribute to our respective families for giving us the needed support and encouragement throughout the many months it took to write the text. Their contributions were probably the least tangible but the most valuable.

Roger M. Tarpy   Richard E. Mayer
Lewisburg, Pennsylvania   Santa Barbara, California

Table of Contents

13/Concept Learning   374

1/ Introduction

Preview

We begin our study of learning by defining it as **an inferred** change in the organism's mental state which results from **experience** and which influences in a relatively permanent fashion the organism's potential for subsequent adaptive behavior. Then we briefly discuss some of the basic methodologies that characterize learning research today—conditioning models (instrumental and classical conditioning), verbal learning techniques, and methods for studying information processing.

1

INTRODUCTION

It is clear that learning is a pervasive and important ability. In fact, there are few abilities that are considered to be as basic or critical to the survival of an organism. Without the capacity to learn, to modify behavior in response to changing environmental conditions or demands, behavior would lack flexibility and foresight; organisms would be unable to adapt rapidly to new situations and their ability to establish control over the environment would be minimal.

One point to note is that the term *learning* applies to a remarkably vast range of behaviors. For example, consider the work of Kandel (e.g., Kandel & Spencer, 1968). He isolated a single nerve cell in the sea hare, a nonshelled member of the mollusk family. Whenever that cell became active, Kandel provided "reward" by electrically stimulating the cell. After a time, the average level of activity for that particular nerve increased. In a sense, Kandel "taught" a single cell a response that it did not perform previously—that of firing at a higher-than-usual rate.

Another kind of learning research was done by Gardner and Gardner (1969) on language learning in chimpanzees. Washoe, a young female chimpanzee, was trained to communicate by using a sign language; she acquired at least a rudimentary vocabulary. In fact, in less than two years Washoe learned about thirty different signs, including "smell," "me," "clean," "toothbrush," "tickle," and so forth (she eventually learned well over one hundred signs). Washoe used these signs appropriately in novel situations and often combined several signs to make a more complex message. For example, she was observed to sign "listen eat" when she heard an alarm clock that signaled the evening meal and "open food drink" when referring to the refrigerator. According to the Gardners, Washoe definitely had learned to communicate.

Finally, consider the countless times each of us has demonstrated complex learning: memorizing poems or telephone numbers, learning and retaining the names and faces of hundreds of people, learning to play a musical instrument, mastering a foreign language, identifying a rare plant as a plant and not a fence post and yet recognizing the subtle differences between that plant and more familiar plants. The list of learning tasks for humans as well as lower animals could go on endlessly. Obviously, learning research must encompass a wide range of behaviors. Yet the psychologist's hope is that these diverse activities share a common base, that they all are related to each other in some fundamental way, or that they may be explained by a limited number of general principles. Two basic tasks of learning psychologists, therefore, are to describe the general conditions that produce learned behaviors, and to induce general principles that might explain all or most of these learned behaviors regardless of their dissimilarities.

Definition of Learning

While there have been many definitions of learning, we shall define it as follows: *Learning is an inferred change in the organism's mental state which results from experience and which influences in a relatively permanent fashion the organism's potential for subsequent adaptive behavior.* In other words, certain forces or conditions in the environment produce a fundamental change in the organism which, in turn, leads to a relatively long-lasting alteration in the organism's potential to respond adaptively. The psychologist, of course, is interested in describing the laws by which these forces or conditions operate as well as the physical and conceptual changes that take place in the organism, and generally, the alterations in behavior that reflect, over time, the learning process.

The definition of learning given above involves five important concepts. First, and most obvious, is that *learning is inferred from the behavior* of the organism. If a behavior is not overt or evident, or if verbal reports are not available, the fact that learning took place cannot be substantiated. For example, Washoe's acquisition of language could only be inferred from her performance—the signs that she made.

A second point is that *learning involves an inferred change in the mental state* of the organism, such as the creation of a new memory or a change in cognitive functioning. (Incidentally, many psychologists believe that the change in mental state is fundamentally a structural or biochemical one and there is impressive evidence for such a belief in the physiological literature.) Changes in performance that reflect learning must be initiated or guided or determined by underlying changes in cognitive functioning. For a number of years it was fashionable in learning research to ignore this point, that is, to assume that learning (except in humans) could be discussed without acknowledging an underlying mental state. However, the muscle fibers themselves, whose contractions constitute overt performance, do not learn; the contractions are initiated or determined by a more central, cognitive state.

A third concept contained in our definition of learning is that *learning stems from experience.* For example, one would not claim that a person had learned to throw a softball if the "new" response merely depended on the healing of an injury to the thrower's arm. Similarly, the deterioration in the quality or speed of a skilled movement as a result of fatigue or the acquisition of a new ability through maturational growth are not instances of learned behaviors.

A fourth point is that *learning is relatively permanent*; it involves a memory or cognitive state that persists through time. Changes in behavior as a function of fatigue are particularly good examples of transient changes that do not reflect learning. Depending on the experimental arrangements and the control conditions used to assess those arrangements, the persistence of learned behavior can vary from seconds to years.

A fifth consideration in our definition is that learning influences a *change in behavior potential.* If a person were to learn from a map the location of a friend's residence, a new mental or cognitive state would have been created even though the person didn't actually make the trip. The fact that learning had taken place, that the *potential* for new behavior had been created, of course, would have to be verified later when the person actually made the trip successfully. Therefore, while learning ultimately is inferred from (and verified by) performance, the potential for a change in mental state to affect behavior is independent of the actual performance.

In the laboratory, many studies have demonstrated quite clearly that learning may occur without performance. For example, in the latent learning studies (see Thistlethwaite, 1951), rats are allowed to explore a maze but they are not fed; later, when food is provided in the goal box, the animals instantly perform the correct response. In fact, the suddenness of the improvement in performance suggests that the subjects were learning all along but were simply not demonstrating it overtly. The potential to perform the response was present but it remained latent until food was provided at a later time.

Examples of Simple Learning Tasks

It would be very useful at this point to illustrate how the above definition of learning corresponds to simple experimental situations or, stated differently, how we use simple situations to study a complex process such as learning. Although there are a vast number of situations that we could mention, two of the simplest (that are prototypical of many other situations) are lever pressing in white rats and nonsense syllable learning in humans. Consider these situations and how the five aspects of the learning definition are reflected by them.

A white rat, when first placed in the lever box, will move around the cage, sniffing and exploring, apparently in an aimless fashion. A typical lever apparatus is shown in Figure 1-1. After a certain amount of time the rat will inevitably push the lever (perhaps the rat will attempt to explore the roof of the apparatus by standing on the lever). When this happens, a food pellet is automatically delivered to the feeding trough. Learning theorists claim that the food acts as a reward; that is, it strengthens the habit of pressing the lever (see Chapter 3). At the very least, the sequence of lever press-food presentation reoccurs at an increasingly frequent rate. Ultimately, the rat is usually observed to be pressing very rapidly, pausing only to eat the food pellet.

Another simple situation is the learning of a serial list of nonsense syllables. The stimuli are presented on a memory drum such as is shown in Figure 1-2. This apparatus contains a cylinder and a motor which rotates the cylinder at a fixed speed. As the figure shows, the paper loop on which the stimuli are printed advances as the motor turns the cylinder. The subject's task is to anticipate each item before it appears in the window. Usually, the number of errors (number of incorrect anticipations) decreases

FIGURE 1-1.

A typical apparatus for training a lever press response.

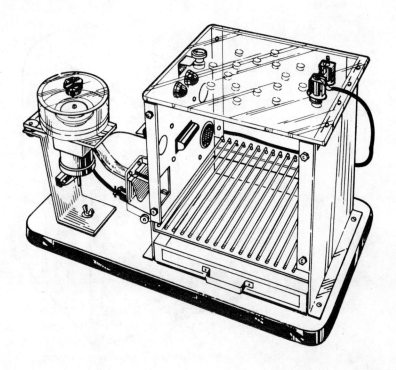

as a function of the number of exposures to the entire list of syllables. Although the rate of improvement varies according to many factors such as the length of the list, the meaningfulness of the stimuli, and so forth, mastery is eventually obtained.

In both the situations cited above, a simple response was learned— lever pressing by the white rat and the memorization of nonsense syllables by a human subject. We can make this statement, "learning occurred," because both situations comply with the stipulations of our definition of learning. First, the learning was not observed directly; it was inferred from the behavior of the subject. In the case of the rat, learning was inferred from the increasing frequency of lever pressing; in the other study, learning was inferred from the decreasing number of errors made over trials. Second, the change in behavior which reflects learning must have involved a change in mental state. The rat surely must have anticipated the presentation of food just as the human subject was able to anticipate the next item in the list of syllables. Third, learning in these two simple situations stemmed from experience. Lever pressing and memorization were not products of maturation, physical change, fatigue, or whatever; they occurred because specific environmental conditions were imposed,

FIGURE 1-2.

A memory drum used to present a list of stimuli, usually words or nonsense syllables, at a fixed rate.

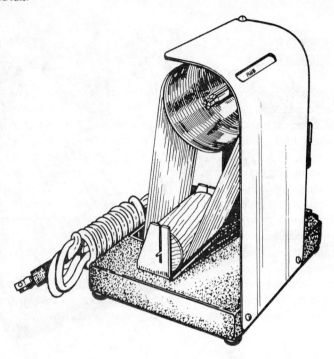

namely, the immediate presentation of food to the rat and the repeated presentation of the syllables to the human. Fourth, the change which we call learning was relatively permanent. Although we did not note this fact directly in the examples we discussed above, we could easily have done so. Specifically, one could return the rat to the lever apparatus on the next day or week and observe that the lever pressing response was retained over that time period. Similarly, the human would display retention of learning over some length of time. At the very least, learning was not transient; it did not dissipate quickly as it might with fatigue (where the behavior would be restored after a rest period). Finally, the simple situations used here to illustrate the definition of learning show, indirectly at least, the fifth facet of the definition: learning is a change in behavior potential. If we had asked our human subjects not to speak the answers, for example, that is, not to inform us of their anticipations but merely to memorize the syllables silently, they still would have learned. We would not have had evidence of this but we could have asked them to recite the list later and confirmed our suspicion that memorization had occurred. Thus, while learning is usually measured directly at the time of practice, it may take place whether or not direct confirmation is obtained at the time of learning. Obviously, confirmation of learning must ultimately be made from the performance but the learning per se may proceed independently of the performance. We shall return later in this chapter to other simple situations commonly used in the learning laboratory. First, however, we will review some of the historical antecedents to learning research.

HISTORICAL FOUNDATIONS OF LEARNING RESEARCH

Research in learning sprang from the behaviorist tradition. This tradition, as popularized by John Watson (1878–1958), was devoted to the study of overt behavior (as opposed to consciousness or mental experience which had preoccupied earlier psychologists—see Boring, 1957; Wertheimer, 1970). The behaviorist revolution changed the way psychological investigation was conducted. As a methodological contribution, behaviorism flourished; indeed, the vast majority of psychologists today are behaviorists in that they *study overt behavior in a systematic and objective way* (see Skinner, 1963). As a theory, however, behaviorism did not survive largely because the scheme was too inflexible; the insistence that all psychological processes could be explained in terms of muscle contractions and the like proved to be both restrictive and fallacious.

In this context of behaviorism, a number of specific historical conditions or developments converged to produce an interest in learning research. Three such foundations deserve special consideration.

Associationism

The Britist Empiricists, or Associationists, as they were also called, influenced modern psychology as much as any other school or doctrine. In fact, Boring (1957), a well-known historian of psychology, called the movement "the philosophical parent of experimental psychology." The empiricist tradition formalized and broadened the study of psychology by stimulating an interest in mental processes and by deriving certain concepts which proved to be the cornerstone of modern learning theory.

The basic doctrine dealt with how knowledge of the world was ac quired. Early empiricists like John Locke (1632–1704) challenged Descartes' notion of innate ideas: the content of the mind (ideas, elements of experience) was not inborn but was derived from experience. Locke clearly favored the most extreme form of this position, for he suggested that the mind, at birth, was like a tabula rasa (blank slate), devoid of any content whatsoever until experience acted on it. By experience, Locke meant primarily sensations but he also included reflection or thought. In sum, the fundamental claim of the associationists was that ideas or mental elements were created from experience. This notion was tantamount to suggesting that the units of mind, the ideas, were learned.

The associationists, particularly David Hartley (1705–1757), developed laws to account for this "learning" process, that is, for the cohesion between sensations and ideas. Each sensation elicited a corresponding idea; when several sensations reoccurred together, the later presence of any one sensation could excite the memory of all the ideas. For example, if sensations A, B, and C were presented together a sufficient number of times, each giving rise to ideas *a*, *b*, and *c* respectively, the subsequent presentation of only one sensation, say B, would elicit all of the associated ideas—*a*, *b*, and *c*.

Associations developed because of the relationship between sensations. Sensations that were *contiguous*, that is, occurred close together in time, were somehow bonded together while sensations that were more remote failed to become associated. Thus, contiguity, the most basic of the laws of association, represented a critical condition for the acquisition of mental experience.

These laws of association directly influenced the study of learning, and in fact, they came to occupy a central position in modern learning theory. One reason was the work of Hermann Ebbinghaus (1850–1909). As we shall see in Chapter 9, Ebbinghaus attempted to investigate the laws of association in his studies on memory. First, he invented the nonsense syllable; he believed that these verbal stimuli (e.g., BIJ, LUZ, etc.) were "pure" stimuli, devoid of any prior association. Ebbinghaus then memorized lists of these syllables in order to study many of the questions related to the laws of association. For example, would the sight of one syllable later during a memory test evoke the memory of the entire list? Would stimuli that occurred closely together in time be more firmly associated (remembered) than syllables that were not contiguous? Ebbinghaus was able to confirm experimentally many of the ideas discussed by Hartley: contiguity is the basic condition for associations; forward associations are stronger than backward ones (i.e., if A preceded B, A will later evoke the memory of B more easily than B will evoke the memory of A); repetition of stimuli strengthens the corresponding association. Thus, contiguity, or more generally, association theory, became an important explanatory concept in studies on learning and memory.

Associationism was tested less directly in another setting. Pavlov had discovered that dogs could learn to associate two stimuli, such as the sound of a metronome and food. After repeated and contiguous presentation of these stimuli, the click of the metronome itself could elicit the reflex of salivation as the dog anticipated food. Here again, a mental idea or element (or memory) must have been created (metronome—memory of food—salivation reflex); the principles that determined such an association were contiguity, repetition, and so forth.

The study of learning, then, began with the belief that knowledge, ideas, mental elements, and the like were derived from experience (the environment). Added to this position were the laws of association. These laws concerned the formation of knowledge; they were principles by which the inherent structure of the environment promoted the formation of mental associations. Finally, specific tests of the laws of association in the laboratories of Ebbinghaus and Pavlov gave rise to a methodology and confirmed the importance of these laws to the study of learning. In one sense, much of modern research on learning is a formalized study of associations in the general context of the laws of associations.

Darwinism

A second specific impetus to the study of learning was the work of Charles Darwin (1809–1882) on evolution. According to Darwin, survival depended upon adaptation; adaptive behavior, in turn, surely encompassed learning. In other words, rapid adaptation to the environment by means of learning represented an important mode of survival. Animals who were able to learn effectively about predators, food supplies, and the like were better able to survive and have offspring. Just as biologists were discovering the principles of genetics as mechanisms of adaptation, psychologists were interested in describing the principles of learning that gave rise to adaptive habits. The study of learning, therefore, provided a way of understanding a central issue in evolutionary theory, namely, adaptation.

Darwin's theory was important to the study of learning for a second reason: the fact that humans evolved from lower forms of life implied an underlying continuity between species. Just as the principles of genetics that were discovered by studying lower animals could be applied to human beings, it was believed that the laws of learning that were discovered using lower animals as subjects might also be applicable to all organisms, including humans. In short, because of a common evolutionary history, principles of animal learning might be similar to principles of human learning. At the very least, Darwin's theory suggested that humans are not totally unrelated to other animals and that the explanation of adaptive behavior (or learning) in humans might be facilitated by the study of lower organisms.

Gestalt Psychology

Gestalt psychology was another, more modern tradition that influenced learning research, particularly in the area of human perception and cognition. The Gestalt movement began in Germany under the direction of Wertheimer, Koffka, and Kohler, all of whom later emigrated to the United States.

Wertheimer's original observations, termed the *phi phenomenon*, involved the perception of movement: when two lights were turned on and off in an alternating fashion, subjects reported that they saw a single point of light "move" across the surface from one location to the other and back again. The perception of movement, of course, posed a paradox since the lights, in fact, did not move, that is, the retina was being stimulated by light sources at two locations. The phi phenomenon is a common one: examples are the motion perceived in moving pictures, or the motion in neon signs that adorn theater marquees and restaurants.

To Wertheimer, the phi phenomenon was more than a simple perceptual illusion. It suggested the need for an entirely new set of principles or laws of human experience. The apparent movement was a "real" experience, yet it could not be explained in terms of physical principles. In other words, the physical aspects of the situation, the two alternating light sources that impinged on the retina, could not account for the psychological reality of the situation—the fact that movement was perceived.

Gestalt psychology differed from other approaches to psychology by insisting that psychological experience could not be explained in terms of the summation of individual, discrete units of experience; that is, the totality of experience could not be synthesized from smaller, elemental parts. The *Gestaltqualitat* (translated as "wholeness") of a given situation was greater than the sum of the components in that situation. For example, a melody was more than a collection of musical notes, a painting evoked perceptions that involved more than just points of color, and alternating lights gave rise to a sense of movement or perception that could not be explained in terms of retinal image.

The early proponents of Gestalt psychology, who were concerned primarily with perceptual experience, developed a number of laws to account for the *Gestaltqualitat*. At the center of their theory was the notion that cognitive forces shaped perceptions; that is, the wholeness of perception was determined not by sensory elements in the situation but rather by cognitive forces in the brain. This emphasis on cognition later became important in learning research as well. It was argued, for example, that learning and memory, like perception, also were influenced by cognition. The processing of information during learning, and the later memories, were not merely atomistic associations (as suggested in Ebbinghaus' work); rather, memories were dynamic and changing as a result of the cognitive forces that shaped them.

The influence of Gestalt psychology in learning research was highly visible in Bartlett's (1932) important book on memory. As discussed in Chapter 11, his experiments involved asking subjects to recall a passage that had been read to them once. The particular story, an Eskimo folktale called "The War of the Ghosts," contained a number of references or concepts that were unfamiliar to the subjects. Bartlett found that his subjects remembered only parts of the original story. More important, the recalls were usually distorted; information contained in the original version was modified in such a way that the elements of the story were more compatible with the subjects' own cultural experiences. In other words, the subjects, in failing to remember many of the exact details of the story, substituted new (but related) information from their own past experiences.

Bartlett concluded that memory was a reconstruction of past learning according to the existing attitudes and cognitions of the subject. Specifically: "Remembering is not the re-excitation of innumerable fixed, lifeless and fragmentary traces. It is an imaginative reconstruction, or construction, built out of the relation of our attitude towards a whole active mass of organized past reactions or experience" (p. 213). Without doubt, Bartlett's work defined a new direction for the psychology of learning that was totally unlike the one established by the British Empiricists.

Bartlett's cognitive approach to memory research received only a modicum of attention for several decades. Rather, the empiricist doctrines (the Ebbinghaus tradition) were more prevalent in both the animal and human learning literature. However, recent learning research, particularly in the area of human information processing and memory, has begun to rely heavily on the earlier cognitive (Gestalt) concepts and theories.

BASIC EXPERIMENTAL STRATEGIES IN LEARNING RESEARCH

Due to the efforts of the empiricists and to Darwin and Watson, among others, American learning psychologists fell heir to some theoretical terms and a sketchy methodology.

The break with the classical European tradition was more than a strategic one. For example, an interest in learning (in adaptive behavior) was consistent with our society's emphasis on education. The vast numbers of people who were immigrating to the United States at the turn of the century were convinced that opportunities for personal and material growth were available to those who could learn and develop new skills. This sense of individualism, this optimistic belief in the value of education, contrasted sharply with the historical patterns in European societies where opportunities for formal education too often were limited to a privileged few and social and economic levels were relatively fixed at birth. In America, however, education was the vehicle for social and economic mobility. The study of learning, therefore, was not only tolerated but encouraged.

Accordingly, the goal of learning research became the discovery of general laws—universal and basic principles that describe and explain the essence of the learning process. Presumably, learning to speak a foreign language or drive a car, memorizing school lessons or acquiring typewriting skills are all determined by the same basic laws. It was believed that the discovery of these basic principles could be realized only if the psychologists studied behaviors that were simple and arbitrary. Laws that described the learning of unique, idiosyncratic behaviors were limited in value because those laws would be idiosyncratic as well; they would not generalize to all instances of learning. However, the laws that govern the learning of simple, arbitrary responses would be more universal precisely because the responses are arbitrary. Therefore, the task for the psychologist became the study of simple and arbitrary responses; the emerging principles of learning would apply to all forms of complex behaviors and to all species capable of learning.

The practical consequences of this view was a stylized methodology: a preoccupation with maze learning or lever pressing in white rats, nonsense syllable memorization by college students, or salivation reflexes in dogs. In each case, the behaviors were simple ones believed to be prototypical of more complex instances of learning. We must emphasize that psychologists have no interest in the behaviors themselves; that rats learn to press levers to receive a pellet of food is trivial and incidental to the real purpose of the investigator, namely, the formulation of general principles that govern the learning process.

The study of lower animals, of course, is consistent with the view that their simple and arbitrary behaviors are influenced by the same basic laws of learning that apply to humans. However, some animals, such as white rats, are useful in learning research for other reasons. For one thing, they are easy and inexpensive to maintain. More important, the investigator can better control the conditions of the experiment, such as past learning history of the subjects, their genetic makeup, the degree of their motivation (such as hunger or thirst), the particulars of the experimental apparatus, and the social interactions between subjects.

In summary, many psychologists believed that complex learning processes should not be studied directly—the simpler elements of complex behavior should be identified and studied first. If these simpler constituents or responses were arbitrary, the basic principles that determine their formation would be general ones capable of explaining more complex instances of learning. Thus, the strategy was first, to reduce the learning process into components, second, to study the laws governing those components, and finally, to apply the laws to all learning situations using the components as basic building blocks.

The remainder of this chapter is devoted to a very brief discussion of three basic approaches to learning research. Most studies in learning fall into one of these categories. In all cases, the research is directed toward investigating simplified and well-controlled situations. It is the psychologists' hope that the ensuing principles of learning will generalize to more complex situations.

Conditioning Models

Most learning research using nonhuman subjects is designed within the context of the two basic conditioning models: instrumental and Pavlovian (or classical) conditioning. Instrumental conditioning, a simple learning paradigm associated with Thorndike (1898), reflects a very common example of learning (our earlier example of a rat learning to press a lever exemplified this type of learning, but see Chapter 3 for a more complete discussion). Anyone who has taught a pet to "sit" before receiving food, to "shake hands" to obtain a biscuit, or to perform other tricks for a reward has employed the concepts of instrumental conditioning. Generally, instrumental training involves the learning of some simple motor response in order to receive a reward. Thus, the essential structure of this type of experiment involves the appropriate apparatus (e.g., maze, lever box) for recording the desired motor response (e.g., running, lever pressing) and the provision for presenting a reward once the response is executed.

The nature of the reward is extremely important. Usually it is in the form of water or small pellets of food, if thirsty or hungry animals are used as subjects, or tokens, candy, and even approving verbal reactions if humans are used as subjects. However, reward in instrumental conditioning may also involve the cessation of an unpleasant or aversive stimulus. For example, a subject may learn to execute a simple response (e.g., lever press) in order to turn off a mildly painful electric shock.

The second major conditioning paradigm, developed primarily by Pavlov (1927), is termed classical or Pavlovian conditioning (see Chapter 2 for a more complete discussion). This technique draws most directly from the work of the empiricists in that associations between stimuli are evaluated with respect to, say, their temporal contiguity. The operational distinction between instrumental and Pavlovian conditioning is extremely important. In the former case, the subject must respond *before* the reward is presented, but in the latter case, the presentation of stimuli proceeds independently of the subject's behavior.

As most people know, Pavlov studied the salivation reflex in dogs. He did this by surgically isolating their salivary ducts and measuring the drops of saliva that collected in a tube following presentations of metronome clicks and food. He found that after repeated presentations of the metronome and food, the dogs would salivate to the sound of the metronome alone. Although very few contemporary psychologists study the conditioned salivary reflex (primarily because of the time, expense, and space required to maintain the dogs), Pavlov's basic experiment is the methodological prototype for all modern experiments in classical conditioning.

What does the measurement of lever pressing or drops of saliva tell us? Much of this text will attempt to answer just this question. Briefly, it is the various learning processes we are interested in, not just the simple responses themselves. For example, the period during which the subject acquires a new behavior—learns the lever press, say, or the salivation response—is called *acquisition*. Another concept is *extinction* (see Chapter 5). Here, after the subject has learned a given response, the experimenter stops presenting the reward; the result is a gradual elimination of the learned behavior. In addition to these basic processes, we are also interested in studying more complex processes such as *generalization* and *discrimination* (see Chapter 6). Generalization occurs when a subject responds to a new stimulus as it did to the training cue because it was similar to the training cue used in acquisition. Discrimination is the process whereby the subject detects the difference between stimuli.

Verbal Comprehension Paradigms

The instrumental and classical conditioning models are applicable to the study of both human and animal learning. However, since language is so integral to human behavior, a second important and basic topic in learning research is verbal learning (see Chapter 9).

Three general techniques for studying verbal learning, memory, and/or comprehension have been popular. The first procedure, originally used by Ebbinghaus (1913), is *serial learning* (our earlier example involved serial learning). Here, verbal stimuli, such as nonsense syllables, are presented sequentially in time on a memory drum (see Figure 1-2).

With the anticipation technique, each item appears for a fixed duration of time followed by a brief pause. The subject's task is to view the item, rehearse, and anticipate the next response. A variation of this procedure is the free recall technique in which the list is presented with no pause between items and the subject is asked to recite the items at the end of the list. There is some evidence (e.g., Battig & Lawrence, 1967) that the recall method leads to faster memorization; that is, using the free recall technique, fewer presentations of the entire list are required on the average before the subject is able to recite all the correct items in their proper order. Of course, simply asking subjects not to anticipate each item out loud before it appears does not preclude the possibility that they are, in fact, using anticipation to facilitate memorization.

Serial learning tasks have been used widely to study verbal learning and memory. However, many theorists currently believe that the technique has limited generality and that a more useful approach is the *paired-associate task*. In paired-associate learning, a list of paired verbal items (e.g., nonsense syllables) is used. The first item (or stimulus) is given alone and the subject is asked to respond to it by giving the second item (response). The second item is then shown and the subject's anticipation of it is thus confirmed or corrected. The paired-associate task focuses on the association between two stimuli and therefore it is analogous to the classical conditioning model.

As with serial learning, the paired-associate experiment can be conducted in several ways. With the anticipation technique, the subjects are presented the stimulus item for several seconds during which they are asked to anticipate the correct response item. Failure to do so is recorded as an error. The response item is then presented along with its stimulus and the subjects can rehearse the association. Learning is measured either by the number of trials (the number of presentations of the entire list of paired-associates) required before the subject is able to anticipate each response correctly, by the decrease in errors per trial, or by the speed of anticipation (e.g., Peterson, 1965).

The second basic technique in paired-associate learning is the test trial method. Here, the subjects are not asked to anticipate each response but are presented with the paired items, given several seconds in which to memorize the association, and then, after all the items on the list have appeared, are tested. The memory test consists of presenting each stimulus and asking the subjects to provide the correct response. The basic feature of this method is that the subjects receive the entire list of paired-associate items (i.e., a complete trial) before giving their responses. As with the anticipation technique, learning may be assessed in terms of either the number of trials required for a perfect recitation or the decreasing rate of errors per trial.

The third important method for studying verbal memory (or comprehension) is the *free recall* technique. Verbal material is presented which may involve single or paired items, or longer prose passages like those used by Bartlett (1932). After one or more exposures to the material, the subjects' memory of it is tested in one of two ways. The subjects may be asked to recall the items or, alternatively, the correct response may be embedded in a matrix of choices and the subjects' task is to identify which of the items is correct.

Research on the differences between recognition and recall is extensive. Traditionally, it has been found that memory for certain items as measured by a recognition task is superior to memory for those same items as measured with a recall task. Such findings have led some investigators (e.g., Tulving & Thomson, 1973) to claim that the recognition method is simply a more sensitive measure of memory than the recall task. Others, however, believe that the two methods are based on different memory processes (Martin, 1975). Regardless, each method is widely used; the differences in performance as a function of which method is employed provides for a complex yet more complete analysis of memory.

There are other ways to measure memory. For example, if the subject remembers the response or associations reasonably accurately after some period of time (i.e., after the retention interval), few relearning trials would be required before a high level of performance was reestablished. In contrast, if substantial forgetting had occurred, significantly more relearning would be needed. Memory, therefore, may be quantified in terms of the degree of relearning necessary. This measure is termed "savings"; it is defined as (O-R)/O where O refers to the number of trials during original learning and R refers to the number of trials required to relearn the behavior to the same criterion of proficiency. In short, savings reflects memory by measuring the extent to which relearning is facilitated by the prior learning.

Information Processing Paradigms

Finally, a third general paradigm in learning research involves models of information processing. The verbal learning tradition established by Ebbinghaus has undergone dramatic changes in recent years (see Chapter 10). Specifically, the recognition that cognitive factors similar to those first described by Bartlett play an important role in memory has provoked many psychologists to abandon the simpler strategies in verbal learning (such as serial and paired-associate designs) in favor of more complex techniques. As Bartlett claimed, associations or memories are not "fixed, lifeless and fragmentary traces." Rather, information received by a subject is acted on, or processed, by the brain. These information processing components, then, are important to an understanding of memory.

Information processing designs vary widely. Many involve the use of reaction time to assess stages of memory such as the perception, storage, and retrieval of the material. For example, a subject might be instructed to press one button as quickly as possible to answer Yes and another button as quickly as possible to answer No. Then, the subject is asked two questions: "Is a canary a bird?" and "Is a canary an animal?" In experiments such as these, differences in reaction time are often observed. The subject usually presses the Yes button much faster to the former question than to the latter one. Results of this sort, therefore, may indicate a number of things about how the brain processes information, that is, how information is perceived and stored as memories. The information processing approach to the study of memory focuses on many other techniques and issues. For instance, prose material may be read to the subject. Then, by analyzing how that material is later recalled, important insights may be obtained as to how the information was encoded and stored by the brain—that is, the organization of memory.

SUMMARY

This chapter has provided a brief historical background to the study of learning as well as an introduction to several topics we shall cover more thoroughly in this text. First, we defined learning as an inferred change in the mental state of an organism which results from experience and which influences in a relatively permanent fashion the organism's potential for subsequent adaptive behavior. One important aspect of this definition is the learning-performance distinction: learning may occur, that is, the mental state of the organism may change, even though the performance index does not show it.

Then we discussed the historical foundations of learning research. Three movements were noted as being particularly important: empiricism or associationism, the study of mental associations; Darwinism, emphasizing adaptive behaviors which, of course, may be acquired through learning; and Gestalt psychology.

Finally, we discussed three broad experimental strategies in learning research. The conditioning models are used to study associative (classical conditioning) and motor or skill (instrumental conditioning) learning in humans and lower species. The verbal learning paradigms included serial learning and paired-associate techniques. The more modern direction in the study of human learning and memory is the information processing approach.

2/ Classical Conditioning

Preview

In this chapter, we consider one of the basic conditioning paradigms—classical conditioning. Some learning theorists believe that the classically conditioned reflex reflects a distinct and fundamental learning process that is the essential building block of more complex forms of learning. Regardless, the learning of associations, as first demonstrated by Pavlov, is an important focal point for modern learning theory. We shall also consider how certain environmental factors influence the acquisition of Pavlovian associations and various phenomena that occur within the Pavlovian conditioning framework. Finally, we shall review how this type of learning explains certain human conditions. For example, many irrational fears could be described as resulting from an object's being associated with a trauma. Similarly, psychosomatic illnesses could originate from classical conditioning.

INTRODUCTION

Classical conditioning is one conditioning paradigm or model; that is to say, it is a procedure that stipulates the essential conditions for the acquisition of associations. Consider this simple example: you watch someone cut a lemon in half; the very sight of the lemon makes you salivate (even the mention of it here may evoke this response). Other spherical yellow objects don't produce this reaction—just lemons. The basic idea is that the sight of the lemon can elicit salivation because you have associated it with a sour taste. The remainder of this chapter will attempt to explain how this type of learning takes place.

Definition of Classical Conditioning

A great deal of learning research has used Pavlovian conditioning procedures to investigate the learned association between stimuli. Classical conditioning may be defined operationally as any situation in which a subject is presented with two stimuli relatively closely in time. While the exact temporal relationship is extremely important, it may vary greatly. In this kind of conditioning, the subject's behavior is recorded but it has no effect on the presentation of the two stimuli. That is, the experimenter presents the stimuli independently of the subject's response. In this regard, the subject is a passive recipient whose behavior, in theory at least, does not alter the course of the experiment.

PAVLOV'S EXPERIMENT

Basic Procedure

Classical conditioning may be illustrated by a description of Pavlov's original work (Pavlov, 1927). Near the turn of this century, Pavlov was engaged in studying the digestive processes, with dogs as his experimental subjects. Much to his dismay, he discovered that the animals would begin to salivate as soon as he walked into the laboratory, that is, before he could even begin the experiment he had scheduled for that day. Apparently, the sight of a person in a lab smock was enough to cause salivation, a response Pavlov believed could be caused only by food. Fortunately, Pavlov was perceptive enough to recognize the importance of this fortuitous finding and in the years that followed, he devoted himself to the study of these "psychic secretions."

In a typical experiment, Pavlov first surgically implanted glass fistulas into the salivary ducts of several dogs to measure their salivation. Then, during conditioning, the animals were restrained in a harness and presented with two stimuli: the sound of a metronome and, several seconds later, a ration of meat. Initially, the metronome tick was "irrelevant" to the dog and there was no salivation response when it occurred. However, copious salivation occurred within a few seconds of the presentation of food. After several pairings of the metronome and food, Pavlov showed that the sound of the metronome itself was sufficient to provoke salivation. Quite clearly, something had been learned: the dogs had learned to anticipate food at the sound of the metronome. The two stimuli had become associated to the extent that the irrelevant stimulus, the metronome, acquired the ability to elicit a physical response, salivation, by virtue of being paired with food.

Terms

Pavlov's experiment involved four basic concepts which are crucial to all contemporary studies using classical conditioning procedures. The *unconditioned stimulus* (US) is any strong, biologically important event that elicits a predictable and reflexive reaction. In Pavlov's experiment, the US was the food but other studies have used a variety of stimuli including electric shock, puffs of air to the cornea, or weak acid placed on the tongue. The *unconditioned response* (UR) is that regular and measurable reaction given in response to the US. In Pavlov's experiment, the UR was salivation but many other unconditioned reflexes may be studied, such as the galvanic skin response* (GSR) or heart rate changes, and motor responses such as limb flex or eyeblink reactions. Often more than one UR is elicited by a US; for example, a mild shock (US) delivered to a dog's paw will elicit a reflexive withdrawal response (UR) as well as changes in respiration, heart rate, GSR, and so on. The important point is that the UR is an unlearned reflex reliably given by the subject whenever the US is presented.

The *conditioned stimulus* (CS) is an originally neutral cue that acquires the ability to elicit the reflex after being repeatedly paired (associated) with the US. In the studies we have referred to here, Pavlov used a metronome but many different stimuli may be employed, provided that the subject *perceives the event*. Although the CS is weak relative to the US—it does not produce a massive and reliable UR—it does elicit a response. The organism, in the process of perceiving the stimulus, inevitably makes an investigatory or orienting reaction (OR) such as a head turn, an eyelid closure, or a postural adjustment. This "what-is-it" reflex, as Pavlov termed it, is extinguished relatively quickly if the US is not presented soon afterward.

Finally, the *conditioned response* (CR) is the learned behavior, the reflex given in response to the CS alone. Although the CR is *nearly* identical to the UR, important differences have been noted. For example, while the UR to food may involve salivation and chewing, the CR may only be salivation (Zener, 1937). Similarly, a shock to the dog's paw may elicit both

---

*The galvanic skin response is a change in the electrical conductivity of the skin, detected by a galvanometer.

withdrawal and vocalization while the conditioned form of the reflex may involve only the withdrawal component. Thus, the CR closely resembles the UR but often it is weaker, its onset is slower than the UR, or it contains only fractional components of the complete UR (e.g., Wickens et al., 1969).

CR Measurement

The CR is a reflex that is elicited by the CS. Demonstration of the CR during the acquisition phase may be accomplished in two general ways. First, the CR may be shown to precede the US presentation. Here, the CS duration often is lengthened on those test trials to facilitate such a demonstration. This anticipation technique, however, has certain drawbacks. For example, different responses may vary in their "sluggishness," that is in how quickly they are elicited by the CS. The CS and US may become associated yet the evidence for this may be lacking because the CR is slow to appear following the CS presentation. Therefore, an increase in the CS duration, for the purpose of demonstrating that the CS itself will elicit the CR in anticipation of the US, may alter the optimum conditions for producing an association.

A second method is the test-trial technique. Here, the specified CS-US temporal relationship is maintained throughout the experiment except for test trials which involve the presentation of the CS only. These test trials are interspersed during the course of training. This method too presents problems of interpretation. For example, each test trial is really an extinction trial because no US is presented. Therefore, the CR is presumably weakened on those trials, thus giving a spurious indication of the strength of association.

The methods described above are direct measures of the CR. The dog's saliva was actually collected in a tube, and leg flex, heart rate or skin resistance changes, and eyelid blinks all are assessed directly. There is, however, another technique for measuring the strength of a Pavlovian CS. This is an indirect method involving a *conditioned emotional response* (CER). The CER technique may vary somewhat but the basic procedure involves the same several stages. First, the subject is trained to press a lever to obtain food. Then Pavlovian pairings are given; usually, a light or tone (CS) is followed by a shock pulse (US), independent of the animal's behavior. As the CS gains strength, it disrupts the lever pressing. In other words, the reduction (suppression) of the lever pressing rate by a CS is the index of CS strength. The greater the emotional reaction to the CS (due to the fact that it is followed by shock), the greater the disruption of lever pressing. Thus, Pavlovian conditioning may be assessed indirectly by measuring the degree to which the CS affects some ongoing behavior.

Disruption of lever pressing in CER experiments (i.e., the measure of the strength of the Pavlovian CS) is usually measured by the suppression ratio B/A + B, where B is the number of responses during the CS period and A is the number during a comparable period of time just before the CS is presented. A ratio of .5 indicates no change in the rate of lever pressing (no disruptive effect of the CS) while lower ratios indicate that emotional conditioning has occurred.

Principles

The most important feature of Pavlovian conditioning, its defining characteristic, is the *contiguity* or closeness in time of the two stimuli. Stimuli become associated or linked in part because they occur contiguously in time (but see subsequent sections of this chapter for modifications of this position).

Pavlov's experiment, or more precisely, the general principle of contiguity, is illustrated in Figure 2-1. The CS and US are presented closely in time and each stimulus elicits an appropriate reaction (OR and UR, respectively). After a sufficient number of pairings, the CR is given to the CS itself, that is, acquisition of the acquired reflex is demonstrated. Finally, if the experiment is extended to include extinction by repeated presentation of the CS without the US, the CR is gradually suppressed until the subject no longer makes the response.

FIGURE 2-1.

Phases in Pavlovian conditioning; CS-US pairings, demonstration of an acquired CR, suppression of the CR during extinction.

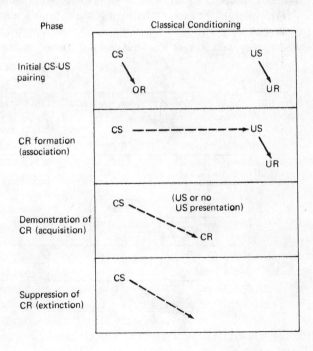

PROCEDURES AND CONTROL CONDITIONS

The principle of contiguity implies very little about the specific arrangement of stimuli in a Pavlovian experiment. In fact, the exact sequence of stimuli over time can vary. Several of the more common procedures are illustrated in Figure 2-2. Each represents a different form of contiguity.

In a *delayed conditioning* situation, the CS is presented prior to the US and it remains on (the CS offset is delayed) at least until the US occurs. In actual experiments, the CS offset may terminate with US onset or the CS may continue to some later time. The second main procedure, *trace conditioning*, is similar except for the fact that the CS offset occurs before the US onset. By virtue of this arrangement, an "empty" interval occurs between the two stimuli over which the CS trace (the decaying neural activity) must span. In other words, in trace conditioning, the CS does not impinge directly upon the sense receptors at the time the US is presented; rather the trace of the CS—the memory of or the neurological "reverberation" established by the CS—persists in time and is present at the US onset.

Numerous studies have compared these two procedures but the evidence as to which produces superior conditioning conflicts. Ross and Ross (1971) and Wilson (1969), among others, found that trace and delayed designs were equally effective in producing conditioned eyeblink and heart rate changes. In contrast, other studies (e.g., Black et al., 1962; Schneiderman, 1966; Manning et al., 1969) have shown that the delayed procedure often leads to stronger CRs as compared with trace conditioning. The discrepancy in these findings may stem from differences in the CS-US interval. For example, in the study by Manning et al. (1969), no difference between procedures was observed when short CS-US intervals were used; with longer intervals, where the empty period was relatively

FIGURE 2-2.
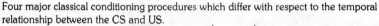

Four major classical conditioning procedures which differ with respect to the temporal relationship between the CS and US.

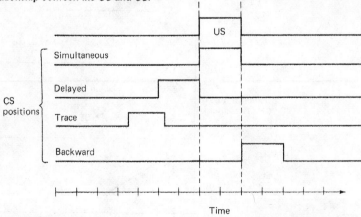

extended, the trace design was significantly inferior to delayed conditioning.

Both trace and delayed arrangements represent forward conditioning procedures; in each case, the CS onset precedes the US onset. Pavlov recognized that such a procedure was essential for conditioning to occur: "Further, it is not enough that there should be overlapping between the two stimuli; it is also and equally necessary that the conditioned stimulus should begin to operate before the unconditioned stimulus comes into action" (Pavlov, 1927, p.27).

The remaining two procedures cited in Figure 2-2 clearly do not provide for this feature. Therefore, each of these may be used as a control condition for assessing Pavlovian learning. That is, the level of "true" conditioning resulting from a forward presentation, such as in the trace or delayed procedures, may be compared to the CR level obtained with these control procedures. The latter provides a baseline to which performance under trace or delayed conditioning may be compared.

Some investigators (e.g., Beecroft, 1966) have claimed that a simultaneous presentation of the CS and US provides the best control condition since, for many responses, little, if any, conditioning occurs.

According to the quotation from Pavlov given above, the backward design (Figure 2-2) also should produce no conditioning. Most investigators believe this to be the case (e.g., Gormezano & Moore, 1969; Plotkin & Oakley, 1975) although some have obtained evidence that conditioned responding, albeit weak, may occur with this backward procedure. Spooner and Kellogg (1947), for example, studied conditioned flex or withdrawal in human subjects by delivering a mild shock US to the finger. They found that the subjects who received backward pairings—that is, the shock came *before* the buzzer—did respond to the CS, but the level of conditioning was very marginal compared to those who experienced the usual forward training procedures. Thus it appears that some backward conditioning is possible (hence it is a poor baseline control procedure), but it is certainly not an effective arrangement relative to the trace or delayed designs (see further discussion on controls in a subsequent section).

TYPES OF CLASSICAL CONDITIONING

Excitatory Conditioning

There are two general classifications or types of Pavlovian conditioning. All the studies discussed above, including those by Pavlov, are examples of *excitatory conditioning*. In this situation, the CS acquires the same ability that characterizes the US to excite or elicit the reflex; the learned response is an overt behavior that the subject actively performs when given the CS.

Inhibitory Conditioning

There is another general type of Pavlovian learning which is termed *inhibitory conditioning*. The associative learning that stems from this type of conditioning is less obvious than with excitatory conditioning because the CR is assessed indirectly. Yet inhibitory conditioning is critical to current theories of Pavlovian conditioning and it represents a major paradigm for associative learning (see Rescorla, 1969, for a review).

Inhibitory conditioning procedures differ from excitatory procedures in one important respect: the CS is explicitly paired with no US. That is, a CS such as a buzzer is deliberately *not* followed by shock. Under these circumstances, the CS comes to inhibit the CR rather than to excite or elicit it. An inhibitory CS (noted as CS− in contrast to CS+ which is an excitatory cue) does not simply remain neutral during conditioning nor is it a distractor. Rather, a CS− acquires associative strength by signaling the nonoccurrence of the US; this associative strength is a response tendency opposite to that of conditioned excitation and is measurable in terms of the cue's ability to suppress or inhibit an excitatory CR.

Conditioned inhibition has been demonstrated in several ways. One technique is termed the summation test. The basic procedure of this test involves presenting an excitatory CS+ and an inhibitory CS− together followed by no US; if the CS− is indeed a conditioned inhibitor, then the excitatory CR, elicited by the CS+, will be weaker because of the CS−. In other words, the joint presentation of the CS+ and CS− involves the summation of both an excitatory and an inhibitory state; the net effect, in terms of CR strength, is lower than if the CS+ were presented alone. You may think of it in the same way as the summation of positive and negative numbers in mathematics.

A number of studies have used this general approach, including some early experiments reported by Pavlov (1927). A demonstration by Hammond (1967) used the conditioned emotional response (CER) technique. As discussed previously, the CER method is an indirect assessment of the strength of Pavlovian CSs. First the subject learns to press a lever for food; then, while the animal continues to lever press, the Pavlovian stimuli are presented independent of the subject's behavior; finally, the degree of disruption of lever pressing which occurs to the CS alone serves as an indirect measure of conditioning strength.

In Hammond's study, rats first received ten days of training in the acquisition of lever pressing. Subjects in Group I (inhibitory) were given a tone CS+ that was followed by a shock US, and a light CS− that was explicitly not paired with shock. In contrast, subjects in Group R (random) received the tone CS+ and shock pairings but, for them, the light CS− was presented randomly with respect to the shock. In other words, both groups received excitatory conditioning to the CS+ as well as CS− presentations. However, for Group I, the light CS− was explicitly *not* paired with shock (inhibitory training) whereas the subjects in Group R received the CS− at random intervals (sometimes close in time to the US, sometimes not). The results of this acquisition phase are shown on the left of Figure 2-3. It is clear that the tone CS+ was excitatory—it produced a marked disruption of lever pressing. The CS−, in contrast, did not influence responding very substantially.

Following this acquisition phase, a summation test was used to demonstrate the conditioned inhibitory strength of the light CS−. Both groups were treated in the same fashion during these five sessions: specifically, the CS+ and CS− were presented together and the net effect was observed.

The results of the summation test are shown in the right panel of Figure 2-3. The combination of CS+ and CS− produced less suppression in Group I than in Group R. Clearly, the excitatory effect (suppression) of the CS+ was reduced by the inhibitory CS− in Group I but much less so in Group R. (The fact that the CS− was somewhat inhibitory in Group R was probably because the CS− had been paired with shock during acquisition on some occasions.) In summary, the difference between groups on the summation test indicated clearly that inhibitory tendencies were conditioned to the CS− in Group I because they were given *explicit* unpairings of the CS− and US.

Another technique for demonstrating conditioned inhibition was shown in a study by Marchant and Moore (1974). The method used by those authors involved measuring the inhibitory strength of the CS− in terms of whether later excitatory conditioning to the CS was retarded. In other words, if a cue had become a conditioned inhibitor, then more excitatory training should be needed later to change it into a conditioned excitor than it should to make a neutral cue into a conditioned excitor.

One group of rabbits was given 50 excitatory trials (light CS+ fol-

FIGURE 2-3.

Mean suppression ratio for the Inhibitory (I) and Random (R) Groups during acquisition and on the summation test.

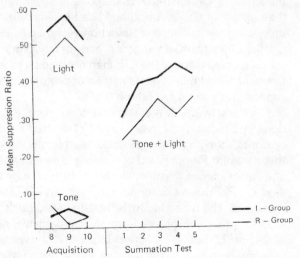

lowed by a brief shock US) intermixed with 50 inhibitory trials (light CS+ plus tone CS−). (Note that the CS+ was also presented on these inhibitory trials. The critical feature, however, was the absence of the US. Therefore, during acquisition the subjects did not respond to the CS+CS− compound because whenever the CS− occurred, regardless of the fact that the CS+ also occurred, shock was never presented.) The control group in this study was simply restrained in the apparatus during this initial acquisition phase; no inhibitory training was given to those animals.

The test for conditioned inhibition to the CS− followed. Both groups of rabbits received excitatory conditioning to the tone (the former CS− for the experimental subjects). For the experimental group, the tone was presumably a conditioned inhibitor since it had been explicitly not paired with the shock US in the first phase of the study; for the control group, the tone was neutral. Marchant and Moore's hypothesis was confirmed: the mean number of trials required to produce excitatory conditioning to the tone (CRs on 80 percent of the trials) was 81.6 for the control group but 134.4 for the experimental subjects. Clearly, the CS− had become a conditioned inhibitor during prior acquisition for the experimental subjects since later excitatory conditioning using that tone CS− was retarded.

A third situation in which inhibition occurs is extinction. As we have said previously, extinction of a Pavlovian response occurs when the CS is repeatedly presented without the US. This results in a gradual reduction in the strength of the CR. The process that weakens the CR, or the reason for the reduction in CR strength, however, is not unlearning; that is, the associative bond between a CS and US is not permanently broken during extinction. Rather, the extinction causes the subject to suppress or inhibit the CR.

The operation of inhibition during extinction is supported by the concept of *spontaneous recovery*. If the subject is given a rest period following extinction and then again tested for CR strength, it is usually observed that the subject's CR has recovered spontaneously during the rest interval. If the associative CS-US bond had been broken during extinction, that is, if unlearning had taken place, then no CR should be evident on the later test. On the other hand, if extinction had merely produced a temporary suppression or inhibition of the CR, then responding should be evident at a later time when the inhibition has had an opportunity to dissipate. The findings support this second hypothesis.

A study which illustrates spontaneous recovery of a Pavlovian CR was done by Burdick and James (1970). They used a CER procedure to assess response strength (although, unlike the Hammond study discussed above, they measured suppression of drinking rather than lever pressing). Burdick and James trained thirsty rats to lick a drinking tube for water during which time the Pavlovian CS (noise and light) and US (shock) were repeatedly presented. The 8 training trials were followed by 40 extinction trials. Then separate groups of subjects were given a particular rest interval: .058, .5, 1, 3, 24, or 72 hours. Finally, Burdick and James tested for spontaneous recovery by returning the subjects to the testing apparatus, presenting the

CS only, and observing the degree to which drinking was suppressed by the CS.

The results of their experiment are shown in Figure 2-4. It is clear that the CS became excitatory during acquisition: drinking was markedly suppressed by the end of training as evidenced by the low suppression ratio. More significant, as shown by the spontaneous recovery data, the extinguished CR reappeared in all but the .058-hour subjects. In other words, the experiment illustrated the fact that extinction of the Pavlovian CR involved an inhibitory process; the CS-US bond was not permanently broken during extinction since recovery of the response was observed after the rest interval.

The results of spontaneous recovery experiments strongly suggest that the underlying process affecting the CR during extinction is one of inhibition. However, this argument poses a paradox: if the CS, during extinction, loses its excitatory strength and gains inhibitory strength, why is the CS later excitatory? In other words, spontaneous recovery indicates that the CR is inhibited during extinction, but it also indicates that the CS reverts back to an excitatory state after the rest interval.

No clear resolution of this point has been reached. Pavlov (1927) assumed that inhibitory states are simply more temporary or transient than excitatory ones; they are more susceptible to disruption. Rescorla (1967a), on the other hand, offered a different viewpoint. He claimed that a CS does not become a *conditioned* inhibitor during extinction but rather reverts to its preconditioned status (i.e., neutrality). According to this theory, the fact that a CS is again excitatory, as opposed to neutral, on a spontaneous recovery test is because the animal quickly pays close attention to

FIGURE 2-4.

Mean suppression ratio during acquisition and the spontaneous recovery test as a function of the length of the recovery interval.

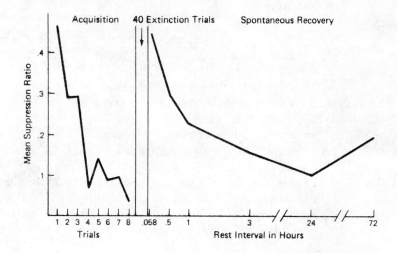

the stimulus. The proper conclusion therefore appears to be that extinction does involve an inhibitory process but that, unlike other situations discussed previously, where a CS becomes a conditioned inhibitor because it is paired with no US, the CS, during extinction, does not become a conditioned inhibitor (see Rescorla, 1969).

FACTORS IN PAVLOVIAN CONDITIONING

The acquisition of Pavlovian CRs is subject to a number of environmental conditions. Several of the more important factors affecting CR strength are discussed in the following sections.

US Intensity

One of the most important parameters in classical conditioning is the US intensity. In general, it has been found that more intense or larger USs produce stronger CRs. This generalization appears to hold for a wide variety of responses and species. For example, the strength of salivary conditioning is related to the magnitude of a food US (Wagner et al., 1964) and the concentration of an acid US (Ost & Lauer, 1965). Similarly, conditioned eyelid (Smith, 1968) or jaw movement CRs (Sheafor & Gormezano, 1972) in rabbits, and conditioned eyelid reactions in adult humans (see Spence & Platt, 1966) increase as a function of the US intensity (shock in the former cases or air pressure in the latter instance). Numerous studies have indicated that suppression of rats' lever pressing in a CER experiment also increases with higher shock levels (e.g., Annau & Kamin, 1961). Finally, Fitzgerald and Teyler (1970), among others, have found that conditioned heart rate (amplitude of the change in beats per minute) generally increased as a function of shock intensity.

US Duration

Although the effect of US duration was somewhat unclear in many of the earlier studies, more recent work has shown that conditioning is more effective with longer USs. Frey and Butler (1973), for example, trained an eyeblink response in rabbits with US durations of .05, .1, and .2 seconds in length. All the animals acquired the response but the .05-second group was the slowest to do so.

Similar results were obtained by Riess and Farrar (1973) who used a CER technique. Those authors administered three CS-US pairings per day for six sessions where the 1-minute light CS was followed by a shock US lasting either .05, .2, .5, 1.0, or 3.0 seconds (for different groups). The results for acquisition of the CR are shown in Figure 2-5. The mean CER suppression ratios (A/A+B, where A is the number of lever presses during the CS and B is the number of presses during a comparable time period

FIGURE 2-5.

Mean suppression ratio as a function of five CER sessions for groups receiving .05, .2, .5, 1.0, or 3.0-second US durations.

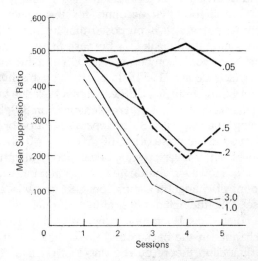

just prior to the CS) suggest virtually no conditioning in the .05 subjects, moderate conditioning in the .2 and .5 groups, and almost total suppression by the end of training in the 1.0 and 3.0-second groups. Recent evidence, therefore, appears to support the generalization that the strength of a Pavlovian CR is a positive function of US duration.

US Omission

The effect of omitting the US presentation during acquisition has been investigated in a great number of studies. In summarizing much of the research on human eyelid conditioning, Ross and Hartman (1965) reported that US omission led to weaker conditioning. Similar results have been found in salivary conditioning experiments: specifically, Fitzgerald (1963), Sadler (1968), and Wagner et al. (1964) all have shown that omission of the US on a portion of the acquisition trials reduces the strength of the CR. Thus, it seems that the acquisition of a classically conditioned response is a positive function of the percentage of CS-US pairings (but see Vardaris & Fitzgerald, 1969; Thomas & Wagner, 1964; Willis, 1969).

CS Intensity

The effect of CS intensity on Pavlovian conditioning is similar to that of US intensity, although the reasons for the effects differ. In general, more intense CSs lead to stronger CRs (see Gray, 1965; Grice, 1968). This fact has been demonstrated in a variety of experimental settings. For example,

Beck (1963) and Moore (1964) have shown that human eyelid conditioning is a positive function of CS intensity and Kamin and Schaub (1963) found a similar result for CER training in rats.

One theory that accounts for this effect is the adaptation level hypothesis. Here, it is proposed that intense CSs are more effective in conditioning than weak CSs because they are more easily discriminated; there is less confusion between the CS and the level of background stimulation (see Logan, 1954). In support of this hypothesis, Kamin (1965) varied CS intensity in a CER experiment relative to the background level of stimulation. Specifically, rats experienced an 80-db white noise throughout training; the explicit CS, for separate groups of subjects, consisted of a reduction in the noise of 70, 60, 50, 45, or 0 db. As shown in Figure 2-6, suppression of lever pressing developed in all groups over the six days of training. However, the degree of suppression was directly related to the amount of change in stimulation: subjects who experienced a more "intense" CS (the actual physical intensity was less but the relative change was greater) displayed more suppression than subjects who received smaller changes in the background noise. Kamin's study clearly supports the discrimination theory by showing that relative changes from a specified background level of stimulation are indeed important to conditioning.

CS-US Interval

The interval between the CS and the US is one of the most important parameters in classical conditioning and, accordingly, it has been studied extensively. The reason for its importance is that the interval essentially defines the degree of stimulus contiguity. It is clear that Pavlovian CRs develop when the CS-US interval is very short, i.e., defined in seconds rather than hours (but see Chapter 7), although the interval that is optimum for conditioning varies greatly with the type of CR studied.

Much of the earlier literature suggested that an interval of .5 seconds was optimum (e.g., Kimble, 1961) but that figure appears to be accurate only for a few responses. In general, two major divisions or categories of CRs are relevant to a discussion of the CS-US interval: motor or skeletal responses like the eyeblink and autonomic or visceral responses.

Eyelid conditioning, in humans, does appear to be maximum when the CS-US interval is .5 seconds. Ross and Ross (1971), for example, using college students for subjects, found this to be true using both trace and delayed procedures. Conditioned responding decreased sharply with intervals shorter than .5 seconds but somewhat more gradually with longer intervals (ranging to 1.4 seconds).

The optimum CS-US interval for eyeblink conditioning in rabbits appears to be only slightly less. Smith, Coleman, and Gormezano (1969) found that conditioning was superior with intervals of .2 and .4 seconds. Virtually no improvement over training was noted with a CS-US interval of .05 seconds. Similarly, Smith (1968) found that the optimum interval was

FIGURE 2-6.

Median suppression ratio over six CER sessions for different CS "intensities" (reduction of the background noise).

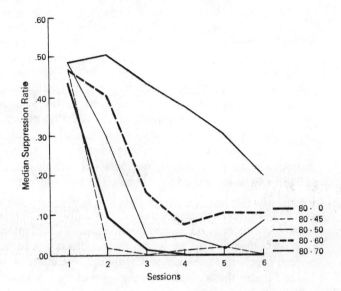

about .25 seconds, although such results may depend, in part, on the number of trials given per acquisition session (Levinthal, 1973).

Conditioning of another skeletal response, the jaw movement CR in rabbits, differs appreciably from eyeblink conditioning in terms of the optimum CS-US interval. Gormezano (1972) has shown that the percent CRs over a series of 240 trials was maximum for an interval of 1–4 seconds; for shorter intervals of .5 and .25 seconds (i.e., those optimum for eyelid conditioning in humans and rabbits, respectively), conditioning was relatively poor.

The second category of CRs includes the autonomic (involuntary) responses; here it has been found that conditioning is superior with relatively long intervals. For example, in heart rate conditioning, optimum intervals of 6 seconds in rats (Fitzgerald & Martin, 1971; Fitzgerald & Teyler, 1970), 2 to 6 seconds in rabbits (Deane, 1965), 2.5 to 10 seconds in dogs (Black et al., 1962), and 13 seconds in humans (Hastings & Obrist, 1967) have been reported. In salivary conditioning, Ellison (1964) demonstrated effective conditioning when the interval between the offset of the 1-second tone CS and the presentation of the US was 8 seconds; some conditioning was apparent even when that interval was 16 seconds. Paradoxically, the optimum interval for GSR conditioning, also an autonomic response, appears to be .5 seconds (Prokasy et al., 1962; but see Badia & Defran, 1970).

The reason for differences in the effect of the CS-US interval on skeletal versus autonomic responding is not entirely clear. One important factor may be the "sluggishness" of many autonomic CRs. The onset of these reactions, for example, is markedly longer than most skeletal responses such as the eyeblink.

Instructions

In experiments with human subjects, instructions designed to produce greater or lesser participation or effort in the experiment have been shown to influence conditioning. This result is somewhat surprising since Pavlovian conditioning is generally associated with the acquisition of reflexive-like responses over which subjects seemingly lack control.

There have been two lines of research. The first concerns the effect of instructions on the eyeblink response. The results of Norris and Grant (1948), who encouraged their subjects to try not to blink when they felt a puff of air, showed that these negative instructions reduced the level of blinking considerably as compared with a group that received no instructions. More recently, Gormezano and Moore (1962) investigated the effect of positive instructions by telling their subjects not to try to control their natural reactions to the air puff. Although the eyeblink response was enhanced under these conditions, the form of the response suggested to the authors that the positive instructions merely increased the incidence of voluntary eyeblinks. Therefore, the effect of instructions on conditioned eyeblink responding appears to be unidirectional: negative instructions suppress CRs while positive instructions cause an increase in voluntary responses rather than better conditioning of true CRs.

A second line of research has focused on GSR conditioning. Several investigators have found that the conditioning of this autonomic CR also may be influenced by instructions. For example, in an experiment that used a tone followed by a shock, Dawson and Reardon (1969) used three groups of subjects. One group was told that becoming conditioned would be "adaptable, sensible, and intelligent"; a second group was informed that it would be adaptable, sensible, and intelligent *not* to become conditioned; and the third group was given neutral instructions. The mean GSR responding on the test trials was higher for the first, facilitatory instruction group and lower for the second, inhibitory instruction group relative to the neutral control subjects.

The reason verbal instructions influence the conditioning of an apparently involuntary response is not entirely clear. Harvey and Wickens (1971, 1973) replicated the Dawson and Reardon finding and included a number of US-only trials during training. They discovered that the UR elicited on these US-only trials was larger in the facilitatory subjects and weaker in the inhibitory instructions group. Therefore, these authors concluded that instructions alter the magnitude of the UR which, in turn, influences the strength of the CR.

THEORIES OF PAVLOVIAN CONDITIONING

The important task for any theorist is to explain how CRs are acquired or, alternatively, what function the CS serves in conditioning. Two major theories of classical conditioning are discussed below.

Stimulus Substitution

The traditional theory of classical conditioning, which originated with Pavlov, is the stimulus substitution theory. According to this formulation, mere contiguity of the CS and US is sufficient to produce an association. Presumably, the nervous system is structured in such a way that the contiguous occurrence of these two events, represented as impulses to the brain, allows for the creation of a bond between them. Stated differently, the CS comes to substitute for the US; it becomes a "surrogate" US. Whereas the US initially elicits a UR, the CS, after repeated CS-US pairings, eventually substitutes for the US and itself is capable of eliciting a "substitute" form of the UR, namely the CR.

There is sufficient reason to question this theory. Evidence based on a consideration of the essential predictions of the theory has not always been supportive. For example, the theory predicts that (a) virtually any UR may be converted into a CR (i.e., conditioned) provided that the CS and US are contiguous, and (b) if the CS substitutes for the US, then the conditioned form of the reflex, the CR, should be identical to the unconditioned form of the reflex, the UR.

With regard to the first prediction, it is clear that some URs, such as pupil constriction in response to light, cannot be conditioned (Young, 1958, 1965). This finding contradicts the stimulus substitution theory since CS-US contiguity and a viable UR were present in those experiments.

Evidence more damaging to the theory has been obtained in studies concerned with the second point—the CR-UR equivalence. According to the theory, if the CS substitutes for the US, then both stimuli should elicit comparable responses. However, the CR is usually different from the UR. For example, Black (1971) noted that the heart rate UR to shock always accelerates while the conditioned form of that response, the CR, may either decelerate or accelerate. Zener (1937) studied salivary conditioning in dogs and observed that the CR contained numerous components not found in the UR. Specifically, the animals made orientation responses to the food tray or the CS which Zener judged were preparatory responses; these components were not part of the UR. Zener also observed conditioned movements, such as panting and yawning, but these behaviors were not characteristic of the UR. Finally, it is well known that a shock US produces jumping and flinching in rats (i.e., highly activated behavior) but the CR is usually freezing and immobility (Bindra & Palfai, 1967; Blanchard & Blanchard, 1969).

Information Theory

A recent theory by Rescorla (1967b) has provided a new perspective on classical conditioning that can accommodate many of the discrepancies cited above. Rescorla's claim is straightforward: a CS acquires information value, that is, it provides information concerning whatever event follows it in time. That CSs convey information to animals is highly plausible; it is very common, for example, to observe dogs jumping about in a frisky manner when their caretaker is opening a can of dog food. In the case of excitatory conditioning, the subject may use the CS to predict the occurrence of the US, while for inhibitory conditioning, the CS is contiguous with no US and therefore signals its absence. Rather than CS-US contiguity, Rescorla refers to CS-US correlation. A CS, presented randomly with respect to the US, acquires no "meaning" for the animal because it fails to predict any consistent outcome. However, as the correlation between the CS and a given consequence increases, the CS takes on associative value.

An experiment that demonstrated the role of CS outcome correlation in associative learning was done by Rescorla (1968). He asserted that no conditioning would take place when the US occurred equally often in the presence and absence of the CS. However, as the probability increased that the US would occur during the presence of the CS (relative to during the absence of the CS), excitatory conditioning would increase. Conversely, as the probability increased that the US would occur in the absence of the CS, inhibitory conditioning would increase.

Rescorla used the CER technique (suppression of lever pressing) to assess conditioning. In one part of the study, four groups of rats were trained to press a lever for food. After their behavior had stabilized, Rescorla removed the lever from the cage and initiated the Pavlovian conditioning procedures. For all subjects, the probability of receiving the shock US during the presence of the 2-minute tone CS was .4. The probability of receiving the US during the absence of the CS was .4, .2, .1, and 0 for separate groups of subjects. After the Pavlovian sessions, the lever was reintroduced into the cages and lever pressing was again stabilized; then, the tone CS was presented on the next six sessions and the suppression was noted.

The results are shown in Figure 2-7. As we noted earlier, the suppression ratio is B/A+B, where B is the number of responses during the CS and A is the number of responses just prior to the CS. Responding was not suppressed in the .4 subjects for whom the probabilities of shock during presence and absence of CS were equal. The inhibitory component which stemmed from the CS-no US occurrences counterbalanced the excitatory component that was derived from the CS-US pairings. In contrast, marked reduction of lever pressing was noted in the other groups, and although this effect later extinguished, the initial degree of suppression was inversely related to the probability of the US in the absence of the CS. For example, subjects in Group 0, who had excitatory CS-US pairings but no inhibitory

FIGURE 2-7.

Median suppression ratio for the four groups as a function of test sessions. The probability of US during the CS was .4 for all subjects; the probability of US during the CS absence is noted for each group.

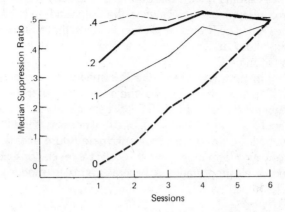

conditioning to counterbalance the effect, showed the greatest suppression. Rescorla concluded that conditioning depends on the disparity between these two probabilities: excitatory conditioning is effective when the CS-US occurrences "outweigh" the CS-no US occurrences; inhibitory conditioning is strong under the reverse conditions.

The notion of "disparity" should be emphasized here since suppression depended not on the number of CS-US pairings per se but rather on the disparity of the probabilities. For example, in a different portion of the study, Rescorla used probabilities of .1 (shock during CS) and 0 (shock during CS absence). The absolute number of CS-US pairings in this group was much less than for the .4-.4 Group noted in Figure 2-7, yet conditioning (i.e., suppression) was much stronger. The stimulus substitution theory, which claims that CS strength is a function of the number of CS-US pairings alone, cannot account for such a finding.

One specific outcome of Rescorla's work was the recommendation that a truly random presentation of CSs and USs provides the most appropriate control condition in Pavlovian experiments. The CS-outcome correlation in this case would be zero; that is, the CS would reliably predict neither the US nor its absence. Stated differently, if a CS acquires "meaning" according to the outcome which it reliably precedes, then it should remain neutral, that is, it should fail to acquire either excitatory or inhibitory strength when a truly random relationship exists between the CS and its outcome.

The validity of this recommendation was certainly supported in Rescorla's own work but more recent investigators have disagreed on the grounds that a truly random control group may display conditioning. Kremer (1969), Kremer and Kamin (1971), and Benedict and Ayres (1972), for example, found positive evidence of conditioning in a random control group. Similarly, Furedy (1971) and Furedy and Schiffmann (1973) failed to note any difference between a truly random control group and one that received explicitly unpaired CSs and USs. According to Rescorla, differences should have been observed since conditioning in the unpaired controls was inhibitory relative to the truly random subjects. These discrepancies noted by Kremer and others suggest that a precise understanding of the conditions under which CSs acquire either excitatory or inhibitory valence is lacking.

In summary, Rescorla's information theory accounts for CS "meaning" or strength in terms of the consistency of the CS-outcome correlation rather than in terms of CS-US pairings alone. In this respect, Rescorla's theory is a cognitive theory, one that addresses itself to the question of how animals come to expect or anticipate future events. The notion that CSs convey information, that they elicit expectations about future events, is extremely important for several trends in modern learning theory (see Chapter 8).

PAVLOVIAN PHENOMENA

A great deal is known about Pavlovian conditioning beyond the simple fact that CS-outcome correlation leads to associative learning. The various phenomena discussed below are extensions of Pavlov's work and often represent special instances of learning that don't conform directly to Pavlov's original experimental design.

Second-Order Conditioning

Second-order conditioning occurs when an excitatory CS—one that has been consistently paired with a US—is paired with a second, neutral CS. This new CS, then, acquires the ability to elicit the CR even though it was never paired directly with the US. Once a CS gains excitatory strength, it can be used as a "US" for another CS; after repeated pairings of the second CS and the original CS, the new CS alone is capable of eliciting the CR.

In a recent study on this phenomenon, Holland and Rescorla (1975) measured CS strength in terms of general activity to the cue. (Rats typically increase their activity during a CS that signals food.) Three groups of subjects were used. The rats in Group PP received 12 CS_1-US pairings in phase 1 (10-second light, then food) followed by 16 CS_2-CS_1 pairings in phase 2 (CS_2 was a clicker). The authors predicted that during this latter phase, the neutral CS_2 would become excitatory (because it was paired with the excitatory CS_1) and would thus elicit an increase in activity of the rats. Groups UP and PU served as controls. In the former case, the CS_1 and US (light and food) were explicitly unpaired during phase 1 but the CS_2 and CS_1 (clicker and light) were paired in phase 2. The reverse was true for the subjects in Group PU; the CS_1-US pairings were given but no CS_2-CS_1

FIGURE 2-8.

Mean responses per minute (activity) during the second-order CS_2 as a function of blocks of 4 CS_2-CS_1 trials.

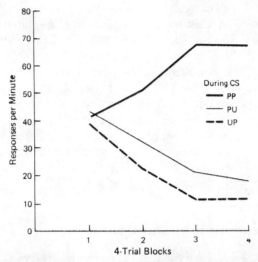

trials occurred in phase 2. No second-order conditioning was predicted in either of these control groups since the UP group lacked a paired relationship between the CS_1 and US and the PU group lacked the CS_2-CS_1 pairings. The results of the study are illustrated in Figure 2-8. During the first four CS_2-CS_1 trials (see block 1), all groups demonstrated a comparable activity level. However, the activity in the two control groups declined over the next three blocks while the mean activity of the experimental subjects rose significantly. Therefore, the study clearly demonstrated that the neutral CS_2, in this case the clicker, had become excitatory when paired with the original excitatory CS_1, the light. Moreover, the fact that activity did not increase showed that second-order conditioning failed to occur when either the CS_1-US or the CS_2-CS_1 pairings were not presented. Similar results have been reported by Kamil (1968, 1969), and Rizley and Rescorla (1972), who used an aversive conditioning procedure (CER technique).

One interesting aspect of this phenomenon was that the strength of the second-order CS did not depend on the integrity or strength of the original CS_1 (see Rescorla, 1973b; Holland & Rescorla, 1975). When extinction of the CS_1 was given following the CS_2-CS_1 pairings, the strength of the CS_2 was unaffected. This finding is quite unlike first-order conditioning where the potency of the original CS_1 is known to depend on the integrity of the US (Rescorla, 1973a).

The theoretical reasons for the qualitative difference between first- and second-order conditioning are not yet clear (see Rescorla 1973a, b). However, these findings are extremely important for a number of reasons. First, the phenomenon of second-order conditioning suggests a mechanism by which environmental stimuli acquire strength even though they are not paired originally with a potent US. In fact, it is reasonable to suggest that, in higher organisms at least, a vast network of higher-order relationships exists. The US is important in strengthening the initial CS, but thereafter, CSs, not biologically active USs, serve to strengthen other novel cues. Second, Rescorla's finding, that CS_1 extinction did not weaken the strength of the CS_2, has important implications for the treatment of phobias. For example, if a person were irrationally afraid of a particular object (i.e., the CS), and if that object had gained its fear-provoking properties because it was paired with another fear-eliciting CS, then extinction of this latter stimulus, the original source of fear, would have no effect on the person's fear of the former object; the phobia would remain strong. Such considerations are important in understanding the etiology and treatment of certain behavior disorders (see the last section in this chapter for more discussion of this topic).

Sensory Preconditioning

Sensory preconditioning, as first outlined by Brogden (1930), is an association between two neutral CSs. Demonstration of this phenomenon involves three phases: first, the two neutral CSs are paired; second, one of the CSs is paired with a US in a normal conditioning arrangement; finally, the other CS is substituted and CR measurements are made. Clearly, this type of experiment is similar to second-order conditioning except that the order of presentation of phases 1 and 2 is reversed. The general result in sensory preconditioning studies is that both CSs, even the one never paired with the US, are capable of eliciting a CR (see Seidel, 1959; Thompson, 1972 for reviews).

An illustration of this phenomenon was a study using a CER technique by Prewitt (1967). In phase 1, either 0, 1, 4, 16, or 64 CS_B-CS_A pairings were given to five experimental groups of rats. For half the subjects in each group, CS_A was a 10-second tone and CS_B was a 10-second light; these conditions were reversed for the other animals. Four groups of control subjects were given both stimuli in phase 1 but they were randomly presented, one stimulus every 30 seconds. Thus, for the experimental groups, some type of associative bond between CS_B and CS_A was expected to develop during phase 1, whereas for the control subjects, the stimuli were not expected to become associated.

In phase 2, all the subjects received normal forward conditioning during which the CS_A and a mild shock US were paired.

Finally, a test for the effects of sensory preconditioning was given. The rats were deprived of water and then were given access to a drinking tube containing sugar water. While the animals were drinking, the CS_B was presented for 10 seconds about once per minute; suppression of drinking during this phase was used to measure the strength of CS_B.

Prewitt demonstrated a clear effect of sensory preconditioning and, as shown in Figure 2-9, the strength of CS_B increased as a function of the number of CS_B-CS_A trials in phase 1. Even though the CS_B was never paired directly with the US, it was able to elicit a conditioned reaction. In contrast to the experimental subjects, the control groups showed only a slight amount of suppression (CER ratio was nearly .5), indicating that CS_B-CS_A contiguity during the preconditioning phase was critical for obtaining the effect. Although Prewitt did not have control groups who received random CS_A and US presentations in phase 2, it has been shown that CS_A-US contiguity also is critical for demonstrating CS_B strength (Rizley & Rescorla, 1972). As illustrated in the upper portion of Figure 2-10, during the preconditioning phase, the CS_A functions like a weak US; the orienting reaction (OR) elicited by CS_A, therefore, could be considered analogous to a UR. Through repeated CS_B-CS_A pairings, the CS_B comes to elicit a conditioned form of this "UR."

In the second phase, a second classical procedure is introduced, namely, the CS_A-US pairings; here, CS_A acquires the ability to elicit a CR. However, it may be assumed that (a) the CS_A also continues to elicit the orienting reaction and that (b) this orienting response produces a sensory feedback stimulus, S_M, which (c) acquires the ability to elicit the CR (but see Cousins et al., 1971). Thus, the sequence or chain created during this second phase would be $CS_A \rightarrow OR \rightarrow S_M \rightarrow CR$.

Finally, in the test of preconditioning, the CS_B elicits the OR (as a result of the preconditioning phase) which in turn elicits the S_M-CR sequence (as a result of the S_M-CR bond established in phase 2). In summary, both the preconditioning and conditioning phases are examples of classical conditioning which share a common element, namely, the CS_A. The reason that the CS_B later is effective in evoking the CR is because the initial conditioned response to it (i.e., the conditioned form of the OR elicited by CS_A) provides, at the same time, a stimulus S_M that elicits the CR.

FIGURE 2-9.

Mean suppression of licking as a function of number of sensory preconditioning trials for the experimental (paired) and control (unpaired) groups.

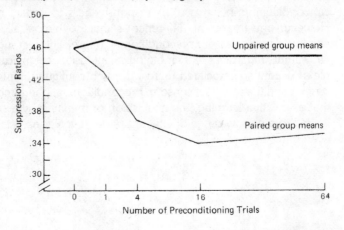

FIGURE 2-10.

A schematic drawing showing the way in which the implicit responses and stimuli may mediate sensory preconditioning.

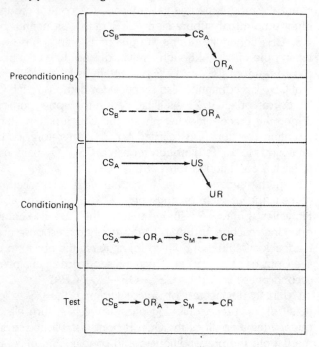

One important test of this theory would be to see if the variables that influence "regular" conditioning during phase 2 similarly affect the sensory preconditioning during phase 1. It appears that many do (but see Thompson, 1972). For example, forward conditioning during the preconditioning phase is necessary for producing a strong effect; that is, like other Pavlovian studies, reversal of the order of stimuli, a backward design, leads to poor sensory preconditioning (Coppock, 1958).

In conclusion, sensory preconditioning appears to be similar to classical conditioning in terms of its responsiveness to certain manipulations. However, the important difference is that no biologically-potent US is employed in the sensory preconditioning phase. This fact suggests that any two stimuli, regardless of their biological intensity or significance, are capable of becoming associated merely through contiguity. Thus, like second-order conditioning, the sensory preconditioning phenomenon suggests that associative learning, the acquisition of meaning by a stimulus, is not limited to a narrow range of USs but rather involves associations between even innocuous stimuli.

FIGURE 2-11.

Mean percent conditioned leg flex as a function of blocks of 20 trials for groups receiving 0, 20, or 40 CS preexposures.

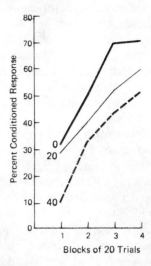

Latent Inhibition

Latent inhibition is defined as the retardation of conditioning to a CS because the subject was preexposed to that CS prior to conditioning (see Lubow, 1973, and Siegel, 1972). The major procedural difference between latent inhibition and conditioned inhibition is that in the latter case, the CS− signals no US in the context of a CS+ (i.e., during excitatory training), while in the former instance, the CS− is presented without the US prior to the actual conditioning phase of the experiment.

An experiment by Lubow (1965) illustrated this phenomenon. Lubow divided a number of goats and sheep into three groups. During the preexposure phase of the experiment, the light CS was presented alone for either 20 or 40 times to two of the groups and zero times for the third group. Following this procedure, all the subjects were given 80 Pavlovian conditioning trials (20 per day for four days) in which the light, the preexposed CS, was paired with a shock to the foreleg of each animal.

The mean percent leg flex CRs elicited by the light CS is shown in Figure 2-11. Conditioning was inversely related to the number of CS preexposures; that is, the more experience an animal had with the light prior to conditioning, the more retarded was the leg flex conditioning. Stated differently, prior exposure to a CS, but not a US, made the CS relatively insensitive to later excitatory conditioning—that is, it delayed and inhibited the conditioning.

Several investigators have tried to explain the latent inhibition phenomenon. Most agree that a latent inhibitor is not a conditioned inhibitor; that is, during preexposure, the CS− does not acquire conditioned inhibitory properties that are antagonistic to excitation. Several studies (Reiss & Wagner, 1972; Rescorla, 1973a; Solomon et al., 1974) have presented the latent inhibitor with a known excitatory CS+. If the latent inhibitor were a conditioned inhibitory cue, then the excitatory strength of the CS+ should be reduced. The studies cited immediately above, however, failed to show such an effect. Similarly, Halgren (1974) found that explicit inhibitory conditioning to a latent inhibitor (i.e., a preexposed CS) was just as retarded as explicit excitatory conditioning to that cue; presumably if the cue had become a conditioned inhibitor during preexposure, additional inhibitory training would have been even easier to accomplish. The fact that it was not suggested that CS preexposure involves a decline in the subject's attention to the stimulus. Stated differently, preexposure of a CS does not entail conditioned inhibition; rather the subjects come to attend to the cue so that the CS has less impact at a later time. However, if (a) precautions are taken to maintain attention to the CS during the preexposure phase (Lubow, Schnur, & Rifkin, 1976), or (b) the environmental context in which the preexposed cue is presented is changed (Lubow, Rifkin, & Alek, 1976), or (c) more intense CSs are used, ones that demand greater attention from the subject (Solomon et al., 1974), then later conditioning is not retarded. All of these findings support an attention theory of latent inhibition.

Inhibition of Delay

As we said earlier, when a CS is not followed by a US, inhibitory processes are generated. For example, a CS that is explicitly paired with no US in the context of excitatory conditioning becomes a conditioned inhibitor. Indeed, the defining characteristic of a CS− is that it is explicitly paired with no US. However, there is an important inhibitory procedure during which, unlike conditioned inhibition, CS-US pairings are maintained. This phenomenon is termed inhibition of delay. Here, if the US onset is delayed for a substantial period of time following the CS presentation, then, over training, the subject gradually learns to withhold or inhibit the CR for longer periods of time. An excitatory CR is made eventually but it appears just before the US presentation after a period during which it is suppressed.

A recent study by Lynch (1973) illustrated inhibition of delay. Dogs were trained to make a flex response using a 42-second tone CS and a 1-second shock US. Ten pairings per day for thirty days were given during acquisition and the latency of response, that is, the time of the CR as measured from the CS onset was recorded. First, Lynch noted for each CR whether its latency fell within one of four categories: 1−10, 11−20, 21−30, or 31−40 seconds; then he computed within each category the percentage of those CRs that involved a full or maximum leg flex. The inhibition of delay phenomenon would predict that, over training, a higher percentage of maximum CRs would occur in categories 21−30 or 31−40

FIGURE 2-12.

Mean percent maximum leg flex CRs, executed with latencies of 1-10 (a), 11-20 (b), 21-30 (c), or 31-40 (d) seconds, as a function of blocks of 50 training trials.

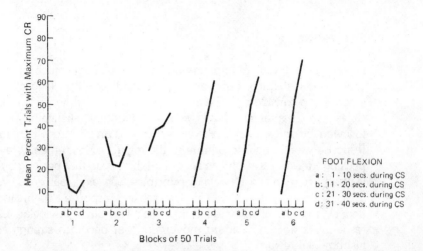

and, correspondingly, a smaller percentage of CRs in the 1−10- or 11−20-second categories would be a full or maximum leg flex.

Inhibition of delay was clearly demonstrated, as shown in Figure 2-12. During the first 50 trials, most of the full or maximum CRs were executed with a relatively short latency. However, as training progressed, more and more of the full conditioned responses were delayed following CS onset; that is, the latency of these responses fell into the 21−30- and 31−40-second categories.

The fact that the latency of a classical CR increases with training does not, in itself, indicate that such a temporary withholding of the response to the CS is due to a state of inhibition. However, research has indicated that the inhibition of delay phenomenon does indeed involve an inhibitory process. For example, if a novel cue is presented during the CS (i.e., during the period the CR is being suppressed), the response is immediately disinhibited. Stated differently, a novel cue, presented during inhibition of delay, disrupts the subject to the extent that the CR is evoked almost immediately. The CR was available all the while but was being suppressed temporarily.

An example of disinhibition comes from Pavlov's (1927, p. 93) own work. He gave dogs a 3-minute tactile CS followed by the presentation of a weak acid solution to the tongue (US). Inhibition of delay was observed: after several CS-US pairings, a weak salivary response (2 drops) began to appear after about 90 seconds; the maximum CR (9 drops) wasn't given until just prior to the US. However, once this pattern was well established, Pavlov presented a new stimulus in the form of a rotating object in addition to the tactile CS. The effect of this novel cue was to disinhibit the CR as evidenced by the fact that a moderately strong CR (6 drops) was given within the first 30 seconds.

Autoshaping

Finally, a Pavlovian phenomenon that has received much attention recently is autoshaping. For many years, conditioned pecking of a disk by pigeons was considered to be acquired through instrumental learning principles (see Chapter 3). That is, such a "voluntary" skeletal response was followed by reward, and, therefore, acquisition or strengthening of the response was thought to be due to the impact of instrumental reward on pecking. Recent research has suggested, however, that pecking by birds is learned according to Pavlovian principles (see e.g., Gamzu & Williams, 1975; Wasserman et al., 1975). The pecking response appears to be elicited by the CS (illuminated disk) much like other Pavlovian CRs; the response is not an arbitrary movement that becomes strengthened via instrumental reward.

The first evidence for this paradoxical phenomenon was obtained by Brown and Jenkins (1968). Pigeons were placed in a cage containing a plastic disk on the wall (the pecking of which was recorded on a counter) and a grain hopper. During the experiment, the disk was illuminated just prior to food presentations. Nothing was required on the part of the animal; as in all Pavlovian experiments, the presentations of the CS (illuminated disk) and US (food) were independent of the subject's behavior. The authors found that such pairings were, in themselves, sufficient for establishing approach and contact behavior; that is, the pigeons approached the disk and pecked at it even though their pecks had no effect whatsoever upon the presentation of food. This so-called autoshaping effect is so strong that pigeons will continue to peck the disk even when such a behavior delays or postpones food (e.g., Williams & Williams, 1969).

Many other studies have supported the notion that the acquisition of pecking by pigeons is a Pavlovian CR. For example, it is clear that the CS and US must be paired in a forward design; backward or random CS-US relationships do not produce the pecking CR (e.g., Wasserman, 1973; Wasserman et al., 1974). In fact, when the CS follows the US presentation, the subjects physically position themselves far from the disk (a withdrawal response that is antithetical to pecking).

Perhaps the strongest evidence for the Pavlovian control of pecking was presented in a remarkable study by Jenkins and Moore (1973). Pigeons were autoshaped under various conditions while, in addition, the form (physical characteristic) of their pecking response was recorded by a high-speed movie camera. In one study, the illumination of the disk (CS) was followed by a water US for the thirsty pigeons; hungry subjects, however, received a food US. All subjects pecked the disk (although food and water were not dependent upon the responding) but the form of the peck

FIGURE 2-13.

Illustrations of the form of a peck when food (left) and water (right) were used as the US. These CRs resemble the pigeon's natural URs to those USs.

varied according to the type of US. Specifically, the food-US subjects made sharp, vigorous pecks at the disk, responses that were characteristic of the animals' natural eating movements. In contrast, the thirsty subjects that received the water US made slower, more sustained pecks with their beaks open; often their drinking-like movements were accompanied by swallowing and licking. An illustration of each type of peck (at the point of impact with the disk) is shown in Figure 2-13.

In subsequent experiments, Jenkins and Moore demonstrated that the motivational state was not responsible for the form of the autoshaped peck; rather, the form was dependent only on the type of US. In fact, when simultaneously hungry and thirsty birds were given two disks, one that had preceded food and one that had preceded water presentations, they executed both the "drinking" peck and the "eating" peck to the appropriate disk. In summary, the overall results indicated that pigeons will peck a disk (CR) in a way that closely resembles their natural consummatory response (UR) to the US. Although other investigators have shown that autoshaping may occur even when the CR and UR are quite different (e.g., Wasserman, 1973), the Jenkins and Moore data strongly confirm the notion that the acquisition of pecking, fundamentally, is a Pavlovian phenomenon. Additional implications that the autoshaping literature poses for learning theory in general are discussed in Chapters 7 and 8.

APPLICATION OF CLASSICAL CONDITIONING PRINCIPLES

Thus far, we have concentrated on the acquisition of easily identified CRs, such as salivation and eyeblink. Pavlovian conditioning, however, also applies to other types of responses, several of which are related to important human conditions. First, just as heart rate or skin resistance changes may be classically conditioned, other highly specialized, covert physical reactions, such as the change in glucose concentration in the blood, for example, are also subject to conditioning. These conditioned reflexes suggest a basis for psychosomatic illness—those baffling physical ailments which do not appear to have any physical basis.

Second, classical conditioning may result in emotional reactions on the part of the subject (see Chapter 8). In fact, if the US is sufficiently aversive, severe anxiety may develop as a result of exposure to the CS. Thus, classical conditioning also has been used as a model for explaining the acquisition of certain phobias—maladaptive, irrational fears. The last section of this chapter deals with some of the work pertaining to this relationship between Pavlovian conditioning and phobias.

Psychosomatic Illness

In interoceptive conditioning, either the CS or the US (or both) are applied directly to the viscera of the organism. That is, the subject experiences one or both of the stimuli internally rather than via the usual sense receptors. Much of the work on this kind of conditioning, done in Russian laboratories, was summarized by Razran (1961) who noted three types of procedures: *intero-exteroceptive*, where the CS is internal and the US is externally applied; *extero-interoceptive*, where the CS is an external cue and the US is internal; and *intero-interoceptive*, where both the CS and US occur internally.

Intero-exteroceptive conditioning was illustrated in the following way: first a balloon was surgically implanted in the uterus of a dog. Infusing the balloon with cool water provided a CS which was followed by a US (food). After repeated pairings, the CS alone was capable of eliciting salivation. Moreover, the subjects were able to discriminate that particular CS from others as they salivated to the infusion of cool water but not to warm water. Thus, it appears that the animals were able to associate an internal event, the change in the temperature of the uterus, with an external biologically important US.

Intero-interoceptive conditioning has also been demonstrated in a study in which an intestinal balloon was inflated slightly to distend the stomach (CS); at the same time, a 10 percent carbon dioxide mixture was delivered via a second fistula down the trachea (US). This US normally produces defensive respiratory reactions such as rapid breathing or panting. After several pairings, simply inflating the balloon could elicit the defensive breathing reaction.

Finally, Razran also noted instances of extero-interoceptive conditioning. In one study, fistulas were placed in the bladders of a group of human subjects for the purposes of medical treatment. Expanding the bladder (US) by infusing water through the fistula produced an urge to urinate (UR). This presentation followed an external CS in which the subjects viewed a dial with pointer that moved (CS) in accordance with the infusion of water into the bladder fistula (US). After the subjects had experienced repeated pairings of the moving pointer and infusion, the experimenter tested for a conditioned reaction: the pointer on the dial was made to move in the usual fashion (CS presentation) but no infusion of water was given. On these test trials, the subjects reported a strong urge to urinate. Conditioning of an internal, physiologically based reaction, therefore, was clearly evident in this experiment. Initially the CS could not elicit the response but through repeated association with the US, it acquired the ability to do so. The interesting point to note is that if such a response were made by a medical patient in the absence of any organic cause, the symptom would be labeled "psychosomatic."

Recent research has provided even more impressive demonstrations of extero-interoceptive conditioning. In many of these studies, physiological reactions per se, not merely verbal reports such as the stated need to urinate, have been shown to change markedly to an external CS. For example, Hutton, Woods, and Makous (1970) conditioned a change in blood sugar in rats by pairing an external CS with an injection of insulin, the US, the UR to which is *hypoglycemia*, a decrease in the sugar in the blood. During the conditioning trials, the researchers drew a blood sample from each animal, gave each an injection, and placed it in a holding cage that was permeated with the odor of menthol. This procedure (blood sample, injection, placement in the cage) constituted the CS. After a 20-minute waiting period, a second blood sample was taken for the purpose of measuring any change in blood sugar that had occurred while the rat was in the cage.

Two groups were used in this research. The experimental subjects were injected on the five conditioning trials with insulin, the US. On other occasions, placebo injections (injections of an innocuous substance) with no accompanying CS presentation, were given these subjects. The control subjects received the same treatment as the experimental group (i.e., the same number of placebo and insulin injections), except that their five insulin injections were not associated with the CS presentation. In summary, the CS (blood sample, injection, placement in the holding cage) was paired five times with the US (insulin) for the experimental animals; the control subjects, however, received a placebo on the five CS trials and insulin injections at times other than after the CS presentation. After this training procedure, all the subjects were tested for a conditioned blood sugar response to the CS.

The results of the experiment are illustrated in Figure 2-14. On the five training trials (left portion of Figure 2-14), a change in blood sugar was noticeable in the experimental subjects. This finding reflects the fact that the UR to insulin was a decrease in blood sugar. In contrast, the control subjects demonstrated little change in blood sugar on any of these acquisition trials. This was the predicted outcome since the controls always received a placebo injection on the CS trails.

The more interesting outcome was on the test (right portion of Figure 2-14) where all the subjects received the CS plus an injection of placebo.

FIGURE 2-14.

Mean change in blood glucose levels for the experimental and control groups over the CS-US and test trials.

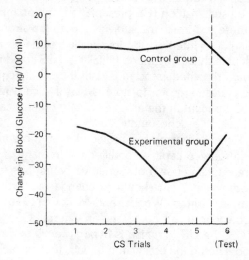

Here, the control subjects, for whom the CS had never been paired with insulin, showed no decrease in blood sugar. However, the experimental animals did show a decrease even though the injection on the test trial had been placebo. In other words, the physiological change in the experimental subjects during the test was brought about by the CS alone; it was a *conditioned* blood sugar reaction, not merely a UR to insulin.

As we have said earlier, the results of interoceptive conditioning studies have important implications. First, it is clear that internal physiological states can be elicited or controlled by external cues. These conditioned responses may constitute part of the complex set of reactions observed in certain clinical syndromes. That is, the origin of many psychosomatic symptoms may be explained in terms of classical conditioning principles. These psychosomatic symptoms are "real," just as the blood sugar changes in the Hutton et al. study were real, yet they are produced by a conditioning procedure rather than an organic agent that is present at the time of observation.

Second, conditioned internal responses, such as those cited above, usually occur without the subject being aware of them. This suggests that these subtle, conditioned reactions may comprise an important portion of unconscious behavior and experience.

Phobias

For our purposes, phobias may be defined as maladaptive, irrational fears. They are maladaptive and irrational in the sense that the fearsome stimulus, the CS, is no longer followed by the traumatic US. Clearly, a detailed understanding of phobias would be an important contribution to our society because we would be in a better position to treat people who suffer from them.

For many years, psychologists have claimed that phobias are acquired via classical conditioning principles: innocuous stimuli (CSs) get paired with traumatic events (aversive USs) and later cause anxiety. One famous demonstration of this process was done by Watson and Raynor (1920). The subject in the study, Albert, was an 11-month-old infant who initially had no fear of white rats. However, he developed a fear of them through conditioning. The experimenters sounded a loud noise (US) every time the child approached the rat (CS); since loud sounds are aversive to young children, a fear reaction was conditioned. Furthermore, the phobia generalized to other white CSs such as a rabbit, a dog, and cotton wool.

Watson and Rayner's intention was to show that phobias such as these originate from a simple classical conditioning experience and not from a psychosexual conflict (which, perhaps, a Freudian theorist would claim was the cause). Although experiments on the acquisition of phobias in humans are rarely done (for the obvious ethical reasons), the vast research using animal subjects seems to provide compelling support for a behavioral theory of phobias. Moreover, when we consider that anxieties are often accompanied by physical symptoms, such as heart palpitations, excessive sweating, and so on, the Pavlovian model of phobias assumes even greater credibility. Emotional as well as physical reactions may be classically conditioned and both combine to provide the full-blown phobia syndrome—irrational fear and physiological symptoms. (A discussion of possible treatments for neuroses is provided in Chapter 3.)

SUMMARY

In this chapter, we discussed classical conditioning—the type of learning in which an association develops between two stimuli because they are presented closely in time. Some claim that Pavlovian conditioning represents a basic building block for more complex learning tasks; in any case, it is a major technique for studying associations.

The general method for obtaining excitatory conditioning is the pairing of a conditioned stimulus and an unconditioned stimulus which elicits an unconditioned reflex. After training, the CS itself is able to elicit a conditioned form of the reaction. CRs are also learned when the CS signals no US but the nature of the CR in this case is one of inhibition rather than excitation. Of course, the strength of conditioning is related to a number of environmental factors, including the intensity and duration of both the CS and the US.

The traditional theory of associative learning claimed that the CS comes to substitute for the US. However, more recently, Rescorla has suggested that the function of the CS is to convey information about impending outcomes. Research has supported this latter theory by showing that the CS-outcome correlation is more important than the simple contiguity of the CS-US.

We have also discussed a number of Pavlovian phenomena. Second-order conditioning occurs when a CS that had already been strengthened by being paired with a US serves to condition a second, neutral stimulus. Sensory preconditioning is similar: the two CSs are associated prior to conditioning with one of them; during the test, the other CS, the one never paired with the US, is also able to elicit the CR. Latent inhibition is the retardation of learning due to CS-only preexposure; presumably the preexposure causes the subject to stop attending to the cue. Inhibition of delay is observed when a long CS is used. Specifically, the subject temporarily inhibits the response until just prior to the US presentation. Finally, the autoshaping literature shows that disk pecking by pigeons really is a Pavlovian CR and not a voluntary response that is strengthened through instrumental reward.

We ended this chapter with a discussion of how Pavlovian conditioning is pertinent to several important human behaviors. First, research has shown that rather specific internal reflexes can become conditioned. These CRs could form the basis for psychosomatic illness. Second, it is widely believed that phobias are classically conditioned; the irrational fear stems from the conditioning of a CS and a traumatic US.

3/ Instrumental Conditioning

Preview

This chapter is about an entirely different technique for training behavior—instrumental conditioning. It differs from classical conditioning in that the organism actively participates in the conditioning process; the award of a US depends on what the subject does. There are four basic types of instrumental training procedures: *reward*, where a positive US follows the behavior; *omission*, where the positive US, such as food, is omitted if the animal makes the designated response; *avoidance/escape*, where an aversive stimulus is terminated or avoided by the response; and *punishment*, where an aversive US follows the designated performance. In all these designs, the notion of *reinforcement contingency* is paramount. Contingency, in this context, means that the reinforcement presentation is contingent on the prior execution of the response, that is, it is withheld until after the response occurs. We shall also look at some of the more important factors that affect learning of instrumental behaviors, especially the schedule of reinforcement. And finally, we shall discuss how the concepts of instrumental conditioning have been applied to a number of complex human concerns such as the programming of instructional material and the treatment of certain behavior disorders.

INTRODUCTION

We suggested in Chapter 2 that classical conditioning represents a fundamental type of learning. There is another conditioning model, *instrumental conditioning*, that may also reflect a basic learning process or simple unit of learning on which more complex behaviors are based.

Have you ever seen one of the popular dolphin shows at Sea World or some other aquatic zoo? The dolphins perform their incredible tricks for the sake of a small reward. This type of learning clearly differs dramatically from the reflexive conditioning described in Chapter 2. We do not know for sure whether classical and instrumental conditioning involve separate and distinct learning processes or whether they are merely different demonstrations of a single process. Nevertheless, instrumental learning procedures provide an important and different perspective in the study of learning.

Definition of Instrumental Conditioning

Like classical conditioning, instrumental conditioning is defined operationally; that is, the paradigm specifies a set of general procedures for producing learned behavior. Instrumental conditioning occurs when a strong stimulus (i.e., a US) is contingent on the subject's response. The experimenter must wait until the subject has made the designated response before administering the US. In this respect, the subject's behavior is not independent of the presentation of stimuli, as in classical conditioning. Instead, the subject, whose behavior is *instrumental* in obtaining the US, is an active participant in the experiment.

THORNDIKE'S EXPERIMENT

Basic Procedure

The discovery of instrumental learning is often attributed to Thorndike (1898) although, in reality, the procedures we now identify as instrumental conditioning have been utilized for centuries. Thorndike, however, was the first person to explore the paradigm, systematically and in depth, in the light of the emerging traditions of American functionalism and behaviorism. In doing so, he was able to suggest a number of laws which formed the basis for a new learning theory. Thorndike also became an important influence in education because of his interest in basic learning phenomena.

Thorndike's original procedure was very simple and it has served as the prototype for all subsequent research in instrumental conditioning. He put hungry cats in a cage, the door of which had a latch on the inside. When they were in the cage for the first time, the cats made a number of responses (which Thorndike thought were random responses), including scratching at the walls and the door. Sooner or later they hit the latch (the "correct" response) which opened the door and allowed them access to food. When this procedure was repeated several times, Thorndike observed that the time the subjects required to manipulate the latch after they were put in the cage decreased with each successive trial. This time interval between the start of the procedure and the correct response is called the *response latency*. Correspondingly, the number and duration of each extraneous behavior also decreased with training. In other words, the subjects had learned to execute, quickly and efficiently, a single response which was instrumental in letting them obtain food.

Terms

The terms used to designate the events in instrumental conditioning are generally the same as those in Pavlovian conditioning. The US is the reinforcing stimulus, usually a biologically important stimulus such as food. However, any stimulus that changes the probability of the instrumental response when made contingent on that response may be termed a reinforcer. In instrumental conditioning, the US may produce a UR but it does not necessarily have to do so; in fact, the Pavlovian URs in instrumental conditioning are rarely measured. Thus, a reinforcing US in instrumental conditioning is defined a posteriori, in terms of its effect on the learned response, rather than a priori, relative to its ability to elicit a classical UR.

The CR in instrumental conditioning is the learned response. Usually it is an arbitrary and voluntary motor response, such as pressing a lever in a box, that is designated by the experimenter as being correct. Here the difference between instrumental and classical conditioning is more significant. The CR is nearly identical to the UR in classical conditioning; the type of response that can be learned in classical conditioning is necessarily restricted by the type of UR that is elicited by the US. On the other hand, the designated CR in instrumental conditioning is not limited to the UR, although the CR must reflect the physical capabilities of the subject; given those constraints, the range of CRs that can be conditioned is broad.

Finally, instrumental conditioning experiments may or may not involve an explicit CS. In Thorndike's original study, no obvious and intentional CS was presented, but in other situations, explicit stimuli are given. However, unlike Pavlovian conditioning, the contiguity between the instrumental stimuli and the rewarding US may vary greatly because the CS-US interval depends on when the subject chooses to respond in order to produce the US. More specifically, an S+ (called a "discriminative" stimulus) is a neutral cue that precedes the CR. It indicates to the subject when reinforcement is available; that is, the S+ is a signal that tells the subject when response will elicit reward. In contrast, an S− may be compared to a Pavlovian conditioned inhibitor in that it signals to the subject when reward is unavailable, that is, when it is appropriate *not* to respond.

FIGURE 3-1.

Phases in instrumental conditioning: Initial performance of R_1—R_N in the environmental context S_1—S_N (A); acquisition of a general S-R bond (B); acquisition of a specific S-R bond (C).

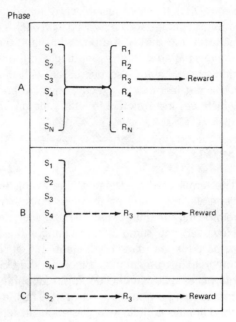

Principles

The fundamental principle in instrumental conditioning is reinforcement contingency. The probability or frequency of a designated CR will increase only if its execution is required to produce the reinforcing stimulus. Such an increase in performance reflects learning. If the US availability is not dependent or contingent on the CR, no improvement in performance will take place.

The principle of reinforcement contingency may be conceptualized as shown in Figure 3-1. First the subject is put into an environment denoted in the figure by S_1 to S_N. Most of these stimuli are not specified by the experimenter; they are the environmental context, both external and internal, in which the experiment is conducted. During the initial phase of training (phase A), the subject makes a variety of responses, only one of which is consistently followed by the reward.

After a sufficient number of rewarded trials, a bond develops between the stimuli and the CR such that when the subject again is introduced into the environment, the stimuli evoke the previously rewarded behavior (Phase B in Figure 3-1). Conversely, if extinction procedures follow the formation of the S−R bond with no reward given for the CR, then the stimuli will gradually cease to evoke the response.

The S-R bond may be more specific, as Phase C in Figure 3-1

shows. If an explicit S+ is provided (say, S_2), then that cue consistently signals the availability of reward; as a result, it is later able to evoke the response.

Implicit in the above discussion is the notion of stimulus control. When a specific S-R bond is strong compared to other bonds, that is, when one stimulus reliably evokes the response but others do not, then the subject's behavior is said to be controlled by that stimulus. Stated differently, stimulus control, the ability of a specific cue to evoke the CR, demonstrates the strengthening of one S-R bond relative to others.

Covariation of Classical/Instrumental Designs

The reason a stimulus acquires the ability to control or evoke behavior is that it is correlated with the availability of reward. Conversely, an S− may come to control nonresponding for much the same reason: the cue consistently signals no reward. The notion of stimulus-outcome correlation, therefore, is essential to the strength or power of the stimulus.

This is basically the same conclusion we reached in Chapter 2: Pavlovian CSs acquire strength because of their correlation with a specific outcome. Although the behavior of the subject in instrumental conditioning intercedes between the discriminative stimulus and the US, an S-outcome correlation does exist. In other words, in instrumental conditioning, the exact timing of the S and US is not fixed because the subject must voluntarily make the CR at any time after the S but prior to the US, yet a general correlation between the stimulus and reward is still present.

It should be clear from this discussion that discriminative cues in instrumental conditioning experiments also function as Pavlovian CSs. By signaling the availability of reward, and, accordingly, controlling the behavior, they are implicitly paired with the US. Stated another way, classical conditioning procedures which involve the presentation of two stimuli independent of the subject's behavior are always present in instrumental conditioning experiments; it is impossible to conduct a "pure" instrumental learning experiment without, at the same time, the presence of Pavlovian S-US pairings.

Incidentally, the opposite claim also seems justified, at least in most cases: in classical conditioning experiments, the subject's behavior may affect the US presentation and produce a more or less rewarding outcome as it does in instrumental conditioning. Therefore, it is very difficult to conceive of a "pure" Pavlovian experiment without some intrusion of an instrumental contingency. For example, in Pavlovian experiments using a shock US, postural adjustments on the part of the subject might minimize, to some degree, the intensity of the shock and therefore be instrumentally rewarded. Similarly, in salivary studies, the dogs may learn certain postural responses to avoid spilling the food US.

In summary, Pavlovian pairings are always present in instrumental experiments and instrumental reinforcement contingencies are usually involved in Pavlovian designs. The fact that the two types of conditioning procedures occur together so frequently makes it exceedingly difficult to judge whether one or two separate and underlying learning processes are involved.

TYPES OF INSTRUMENTAL CONDITIONING

Before we go on to discuss the nature of reward and the various factors which influence instrumental learning, it would be useful to clarify briefly the four major categories of instrumental conditioning. As Figure 3-2 shows, the designs are classified according to the outcome of the CR (production or prevention of the US) and the type of US (aversive or appetitive).

Reward Training

The most common type of instrumental conditioning is reward training. Here, the response produces a positive reinforcement which is usually an appetitive stimulus such as food. Many situations are used in the laboratory to study reward training. The typical lever press apparatus shown in Figure 1-1 is one of the most common. Other situations include mazes and alleyways. All these experimental arrangements presumably are analogs for a vast number of everyday situations, from teaching circus tricks to animals to rewarding prosocial behavior in children.

Reward training, of course, may be conducted with a variety of positive USs, not just biologically related stimuli like food. Praise, sensory stimulation, and social approval all may be strong reinforcers for some responses (see below for discussion).

FIGURE 3-2.

Types of instrumental conditioning based on the consequence of the CR and the type of US.

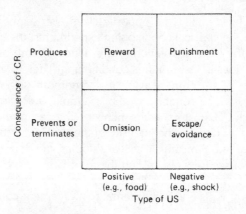

Omission

Omission training has not been investigated as extensively as other types of training. It is defined as the situation in which the response precludes a positive, or appetitive, reward. The subject is rewarded foɪ not responding but is not reinforced for making the previously trained CR. The effect of omission training is opposite to that of reward training and the subject gradually stops performing.

In some respects, extinction procedures are a form of omission training. During extinction, the US is withheld following the response, thus causing a gradual reduction in CR strength (see Chapter 5). However, extinction usually entails the complete withdrawal of the reinforcement contingency whereas omission training usually involves rewards for non-responding.

One study which compared the effectiveness of extinction with omission techniques in suppressing a well-learned response was done by Uhl and Garcia (1969). First, they trained rats to press a lever at a relatively high and stable rate. Then they gave either extinction or omission procedures to separate groups of subjects for three days. For the extinction subjects, none of the lever presses were ever followed by reinforcement; for the omission subjects, reward was given after a certain period of time only if no lever press was executed during that time. In other words, if the omission subjects refrained from lever pressing for a certain period of time, they eventually received the food reward; however, if they made a lever press during the omission period, reward presentation was delayed even further. The third phase of the experiment consisted of reestablishing the lever press through contingent reinforcement; here, the authors were interested in evaluating the permanence of the suppression caused by the prior omission and extinction procedures.

The results of the study indicated that suppression of lever responding was less rapid with omission procedures than with extinction. According to Uhl and Garcia, the reason for this finding was that conflicting habits developed in the omission subjects: the presentation of food during the initial training had become a S+ for additional lever responding. Since that event always had signaled reinforcement availability, it came to control the behavior. During omission training, the animals were learning not to respond (responses resulted in no reward for a certain time period) yet when reward eventually was presented, the tendency for the food to evoke additional lever pressing counteracted the suppression caused by the omission procedure.

The second finding in this study was that resumption of lever pressing was slower following omission training than it was after extinction. The authors theorized that extinction had resulted in the cessation of responding without the acquisition of specific alternative behaviors. Therefore, those subjects merely had to relearn the lever press. The omission subjects, on the other hand, had learned specifically *not* to lever press; during relearning, they not only had to relearn the previous habit of lever pressing but they also had to overcome their newer habit of not pressing the lever. In a sense, the omission procedure had taught the subjects to "resist temptation" when they were later confronted with the availability of reward through lever pressing.

Another technique that involves omission of reward for responding is *time-out* (see Coughlin, 1972; Leitenberg, 1965). Time-out is a period during which the lights in the experimental chamber are turned off and reinforcement is unavailable. Often, time-out is given following a response to the S−. In general, it has been found that time-out periods suppress responding. Suppression is greater with longer time-out periods (Ferster & Appel, 1961; Kaufman & Baron, 1968), with more frequent time-outs per response (Thomas, 1968), and with more immediate time-out periods (Carlson, 1972). In addition, it has been shown that time-out periods are aversive to the subject in the same way that a noxious punishment such as shock is aversive. For example, subjects will learn to terminate the time-out period if they are allowed to do so (Kaufman & Baron, 1966).

Punishment

The third basic method in instrumental conditioning is punishment, where the response produces an aversive stimulus such as shock. The effect of contingent punishment is to suppress responding. As with reward training, punishment may be preceded by a discriminative stimulus which signals periods during which punishment will be given following the response (see Chapter 4 for a more detailed account of punishment).

Escape/Avoidance Learning

The fourth basic procedure in instrumental learning is escape/avoidance. In escape training, a noxious stimulus is presented which the subject may terminate by executing the correct instrumental response.

Avoidance learning is similar to escape but with one important difference: the subject is able to avoid the noxious stimulus altogether. Usually a warning stimulus is given for a few seconds prior to the noxious US. If the subject makes the response during this cue, the stimulus is turned off and the US (e.g., shock) is omitted for that trial. If an avoidance response is not made, that is, if the subject fails to respond during the signal, then the shock is presented and the subject is allowed to make an escape response. Therefore, the early trials in an avoidance experiment typically involve escape responses; however, as the subject learns that the S+ signals the onset of shock, avoidance responding begins to occur with some regularity during the S+.

A somewhat different avoidance procedure is called Sidman or free-operant avoidance. No explicit warning signal is used in this paradigm; rather, a shock pulse is programmed to occur at fixed time periods if the subject sits passively. However, if the subject makes a response (the temporal interval itself is an S+), the timing apparatus is reset and presentation of the next scheduled shock pulse is delayed. By responding at a high enough rate, or by consistently responding just before shock is to be delivered, the subject may postpone, and thus avoid, shock indefinitely. The free-operant procedure, therefore, involves continuous avoidance behavior, measured in terms of rate of responding, rather than discrete trials for which speed of response is the index of learning.

NATURE OF REWARD

It is clear that a contingent reward produces an increase in performance of an instrumental response. This statement, however, is merely a description of an empirical fact; it makes no reference to underlying mechanisms for learning, to possible causes for the change in performance, or to the conditions under which the learning can be predicted a priori. A number of psychologists have attempted to account for instrumental learning in theoretical, or even physiological, terms. Several of these systems are considered below.

Thorndike was the first major theorist to speculate about the nature of reward. He proposed that responses were "stamped in" or strengthened because reinforcement was satisfying to the subject. Conversely, habits were gradually eliminated by punishment because punishment was annoying. These two terms—"satisfaction" and "annoyance"—were, in a sense, the mechanisms by which reward and punishment operated; they defined the nature of reward and punishment.

A more formalized statement about instrumental learning was contained in Thorndike's law of effect. This law stated that when a response was followed by a satisfying state of affairs (one that the subject tried to obtain), it became stronger and, therefore, tended to be repeated in the future. The negative law of effect dealt with punishment: a response that was followed by an annoying state of affairs (one that the subject avoided) became weaker and tended to be suppressed.

Although the empirical relationship between responses and reinforcers was clear, Thorndike's law of effect, based on the "mechanism" of satisfaction and annoyance, was never strongly influential with later theorists. The main reason was that the terms satisfaction and annoyance were subjective and were not specific or operational; the nature of reward was not clarified in the least by the assignment of such labels.

Drive/Need Reduction

A more successful attempt to specify the mechanism underlying reward was made by Hull (1943). First, it should be noted that in Hull's basic system performance was attributed to the joint interaction of two variables:

habit and drive. *Habit* referred to the S-R bond, the strength of which was determined by the number of reinforcements. Generally, habit accounted for the direction of behavior, the specificity of the response given an appropriate stimulus context. *Drive*, on the other hand, referred to the biological need conditions of the subject; it was defined operationally in terms of hours of food or water deprivation, intensity of shock, and so forth. The function of the concept drive was to account for the energy or impetus behind responding, the motivation of the subject toward action. Thus, Hull's system contained both a learning component (habit) and a motivational component (drive), with performance resulting from the interaction of these two factors.

Returning now to the nature of reward, Hull believed that any stimulus that reduced drive (or need) was reinforcing. In other words, a response or habit was strengthened by a US when that stimulus resulted in the reduction of drive. Hull's theory seemed to account for many, if not most, of the typical cases of instrumental learning; the presentation of food or water, for example, reinforced an instrumental response in hungry or thirsty subjects.

Although Hull actually did not make a strong distinction between drive and need, the most compelling support for his position was the demonstration that learning could take place when the reinforcing stimulus reduced the need directly. Coppock and Chambers (1954) conducted such a study. Hungry rats could move their heads to interrupt a photoelectric beam. The experimental subjects were trained to make a head turn to one side in order to be infused, directly into the vein, with glucose. The controls received the same training except that their reward was physiological saline (placebo). The need or drive reduction theory, of course, predicted that the experimental subjects would learn this response because glucose restores the nutrition balance but the control subjects would not because physiological saline has no appreciable effect on the body. Coppock and Chambers confirmed this prediction: over the course of three 30-minute training periods, the experimental subjects performed the head-turning response at a significantly higher level than the controls. Similar experiments, in which an injection of milk directly into the stomach taught rats to make a correct turn in a T-maze, were done by Miller and Kessen (1952).

Although the results cited above provided strong support for Hull's drive (need) reduction theory, there is now sufficient evidence to question the theory; in fact, most theorists believe that the nature of reward is far more complex than the need reduction theory implies. Many of the studies that are contrary to Hull's position have shown that reinforcement may occur even when no biological need is reduced (see Eisenberger, 1972, for a review). For example, it is well known that saccharin can reinforce instrumental behavior even though it cannot reduce biological need because it is nonnutritive (e.g., Sheffield & Roby, 1950). Kish (1955) found that mice would press a lever merely to turn on a light. Similarly, it has been shown that monkeys will learn a response in order to be able to look from their cages into the colony room (Butler, 1953), and that rats will make a correct turn in a T-maze to gain access to a complex environment (Montgomery, 1954). All of these studies suggest that biological need reduction is too limited a mechanism to explain all instrumental learning.

Recently, the drive reduction position has been modified in several ways to meet the challenge of many of these findings. The essential and common element in most of these modified theories is that organisms have an exploratory drive. That is, organisms need to maintain an appropriate level of stimulation (just as they need to maintain proper nutrition) even though their immediate, biological health is not in jeopardy (Fiske & Maddi, 1961; Glanzer, 1953, 1958). Alternatively, it has been suggested that organisms develop a "boredom" drive that, like hunger, goads them into action; the boredom drive presumably is reduced when the subject explores, that is, changes the environment by making a response (Myers & Miller, 1954).

There is substantial evidence to support these theories. For example, many experiments have shown that a period of sensory deprivation increases the tendency of subjects to seek stimulation. Fox (1962) placed monkeys in a lightproof box for 0, 1, 2, 3, 4, or 8 hours. Then, during a test period, he presented a .5-second light each time a monkey pressed a lever in the box. The results of this experiment are shown in Figure 3-3. Responding, averaged over the four 15-minute observation periods, increased as a function of the length of time the subjects were light deprived. Fox concluded that an exploratory drive had been enhanced by deprivation and, therefore, that this effect was analogous to the hunger drive. Similar results have been obtained by other investigators using rats (e.g., Fowler, 1967) and hamsters (Schneider & Gross, 1965).

The assumption that animals get bored and consequently seek stimulation, or that they have an exploratory drive, provides far more latitude and flexibility than Hull's original formulation. Nevertheless, many recent

FIGURE 3-3.
_____

Mean lever responses for a .5-second light as a function of hours of light deprivation.

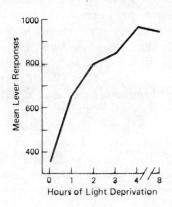

theorists are still very cautious in accepting this extension. First, several experiments have failed to demonstrate the relationship shown by Fox (1965) between length of sensory deprivation and responding (e.g., Haude & Ray, 1967). More importantly, the nature of an exploratory or boredom drive itself is somewhat ambiguous. Therefore, theorizing that an exploratory drive reduction is the mechanism by which light onset affects performance in a sensory deprived subject is simply to name the phenomenon rather than to explain it.

In summary, the drive reduction theory has been one of the more important and enduring accounts of the nature of reward. Although much of the research using nonbiological reinforcers (e.g., opportunity to explore or initiate sensory change) is compatible with the general drive reduction position, further evidence is required. Unfortunately, few alternative theories have been proposed that successfully integrate the vast literature on reward.

Physiological Theories

In recent years, many learning psychologists have attempted to explain the nature of reward in physiological terms. The impetus for this research was an important paper by Olds and Milner (1954). First, they implanted tiny electrodes of thin wire in the brains of rats. Once in place, the electrode was permanently fixed to the skull and head surface by a special cap. Rats who underwent this routine surgery were in no discomfort and were able to function normally in every respect for many months. The purpose, of course, of implanting an electrode was to be able to stimulate particular regions of the brain electrically and then observe the changes in behavior that were caused by activating those regions.

Following the recovery from surgery, Olds and Milner placed the rats into a testing cage containing a lever and delivered a brief, extremely mild pulse of current to the implanted electrode after each lever response. They found that the rats were reinforced by the brain stimulation; that is, the rate of lever pressing increased dramatically. Olds and Milner, therefore, concluded that they had located a "pleasure center" since the subjects responded vigorously to obtain the stimulation.

The self-stimulation phenomenon has been replicated in hundreds of studies; it is found in a wide variety of species (from fish and birds, to dogs and rabbits, to humans) and the effect of the stimulation is extremely potent. For example, Olds (1958) demonstrated that rats will perform thousands of responses per hour, until they are physically exhausted, in order to produce the stimulation.

Many investigators have explored thoroughly the anatomical locations and biochemical agents of the phenomenon (e.g., see Olds & Olds, 1963; Olds, 1969). Briefly, they have found that the brain areas critically involved are the medial forebrain bundle, a fiber tract traveling through the midbrain, the hypothalamus, and the septal regions. One biochemical agent that seems to be involved is norepinephrine, a substance which mediates the transmission of neural impulses (see Stein, 1969), although other transmitters likely are involved.

Although Olds and Milner (1954) stimulated the reward system directly, theoretically all stimuli that reinforce an organism do so because they activate these same centers of the brain. Therefore, the important point for the present discussion is that Olds and his colleagues were able to locate the anatomical substrate of reward; that is, they identified, in specific physiological terms, the mechanism underlying the reinforcement process. What is implied, of course, is that the stimuli we find pleasurable (i.e., reinforcing), from pats-on-the-back, to sexual gratification, to ice cream sodas, are pleasurable or reinforcing *because* they ultimately involve the stimulation of the reward centers in the brain.

Predictive Theories

A third category of theories in learning concentrates on the prediction of behavior rather than on the specification of underlying mechanisms of reward. Skinner (e.g., 1950) has long advocated that the proper focus for learning research is the investigation of functional relationships between manipulations of the environment and performance. According to this point of view, prediction and control of behavior can be achieved without speculation about internal mechanisms (e.g., reward sites in the brain) or theoretical processes (e.g., drive reduction). Thus, an entire tradition has developed within the area of learning that is devoted to the study of functional relationships on a descriptive, as opposed to a theoretical, level. The outcome of this collective effort has provided an important perspective in learning research as well as a wealth of valuable phenomena and principles.

One problem with this general approach, however, is that often one cannot predict in advance whether a stimulus will function as a reinforcer. Unlike the drive reduction and physiological positions discussed previously, where a stimulus could, in theory, be identified as a reinforcer before an actual test of that fact, the Skinnerian approach, because it makes no assumptions about the underlying nature of reward, cannot easily predict a reinforcement relation. However, several theories that stem from the Skinnerian tradition are able to make such predictions. These theories make no reference to the underlying nature of reward but they do specify certain principles that are critical to a reinforcement relation.

The most successful predictive theory was formulated by Premack (1959, 1965); it involves two basic principles. First, Premack asserted that a subject's total activity pattern can be analyzed in terms of component activities. That is, in a given environment with no restrictions placed upon access to the various activities, the subject will engage in most, or perhaps all, of the activities a certain percentage of the time. For example, in a cage containing a lever, a running wheel, light, and food, a rat probably would respond periodically to each activity over the course of an observation period. If the rat were deprived of food, eating would predominate when food became available whereas if the animal were deprived of illumination (as in the Fox, 1962 study), time spent attending to the light might prevail.

The implication of Premack's argument is that the percent of the total time in which the subject engages in a given activity reflects both the probability of that activity and, correspondingly, the preferability of the activity. Clearly, the assignment of preferability does not depend on the number or type of activities; rather, the preferability of any given response may be calculated relative to the available options. In the example given above, a satiated animal may spend 30 percent of its time eating, 60 percent running in an activity wheel, and 10 percent lever pressing; conversely, a hungry rat may eat for 70 percent of the test, run for 15 percent, and lever press for 15 percent. In each case, the percentage values reflect the preferability of the activity.

The second principle in Premack's system relates to the reinforcement relationship which always involves two behaviors. Specifically, a more preferable activity will reinforce the performance of a less preferable one if access to the preferred response is made contingent on execution of the less preferred activity. In the typical situation, eating (a highly probable activity for a hungry animal) will reinforce lever pressing (a less preferable activity) if the subject's access to food is contingent on the lever response.

Premack's theory has considerable predictive power. All that is required to predict whether a stimulus (or the activity related to that stimulus) will be reinforcing is to estimate its preferability relative to some other response. For example, in one study, Premack (1963) observed rats for a series of 600-second sessions during which the subjects had the opportunity to run in a wheel weighted either 18 or 80 grams or to drink either a 16, 32, or 64 percent sucrose solution. From the last four sessions, Premack computed a probability for each activity (time spent engaging in the activity divided by 600 seconds).

Following this procedure, Premack positioned a lever in the cage and required the rats to press it three times in order to release the brake on the activity wheel or to gain access to the drinking tube. The results of this phase are shown in Figure 3-4. Lever pressing performance was positively related to the preferability of the reinforcing activity; although access to an 18-gram wheel (probability of about .275) reinforced lever responding, being able to drink a 32 percent sucrose solution (probability of about .4) was more effective. Thus, the strength of the reinforcement relationship depended on the probability of the reinforcing activity.

An interesting and important feature of Premack's system is that reinforcing stimuli are defined in relative terms. The reinforcement value of an activity is not limited to a certain class of behaviors (e.g., activities that reduce biological needs). The implication is that any activity could reinforce any other behavior provided that the probability of the reinforcing activity was greater. Premack (1961) clearly demonstrated this by showing that the usual reinforcement relation could be reversed. Specifically, he

FIGURE 3-4.

Mean lever responses when each of the five activities, differing in preferability, were made contingent on lever pressing.

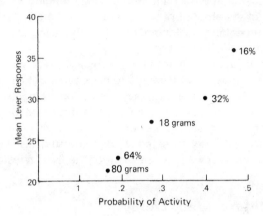

rationed either water or access to a running wheel. When the rats were deprived of water, the preferability of drinking increased and, correspondingly, drinking reinforced running when made contingent on running. Conversely, when the subjects were deprived of access to the wheel, the reinforcement relation was reversed: wheel running (now the more preferable activity) reinforced drinking.

Although Premack's theory does not speculate about the underlying nature or mechanism of reward, it does suggest both a procedure for predicting, a priori, a reinforcement relationship and it indicates an essential principle underlying this relationship, namely the contingency of a probable response on a less probable behavior.

FACTORS IN REWARD CONDITIONING

The principles of learning extend well beyond the simple notion of reinforcement contingency. The following sections give an account of many of the important environmental factors which influence reward learning. (See Chapter 4 for a discussion of the parameters affecting escape, avoidance, and punishment.)

Reinforcement Magnitude

Many experiments have indicated that reward learning is positively related to the size of the reinforcement (e.g., Kintsch, 1962; Meltzer & Brahlek, 1968; Roberts, 1969) as well as the quality of the reward (e.g., sucrose concentration, Kraeling, 1961). For example, in the Kintsch study, rats were rewarded with .25, 1.75, or 3.5 cc water for traversing an alley. Although the performance of all three groups improved with training, both the rate of improvement and the final running speed increased as a function of the amount of water received. The effect of reward magnitude in instrumental conditioning, therefore, is analogous to the effect of US magnitude in Pavlovian conditioning.

An interesting result was obtained recently by Essock and Reese (1974). Pigeons were taught to peck either of two disks to obtain access to grain. Pecks on one disk produced a fixed amount of reward (i.e., a fixed duration of access to the grain) while responses to the other disk produced a variable amount of reward (the average duration equaling the fixed duration). Under these conditions, the subjects showed a preference for the variable reward rather than for the fixed reward.

Reinforcement Delay

The degree to which reinforcement is delayed is an important factor in reward learning; this parameter is analogous to the CS-US interval in classical conditioning. Generally, performance is inversely related to reward delay; even small intervals between the response and reinforcement lead to substantial decrements in performance (see Renner, 1964; Tarpy & Sawabini, 1974, for reviews).

Many investigators have tried to specify the exact relationship between performance and delayed reinforcement. Although most of the studies have confirmed that the relationship is a graded one, the extent of the gradient has differed. One early study by Wolfe (1934) found that rats could acquire the correct turn in a T-maze even when the reward was withheld for two minutes. Later research, in contrast, found that delay gradients extended to only about 30 seconds (Perin, 1943) or even five seconds (Grice, 1948).

This issue is an important one: the delay gradient specifies how long a response trace can exist before it must be acted on by a reinforcer. (A response trace is the declining level of neural activity resulting from a response.) In other words, the extent of the delay gradient defines the time limits for strengthening an S-R bond by a reinforcer; the US must be presented within those limits if it is to be effective.

One reason for the discrepancy in the gradients noted above is that in some situations, subjects can "bridge" the delay by utilizing existing cues as sources of information. For example, certain apparatus cues (e.g., in the goal box) eventually are paired with reward; then, during the delay interval, they operate as temporary, surrogate rewards or as sources of information signaling to the subject that the reward is pending. If such cues occur naturally in the experiment (as in the Wolfe study) or if they are explicitly presented during the delay interval (e.g., Tombaugh & Tombaugh, 1971), then performance improves dramatically. In contrast, when precautions are taken to minimize the impact of these cues or secondary reinforcers (e.g., Grice's, 1948, study), performance is debilitated by delays of even a few seconds. In summary, performance is related to delay in a graded fashion but the extent of the gradient is only a few seconds. In some cases, where cues that are associated with reward occur during the delay interval, the subject utilizes these cues as rewards or as sources of information about reward and can thus tolerate much longer delays.

Delay of reinforcement has a variety of effects on behavior. One study of how delay affects discrimination learning was done by Carlson and Wielkiewicz (1972). Four groups of rats were taught to press one lever in the presence of a tone and a different lever during a clicking sound. Subjects in the No Delay condition were immediately rewarded after each response while those in the All Delay group received a 5-second delay after each lever press. In the Random Delay condition, the subjects received a 5-second delay on half of the trials (the trials were determined randomly) whereas the delay for the Correlated group was given consistently following one, but not the other, response.

The results are shown in Figure 3-5. Delay following both responses retarded discrimination learning relative to the No Delay condition. However, the more interesting comparison is between the Correlated and Random groups. Although subjects in both groups received the same number of delayed rewards, those in the Random group performed as poorly as

FIGURE 3-5.

Mean percent correct responses over 30 training sessions for the four delay conditions.

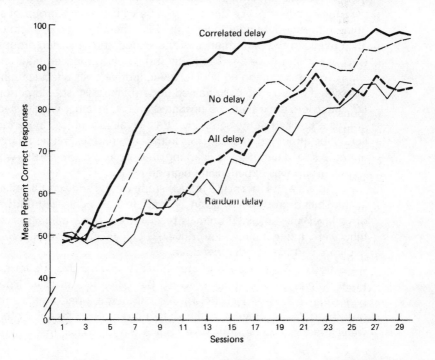

the All Delay subjects while rats in the Correlated group learned the discrimination faster than the No Delay subjects. The study, therefore, confirms that delay generally retards discrimination learning (also see Culbertson, 1970). However, when the subject can reliably use the delay interval itself to predict pending reward (as in the Correlated group) performance, paradoxically, is improved beyond the level of a No Delay condition.

Drive Level

A third important variable in reward learning is the drive level of the subject. You will recall that drive is the motivational impetus for responding; in learning research it is usually defined in terms of the operations which produce the underlying need state, for example, hours of food or water deprivation (see Weinstock, 1972). Many studies have shown that the stronger the motivation, the better the performance (e.g., Pavlik & Reynolds, 1963; Zaretsky, 1965).

In Hull's (1943) theory, drive served simply to energize the existing current habits but otherwise was independent of learning. However, recent evidence indicates that drive does more than simply energize behavior. Apparently, habits learned under high drive—when the subjects are very hungry or thirsty—are stronger than those learned under a lower motivational level. This has been demonstrated in a number of experiments (e.g., Eisenberger et al., 1973; Capaldi, 1971; Capaldi & Hovancik, 1973) that trained subjects under high drive, tested them under low drive, and compared their performance under low drive with that of a group of subjects trained throughout under low drive. Hull's theory would predict no difference between the performance of the shifted and unshifted groups; drive level would not have affected habit and so performance under low drive should be uniform and equal. However, if drive does affect learning, then the shifted group, originally trained under high drive, should perform better under low drive than the unshifted group. In other words, since both groups are tested at the same low drive level, differences in performance cannot be attributed to differences in the current drive; rather they must be attributed to differences in learning that occurred previously when the shifted group was experiencing high drive.

Capaldi and Hovancik's (1973) study clearly showed this effect. Rats in the shifted group were given 34 trials in a straight alley under a high drive level; the unshifted animals received the same training except that they were trained under low drive. Then, all the subjects received an additional 34 trials under low drive.

The results of this study are shown in Figure 3-6. Performance in Phase 1 was strongly influenced by the difference in drive level (note performance at P1 in Figure 3-6). More important, performance throughout Phase 2 was superior in the shifted group even though both groups were under the same drive level. Since the difference in running speed

FIGURE 3-6.

Mean speed of running to goal area for the shifted and unshifted groups on the last day of Phase 1 (P1) and sessions of Phase 2. One trial was given on sessions 1 and 2, two on session 3, and 3 on the remaining sessions.

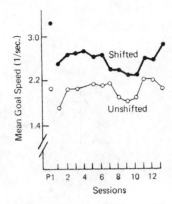

could not be attributed to the drive level in Phase 2, it must have reflected a difference in habit strength acquisition that occurred in Phase 1.

Performance in instrumental learning, then, is a positive function of drive level. Furthermore, there is ample evidence that drive affects learning. It is possible that habit is strengthened by high drive, or that subjects learn qualitatively different habits under different motivational conditions (e.g., see Logan, 1956).

Incentive

While the principal motivational construct in Hull's system was drive, subsequent research indicated that a second source of motivation, incentive, was also important to behavior (see Bolles, 1967).

Incentive refers to the motivational properties of reward objects; that is, reward not only strengthens an S-R bond, it also motivates performance. For Hull, drive was momentary, based on a biological need; drive "pushed" or goaded the subject into action. In contrast, incentive is learned; it is an enduring state based on the subject's past history with reward. Incentive "pulls" or entices the subject toward the goal object. Therefore, although both drive and incentive energize or motivate behavior, drive is a primary source based on need whereas incentive is a secondary source based on learning. In everyday language, we could say that we are goaded by hunger (drive) but lured or enticed by an ice cream cone (incentive); either way, our behavior is being energized.

Evidence that a reinforcing stimulus may energize behavior was obtained by Marx and Murphy (1961). Two groups of rats were trained to poke their noses into a small hole to obtain food. A buzzer was paired with

FIGURE 3-7.

Mean start box latency for the experimental and control subjects on extinction trials 1-14.

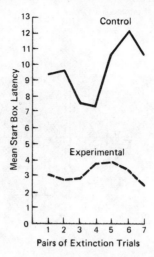

Pairs of Extinction Trials

food for one group (Experimental) but not for the other group (Control). In part two of this study, 20 acquisition trials were given in an alley followed by extinction; from trial 16 of acquisition on, the Pavlovian CS (buzzer) was presented when the rats were placed in the start box.

As illustrated in Figure 3-7, the times that elapsed before the rats began to run—the start box latencies—for the Experimental group were much shorter than for the Control subjects. This result indicated that the new behavior, running in the alley, was energized by the Pavlovian CS. In other words, by being contiguously associated with food in the first phase of the study, the buzzer acquired incentive properties; later it was able to enhance the motivation for running. Differences in performance on the running task were clearly due to differences in incentive since the drive (deprivation) and learning (reward) parameters at that time were the same for both groups.

The incentive concept was an important feature of Spence's (1956) theory. The mechanism for its operation, which Spence developed, is diagrammed in Figure 3-8. As acquisition proceeds (Phase 1), the stimulus complex (stimuli S_1-S_N) comes to elicit the CR of running; the start box, arbitrarily noted as S_3, is particularly important in this regard. In addition, the goal box, S_G, is classically paired with reward. In other words, two processes are occurring: the start box becomes an S+ for the instrumental running response while the goal box is a CS that is paired with reward and, presumably, acquires the ability to elicit a Pavlovian CR such as licking or salivation.

The motivational effect operates as shown in Phase 2. When the subject is placed in the start box, the goal box stimuli generalize to the start box and a fractional component of the goal response (r_g) is elicited. This

FIGURE 3-8.

Diagram of the r_g—s_g mechanism. In Phase **1**, S_3 comes to control R while S_G is paired with reward. Later, in Phase 2, R is elicited by both S_3 and s_g.

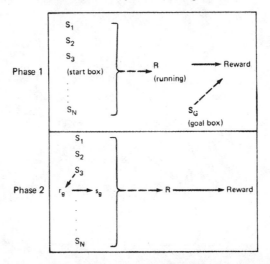

occurs because the start box, S_3, is similar to the goal box, S_G. The fractional r_g response, in turn, generates an internal feedback stimulus (s_g). It is this element, the s_g, that becomes an added part of the overall stimulus complex. Stated differently, after a Pavlovian CR has developed, the start box, which is a generalized stimulus, elicits an r_g – s_g sequence; as a result, the directive, eliciting, or controlling properties of the stimulus complex are enhanced. The running response is now elicited both by the start box and by internal feedback.

Contrast Effects—Reward Magnitude

According to the concept of incentive, the differential effects on performance of the magnitude of the reward, discussed previously, are due to differences in motivation. Evidence for this is found in studies on *contrast*. Contrast is the term for what occurs when a subject learns a behavior under one set of reward conditions and is then switched to a different level of reward. In a typical experiment, two groups of subjects are trained to make a response for a small reward while two more groups are given a large reward. Once the behavior is stabilized, one group in each of the reward conditions is shifted to the alternate reward magnitude; the other group in each condition continues with the same reward size. As illustrated in Figure 3-9, performance in the shifted groups changes appropriately: the subjects who are shifted from low to high improve while performance in the subjects shifted from high to low deteriorates. The more important result is that the shifted subjects tend to overshoot the level of the control

FIGURE 3-9.

Hypothetical data showing positive and negative contrast. The shift in reward magnitude occurs at arrow.

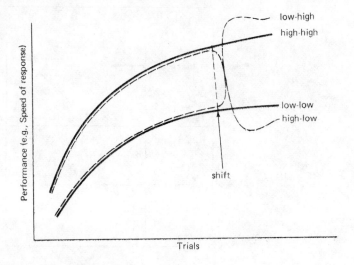

groups. That is, after the shift, the low-high subjects perform even better than the high-high group and the high-low animals are worse than the low-low subjects. The positive contrast effect is the tendency to overshoot and the negative contrast effect is the tendency to undershoot (see Dunham, 1968, for a review).

Two main characteristics of the contrast phenomenon indicate that the performance changes are caused by an incentive motivational change. First, the over- and undershooting per se must be due to differences in motivation. The alternative explanation would postulate differences in learning, yet the low-high group clearly could not have a stronger habit than the high-high group, and similarly, the high-low group cannot be "unlearning" their habit relative to the low-low controls. Second, the positive and negative contrast effects occur very rapidly (often after a single trial), far too quickly to be accounted for in terms of additional learning (for the low-high condition) or gradual unlearning (for the high-low group).

It is puzzling that, following the original demonstration of contrast by Crespi (1942), many studies have *not* shown positive contrast (e.g., Di-Lollo, 1964; Spear & Spitzner, 1966). Black (1968) concluded that positive contrast was in fact not a reliable phenomenon and he developed a theory to account for this discrepancy based on the interaction of excitation and inhibition. Bower (1961), on the other hand, claimed that the problem was merely an inability to demonstrate positive contrast due to a ceiling effect: performance of the high-high subjects was already at near-maximum level; therefore overshooting by the low-high subjects would not be expected to occur due to the physical limitations on response speed. In other words, Bower speculated that positive contrast might indeed occur

FIGURE 3-10.

Mean number of licks per minute for 32% or 4% sucrose as a function of averaged sessions.

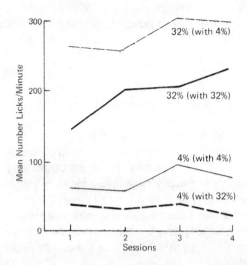

yet remain undetected if subjects in both the low-high and high-high conditions were at their maximum level of performance.

Recent evidence appears to confirm, in part, Bower's hypothesis. For example, Marx (1969) successfully demonstrated positive contrast by using a much larger reward differential to enhance the shift in incentive. Another technique used by Mellgren (1971, 1972) and Shanab, Sanders, and Premack (1969) to avoid the problems of a ceiling effect was to train all groups with a delayed reward. The overall performance level for the subjects, therefore, was reduced, and when the shift in reward magnitude was given, performance of the low-high subjects overshot the level of the high-high animals. Finally, measures other than running rats in an alley have been used to assess changes in reward magnitude. Flaherty and Largen (1975) allowed rats to drink a sucrose solution daily for six minutes from two bottles. The bottles were alternately presented, once per minute. For one session in four, both bottles contained a solution of 32 percent sucrose, highly preferred by the rats; on another session, the solutions were a 4 percent concentration (less preferable); and on two of four sessions, one bottle contained a 4 percent concentration while the other contained a 32 percent solution.

Flaherty and Largen measured the mean number of licks per minute on each bottle. As shown in Figure 3-10, the subjects generally responded more to the 32 percent solution than to the 4 percent solution. However, the rate of licking the 32 percent sucrose was higher when the contrasting solution was 4 percent than when it was 32 percent, i.e., compare the 32 percent (with 4 percent) condition with the 32 percent (with 32 percent) condition. This finding clearly demonstrated positive contrast. Of course, negative contrast was found as well. The drinking rate of the 4 percent solution was lower when the contrasting fluid was 32 percent, i.e., 4 percent (with 32 percent) condition, than when the alternative fluid was 4 percent, i.e., 4 percent (with 4 percent) condition.

In summary, both positive and negative contrast appear to be reliable phenomena, although the demonstration of positive contrast often requires special procedures.

Contrast Effects—Reward Delay

Positive and negative contrast illustrate the fact that reward has motivational properties. In the studies discussed above, the important characteristic of reward which proved to be an underlying dimension of incentive motivation was reward magnitude. However, another defining characteristic of reward is its immediacy of presentation. Many investigators have postulated that incentive should vary inversely with reward delay. Their prediction is that positive contrast should occur when the delay of reward is reduced while negative contrast should be observed when delay is increased.

Results of studies in which the delay of reward was shifted are not entirely consistent with the above prediction. Although most of the experiments have successfully demonstrated negative contrast (i.e., subjects in a short-long group perform worse after the shift in delay than the long-long controls) none has shown positive contrast (e.g., Beery, 1968; McHose & Tauber, 1972; Shanab & Biller, 1972). In the Shanab and Biller study at least, the demonstration of positive contrast was not precluded by a ceiling effect. Their findings led Tarpy and Sawabini (1974) to question the role of delay of reward in relation to magnitude. The belief that both delay and amount are underlying parameters of incentive implies that positive contrast would be obtained in both cases. However, the fact that positive contrast appears following shifts in magnitude but not following shifts in delay could mean that delay and amount of reward are not different components of a single incentive state.

SCHEDULES OF REINFORCEMENT

Perhaps the most important influence on instrumental conditioning is the reinforcement schedule. Most of the literature discussed in previous sections dealt with continuous or 100 percent reinforcement of a discrete instrumental response. However, the schedule of intermittent reward deserves separate treatment for two reasons. First, it has a profound and intricate impact on the rate and probability of behavior. Second, complex behavior in a natural setting is rarely reinforced for each response. Think a moment, for example, of the many rewards we constantly experience in our environment. Only a few are ever made on a continuous, regular basis. Most occur intermittently—once a month, as with a pay check, or after a variable number of days, as with a letter from a friend, and so forth. Even such "reliable" rewards as candy or soda from a vending machine occasionally fail to appear when we deposit our money; they too are delivered according to an intermittent schedule of reward. Delineating the pattern and frequency of intermittent reward is integral to understanding the factors that control our behavior.

There are four basic types of reinforcement schedules. For two of them, ratio schedules, reward is based on the number of responses the subject makes; for the other two, interval schedules, a response is rewarded after a certain period of time has elapsed. Ratio and interval schedules are further classified according to whether the number of responses or the interval of time required to produce a reward is fixed or variable.

Fixed Interval Schedules

Under a fixed interval (FI) schedule, the subject is rewarded for a response after a fixed period of time has elapsed. Clearly, the most efficient behavior for the subject would be to wait until the interval had passed and then make a single response to earn the reward. However, subjects normally respond at a higher rate although the rate is lower than under the other three types of schedules.

The most salient response characteristic under an FI reward schedule is that the rate is a positive function of reward immediacy. After the subject has received the reward, the rate of response is extremely low; in fact, there are appreciable pauses in responding. As the availability of the next reward draws closer in time, the response rate gradually increases to a maximum until just before the reward. Schneider (1969) reported that the length of the postreinforcement pause is related both to the length of the FI requirement (longer intervals between rewards produces longer pauses) and to the degree of training (after extended experience with the schedule, long pauses followed by the rapid resumption of a high rate are observed).

Several investigators have tried to explain this pattern of responding under an FI schedule. One hypothesis (see Dews, 1962; Morse, 1966) is that the strength of the response depends primarily on the response-reward interval. Responses made early in the FI sequence are more remote from reward than responses given later. The strength of these early responses, then, is less compared to later responses which are more immediately reinforced.

A more successful explanation of the change in the FI response rate is that the subjects learn to discriminate (although somewhat imperfectly) the temporal interval. Early in the interval, the temporal discrimination is relatively easy since the probability of additional reinforcement is lowest right after the reward. However, as the next scheduled reward draws closer in time, an exact discrimination gradually becomes more difficult and an increase in response rate occurs.

This theory has considerable support. It is known, for example, that pigeons and rats are able to make accurate temporal discriminations (e.g., Reynolds & Catania, 1962; Tarpy, 1969). Moreover, as discrimination increases with training, the postreinforcement pause also increases (Schneider, 1969). Finally, several studies (e.g., Kello, 1972) have shown that after merely exposing a subject to FI reward, without requiring a response, the typical postreinforcement pause is observed later when the subject is allowed to respond on an FI schedule. This finding strongly suggests that the FI pattern of responding was based upon a temporal discrimination acquired prior to the test.

Fixed Ratio Schedules

Under a fixed ratio (FR) schedule, the subject must execute a fixed number of responses before receiving reinforcement. The overall rate of responding is markedly higher than under an FI schedule although with very high FR values, the performance often deteriorates. The ability to tolerate a low-payoff ratio schedule depends upon the type of subject: FR-10 (reward after ten responses) appears to be optimal for a rat while FR-50 is best for pigeons.

The response pattern for an FR schedule is similar to that for an FI schedule in that marked pauses are observed immediately following reward. Felton and Lyon (1966) showed that the length of the pause was related directly to the FR requirement. Pigeons responding on an FR-25 schedule stopped pecking for about 1.5 seconds after each reinforcement but, when under a FR-150 schedule, they paused for nearly a minute.

The fact that pauses occur is somewhat paradoxical since the availability of the next reward depends not on the passage of time, as with an FI schedule, but on the speed of responding. There is no advantage for an animal to pause from the viewpoint of earning a reward sooner. However, with an FR schedule, the first few responses are never followed by reward; that is, the period of time immediately after reward is never associated with the subsequent reward. Therefore, responding declines due to a temporal discrimination much as it does under an FI schedule of reward (see Neuringer & Schneider, 1968).

Variable Interval Schedules

The variable interval schedule (VI) is similar to the FI with one major difference: the length of the interval between periods when reinforcement is available varies. The value stated for the VI schedule is the mean of these periods. Thus, for a VI-.5 schedule, the average length of the interval between rewards is 30 seconds although the actual intervals experienced by the subject may vary from 10 to 50 seconds.

The rate of responding, under a VI schedule, is a direct function of the rate of reinforcement. In a study by Catania and Reynolds (1968), subjects were given 61 reinforcements per session; the average VI length varied from 12 to 427 seconds. The authors found that the rate of responding increased as a function of the rate of reinforcement. Most of the subjects were making about 60 to 100 responses per minute under the VI-.2 schedule (300 reinforcements per hour) but the rate dropped to about 20 to 70 responses per minute for the VI-7.1 schedule (8.4 reinforcements per hour).

Catania and Reynolds (1968) also found that the rate of responding increased somewhat between reinforcements. Postreinforcement pauses were not observed but, for all subjects, rate increased to a maximum just before the next reward.

The reason for these variations in rate, in terms of differences between schedule means as well as within a given schedule (i.e., local changes from one reinforcement to the next), is related to the probability of reward. The probability that a given response will be reinforced increases as time passes. Therefore, a temporal discrimination is linked to changes in probability and the result is a change in response rate. For an FI schedule, the temporal discrimination is relatively easy and the increase in rate, as a function of the constant increase in reward probability, is dramatic. However, for VI schedules, the temporal discrimination is more difficult and the increase in response rate, as a function of the average increase in reinforcement probability across time, is lower.

Variable Ratio Schedules

The fourth basic schedule is a variable ratio (VR). Here, the subject must execute a given number of responses before reward is presented but the actual number varies. The VR schedule is noted by the average number of responses. For example, an animal may obtain reward, on the average, after 10 responses but the actual requirements may range from 1 to 20.

The response rate under a VR schedule characteristically is high (higher than the other three basic schedules) and stable. Unlike with the FR schedule, a postreinforcement pause is not found although if the VR requirement is very high, subjects will stop responding for short periods of time (see Ferster & Skinner, 1957).

Theory of Ratio and Interval Schedules

Ratio and interval schedules differ in several important ways. First, the overall rate of responding is lower for interval schedules than for ratio schedules. The reason for this stems from the relationship between the response and reinforcement rates. For interval schedules, the rate of response actually does not affect the immediacy of reward presentation; the reward is scheduled for a particular time regardless of how rapidly the subject responds prior to that point. In contrast, reward may be earned more quickly under a ratio schedule if the subject chooses to respond at a high rate.

A second difference between interval and ratio schedules is that the transition from continuous to intermittent reward is much easier if the intermittent schedule is an interval, rather than a ratio, schedule. The reason for this difference is related to the changes in probability of reward as a function of time of responding. For interval schedules, the probability that a response will be rewarded increases over time; a low response rate, therefore, is associated with a high reinforcement-per-response payoff. In other words, if the subject responds slowly when first confronted with an intermittent schedule, the probability is very high that any given response will result in reward. Even a single response is sufficient provided that the interval requirement has been met. The fact that the probability of reward per response is very high, of course, strengthens responding.

For ratio schedules, the situation is different. The probability of reward increases with each response rather than with time. Slow responding under ratio reward only prolongs the increase in reward probability.

Several hypotheses have been proposed to explain the rate differences between interval and ratio schedules. One of these suggested that responding is influenced by frequency of reward: a high rate, as found, for example, with a ratio schedule, is maintained because it produces a high reward frequency. This explanation, however, has been largely discredited by Killeen (1969). In that study, one subject was reinforced under an FR schedule (either FR-25, -50, -75, or -100) while a response by a second subject was rewarded only after the first subject had earned a reward. Thus, the reward for the second subject was administered according to an interval schedule. The important point of the experimental design was that both subjects, the ratio and interval animals, received the same frequency of reward but the nature of the response requirement differed.

Killeen found that the ratio schedule produced a much higher rate of responding than the interval schedule; in fact, the rate of the FR subjects was almost twice that of the interval subjects. Therefore, the study clearly showed that frequency of reward is not the feature of the schedule that controls response rate.

The theory that appears to be a better explanation of response rate concerns the differential reinforcement of interresponse time (IRT). For an interval schedule, the reinforcement probability increases with longer IRTs. Therefore, a rate that is characterized by long IRTs would be selectively reinforced. Dews (1969) has shown this to be the case: IRT values just prior to reward were relatively long, and conversely, short IRTs were never followed by reward.

The situation is the reverse for ratio schedules. Here, the probability of reinforcement increases as a function of short IRTs and, therefore, short

IRTs are selectively reinforced. The fact that subjects can learn to respond with a particular IRT value has been confirmed by Shimp (1967).

Other Schedules

It is possible to design a great many complex schedules and most are a combination of one or more basic schedules. For example, a concurrent schedule is when the subject can make two responses; different schedules pertain to each response and the subject is free to respond according to either or both schedules (see Catania, 1966). Normally, subjects respond to both schedules, maintaining the characteristic patterns (e.g., rate, pauses) usually found for each schedule.

Other complex schedules involve only one response but a sequence of more than one basic schedule. For example, under a compound schedule, the subject must fulfill two requirements, as, say, 10 lever presses (FR requirement) produces a reward only after 1 minute (FI requirement) has elapsed.

An interesting type of schedule is termed the differential reinforcement of low rate (DRL) schedule (see Kramer & Rilling, 1970). Here, the subject must withhold the response until a certain period of time has elapsed. If no response occurs during that time, the next response earns reinforcement. On the other hand, if the subject responds prior to the end of the period, the timing apparatus is reset and the interval begins again. Initially, at least, performance under a DRL is inefficient: the response rate is increased due to reward, then suppressed by omission procedures, causing fluctuations and occasional bursts of responding. Later, however, responding becomes more stabilized.

An interesting characteristic of DRL performance is that the animals engage in collateral behavior between responses; they may assume various idiosyncratic postures or show reactions such as nuzzling the food cup, sniffing, or even tail-chasing (Laties et al., 1965). Some evidence has suggested that this collateral behavior mediates the DRL period; that is, the collateral behavior constitutes a chain of reactions in a continuous sequence leading up to and controlling the rewarded response (Laties et al., 1969).

APPLICATIONS FOR INSTRUMENTAL CONDITIONING PROCEDURES

The ultimate purpose in studying learning phenomena in lower organisms such as rats and pigeons is to generate basic principles that apply to more complex human behaviors. The work in instrumental conditioning has been particularly successful in this regard (but see Chapter 7). Numerous investigators have shown that important human behaviors may be altered through reinforcement contingencies; often this conditioning has resulted in behaviors that are more useful or adaptive to the individual. Several areas in which reward contingencies have been applied to human responding are discussed below.

Verbal Conditioning

According to some theorists, verbal utterances may be viewed as responses not unlike skeletal motor behavior (but see Chapter 7). Therefore, it should be possible to modify vocal responses with instrumental conditioning methods. Indeed, several investigators have demonstrated that vocalizations can be conditioned in organisms such as the cat (Molliver, 1963) and in humans (e.g., Greenspoon, 1955).

In the Greenspoon experiment, the subjects were asked to "say all the words you can think of" but not sentences. For some groups of subjects, plural nouns were reinforced by the experimenter saying "mmm-hm" or "huh-uh"; control groups were not given this reinforcer. Greenspoon found that the frequency of speaking plural nouns increased in the experimental subjects relative to the controls. Furthermore, there was some evidence that this conditioning took place without any awareness of the reinforcement contingency on the part of the subjects. Other studies, however, have questioned this latter result by showing that subjects are able to report their awareness of the contingency if they are questioned in the proper way (e.g., see Verplanck, 1962).

Control of verbal behavior has been demonstrated in other settings. Several studies, for example, have shown that the frequency of vowel utterances may be influenced by VI and DRL reinforcement schedules in the same way that skeletal behavior in lower organisms is controlled by those schedules (Lane, 1960; Lane & Shinkman, 1963).

Finally, verbal conditioning techniques have been used to improve the fluency of speech in stutterers. For example, Flanagan, Goldiamond, and Azrin (1958) punished instances of stuttering with the contingent presentation of a loud noise. They found that during the period of response-contingent punishment, the frequency of stuttering declined. Although stuttering behavior was resumed at a high rate after this treatment, the implication is that permanent improvement could be achieved with a longer treatment period.

In summary, the work cited above suggests that many complex human behaviors may be modified by reinforcement contingencies (see Holz & Azrin, 1966; Krasner, 1958 for reviews of verbal conditioning) and that these changes may reflect an integral part of normal social interaction.

Biofeedback

The discussion above has focused on a global human behavior—verbal utterances. Within the last decade, however, there has been considerable interest in exploring the degree to which other response systems, namely, internal autonomic behaviors such as heart rate, GSR, blood pressure, and the like, can be controlled by instrumental reward contingencies. These research programs all have used the so-called "biofeedback" technique: the procedure of rewarding the subject following the execution of the appropriate autonomic response. In the case of humans, the contingent reward often has been praise, money, avoidance of shock, or information concerning the correctness of the behavior; for lower species, a variety of rewards has been employed including food, shock avoidance, and pleasurable brain stimulation.

The vast number of studies have shown that visceral, or autonomic, responses can, indeed, be modified with instrumental conditioning techniques. For example, one important study was done by Crider, Shapiro, and Tursky (1966). College students were fitted with a device for measuring electrodermal activity (i.e., electrical potential on the palm). Then, each subject was instructed to "recall and actively think about situations in your life in which you have felt especially emotional" (p. 21). During the next 30 minutes, reinforcement procedures were in effect. Specifically, one group of students was presented with a tone (the reward) each time an electrodermal response was made; the control group received the same tone but on a noncontingent basis. The tone was expected to function as a reinforcer since all the subjects were told that they would receive five cents each time it was sounded.

As illustrated in Figure 3-11, conditioning was clearly evident. The control subjects, who did not experience the response-reward contingency, showed a decline in electrodermal activity over the testing period; such a change is the normal pattern of behavior in this situation. The contingent subjects, on the other hand, maintained their original level of electrodermal activity due to the contingent reward.

Two points should be noted. First, subsequent studies by Crider et al. (1966) indicated that the instructions "to think emotional thoughts" were in no way critical to the conditioning effect. Indeed, many experiments have demonstrated instrumental autonomic conditioning in humans who were told merely to "keep the light on," and in lower species who, obviously, could not be influenced by verbal instructions. Second, conditioning has been demonstrated many times with the other basic instrumental paradigms, namely, escape/avoidance, punishment, and omission training.

The widespread interest in biofeedback in recent years has been on two levels. First, there has been a theoretical interest in the finding that autonomic functions can, indeed, be modified by instrumental conditioning procedures. Traditionally, it was believed that involuntary responses such as heart rate and GSR were subject only to classical conditioning procedures. After all, it was hard to imagine how these behaviors could be performed voluntarily in order to achieve an instrumental reward. Some psychologists suspected that conditioned visceral behavior really was a by-product of skeletal movement (e.g., Katkin & Murray, 1968). Specifi-

FIGURE 3-11.

Mean spontaneous skin potential responses as a function of 5-minute intervals for the contingently rewarded and noncontingently reinforced subjects. Response level at "R" indicates the initial resting level.

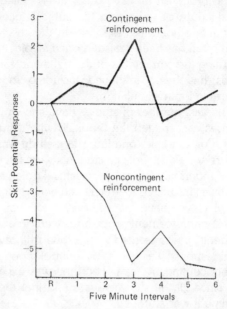

cally, skeletal behaviors could be getting conditioned instrumentally; these behaviors, in turn, might be reflexively producing the autonomic responses. Of course, it was well accepted that skeletal behaviors can be controlled by instrumental rewards and that such behaviors can change visceral functioning (e.g., muscle tension increases heart rate). Other psychologists (e.g., Crider et al., 1969; Miller, 1969) took the opposite position: instrumental reward was acting *directly* to change the autonomic responses; visceral changes were not a by-product of conditioned skeletal behavior. Although this debate continues in some quarters, it now is generally recognized that instrumental autonomic conditioning does, in fact, involve skeletal movement (see Black & DeToledo, 1972; Miller & Dworkin, 1974; Schwartz, 1975). In other words, it has not been conclusively proven that the contingent instrumental reward acts *directly* to condition visceral behaviors.

The conclusion about theory stated above does not, of course, deny either the finding that instrumental autonomic conditioning can be achieved in the unconstrained subject or the potential importance of that finding. In fact, the second major impetus for research in biofeedback has been the potential for treating medical symptoms. For example, if blood pressure could be modified through instrumental reward training, perhaps seriously hypertensive patients could learn to lower their blood pressure and thus allay the threat to their general health. To date, a great number of symptoms, such as hypertension, headaches, cardiac arrhythmias, and so forth, have been treated with biofeedback techniques but, unfortunately, the promise of a rapid and lasting therapy remains unfulfilled (see e.g., Blanchard & Young, 1973; Schwartz, 1973). In many of the attempts, a statistically significant change in autonomic functioning was achieved but the change was not clinically meaningful. That is, the improvement in visceral functioning was either too small or too transient. For example, some investigators have found marked improvement in the laboratory (e.g., Benson et al., 1971), but often the patients were unable to maintain control over their visceral responding when living in the hectic and rapidly changing environment outside the laboratory (e.g., Schwartz, 1973). In summary, biofeedback is an important area in learning from both a theoretical and practical viewpoint. Although the earlier claims for biofeedback appear to have been somewhat premature, future research may indicate with greater clarity the proper theoretical and practical utility of biofeedback training.

Programmed Instruction

The principle of reinforcement contingency has been applied to many other behaviors, including classroom performance. Skinner (e.g., 1958) had a major impact on both educational philosophy and practice when he suggested that academic training could be improved by instituting instrumental procedures in the classroom. The result of his efforts was the advent of programmed learning materials and the somewhat more structured "teaching machine."

The basic tenet of this approach is that if one can identify the correct responses, the concepts and facts to be learned by the student, then appropriate reinforcement can be given, explicitly and efficiently, when those responses are made. Thus, a programmed text divides the material into small, discrete units often posed as questions. The student's task is to anticipate the answer: if the answer is correct, it is immediately confirmed (rewarded); if the answer is incorrect, the student is allowed to review or begin again. Since each small step in a programmed text is easy, the student experiences a high rate of success (reinforcement) and proceeds to new material only after mastery is achieved.

The teaching machine is simply an apparatus for the automated presentation of programmed units. Usually, several buttons are provided which correspond to alternative answers. If the correct button is pushed, the student is rewarded by the machine's advancing to the next unit.

Programmed materials have been extremely successful in many cases and although programmed learning may not improve retention, it does appear that the time required to master programmed material is reduced relative to other conventional techniques (see Nash et al., 1971, for a review).

A more recent innovation (Keller, 1968) has been the programming of an entire course. Here, the overall material is reduced into discrete units, such as a textbook chapter, and study guides which identify the important concepts of the unit are used. After mastering the unit, the student may volunteer for a quiz. If successful, the student continues to the next unit; if not, the proctor gives immediate feedback (diagnosis of the strengths and weaknesses of the student's work on the quiz) and the student is allowed to try again. Since no penalty is levied for failing a quiz, the student may proceed at any pace, making sure that all the material in one unit is mastered before going on to a new unit.

This personalized system of instruction is now common in many schools and some research has indicated that students enjoy and learn more when this teaching method is used (e.g., McMichael & Corey, 1969). The reason for this success, as with teaching machines, is that each student is an active participant and that a contingent reward for correct performance is abundantly and efficiently utilized.

Behavior Modification

Instrumental conditioning procedures have been applied to larger segments of human behavior. Some of these efforts have involved the management of classroom behavior such as disruptive behavior or study habits (see O'Leary & Drabman, 1971, for a review). Generally, the method used in these programs is the systematic and frequent awarding of prizes and rewards for correct responding. In one study, for example (O'Leary et al., 1969), the elementary classroom teacher was instructed to ignore disruptive behavior and to praise good behavior. This procedure proved to be only moderately successful. However, when good behavior was rewarded with a token (exchangeable for candy), disruptive behavior declined markedly.

The token reward method, as well as other instrumental procedures, has been applied to so-called abnormal behavior. Since the literature on behavior therapy is voluminous, only a brief discussion is presented below (see Krasner & Ullmann, 1965; Franks, 1969; and Lazarus, 1971, for reviews).

According to behavior therapists, abnormal behaviors are not unique; the principles by which they are acquired and eliminated are the same as those principles that apply to other behaviors. The therapist's task, therefore, is to identify the behavior, extinguish it, and attempt to recondition a more adaptive substitute behavior. It should be emphasized that behavior therapists treat maladaptive behavior per se; they don't consider possible internal states such as "id," "will," or "superego," which do not lend themselves to objective analysis.

A study by Kushner (1965) involved a patient who had developed a phobia about cars after an auto accident. In the therapy session, the person, while deeply relaxed, was asked to visualize a car. When the patient could do this without discomfort, the therapist required the visualization of more explicit images until gradually the patient was able to cope with the visualization of the accident itself. As a consequence, anxiety was extinguished, and the person later was able to resume a normal pattern of behavior, including driving an automobile.

In another example reported by Barrett (1962), the patient was afflicted with multiple tics: contractions of the neck and chest muscles, blinking, opening of the mouth, and other facial movements. First, the patient was seated in a chair that had special sensing devices for the detection of even small muscle movements. Then, during the treatment phase, pleasant music was turned off (omission training) and a noxious noise was turned on (punishment) whenever the patient's tics were sensed by the apparatus. The results were very encouraging: over a number of sessions, the frequency of this maladaptive behavior subsided dramatically.

Behavior therapy techniques also have been used to treat psychotic patients. In one important study, Ayllon and Houghton (1962) extinguished, in schizophrenics, dependent eating habits (the tendency to require spoon-feeding) by providing food only to those patients who came to the dining hall for dinner. At first, the patients could obtain food for a 30-minute period but later this period was reduced. The success of the program was remarkable: after a period of several weeks, virtually all of the patients were feeding themselves.

Ayllon and Houghton extended their work to include the training of social cooperation. In order to be admitted to a meal, two patients simultaneously had to press separate buttons. By successfully cooperating at this task, each was awarded a token which permitted access to the dining hall. Not only did the patients learn this simple behavior, but the frequency of verbal exchanges with nurses and other patients increased as well.

In conclusion, behavior therapy has become an important concept and tool in the area of mental health treatment. Although the techniques are relatively new, their success is well documented. Of interest here is that the principles underlying behavior therapy stem directly from the findings in the laboratory on instrumental conditioning, particularly the concept of reinforcement contingency.

SUMMARY

Instrumental conditioning occurs when an important outcome, usually a rewarding US, is contingent on the behavior of the organism. The particular type of instrumental learning may vary: in reward conditioning, an appetitive US is presented following the criterion response whereas in omission training, the reward is explicitly withheld when the behavior is executed. In escape/avoidance, the subject may terminate or avoid the presentation of a noxious US whereas punishment involves the presentation of an aversive stimulus contingent on the subject's response.

We know a fair amount about how reward learning is affected by environmental factors including the reward magnitude, delay, and schedule. However, we know much less about the underlying nature of reward. Some have postulated that reward occurs whenever a biological need is fulfilled; others have suggested that reward actually culminates in the stimulation of certain "pleasure centers" in the brain; still other theorists have devised systems for predicting reward relationships without attempting to say why they work.

We noted in this chapter that the concepts of instrumental conditioning are integral to many complex human behaviors. For example, we can condition general behaviors such as verbal utterances or more specific behaviors such as changes in heart rate or blood pressure. In addition, instrumental conditioning techniques may be used to modify other human behaviors of considerable importance. Thus, teaching machines (or programmed learning techniques) were devised to facilitate educational instruction, and behavior therapy methods were developed to treat behavior disorders of various kinds.

4/ Aversive Control of Behavior

Preview

Unfortunately, our everyday world involves many unpleasant, aversive experiences; in fact, a good deal of the time and energy of each one of us is directed toward avoiding or reducing painful threats, either physical or psychological, of a great many kinds. This chapter examines the basic research on aversive control—that is, instrumental learning situations in which the subject performs to avoid unpleasant consequences. The basic principles of learning which apply to aversive situations deserve special attention since without an adequate understanding of these principles, unwanted side effects, such as neurosis or physical illness may arise. Although we do not know a great deal about aversive control and its side effects, some patterns are becoming clear. This chapter will describe some of the factors that influence learning under aversive stimulation, the theories that attempt to account for this learning, and the results of studies on punishment and neurosis.

INTRODUCTION

Consider a few of the many behaviors that we normally perform in order to avoid aversive consequences: a child learns not to touch a hot stove—perhaps because of being burned on an earlier occasion; a sunbather applies tanning lotion to avoid a painful sunburn; children may stop jumping on the furniture if they are spanked for doing so; drivers obey traffic signs to avoid automobile accidents. In all these common instances, behavior is functioning to terminate or avoid painful experiences. In fact, it is clear that punishment or the threat of punishment controls behavior on virtually all levels of human interaction, despite the fact that the consequences of punishment are poorly understood.

Because the use of punishment is so widespread, and because we don't have a complete understanding of how punishment works, the research in this area may have enormous potential importance. Obviously this is not an aspect of psychology which can be studied by experimenting upon human beings and thus most of the research has been done with animals—primarily with the rat. It is worth keeping in mind, however, that the importance of the experiments is not how aversive experiences affect the animal subjects, but how the results further our understanding of human behavior.

A clear understanding of the principles that govern behaviors elicited by punishment would be a valuable achievement for psychology. In fact, we might go so far as to say that the future use, if any, of aversive paradigms should be contingent on such an understanding. Johnston (1972) summarized this sentiment: " . . . unconditioned and conditioned punishing stimuli as consequences to behavior delivered by our social and physical environment are as much a natural part of our lives as are positively reinforcing consequences. This being the case, behavioral science should undertake to understand and to control the results of their use" (p. 1051).

Like reward training, which we discussed in Chapter 3, aversive control of behavior represents instrumental conditioning. However, many of the parameters of training and theoretical concepts used to explain aversive learning differ markedly from those of reward training. There are three important designs of this type of instrumental conditioning: escape, avoidance, and punishment.

Aversive control of behavior involves a US that is unpleasant or *noxious*, one that a subject will terminate if given the opportunity. In the case of escape and avoidance training, terminating or avoiding an aversive US by the subject results in the increased probability of the response; that is, subjects are negatively reinforced (negative referring to the quality of the US) for performing the instrumental response. In the case of punishment, the response is suppressed by a contingent, aversive US.

FACTORS IN ESCAPE CONDITIONING

US Intensity

The severity of the noxious US is one of the most important variables affecting escape learning. The stronger the unpleasant US, the greater the improvement in performance, as many studies have shown. Most of these experiments involved a shock US; in fact, this stimulus is used widely in studies on escape, avoidance, and punishment because both the delivery of shock and its intensity can be specified accurately. However, a number of investigators have used escape from cold water (Woods et al., 1964), loud noise (e.g., Bolles & Seelbach, 1964; Masterson, 1969), and intense light (e.g., Kaplan et al., 1965).

An experiment by Trapold and Fowler (1960) demonstrated the effect of shock level on escape behavior. Rats were placed in the start box of an alley and given 29 trials of escape conditioning. When the start box door was raised, rats in separate groups received a footshock of 120, 160, 240, 320, or 400 volts (through a 250-K ohm limiting resistor*) which remained on until they reached the goal box. The authors found that performance in the alley increased over trials in all groups. More important, the final, stabilized level of performance was a direct function of shock intensity: it took the 120-volt animals about 1.4 second (mean time) to cross the 4-foot alley while the 400-volt subjects ran across in about .8 seconds.

Amount of Reinforcement

Escape learning, as it is typically studied, differs from reward training in several ways. One difference is the fact that drive (or, more precisely, the noxious US) is reduced to zero following an escape response; in contrast, the hunger drive is rarely eliminated completely by a single reinforcement in reward training. In studying the effect of reward magnitude in escape learning where the escape and reward procedures are equated as nearly as possible, some investigators have varied the degree of shock reduction. Campbell and Kraeling (1953), for example, trained rats to escape a 400-volt shock (through a 250-K ohm limiting resistor) in an alley. When the subject entered the goal box, the shock intensity was switched from 400 to 0, 100, 200, or 300 volts for separate groups of animals. The subjects received this new shock level for 30 seconds after which they were removed from the goal box and another trial was initiated. Performance was found to be a positive function of the degree of shock reduction: the median stabilized running time for the 400–300 subjects was about 5.2 seconds while the median times for the other groups decreased in a graded

---

*Often volts and resistance in ohms are cited. From these terms, the amount of shock that a subject receives, namely amperes, can be calculated.

fashion with the 400 – 0 subjects making the response in about 1.2 seconds. In summary, escape and reward training do appear to be similar in that greater amounts of reward (percentage of shock reduction in the case of escape) produce better performance.

Contrast Effects

In Chapter 3, we discussed what happens when subjects learn a behavior under one set of reward conditions and are then switched to a different level of reward: the behavior overshoots the performance level of subjects maintained all along on the new reward. These contrast effects have been obtained in experiments on aversive learning too.

However, since drive level and reward magnitude are so intricately related in escape conditioning (a change in one variable inevitably produces a change in the other), contrast effects are difficult to interpret. Either a change in the amount of reward or the drive level (or both) could be operating to produce the shifts in behavior.

In one study by Bower, Fowler, and Trapold (1959), rats learned to escape shock (250 volts through a 250-K ohm limiting resistor) in an alley. For the first 15 trials, shock in the goal box, in which the subjects were confined for 30 seconds after each response, was set at 50, 150, or 200 volts. On trials 16 – 30, the percentage of shock reduction was changed for some groups: goal box shock for the 200-volt group was shifted to either 200, 150, or 50; the 150-volt subjects continued with no change; and the 50-volt subjects were shifted to either 50, 150, or 200.

Several results, shown in the left panel of Figure 4-1, were obtained

FIGURE 4-1.

Left panel: Mean alley speed as a function of blocks of three trials. All subjects received 250 volts in the start box and alley and either 50, 150, or 200 volts in the goal box as indicated in the figure. Right panel: Mean alley speed as a function of blocks of four trials. Subjects receiving .2, .4, or .8 milliamp shock in the start box and alley were shifted to .4 following trial block 5.

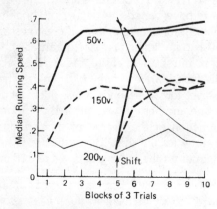
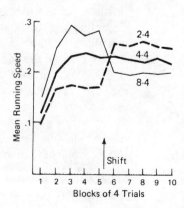

in this study. First, the authors confirmed Campbell and Kraeling's finding that performance was a function of the percentage of shock reduction: on trials 1 – 15, group 50 performed the best followed by group 150; subjects in group 200 showed no improvement over the training trials. Second, when reward magnitude was shifted to another value, rapid adjustments in performance were observed. On trials 16 – 30, all groups that received a given percentage reduction in shock performed at an equal level regardless of the reinforcement conditions on the earlier trials. Third, no over- or undershooting (contrast) was found; this result, therefore, conflicted with the studies on reward training we discussed in Chapter 3.

However, contrast has been observed in more recent escape studies in which the drive level was shifted. For example, in an experiment by Nation, Wrather, and Mellgren (1974, Experiment 1), rats were trained to escape a .2-, .4-, or .8-milliamp shock. After 20 trials, the shock level was shifted to .4 milliamps for all of the subjects and training was continued for an additional 20 trials. The results of this study are illustrated in the right panel of Figure 4-1. The facilitative effect of high drive level on the preshift performance (trial blocks 1 – 5) clearly supports the findings discussed previously. The more important result, however, was the demonstration of both positive and negative contrast: The .2-.4 subjects overshot the control group's performance level whereas the .8-.4 subjects undershot. It appears that escape training is similar to reward learning in that positive and negative contrast effects have been shown in both paradigms. What remains unconfirmed is whether contrast in escape conditioning results from a shift in drive (Nation et al. study) but not reinforcement magnitude alone (e.g., Bower et al. study).

Delay of Reward

A delay in the offset of the US has profound effects on escape performance (see Tarpy & Sawabini, 1974, for a review), with, as we might expect, poorer performance with longer delay. Fowler and Trapold (1962) showed this in a study in which rats were trained to escape shock by running down an alley. As they entered the goal box, they received either 0, 1, 2, 4, 8, or 16 seconds of additional shock (i.e., the offset was delayed). As shown in Figure 4-2, alley performance was negatively related to delay in a graded fashion: whereas performance by the 0-delay subjects was high, performance levels declined as a function of delay, with the 16-second subjects showing little improvement over training.

Very different delay gradients have been found in other studies. For example, Tarpy and Koster (1970) required rats to press a lever to terminate shock. When even a small delay of three seconds was used, no improvement in performance over the training period was observed.

The difference in gradients cited above is probably due to several factors. One is the influence of external cues. Escape performance with delay, like reward training, is dramatically influenced by the presentation of cues

FIGURE 4-2.

Mean running speed in the alley as a function of training trials for the different delay of reinforcement groups.

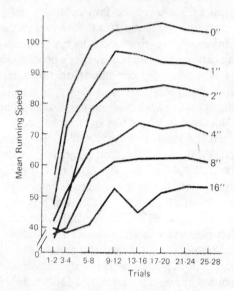

during the delay interval. These informative or rewarding cues are present in the goalbox immediately following the running response in the alley (i.e., they are consistently paired with shock offset, albeit delayed, and thus serve to "bridge" the delay in the temporary absence of shock offset). Such differential reward-assisted cues, however, do not normally exist in the lever press situation although when they are specifically added, performance under delay improves markedly (Milby, 1971; Tarpy, 1969; Tarpy & Koster, 1970).

In summary, delay of US offset debilitates shock escape performance. Rats are unable to tolerate even very short delays, although if reward-related cues are presented during the delay interval, they are able to respond effectively with delays as long as 16 seconds.

FACTORS IN AVOIDANCE LEARNING

Avoidance conditioning has been one of the most thoroughly investigated paradigms in learning research. The purpose of this section is to provide an account of the major factors that influence avoidance behavior.

US Intensity

One of the most important parameters in avoidance conditioning is the intensity of the US. The reason is that the motivational basis for avoidance depends upon the severity of the US. The obvious prediction is that avoidance learning, like escape behavior, would be positively related to US intensity with higher shock levels producing better responding. The actual results, however, are far more varied and complex.

Some earlier studies (e.g., Boren et al., 1959; Kimble, 1955) indicated that avoidance acquisition was, indeed, better with higher shock intensities. More recent experiments, however, have suggested that this relationship applies only to a lever pressing task (or a similar task, such as turning a small wheel, as in Kimble's study). Why the positive relationship between responding and shock intensity holds only for lever responding is discussed more extensively below.

An example of the positive relationship between responding and US intensity is found in a study by Riess and Farrar (1972). These authors used a Sidman avoidance task in which rats could postpone a .15-second, unsignaled shock for 20 seconds by lever pressing; failure to press the lever resulted in shock being delivered every three seconds. Shock intensity was set at .25, .5, 1.0, 2.0, or 4.0 milliamps for separate groups of subjects. The results indicated that acquisition of the lever response improved with higher shock intensity. Although the subjects who received the three highest shock levels performed at a comparable rate (about 5 to 6 responses per minute after eight 1-hour training sessions), those who received the three lowest intensities failed to show any improvement in response rate over training.

The stable, asymptotic level of avoidance performance (i.e., following the acquisition phase) appears to be especially responsive to shock intensity. Riess (1970), for example, used rats that had acquired the avoidance behavior to a minimal degree with a .25 milliamps shock. Each subject then was given additional training with a .5, 1.0, 2.0, and 4.0 milliamps shock. As shown in Figure 4-3, the rate of responding increased as a function of shock level. Although the original acquisition under .25 milliamps was marginal, appreciable responding was observed under the other shock conditions. The relationship, illustrated in Figure 4-3, was especially compelling since the variability in responding between the subjects was quite low. Similar improvements in avoidance following an increase in shock intensity were found by D'Amato, Fazzaro, and Etkin (1967, for signaled shock using rats) and Klein and Rilling (1972, using pigeons).

When we consider the acquisition of other types of avoidance behavior, especially the shuttlebox response, we find that shock intensity has quite different effects from those discussed above. Shuttle avoidance is where the subject runs from compartment A of the apparatus to compartment B, and then back again on the next trial. The general finding has been that shuttlebox performance is an inverse function of shock intensity; higher levels of the US produce inferior responding (e.g., Bauer, 1972; Bintz, 1971; Moyer & Korn, 1964; Levine, 1966). For example, Moyer and Korn (1964) trained separate groups of rats to make a shuttle avoidance response using a .5, 1.0, 1.5, 2.5, 3.0, 3.5, or 4.5 milliamp

FIGURE 4-3.

Mean lever responses per minute during avoidance maintenance as a function of shock intensity.

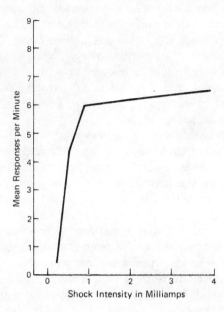

shock. Figure 4-4 shows the mean percentage of avoidance responses executed by each intensity group over the 120 training trials. It is clear that avoidance performance deteriorated at higher shock intensities, a finding that is in opposition to the one shown in Figure 4-3.

The reason for this inverse relationship has been the focus of recent investigations. Moyer and Korn argued that high shock intensities disrupted or disorganized behavior. Their hypothesis, however, appears to be untenable since the same inverse relationship has been found in studies using much weaker shocks (e.g., .2 to .8 milliamps, Levine, 1966).

An alternative theory, proposed by Moyer and Korn (1966) and Theios, Lynch, and Lowe (1966), was that shuttle responding involved two conflicting tendencies: the movement away from the locus of shock on the current trial, and a tendency to refrain from returning to the locus of shock on the previous trial. The reluctance of the subject to return to the compartment in which shock had been given on the previous trial is called passive avoidance. This theory suggests that high shock levels increase the passive avoidance component and thus weaken the performance of the active (running) response.

To test this theory, Theios et al. (1966) varied shock intensity in both a shuttlebox and a one-way avoidance situation. As we said earlier, a shuttle avoidance response is one in which the animal responds in both directions: the rat runs from compartment A of the apparatus to compartment B and then back again on the next trial. In one-way avoidance, however, the

FIGURE 4-4.

Mean percentage shuttle avoidance responses as a function of shock intensity in milliamps.

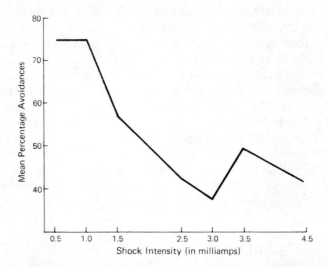

animal runs in one direction only, from the start box (usually painted a distinctive color) to a separate goal box. Then the animal is removed from the goal box and replaced in the starting area for the next trial. Theios et al. confirmed that shuttle performance was inversely related to intensity. One-way avoidance, however, where there was no opposing passive avoidance component to compete with running, improved as a positive function of shock intensity.

The Theios et al. theory has been further confirmed by Freedman, Hennessy, and Groner (1974). Three groups of rats were trained to make a shuttle avoidance response under a high, medium, or low shock intensity. Three additional groups were treated in the same way except that the shock intensity consistently associated with one side of the apparatus differed from the intensity on the other side. The authors hypothesized that the passive avoidance component would be weaker when the response involved moving to a place where the previous shock had always been lower than when the response involved running to a place associated with the same shock level. The hypothesis was confirmed: a subject performed an active avoidance response much better when it was required to run to a chamber associated on the previous trial with a lower shock intensity. That is, the reluctance of the animal to enter the previously shocked compartment interfered with shuttle responding and the degree of the interference was a function of the shock intensity in that compartment.

In addition, several studies have shown that rats respond to apparatus cues associated with shock with freezing or immobility reactions (e.g., Blanchard & Blanchard, 1969; Bolles & Collier, 1976). In these experiments, simply shocking an animal produced the passive avoidance response of freezing when the rat was subsequently placed inside the familiar apparatus, but when it was tested in a different apparatus, the freezing behavior was eliminated.

The two major conclusions discussed above—that shuttle avoidance is impaired by a passive avoidance tendency and that the nature of this tendency is freezing elicited by the apparatus itself—appear to account for the effect of shock intensity on shuttle avoidance learning (but see Chapter 7). When the passive avoidance component is eliminated, shuttle performance and shock intensity appear to be positively related (McAllister et al., 1971; Theios et al., 1966). Therefore, some investigators (e.g., Riess & Farrar, 1972) have suggested that the lever response situation, where the relationship between responding and US intensity is positive to begin with, is probably devoid of this added, passive avoidance component. This notion is plausible since the lever, like the goal box in a one-way avoidance experiment, is a discriminable locus within the apparatus which the animal can associate with shock reduction.

US Duration

The effect of US duration is closely related to that of intensity in that the general aversiveness of a shock US, and thus the overall drive level, depends on both the severity and the length of the US. The relationship between duration and performance has been studied predominantly with a Sidman avoidance since shock duration can be accurately controlled by the experimenter. In other situations, where a continuous shock is used which the subjects must escape following their failure to avoid, the length of the shock varies according to the subject's escape latency.

In general, it has been found that the longer the US lasts, the higher are the rates of avoidance responding. This was shown by Riess and Farrar (1972), who trained rats to postpone a 1.3 milliamp shock by pressing a lever. Failure to do so resulted in inescapable shock presentations (every three seconds), each lasting .05, .15, .2, or .3 seconds for different groups. As shown in Figure 4-5, responding improved over the seven 1-hour sessions for all groups. The rate of improvement, however, was a positive function of shock duration. Therefore, US duration appears to have had the same effect on lever press avoidance as intensity.

CS Intensity

Although relatively few studies have investigated the effect of CS intensity on avoidance learning, the usual finding is that performance improves with more intense CSs. The relationship, however, is a complex one. Bauer (1972), for example, observed that avoidance performance increased with more intense CSs but found this effect only when intense shock was used. In a study by Myers (1962), both the intensity and quality of the CS were found to be important: loud tones were more effective than soft tones but a

FIGURE 4-5.

Mean lever responses per minute over seven training sessions for groups receiving .05, .15, .2, or .3 seconds of shock.

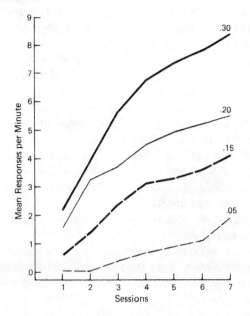

harsh buzzer produced even better responding even though it was less intense than the tones. Finally, James, Ossenkop, and Mostoway (1973) found that more intense CSs improved performance only when the CS increased in intensity. They trained rats to make a shuttle response for which the CS was an increase or decrease in the intensity of white noise. The noise remained on until the next trial, when its intensity shifted to a different value. Thus, the effect on performance of increases and decreases in the CS intensity could be assessed. The authors found that avoidance was not influenced when the changes were a reduction in noise but the avoidance rate improved as a function of the degree of change when the changes were increases in noise.

CS-US Interval

The length of the warning signal prior to shock is an important parameter in avoidance. Low and Low (1962) gave separate groups of subjects either a 2-, 4-, 6-, 8-, or 10-second CS prior to the onset of the US. Although shuttle performance was faster with shorter CS-US intervals, the number of avoidance responses and the rate of learning increased as a function of the CS duration. Presumably, the more time the subject has to respond, the more likely it is to make an avoidance response (but see Bolles et al., 1966; Cicala et al., 1971).

TWO-FACTOR THEORY OF AVOIDANCE

The problem of explaining avoidance learning has provoked more theorizing than perhaps any other single issue in animal learning research. For nearly four decades, the avoidance paradigm has provided the testing ground for large-scale theories regarding the existence of separate instrumental and classical learning processes as well as for more limited theories involving, for example, the principle of drive reduction.

The initial reason for such an interest in avoidance was that the motivational basis for responding and the nature of the reinforcement were not clear. According to Hull's (1943) drive reduction theory (which was widely accepted in the 1940s), the nature of the motivation and reward were intuitively obvious in the case of reward learning: subjects were trained under a deprivation or drive state and the reward reduced this drive state. The situation was equally clear for escape learning: pain from an aversive US motivated the subject and the offset of the US reinforced the behavior which produced the offset. In contrast, the source of motivation and the nature of reward for avoidance conditioning could not easily be identified. On avoidance trials, when the US did not occur, the subject, paradoxically, was motivated. Since the source of drive couldn't be identified accurately, the nature of reward (i.e., the source of drive reduction) was in doubt as well.

Two-Factor Theory

A resolution to this problem was provided in a well-known paper by Mowrer (1947). Basically, he suggested that both classical and instrumental learning contributed to or were involved in the acquisition of avoidance.

During the early training trials, before the subject had learned to avoid the shock (i.e., when the subject was still making escape responses), the CS was being paired with the aversive US. Since this was a clear example of Pavlovian conditioning, the CS acquired the power to elicit Pavlovian CRs. The nature of the CR was not just the motor escape response but also visceral reactions, such as heart rate or GSR, and conditioned fear. In other words, it was reasonable to assume that subjects would react to the CS with fear as well as with increased involuntary physical reactions since the CS signaled the presentation of an aversive event.

The second stage or factor in Mowrer's theory involved instrumental conditioning. During the early portions of avoidance training, he suggested, the subjects were motivated to escape shock and were reinforced for doing so by the offset of the US. Thus, motor responding, initially at least, was a straightforward example of instrumental escape conditioning.

According to Mowrer, the classically conditioned fear state, the first factor, and the instrumentally conditioned escape response, the second factor, combined to produce avoidance behavior. When the animal was given the CS, it became fearful; this was a form of secondary (learned) motivation which energized behavior. The response that was energized the most by fear was the escape reaction since that CR had been strengthened through instrumental conditioning while other responses had not been reinforced. In other words, the dominant escape response was elicited earlier in time (prior to shock) by the fear CS.

The final argument in Mowrer's theory dealt with the nature of the reinforcement for an avoidance response. Stated simply, the avoidance response was motivated by fear (as discussed immediately above) and was reinforced by the reduction of fear.

Mowrer's theory was extremely important. First, it provided an explanation for the source of motivation and reward for avoidance trials. Previous theorists had been unable to identify these elements based on the more conventional reward and escape paradigms. Second, Mowrer's theory suggested that there were two separate learning factors or processes; both were necessary components for avoidance behavior. The classical component, based on CS-US contiguity, accounted for the motivation of avoidance while the instrumental component, based on drive reduction, accounted for the reinforcement of the motor response.

Before reviewing the evidence for and against Mowrer's position, we should discuss Schoenfeld's (1950) modification of the two-factor theory. Schoenfeld objected to the mentalistic language of Mowrer, the imprecise nature of fear and of fear (drive) reduction. He argued that early in avoidance training the CS became aversive through association with the noxious US. Eventually the subjects simply responded to terminate the CS, thereby avoiding shock. For Schoenfeld, then, the avoidance response was actually an escape reaction (i.e. the termination of the aversive CS).

Schoenfeld's version of the two-factor theory was a marked improvement over Mowrer's formulation mainly because it identified more specifically the nature of the avoidance response and the reinforcement. If the subjects were escaping the noxious CS, just as they had escaped the noxious US, then the offset of the CS should be the locus of reward, just as the offset of the US was the reward on shock escape trials. Mowrer's theory predicted instead that the reward was the reduction in fear motivation—an event that could not be specified or measured easily. In summary, Schoenfeld retained the classical component in his theory (that the CS did become aversive and thus energize the escape response), but improved on the general two-factor position by suggesting that avoidance behavior really was an escape-from-the-CS response and therefore that CS offset on avoidance trials constituted the locus of reward.

Supporting Evidence

Evidence supporting the two-factor theory focused on a number of issues. First was the notion that acquired fear motivates or energizes behavior. To test this, Miller (1948) placed rats in the black compartment of a shuttle box and, after turning on a shock, allowed them to escape into the white half of the chamber. After repeating this a number of times, Miller tested to see whether the animals had acquired fear motivation. He installed a small wheel near the door, placed the subjects into the black compartment without shock, and allowed them to rotate the wheel to open the door and escape into the white side of the box. Miller found that the rats learned this new response. Since there was no shock during the test, Miller concluded that fear, aroused by the black box, had motivated the behavior; escape from or termination of the fear CS had been the reinforcement. Miller's experiment indicated that fear could be learned via Pavlovian contiguity (black box paired with shock) and that the fear served as a source of motivation for new learning.

More support for the two-factor theory was the extensive work of Kamin (1954, 1956, 1957a, 1957b) concerning the nature or locus of reward in avoidance learning. In one series of studies, Kamin (1957a, 1957b) hypothesized that if the CS offset were the point at which subjects received reward for their avoidance response, then a delay in that event should attenuate performance. Delay of reward, of course, was known to debilitate learning; thus, if the CS offset was indeed the reinforcing event for avoidance learning, an inverse relationship between CS-offset delay and avoidance performance should be observed.

Kamin trained rats to make a shuttle avoidance response. Separate groups of subjects received either 0, 2.5, 5, or 10 seconds delay in the CS offset following each response. That is, after the animal had crossed into the other compartment, the CS was continued for those periods of time. As illustrated in Figure 4-6, the 0-second delay group performed at a high level, about 90 percent avoidance responding by the end of training. In contrast, delay of CS offset seriously affected the other groups. Whereas a short delay of 2.5 seconds retarded learning somewhat, a 10-second delay precluded improvement in performance altogether. Kamin concluded that the CS offset must indeed be the source of reward for avoidance learning since he obtained the usual delay-of-reinforcement gradient. In other words, the study strongly supported the two-factor theory (and Schoenfeld's modification of that theory) by showing that immediate CS offset was critical for effective avoidance learning.

Conflicting Evidence

Many recent investigations have challenged the adequacy of the two-factor theory, or at least the specific version that deals with the role of the CS and CS offset (see Bolles, 1970; Herrnstein, 1969 for reviews). For example, Sidman (1955) and Keehn (1959) hypothesized that if the CS were aversive, then subjects, if given the opportunity, should learn to postpone the CS. In other words, the animals do use a temporal CS in Sidman avoidance to predict shock presentations and thereby pace their responses in order to postpone shocks efficiently. If the CS were also aversive, the

FIGURE 4-6.

Mean percentage avoidance responses over blocks of 10 trials for the separate groups of subjects receiving a delay of CS offset.

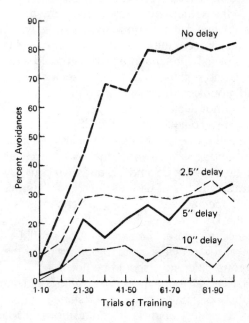

subjects should be motivated to postpone CS onset as well. In each study, however, subjects waited until the CS came on before they responded to postpone the US. They showed no avoidance of the CS itself.

A related series of studies (Bolles & Grossen, 1969; Bower et al. 1965; D'Amato et al. 1968) dealt with the nature of the CS offset. The basic design of these experiments involved three groups of subjects: one was given normal avoidance training with the response producing immediate CS offset. For a second group, the CS offset was delayed. A third group was also given CS-offset delay but, in addition, a second cue was presented during the delay interval. The authors confirmed Kamin's (1957a) result that CS-offset delay retarded avoidance performance. However, they found that responding in the third group (additional cue during the delay interval) was equal to the first group (no CS-offset delay); the second cue restored performance to normal levels. This result suggested that the function of the CS offset was not reinforcement—if it were, *both* groups receiving the CS-offset delay should have performed poorly—but rather a source of information. Such information would be critical to subjects who, on avoidance trials when no US occurs, have no other cue to signal their successful avoidance of shock.

Another important result dealing with the issue of CS offset was obtained by Bolles, Stokes, and Younger (1966). They reasoned that there were three potential sources of reward for avoidance: termination of the CS (i.e., Schoenfeld's theory), escape from or termination of the US, and avoidance of the US. Each of these represented a contingency between the response and a potential reward. By allowing subjects one or more of these options, the authors were able to measure which was the most important option for avoidance performance, that is, which potential source of reward was, indeed, the most effective. In their study, rats were allowed to run in a wheel. One group of subjects could terminate the CS by running but could do nothing to avoid the shock or escape it once it came on. A second group could terminate both the CS and the shock US (if it was on) but could not avoid the shock by responding before it came on. A third group of rats could terminate the CS and avoid the US but they could not terminate the US once it came on (it lasted a fixed period of time). Finally, a fourth group was given normal avoidance training, that is, they could terminate both the CS and US and they could avoid the US. It should be emphasized that, in all cases, subjects could terminate the CS (presumably the reinforcer, at least according to Schoenfeld's theory) but their ability to affect the US varied. If the CS offset were the source of reward for the avoidance response, then the groups should not differ, but if another source of reward were more important (e.g., the ability to avoid shock), then group differences should be noted.

Bolles et al. found that subjects who could terminate the CS and avoid shock but not escape shock once it started performed nearly as well as the normal avoidance animals; in contrast, rats who lacked the ability to avoid shock performed poorly even though it was possible for them to terminate the CS. In short, the results indicated that CS termination alone was only minimally related to avoidance performance; the ability to avoid shock itself was the most important factor in determining avoidance performance.

Finally, another line of research that has seriously challenged the two-factor theory was conducted by Herrnstein and Hineline (1966). Rats were given brief shocks at various time intervals (schedule A). No warning signal preceded these shocks nor could the subject avoid the shocks or terminate them once they occurred. However, if the animals pressed a lever, the next shock was delivered according to a different time schedule (schedule B). Once the next shock was given, the shock regimen reverted back to the original schedule A. Thus, by pressing consistently, the subjects would receive all shocks according to schedule B.

The critical element of the design was that the frequency of shock for schedule A was higher than for schedule B. Pressing the lever achieved nothing for the animal except a reduction in the frequency of shock. Since Herrnstein and Hineline found that their rats learned this response, they questioned the two-factor theory. First, there was no warning signal CS and thus no CS offset to reinforce the behavior. Second, no escape responses occurred so such an instrumental CR could not have moved forward in time, energized by fear. Third, no avoidance of shock was possible (at least in the conventional sense). Finally, shock delivery was not necessarily delayed following a lever response although the average delay of shock was greater for the rats who pressed the lever than for those who did not. Herrnstein and Hineline concluded that avoidance learning can best be explained in terms of a single principle—reduction in shock frequency.

In summary, the two-factor theory was an extremely important theoretical contribution which elicited much research. Some aspects of the theory, however, appear to be inaccurate, especially the notion that fear occurs, then disappears, with the onset and offset of the CS. The current belief is that the CS is a discriminative cue for the response and its offset provides information about the effectiveness of the avoidance behavior. Although the immediacy of the CS offset is important for efficient avoidance performance, the ability to avoid shock per se is the important source of reward for avoidance acquisition. The notion proposed by Herrnstein (1969), that changes in the delay and/or frequency of shock support avoidance responding, certainly forms a compelling descriptive account of avoidance behavior. However, a third direction in theory, dealing with biological factors in avoidance, is perhaps more useful (see Chapter 7).

FACTORS IN PUNISHMENT

In experimental psychology, punishment is the procedure in which a response is followed by an aversive US. It is, as we have said before, an important and pervasive instrumental paradigm. Accordingly, a considerable number of studies have attempted to identify the basic principles regarding the effects of punishing stimuli on behavior. The following sections of this chapter highlight many of these important findings (see Azrin & Holz, 1966; Church, 1963; Dunham, 1971; and Solomon, 1964 for reviews).

Contingency

In Thorndike's original theory, the law of effect was symmetrical: rewards "stamped in" a response while punishments had the opposite effect: they weakened or "stamped out" behavior. Later, Thorndike (1932) altered his theory by eliminating the negative law of effect dealing with punishment and retaining only the positive side of the law. He did this because he observed in several experiments that punishers, unlike rewards, did not have a strong effect on behavior. Thorndike found that the probability of a given response was increased if it was immediately rewarded—the habit was strengthened—but, in contrast, the probability of a punished response did not change. Subjects were not less likely to perform a punished response in the future (they would continue to choose that response along with other nonrewarded behaviors) but they were more likely to perform a positively rewarded response.

Some of the early research supported Thorndike's claim. Skinner (1938) and Estes (1944), for example, found that while punishment suppressed behavior, the effect was transient. Furthermore, contingent punishment—aversive stimuli presented immediately following a response—appeared to have the same temporary effect on behavior as noncontingent punishment—punishers presented randomly with respect to the execution of the response. Since this finding differed from the results of reward, where contingent positive reward was found to be far more effective than noncontingent reward, an asymmetry between reward and punishment was claimed.

Although Thorndike's contribution was very important (indeed, he had a major impact on educational practices in the 1920s and '30s), recent evidence has confirmed that contingent punishment is more effective in suppressing behavior than noncontingent punishment (see Church, 1969). For example, in one study by Boe and Church (1967), three groups of rats were trained to press a lever to obtain food. After responding had stabilized, Boe and Church punished the subjects in one of three ways: a noncontingent shock presented every 30 seconds, a shock contingent (immediately following) a response at about 30-second intervals, or no shock. Following the punishment period, additional sessions without shock were given to observe the recovery from the suppressive effects of shock. The authors found that rats in the contingent group resumed lever pressing soon after the shocks were discontinued and their rate of pressing was nearly the same as that of the nonshock control subjects. However, marked suppression of lever pressing in the contingent shock group was observed throughout the remaining sessions of the experiment.

The Boe and Church article raised another issue, namely, the nature of the conditioned emotional response (CER). This procedure has been described frequently in preceding chapters as a method for measuring the strength of a Pavlovian CS. In a CER design, the Pavlovian CS is paired with an aversive US and the CS is later able to disrupt an ongoing instrumental response such as lever pressing (the degree of suppression is a measure of fear or CS strength; see Chapter 8). During CER training, the aversive US is contingent on the signal (a case of Pavlovian conditioning) and not on the lever response as in the instrumental punishment procedure of Boe and Church. Accordingly, important differences should be observed between suppression via a CER method and suppression via response-contingent punishment since response-US contingency is so critical to instrumental conditioning.

The CER (signal-contingent) and punishment (response-contingent) procedures were compared directly by Church, Wooten, and Matthews (1970). Rats were trained to press a lever to obtain food on an VI-1 (variable interval) minute schedule. Then, during five treatment sessions, 3-minute noise CSs were presented. One group (CER condition) was given several random shocks during the signal while a second group (punishment condition) was given an equal number of shocks but their delivery was contingent on a lever press. As shown in Figure 4-7, both groups demonstrated

FIGURE 4-7.

Mean suppression ratio as a function of treatment sessions for the CER and punishment (response-contingent) groups.

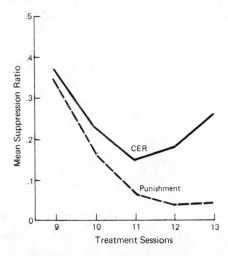

suppression of lever pressing (a ratio of .5 indicates that the signal had no effect on rate of responding). However, the punishment condition resulted in significantly more suppression than the CER condition. This finding clearly illustrated that the subjects were less willing to make a response that was directly punished than to make the same response merely in the presence of a fear-eliciting cue.

Schedules of Punishment

The notion discussed above, that contingent punishers are more effective in suppressing behavior than noncontingent ones, suggests that the schedule of presentation of punishment would be important. Certainly it is in the case of reward training. Several studies have confirmed this notion. Azrin (1956), for example, maintained a pecking response in pigeons on a variable interval food reward schedule while superimposing several punishment schedules. In one condition, the birds received response-contingent shock on a variable interval basis. Azrin found that overall response rates were much lower with punishment than without, but they remained fairly stable. In contrast, when the birds were punished according to an FI (fixed interval) schedule, where the temporal interval could easily serve as a discriminative cue for shock, the response rate changed between successive shocks. Specifically, the subjects' pecking rate was very high following shock but it slowed down appreciably as the time for the next shock drew near. Azrin concluded from these data that punishment schedules had the same effect on responding as reward schedules but that

FIGURE 4-8.

Mean suppression ratio as a function of the product of shock intensity and duration.

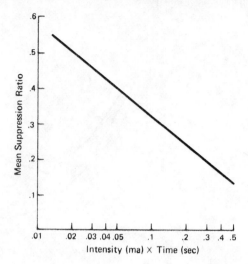

the effects were in the opposite direction. Such a conclusion has been confirmed in many studies in which FR (fixed ratio) punishment schedules were used (e.g., Azrin et al. 1963) or in which interval and ratio schedules were compared (e.g., Camp et al., 1966).

US Intensity and Duration

Many studies have shown that suppression of behavior is directly related to the intensity of the punisher (e.g., Camp et al., 1967; Church, et al., 1967; Filby & Appel, 1966; Powell, 1970) as well as to the duration of the US (e.g., Campbell, et al., 1966; Church et al., 1967). The relationship between these two variables was especially clear in the Church et al. (1967) study. Rats, trained to press a lever for food, were given a response-contingent shock delivered on a VI-2 minute schedule. For separate groups of subjects, the intensity was either .05, .15, or .25 milliamps in combination with shock durations of either 0, .25, .3, .5, 1, or 3 minutes (all intensity/duration combinations were studied). The usual B/A+B ratio was used to measure the combined effects of shock intensity and duration on responding.

Church et al. found that suppression was greater with longer or more intense shocks. The exact relationship is shown in Figure 4-8. Behavior was suppressed a constant unit (measured in terms of the suppression ratio) each time the intensity times duration product doubled. This relationship between the suppression of appetitive behavior and the intensity/duration of punishment is remarkably similar to the relationship

FIGURE 4-9.

Median response latency to enter the black compartment as a function of the delay of punishment.

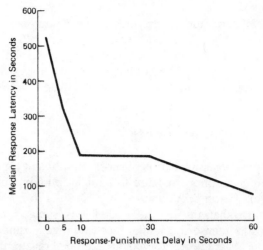

between the maintenance of avoidance behavior and the intensity/ duration of the US (see Leander, 1973).

The absolute intensity of the punisher is not the only characteristic affecting performance; the variability in intensities also is important. This principle was documented in a study by Boe (1971) who found that when the intensity of the punishment was varied, responding was suppressed more than when the shock was constant; that is, the variable group showed greater suppression than the constant group even though the average shock intensity was the same in both conditions. Since the variable group's performance was comparable to the group which received the greatest shock, Boe concluded that overall aversiveness of variable punishment is better described by the highest shock level rather than the average shock level.

Delay of Punishment

It is not surprising that delaying the presentation of a punisher weakens its suppressive effects. This principle has been demonstrated clearly in a variety of situations. For example, Randall and Riccio (1969) punished rats with a 1-second shock for entering a black compartment, a response which nocturnal animals such as rats usually perform readily. The shock presentation was delayed either 0, 5, 10, 30, or 60 seconds for separate groups of subjects. After a 30-minute rest period, the rats were tested for their fear of the black box, that is, the degree to which the punishment had suppressed the response of entering the black compartment. As shown in Figure 4-9, immediate punishment resulted in a long latency; the subjects' natural tendency to enter the black box had been highly suppressed. However, the suppressive effect of punishment was inversely related to the response-shock delay so that the 60-second group reentered the black box relatively quickly.

Other studies that investigated suppression of lever pressing (e.g., Camp et al., 1967), alley running (Baron, 1965), or avoidance responding (Baron, et al., 1969; Kamin, 1959; Misanin, et al., 1966), as a function of the delay of punishment have found essentially the same result: the effectiveness of punishment is inversely related to delay in a graded fashion.

Prior Punishment

The suppressive effects of shock punishment can be minimized if subjects are given prior exposure to a milder punishment. In fact, several studies (e.g., Baron & Antonitis, 1961; Karsh, 1963; Miller, 1960) have demonstrated that, under certain conditions, subjects may be relatively impervious to intense shock after receiving preexposure to mild shock.

Miller (1960), for example, trained rats to run in an alley. In addition to the food reward, one group was given shock punishment in the goal box while another group was not. The intensity of the shock for the first few trials was mild but it increased gradually throughout training. During a second phase of the study, both groups were subjected to intense shock in the goal box. Miller found that running was almost completely suppressed in the group that received intense shock for the first time. In contrast, performance in the experimental group, the subjects that had experienced gradually increasing shock, was not affected. Miller concluded that the "gradual" subjects had learned to tolerate stress; that is, their running response had been strengthened by food reinforcement despite the increasing shocks.

More recently, Church (1969) expanded our knowledge of this phenomenon by investigating the effects of both mild and intense prior shock on the effectiveness of moderately intense punishment. Like Miller, Church found that prior exposure to mild shock later attenuated the suppressive effects of a stronger shock. Church also observed, however, that prior exposure to strong punishment had the opposite effect—later suppression due to less intense shock was increased. In other words, mild shock reduced the effectiveness of moderate shock whereas preexposure to intense shock increased the later effectiveness of moderate shock. Church explained his results in terms of *generalization*: the subjects generalized from previous shock levels to later levels which caused them to respond to the later levels of stimulation somewhat as they had responded to previous levels. Presumably, the prior shock level served to establish a norm against which later levels were compared. Thus, moderate shock elicited less aversion if the prior shock was weak or more aversion if the prior shock was strong.

THEORIES OF PUNISHMENT

Unfortunately, as little is known about why punishment suppresses behavior as is known about why positive reward strengthens responding. Although the conditions under which each effect occurs are fairly well documented, theoretical explanations concerning the underlying mechanisms of punishment and reward lack firm support.

Competing Response Theories

One important class of theories involves the notion of competing responses. These theories suggest that punishment suppresses behavior because the subject performs either conditioned or unconditioned reactions to shock that interfere or compete with the conditioned response that is specifically being punished. Thus, punishment operates indirectly to suppress responding; it creates a situation in which the behavior is interfered with rather than unlearned.

One competing response theory, proposed by Guthrie (1934), accounted for punishment in terms of classical conditioning principles. Guthrie suggested that punishment elicited a number of unconditioned reactions (such as flinching, jumping, or freezing) that interfered with the execution of the punished response. Moreover, these competing URs often were conditioned to surrounding cues and thus interfered with the behavior even in the absence of shock.

Guthrie's theory has been supported in several experiments. In one study, Fowler and Miller (1963) punished rats in the goal box after they had traversed an alley. One group of subjects received shock on the forepaws (only the metal rods just in front of the food cup were electrified) while the other subjects experienced shock on the hindpaws (shock was delivered only to the rods closest to the entrance to the box). The authors found that running performance was facilitated in the rats shocked on the hindpaws but retarded in the animals punished on the forepaws. They theorized that the unconditioned reaction to shock on the hindpaws was lurching forward, a response compatible with running, while shock to the forepaws elicited a flinching reaction that was incompatible with (i.e., competed with) running.

Guthrie's competing response theory, however, cannot account for other important findings. For example, it is not clear why response-contingent shock is so much more effective in suppressing behavior than noncontingent shock. In each case, the US to shock should be the same. Thus, Guthrie's theory, emphasizing incompatible skeletal reactions to punishment, may be too limited an explanation.

Another competing response explanation is the two-factor theory of avoidance as applied to punishment (see Dinsmoor, 1954, 1955; Mowrer, 1947). According to this theory, Pavlovian fear conditioning takes place when shock punishment is delivered; the apparatus cues and particularly the response-produced stimuli come to elicit this fear. The animal will then attempt to make avoidance responses which terminate the fear (or aversive CSs). The most adaptive behavior in this regard is simply not to respond; that is, by not responding, the subject is able to avoid the response-produced cues that are associated with the aversive punishment. Unlike Guthrie's theory, which claims that particular skeletal responses *physically* compete with the instrumental response, the two-factor hypothesis stated that *any* response, other than the punished response, increases in strength due to shock avoidance. Since the subject cannot respond and perform a nonresponse at the same time, responding declines.

There are two major problems with Mowrer's two-factor theory of punishment. First, it is extremely difficult to identify which specific competing behaviors are being conditioned; if the theory were correct, competing behaviors must be present. Second, even if an increase in a specific competing response were shown, it may not be an avoidance response; the reaction could be a classically conditioned response or merely a by-product of response suppression. In other words, demonstrating that one response increases while the punished response is suppressed does not necessarily imply that the suppression of the punished behavior is directly due to the increase of (competition from) that new behavior.

In summary, punishment suppresses behavior but we do not know exactly why. Classically conditioned skeletal responses or voluntary instrumental avoidance reactions may represent important sources of interference yet none of the major theories, by itself, appears to be a sufficient explanation of how or why punishment works as it does

PUNISHMENT AND NEUROSIS

It often has been claimed that punishment and neurosis are invariably linked, with the former producing the latter. Actually, relatively little is known about this relationship. One reason is that neurosis (here defined as maladaptive behavior based on fear) is difficult to define in the laboratory. Although animals may perform certain responses that, from the experimenter's viewpoint, *appear* to be highly maladaptive, there is no guarantee that the responses are, in fact, like human neuroses. Nevertheless, several lines of research have been explored and a few generalizations regarding the relationship between punishment and neurosis have been formed.

Self-Punitive Behavior

One area of research is on self-punitive behavior, a phenomenon in which punishing an avoidance or escape response during extinction may increase responding rather than suppress it. Since shock is never given during avoidance extinction, the animal eventually should stop responding; in

FIGURE 4-10.

Mean running speed in the first segment of the alley as a function of blocks of 10 extinction trials for the No Shock group (no punishment in the alley). Short Shock group (punishment in the last segment of the alley), and the Long Shock group (shock throughout the ailey).

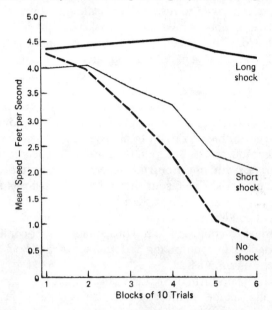

fact, punishment for responding during extinction should, if anything, help to eliminate the avoidance behavior. Paradoxically, though, the subjects persist, and by doing so inflict more punishment upon themselves. Continued responding in this situation therefore is maladaptive in the sense that it is self-punitive; it merely leads to further shock (see Brown, 1969, for a review).

An example of the phenomenon was shown by Brown, Martin, and Morrow (1964). They gave rats 20 shock-escape trials in an alley, followed by 60 extinction trials during which the start box was not electrified. One group of subjects, the No Shock group, was not punished during extinction. A second group of animals, the Short Shock group, were given shock in the last section of the alley, just before they reached the goal box. The third group of subjects, the Long Shock group, experienced shock throughout the entire six feet of the alley. As shown in Figure 4-10, speed of running was markedly affected by the punishment conditions during extinction. The No Shock group (regular extinction) gradually slowed down over the extinction sessions. In contrast, the groups punished for leaving the uncharged start box continued to run fast, especially the Long Shock subjects who were punished throughout the entire alley. Thus, the Brown et al. results suggested that punishment delivered during extinction of an aversively motivated response produced a form of self-punitive, or masochistic, behavior.

Brown's explanation for the self-punitive responding was based on Mowrer's (1947) two-factor theory of avoidance. He suggested that responding during extinction was based on fear motivation; punishment of the response maintained or heightened fear. Therefore, subjects were even more motivated to respond following punishment.

A number of investigators challenged the fear theory of self-punishing behavior. They claimed that subjects simply failed to discriminate the difference between acquisition and extinction contingencies. Punished subjects were confused and continued to respond as if the acquisition procedures were still in effect.

The confusion hypothesis has received compelling support. For example, Campbell, Smith, and Misanin (1966) conducted an experiment similar to that of Brown et al. They used three groups of rats: a regular extinction group; one punished in the first segment of the alley near the start box; and one group that received shock in the alley segment closest to the goal box. The results showed that the self-punitive response occurred only in the subjects punished near the start box. In that group, the punishment conditions were nearly the same as the acquisition conditions, thus leading to confusion and, consequently, to a continuing high rate of responding. In contrast, the performance of rats shocked just prior to the goal box was suppressed.

The problem of deciding which theory is correct has been complicated by the fact that supporting evidence has been obtained for both positions. However, the theoretical controversy appears to have been resolved in an insightful paper by Dreyer and Renner (1971), who argued that the fear and confusion hypotheses actually are compatible. Punishment certainly should enhance fear yet continued responding may be due to confusion. The fear theory implies that subjects discriminate between acquisition and punished extinction conditions, and therefore, that persistent responding reflects the subject's choosing to perform a masochistic behavior. However, there is no independent evidence indicating that subjects do, in fact, discriminate; procedures used to demonstrate the self-punitive phenomenon are precisely those that would retard such a discrimination. Indeed, when human subjects are used in experiments that are comparable to those described above, a masochistic-like behavior is observed but the subjects report that they lack knowledge about the change in the response contingency (Dreyer & Renner, 1971).

In conclusion, the self-punitive phenomenon does not appear to be a true analog for masochism but it does illustrate that, under certain circumstances, punishment may produce highly maladaptive behaviors if precautions are not taken to clarify the response-punishment contingencies (see O'Neil et al., 1970).

Punishment of Conflict

Another line of research indicated a more direct relationship between conflict (or confusion, as in the case of self-punitive behavior), punishment, and neurosis. Maier (1949) trained rats to jump across an open space to one of two doors. If the subject jumped to the correct side, the door swung open and it was given a food reward. If the rat jumped to the wrong door, the door remained closed and the animal fell into a net several feet below One group of subjects in Maier's study was taught to jump to one side rather than the other, a response they learned easily. The other group was given random rewards not correlated to either side. These latter subjects soon stopped jumping since they were thwarted on half of the trials from obtaining reward. When the random subjects were punished by shock or an air blast for not responding, they began to jump but in a fixated manner—always to one side.

In a second part of the study, Maier attempted to train all the animals to jump to a black door rather than a white one. The first group had little trouble in learning this new discrimination, but the previous random subjects, who had developed a fixated pattern of responding, were unable (or unwilling) to learn this new response. Instead, they continued to make their previous stereotyped reactions, even when the jumping platform was placed next to the correct door and they were allowed to inspect the food reward. Thus Maier's work was important in suggesting that subjects may fixate and later be unable to master simple tasks if they are punished while in a state of conflict or when confronted with an insoluble problem. Although one must always be cautious when making comparisons to human behavior, the implications of this research are evident. If a person were motivated to resolve an important conflict but could find no clear resolution, punishment could possibly have the undesirable side effect of producing fixated behavior without the subject attempting to learn new, adaptive behaviors.

Punishment of Consummatory Behavior

Neurosis may also appear when certain types of responses are punished. For example, some early research (e.g., Lichtenstein, 1950; Masserman, 1943) suggested that punishing some innate reactions, such as eating or drinking, leads to neurosis whereas punishing a single instrumental behavior does not (see Bertsch, 1976). In Lichtenstein's experiment, for example, dogs were given electric shock either during food delivery or while they were actually eating. Punishing the eating response had a profound and lasting effect: most of the dogs stopped eating, many became lethargic while others became unusually aggressive, and some even developed tremors and tics and later retched in the presence of food. None of these neurotic symptoms was observed in the dogs who were given shock during food delivery.

FIGURE 4-11.

Mean suppression ratio as a function of training sessions for the groups punished for licking or lever pressing. The ratio was computed by dividing the total responses on the punishment session by the average number of responses on the two preceding baseline sessions.

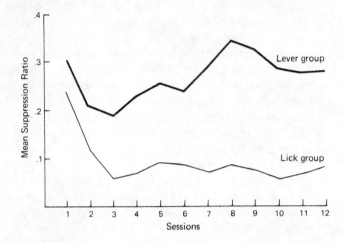

More recently, a study by Bertsch confirmed that eating and drinking—the consummatory responses—are more sensitive to the suppressive effect of punishment than are instrumental behaviors. Bertsch reinforced rats with water on an intermittent schedule for licking a drinking tube or for pressing a lever. Contingent shock punishment was presented after the licking (consummatory) or lever pressing (instrumental) response to separate groups of subjects. As Figure 4-11 shows, licking was suppressed far more by punishment than was lever pressing. Although the experiment was not designed to assess other consequences of punishment, like the symptoms noted by Lichtenstein, such heightened sensitivity to the effects of punishment may be a precursor to neurosis (see Solomon, 1964; Bertsch, 1976, for reviews).

Physiological Consequences of Punishment

In connection with punishment and neurosis, it should be noted that stress or intense punishment per se may have deleterious consequences for the physical health of an organism. Many experiments, for example, have shown that animals may develop gastrointestinal ulcers as a result of stress. In some cases, the ulcers were due to prolonged periods of shock followed by relief (Desiderato et al., 1974), being tightly restrained (e.g., Mikhail, 1973), or conflict situations in which food acquisition was punished by unavoidable shock (e.g., Moot et al., 1970). Other investigators have noted ulcer-producing (ulcerogenic) factors that were more consistent with principles discussed previously. For example, unsignaled shock—shock which the subject cannot predict—has been shown to be less preferable to rats than predictable shock (e.g., Miller et al., 1974); subjects who could not actively choose signaled versus unsignaled shock, or who received unsignaled shock, developed ulcers (Caul, et al., 1972; Gliner, 1972). Weiss (1971a, 1971b) explained this phenomenon in terms of coping behavior and feedback. Specifically, the animals try to cope with stress by avoiding or reducing it; they develop ulcers when they do not receive information about their successful coping attempts. In other words, if, following an avoidance response, subjects receive stimuli that are associated with no stress and therefore signal a successful coping attempt, they do not develop ulcers. On the other hand, responses to stress that do not result in relevant feedback lead to severe ulceration. Thus, Weiss' work appears to suggest principles similar to those stemming from Maier's research: punishment during periods of uncertainty leads to behavioral anomalies such as fixation (Maier) or even to physical pathologies like ulceration (Weiss).

Research on ulceration has also focused on the difference between instrumental and consummatory behaviors. Paré (1972) confirmed that punishment of consummatory responding (which is especially sensitive to suppression by punishment—Bertsch, 1972) produced ulcers more readily than did punishment of instrumental behaviors. Rats were rewarded with food for pressing a lever. Shock was presented either after a nonrewarded lever response, a rewarded response, after the animal had secured the food pellet, or while it consumed the reward. Paré found a higher incidence of ulcers in the subjects who were shocked while eating the food reward.

Aggression

Finally, punishment may induce forms of behaviors that are socially undesirable or inappropriate. Many experiments have demonstrated that noncontingent shock punishment may induce aggressiveness. An important study on this topic was done by Ulrich and Azrin (1962) who observed that shock elicited a reflexive-like fighting behavior between two rats. In addition, aggressiveness increased with more frequent or more intense shocks, when the subjects were tested in a smaller apparatus, or, as shown by Azrin et al. (1946b), with longer shocks. Although fighting was closely dependent on the actual shock presentation in Ulrich and Azrin's study, other investigators (e.g., Baenninger & Ulm, 1969) have shown that aggression (mouse killing by rats) will take place even when the "opponent" animal is introduced into the cage *after* the shock has been terminated.

Other studies have shown that shock-induced aggression occurs in a wide variety of species including squirrel monkeys (Azrin et al., 1963). In fact, the fighting between these primates was far more vicious, less stereotyped, and longer lasting than that between rodents. Monkeys have been shown to attack and bite inanimate objects such as a stuffed doll or tennis ball (Azrin et al., 1964a). Finally, Azrin (1970) demonstrated that a punishing shock contingent on a biting attack suppressed the aggression of monkeys, but the same shock delivered on a random or noncontingent basis elicited aggression.

These sobering results suggest that noncontingent punishment may have highly undesirable social consequences as well as physiological side effects. Although considerable work is needed to clarify the relationship between punishment and neurosis, it appears that unless aversive control procedures are contingent on unambiguous instrumental behaviors and involve appropriate feedback, anomalous behavioral and physiological reactions may occur.

SUMMARY

The principles of aversive learning are important because so much of our everyday behavior is directed toward terminating or avoiding noxious or threatening stimuli. The simplest aversive paradigm is escape conditioning which, in many respects, is similar to reward training in that faster learning occurs with larger and more immediate reinforcements. The difference is that in aversive learning the reward is the termination of a painful or unpleasant stimulus.

Avoidance conditioning is somewhat more complex. Here, the subject must respond during a CS in order to avoid an aversive US. Mowrer's two-factor theory claimed that fear was first conditioned to the CS via classical conditioning; this fear then motivated the instrumental avoidance response, with fear reduction (at the point where the CS is turned off) providing the reinforcement. It now appears that the CS offset provides information to the subject rather than reinforcement by confirming that the correct response has been made.

Punishment is an aversive stimulus following an instrumental response. Responding can be increasingly suppressed with longer, more intense, and more immediate punishers; moreover, punishers suppress behavior in characteristic ways depending on the schedule of delivery. One of the most important areas of concern and one for which we have relatively few firm answers is whether punishment necessarily leads to neurosis—defined here as maladaptive behavior based on fear. It appears that if subjects are punished when they are in a high state of conflict, such as trying to deal with an important but insoluble problem, or engaging in innate behavior of the kind that is biologically important for survival, neurotic-like behaviors may result. Furthermore, punishment may produce undesirable side effects, both physiological in the form of disease, such as ulcers, and behavioral in the form of disturbances, such as aggression.

5/ Extinction

Preview

In this chapter, we consider what happens to a conditioned response when
it is no longer followed by an unconditioned stimulus: the subjects gradually
stop performing the learned behavior. In learning psychology, this process
is called *extinction*. We shall consider a number of factors that influence the
extinction behavior as well as the theories that try to explain
why organisms stop performing behavior which no longer produces a
rewarding US. Part of the interest in the topic of extinction is due to the fact
that some very interesting and paradoxical effects occur. For example,
partially reinforced habits **are** more resistant to later extinction than habits
that had been continuously reinforced (according to some theories, at least,
the latter habits should have been the stronger ones). Another topic is the
extinction of fear-motivated behavior. This area of inquiry is especially
important to behavior therapists with respect to the treatment of behavioral
disorders in human beings.

117

INTRODUCTION

Our discussion of the principles of learning in the previous four chapters has been limited almost entirely to the acquisition of behavior. This chapter will discuss factors that influence the rate of extinction and the various theoretical accounts of the extinction process.

Extinction, like acquisition, refers to an experimental procedure, which, in this case, is the withholding of reinforcement following the execution of a response. In classical conditioning, extinction occurs when a CS presentation is not followed by the US. In contrast to other processes such as forgetting (where a response is eliminated after a period of disuse), omission of the reward is the defining characteristic of extinction.

Consider the following hypothetical example: you ring the doorbell of a friend's house but get no answer; after ringing several times, you stop and walk away. Or this example: you check your mailbox for an important letter you are expecting but find the box empty; under some conditions, you might check the box repeatedly for several hours and stop only when you have thoroughly convinced yourself that the letter will not be delivered.

Clearly, the outcome in these instances, as it is whenever a US is no longer presented following a response, is the reduction, often gradual, in responding. The rate of reduction in responding, or conversely, the persistence of the response (called *resistance to extinction*) despite the conditions of no reward, depends on the particular conditions present during the extinction trials and on the factors present during the prior acquisition phase. Extinction is an important and adaptive process; without the possibility of eliminating behaviors that no longer produced reward, our lives would be a clutter of useless activities.

For a number of years, learning psychologists considered resistance to extinction as an alternative measure of response strength; stronger habits had greater resistance to the effects of nonreinforcement than weaker habits. As a result, the investigation of extinction per se was often secondary to an analysis of the various conditions that promoted acquisition. However, resistance to extinction does not appear to be merely another way to measure habit strength; in fact, it is often poorly correlated to other measures of habit that are assessed during prior acquisition. Extinction really is a form of learning in that the subject modifies its behavior based on the elimination of the reward contingency. Resistance to extinction, therefore, provides an alternative focus for the study of learning.

EXTINCTION OF PAVLOVIAN CRs

Factors in Extinction

Since the strength of Pavlovian CRs depends so directly on the number of contiguous CS-US presentations, we would expect that extinction in turn should take place when CS-only trials are given. Several experimenters, for example, have shown that conditioned responding declines as a function of the number of CS-only presentations (e.g., Kalish, 1954). The number of CS-only trials in extinction is not the only factor that influences the rate of suppression; the duration of the CS also is important. The interaction of these two components was demonstrated by Shipley (1974). During acquisition, rats were given either a 25- or 100-second tone CS followed by a shock US. Then, the strength of the CS (or, rather, the extinction of the strength) was assessed by a CER technique. During extinction the subjects in each acquisition condition were divided into six separate groups. Three of the groups continued to receive CS-only trials where the duration of the CS remained the same as in acquisition (25 or 100 seconds). The remaining three groups received the other CS duration during extinction, that is, the CS duration was changed from 25 to 100, or from 100 to 25 seconds. The number of CS-only trials in extinction also was varied so that one group in each of the extinction-duration conditions received 200 exposures to the tone, a second group received 400 trials, and a third, 800 exposures. Shipley found that neither the number of extinction trials nor the duration of the CS *alone* accounted for the extinction of response. Rather, extinction was determined by the combination of number and duration of CS-only trials; the greater the total exposure to the CS, regardless of whether the exposure was due to more trials, or fewer but longer trials, the faster the extinction of suppression to the CS. Shipley's results challenge a number of extinction theories, most of which focus on either the number of extinction trials or on the duration of the CS in extinction but not on both (see below).

In addition to the number and duration of CS-only trials, instructions concerning the change in CS-US relationship have been shown to promote extinction (Bridger & Mandel, 1965; Notterman et al., 1952a). For example, Notterman et al. conditioned a heart rate CR in human subjects. They then gave regular extinction but told half the subjects that they would not be given the shock US. The results confirmed the notion that prior knowledge of the new CS-no US relationship facilitated a change in responding: the subjects who knew of the extinction procedure extinguished more rapidly than the regular group. This finding, of course, explains why the extinction of many human behaviors is so rapid. Often we have knowledge of the new CS-no US relationship (for instance, in the example of doorbell ringing given in the introduction—if you knew your friend was not at home, you would stop pressing the button as soon as you remembered that fact).

Theory

The earliest theory of extinction was offered by Pavlov (1927). He argued that the suppression of the CR during extinction was due to inhibitory tendencies that competed with conditioned excitation (see Chapter 2). The main evidence for this argument was the fact that responding spontaneously recovered after a rest interval. Presumably, the inhibition that had accumulated during the extinction trials dissipated during the rest interval.

Pavlov also demonstrated that suppression of responding during extinction could be disinhibited, that is, the full, excitatory CR could be restored if a novel cue were presented during the extinction procedures. The novel cue apparently distracted the animal from the inhibitory process that was building up during extinction, thus allowing the underlying excitation to be expressed immediately. In summary, the phenomena of spontaneous recovery and disinhibition led Pavlov to hypothesize that extinction involved an inhibitory process that was superimposed upon excitation; since increments in excitation could not take place during extinction (the CS was not followed by the US), the inhibition gradually became dominant and responding declined.

The main problem with Pavlov's theory is that if inhibition were developing during extinction as Pavlov claimed, then the CS should be a conditioned inhibitor. However, apparently it is not.

An alternative to Pavlov's viewpoint stems from Rescorla's (1967b) theory of Pavlovian conditioning. Rescorla suggests that extinction procedures involve a change in the CS-US correlation and an alteration of the association correspondingly develops during acquisition. Stimuli come to signal particular outcomes during acquisition (i.e. the US). Then, during extinction, because these same cues signal no US, the CS-outcome correlation is maximally changed. As a result, the conditioned behavior, which reflects the underlying CS-outcome association, declines.

It should be noted, however, that Rescorla's theory, as applied to extinction, is not clear about some facets of the extinction process, such as the nature of spontaneous recovery. Theories of extinction of Pavlovian CRs generally are not yet sufficiently clear or detailed beyond the fact that the CS-outcome correlation is important to the development and maintenance of associations. Fortunately, extinction theories dealing with instrumental responding are more fully developed (see subsequent sections).

FACTORS IN EXTINCTION FOLLOWING INSTRUMENTAL REWARD TRAINING

The following sections indicate the general effects on extinction of the various experimental conditions present either during the extinction series or during prior acquisition of an instrumental response.

Reward Magnitude

A number of investigators have found that the size of the reward during the acquisition process affects later resistance to extinction. Larger rewards decrease later resistance to extinction (Campbell et al., 1972; Roberts,

FIGURE 5-1.

Mean percentage of asymptotic (terminal performance during acquisition) start speed during extinction as a function of blocks of three extinction trials for groups that received 1, 2, 5, 10, or 25 pellets of reward during acquisition. The mean acquisition asymptote is shown at R.

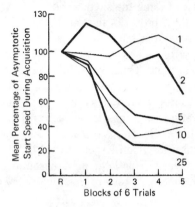

1969; Wagner, 1961), that is, the larger the reward during the acquisition of the behavior, the less time it takes to eliminate the behavior. Note the contrast of this finding to acquisition studies where large rewards *increase* response strength as compared to small rewards.

In the Roberts (1969) study, rats were trained to traverse an alley for either 1, 2, 5, 10, or 25 food pellets. During the extinction trials, the food reward was not given in the goal box. The results are illustrated in Figure 5-1. Mean running speed in the start box during the last 30 extinction trials is expressed as a percentage of the terminal performance level in acquisition (shown in Figure 5-1 at "R"). It is clear that performance declined as a function of the reward magnitude during acquisition; that is, the larger the acquisition reward, the faster the extinction.

The variability in reward magnitude has also been shown to influence resistance to extinction. Sytsma and Dyal (1973) trained a running response in rats using two alleys. All the subjects were given 40 trials in each alley but the sequence of the alleys was randomized across trials. One group received 10 food pellets in the goal box of both alleys following the running response. The second group received a constant amount of reward (10 pellets) in one alley but a variable amount (1 or 10 pellets) in the goal box of the other alley. During extinction, all the rats were tested in the alley in which they had previously received consistent reinforcement. Sytsma and Dyal found that variable reward markedly increased resistance to extinction. Running speed in the constant-amount alley was high in the subjects that had experienced variable reward, during acquisition, in the other alley.

Other experimenters have examined the effect of patterns of variable reward magnitude (e.g., Wike & Atwood, 1970; Wike & King, 1973). In the Wike and King study, the reward magnitude was increased over three daily trials from 0 to 45 to 500 milligrams of food for one group of rats; for a second group, the amount of reward was decreased. The authors observed patterned responding, that is, during both acquisition and extinction, the increasing-reward group responded progressively faster over the daily block of three trials while the decreasing-reward group decreased in speed. A third group in this study, for which the amount of reward was randomized across trials, ran at a fast and consistent speed. In fact, those subjects performed as well on all three trials as the other two groups did in their fastest trials. Thus, Wike and King's study suggested two important principles. First, the degree to which varied amounts of reward are randomized during training is critical to the subject's resistance to extinction: randomization produces faster performance and slower extinction than fixed patterns. Second, resistance to extinction increases following a reward pattern in which larger reward is followed by a less preferred (i.e., smaller) reward. This later generalization also appears to be true when other parameters of reward, such as delay or quality, are varied (see below).

Response Effort

A number of experiments have shown that extinction occurs more rapidly when the response during extinction (Fischer et al., 1968) and/or acquisition (Johnson & Viney, 1970) requires more physical effort from the subject. In the Fischer et al. study, for example, rats were given 60 acquisition trials in an alley. For 20 trials (randomly determined), the alley was horizontal, but for the remaining 40 trials (also randomly determined), the alley was tilted either 20 or 40 degrees. Thus, effort was defined in terms of the angle of slant the subject had to climb. During extinction, the subjects were tested with either the 0-, 20-, or 40-degree alley. Fischer et al. found that resistance to extinction was an inverse function of the response effort. The mean number of responses executed by the 0-degree group during the 30-minute extinction series was about 35, compared to 25 and 22 for the 20- and 40-degree conditions, respectively. It is interesting to note that response effort did not affect running speed during acquisition. This finding eliminated the possibility that differential resistance to extinction merely reflected different habit strengths at the end of acquisition.

Delay of Reward

Although delay of reward has a pronounced and unitary effect on the acquisition of behavior, the effect of delay on resistance to extinction is varied (see Tarpy & Sawabini, 1974). Several studies have shown that resistance to extinction is not affected by a constant delay during acquisition (e.g., Habley et al., 1972; Renner, 1965; Sgro et al., 1967). In contrast, other investigators have found that resistance to extinction is an inverse

FIGURE 5-2.

Left panel: Mean speed in alley during extinction as a function of reward delay during acquisition. Right panel: Mean trials to criterion (resistance to extinction following a correction of the data for differences in terminal acquisition levels) as a function of reward delay during acquisition. In each panel, different groups of subjects are identified according to the acquisition delay (left number) and the goal box confinement period following an extinction response (right number).

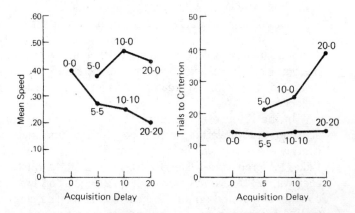

function of delay, with greater constant delays during acquisition leading to faster extinction (Tombaugh, 1970; Tombaugh & Tombaugh, 1969).

One important study that helped to resolve this issue was done by Tombaugh (1966). Rats were given 70 acquisition trials in an alley for which the reward in the goal box was delayed either 0, 5, 10, or 20 seconds. On the 60 extinction trials, four groups of rats were confined in the goal box following a response for the same length of time as the acquisition delay, that is, 0, 5, 10, or 20 seconds. Three other groups received a zero-second confinement period, regardless of the previous delay condition.

The results of Tombaugh's experiment are shown in Figure 5-2. Mean speed of response during extinction (left panel) declined as a function of acquisition delay when the confinement period following an extinction trial equalled the previous delay value. However, as shown in the right panel of Figure 5-2, when the extinction data were equalized according to terminal acquisition levels (Anderson, 1963), no differences in extinction were observed between those groups. This latter finding suggests that acquisition delay merely influenced the terminal performance levels and not the rate of extinction itself.

In summary, the greater the constant delay of reward during acquisition, the less the resistance to extinction (although this relationship was not found by Tombaugh, 1966, when terminal acquisition levels of performance were equated). If the confinement period following an extinction response is reduced relative to the acquisition delay, resistance to extinction increases; alternatively, if the extinction confinement is lengthened relative to acquisition delay, extinction takes place more quickly (Wike & McWilliams, 1967).

The effect of intermittent delay of reward on extinction has been thoroughly studied. Most investigators (e.g., Knouse & Campbell, 1971; Tombaugh, 1970) have confirmed that partial delay during acquisition increases resistance to extinction. For example, in the Knouse and Campbell (1971) experiment, rats were trained to traverse an alley for food reward. On 50 percent of the acquisition trials, the reward was delayed for 0, 8, 16, 24, 32, 40, 48, or 56 seconds for separate groups. Although there was only minimal evidence that delay affected acquisition performance, resistance to extinction increased as a linear function of delay duration, with the greater delays leading to faster running speeds in extinction.

In the Knouse and Campbell study, the delay values were varied across groups while the percentage of acquisition trials on which the reward was delayed was held constant. The opposite strategy was used by Wike, Mellgren, and Wike (1968). In their study, rats were trained in an alley with a 20-second delay on the 72 acquisition trials and a 20-second confinement period on the 32 extinction trials. The percentage of delayed trials, both in acquisition and extinction, was varied. That is, different groups received a 20-second delay on either 0, 33, 67, or 100 percent of the acquisition trials; then, during extinction, some animals in each of the percentage conditions continued to receive the same percentage of confinement trials while others were shifted to a different percentage.

First, Wike et al. found that resistance to extinction was an inverse function of the percentage of confinement trials during extinction: the greater the percentage of confinement trials, the faster the extinction. The same general relationship, although less exact, was observed between resistance to extinction and percentage of delay during acquisition. Second, the authors noted that changes from one acquisition percentage value to a different percentage of confinement trials during extinction affected resistance to extinction. Shifts to a higher percentage of confinement trials promoted faster extinction whereas shifts to a lower percentage increased resistance to extinction. Thus, the effect of varied percentage of delayed trials on resistance to extinction is similar to the effect of varied duration of constant delay: A shift to longer constant delays or to a higher percentage of delayed trials results in more rapid extinction.

Number of Acquisition Trials

The traditional view was that resistance to extinction increased as a function of the number of acquisition trials (Williams, 1938), that is, a well-trained habit would persist longer during the extinction process than a weaker response. However, recent evidence indicates that this positive relationship between training level and extinction only occurs when small rewards are used (e.g., Ison, 1962; Ison & Cook, 1964). For example, Ison

FIGURE 5-3.

Mean running speed in the alley as a function of blocks of five trials during acquisition and extinction for groups that received 30 or 75 acquisition trials combined with 1 or 10 food pellets.

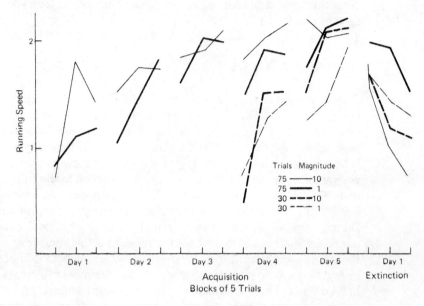

Trials Magnitude
75 ————10
75 ———— 1
30 ——————10
30 ———— 1

Running Speed

Day 1   Day 2   Day 3   Day 4   Day 5   Day 1

Acquisition
Blocks of 5 Trials

Extinction

and Cook rewarded a running response in an alley for 30 or 75 trials (15 trials per day). Half the subjects in each group received 1 or 10 food pellets in the goal box. Then, 15 extinction trials were given. As shown in Figure 5-3, response strength during acquisition increased both as a function of the magnitude of reward and the number of trials (the 30-trial subjects were trained on the last two trial blocks). During extinction, however, the outcome was more complicated. For the subjects that received the small reward, extinction was a positive function of the number of training trials: the more the trials, the greater the resistance to extinction. In contrast, after receiving a large reward, extinction speeds declined more quickly with extended training.

In summary, resistance to extinction increases as a function of training level when small rewards (or low drive—Traupmann, 1972) are used during acquisition; however, with large rewards, resistance to extinction is an inverse function of the number of acquisition trials (see Sperling, 1965 for a general review of this phenomenon).

GENERAL THEORIES OF EXTINCTION

Although several of the more recent and influential theories of extinction were designed primarily to explain the partial reinforcement effect (see a later section of this chapter), they also serve as general theories of extinction, attempting to explain the cause for response suppression following nonreinforcement. First, however, it would be useful to review a somewhat older theory of extinction which provided much of the foundation for the current positions.

Inhibition Theory

One of the earliest and most formalized theories of extinction was proposed by Hull (1943). Hull suggested that two processes were affected when an animal responded to obtain a reward. First, habit strength increased due to the reward, and second, *reactive inhibition* increased. This latter term was analogous to fatigue; the act of responding per se required energy expenditure which was, in a sense, aversive to the subject. Therefore, while habit was strengthened during acquisition, an inhibitory component, a potential for the suppression of the response, also developed. During acquisition, performance remained at a high level because the dominant effect of reinforcement outweighed the inhibitory tendency. However, during extinction, conditions favored inhibition. That is, when responding was no longer rewarded, fatigue continued to increase whereas habit did not. The consequence was a decline in responding.

Hull's theory was supported by a variety of findings. For example, the effect of increasing the effort required of the subjects was shown to hasten extinction. Since fatigue would be greater with more effortful responses, the reactive inhibitory component should also increase as a function of response effort, producing faster extinction. Hull's theory also accounted successfully for spontaneous recovery. Here, the reactive inhibition that had developed during extinction dissipated during the subsequent rest interval, allowing for the conditioned excitatory tendencies to be expressed.

Hull had considerable trouble accounting for some facets of extinction behavior. Although he postulated additional concepts such as conditioned inhibition which improved the generality of his theory, some phenomena still could not be explained very adequately. For example, the theory could not explain the extinction of effortless responses, such as GSR, where little fatigue would develop. Second, a number of studies have demonstrated that merely placing an animal in the goal box of an alley, without providing reward as is usually done during acquisition, promotes later extinction of the running response (see Moltz, 1957). Such a latent extinction phenomenon questions Hull's theory because, again, responding is not required (during which fatigue would develop) for suppression of behavior during extinction. Finally, and most important, Hull's theory cannot easily explain the partial reinforcement effect. Reactive inhibition should be the same in both continuously and intermittently reinforced subjects, yet a vast number of experiments have shown that intermittent reward leads to greater resistance to extinction.

Interference Theory

Hull's inhibition theory is based on the notion that responding itself is suppressed during extinction, i.e., that inhibition subtracts from performance. An alternative approach, interference theory, is that subjects learn a new response during extinction, one that competes with the behavior learned previously during acquisition. Theories of this sort have great intuitive appeal. First, it is clear that subjects do perform other behaviors during extinction, although it is not always certain that these alternative behaviors necessarily cause extinction through competition. Second, when the subjects explicitly do not engage in alternative behaviors during extinction, the rate of decrease of their responses lessens or slows down (e.g., Davenport, 1964).

The most widely supported interference theory is the *frustration hypothesis* (see Amsel, 1958, 1962, 1972). This theory states that subjects come to expect reward during acquisition; then, during extinction, the experience of nonreward produces frustration. Frustration is an aversive drive state and, thus, behavior which reduces frustration, such as cessation of responding or the adoption of other competing behaviors, will be reinforced. Imagine, for example, the feeling of frustration you might experience if you lost a quarter in a soda pop machine that had always worked for you in the past. In an effort to reduce your aversive drive state, you may end up banging your fist on the machine, or walking away in disgust.

The notion that frustration stemming from nonreward *energizes behavior*, that it is a source of motivation or drive, was confirmed in a classic study by Amsel and Roussel (1952). Rats were trained to run down a double alley. On the first 28 days of acquisition, they ran in the first alley to one reward and then in a second alley for another reward. Later, during the test trials, the subjects received reward in the first goal box on half the trials but not on the remaining trials. The failure to receive reward, of course, was presumed to be frustrating (but see Scull, 1973).

Amsel and Roussel measured the frustration effect in terms of speed of running in the second alley. As shown in Figure 5-4, running speed in the second alley following nonreward in the first goal box was appreciably faster than speed following reward. In other words, the experience of nonreward in the first goal box energized behavior, causing a subsequent increase in running speed in the second alley.

The motivating characteristics of nonreward have been documented in many other studies. The amount of frustration, as measured by the relative increase in running speed in the second alley, has been shown to reflect the relative reduction in reward magnitude in the first goal box (e.g., Bower, 1962; Daly, 1968; Peckham & Amsel, 1967). Other experiments have demonstrated that the intensity of frustration is a function of the delay of reward in the first goal box (Sgro, 1969) and the degree of prior training (the more acquisition trials, the greater the expectation of reward, and, thus, the greater the frustration from nonreward—Stimmel & Adams, 1969; Yelen, 1969).

FIGURE 5-4.

Mean running time in the second alley as a function of training. On the test trials, performance, in the second alley, for rewarded and nonrewarded trials (in the first goal box) is plotted separately.

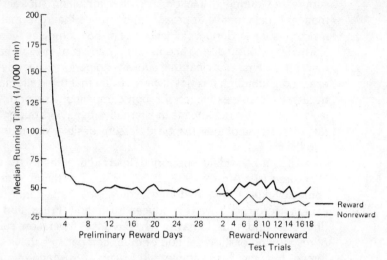

The studies by Amsel and others showed that frustration was a drive state; it energized the dominant behavior of running in the second alley. One problem not addressed by those results was that increased running in the second alley didn't necessarily compete with the learned response and, thus, promote extinction; in fact, the frustration effect observed by Amsel and Roussel (an increase in running speed in the second alley) was compatible with continued responding.

The notion that frustration from nonreward can produce explicit competing responses during extinction was demonstrated in an important study by Adelman and Maatsch (1955). Rats first were trained to run down an alley to secure food in the goal box. Then, during extinction, three treatment groups were designated: subjects in the "Normal" group remained in the goal box without food for 20 seconds following their response. A second group of subjects, the "Jump" group, was allowed to jump out of the goal box into a neutral holding cage. Presumably, the aversive nature of the frustration drive would promote such escape behavior. Rats in the third group, the "Recoil" subjects, were allowed to retrace their steps back into the alley after they had discovered there was no food in the goal box.

Adelman and Maatsch found that extinction was fastest in the Recoil group. To explain their findings, the authors postulated that running back into the alley had been reinforced by a reduction in frustration. Since running *from* the goal box was incompatible with the original acquisition task of running *to* the goal box, this new behavior competed with the original response and caused a rapid decline in running during extinction. The major implication of this finding is that the same process (competing responses learned via frustration reduction interfere with the acquisition behavior) occurs under normal extinction conditions. The actual competing behaviors, of course, are usually not known by the experimenter; indeed, Adelman and Maatsch had to take special steps to insure that the Recoil animals could make an easily-specified competing response.

In conclusion, the frustration theory suggests that extinction results from the action of competing responses, energized by frustration following nonreward. Although it is not clear at this time why extinction is relatively permanent (frustration should decrease with continued experience with nonreward, thus allowing the original habit to be reestablished), the frustration theory does account successfully for many of the findings cited previously.

Generalization Decrement Theory

Like the frustration hypothesis, generalization decrement theories have been formulated primarily to explain the partial reinforcement effect. However, they also serve as general theories for extinction.

The basic notion can be explained most easily by noting three stages through which subjects progress. First, during acquisition the subjects learn to respond to a complex of discriminative stimuli. One very important source of stimuli is the reward; that is, the reward, its aftereffects, and the stimuli generated by those aftereffects come to serve as controllers or elicitors of the conditioned response (see the discussion on the r_g-s_g mechanism in Chapter 3). Second, during extinction, the stimulus complex changes substantially since no reward or reward aftereffects are provided. A different, although overlapping set of cues comprises the stimulus complex during extinction. Third, responding declines during extinction because the controlling stimulus complex differs noticeably from the complex to which the subject was conditioned during acquisition. The extent of the decrease during extinction is positively related to the discrepancy between the acquisition and extinction stimuli. In other words, if the stimulus complex during extinction is relatively similar to the complex during acquisition, the conditioned response will continue to be made—there will be strong resistance to extinction. On the other hand, if the complexes differ appreciably, the response will rapidly disappear during extinction—low resistance to extinction. In summary, extinction takes place when the cues involved in extinction are dissimilar from those in acquisition. Normally, withdrawing the reward constitutes a salient and important enough change in the stimulus complex to produce a decrease in the elicited behavior; changes in other stimuli may be less critical.

The generalization decrement theory successfully accounts for many of the findings discussed previously. For example, the discrepancy between constant large reward and no reward is greater than between small reward and no reward. According to the theory, therefore, extinction should be more rapid following large reward in acquisition than following small reward because there is more difference between the stimuli complexes; the results confirm this prediction. Second, changes from acquisition to extinction in certain parameters of training establish a different stimulus complex and, thus, promote extinction.

Procedures that increase the discrepancy between the acquisition and extinction conditions hasten extinction while procedures that minimize the differences increase resistance to extinction. Intermittent reinforcement during acquisition, of course, is one example. However, other strategies have been used. Rescorla and Skucy (1969) presented reward during the extinction of lever pressing independent of the subject's behavior. This was to help maintain the general stimulus conditions the subject associated with the acquisition series, principally reward and reward aftereffects. The authors found that extinction was retarded even though the subject was no longer contingently rewarded for responding. Specific formulations of the generalization decrement theory, designed to account for the partial reinforcement effect, are provided in a later section.

FACTORS IN EXTINCTION FOLLOWING INTERMITTENT REWARD TRAINING

One of the most reliable phenomena in learning research is the partial reinforcement effect—the fact that resistance to extinction is stronger following intermittent, as compared to continuous, reinforcement during acquisition. Humphreys (1939) was one of the first investigators to note this apparent paradox: omission of reward during acquisition should lead to a lower level of habit strength; yet, in terms of resistance to extinction, habit strength is more durable following intermittent reward. Current theory has resolved this paradox by noting that resistance to extinction is not merely an alternative index of habit strength. Moreover, many factors that influence resistance to extinction following partial reward can be accounted for with some precision by more modern concepts. The following sections describe some of these factors that form a basis for theory (see Robbins, 1971, for a review).

Percentage of Rewarded Trials

The effect of overall percentage of rewarded trials during acquisition is one parameter that affects resistance to extinction. Several investigators have found that resistance to extinction was an inverse function of the percentage of rewarded trials; the greater the percentage, the faster the extinction (e.g., Ratliff & Weinstock, 1958). However, another finding was that resistance to extinction was an inverted U-shaped function of percentage of reward during acquisition (e.g., Bacon, 1962; Coughlin, 1970; see Lewis, 1960); that is, extinction occurs rapidly following very low or very high percentages of rewarded trials but greater resistance to extinction is found following intermittent levels of reward. Bacon, for example, trained rats to run in an alley; percentages of reinforced trials, for separate groups of subjects, were 30, 50, 70, or 100. During extinction, Bacon found that the 30 and 100 percent subjects ran slower than the subjects in the other two groups, that is, the resistance-to-extinction curve was an inverted U-shaped function of percentage. However, when the rate of decrease in responding is considered, resistance to extinction declined progressively as a function of percentage of reward.

Reward Magnitude

Many studies have shown that resistance to extinction depends on both the schedule and magnitude of reward during acquisition. As noted earlier, following continuous reinforcement, resistance to extinction decreases as a function of reward magnitude but, conversely, following partial reinforcement training, resistance to extinction increases with reward magnitude (Capaldi et al., 1968; Leonard, 1969; Ratliff & Ratliff, 1971; Wagner, 1961). For example, Ratliff and Ratliff (1971) trained rats to traverse an alley. During the 64 acquisition trials, separate groups of subjects were rewarded on 25, 50, 75, or 100 percent of the trials; on the rewarded trials, separate groups in each of the percentage conditions received either 2, 4, 8, or 16 food pellets in the goal box. Thus, the experiment combined four levels of reward magnitude with four levels of partial reward training.

Figure 5-5 illustrates the results obtained on the 64 extinction trials. It

FIGURE 5-5.

Mean resistance to extinction (rate of decrease from terminal acquisition performance) as a function of percentage of rewarded trials during acquisition for groups differing in reward magnitude.

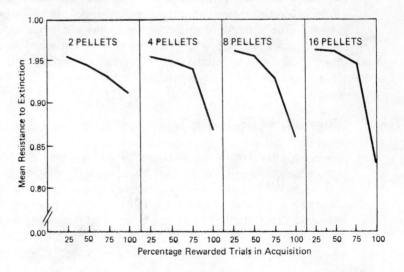

FIGURE 5-6.

Mean running speed as a function of blocks of extinction trials for groups that received differing numbers of partial reinforcement training trials. Data at A represent terminal acquisition performance.

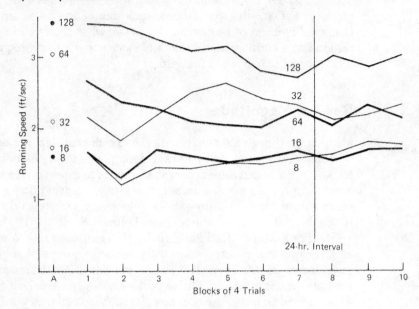

is clear that the averaged resistance to extinction for the continuous groups, measured in terms of a rate decrease from the terminal acquisition level (Anderson, 1963), decreased as a function of reward magnitude. However, for the partial reinforcement conditions, resistance to extinction was an increasing function of reward magnitude. In fact, extinction was slowest in all of the 16-pellet, partially-reinforced groups and fastest in the 2-pellet, partially-rewarded groups, regardless of the actual percentage of reward. In summary, reward magnitude has a differential effect on behavior depending upon, among other things, the schedule of reinforcement. Following continuous reward, resistance to extinction decreases with larger rewards, but following partial reinforcement, the reverse is true.

Number of Training Trials

Resistance to extinction following partial reinforcement increases as a function of the number of acquisition trials (e.g., Hill & Spear, 1963; Wilson, 1964). In the Hill and Spear study, five groups of rats were given partial reward training in an alley for either 8, 16, 32, 64, or 128 trials. The extinction data, shown in Figure 5-6 indicated that resistance to extinction was a positive function of the degree of training. Subjects that received 128 trials continued to run the fastest during extinction while the subjects that had 8 or 16 trials were the slowest. Thus, the relationship between the extent of acquisition and resistance to extinction is a positive one following partial reinforcement, but a negative (inverse) one following continuous reinforcement (see previous section).

It should be noted that partial reinforcement increases resistance to extinction, relative to continuous reward, even after a very few training trials (e.g., Capaldi & Deutsch, 1967; McCain, 1966). This finding has important implications for theories of the partial reinforcement effect and is discussed in a later section.

Patterns of Reward

Patterns of reward and nonreward trials are extremely important to the issue of resistance to extinction. Early research (e.g., Tyler et al., 1953) indicated that alternating patterns of reward during acquisition reduced later resistance to extinction compared to random patterns. This effect has been documented in many other studies (e.g., Capaldi, 1958), although with a small number of training trials, an alternating pattern leads to greater resistance to extinction (Capaldi & Hart, 1962). The reason for this discrepancy is discussed more fully in a later section.

Capaldi (1958) and others explained their results by suggesting that the difference in the reward-nonreward condition during extinction was greater following alternating than following random patterns and thus performance declined more quickly; that is, continuous nonreward during extinction was more apparent to the subject when the previous reward-nonreward pattern was fixed than when it was variable. This hypothesis was confirmed in a study by Rudy (1971) who found that single alternation of reward and nonreward trials during acquisition decreased resistance to extinction as compared to a random pattern of reinforcement. More important, however, was the finding that subjects who received a random schedule but for whom a light in the alley was turned on during the nonrewarded trials extinguished as fast as the alternation group. In other words, when subjects could easily discriminate the pattern of reward during acquisition, extinction was quite rapid (alternation group). If the pattern was less easy to discern (random group), responding was prolonged unless, at the same time, an additional factor was present (in this case, the light stimulus) which aided the subject in making the discrimination.

THEORIES OF THE PARTIAL REINFORCEMENT EFFECT

Among the many theories of the partial reinforcement effect, two recent major positions have received considerable attention. The following sections review the frustration and sequential theories and the supporting evidence.

Frustration Theory

When we expect a reward and do not get it, we experience frustration. Presumably, this is true for animals too, and studies have shown frustration is aversive, that is, similar to punishment (see Wagner, 1969) and it energizes responding (e.g., Amsel & Roussel, 1952). In general, the reason partially reinforced subjects persist in making responses longer during extinction than continuously rewarded subjects is that they have been conditioned to perform in the presence of frustration. In contrast, the continuously reinforced subjects experience the full impact of the aversive frustration for the first time during extinction; therefore, they cease to respond rather quickly.

Amsel's frustration hypothesis uses many of the same arguments posed by incentive theory (see Chapter 3) except that the goal event here is one of nonreward. When an animal runs to the goal box expecting reward (based on the fact that reward was available on previous trials) but receives no reward, a frustration response occurs. On subsequent trials, the start box and alley evoke a fractional component of the primary frustration response, r_f. Like all responses, r_f, in turn, generates an associated stimulus, s_f (the frustration reaction, elicited by the alley prior to the goal box, is also a source of an internal stimulus). If the rat enters the goal box and is fed while experiencing the r_f-s_f sequence, then it is reinforced for running in the presence of the frustration cues. In other words, s_f comes to be part of the overall stimulus complex that elicits running since the subject receives reinforcement in the presence of s_f; the elicitation of r_f-s_f provides an opportunity for s_f to become associated with reward and, thus, to control behavior. Continuously reinforced subjects, of course, do not experience frustration during acquisition so they are never reinforced for running in the presence of the s_f cue. Continued occurrence of frustration (r_f-s_f) during extinction leads to continued performance by the partially rewarded animals. The continuously reinforced subjects, on the other hand, experience frustration for the first time during extinction; they have not been rewarded for running to s_f, so when frustration occurs, their responding declines rapidly.

The frustration theory easily accounts for many of the factors discussed previously. For example, it is clear that the strength of conditioned responding to frustration cues during extinction would be a positive function of the percentage of nonreward trials during acquisition; that is, the opportunity for an intense frustration to develop, and, thus, for a strong r_f-s_f sequence to be conditioned by reward, would be greater with more nonrewarded trials. In the case of reward magnitude, a larger, continuous reward during acquisition would lead to more rapid extinction than a small reward because greater frustration (disruption) would be elicited during extinction. In contrast, a large, partial reward would increase resistance to extinction, relative to a small reward, because the r_f-s_f sequence would be more strongly conditioned by the large reward during acquisition. Finally, a similar argument can be made in the case of number of training trials: more extended partial reinforcement training would increase the strength of running to r_f-s_f (i.e., produce strong resistance to extinction) whereas a large number of continuous reinforcement trials merely would accentuate the disruptive effects of frustration during extinction.

The notion that nonreward produces an emotional reaction is critical to the frustration theory. One prediction is that methods that eliminate emotionality also should eliminate, or at least reduce, the partial reinforcement effect. Several studies have attempted to confirm this prediction (e.g., Gray, 1969; Ison & Pennes, 1969). In Gray's study, rats were trained under either a continuous or partial reinforcement schedule to traverse an alley for 64 acquisition trials. Prior to the acquisition trials, half the subjects in each group were injected with amobarbital (a tranquilizing drug that reduces emotionality) whereas the other half received a placebo injection. During extinction, all the subjects received placebo. Gray found that the partial reinforcement effect was greatly lessened in the subjects that had been given amobarbital. According to the frustration theory, neither the partial-injected nor the continuous groups experienced strong frustration during acquisition: continuously rewarded subjects never experienced nonreward, and frustration in the partially reinforced animals was reduced by the amobarbital. Therefore, conditioning of the approach response to frustration cues was relatively weak in the partial subjects. However, during extinction, when intense frustration was present in both groups for the first time, both groups extinguished at a comparable rate.

Although the evidence from drug studies provided strong support for the frustration theory, other investigators have failed to obtain comparable results. Ziff and Capaldi (1971), for example, conducted an experiment like Gray's except for the fact that only a few (3 or 6) acquisition trials were used. Ziff and Capaldi found that amobarbital administration during acquisition did not eliminate or even reduce the partial reinforcement effect during extinction; partially rewarded subjects still were more resistant to extinction than continuously rewarded animals.

Ziff and Capaldi's study raised an important criticism of the frustration theory, namely that the aftereffects of nonreward on the first few trials are not emotional in nature. Numerous other studies have demonstrated the partial reinforcement effect after only a few acquisition trials; under such training conditions, it is unlikely that frustration could have developed (and have been conditioned) so rapidly.

The argument, that frustration theory is inadequate because the partial reinforcement effect occurs after only a few acquisition trials, was supported recently by Capaldi and Waters (1970). They compared the performance of continuously reinforced subjects (5 or 10 acquisition trials) during extinction to the performance of a group of partially rewarded subjects. This group received five nonrewarded (N) trials, followed by five rewarded (R) trials. Capaldi and Waters found that the partially reinforced animals were more resistant to extinction than the continuous subjects even though frustration could not have been conditioned. Those subjects could not have expected reward during the N trials since they never experienced reward prior to the N trials; if they did not expect a reward, they could hardly have been frustrated at not receiving one. Thus, conditioning to frustration cues could not have taken place. Although several investigators have attempted to adjust the frustration theory to account for the partial reinforcement effect after limited training (e.g., Amsel et al., 1968; Brooks, 1969), the general consensus is that frustration theory may be appropriate only when extended training is used; otherwise, a theory that relies on the conditioning of nonemotional aftereffects appears to be more useful (see following section).

Sequential Theory

The most widely-accepted theory of the partial reinforcement effect is Capaldi's sequential aftereffects hypothesis (see Capaldi, 1966, 1967; Koteskey, 1972). The basic concepts which the theory uses to explain extinction are nearly identical to those of the frustration theory. The principal difference is that the sequential theory does not assume that the aftereffects of nonreward are emotional. Rather, reward and nonreward generate distinctive, nonemotional stimuli that are capable of persisting through time via memory. If the aftereffects stemming from nonreward are present on a subsequent rewarded trial, they become conditioned by reward and thus form part of the overall stimulus complex that controls behavior. Partially-reinforced subjects are reinforced, on rewarded trials, for performing in the presence of distinctive aftereffects from nonreward (that occurred on previous trials); during extinction, the aftereffects from nonreward continue to elicit the behavior because they are part of the stimulus complex that had been conditioned during acquisition. Continuously-reinforced animals, on the other hand, never experience nonreward aftereffects during acquisition. During extinction, nonreward aftereffects occur for the first time and since they were not conditioned during acquisition, they contribute to a marked change in the stimulus complex, a generalization decrement, and, in turn, produce a rapid decline in performance.

As we said above, the central notion in the sequential theory is that stimuli from nonrewarded (N) trials get conditioned on subsequent rewarded (R) trials. In more specific terms, conditioning of N aftereffects always involves N-R transitions; that is, an N trial, on which nonreward aftereffects occur, must eventually be followed by an R trial, during which the N aftereffects get conditioned. The reverse transitions (R-N) are relatively ineffective in this regard since N aftereffects are not followed by reward, and, thus, are not conditioned.

Given the importance of N-R transitions, Capaldi has been able to specify three crucial factors or conditions that determine later resistance to extinction. These are: (a) the N-length, that is, the number of consecutive nonrewarded trials prior to an R trial, (b) the number of times a particular N-length occurs; and (c) the variety of N-lengths.

The importance of all three factors was demonstrated in a study by

FIGURE 5-7.

Log median time for the running response during acquisition (sessions 1-8) and extinction (sessions 9-11) for the N_1 and N_2 groups (N-lengths of 1 and 2, respectively).

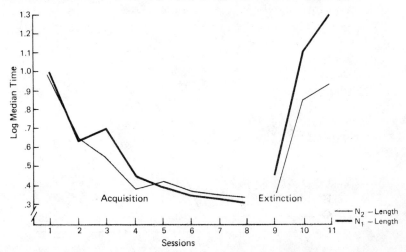

Capaldi (1964). In one experiment dealing with N-length, two groups of rats were trained to run in an alley for food. Both groups received the same sequence of reward and nonreward trials (e.g., RNNRRNNR). In addition, intertrial rewards (r) were administered. On those occasions, the subjects were merely placed in the goal box during the intertrial interval and given food; no instrumental running response was required. The purpose of giving an intertrial reward was to change the aftereffects from N to R; that is, an r experience would abolish any N aftereffects by producing the same aftereffects as an R trial, but r itself would not strengthen the running behavior since r was not contingent on running.

Subjects in group N_1, for whom the N-length was one, received intertrial rewards just prior to the last trial (e.g., RNrNRRNrNR) whereas the subjects in the N_2 group, for whom the N-length was two, received their intertrial rewards prior to the last two N trials (e.g., RrNNRRrNNR). The only difference between the two groups during acquisition was the N-length prior to a rewarded trial.

The results, for both acquisition and extinction, are shown in Figure 5-7. Although the two groups did not differ during acquisition, a marked difference was obtained on the extinction trials. Specifically, subjects in group N_2 were significantly more resistant to extinction than those in Group N_1. Capaldi explained these results by claiming that aftereffects from nonreward trials built up over successive N trials. The conditioned aftereffects, as part of the controlling stimulus complex, were stronger in Group N_2 than N_1; consequently, the conditioned aftereffects in Group N_2 generalized more readily to the extinction situation than those of Group N_1.

The second two principles (resistance to extinction increases as a function of the number and variety of N-lengths) also were investigated by

FIGURE 5-8.

Mean log running time as a function of extinction sessions for groups given 24, 60, or 120 training trials and an N-length of 3 or varied N-lengths of 1, 2, and 3.

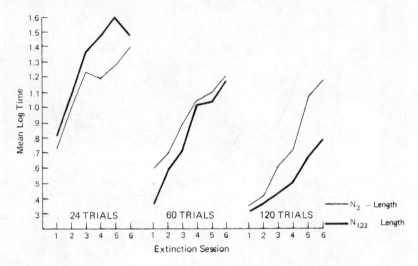

Capaldi (1964, Experiment 3). Again, a running response in an alley was trained, then extinguished. Two groups received 24 trials, two received 60 trials, and two were given 120 training trials. One group in each of the above conditions consistently had an N-length of three (e.g., RNNNRR); the other group in each condition experienced N-lengths of 1, 2, and 3 (e.g., the patterns were RNNNNRR, or NRNNRR). Thus, the six groups differed only in terms of the number of reinforced N-lengths (24, 60, or 120 trials) and the variety of N-lengths (always 3, or 1, 2, and 3).

Extinction performance for the six groups is shown in Figure 5-8. After 24 training trials, Group N_{123} was less resistant to extinction than Group N_3. According to Capaldi, the conditioning of a single N-length in the N_3 subjects was stronger than the cumulative conditioning to the separate N-lengths of 1, 2, and 3 in the N_{123} subjects. However, after extended training, results were the reverse: Group N_{123} was more resistant to extinction than Group N_3. This occurred because conditioning to a single N-length of three generalized to the extinction trials less than the cumulative conditioning to N-lengths of 1, 2, and 3. In other words, by the end of 24 acquisition trials, the strength of the counterconditioning in the N_3 subjects had increased nearly to its maximum level; in contrast, each of the N-lengths in Group N_{123} had been reinforced only a few times and their combined effect was still relatively weak. However, after 120 trials, each of the N-lengths in Group N_{123} had reached its maximum level and the cumulative effect at that point was greater than the strength of the single N-length in Group N_3.

By considering N-length and the number and variety of N-lengths, Capaldi's theory can account for nearly all of the factors that affect extinction after partial reinforcement. For example, large partial rewards increase resistance to extinction because the N aftereffects are more strongly conditioned during acquisition; in contrast, animals that are given continuous large rewards experience a more intense generalization decrement at the outset of extinction (their behavior is not controlled by nonreward aftereffects) and thus extinguish quickly. In addition, Capaldi and Capaldi (1970) and Capaldi and Lynch (1968) have shown that resistance to extinction is influenced by the reward magnitude following an N trial, not by the discrepancy between the anticipated and actual reward on the N trial. As discussed previously, frustration theory claims that such a discrepancy would be critical to the intensity of frustration and thus to resistance to extinction.

In summary, Capaldi's sequential theory successfully accounts for most of the partial reinforcement phenomena. It is particularly suited for explaining increased resistance to extinction following a very limited number of partially reinforced trials, differences in extinction following partial versus continuous training with extremely long intertrial intervals, and increased resistance to extinction following a partial delay of reward in acquisition. Since none of the above effects is as easily handled by frustration theory, the sequential aftereffects view appears to be the most suitable approach.

EXTINCTION FOLLOWING AVERSIVELY MOTIVATED LEARNING

The general issue of avoidance extinction has been the subject of many investigations. It is especially interesting because the elimination of fear-motivated behavior is central to many behavior therapies (see Chapter 3).

Think, for example, how drastic the consequences might be if we couldn't easily extinguish fear-motivated behavior: the behavior would persist and, if the unpleasant stimulus no longer occurred, would become not only useless but maladaptive. Therefore, an understanding of the fundamental principles of fear and avoidance extinction should aid in the design of more effective behavior therapies.

As we have said before, extinction following appetitive training involves either withholding the reward or presenting a noncontingent reward—in any case, terminating the response-reinforcement relationship (e.g., Rescorla & Skucy, 1969). In terms of avoidance behavior, the analogous procedures would involve disallowing the subjects to avoid shock, or perhaps using a schedule in which shock avoidance was not directly contingent on the subject's response. Surprisingly few experiments have used these procedures. However, in those that have (e.g., Bolles et al., 1971; Reynierse & Rizley, 1970), the findings have been clear: the inability to avoid the unpleasant stimulus is especially important in promoting extinction; when a subject's response no longer avoids shock, the extinction rate declines.

Extinction Using US Omission

The usual procedure used in avoidance extinction has been to present the CS but omit the US. This method poses a special problem: if a subject continues to make successful avoidance responses during extinction, then the fact that the US will not be presented will never be experienced by the subject. Only by failing to make an avoidance reponse will the subject be able to experience the new contingency (no US presentation) during extinction. This problem can be stated in a different way: how can a subject come to experience the fact that shock will not be presented (that extinction procedures are not in effect) if the subject already is responding before shock was scheduled to occur during acquisition? From the subject's viewpoint, the US is omitted in either case. Unless a noticeable change in the reinforcement contingency is present, no change in behavior (i.e., no extinction) can be expected.

The implication, that avoidance extinction may be prolonged with the US omission procedure, was noted by Solomon, Kamin, and Wynne (1953). Dogs were trained to jump from one compartment to another, then back again on the next trial, to avoid a very intense shock. During extinction, the avoidance behavior continued unabated for hundreds of trials; that is, the extinction procedure, no US presentation, had virtually no effect on responding and the dogs continued to jump.

Solomon and Wynne (1954) later attempted to explain this result with the concept of "conservation of anxiety." According to their theory, since avoidance responding was motivated by fear (Mowrer's two-factor theory—see Chapter 4), extinction of avoidance would take place only if the fear on which the avoidance depended was extinguished first. Yet during extinction, fear was preserved because the nonoccurrence of shock was never experienced by the subjects. The consequence of this conservation of anxiety was the perpetuation of rapid "avoidance" behavior and the continued protection of fear from extinction.

The solution to the problem required the extinction of Pavlovian fear first; presumably, avoidance behavior then would decline also since the motivating impetus behind the avoidance would be absent. Solomon et al. (1953) used several techniques to extinguish fear, the most effective of which was *response blocking*, also called *flooding*. Here, the subject was prevented from responding during the CS by the insertion of a plastic barrier between compartments. The subject, therefore, was compelled to "reality test," that is, was forced to learn that the painful stimulus would not be presented. The consequence of flooding was a decrease in the resistance to extinction.

Parameters of Flooding

Flooding, or response prevention, has been studied extensively (see Baum, 1970; Smith et al. 1973 for reviews). It is an important topic in learning research because it relates directly to several human behavior therapies. In other words, the research on flooding has attempted to assess directly the most effective way of extinguishing fear-motivated behavior; that is, the main goal for investigators who study flooding has been to provide an analog to the problem of fear extinction in humans.

The typical procedure is to train an avoidance response, then "flood" the subject with the CS during which time the avoidance response is blocked. Subsequently, when extinction trials are given, the flooded subjects are invariably less resistant to extinction than nonflooded controls; that is, their responses are extinguished more easily.

The efficacy of the flooding procedure has been shown to be related to a number of factors. For example, Baum (1969a) trained rats to avoid shocks of .5, 1.3, or 2.0 milliamps. Later measures of resistance to extinction indicated that a 3-minute flooding procedure was less effective in the more intense shock groups. In other words, the ability for flooding to promote extinction was inversely related to prior shock intensity.

The number and duration of CS exposures have also been investigated. Bersh and Keltz (1971) trained rats in a shuttlebox to a criterion of three consecutive avoidance responses. The subjects then received five flooding sessions during which the CS was presented to four separate groups for 5, 15, 120, or 300 seconds. Resistance to extinction was reduced in all groups (relative to an unflooded control group) but more so in the 120- and 300-second groups. In addition, a single CS-US pairing after extinction restored the response in all of the groups except the 300-second subjects. Thus, extended exposure to the CS during response blocking promoted extinction and precluded the reinstatement of responding following an additional CS-US pairing.

The interrelationship between the number of flooding sessions and the duration of the CS per session was investigated by Schiff, Smith, and Prochaska (1972). Rats first were trained in an alley to avoid shock. Then, during the flooding phase, separate groups of subjects received either 1, 5, or 12 blocked trials each lasting either 0, 5, 10, 50, or 120 seconds (there are 15 possible combinations of number of trials times duration of trial, one combination per group). Finally, all subjects then were extinguished to a criterion of three consecutive trials for which the response latency exceeded 120 seconds. The authors found that a few, long-lasting blocking trials were as effective in promoting extinction as many, shorter-lasting trials.

Although Schiff et al. showed that increased duration and number of flooding trials were equally effective in reducing resistance to extinction, there was some indication in their data that the number of trials was more critical to extinction than was the duration. Indeed, other investigators (e.g., Baum & Myran, 1971; Franchina, et al., 1974) have shown that the presentation of several flooding trials is more effective in promoting extinction than a single, long-lasting trial. In the Baum and Myran study, for example, the mean number of extinction responses, executed by subjects who had received three minutes of flooding for three consecutive days, was .9; in contrast, the mean number of responses for subjects given a single, 9-minute flooding session was 6.7. Both duration of flooding and the number of flooding trials affect extinction responding; the greater the total time, the less the resistance to extinction. However, the number of trials, rather than the duration of the trials, appears to be the more important factor in this relationship.

Several other factors during flooding have been shown to influence extinction. Lenderhendler and Baum (1970) found that gentle prodding of the subjects, so that they became active, increased the effectiveness of flooding. Conversely, Baum and Myran (1971) showed that confining the animals so that their activity was restricted decreased the efficacy of the flooding procedure. Finally, Baum (1969b) found that if nonfearful rats were placed in the apparatus with the test animal during flooding, the flooding was more effective.

Theories of Flooding

One important theory of flooding is based on Mowrer's two-factor theory of avoidance learning. According to this position, avoidance is motivated by fear. When fear is extinguished (CS followed by no US) during the flooding session, motivation for the avoidance response is reduced, and, accordingly, avoidance extinction occurs rapidly.

The fear theory is supported by several of the findings cited previously. For example, the inverse relationship between shock intensity (greater shock produces more intense fear) and the effectiveness of flooding is consistent with the fear theory. Similarly, the fact that longer flooding sessions, or a greater number of sessions, promotes extinction also can be explained in terms of fear reduction. Indeed, some investigators have shown that subjects are less fearful (measured in terms of their passive avoidance of the shock compartment) if they were given flooding than if they were not (e.g., Bersh & Paynter, 1972; Linton et al., 1970; Wilson, 1973). Finally, Morokoff and Timberlake (1971) directly observed a reduction in fear behavior (freezing) from one flooding session to the next. Thus, it appears that Pavlovian fear reduction, during flooding, plays a significant role in later avoidance extinction.

However, other investigators have been critical of the fear theory, at least as the sole explanation of flooding. For example, Coulter, Riccio, and Page (1969) found that although response prevention decreased later resistance to extinction, considerable fear (avoidance of the shock compartment) was still present at the end of extinction. In another experiment, Linton et al. (1970) flooded one group following avoidance acquisition but not the other. The responses of both groups were then extinguished to the same criterion (failure to leave the startbox within 10 seconds on three consecutive trials). The authors found that flooding reduced resistance to extinction; however, on a passive avoidance test, designed to measure residual fear to the CS, the previously blocked subjects paradoxically were more fearful than the animals who were not flooded.

Alternative viewpoints have emphasized the role of competing responses. However, the exact nature of the competing behavior is not entirely clear. Coulter et al. (1969) argued that subjects developed freezing responses during flooding; later, these responses competed with avoidance extinction. According to this theory, the decrease in resistance to extinction was not due to a loss of fear, but rather to competition with freezing behavior that was acquired during flooding. Only minimal evidence has been provided in support of this theory: Linton et al. (1970) found that six out of ten blocked subjects, who explicitly froze during flooding, failed to leave the start box during extinction.

Other investigators have suggested that a radically different type of competing response occurs. For example, Baum (1970) observed that animals engaged in locomotor behavior during flooding. Therefore, Baum claimed that general activity, which increased over the flooding session, was reinforced by the nonoccurrence of shock (i.e., became conditioned to the surrounding apparatus cues). During extinction, these "relaxation" responses were elicited causing competition with the avoidance response (i.e., rapid avoidance extinction).

The evidence for this type of competing response theory is more compelling. First, general activity (not freezing) has been shown to increase during flooding (Baum, 1970). Second, if the subject was prodded into being more active, extinction was even more rapid (Lenderhendler & Baum, 1970); conversely, if activity during flooding was restricted, that is, if the opportunity for developing competing "relaxation" responses was reduced, extinction responding was prolonged (Baum & Myran, 1971). Finally, and most important, a number of investigators have shown that when competing locomotor responses had ample opportunity to become conditioned during flooding, resistance to extinction was decreased. Specifically, positively reinforcing brain stimulation during flooding was shown to increase the efficacy of the flooding session (Gordon & Baum, 1971), not because it induced general activity (Baum et al., 1973) but because it reinforced competing behaviors. Prado-Alcala et al. (1973), for example, showed that flooding was even more efficient in promoting extinction when pleasurable brain stimulation, during the flooding, explicitly was contingent on a competing behavior.

In summary, extinction following flooding appears to be a function of the interaction between fear reduction and competing responses. Changes in fear occur during a flooding session and the amount of fear reduction depends upon several important parameters of training. However, at the same time, competing responses acquired during flooding also play a role in facilitating later extinction. It is hoped that these issues will be clarified even further by future research, and that it will be possible to use any improvements in flooding techniques in actual therapy programs.

SUMMARY

Extinction involves withholding the reward after the subject has made the conditioned instrumental response. In Pavlovian conditioning terms, extinction occurs when the US does not follow the CS. In both cases, the result is a decrease in the conditioned response.

The rate of response decrease, or conversely, the resistance to extinction procedures, is influenced by many factors. For example, constant large reward decreases the resistance to extinction as compared to a constant small reward. In contrast, large reward presented intermittently during acquisition increases later resistance to extinction as compared to a small intermittent reward. Other factors that influence extinction behavior include the response effort, reward delay, and the number and pattern of rewarded trials during acquisition.

One of the most interesting extinction phenomena is the partial reinforcement effect—subjects who received reward intermittently during acquisition persist in responding longer during the extinction procedure than subjects who received continuous reward. The frustration and aftereffects theories account very nicely for this finding. Both positions claim that stimuli that occur on the nonreinforced trials during acquisition persist to the next rewarded trial and thus become counterconditioned. In one sense, the subjects are rewarded for responding in the presence of internal, nonrewarded stimuli. During extinction, then, the partially-rewarded subjects persist longer due to this prior conditioning (continuously-rewarded subjects, of course, never experienced nonreward during acquisition and therefore could not have been counterconditioned to respond to nonreward stimuli).

Another interesting issue in extinction involves the extinction of aversively motivated behavior. Research has shown that flooding procedures—that is, presenting a fear CS without allowing the animals to make their previously learned avoidance response—promotes extinction. This finding has very important implications for the treatment of human neurosis. The therapy aims to suppress fear-motivated behavior which is no longer adaptive by applying flooding techniques.

6/ Generalization and Discrimination

Preview

In this chapter, we discuss behavior that is somewhat more complex than a simple conditioned response: discrimination and generalization. Here, we are concerned with the degree to which a subject tells the difference between two stimuli—discriminates between them—and the degree to which the subject reacts to the similarity between two stimuli—generalizes from one stimulus to another. To understand these processes, we shall consider how various factors influence generalization and, similarly, discrimination; also we shall consider several theories that explain how or why we behave this way. One interesting aspect of this topic is that human problem solving, that is, making a correct response to one stimulus rather than to another, is fundamentally based on discrimination behavior. As we shall discover in this chapter, research which uses animals in controlled situations has, at the very least, generated some useful, basic concepts which help us to understand problem solving behavior in humans (for an extension of this work, see Chapter 13.)

INTRODUCTION TO GENERALIZATION

In Chapters 2 and 3, we noted that a CS acquires the ability to elicit a CR due to its association with a US. In the case of a discriminative stimulus it is the fact that the S+ signals reinforcement availability which can elicit the CR. However, CRs are not necessarily restricted to a single CS; other stimuli, which were not employed in the original training, also can evoke a CR. Consider the following example. A child walks into a store with her parents and sees a ceiling fan slowly revolving. Previous to this shopping trip, the child had been given a record player and learned to say "record" when she saw the turntable revolve. Now, in this new situation, the child sees the revolving fan in the store for the first time and says "record." Clearly, she has responded to an entirely novel stimulus with a response she had learned to a different stimulus. The child had generalized from the turntable to the fan based on the fact that both were circular objects that rotated.

The important phenomenon illustrated in the example above is termed *stimulus generalization*: after a particular response has been conditioned, a novel, yet similar CS is able to elicit the CR. The magnitude of the generalized response is usually a function of the degree of similarity between the original and the test CSs; that is, the more similar a novel CS is to the original stimulus, the larger the reaction on the generalization test. This orderly, graded relationship between the CR magnitude and the similarity of the training and test stimuli is the *generalization gradient*. (See Kalish, 1969; Mednick & Freedman, 1960; Mostofsky, 1965; and Prokasy & Hall, 1963 for reviews of generalization.)

Generalization is important because it allows us to behave adaptively in our environment. We could not possibly survive for very long if we had to learn the significance of each and *every* stimulus separately. Given that generalization from one stimulus to another is possible, we can often make an appropriate (adaptive) response to novel stimuli; that is, we can take advantage of past learning.

Much of the basic research on generalization uses pigeons as subjects. A note about research strategy: pigeons have extraordinary color vision, thus making it relatively easy to collect certain kinds of data. As with other research in which animals are used as subjects, the important goal is to discover basic laws which can then help us understand similar processes in humans.

Excitatory Gradients

Most of the research on generalization has involved *excitatory conditioning*, in which the conditioned stimulus signals the presentation of the US (see Chapter 2). One experiment was done by Guttman and Kalish (1956) who trained hungry pigeons to peck a small translucent disk, located on the side of the testing cage, to gain access to grain. A light was placed

FIGURE 6-1.

Mean total responses on the generalization test as a function of the wavelength of the stimuli for four groups for whom the original CS was either 530, 550, 580, or 600 nanometers.

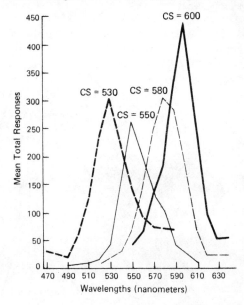

behind the disk so that, with the use of filters, the color of the disk could be controlled accurately. Four groups of subjects differed only in terms of the wavelength of this disk, which was the discriminative stimulus: 530, 550, 580, and 600 nanometers.

During periods when the light CS was on, the pigeons were rewarded for pecking on a VI-1 minute schedule of reinforcement. Following acquisition, a generalization test with no rewards was given by showing the original CS wavelength plus 10 other stimuli (both higher and lower on the spectrum) for 30 seconds; each set of 11 randomly ordered test stimuli was repeated 12 times.

The results of this study are shown in Figure 6-1. Mean total responses to each stimulus are plotted separately for the four groups. Maximum responding in each group of subjects was, appropriately, to the CS experienced during training. However, other novel stimuli also elicited the pecking response with the magnitude of performance reflecting the similarity between the training and test stimuli. These symmetrical gradients were a striking feature of the data.

Inhibitory Gradients.

A number of studies have demonstrated generalization of inhibitory stimuli (e.g., Hearst et al., 1970; Jenkins & Harrison, 1962; Weisman & Palmer,

FIGURE 6-2.

Number of responses on the generalization test as a function of line orientation of the test stimuli (S- was zero degrees) for five subjects. Responding to S+ is shown at right of each individual gradient.

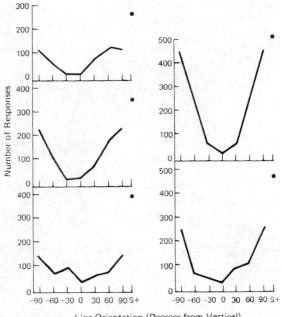

Line Orientation (Degrees from Vertical)

1969). As you probably remember, an inhibitory CS is one that is paired with no US, that is, it signals the absence of the US. You may recall also that we measure the conditioned inhibitory tendency by combining the CS— with an excitatory CS+; if excitation is reduced, then the CS— must be an inhibitor. Here, the idea is to combine generalized stimuli (that are novel yet similar to a CS—) with a CS+. The prediction, of course, is that if inhibition generalizes like excitation, an inhibitory generalization gradient (really the mirror image of an excitatory gradient) will be found.

In the Weisman and Palmer study, pigeons were trained to peck a disk for food (delivered on a variable interval 1-minute schedule). Then, all the subjects were given discriminative training: pecking a green disk was reinforced whereas pecking the green disk with a white vertical line projected onto it was not rewarded. This procedure was designed to establish the green disk as the S+ and the white line as the inhibitory S—. In a third phase of the study, each subject was given a generalization test during which the vertical line (S—) plus six other lines, departing from vertical by −90, −60, −30, +30, +60, and +90 degrees, were randomly presented.

The individual inhibitory gradients for five of the subjects are shown in Figure 6-2. A comparison of the number of responses elicited by each stimulus, relative to the number of responses to the S+, indicates that

FIGURE 6-3.

Total responses during generalization as a function of line tilt for groups of pigeons that received 2, 4, 7, or 14 50-minute sessions of VI training. The S+ was a vertical line.

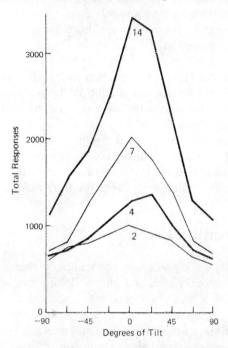

responding was suppressed by the presence of a white line on the disk. However, the degree of suppression varied: A vertical line of 0 degrees (the original S−) produced the greatest inhibition of pecking whereas tilted lines caused less suppression. The amount of response suppression caused by the generalized stimuli was a positive function of the similarity between the training and test stimuli: the greater the tilt from vertical, the less the stimulus produced generalized inhibition.

FACTORS AFFECTING GENERALIZATION

The degree to which generalization occurs is indicated by the height and steepness of the generalization gradient. A steep gradient reflects little generalization: even stimuli that are very similar to the original CS evoke a low level of responding. This section discusses some of the important factors that affect generalization.

Degree of Acquisition

A number of investigators have shown that generalization decreases (the gradient becomes sharper) following more extended acquisition (e.g.,

Brown, 1970; Hearst & Koresko, 1968). In the Hearst and Koresko study, for example, groups of pigeons were given 2, 4, 7, or 14 50-minute training sessions; pecking during the S+ (vertical line on disk) was rewarded on a VI-1 minute schedule. Six generalized stimuli, differing from the S+ in terms of tilt, plus the original S+, were presented randomly during extinction. As shown in Figure 6-3, the overall height of the generalization gradient increased as a function of training level. In addition, Hearst and Koresko found that the gradients became steeper with more acquisition; that is, responding to the generalized stimuli, relative to the S+, was less with extended training than with limited acquisition. Therefore, the absolute level of responding to generalized stimuli increased as a function of training whereas the relative response rate to generalized stimuli decreased. Similar results (steeper generalization gradients), also have been found in studies that varied the degree of extinction (e.g., Friedman & Guttman, 1965; Kalish & Haber, 1963).

Motivation Level

The effect of drive level on generalization has been studied by a number of investigators. Kalish and Haber (1965) trained a pecking response in pigeons that had been deprived of food to 90, 80, or 70 percent of their normal body weight. During the generalization test, they were maintained at that same weight level. The authors found that the slope of the generalization gradient varied as a function of drive level; the 90 percent group (low deprivation condition) displayed a relatively flat gradient whereas the 70 percent group (high deprivation) showed a steep gradient. In a similar study by Newman and Grice (1965), acquisition was conducted while all subjects were 24-hours food-deprived; then, generalization testing was done while the subjects were either 12 or 48 hours hungry. The authors observed that the overall response level during generalization as well as the steepness of the gradient were higher for the hungrier subjects who had the more intense drive level. In summary, it appears that the greater the drive level, the less likely the subject is to generalize (but see Coate, 1964; Sidman, 1961).

Training-Test Interval

An interesting and important finding is that generalization increases over time, that is, the generalized stimuli elicit relatively more responding after a delay than immediately after training. A number of investigators have documented this phenomenon, using either an appetitive task (e.g., Burr & Thomas, 1972; Perkins & Weyant, 1958; Thomas & Lopez, 1962) or an aversive task (e.g., Desiderato et al., 1966; McAllister & McAllister, 1963).

In the Thomas and Lopez experiment, pigeons first were trained to peck a disk. The S+ during the ten 30-minute session of VI reinforcement was illumination of the disk by colored light (550 nanometers). Generalization testing then was administered either immediately, one day, or one week later (separate groups of subjects); the test consisted of the repeated and random presentation of 11 stimuli varying in wavelength. The results indicated that generalization increased with the passage of time, that is, the gradient was "flatter" after a one-day or one-week rest interval than it was on the immediate test. In short, the relative number of responses to generalized stimuli, even those quite discrepant in wavelength from the original S+, increased with time.

One theory of this result is that forgetting of the S+ occurs during the rest interval. In other words, although the subjects remember the general task of pecking the disk, they forget within 24 hours the specific features of the situation, in this case, the exact color of the S+. When tested immediately, of course, the subjects had no difficulty remembering the exact color of the S+, so there was a greater percentage of responding to that stimulus than to the generalized stimuli. It is interesting to note that Desiderato, Foldes, and Gockley (1966) found a similar result using human subjects which they also interpreted in terms of a retention loss.

Early Sensory Experience

Several studies have shown that generalized stimuli elicit CRs even in subjects who had very limited experience, from birth, with the stimulus dimension varied on the generalization test (e.g., Mountjoy & Malott, 1968; Riley & Leuin, 1971; Rudolph et al., 1969; Tracy, 1970). The finding is important because it suggests that prior exposure to the generalized stimuli is not a necessary condition for a response to those stimuli.

In Riley and Leuin's study, chicks were raised in an environment illuminated by a light of one wavelength only (589 nanometers). Thus, their experience with different colors which could influence later responding to those colors on a generalization test was absent. At 10 days of age, all the chicks were trained to peck a disk that was illuminated by the same color light (589 nanometers). Then, after about seven days of training, the subjects were tested for generalization. The birds were given the S+ (the 589 nanometer light) and two similar colors (569 and 550 nanometers) in a random order. The authors found that responding occurred to the generalized stimuli although the original S+ elicited a greater rate of responding; that is, a normal generalization gradient was observed. Riley and Leuin, therefore, concluded that some animals (notably birds) have an innate ability to distinguish between colors; if the ability to discriminate color depended on experiencing different colors, then subjects who were not given this experience should not show any differential responding to the test stimuli, that is, they should show complete generalization by responding to all the wave lengths. The fact that Riley and Leuin observed differential responding to the S+ and generalized stimuli in the color-restricted birds indicated that the color differentiation was innate.

FIGURE 6-4.

Mean total responses on the two generalization tests as a function of the stimulus wavelength for the Experimental (prior discrimination training) and Control (no discrimination training) groups.

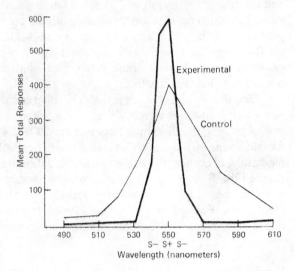

Prior Discrimination Training

Finally, the effect on generalization of prior discrimination training has been studied extensively. One reason for the interest in this area was the finding that generalization gradients may be predicted from the discriminative capacities of the subject; the greater the ability to distinguish between stimuli, the less the generalization (e.g., Kalish, 1958; Thomas & Mitchell, 1962). The notion that generalization is the inverse of discrimination suggests that explicit discrimination training, prior to the generalization test, should sharpen the gradient, that is, produce less generalized responding. A number of studies have shown this effect (e.g., Hanson, 1959, 1961; Friedman & Guttman, 1965; Jenkins & Harrison, 1960; Thomas, 1962). For example, Hanson (1961) trained pigeons to peck a disk for food on a VI schedule. The S+ was the illumination of the disk by colored light (550 nanometers) which signaled that food was available. After five days of acquisition, the Control subjects continued with the same regimen whereas the Experimental subjects were given discrimination training. Here, responding to the S+ was reinforced but responding during either of the S− stimuli (light of 540 and 560 nanometers) was not reinforced. After reaching a criterion of discrimination, both groups of pigeons were given two generalization tests. The S+, both S− cues, and eight other generalized stimuli were presented randomly, twelve times on each test. As shown in Figure 6-4, the mean total responses to the generalized stimuli, that is, the gradients, differed between groups. The control subjects showed a flat

FIGURE 6-5.

Mean responding to the S+, S-, and generalized stimuli by the control and prior discrimination groups (labeled according to the value of their S-).

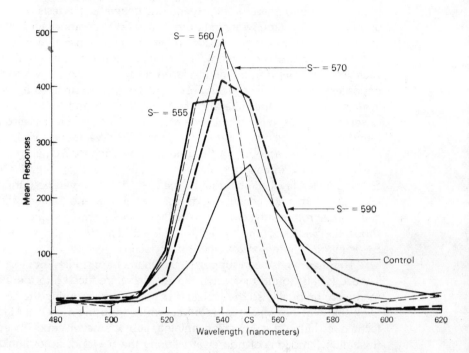

gradient; their responses to generalized stimuli declined gradually as a function of the differences between those stimuli and the original S+. In contrast, the gradient for the Experimental subjects was much steeper: responding to the S+ was high but quite low to the S- colors and the other generalized stimuli. In summary, prior discrimination training produces less generalization and a steeper gradient. This effect occurs not only when the discrimination training involves the same stimulus dimension as the generalization test (e.g., color as in Hanson's study) but also when the two dimensions are entirely different. Mackintosh and Honig (1970), for example, showed that discrimination training, using tilted lines as the stimuli, later influenced the generalization gradient for wavelength. Specifically, the wavelength gradient was steeper (less generalized responding) for subjects who were given prior line-tilt discrimination training than for subjects who did not receive prior discrimination training.

One interesting phenomenon that occurs in this context was demonstrated by Hanson (1959). He studied generalization following discrimination training and observed a displacement of the peak of the gradient away from the S+ in the direction opposite to that of the S-. This peak shift (see Purtle, 1973, for a review) could be predicted, generally, from the interaction of excitatory and inhibitory gradients (also see Marsh, 1972).

In Hanson's experiment, pigeons were trained to peck a disk during an S+ (550 nanometers). Later, four groups were given discrimination training for which the S+ was 550 and the S− was either 555, 560, 570, or 590 nanometers; a fifth control group did not receive discrimination training. In a third phase of the experiment, generalization tests were given during which 13 stimuli, ranging from 480 to 600 nanometers were used.

The results on the generalization test are shown in Figure 6-5. Compared to the control group gradient, the peak of the excitatory gradients for each experimental group was displaced away from the S+ on the side opposite to the S−. The degree of the peak shift, furthermore, was an inverse function of the difference between the S+ and S−; that is, the closer the S− was to the S+, the greater the peak shift. This has also been found more recently by other investigators (e.g., Weinberg, 1973).

How can we account for this unusual phenomenon? One prominent theory is that the inhibitory gradient represents emotional reactions to the S− and generalized stimuli; that is, the S− becomes aversive during discrimination training because it is associated with no reward. During generalization, the subject tries to "avoid" the S− and in doing so, overshoots the S+. Since the subject really is avoiding the S−, the closer the S− is to the S+, the greater the overshooting.

This theory has been supported by a number of studies. For example, Terrace (1963) found that when the S− was introduced into the experiment very gradually, so that subjects made no errors during the S−, the peak shift was not obtained. In other words, by using a special "fading" technique during discrimination training, subjects never experienced the frustration (emotion) of nonreward during the S− and, accordingly, did not overshoot the S+ on the generalization test. Second, Terrace (1966) observed that the peak shift was abolished if prior discrimination training was extended. Here, the emotional reaction to the S− abated over the extended course of discrimination. Third, Lyons, Klipec, and Steinsultz (1973) found that the administration of chlorpromazine, a tranquilizer, during the generalization test eliminated the peak shift. Again, it was concluded that the peak shift was absent because the emotional reaction to S− had been reduced by the drug.

Although the evidence cited above is compelling, other investigators have found contradictory results. Hoffman (1969) reported that the peak shift could be obtained following "errorless" discrimination training. Similarly, Ellis (1970) demonstrated the peak shift even after extended discrimination training was provided. Therefore, the exact nature of the peak shift penomenon is not yet clear.

THEORIES OF GENERALIZATION

Two major theories of generalization have been dominant in learning psychology for several decades. We shall discuss these first and then cover a third position which is especially relevant to the generalization of meaning of verbal material in humans.

Hull's Theory

Hull (1943) hypothesized that generalization was a primary process in learning that was an inherent part of conditioning rather than a by-product of some other process. More specifically, he suggested that responses during acquisition were conditioned, not to a single stimulus, but actually to a "zone" of stimuli. All the stimuli in the zone were similar, that is, they were related along a particular sensory continuum as various intensities of a sense modality and all became bonded to the response. The fact that more than one stimulus was able to elicit a response became evident only on a generalization test where the various stimuli along the sensory continuum were presented.

Given that most experimenters used a single S+ during conditioning, Hull's notion (that a stimulus zone gets conditioned) was not, on the surface, very obvious. Hull tried to clarify his ideas by suggesting that the environment was constantly in flux; subjects never experienced *exactly* the same stimulus twice. In fact, habits developed to each stimulus in a zone, the many individual habits actually summating to produce the "typical," large CR. On the generalization test, since most of the fluctuating stimuli in the zone cluster around a mean value, namely the S+, the strongest response is to the S+. However, habits also had formed to other stimuli in the zone that were more distant from and therefore less similar to the S+. Thus, generalized CRs, although weaker because they were the summation of fewer components in the zone, were given as well.

A fair amount of evidence has supported Hull's theory. For example, the overall height of the generalization gradient has been shown to increase as a function of training trials. Here, it is claimed that the response strength evoked by each stimulus in the zone, and thus the summation of habits, increased with training. Similarly, several investigators have shown that the overall height of the generalization gradient is elevated following an increase in motivation. Since Hull's basic theory of behavior (see Chapter 3) claimed that drive interacted with habit to produce performance, such a finding would be predicted, that is, an increase in drive also should energize generalized habits.

Lashley-Wade Theory

A somewhat more successful theory of generalization was suggested by Lashley and Wade (1946). According to their hypothesis, generalized CRs were given merely because the subjects could not discriminate adequately between the original training S+ and the generalized stimuli. If the subject could distinguish between the stimuli, they would not confuse them and, consequently, they would not generalize.

One implication of the Lashley-Wade position was that variations along the stimulus dimension, that is, the dimension that is varied on the generalization test, were not known by the subjects until they had acquired some experience with the dimension. In other words, only through exposure to the generalized stimuli could the subjects gradually come to recognize, or discriminate, the generalized stimuli. Prior to such exposure, generalization (or confusion) would be relatively strong, whereas after sufficient exposure to the relevant dimension, less generalization (better discrimination) would be evident. The evidence relating to generalization and training level has supported this prediction from the Lashley-Wade theory (see Figure 6-3).

Another issue used to support this hypothesis involved predicting the generalization gradients from known discrimination abilities or, conversely, predicting discrimination capabilities from previously derived generalization gradients. Presumably, if generalization were the inverse of discrimination, generalization gradients and discriminative abilities should covary. Although several experiments failed to find a strong relationship between generalization and discrimination (e.g., Guttman & Kalish, 1956), other studies have demonstrated such a covariance (e.g., Kalish, 1958; Thomas & Mitchell, 1962).

For example, in a study by Kalish and Haber (1965) which we previously discussed with regard to generalization and drive level, groups of pigeons were taught to peck a disk (S+ color was 550 nanometers) and were then given a generalization test with stimuli ranging from 490 to 550 nanometers (approximately green to greenish yellow). In a second phase of the study, separate groups learned the same pecking response (S+ was again 550 nanometers) and were then given discrimination training for which pecking during the S+ (550) was reinforced but pecking during the S− (540) was not. Using the latter subjects, the authors computed a relative measure of responding: the ratio of response during the S− over responses to the S+. Then they compared those ratios to the ratio scores found in the first phases of the experiment on the generalization test. The ratios turned out to be nearly equal in both phases of the experiment. In other words, the ratio of responding in phase 1 (S− /S+ responding for the generalization subjects) was the same as the ratio in phase 2 of the study (S− /S+ responding for the discrimination subjects). Thus, discrimination behavior was predicted accurately from independently derived generalization behavior.

Finally, many of the effects of prior discrimination on generalization failed to conform to Hull's analysis. An inhibitory gradient following discrimination training, according to Hull and Spence, should reduce the overall postdiscrimination generalization gradient because the inhibition subtracts from excitation for each generalized stimulus, yet the data failed to substantiate Hull's prediction. Overall level of responding to generalized stimuli was stronger after discrimination training (see Figure 6-5), which was contrary to the predictions of the Hull-Spence model.

In summary, neither the Hull nor the Lashley-Wade theories appear to account for all the findings in the generalization literature. To some extent, both positions may be compatible. Generalization may occur when the subjects do not perceive the differences between stimuli.

Alternatively, generalization may involve the conditioning of, say, background cues that are not identified by the experimenter as part of the S+ but do influence responding on the generalization test.

Mediated Generalization

Before we review a third theory of generalization, it would be useful to note several studies with human subjects for which the generalization dimension was the meaning of verbal material rather than a physical continuum such as color or tone intensity. In one study, Lacey and Smith (1954) presented a list of words and requested that each subject give associations to those words for about 15 seconds. The words "cow" and "paper" appeared several times on the list in addition to other rural words like "tractor" and "farmer," and neutral words like "clock" and "blue." Some of the subjects were given a mild shock to the forearm following their associations to "cow"; others received the shock following "paper." The authors found that a Pavlovian heart rate CR was conditioned to the word CSs; that is, heart rate changed during the 15-second period after "cow" or "paper" depending on which word was followed by shock. More important to the topic of generalization, heart rate reactions also were given to semantically related words. For example, "tractor" and "chicken" elicited generalized responses in subjects who experienced shock after "cow." Clearly, the Pavlovian CR had generalized from "cow" to other words related in meaning. Similar results on semantic generalization have been found in numerous other studies (e.g., Abbott & Price, 1964; Lacey et al., 1955; Razran, 1939; Riess, 1940).

The explanation for semantic generalization involves the operation of implicit, mediating responses (see Jenkins, 1963; Osgood, 1953). According to this position, words with a common meaning elicit the same internal mediating reaction. This reaction can be characterized as a thought, an implicit response to the meaning or semantic category of the words. As Figure 6-6 shows, for example, the two semantically related word CSs, labeled S_1 and S_2, both elicit the common mediating reaction r_m—s_m. During acquisition, one of the stimuli, S_1, comes to elicit a conditioned response, R_1. However, part of the conditioning process involves a bonding between s_m and R_1; that is, R_1 is elicited by S_1 via s_m. Finally, on the generalization test, S_2, the word never previously associated with the US, is able to elicit a generalized response, R_1, because S_2 unconditionally evokes the r_m—s_m sequence that is bonded to R_1.

In the case of semantic generalization, it is assumed that synonyms, or even homonyms, naturally elicit a common mediating response sequence. However, the existence of such mediators has been demonstrated more directly in other experiments (e.g., Grice & Davis, 1958, 1960; Jeffrey, 1953; Mink, 1963). For example, in the Grice and Davis (1960) study, subjects were instructed to push a lever with the right hand when tones A and B were sounded and to push a different lever with the left hand when

FIGURE 6-6.

Schematic diagram showing the mechanism for mediated generalization.

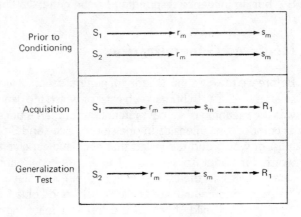

tone C was presented. Tone B was intermediate in frequency and it was followed by a puff of air to the eye which made the subjects blink. After a period of eyeblink conditioning, the authors measured eyeblinks to tone B, that is, the CRs, as well as to tones A and C, the generalized responses. They found that tone A elicited a significantly greater number of generalized CR blinks than tone C even though neither stimuli had been followed by the US air puff. This finding was attributed to the deliberate conditioning of mediating responses to A. That is, through training, both tones A and B came to elicit the same mediating thought ("push lever, right hand") whereas tone C evoked a different reaction ("push lever, left hand"). Superimposed on the development of those mediating responses was the conditioning of a Pavlovian CR to tone B. On test trials, then, tone A elicited more generalized responding than tone C because the mediating reaction (s_m, see Figure 6-6), conditioned to tone A, was similar to the one for tone B.

In summary, the mediation theory assumes that generalization is due to the presence of common implicit reactions, that is, mediating thoughts. Semantically related words, or stimuli that share certain salient traits such as color or pitch, already elicit a common mediating reaction and, as a consequence, naturally evoke generalized CRs. However, other stimuli may come to elicit a single mediating response via deliberate conditioning procedures as in the study by Grice and Davis. When this is done, those stimuli also may evoke generalized responses.

INTRODUCTION TO DISCRIMINATION

Although the topic of discrimination is intricately related to generalization, discrimination itself is an important phenomenon in learning research. Discrimination behavior in the experimental framework means that the organism is responding to one situation, based on reward availability, but not to another situation, where there is no reward, less reward, or where punishment is provided. Usually, the two situations are identified by discriminative stimuli: S+ for the rewarded condition, S− for nonreward. The extent to which the former, but not the latter, stimulus comes to elicit a response is a measure of discrimination (see Gilbert & Sutherland, 1969, for a review).

We could cite many examples of human discriminative behavior. We put cold milk into the refrigerator, not into the oven; clearly we know the difference between those two stimuli and react differentially to them even though both may be square compartments with white enamel doors. Similarly, children learn to discriminate one letter of the alphabet from others; here, approval is given when the child responds correctly to the differences between the stimuli even though the letters may appear similar in many respects. In short, we are constantly engaged in discrimination behavior—reacting to the differences between stimuli. Without this ability, of course, we would be unable to solve problems, that is, to choose the appropriate stimulus or make the appropriate response and avoid the inappropriate one based on the distinguishing features of those stimuli. Choice behavior or problem solving, then, is one important area of study that is grounded on basic concepts in discrimination research (see Chapter 13).

There are two general methods for studying discriminative capacity. The *simultaneous discrimination technique* presents both the S+ and S− together, thus offering a choice. If the subject consistently chooses the reward option, we say that discrimination has occurred. The second procedure is *successive discrimination*. Here, the subject is given the S+ and S− sequentially in time; the task is to respond only during the rewarded portion of the trial, that is, during the S+, but not during the S−.

FACTORS AFFECTING DISCRIMINATION

Some of the factors that influence the rate at which subjects form discriminations were covered previously in the section on generalization. For example, discrimination improves (generalization declines) as a function of training trials. The following sections provide a brief account of several other parameters that affect discrimination learning.

Problem Difficulty

It is not surprising that discrimination learning occurs rapidly when disparate, easily distinguished stimuli are used, but much more slowly when the cues are similar. For example, a child finds it easier to distinguish between "O" and "I" than between "F" and "E." Similarly, rats quickly learn to choose the correct (rewarded) stem of a T-maze when the doors to the rewarded and nonrewarded stems are painted black and white; when the

FIGURE 6-7.

Mean percent errors as a function of training trials for the three groups. Arrow indicates the transition to the difficult discrimination.

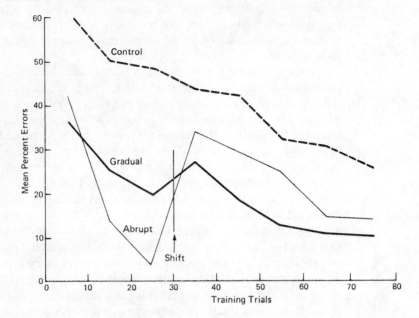

doors are painted different shades of gray, learning is much slower. In short, the ability to respond differentially to two stimuli is limited by the subject's capacity to distinguish one stimulus from another.

One important finding related to discrimination and problem difficulty was shown by Lawrence (1952). Rats were trained to jump from a start box into one of two goal boxes, both of which were visible from the starting point. The inside walls of the goal boxes could be covered with painted inserts that varied from a very light to a very dark shade of gray. The subject's task was to choose, on the basis of brightness, the rewarded box. One group (Control) was given 80 trials with a difficult discrimination (two intermediate grays). A second group (Abrupt) was given 30 trials during which the goal box tones were highly contrasting (easy discrimination) followed by 50 trials with the difficult discrimination. A third group of subjects (Gradual) received 10 trials with the easy problem, 10 with a somewhat more difficult discrimination, 10 with yet a more difficult discrimination, and finally, 50 trials with the hardest (least differentiated) tones. Lawrence's study investigated two questions: did learning a simple discrimination influence later performance on a very difficult problem, and, did a gradual shift in problem difficulty affect the solution of a difficult discrimination more so than an abrupt transition from the easiest to the hardest problem?

As shown in Figure 6-7, the mean percent errors in the Control subjects was relatively high at first but declined gradually over training. In contrast, the initial performance of the other two groups, especially the Abrupt subjects, was superior because the difficulty of discrimination, at that point in the training sequence, was much lower.

The interesting result occurred on the last 50 trials during which all groups received the same difficult problem. The Abrupt and Gradual groups clearly performed the discrimination with fewer errors than the control subjects. In other words, prior training with easily distinguished stimuli facilitated later discrimination of hard-to-distinguish stimuli. Lawrence also found that performance on a difficult discrimination was enhanced even more when the problem difficulty was increased gradually during the prior training, as shown by the superior performance of the Gradual group to the Abrupt group.

Several investigators have tried to explain this facilitation effect. One theory suggested that any experience with discrimination problems whatsoever, regardless of the stimulus dimension, would promote discrimination performance because some general, problem-solving skill would be learned. This hypothesis was not supported in later research by Marsh (1969). In that study, the performance of pigeons on a difficult wavelength discrimination improved when they had prior training on an easy wavelength problem but this improvement was not evident in another group of subjects whose prior exposure was to an easy brightness problem. Thus, the facilitation effect apparently was intradimensional; it occurred only when the stimuli on both the easy and difficult problems were of the same category.

Mackintosh and Little (1970) proposed that the appropriate explanation for the facilitation effect was related to attention (the hypothesis originally offered by Lawrence, 1952): animals trained on an easy problem learned to attend more strongly to the relevant stimulus dimension than those given a difficult discrimination; strong attention to the dimension allowed the "Easy-Hard" subjects to execute the difficult discrimination easily when it occurred without having to continue to master the stimulus dimension at the same time.

Stimulus Information

A great deal of research on discrimination has been devoted to the nature of the stimuli, particularly their information value. One study by Olton (1972) was designed to assess whether the choice behavior depended on information-about-reward or information-about-nonreward. Olton trained thirsty rats in a maze containing three distinctively-painted alleys. On each of 24 days, the subjects were given two forced-choice trials, one to the rewarded alley and one to the nonrewarded stem. Then the animals were given a choice between all three alleys. Olton found that they avoided the nonreward alley on the choice trials but that they chose the previously rewarded alley and the "neutral" stem about the same number of times. He concluded that the information the rats got from the nonreinforced trial influenced their discrimination behavior to a greater extent than did the information from the rewarded trial.

A related finding was obtained by Sainsbury (1971) who rewarded pigeons for pecking at one translucent disk (S+) but not another (S−). Both disks were divided into four areas and each area was illuminated by a red or green circle that was projected from behind the apparatus. On a given trial, seven of the eight circles were the same color while one was the other color. The pigeons had to respond to the S+ on the basis of this single, distinctive feature.

Discrimination learning was quite poor when the distinctive circle was located on the S− disk. However, the subjects readily learned the discrimination when the distinctive circle was part of the S+ display. In other words, given a complex set of stimuli, the pigeons learned to discriminate between the stimuli only when the single distinctive feature that made the discrimination possible was associated with the rewarded cue.

Sainsbury explained these results in terms of differential reinforcement for the distinctive versus the common elements. To make the correct response, the pigeons had to attend to the distinctive element; in fact, Sainsbury noted that they literally pecked at the distinctive circle. When the distinctive element was part of the S+ complex, attending or responding to it was rewarded immediately. The result was the strengthening of the single response that led to effective discrimination learning. However, when the distinctive circle appeared on the S− display, immediate reward was not provided for attention to that element.

Finally, a related study by Hearst (1971) investigated the effect on discrimination of prior conditioned S+ and S− cues. One group of pigeons (Excitatory) was rewarded for pecking an illuminated disk on which a .6-centimeter, vertical line was projected; the S− disk, which gave no reward for a peck response, was blank. A second group (Inhibitory) was reinforced for pecking a blank disk; their S− was a disk on which a 1.8-centimeter vertical line was projected. In other words, during this pretraining phase, one group were given reward for responding to a short vertical line whereas the other group experienced nonreward for responding to a long vertical line. Then both groups were given discrimination training for which the S+ disk contained the short line and the S− disk included the long line.

Hearst found that prior differential exposure to the cues had a strong effect on discrimination learning. The Excitatory group required about 1.5 sessions to reach the discrimination criterion (response rate during S− less than 10 percent of the rate during S+), whereas the Inhibitory group took about 4.0 sessions. That is, the Excitatory group, which had experienced excitatory conditioning to the S+ short vertical line but no exposure to the S− long vertical line, learned the discrimination significantly faster than the Inhibitory group, which had received no reward for responding to the S−

but had not experienced the S+. These results suggest that the excitatory consequences of reward are more important for later discrimination learning than are the inhibitory consequences of nonreward.

Observational Learning

A third factor that may affect discrimination learning is the opportunity for the experimental subject to observe another subject perform the response. This topic is important for understanding human behavior, especially those instances where we appear to learn vicariously from the experience of others. In the animal laboratory, numerous studies have shown that observations of reinforced behavior helped the observing animal to learn a lever press and avoidance response (e.g., Corson, 1967; John et al., 1968). Moreover, seeing errors appears to be more helpful to the observer than merely watching skilled performance without errors (Herbert & Harsh, 1944).

A more recent study by Kohn and Dennis (1972) investigated observational learning and discrimination behavior. Rats were placed in a compartment from which they could observe another animal choose between a vertically- or horizontally-striped door to escape a pulsating shock. One group of subjects (Observe) always saw the model choose the correct pattern, which was the one they later experienced as the S+ on the discrimination task. A second group (Observe-Reverse) watched the model choose the pattern that later was used as the S−; in other words, these rats were observing the reverse of the discrimination they would later have to perform. Two control groups were employed: One (No Observe) was not given the observation learning experience; the second group of subjects (Observe-No Discrimination) saw the model leave the start compartment but they did not see the rat choose (i.e., discriminate) between doors.

Following this pretraining phase, all the subjects were given discrimination training. The task was to enter a goal box via the correct door; failure to respond resulted in the delivery of a mild, pulsating shock. Discrimination training was continued until each animal made nine consecutive correct choices.

Kohn and Dennis found that discrimination learning was facilitated by the opportunity to observe other subjects perform the correct response. Control groups "No Observe" and "Observe-No Discrimination" reached the discrimination criterion in 51.6 and 55.4 trials, respectively. In contrast, the "Observe" group required a mean of only 31.6 trials to meet the criterion. Interestingly, the "Observe-Reverse" group took significantly longer to learn the discrimination (63.0 trials). This result supported the notion that facilitation resulting from observation learning was specific in nature: observation facilitated later discrimination only when the observer was trained to approach the same S+. In other words, the subjects learned through observation specifically which door was the correct one to run toward to escape the shock rather than simply a general response tendency to run toward the doors of the apparatus.

As we said earlier, observational learning is common in human behavior. In fact, a great deal of our behavior is merely a reflection of someone's else's performance, from learning how to play baseball to watching others to learn proper protocol at the dinner table.

THEORIES OF DISCRIMINATION

Two major theoretical positions regarding discrimination learning are reviewed in the following sections.

Hull-Spence Theory

One of the earliest theories of discrimination was formulated by Hull (1943) and Spence (1936). This theory, based on the interaction of excitatory and inhibitory generalization gradients, has held a dominant position in research on discrimination and generalization until recently.

The Hull-Spence theory has three basic tenets: first, reinforcement leads to conditioned excitation to the S+. Second, nonreinforcement leads to conditioned inhibition to the S−; and third, excitation and inhibition that generalize to other stimuli summate algebraically, the net effect resulting in performance. To state it another way, the response to the S+ is strengthened by reward whereas the response to the S− is reduced through inhibition. In addition, differential responding to the S+ and S− is influenced by generalized tendencies. For example, as the S+ increases in strength, excitation generalizes to the S−; similarly, as S− becomes more inhibitory, generalized inhibition subtracts from the excitatory tendency of the S+. The actual level of performance for any given stimulus is the net result of the generalized excitatory and inhibitory tendencies.

Various facets of the Hull-Spence theory have been supported in many experiments (see Spiker, 1970). In one study by Gynther (1957), human subjects were given eyeblink conditioning. For one control group, only excitatory trials were administered; that is, a light CS+ was followed by an air puff US but no CS− was ever presented. A second group received discrimination training with both stimuli; the CS+ was followed by the US whereas another light, the CS−, was not. Gynther predicted, on the basis of the Hull-Spence theory, that excitatory conditioning to the CS+ would be weaker in the discrimination group than in the control subjects because the generalized inhibitory tendency from the CS− would subtract from the excitatory tendency of the CS+. Since the control subjects did not receive inhibitory training, their performance to the CS+ should be unaffected. The prediction was confirmed: performance to the

CS+ by the control subjects significantly exceeded the response level of the discriminative group.

The Hull-Spence theory has been severely criticized in recent years. Much of the support for the theory has been reinterpreted in light of other concepts, such as attention. Various research findings have also challenged the adequacy of the theory. The attention theory of discrimination learning is described in the next section, followed by a discussion of several of the important phenomena that are easily explained by it.

Attention Theory

In their remarkable book, Sutherland and Mackintosh (1971) outlined a theory of discrimination learning based on attention. According to their position, discrimination learning involves two discrete processes: the strengthening of attention to one or more relevant stimulus dimensions, and the attaching of a particular response to the relevant stimulus.

The attention process involves *analyzers*, mechanisms in the brain thought to receive and process sensory information. Some basic analyzers are innate. Hubel and Wiesel (1962), for example, demonstrated that particular cells in the cortex of the brain "trigger" only when visual stimuli in a particular spatial orientation move across the retina. Other, more general analyzers merely receive information in a nonselective manner, that is, they pertain to an entire stimulus dimension rather than to a single stimulus on that dimension.

Each stimulus dimension that characterizes sensory information has an analyzer. For example, a subject viewing a green vertical bar, one inch long, projected onto a gray background, could notice or pay particular attention to each possible dimension in the array: the color of the bar and background, brightness, length and orientation of the bar, and so forth. Initially, the strength of an analyzer is related to the strength of the incoming signal; if the stimulus has a particular potent feature, such as brightness, then the brightness analyzer operates and the subject's attention is drawn toward that dimension.

Analyzers, however, may change in strength. Critical to this ability is the notion that analyzers generate *outputs*, that is, interpretive "decisions" or expectations about the stimuli along the dimension. These outputs are essentially attention responses, dispositions to respond to one stimulus along the dimension and not another. If the outputs from the analyzer correspond to or predict important events for the animal, then the analyzer increases in strength. Using the above example, if the tilt of the line were correlated to food presentation but the brightness and color of the line were not, then the strength of the orientation analyzer would increase whereas the strength of the brightness and color analyzers would decrease. In other words, if the outputs from one analyzer ("pay attention to line tilt") predict an important event, that analyzer will be strengthened ("line tilt is the more important dimension to attend to") while other analyzers will decrease in strength ("color and brightness may be ignored").

The second general process specified by the attention theory is the attaching of a response to a particular analyzer output. That is, a bond or attachment develops between a given response ("press the lever") and a single output generated by the analyzer ("vertical is the correct orientation"). Reward, therefore, has a second function: it directly strengthens the analyzer-response attachment. When a subject is rewarded for responding to a particular line tilt, the connection between that response and that analyzer output is strengthened; at the same time, the attention to the dimension, the analyzer per se, increases in strength because the output, the particular line tilt, correctly predicts food.

To summarize the Sutherland and Mackintosh theory, subjects learn two things during discrimination experiments. First, they learn to attend to particular dimensions of the environment (analyzers are strengthened) on the basis of whether the consequences of their attention (analyzer outputs) correctly predict important events. Second, they learn to attach responses to an analyzer output on the basis of reinforcement.

This theory, of course, involves a number of other formalized principles. Two are particularly important to explain many findings in discrimination research. The authors assert that the strength of an analyzer increases more slowly than that of the response attachments. In other words, although a pigeon, for instance, will readily learn to peck a particular disk in the presence of a certain S+, such as a vertical line, its selective and exclusive attention to that stimulus dimension lags behind.

A second rule is that performance is determined both by the strength of the analyzer and the response attachments to that analyzer. While the strongest analyzer will direct the attention (performance) of the subject, the strongest response attachment to that analyzer will be the behavior that is performed.

There is considerable support for the attention theory of discrimination. For example, the theory easily explains the research we discussed earlier in this chapter on the facilitation of discrimination learning (e.g., Lawrence, 1952; see Figure 6-7). The control subjects, who receive the difficult discrimination right from the start, make many errors; they confuse the stimuli and the analyzer outputs fail to predict reward consistently. Thus, analyzer strength is low for these subjects. In contrast, the subjects who receive an easy problem first make relatively few errors; the analyzer outputs always predict food. The strength of the analyzer for these subjects is much higher. Moreover, following the shift (from easy to difficult) for these animals, performance continues at a high rate because the analyzer is strong (performance is determined by the strength of the analyzer).

Another interesting study that supported these arguments was done by Waller (1973). Rats first were trained to run down an alley for food. Four conditions were used during this first phase: two groups received reward in the goal box on each of 50 trials; the other two groups were rewarded on 50 percent of the trials. For one group in each condition, the alley was painted gray; for the other group, the alley walls were covered with black and white vertical stripes. In the second phase of the experiment, all the subjects were given discrimination training—they learned to choose between two goal boxes for a food reward. One box was covered with stripes slanting 45 degrees to the right; the other with stripes slanting 45 degrees to the left.

The rationale of Waller's study was that the Partially Rewarded-Stripe subjects would pay less attention to the stripes during phase 1 than would the Continuously Rewarded-Stripe group. In the former case, where stripes did not consistently predict reward, the analyzer for that dimension would not become strong; in the latter group, however, since stripes always predicted reward, attention of the rats to the stripe dimension should become strong. If the analyzer strength for stripes differed between groups after the first phase, then the discrimination learning during the second phase should be better for the Continuous-Stripe group than for the Partial-Stripe subjects. The Partial-Gray and the Continuous-Gray subjects, however, who did not experience stripes during phase 1, should not differ in their attention to stripes. Consequently, in phase 2, both of those groups should learn the stripe discrimination equally well in the second phase of the study.

As predicted, discrimination performance did not differ for the two control groups—the subjects trained in the gray alley during phase 1. In contrast, the experimental subjects, who were trained initially in the striped alley, differed on the discrimination task. The Partial-Stripe group required 118.4 trials to meet the criterion whereas the Continuous-Stripe group took only 93.7 trials. Thus, reward consistency did not affect later discrimination learning when the relevant dimension was absent but when the subjects were exposed to stripes under a partial reward schedule, they were less able to learn the stripe discrimination. Waller's experiment clearly supports the attention theory of discrimination learning: the analyzer for stripes was weakened by partial reinforcement but strengthened by continuous reward. The contribution of analyzer strength (attention) was then evident on the discrimination task.

DISCRIMINATION PHENOMENA

There are a number of important phenomena related to discrimination learning. None of the issues discussed below can be explained by the Hull-Spence theory whereas two of them are handled easily by Mackintosh's attention theory. Again, it should be noted that some of these discrimination phenomena provide a basic framework for understanding issues addressed in Chapter 13 on human problem solving and concept formation. That is, the underlying mechanisms or theories that deal with human problem solving are remarkably similar to those discussed in the section on the attention theory.

Overlearning Reversal Effect

Suppose some rats were trained to learn a discrimination response such as picking a black door rather than a white door to obtain food. After all the animals have learned to do this, they are divided into two groups. The rats in one group are given 100 more trials—that is, they practice the same response over and over again. Then the conditions of the experiment are switched: now the rats must learn to pick the white door to obtain the food. Which rats would learn to choose the white door more quickly: the regular group, whose trials ceased when all the rats were choosing the correct door or the overtrained rats who received extra practice?

This experiment was designed by Mackintosh (1965) to answer this question. Mackintosh found that the regular group took about 43.3 trials to learn the new task whereas the overtrained group learned it significantly faster (by 33.8 trials); overtraining facilitated reversal learning. This important phenomenon is the *overlearning reversal effect*. It was first noted by Reid (1953) and Pubols (1956) and it has been replicated by other investigators (see Denny, 1970; Sperling, 1965a, 1965b for reviews).

The Hull-Spence theory of discrimination clearly could not accommodate this paradoxical result. According to that position, overtraining should have strengthened the original habits of choosing the rewarded box and avoiding the nonrewarded box, thus making it even more difficult to learn the reverse discrimination.

For several years after it was discovered, a number of investigators could not replicate the overlearning reversal effect (e.g., D'Amato & Schiff, 1965). However, more recent studies have determined that reversal learning is facilitated by overtraining most effectively when a difficult visual problem is used (e.g., Mackintosh, 1969) and when a large reward is given for a correct response (e.g., Hooper, 1967; Theios & Blosser, 1965). When simple spatial discrimination problems (such as a right-left turn in a T-maze) or small rewards are used, the phenomenon is rarely observed (Mackintosh, 1965; 1969). Any theory of the overlearning reversal effect, therefore, must take into account the fact that both difficulty of discrimination and large reward are necessary conditions.

Several investigators have attempted to explain the effect. One notion (e.g., Hall, 1973) was that overtraining strengthened general observing or orienting strategies so that when reversal learning was given, the overtrained subjects were better able to learn the reversal task. Mackintosh (1963a) questioned this hypothesis on the basis of an experiment which showed that overtraining did not facilitate the acquisition of an entirely new discrimination (e.g., one involving a new stimulus dimension).

A more successful theory invokes the concept of frustration (e.g., Theios & Blosser, 1965; Theios & Brelsford, 1964). This position suggests that the initial reversal trials involve frustration since the subjects expect reward and their inevitable errors result in nonreward. Overtraining and large rewards simply heighten their expectation and thus their frustration when the reward is not forthcoming. During the reversal phase, since the former S+ becomes aversive due to its association with nonreward, reversal of the habit (avoiding this former S+) takes place more quickly following overtraining and large reward than following a normal level of training or small reward.

The frustration theory accounts for a number of facts, notably the need to use large rewards when demonstrating the overlearning reversal effect. However, other data conflict with the theory. For example, it is equally important when demonstrating the phenomena that a difficult visual discrimination is used (Mackintosh, 1969). Second, the addition of one or more irrelevant stimulus dimensions during reversal learning does not affect performance in the overtrained subjects but does retard or disrupt reversal learning in normally trained animals (Mackintosh, 1963b). The frustration theory cannot account easily for either of these facts.

The theory that most successfully accounts for the overlearning reversal effect is the attention theory (see Lovejoy, 1966; Mackintosh, 1969). The increase in the strength of the analyzer over training lags behind the strength of the motor response; that is, the discrimination criterion may be reached without the subject exclusively attending to the relevant stimulus dimension. Overtraining continues to strengthen the analyzer (attention to the relevant dimension). Therefore, during reversal learning, as the original response extinguishes, the overtrained subjects maintain their attention to the relevant dimension; this strong attention facilitates their learning the new task which, of course, involves that same dimension. In contrast, the normally trained animals, who are not giving their maximum attention to the proper dimension when the reversal trials begin, cannot learn the new task as well. Reversing a habit requires that the subjects maintain their attention to the relevant dimension, that is, have a strong analyzer.

Mackintosh (1963b) found further support for the attention theory in a study which showed that when irrelevant stimulus dimensions were added for the first time during reversal learning, the behavior of the normally trained subjects was disrupted. The extraneous dimensions, however, did not affect reversal learning in the overtrained animals. This result suggested that the normal subjects were not attending exclusively to the appropriate dimension; the new dimension competed somewhat for their attention and disrupted their performance. The extra trials must have increased the attention of the overtrained subjects to the relevant dimension since reversal performance, behavior that was related directly to attention to the appropriate dimension, was not disrupted by additional, extraneous dimensions.

The attention theory also accounts for the overlearning reversal effect with regard to problem difficulty. Spatial (e.g., right-left turn) discriminations are so easy for rats to learn that attention to the right-left dimension (analyzer strength) becomes maximal within a few trials, even for normally trained subjects. Therefore, overtraining has little effect on reversal learning because it contributes relatively little to the analyzer strength. As the discrimination problem becomes more difficult, however, analyzer strength is slower to develop and overtraining has a greater impact on analyzer strength and, in turn, on reversal behavior.

Intradimensional and Extradimensional Shifts

A related set of findings involves discrimination shifts using new stimuli within either the same or a different stimulus dimension (see also Chapter 13). Mackintosh (1964) trained rats to jump to one of two doors for food located behind the correct door. For one group of subjects (Intradimensional), the doors were marked either with black and gray squares or white and gray squares; the animal had to make the appropriate response based on the brightness of the door. For a second group (Extradimensional), the choice was between a square or a diamond shape on the door; although each stimulus was painted black or white, it was the shape rather than the brightness which was relevant for those animals. In stage 2, all the subjects were trained to make a brightness discrimination; here, the stimuli were squares, painted either black or white.

Mackintosh found that the Intradimensional subjects took 45.6 trials to reach the discrimination criterion in stage 2. The Extradimensional animals were much slower, requiring about 61.2 trials before they were able to make 80 percent of their responses correctly. Thus, learning a second discrimination was much easier when the initial problem involved the same dimension (brightness) than when the initial task involved a different stimulus dimension (geometric shape). Similar results have been observed for pigeons (Mackintosh & Little, 1969), rats (Shepp & Eimas, 1964), and monkeys (Shepp & Schrier, 1969).

The finding that intradimensional shifts are learned more easily than extradimensional shifts (even though, in both instances, new stimuli are involved in the stage 2 problem), cannot be explained by the Hull-Spence theory or by the hypothesis which proposes that general orienting strategies are learned during the initial discrimination that later facilitate the acquisition of the second discrimination. Like the overlearning reversal effect, the more appropriate explanation is in terms of attention theory. The analyzer for the appropriate stimulus dimension in stage 1 is strengthened during training. Following the shift, intradimensional subjects already possess a strong and appropriate analyzer for the new discrimination problem; all that is required is for those subjects to learn the new response. On the other hand, extradimensional subjects must respond to an entirely new dimension after the shift; their new task involves both suppressing the former relevant dimension (Turrisi et al., 1969) as well as acquiring the new dimension and the new response.

Learning Sets

As we noted above, intradimensional shifts are learned more easily than extradimensional shifts. In fact, performance may improve dramatically with repeated exposures to a reversal task (i.e., intradimensional shifts—Mackintosh et al., 1968; Woodard et al., 1971). However, improvement in discrimination learning is possible when the dimension is shifted. That is,

FIGURE 6-8.

Wisconsin General Test Apparatus used in Harlow's learning set experiments.

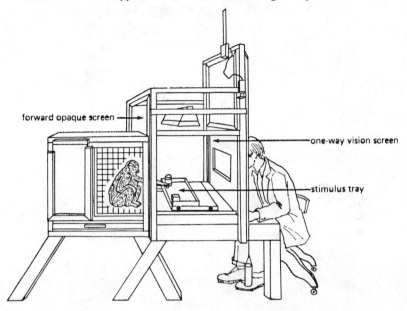

forward opaque screen

one-way vision screen

stimulus tray

exposure to many different discrimination problems produces a marked improvement in discrimination learning of new problems. This latter phenomenon is termed *learning set*; it refers to the progressive improvement in a subject's ability to solve discrimination problems as a function of repeated exposure to many different problems (see Medin, 1972; Miles, 1965; Reese, 1964, for reviews).

The classic study on learning sets was done by Harlow (1949) using rhesus monkeys as subjects. As shown in Figure 6-8, the discrimination apparatus consisted of a flat tray with two food wells on top of which blocks or geometric shapes of various colors were placed. The monkey's task was to choose one of the stimulus objects. If it chose correctly, the monkey was allowed to eat the reward concealed beneath the object but if it chose the incorrect (nonrewarded) stimulus, the objects were rearranged (unseen by the subject) and another trial was administered. A number of trials, ranging from 6 to 50, were given for each pair of stimulus objects; after the monkey had learned the discrimination for one problem, a different set of stimuli, that is, a different discrimination problem, was used. This procedure continued for a total of 344 different problems.

Figure 6-9 shows that learning on each of the first 18 problems was somewhat slow; after six trials, the subjects were correct only about 75 percent of the time. However, learning rate improved gradually as a function of continued exposure to many discrimination problems: on problems 25-32, the subjects were responding correctly 90 percent of the time by the sixth trial whereas their performance was nearly perfect (about 97 percent

FIGURE 6-9.

Mean percent correct responses for the first six trials on each discrimination problem. Different groups of problems are shown in the key.

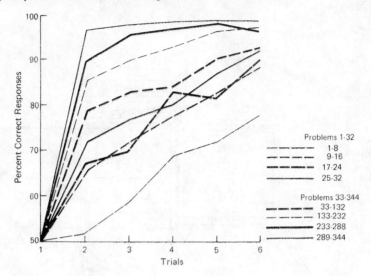

correct) on the second trial for problems 289–344. We could say then, that as the acquisition rate on each discrimination problem improved with successive groups of problems, the monkeys were, in a sense, "learning how to learn."

Harlow's work demonstrated an important principle in learning, namely, that the ability to solve discrimination problems, the ability to learn itself, may be influenced by previous learning experiences. Learning abilities are too often assessed using naive animals as subjects; investigators assume that such abilities reflect pervasive laws of learning that apply even to subjects in their natural environment. However, animals in their normal environment, and certainly humans, are faced constantly with discrimination problems; their ability to cope with any given problem, therefore, is influenced by previous solutions to other problems. Certainly, the investigation of learning sets provides an added dimension to the study of learning, one particularly relevant to organisms in their natural environment.

Another important issue raised by Harlow's results was the possibility that learning sets reflect the general intelligence level of a species. Presumably, the ability to utilize previous experience is related to the evolutionary complexity of the organism. Thus, monkeys would show greater improvement from problem to problem than rats; humans, of course, would show even better learning set performance. A number of experiments suggested that learning sets might, indeed, provide an index of intelligence (see Harlow, 1959; Warren, 1965). However, recent studies have not supported this notion. First, the methodology used to assess learning set formation is important; comparisons of fish and rodent learning set behavior may be erroneous simply because identical procedures cannot be utilized. Some investigators, for example, have shown that two species of monkeys may differ in their learning set behavior merely as a function of differences in methodology (Levine, 1970). Second, the responses that different species are able to execute and, more important, the stimuli to which animals are most responsive, vary enormously. For example, when rats are given discrimination problems involving visual stimuli, they are comparatively poor in forming learning sets. However, when they are required to discriminate between odors, a highly salient and important stimulus dimension for rats, learning set formation is very rapid; the performance is comparable to that reported for primates trained with visual cues (Slotnick & Katz, 1974). In summary, learning set formation does provide valuable information about the learning capacities of various species; the notion, however, that learning sets provide a simple measure of intelligence for comparing different species is not correct.

The learning set phenomenon has provided a formidable challenge to theorists. The Hull-Spence theory (and certain modifications of that theory—see Reese, 1964) was inadequate; improvement in discrimination learning could not be explained merely in terms of the strengthening of some habits by reward and the weakening of other responses by nonreward.

Harlow (1959) suggested that a single process, inhibition, could account for learning set formation. Specifically, subjects learned what *not* to do; the tendency to make an incorrect choice gradually was inhibited during learning set training.

Harlow's hypothesis stemmed from the observation that animals committed systematic errors at the start of training. Some subjects perseverated (continued to choose the incorrect stimulus) because of innate or acquired preferences; other subjects always responded to the right or left side regardless of which object had been placed there. In short, the errors were not random. Later in training, however, these error patterns were suppressed; subjects were learning to make the correct choice by learning what errors not to commit.

A more developed theory was proposed by Levine (1959, 1965). According to this position, animals developed hypotheses about the discrimination problems, that is, general strategies or rules that guided their behavior. If a given strategy (e.g., "respond to left") successfully predicted the reward stimulus, the subject would maintain that behavior pattern. However, the subjects would abandon their current hypothesis if it was disconfirmed by the trial outcome in favor of another strategy (e.g., "win-stay with object, lose-shift to other object").

Levine's theory accounts for two important features of learning set behavior. First, errors are systematic; they appear to be the result of a general plan rather than random variations. Second, the improvement in discrimination learning stems from the eventual confirmation of the appropriate hypothesis (one that is applicable to all of the discrimination problems), not merely from the strengthening of particular habits that have little generality to the other problems.

Research generally has supported Levine's theory (e.g., see Behar & LeBedda, 1974). For example, several studies (e.g., Schrier, 1974; Schusterman, 1964) demonstrated that learning set formation improved following a series of reversal learning problems. That is, repeated reversal learning (intradimensional shifts) facilitated the acquisition of a learning set (extradimensional shifts). This finding supported Levine's theory in that both tasks shared the "win-stay with object, lose-shift to other object" strategy. Presumably, that strategy was reinforced during reversal learning and it carried over to the learning set task.

Again, it should be noted that learning set behavior is similar to the ways in which humans solve simple discrimination problems. That is, humans also appear to follow a "win-stay with object; lose-shift to other object" strategy. The more encompassing problem of discrimination and transfer in humans (how humans solve problems before and after shifting to new stimuli) is discussed in Chapter 13.

SUMMARY

In this chapter, we have discussed two related topics—generalization and discrimination. Generalization occurs when a subject reacts to the *similarity* between stimuli, that is, when stimuli that are novel but similar to the original CS+ elicit a CR. Inhibitory tendencies to a CS− also generalize and, like generalized excitation, a gradient is observed such that the more dissimilar the generalized and original CSs are, the less the CR magnitude.

An early theory by Hull claimed that generalized stimuli really had become conditioned during acquisition because they were part of a "zone" surrounding the nominal CS. There is some evidence compatible with this theory: the overall generalization gradient is elevated with increases in drive and training. However, a more successful theory was formulated by Lashley and Wade who argued that generalization occurred only when subjects confused the original CS with the new test stimulus. The evidence for this theory is a bit clearer. For example, gradients become steeper with more training, which suggests that subjects become less confused as they gain more experience with the various stimuli along the dimension.

The second phenomenon discussed in this chapter is discrimination— the process by which subjects react to the *differences* between stimuli. The ease with which a rewarded CS+ comes to elicit a response (as opposed to a nonrewarded CS−) depends on a number of factors. For example, discrimination learning is faster with easily distinguished stimuli, when the distinctive feature is part of the CS+ display, or after a period of observing another subject learn the discrimination.

Discrimination was explained by Hull and Spence in terms of the interaction of excitation (for the CS+) and inhibition (for the CS−). However, Mackintosh's more recent attention theory appears better able to explain certain phenomena noted in discrimination research. For example, if subjects are given extra training trials on one discrimination problem, they are able to learn the reverse discrimination more easily than if they are given no extra trials. Here, Mackintosh's theory claims that attention to the relevant stimulus dimension becomes especially strong during overlearning, thus making it easy to maintain attention to that dimension while learning the reverse habit.

Finally, the chapter also covered other types of shifts in discrimination including intradimensional and extradimensional shifts. All of this material is important to the issue of human problem solving, especially the discussion of learning set behavior—the finding that subjects can "learn to learn."

7/ Biological Perspectives in Learning

INTRODUCTION

LEARNED TASTE AVERSION

AVOIDANCE LEARNING

BIOLOGICAL PERSPECTIVES IN HUMAN
    LEARNING

SUMMARY

Preview

In this chapter, we shall consider one of the two new trends in learning research. These trends are so major and distinct that it seems appropriate to discuss them separately. The argument here is that learning theorists must consider biological or evolutionary factors if they are to achieve an accurate account of learning. The ability of an animal to learn depends, in part, on the animal itself: the forces of evolution have shaped each species in unique ways, making some kinds of behaviors or responses easy to learn and others hard or perhaps impossible to learn. This argument certainly applies to human beings as well: language use, for example, and even the kind of maladaptive behavior we call neurosis appear to reflect human-specific capabilities. The main result of these new perspectives has been the reexamination of traditional methods and theories in learning research.

INTRODUCTION

Consider the following example taken from the classic work of Tinbergen (1943) on the behavior of the herring gull. If an egg rolls out of the nest, the female will attempt to retrieve it in a very peculiar way: she places her beak beyond the egg and attempts to draw the egg backward toward her breast; that is, the mother bird will attempt to pull the egg into the nest rather than push it. The behavior is odd because the egg is asymmetrical and the bird's beak is narrow, making the task both awkward and highly inefficient. In fact, the egg often slips clumsily to the side, making only slow progress toward the final destination—the nest. Retrieval would be much easier if the bird learned to use a wing or its webbed feet. By positioning itself behind the egg and pushing with a broader surface, the gull could move the egg far more efficiently. This example is of great interest to learning theorists since it is not at all clear why the mother bird does not learn to perform this task more efficiently. Surely there must be many occasions for learning a simpler method for egg rolling and yet these birds do not seem to do so. Anomalies such as this have raised important questions for learning theory.

As we said in Chapter 1, many psychologists have believed that universal principles of learning could be discovered only if they studied a few simple, arbitrary behaviors. If specialized responses that were unique to a single species or a particular situation were investigated, the functional relationships between those responses and environmental factors would be unique and special too. That is, the principles of learning discovered by investigating unique behaviors, by definition, would not apply to all learned behaviors or, at least, not to "typical" learned behaviors.

This view was highlighted by a schism between ethological and psychological research. The ethologists, on the one hand, generally were interested in studying naturalistic behavior, *special* response systems in particular species. To ethologists, the uniqueness of a behavior was a principal justification for its study. On the other hand, learning psychologists emphasized the more general laws of behavior which, apparently, most species shared (at least in prototypical laboratory situations such as the lever box). To psychologists, the vagaries of specialized behaviors were incidental to an analysis of general principles of learning; in fact, they often obscured the study of universal laws of learning.

The adherence by psychologists to this view, however, has diminished in recent years. The main impetus for this change in thinking has been the finding that some behaviors do not appear to be prototypical or arbitrary; the conventional laws of learning, such as reinforcement contingency, do not seem to apply equally well in all situations. Thus, the failure to demonstrate that learning principles are, in fact, general for most behaviors has prompted many psychologists to reevaluate the direction and strategies in learning research. This reevaluation process has spawned an interest in biological or evolutionary factors in learning. In one sense, then, the gap between ethologists and learning psychologists has been bridged to a considerable degree in recent years. The following sections in this chapter illustrate many of the issues and theories that bear on such biological perspectives in learning research.

Evolution and Learning

It is perhaps ironic that Darwin's theory of evolution had a major impact on the development of American psychology but failed to become a central issue in learning research. Although the laws of heredity were believed to be suitable for explaining eye color, body weight, or instinct, most learning psychologists believed that such laws were irrelevant to the analysis of learning principles. In other words, genetic makeup could account for morphology—form and structure of a given species—and in lower organisms, perhaps even for instinctual behavior patterns. Learning in higher organisms, however, was thought to be determined merely by the environment acting upon the highly developed mammalian brain.

It now is clear that all behavior, learned behavior as well as instinctual or reflexive response patterns, is related in a fundamental way to the evolutionary history of the species. The capacity to receive and process sensory information, to utilize that information in executing adaptive responses, depends on the neurophysiological composition of the organism. Therefore, the capacity to change or adapt (to learn) also must be governed by those components. For example, successful reproduction by an organism insures that certain genetic traits will pass to its progeny. One trait may be eye color. However, another trait may be a brain with a greater (or lesser) capacity to learn. If a given organism, in fact, possessed a greater capacity to learn, its chances for survival and for successful reproduction would be increased. Thus, organisms who (for whatever reason) easily learn adaptive behaviors are more likely to survive and reproduce; their offspring are more likely to inherit enhanced learning capabilities. In short, it is not claimed that behaviors in themselves are inherited (that they are "pre-programmed" or reflexive), but, since heredity depends on successful reproduction which in turn often depends on survival through learned adaptive behavior, the capacity for learning may be considered to depend on evolutionary development.

Preparedness

The arguments stated above do not conflict, necessarily, with the general view of learning stated earlier; that is, the notion that learning abilities are related to evolutionary development implies very little about the universality of those learning abilities. However, an important implication does arise in this context: if the morphology of organisms has diversified throughout evolution, it is very likely that the learning capacities among different species or within a single species have diversified as well. Stated differently, the morphological characteristics of different species, such as the pectoral fins of fish versus the wings of birds, or specialized morphological aspects within a given species, such as the elongated bill of the hummingbird, display both uniqueness and diversity; differentiation throughout evolution, from single cells into complex organisms, has occurred because the increasingly unique, specialized characteristics have allowed the species to cope with its environment and, thus, to reproduce successfully. The same argument should apply to learning abilities: the learning capacities of different species, or specialized abilities within a given species, also should display a uniqueness and diversity; differentiation of learning abilities throughout evolution should reflect the specialized environmental demands (requiring learned adaptive behavior) with which the species must contend. The consequence of this argument for the study of learning is that learning laws probably are not universal; a single set of basic and general principles of learning cannot be compiled because learning abilities per se have diversified throughout evolution (see Hinde & Stevenson-Hinde, 1973; Seligman & Hager, 1972; Shettleworth, 1972).

These ideas were discussed in an important paper by Seligman (1970) who claimed that there are three separate categories of learned behavior, *prepared* behavior, *unprepared* behavior, and *contraprepared* behavior, which differ according to the degree to which an organism is biologically predisposed to learn the responses.

Prepared behaviors are learned responses, that is, they are not instincts per se, but since they are invariably related to specialized and basic survival needs of the organism, learning takes place with very minimal training. Here, CS-US association or instrumental motor responses are acquired so quickly that conventional principles of learning do not seem to apply. Thus, prepared behaviors are innate-like; they are usually unique to a given species, reflecting a specialized mode of adapting to environmental demands.

There are many kinds of prepared behaviors, several of which are discussed later in this chapter. Marler (1970) gave a good example using white-crowned sparrows. If young birds are isolated between 10 and 50 days of age so they do not hear the singing of adult white-crowned sparrows, they later sing a poorly developed version of the basic song. However, if the young birds are exposed to their species-specific song during a critical period, they learn to imitate its characteristic features and sing it clearly as adults. Obviously this type of learned behavior is unlike responses such as lever pressing or conditioned salivation. it takes place very rapidly (i.e., the sparrows are biologically prepared to learn their song) and it appears to be impervious to extinction. More important, learning the correct song depends on the presence of a particular set of biological stimuli, namely the characteristic features of the white-crowned sparrow song itself. Seligman's notion is that the laws of learning needed to account for such prepared behaviors are distinct from those principles that pertain to the learning of unprepared responses.

The second category of learning behavior in Seligman's scheme is *unprepared* behavior—responses that subjects learn with moderate difficulty. Unprepared behaviors include most of the Pavlovian and instrumental CRs that are studied in the normal laboratory setting; they are not acquired easily but the subjects do learn them eventually.

Since unprepared behaviors are "typical" laboratory responses, most of the traditional laws of learning (e.g., contiguity, reinforcement contingency, laws of extinction, and retention) apply only to this category. In other words, learning psychologists within the general process tradition have restricted their inquiries to a limited set of (unprepared) behaviors, the learning of which is moderately difficult. Therefore, the traditional principles of learning apply only to the acquisition of such unprepared behaviors and not universally to other sorts of responses.

Finally, Seligman's third type of learned behavior is the *contraprepared* category. Contraprepared behaviors are responses that subjects fail to learn well even with very extended training. Presumably, these behaviors are so different from those that are natural for the animal that no biological predisposition for learning them exists. To put it another way, many species have not inherited the capacity to learn certain types of response (or CS-US relationships) because these responses, or relationships, have never been integral to the survival of the species. As in the case of prepared behaviors, Seligman argues that the conventional principles of learning, derived through the study of unprepared responses, fail to account for the acquisition of contraprepared responses.

Examples of contraprepared behavior were demonstrated in an important report by Breland and Breland (1961; also see subsequent sections of this chapter for a more complete discussion of contraprepared learning). The Brelands were noted psychologists who went into the business of training various animals for circus, movie, and television roles. In one situation, they tried to train a raccoon to deposit tokens in a metal box in order to obtain food reward. The animal accomplished this task when it was given only one token, although it showed some hesitancy in releasing the token into the box. However, when the raccoon had to deposit two tokens, the "simple" instrumental behavior deteriorated markedly. Instead of releasing the tokens, the animal constantly rubbed them together, often dipping them into the opening of the box only to pull them back out immediately. Clearly, the animal had not learned the instrumental task even though the appropriate reinforcement contingency was provided. Apparently the raccoon had resorted to its instinctive food-washing behavior, that is, it performed the rubbing and washing response as if the tokens were food. Breland and Breland claimed that when an animal's strong instinctual behavior patterns were incompatible with the related instrumental task, the learned behavior "drifted" toward the instinctive behavior. To put it another way, many animals are contraprepared to learn some behaviors, and when required to do so, they resort to performing their instinctual patterns rather than the designated instrumental response.

There are other examples of contraprepared associations, of the failure by animals to learn "conventional" laboratory CRs even when the conditions for learning appear to be optimal. In one study (Bolles et al., 1974), rats were given a mild shock at the same time each day for 30 days which they could avoid by jumping onto a platform. Bolles et al. found that the rats did not learn to anticipate (i.e., avoid) the shock. The principal CS for the avoidance response, an internal cue based on the time of day, clearly was not associated with the shock. These results failed to support the general process view of learning since a number of other experiments (e.g., Bolles & Moot 1973; Bolles & Stokes, 1965) had shown that rats readily learned to anticipate a food US when it was presented at the same time each day. Thus, the anticipation of a periodic shock US, based on internal cues stemming from the rat's diurnal cycle, appeared to be a contraprepared association; it was not acquired readily even though the type of stimuli (internal CS) and the experimental arrangements were effective in other learning situations where the animals anticipated food.

In summary, Seligman's suggestion that learned behaviors fall into one of three categories appears to be well documented. On the one hand, innate-like responses are learned quickly without the prolonged training procedures usually required for learning conventional, unprepared behaviors. Reinforcement contingencies or repeated CS-US pairings seem irrelevant to the acquisition of these prepared responses. On the other hand, animals seem to be contraprepared to learn some behaviors or associations, even though the structure of the experiment adequately provides for the learning of unprepared responses. This notion, that reinforcement contingency is not the single, pervasive condition of learning (i.e., that reinforcement contingency fails to account for the very rapid learning of prepared responses and the very marginal acquisition of contraprepared responses) is summarized by Breland and Breland (1961, p. 684):

> Three of the most important of these tacit assumptions [of the general process view] seem to us to be: that the animal comes to the laboratory as a virtual *tabula rasa*, that species differences are insignificant, and that all responses are about equally conditionable to all stimuli.
>
> It is obvious, we feel, from the foregoing account, that these assumptions are no longer tenable. . . . It is our reluctant conclusion that the behavior of any species cannot be adequately understood, predicted, or controlled without knowledge of its instinctive patterns, evolutionary history, and ecological niche.

The remaining sections of this chapter review other important examples of learning that reflect the biological constraints which influence the learning capacities of humans and lower animals.

LEARNED TASTE AVERSION

Probably all of us at one time or another have become nauseated following the consumption of a particular food. We usually find later that we have developed a strong dislike for that food. In fact, it is not unusual for such an experience to result in a lasting aversion to the flavor or smell of whatever it was we associated with feeling ill.

This phenomenon, taste aversion, is true of many other animals besides humans and has provided one of the most important areas of research supporting the notion that organisms have biological predispositions to learn certain adaptive behaviors (see Garcia et al., 1974; Garcia et al., 1972; Rozin & Kalat, 1971, for reviews; and Riley & Baril, 1976, for a bibliography). If an organism consumes a distinctively flavored food or liquid and later becomes ill, it will avoid consuming substances of that flavor in the future because an association develops between the flavor and the poisoning agent. On the surface, acquired aversion to a flavor appears to be a simple Pavlovian CR in that a CS (flavor) is paired with a US (poison or other illness-inducing agent). However, taste aversion differs appreciably from normal Pavlovian conditioning in a number of important ways.

Belongingness

One anomalous finding in the area of acquired taste aversion pertains to the equipotentiality of stimuli. According to the traditional general process view, all USs should be equally potent in becoming associated with a CS and should be interchangeable in this sense. However, a number of investigators have discovered that acquired flavor aversion does not occur with all USs (e.g., Domjan & Wilson, 1972; Garcia & Koelling, 1966; Garcia et al., 1968; K. Green et al., 1974; L. Green et al., 1972).

In the Garcia and Koelling (1966) experiment, for example, thirsty rats were allowed to drink a saccharin-flavored solution while a light/noise stimulus was also presented. The "bright-noisy-tasty" CS then was followed by a US. For one group of subjects, the US was a shock whereas the other animals received an injection of lithium chloride, a substance which produces a feeling of nausea. In a second phase of the study, Garcia and Koelling tested the animals for acquired aversion. Half the subjects in each treatment group were given the light/noise CS while drinking plain water whereas the other half were given the flavor CS. The acquired aversion was measured in terms of the consumption of fluid on the test: the greater the aversion to the CS, the less the consumption.

As Figure 7-1 shows, the poison (lithium chloride) and shock USs did not function in an equivalent fashion. The subjects that received the shock during training demonstrated a strong aversion to the light/noise component but almost none to the saccharin CS. In contrast, the results for the poison-injected subjects were the reverse: they showed strong aversion to the flavor but not to the light/noise CS. In other words, the rats easily learned to associate flavor-poison and light/noise-shock as shown by substantially reduced drinking on the test following those pairings. However, they apparently did *not* learn the flavor-shock or light/noise-poison associations. This important phenomenon, that CSs and USs are not equally

FIGURE 7-1.

Mean licks per minutes (times 100) of the flavored solution (open bars) or the "bright-noisy" solution (filled bars) for the groups that were injected with poison or given the shock US.

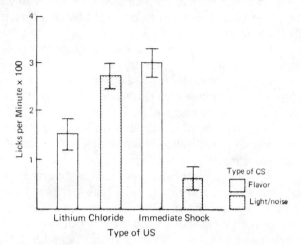

associable, has been replicated in many other taste aversion studies in which the poisoning agent was X-irradiation and the external cue was food-pellet size (Garcia et al., 1968); the shock US was long lasting (L. Green et al., 1972); or the flavor was infused into the oral cavity without requiring the animal to approach the drinking tube (Domjan & Wilson, 1972).

According to Seligman (1970), Garcia and Koelling's experiment required psychologists to reexamine the general process view of learning. First, of course, was the issue of whether all CS become associated with USs to the same extent. Learned taste aversion appeared to involve a gastrointestinal US but not an external US such as shock. Therefore, the general proposition that any viable US may become associated with a CS through contiguity clearly was violated. Second, the taste aversion phenomenon appeared to be an example of prepared learning, i.e., a specialized form of learning reflecting environmental pressures during evolution. Animals with the capacity to identify a flavor that later made them ill were less likely to consume that flavor in the future. Thus the probability of consuming the food again and being fatally poisoned decreased; alternatively, the probability that such animals would reproduce successfully and pass on to their offspring their own capacity to learn flavor-poison relationships increased. Throughout evolutionary history, therefore, flavors and their subsequent gastrointestinal effects came, for certain species, to "belong" together (Revusky & Garcia, 1970).

In this context, the failure by rats to associate flavors and shock, or external cues and poison, is an example of contraprepared learning. Those pairs of stimuli simply do not belong together in the natural environment; the ability to associate them is irrelevant to the task of survival. Although several investigators recently have demonstrated that, under certain circumstances, external cues may become aversive when followed by poison (e.g., Best et al., 1973; Mitchell et al., 1975; Revusky & Parker, 1976), the results are marginal when compared to flavor aversion learning (see Krane & Wagner, 1975).

Flavors and gastrointestinal events belong together to the extent that flavors, for rats, are the primary cues for selecting food. That is, since rats "depend" on flavor for food selection, it is understandable that they have developed a unique capacity to associate the flavor of foods with their gastrointestinal consequences. If such an evolutional argument were correct, then species which depend on a different sense modality for food procurement should show a similar ability to associate poisons with cues in that sense modality.

The above prediction was confirmed in an important study by Wilcoxon, Dragoin, and Kral (1971). Rats and quail became ill after they had ingested a sour solution. Since the blue color of the liquid was visible inside the glass drinking spout, both the color of the solution as well as its taste could function as a CS for aversion learning. Later, the authors measured fluid consumption (the more the animals consumed, the weaker was their aversion). One group of rats and quail were given blue water, that is, they were tested for their aversion to the color CS. Another group of rats and quail were given a colorless sour-flavored fluid, that is, they were tested for their aversion to the flavor. The results clearly indicated that the rats avoided drinking the flavored water whereas the quail avoided the colored water.

These striking results support the notion that certain stimuli have come to belong together throughout evolutionary history. For rats, smell and taste are the important sense modalities for food procurement. Quail, in contrast, utilize their keen visual sense in foraging. Thus, both species have evolved along separate lines yet both have a similar specialized ability to identify poisonous foods. In the case of the rat, taste and illness belong together, whereas for quail, color and illness associations are biologically prepotent.

Long-Delay Learning

A second major finding that highlights the uniqueness of taste aversion learning pertains to the CS-US interval. Although the acquisition of conventional Pavlovian CRs requires a very short CS-US interval (i.e., defined in seconds—see Chapter 2), many studies have shown that taste aversion learning is possible even when the poison US is presented hours after the flavor CS (e.g., Andrews & Braveman, 1975; Garcia et al., 1966; Kalat & Rozin, 1971). For example, in the study by Kalat and Rozin (1971), separate groups of rats were first given sucrose water and then injected with lithium chloride (the poison US) after either .5, 1, 1.5, 3, 6, or 24 hours. Finally, two days after the training session, each subject was tested for an

FIGURE 7-2.

Median percent preference for the sucrose solution as a function of the flavor-poison interval during training.

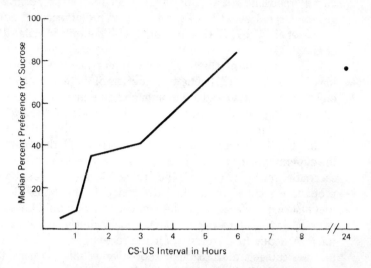

aversion to the sucrose. As shown in Figure 7-2, the percentage preference for sucrose increased as a function of the CS-US interval. That is, a strong aversion was evident for the groups that had received the lithium chloride within one hour after consuming the sucrose. However, aversion to sucrose was much less in the groups that experienced a 1.5- to 3-hour CS-US interval during training. With a 6-hour interval, no aversion was evident (those subjects showed as strong a preference as the 24-hour control subjects). In summary, it is clear that the strength of the aversion CR was inversely proportional to the length of the US delay. The remarkable feature, however, was that the stimuli in the taste aversion paradigm were associable even when the US was delayed for three hours or, under some circumstances, 12–15 hours (e.g., Andrews & Braveman, 1975).

That taste aversion operates even when the US is delayed for several hours following the CS attests to the uniqueness of this type of learning and implies that evolutionary principles are important in the analysis of learning. It seems reasonable that animals who could bridge a long time interval and still associate a novel flavor with subsequent illness were at a selective advantage during evolution. This long-delay feature is additional evidence that acquired taste aversion is a specialized learning ability that has been selected for during evolutionary development.

Acquired Taste Preference

An important variation of the taste aversion paradigm involves acquired taste preferences. Basically, taste preferences are the reverse of taste aversions in that a beneficial (as opposed to an illness-producing) US is used. In a typical study, a flavor is paired with an illness-reducing US—the US is, in fact, a "medicine" or antidote. Pairing a flavor with a positive or beneficial gastrointestinal event results in increased preference for that flavor (e.g., Garcia et al., 1967; K. Green et al., 1974; Zahorik & Maier, 1969; Zahorik et al., 1974).

One important study on taste preferences was done by Zahorik, Maier, and Pies (1974). The basic design of the experiment included several groups of rats who were maintained on a thiamine-deficient diet for 28 days. During this deficiency period, the subjects had access to quinine-flavored water. Since quinine was paired with the deficiency, it was expected that the flavor would become aversive. During a second phase of the experiment, in which the subjects had access to a different flavor (either saccharin, anise, or vanilla), they were injected with enough thiamine to produce a recovery from their deficiency. In this phase, it was expected that a strong preference for the recovery flavor would be acquired due to its association with recovery from ill health. Finally, the subjects were tested for their acquired preference for the recovery flavor. The authors found that the subjects didn't simply choose any "safe" familiar flavor not associated with the lack of thiamine but explicitly preferred the flavor associated with recovery from the deficiency.

The work on acquired taste preferences, combined with the research on aversions, provides important insights into the problem of food selection and diet regulation. Flavors paired with sudden illness or with a more gradually induced diet deficiency may also become aversive (e.g., Rozin, 1967). Animals do not consume those foods in the future on the basis of flavor and thus may avoid fatal poisoning or malnourishment. Such flavor aversions, therefore, are highly adaptive in allowing animals to avoid the deleterious consequences of an improper diet. Avoiding an improper diet, however, is only half the problem for an animal in ill health. Selecting appropriate foods that will enrich the otherwise deficient diet is important as well. Therefore, acquired preferences also allow animals to identify "medicines" on the basis of taste, to learn what foods are appropriate for correcting dietary imbalances through association of the flavor with the beneficial consequences of the food.

If, as claimed previously, the taste aversion/preference paradigm is an example of classical conditioning (leaving out the anomalies of belongingness and long delay), then the flavor CS should elicit a conditioned form of the illness UR. That the CR is nearly identical to the UR is central to all examples of Pavlovian conditioning (see Chapter 2). Several studies have confirmed that illnesslike CRs are indeed elicited by the flavor CS following conditioning. For example, Rozin (1967) found that rats spilled their thiamine-deficient food after a period of thiamine deprivation. Rats typically engage in such behavior only when their food is highly unpalatable. In other situations, where the illness was suddenly induced, the rats engaged in "chin-washing" behavior, a response that rats also performed when required to consume highly distasteful quinine (Garcia et al., 1974).

Factors Affecting Taste Aversions

A great deal of research has been done to clarify the role of a number of variables in taste aversion learning. One of the most important findings concerns the novelty of the flavor CS. Many investigators (e.g., Ahlers & Best, 1971; Revusky & Bedarf, 1967; Siegel, 1974) have shown that aversion conditioning occurs more strongly when novel flavors are used. Although conditioning may in some circumstances occur after extensive preexposure to a flavor CS (Nachman & Jones, 1974), even a single preexposure is usually sufficient to attenuate taste aversion learning (Siegel, 1974). For example, in both the Ahlers and Best (1971) and Revusky and Bedarf (1967) experiments, rats were given two flavors just prior to illness. One of the flavor CSs was novel whereas the other was familiar to the subjects. Preference tests revealed that a much stronger aversion had accrued to the new flavor. In fact, the order of presentation on the training trial (novel-familiar versus familiar-novel) made little difference; the novelty of the flavor CS was far more important than CS-US contiguity.

Although previous research had shown clearly that novelty was critical to taste aversion learning, the question remained whether all novel flavors had an equal tendency to become associated with poison. That is, a second characteristic of flavors that also might be important to taste aversion learning might be their strength or salience. Several investigators have confirmed this notion. For example, Kalat and Rozin (1970) presented their subjects with two novel solutions followed by lithium chloride (the illness-producing US). On the following day, they offered both flavors during a choice test. Kalat and Rozin found that all flavors were not equally potent in eliciting the aversion. Sucrose or casein were the most effective CSs in this regard while, in contrast, vanilla or sodium chloride solutions failed to evidence a strong aversion on the test.

Kalat and Rozin attributed this difference in CS effectiveness to "salience," a term they defined as the tendency of a solution to become associated with poisoning. Salience was an inherent property of the flavor; the associability of the flavor, its salience, did not depend on which other flavors were given during training (the salient flavor always induced a stronger aversion) or on the novelty of the solutions (all the flavors in Kalat and Rozin's study were novel). Thus, salience (and novelty) of a flavor appear to be more crucial to taste aversion learning than CS-US contiguity.

Properties of the US also are important parameters in taste aversion learning. A great variety of illness-inducing agents, over fifty in number, are effective in producing taste aversions, including alcohol and many psychoactive drugs (e.g., Cappell et al., 1973). Also, the strength of taste aversions is positively related to the US intensity. For example, Nachman and Ashe (1973) presented rats with a novel sucrose solution and about five minutes later injected them with lithium chloride. Separate groups of subjects received different concentrations and volumes of the US. Three days later, the subjects were tested for their aversion to sucrose. As shown

FIGURE 7-3.

Mean sucrose consumption as a function of the amount of lithium chloride US present in the injection (expressed in millimoles). Concentrations varied from .15 M to .65 M and injection volumes varied from 0 to 20 ml/kg.

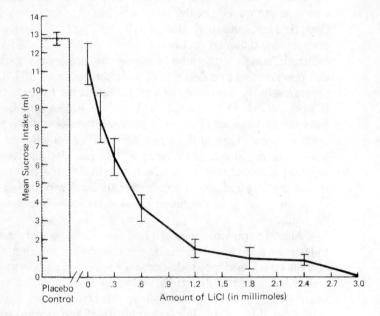

in Figure 7-3, an orderly gradient between sucrose consumption and US intensity was obtained. That is, very low amounts of lithium chloride did not produce appreciable aversions (relative to the placebo control group); however, aversion strength increased dramatically as the amount of lithium chloride present in the injection increased. In summary, the relationship between conditioning and US magnitude was comparable to those found for other Pavlovian CRs (see Chapter 2).

Theories of Taste Aversion

There are several theories that attempt to explain why the US presentation may be delayed for many hours in taste aversion learning. A traditional position in Pavlovian theory, of course, is the contiguity, or trace-decay, theory. This theory assumes that the CS established some sort of neural trace or activation that decreases over time. If the US is presented soon, while the CS trace is still strong, a strong association is formed. However, if the US presentation is delayed until the US is contiguous with only the weak remnants of the CS trace, a weak association develops. Theorists have speculated that the trace-decay theory is not applicable to the case of taste aversion principally because it is unreasonable to maintain that gustatory traces decay only after many hours whereas visual traces decay completely within a few seconds or less.

Some theorists have attempted to salvage a trace-decay position by making special assumptions about flavor CSs. One is that flavors produce aftereffects in the form of sensations in the oral/gastric tract that linger for several hours. When the US eventually is presented, it bonds directly to these sensations. A more specific version of this theory postulates that subjects partially regurgitate the novel substance thereby providing a taste cue contiguous with the delayed US presentation.

There are a number of arguments against this position. For example, Nachman (1970) reared a group of rats with a saccharin solution as their only fluid. During taste aversion training, the animals were given plain water (a novel CS) and lithium chloride. A significant aversion to the water was found even when the US presentation was delayed for four hours. The aftereffects theory clearly was not supported in this study since water does not induce either persisting oral/gastric sensations or regurgitation.

Another special assumption is that novel flavors are free from competition with other stimuli (see Revusky, 1971). Stated differently, the neural trace of a flavor may persist longer than the neural trace of a light or noise simply because interference with the flavor trace from other flavor cues is minimal. This claim cannot be made for external cues such as noise and lights, however. The many extraneous sounds and lights that would impinge on the animal during a long CS-US interval surely would interfere with the original light/noise trace, preventing it from becoming strongly associated with the US.

The interference theory, like the aftereffects position, has been strongly criticized. The theory implies that interference to the CS, if it were provided deliberately during the experiment, would preclude the long-delay learning. Most likely the subjects would develop aversions to the competing or interfering flavors rather than to the original CS. However, several investigators (e.g., Der-Karabetian & Gorry, 1974; Kalat & Rozin, 1970, 1971) have shown that aversions are learned even when other flavors are presented between the CS and US. In the study by Der-Karabetian and Gorry (1974), for example, three solutions, flavored with salt, vinegar, or coffee, were given between the sucrose CS and the lithium chloride US. According to the interference theory, these flavors should have produced marked interference but the sucrose aversion remained strong. It should be noted that these studies also argue strongly against the aftereffects theory since the aftereffects that would get conditioned to the US should be those of the intervening solutions, not the original CS.

A unique theory, the learned safety theory, was proposed by Rozin and Kalat (1971). Those authors argued that the CS trace is not decaying during the CS-US interval, but rather that the subjects are learning that the CS is safe. It appears that subjects react to novel stimuli, especially flavors, with some reluctance: initial consumption is reduced (e.g., Nachman & Jones, 1974) and avoidance of the flavor may be enhanced by prior illness (e.g., Rozin, 1968). It is as if the subjects expect the food to be a potential poison and approach it tentatively at first. Following consumption of the novel substance, its consequences are "evaluated" and, after a period of hours, if no illness has occurred, the flavor is judged to be safe. On the other hand, if the animal does become ill, aversion to the new substance develops.

The learned safety theory accommodates many findings in the taste aversion literature, particularly the fact that aversion strength depends on the novelty of the flavor. However, perhaps the clearest support for the theory was provided by Kalat and Rozin (1973). Three groups of rats were used: one group was given the novel flavor 4 hours before being poisoned (made ill); a second group received the CS ½ hour prior to the poison; and a third group received the flavor both 4 hours and again ½ hour prior to the poison. The trace-decay and the learned safety theories predicted opposite results for the third group. According to the trace-decay position, the aversion strength of the 4-½-hour subjects should be comparable to the ½-hour subjects since the CS-US contiguity relationship was the same in both cases (i.e., ½ hour). In contrast, according to the learned safety position, the aversions for the 4-½-hour subjects and the 4-hour subjects should be comparable: in both groups, the subjects had a total of 4 hours during which they could learn that the fluid was safe. Kalat and Rozin's results supported the learned safety theory. Groups 4 and 4-½ showed approximately the same level of aversion conditioning; that is, the aversion in the 4-½ subjects was reduced to the same level as in group 4 (due to learned safety during the 4 hours) even though the CS had been reinstated only ½ hour prior to the poison.

The learned safety theory has been criticized in recent years. For example, Nachman and Jones (1974) demonstrated aversive learning even when the flavor was thoroughly familiar and safe. Best (1975) found that flavor preexposure rendered the CS "meaningless" rather than beneficial or safe as the learned safety theory suggests. Finally, Domjan and Bowman (1974), who used Kalat and Rozin's (1973) original experimental design but corrected for problems of differential fluid consumption, found that a second CS exposure ½ hour before poisoning did increase aversive learning.

It appears that no single theory of taste aversion is adequate at this time. Notions of belongingness, trace decay, and relative (contextual) novelty all seem to contribute to long-delay learning. Many of these factors are likely to be integrated in the near future. Although no single theory appears adequate, the basic findings in the taste aversion literature certainly highlight the biological or evolutional factors in conditioning.

We should point out that experiments on taste aversion have some interesting applications for problems outside the scientific laboratory. One such application involves the use of conditioned taste aversions to control predatory attacks of coyotes on flocks of sheep. Coyotes are notoriously difficult to trap and many environmental groups have lobbied to prevent their being killed by poison. On the other hand, these animals pose a constant threat to the farmer. The issue then is to control attacks on sheep without endangering the coyote species.

A number of studies have addressed this problem. Gustavson et al. (1974), for example, showed that coyotes would avoid eating lamb flesh if they had been mildly poisoned after eating it previously. Their willingness to eat rabbit meat, however, was undaunted. The implication from this work, therefore, is to lace lamb flesh with lithium chloride (causing sickness but not death) in the natural environment; coyotes who become aversive to the meat will select another diet, namely, rabbit.

AVOIDANCE LEARNING

As we said in Chapter 4, the two-factor theory of avoidance learning (especially Schoenfeld's version of that theory) has not received much support in recent years. Although fear is established when aversive USs are employed (see Chapters 2 and 8), the notion that avoidance learning is reinforced by the CS-offset (as Schoenfeld claimed) appears untenable. Rather, many theorists now believe that the CS-offset is merely a source of information for the subject. Although this belief makes good sense in the light of recent experimental findings, the problem of specifying the rein-forcement for avoidance learning still remains.

A different theory of avoidance (e.g., Herrnstein, 1969, see Chapter 4) attributes avoidance learning to a reduction in shock frequency (just as an appetitive response learning, for example, lever pressing, increases due to the presentation of food contingent upon lever pressing). Herrnstein's position essentially relies on a single "factor," namely reinforcement con-tingency. That is, avoidance behavior is acquired because a reward (e.g., avoidance of shock per se, perhaps a period of acknowledged safety from shock, a reduction in the density of shock over time, etc.) is contingent upon the avoidance behavior.

The problem with such a broad theory that relies solely on the concept of reinforcement contingency is that in some cases, avoidance behavior appears to be quite unrelated to reinforcement contingencies. Just as Bre-land and Breland (1961) reported that contingencies didn't "work" in the acquisition of some appetitive behaviors (see the previous section of this chapter), reward contingencies are not always effective for avoidance be-haviors. For example, a number of studies have shown that rats are ex-tremely poor at learning to press a lever to avoid an unpleasant stimulus (e.g., D'Amato & Schiff, 1964); they can attain moderate levels of perfor-mance only if very special procedures are used (D'Amato & Fazzaro, 1966; Petersen & Lyon, 1975; Scheuer & Sutton, 1973). This finding contrasts sharply with the rapid acquisition of other types of avoidance behaviors like running or freezing.

The case of lever-press avoidance, of course, raises the issue of pre-paredness. Some avoidance behaviors, like running or freezing in rats, for example, are highly prepotent, or prepared, because they are compatible with the natural behaviors that these animals use to cope with threats. These prepared behaviors have evolved as species-specific modes of responding under stress. On the other hand, some avoidance behaviors (e.g., lever press avoidance) are contraprepared; they are unrelated to the natural defense responses of the species to aversive stimulation. In summary, the concepts of preparedness, adaptive specializations through evolutionary development, and biological perspectives all apply to the issue of avoidance learning just as they apply to appetitive behaviors.

Species-Specific Defense Reactions

The ideas discussed above are central to a theoretical proposal by Bolles (1970). Bolles claims that avoidance behaviors actually are innate, unlearned, defensive reactions that are particular to a given species. Survival from predators in the natural environment is too important to be dependent upon gradual, instrumental learning processes. Survival is based on innate reactions that have become stereotyped and specialized in the course of evolutionary development. As Bolles (1970) stated: "The parameters of the [natural environment] make it impossible for there to be any learning [of defensive behaviors]. Thus, no real-life predator is going to present cues just before it attacks. No owl hoots or whistles 5 seconds before pouncing on a mouse. And no owl terminates his hoots or whistles just as the mouse gets away so as to reinforce the avoidance response. Nor will the owl give the mouse enough trials for the necessary learning to occur. What keeps our little friends alive in the forest has nothing to do with avoidance learning as we ordinarily conceive of it or investigate it in the laboratory" (p. 32 – 33).

Bolles proposes that avoidance behavior is the execution of a species-specific defense reaction (SSDR). These SSDRs are innate responses to a new, sudden, or aversive stimulus. Although SSDRs usually involve running or fleeing, freezing or threat display, or aggression, other patterns occur depending upon the species and the situation.

According to Bolles' theory, SSDRs exist in a hierarchy. At the top of the hierarchy are the most prepotent responses, those that occur first during times of threat. Further down are responses that the organism learns with moderate ease after the more natural SSDRs are suppressed. Finally, at the bottom of the SSDR hierarchy are the non-SSDRs, behaviors that are alien to the species' naturalistic defense patterns.

When a subject is confronted with an aversive situation, it reflexively makes the dominant SSDRs first. In the natural environment, of course, these responses are the most effective in coping with stress. If the dominant SSDRs fail to cope with or eliminate the threatening stimulus, they are suppressed in favor of more subordinate SSDRs and, if these also fail, non-SSDRs are executed.

The acquisition of a lever-press avoidance response may be considered in light of this last statement: only after all their natural SSDRs are suppressed will rats learn to press a lever to avoid shock. Indeed, it has taken many investigators (e.g., Herrnstein and Hineline, 1966) who have employed lever-press avoidance in their experiments thousands of trials to achieve acceptable levels of conditioning. These failures to show rapid lever-press avoidance learning argue against Herrnstein's (1969) one-factor theory and in favor of Bolles' (1970) SSDR theory. If reduction in shock density were the mechanism for all avoidance behavior (as Herrnstein suggests), then the acquisition rate for a lever-press avoidance should not be so discrepant from the acquisition rate for a running response since lever pressing is a response that, in other situations, is learned easily.

While the case of lever-press avoidance suggests indirectly the existence of an SSDR hierarchy, numerous studies have provided more direct support for Bolles' theory. For example, Brener and Goesling (1970) trained rats to avoid shock. The subjects in one group could avoid shock by remaining still during a 2-second tone which was initiated by their movement; if they continued to move, a shock was delivered. Subjects in a second group could avoid the shock by being active. Here, if motion was not detected, a warning tone was sounded two seconds after which the subjects were shocked if they had failed to move around during the tone.

Brener and Goesling found that both groups learned to avoid the shock. That is, the contingency between shock avoidance and activity or immobility was effective in both cases. However, the immobile-avoid subjects learned their avoidance task much better than the active-avoid subjects in that they received many fewer shocks during training. In other words, since freezing or immobility was a more prepotent reaction to shock than was activity, the avoidance response involving immobility was learned more readily than the one involving activity. Thus, Brener and Goesling's study indicated that the efficacy of a given reinforcement in conditioning depended on the type of UR elicited in that situation.

Another important study that supported the SSDR theory of avoidance learning was done by Blanchard and Blanchard (1971). Rats were placed in a small wire-mesh cage which was then placed inside a much larger observation chamber. For the experimental subjects, a cat was introduced into the larger chamber; no cat was presented to the control rats. The authors were interested in measuring the type of UR that the cat, a "naturalistic" US, elicited. Specifically, the authors recorded, for each minute of the 10-minute test session, the number of seconds that the rats and cat were in motion. As shown in Figure 7-4, there were no differences in activity between the experimental and control rats before the introduction of the cat. However, when the cat was placed in the larger chamber, the activity level of the experimental rats inside the smaller wire-mesh cage was immediately reduced. The control rats, who were not exposed to the cat, continued the same pattern of motor activity. Thus, the dominant UR to the cat in this situation was freezing or immobility.

In a second study, Blanchard and Blanchard repeated the above experiment with a few important changes. First, the smaller wire-mesh cage was not used; the rats were merely put in one corner of the larger

FIGURE 7-4.

Mean seconds of activity during each minute of the test for the cat and for the experimental and control rats (data on left indicate activity levels prior to the introduction of the cat).

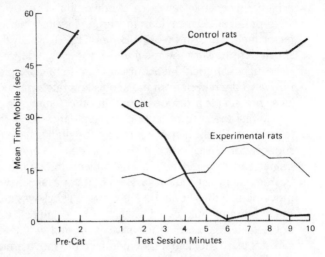

chamber. Second, an escape route in the form of an electrified alley was attached to the side of the chamber. The basic procedure involved exposing the experimental rats to a cat (who sat in another corner of the chamber) and measuring whether the rat would actively escape the situation by crossing the electrified grid in the alley. Control rats were not exposed to the cat and, therefore, no escape behavior was expected.

The authors found that the control animals indeed were unwilling to submit to shock; generally, they remained in the chamber on each trial for the full 5-minute period. The experimental animals, however, escaped through the alley within seconds of seeing the cat, even when the shock intensity in the alley was extremely high. In short, the cat had elicited an active escape response, a UR opposite to that observed in the first experiment. Blanchard and Blanchard reasoned that both types of URs were SSDRs. Running or escaping, however, appeared to be dominant since the animals escaped when this response was possible. On the other hand, freezing was readily elicited when an escape route was not provided. Freezing, therefore, was not merely the absence of a SSDR; it was an alternative SSDR that was appropriate and useful in the situation where escape was not possible.

In summary, there are two related positions with regard to biological perspectives in avoidance learning. Both positions stem from the realization that reinforcement contingencies often fail to produce avoidance learning even though there is absolutely no reason to suspect that the reinforcer, the response, or their contingent relationship are inappropriate for the animal. The first position involves the general notion of preparedness: the potential for learning some instrumental avoidance behaviors has increased in the course of evolution; in contrast, the capacity to learn contraprepared responses which have little bearing on an animal's natural defense needs has decreased.

The related position is Bolles' SSDR theory which claims that avoidance responses are not even learned—they are reflexes that have developed during evolution. If the task required by the experimenter is compatible with the subject's dominant SSDR, learning is very rapid (see Galvani et al., 1975; Grossen & Kelley, 1972). However, if the animal must execute an non-SSDR because none of its SSDRs "work," learning of the avoidance response, if it occurs at all, is very slow.

BIOLOGICAL PERSPECTIVES IN HUMAN LEARNING

The implications posed by the preparedness concept are not limited to nonhuman behavior. Presumably, human learning abilities are also a product of evolutionary selection in that some behaviors are easily learned (prepared) while others are difficult to learn (unprepared or contraprepared). It also follows that the laws that govern human learning vary along the preparedness dimension: no single set of laws pertains to all human behavior nor do the laws for lower organisms necessarily overlap with those for human learning. In short, there are biological perspectives (or conditions, constraints, and so on) in human learning just as in infrahuman learning. The remainder of this chapter reviews some evidence for this notion with reference to two notable types of human activity.

Human Neurosis

As we said in Chapter 3, many psychologists believe that neurotic behavior in humans—maladaptive responding based on fear—is acquired according to the same principles of learning that govern the acquisition of other, normal behaviors. The outcome of this belief has been behavior therapy— the attempt to treat maladaptive behavior *as behavior* by using the same extinction and reacquisition techniques that have been employed in laboratory studies of learning. (Note that this approach to psychological therapy differs from more traditional techniques which regard the neurosis as a *symptom* and attempt to treat the disorder that underlies or causes it.)

Behavior therapy is based on the notion that most, if not all, human behaviors, including *phobias* (irrational fears), are "interchangeable"; the behaviors are strengthened by reinforcement contingency (the single underlying concept for the acquisition of behavior) and they may be suppressed by the removal of that contingency or by punishment. No qualitative difference is noted between behaviors, whether they are simple motor skills, language (e.g., Skinner, 1957), or neurotic behaviors. In short, the behavior therapies illustrate the devotion that many psychologists have had toward the traditional view of learning.

Seligman (1971), however, has argued that many abnormal behaviors, such as phobias, are nonarbitrary behaviors; that is, phobias represent a class of prepared behaviors in human learning. For example, the list of objects toward which humans typically become phobic is quite small. Irrational fears usually develop for specific animals (e.g., snakes) or insects, darkness, and heights. In contrast, it is very rare to encounter a "desk," a "tree," or an "eyeglass" phobia. The set of potentially phobic stimuli—objects with which intense and irrational fears are associated—is small; it seems that not just any stimulus can serve as a phobic object.

Seligman notes several other characteristics of phobias, besides the fact that they are nonarbitrary. First, phobias are learned very quickly, often after only one pairing of the stimulus object and trauma, and they are exceedingly difficult to extinguish. Second, phobias are irrational and, in a sense, noncognitive. That is, consciously knowing that the phobic stimulus will not be followed by the traumatic US does not allay the fear; the person irrationally continues to fear the object.

To summarize Seligman's view, the acquisition of a phobia is not the result of an arbitrary stimulus' getting paired with a traumatic US. Rather, phobias are prepared responses. Irrational fears develop very rapidly to a limited number of objects (which, from an anthropological point of view, probably represented threats to survival during humankind's evolutionary development). Clearly, the implication of Seligman's work is that behavior therapists, when treating phobic patients, should recognize that they are dealing with prepared as opposed to unprepared behaviors.

Research on the biological perspectives in human learning, notably neurosis, has been initiated only recently. However, a number of significant studies have been completed. For example, Ohman, Eriksson, and Olofsson (1975) tested several of Seligman's assertions, namely that some stimuli become phobic more easily than others, and that the acquisition of aversion to these stimuli is very rapid whereas extinction is very slow. College students served as subjects. Electrodes were attached to their index fingers to measure galvanic skin response (GSR) and to deliver a mild shock US. The subjects were first shown ten color slides, five of which were pictures of snakes while the other five were pictures of houses; each subject was asked to rate the pictures on a $1-9$ "discomfort" scale. Then, 5 conditioning trials were given. Half the experimental subjects were shown pictures of snakes followed by shock whereas the other half were presented with pictures of houses plus shock. Separate groups of control subjects were given either the snake or house CSs but, for them, the shock US was delivered at random times between slide presentations. Aversive conditioning to the CS was expected to occur for the experimental subjects but no conditioning was anticipated in the control subjects. Following this training phase, 10 extinction trials were given during which the slide USs (either snakes or houses) were presented alone. Finally, all subjects were asked to rate once again the pictures on the "discomfort" scale.

The results strongly supported the notion that phobic responses are prepared behaviors. As Figure 7-5 shows, very little conditioning was

FIGURE 7-5.

Mean GSR magnitude during the 10 extinction trials for the experimental and control subjects, half of whom received the "snake" CS and half received the "house" CS.

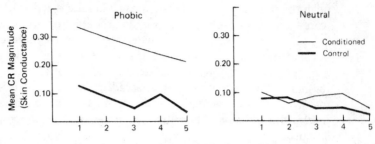

Blocks of 2 Extinction Trials

evident during extinction testing in the random CS-US subjects. Moreover, 5 acquisition trials were not enough to condition a CR to the house (neutral) stimuli; that is, GSR magnitude during the extinction trials was as low in those subjects as in the control subjects. But the important finding concerned the experimental group that received the snake pictures as the CS. Here, conditioning was very strong, even after 5 trials (in fact, the authors gave another group of subjects only a single training trial and found equally strong conditioning) and the CR magnitude declined only minimally over the 10 extinction trials. The final result was that the feelings of "discomfort" provoked by the stimuli increased as a result of conditioning for the phobic subjects but not for the neutral group. In other words, even the self-reports by the subjects indicated that aversion had accrued to the snake pictures during conditioning but not to the house pictures.

In summary, the general theory of preparedness applies to the learned behaviors of all species including humans. One implication is that neuroses are not arbitrary maladies but reflect the outcome of prepared learning. They involve objects that human beings are predisposed to fear. Certainly empirical research like that discussed above supports the notion that only certain objects readily become aversive when paired with trauma.

Language

It is clear that many different species are capable of communication. The systems, of course, vary widely, from noises or songs, to chemical scents, to visual displays. However, only one species, *Homo sapiens*, uses true language to any great extent. This is not to deny the recent, and generally successful, attempts to teach language to chimpanzees Nonetheless, the ability to use highly abstract symbols to communicate meaning in a flexible and pervasive sense is a uniquely human capacity.

This observation has led many psychologists to question how language is acquired. One of the oldest and most widespread positions is based on the concepts of instrumental conditioning. This approach suggests that distant ancestors of modern humankind "discovered" the utility of their utterances when those utterances helped to produce rewards. For example, arbitrary sounds probably served as signals, facilitating social organization and allowing hunting to be more efficient. Since vocal utterances were reinforced, they were repeated in the future. Slowly, according to this theory, the variety and subtlety of sounds increased into a full-blown language which was passed from parent to offspring also by means of reward contingencies; that is, each child was reinforced for producing the utterances that the parents knew were appropriate to their language.

Although this type of theory has been proposed formally by some scientists (e.g., Skinner, 1957), many now believe that language development did not occur in that way (see Chomsky, 1959; Lenneberg, 1967; McNeill, 1970). According to these latter investigators, language is biologically determined, not instrumentally learned. Stated somewhat differently, genes produce the propensity, the unique, species-specific potentiality, to learn language. In terms of Seligman's (1970) theory, language is prepared behavior.

The evidence for this biological theory of language has been accumulating rapidly within the past decade. First, of course, is the fact that humans are most efficient at language learning. If language had developed merely via the reinforcement of arbitrary utterances, then surely other species besides humans would be capable of learning language.

According to McNeill (1970), humans had a particular need for language that was not shared even by other primates. During the course of evolution, the human brain (and skull) increased in size and became quite large in proportion to the size of the body. This increase in brain size was highly adaptive because although humans were smaller, slower, and weaker than many other animals in their environment, their greater intelligence enabled them to cope not only with the existing environment but also with a changing environment, which greatly increased their chances for survival. At the same time, however, humans had also become bipedal—walking upright on two legs. The upright position meant that the birth canal could not enlarge beyond a certain size to accommodate the larger cranium and so a different developmental strategy evolved: human infants were born while their skulls were still small and the brains they housed were still relatively undeveloped. This in turn meant that they were practically helpless. For many months, the immature human could not locomote or gesture to its mother in order to communicate its needs. Offspring of other primates, of course, are physically more developed at birth and are able to function quite well in this regard. However, the human infant, by emitting sounds, could communicate with the mother. Therefore, infants who could vocally indicate their discomfort or hunger were at a distinct biological advantage, both for their immediate survival and for the probability that they would reach maturity and reproduce successfully.

Although we cannot draw a firm conclusion yet, there is evidence that language is a prepared, human-specific behavior. This position is consistent with the more general emphasis on the biological perspectives in learning. As Lenneberg (1967) wrote: "It seems unlikely that genes actually transmit behavior as we observe it in the living animal because the course that an individual takes in its peregrinations through life must necessarily depend on environmental contingencies which could not have been 'programmed and prepared for' in advance. Inheritance must confine itself to propensities, to dormant potentialities that await actualization by extra-organic stimuli, but it is possible that innate facilitatory or inhibitory factors are genetically transmitted which heighten the likelihood of one course of events over another. When put into these terms, it becomes quite clear that nature-nurture cannot be a *dichotomy* of factors but only an *interaction* of factors. To think of these terms as incompatible opposites only obscures the interesting aspects of the origin of behavior" (p. 22).

SUMMARY

The traditional view of learning focused on the arbitrariness of behavior. Universal laws of learning could not be found, according to that view, if specialized or unique behaviors were investigated since the laws, like the responses, would be special and unique to the species being studied. However, the newer attitude in learning research is to acknowledge that learning abilities or propensities have evolved just as physical properties have. In fact, the preparedness theory stipulates that some behaviors are innate-like, that organisms are *prepared* to learn those responses, and that very little effort on the part of the investigator is required before learning takes place. Some *unprepared* behaviors may be learned, but with moderate difficulty. *Contraprepared* responses are learned only with extreme difficulty; these responses are often alien to the natural behavior patterns of the organism.

There are many examples of prepared learning, including bird song learning. One example important for survival is acquired taste aversion. Here, the subject learns to associate a flavor with poison even when the poison (i.e., the US) is presented many hours after the flavor. In the context of the classical Pavlovian experiment, associative learning is not possible with delays of more than a few seconds. Another way taste aversion differs from conventional classical conditioning is that flavors appear to become associated with an internal US, such as poison, but not with an external US, such as shock. Again, the traditional view would predict that both USs would be equally effective. The new approach to learning research, in contrast, emphasizes the adaptive value of learning. In the case of taste aversion, individuals who could associate flavors with a long-delayed gastrointestinal upset were less likely to consume the poison a second time; accordingly, they were more likely to survive and pass on their genes to future generations.

Another important development that illustrates emerging biological perspectives in learning research is work on avoidance learning. It has long been known that rats have difficulty learning to press a lever to avoid shock (as compared to learning to make a running response to avoid shock). According to Bolles, avoidance learning is rapid only if the animal is allowed to make its naturalistic species-specific defense reaction.

Finally, our understanding of human behavior has been enriched by adopting certain biological perspectives. For example, it has been claimed that phobias develop not just to any stimulus but to certain, biologically-relevant stimuli. Some research has shown that pictures of snakes will elicit more emotion after being paired with shock than will pictures of other "neutral" objects. A more fundamental example of the utility of biological perspectives in human behavior is language. Although many animals communicate, humankind is the only species capable of making extensive and flexible use of both written and spoken symbols to convey meaning. Thus, the strong affinity toward language use has been viewed as a human-specific ability.

8/ Cognitive Perspectives in Learning

INTRODUCTION

CLASSICAL/INSTRUMENTAL INTERACTIONS

COMPOUND CONDITIONING

EXPECTANCY THEORY

SUMMARY

Preview

In this chapter, we explore a second major trend in learning research—the increasing use of cognitive concepts to account for basic learning phenomena. This new direction is based on the notion of information processing, the idea that organisms utilize information in their environments. Thus, Pavlovian CSs may provide information about future events (the US presentation, for example) if they are reliably correlated with those events. Given that we can manipulate these CS-US correlations and thus influence the predictive validity of the CS, we can investigate how predictive cues affect behavior in both classical and instrumental settings. These interaction experiments and studies which employ compound CSs have increased our understanding of the learning process. Also in this chapter, we discuss the relationship between helplessness and expectancy. Here we note that responses also may be correlated with outcomes. If an animal learns that response and reward are independent of each other, future learning may be impaired. This state of helplessness also has important implications for human depression.

INTRODUCTION

In recent years, the focus in animal learning research has changed dramatically in at least two ways: first, as discussed in Chapter 7, attention has been given to certain biological perspectives in learning. Second, there has been an increased willingness to use cognitive language when theorizing about the behavior of lower species. Cognition here is used to mean thought processes; more specifically, a cognition is an expectancy, a prediction by the subject of a future event based on a stimulus or response that consistently has preceded that event. Historically, many psychologists have avoided using cognitive language to account for animal behavior because it is impossible for us to know what the animal is really "thinking"; we could be making significant errors by attributing our own thought processes to the animals we are observing. Yet it seems reasonable to say that an animal expects food after it presses a lever, if food has always followed lever presses in the past, or that it expects a shock after a tone is sounded, if the tone-shock sequence has occurred consistently in the past. To the extent that we can observe and control these sequences of response/outcomes and stimuli/outcomes, we may usefully speak of predictions and expectancies; that is, an expectancy can essentially be defined operationally in terms of the correlation between the stimuli and outcome or between the response and the outcome. This trend has enriched the theoretical treatment of many established phenomena in learning. The present chapter reviews much of the work utilizing these cognitive or expectancy concepts.

Expectancy

Perhaps the most important development in learning theory, with respect to the use of cognitive terminology, has been the research in classical conditioning on CS information value, the extent to which a CS reliably predicts the US. One important study was done by Egger and Miller (1962). First rats were trained to press a lever to obtain food. Then, during the second phase, all the subjects were given Pavlovian conditioning involving two CSs (tone and flashing light) and a US (food). For some animals, the first CS (CS_1) was followed .5 seconds later by the second CS (CS_2); both CSs continued for 1.5 seconds until food delivery. According to traditional theory, that is, one based merely on the notion of CS-US contiguity, CS_2 should have become stronger than CS_1 because it occurred closer in time to the US. From an informational point of view, however, CS_2 was redundant (since CS_1 occurred first and always predicted the US) and, therefore, should have failed to become a strong CS during conditioning.

In order to assess the information hypothesis, Egger and Miller tested the strength of the two CSs in a third phase of the study. Here, lever press extinction was followed immediately by reacquisition during which a response produced either CS_1 or CS_2 (for separate groups of subjects). The mean number of lever presses during the 10-minute reacquisition phase was 115.1 for subjects who were given CS_1 following a lever press; in contrast the mean number of responses was 65.8 for the other subjects who received CS_2. Thus, conditioning to CS_2 was much weaker than to CS_1 (i.e., less potent in serving to strengthen lever pressing during reacquisition) even though CS_2 was more contiguous with the US. That is, CS_2 was a redundant source of information about the US and therefore the conditioning procedure was relatively ineffective. The authors concluded that the information value of the CS was more critical to Pavlovian conditioning than CS-US contiguity.

To strengthen their claim, Egger and Miller tested two additional groups of subjects. During the Pavlovian conditioning phase, they gave these animals extra CS_1 presentations during the intertrial interval. Since these CS_1 occurrences were not followed by CS_2 or the US, their effect was to render CS_1 an unreliable predictor of the US (sometimes it was followed by food, other times it was not) and, correspondingly, to eliminate the redundancy of CS_2 (i.e., make CS_2 the reliable predictor of food). During the later test for CS strength, a mean of 76.1 lever presses were executed by the subjects who were given the unreliable CS_1 for their response. However, subjects who were presented with CS_2 for lever pressing responded, on the average, with 82.6 presses in the 10-minute test. Again, the strength of classical conditioning appeared to depend on the predictive value of the CS, not merely on the degree of CS-US contiguity.

Egger and Miller's information hypothesis was an important precursor to Rescorla's (1967b) theory of classical conditioning (see Chapter 2). You may recall that Rescorla also claimed that CSs were potent only when they conveyed reliable information about the US occurrence (or nonoccurrence). Stated somewhat differently, classical conditioning took place only when a predictive relationship existed between the CS and the US (or no US). The exact mechanism by which the CS acquired predictive power was the CS-outcome correlation: if the correlation were high, that is, if the US occurrence (or nonoccurrence) consistently followed the CS, information value (degree of conditioning) was high. Conversely, if the CS and US were presented randomly, no information about the US was conveyed by the CS and, accordingly, CS strength was minimal.

In summary, recent work in classical conditioning has stressed expectancies of the US or no US based on informative CSs. Although contiguity is still an important concept (i.e., CR strength varies as a function of the CS-US interval), it is not a necessary or sufficient condition for classical conditioning. What this really implies is that at least two types of responses are learned during Pavlovian conditioning. In addition to the "overt" CR (e.g., conditioned salivation or heart rate) that develops, an underlying cognitive expectancy about the CS outcome also is formed. Both the overt CR and "covert" or cognitive (expectancy) CR depend on the CS-outcome correlation.

FIGURE 8-1.

A matrix indicating the type of emotions that get conditioned when a CS is paired with either the presence (CS+) or absence (CS-) of an aversive or appetitive US.

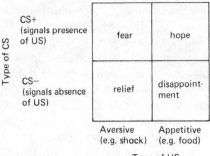

Type of CS

CS+
(signals presence of US)

| fear | hope |

CS-
(signals absence of US)

| relief | disappoint-ment |

Aversive
(e.g. shock)
Appetitive
(e.g. food)

Type of US

Conditioned Emotion

In the section immediately above, it was implied that two types of CRs are acquired during Pavlovian conditioning: the reflexive, overt, behavioral CR such as the leg flex or GSR response, and the cognitive, covert expectancy. Each of these conditioned reactions reflects a different substrate of learning. That is, a subject may react to a CS on several levels: the behavioral (overt response such as salivation) and the cognitive (covert thought or prediction) are two such levels.

Actually, there is a third major type or level of response that can be elicited by an informative CS during Pavlovian conditioning. Depending on the nature of the US, various conditioned emotions may be acquired. The most obvious conditioned emotion is fear: when a CS consistently predicts the occurrence of an aversive US, the CS comes to elicit fear. The conditioned fear, of course, is measured in a number of different ways including a CER suppression ratio or the degree of autonomic arousal that accompanies fear. Regardless, the conditioned emotion is one type of cognitive response and is distinct, theoretically, from both the overt behavioral CR and the other type of cognitive response discussed above, namely, the expectancy based on the CS-outcome correlation.

A more inclusive theory of conditioned emotion was presented by Mowrer (1960). Mowrer claimed that all informative CSs elicited an emotional response, not just fear cues that signaled the onset of an aversive US. The reason CSs come to elicit emotional reactions is because they are paired with potent emotion-producing USs. Since USs are defined as strong, biologically relevant cues, it is not surprising that they provoke emotional reactions which, in turn, become conditioned to CSs. Aversive USs, of course, produce pain, the conditioned emotional response to which is fear. However, appetitive USs also evoke emotion, in this case a sense of pleasure. Therefore, the cues that signal pleasurable USs come themselves to elicit conditioned emotional states of pleasure. In short, all

FIGURE 8-2.

A model of cognitive space. The matrix indicates how the expectancy (CS-outcome correlation) and emotional (hedonic value of the US) components interact during classical conditioning. Various types of CSs, having both signaling and emotional valence, can be located within the cognitive space.

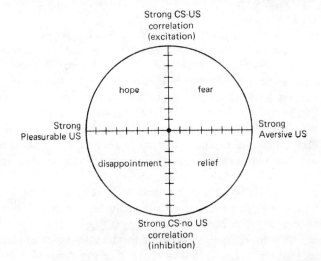

USs have *hedonic valence*; they can evoke an unconditioned emotional reaction along a pleasure/pain dimension.

Mowrer suggested that CSs could elicit one of four basic types of conditioned emotion (diagrammed in Figure 8-1). A cue that is paired with shock or any other aversive US elicits fear. Conversely, a CS− that signals the absence or termination of an aversive US later evokes the emotional CR of relief. On the other hand, the situations in which appetitive (or generally pleasurable) USs are used also involve conditioned emotion. That is, a stimulus correlated with the presentation of food evokes the conditioned emotion of hope, whereas a CS− paired with no food elicits a conditioned state of disappointment.

Cognitive Space

The term "cognitive space" is used here to suggest that both types of cognitive CRs in classical conditioning, the expectancy reaction *and* the emotional response, are independent but covarying conditioned reactions. A proposed model of cognitive space is presented in Figure 8-2. The vertical axis of the matrix represents the strength of the CS-US (or CS-no US) correlation. At the center of the line, the CS and US presentations are random. However, toward the periphery of the axis, the correlation strength increases, producing either excitatory or inhibitory CSs.

The emotion-eliciting capacity of the CS is represented by the horizontal axis. In cases where the US is aversive, the corresponding conditioned emotions will be fear (for excitatory CS-US relationships) or relief (inhibitory quadrant). Conversely, when the US is appetitive or pleasurable, the conditioned emotional states will be hope (excitatory quadrant) or disappointment (for inhibitory CS-no US relationships). At the center of the axis are conditioned stimuli that are hedonically neutral (because the USs are weak).

The model presented in Figure 8-2 has several implications. First, all Pavlovian CSs may be located within the confines of the cognitive space; that is, CSs may be classified along two separate dimensions. If the CSs have excitatory valence, they are located in the upper quadrants. Conversely, if the CSs have inhibitory valence, they are placed on the lower quadrants. The greater the CS-US correlation, (or CS-no US correlation) the closer the CS is to the periphery of the matrix. *At the same time*, CSs elicit emotional reactions based on the type of US used during conditioning. Aversive situations are encompassed in the right quadrants; appetitive situations in the left. In many instances, CSs may be classified simultaneously according to their predictive capacity and their emotional valence; both dimensions vary from neutrality (at the intersection of the axes) to strong (at the periphery).

A second implication of the model is that certain phenomena may be located within the cognitive space. For example, sensory preconditioning (see Chapter 2) might be considered to involve an excitatory CS+ that signals a "neutral US" (actually a second CS). Here, the CS would fall on the vertical axis near the top. Similarly, random control procedures, in which the CSs and USs are not correlated, would involve CSs that are uninformative (hence these would be located on the horizontal axis). Yet, the overall conditioning situations may be pleasurable or aversive, depending upon the character of the US.

In summary, we have claimed in this section that Pavlovian conditioning actually may involve three types of conditioned reactions. First is the overt CR, the behavioral response such as salivation, GSR, or conditioned heart rate changes. In addition, there are two covert reactions that may become conditioned. One is a cognitive response based on the predictive value of the CS; this is an expectancy, a "guess" about what will follow the CS. Another covert reaction is the emotional response. Here, fear, relief, disappointment, or hope can be elicited by a CS depending on the nature of the US. In other words, CSs may mean various things; they may signal the future occurrence of another event and *at the same time* they may elicit an emotional reaction. We are suggesting that these two types of covert CRs (a) are independent of one another, and (b) may occur simultaneously with the overt behavioral CR.

CLASSICAL/INSTRUMENTAL INTERACTIONS

The notion or theory that Pavlovian CSs can elicit both expectancies and emotions is extremely important. First, the theory acknowledges that stimuli derive predictive meaning, emotional valence as well as the capacity to elicit reflexivelike CRs. Thus, the salivation response is only part of the total picture; subjects also experience or acquire certain emotions and thoughts as a result of their training. The inclusion of cognitive language in learning theory, based not on ambiguous criteria but on operationally defined concepts such as the CS-outcome correlation and the hedonic quality of the US, reflects the belief that conditioning situations are far more complex than can be described by an appeal to the reflexive CR alone. The subjects' experience, and indeed, the range and type of CRs, is far richer and more varied than previously acknowledged.

Two-Process Theory

One reason this cognitive viewpoint is important is that it provides a new perspective for the resolution of certain traditional questions in learning research. One specific issue here involves the two-factor theory of avoidance learning (see Chapter 4). Does Pavlovian fear motivate instrumental avoidance behavior (notwithstanding the role of the CS offset and other factors)? A more general formulation of this issue concerns the existence of two separate learning processes. Do Pavlovian and instrumental conditioning procedures reflect, in fact, different underlying processes or are they merely different techniques for demonstrating a single type of learning?

Resolving the two-process position is not easy. We have pointed out before that *all* learning situations involve elements of both Pavlovian and instrumental conditioning. In fact, it is extremely unlikely that any "pure" demonstration of either classical or instrumental conditioning alone is possible. For example, classical CS-US pairings always occur when a subject makes instrumental responses. Similarly, voluntary motor responses executed during Pavlovian training are almost sure to have some impact on the strength of the US, or at least, on a subject's "perceptual" reaction to the US (see Brennan & Riccio, 1975). What this means is that we can't be sure whether there are one or two basic types of learning. If we can't separate them and get a "pure" example of Pavlovian or instrumental conditioning, then we cannot know, at least with confidence, if the processes differ from one another.

The issue of whether there are one or two types of learning has been viewed another way, one which relies on the fact that CSs may elicit cognitive/emotional CRs as well as reflexive reactions. Rather than trying to separate classical and instrumental procedures, this new approach explicitly combines them (see Rescorla & Solomon, 1967).

Think again about whether fear motivates avoidance learning. One could say that the underlying motivational state is "still-in-doubt," although we might guess that the state is fear. If we were to introduce a *known* state of fear which was elicited by a fear CS+ we had conditioned on a previous occasion, and if the avoidance behavior improved, then we could conclude that the avoidance response did indeed depend on fear: the two emotional states, one known and the other "still-in-doubt," were compatible; the former augmented the latter. In other words, if a Pavlovian CS elicits a known state of emotion which is compatible with the "still-in-doubt" state that is presumed to underlie the instrumental behavior, then the instrumental behavior will be facilitated. In contrast, if a Pavlovian CS is presented during instrumental learning and the CS elicits a cognitive or emotional state that is not compatible with the existing "still-in-doubt" state that underlies the instrumental behavior, then the instrumental behavior will be disrupted; performance will decline.

What is being accomplished here is the explicit combination of known Pavlovian emotional states with a "yet-to-be-determined" emotion that is at the base of the instrumental behavior. These studies consider the interaction between Pavlovian and instrumental conditioning. The change in the instrumental behavior is a clue to the underlying motivation for that behavior since the changes reflect the compatibility between the underlying motivation and the explicitly known Pavlovian emotion. In summary, this new approach involves the intrusion of a Pavlovian emotion during an instrumental response which is based on a "still-in-doubt" emotion. Compatibility of emotions leads to an increase in instrumental performance; incompatibility leads to a decrease. Since these changes reflect the influence or mediation of Pavlovian emotion during instrumental learning, they are concerned with what emotional or motivational state underlies the instrumental behavior.

Obviously, fear is not the only Pavlovian conditioned emotion. Other Pavlovian instrumental interactions that include hope, disappointment, and relief as well as fear, are possible. All these predicted effects are indicated in Figure 8-3. The particular type of Pavlovian CS is noted on the vertical dimension; the instrumental learning task, during which the classical CS is presented, is noted on the horizontal dimension.

Interaction Experiments

One common type of interaction study is the conditioned emotional response (CER) design which has been cited frequently as a technique for assessing the strength of aversive Pavlovian CSs (see Chapter 2). Predicting the effect of the Pavlovian CS presentation on the instrumental behavior is straightforward (Figure 8-3, cell 5); when the subject is performing an appetitively rewarded response such as lever pressing and a Pavlovian fear cue is presented at the same time, the response rate goes down. This occurs because the Pavlovian fear or expectancy state counteracts the emotion or cognitive state that underlies the lever pressing. The former is based on an aversive US whereas the latter is based on an appetitive US. Thus, the CER outcome (response suppression) is a particularly clear example of what happens when two conflicting states are elicited simultane-

FIGURE 8-3.

Matrix illustrating the various interactions between Pavlovian emotional states and instrumental behavior. Arrows indicate whether the superimposed Pavlovian CS facilitates (↑) or inhibits (↓) the instrumental performance. Numbers in each cell identify the cell for discussion in text.

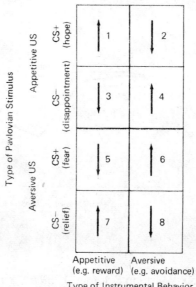

Type of Instrumental Behavior

ously, with the known Pavlovian state being superimposed on the ongoing instrumental behavior.

If an aversive CS+ (fear cue) is a counteractive force in appetitive responding, it should have the opposite effect on aversive responding (Figure 8-3, cell 6). Many experiments have confirmed this prediction. For example, Martin and Riess (1969) trained rats to press a lever in order to postpone shock (Sidman avoidance). After a stable response rate was reached, the subjects were given classical CS-US pairings where the light CS was followed by a shock US. The third phase in the experiment involved presenting the Pavlovian CS during Sidman avoidance responding. The authors found not only that the avoidance response rate was accelerated by the CS presentation, but that the rate of increase in avoidance performance was a function of the shock intensity used during the Pavlovian training session. In summary, then, it appears that Pavlovian fear CSs produce an increase in avoidance responding because they augment the existing fear that underlies the avoidance behavior (Scobie, 1972).

According to the arguments posed above, an aversive CS− should have an effect on instrumental performance opposite to that of a CS+. Numerous studies have shown this to be the case: when a cue that signals no shock is presented during avoidance conditioning (Figure 8-3, cell 8) rate of avoidance declines (e.g., Grossen & Bolles, 1969; Rescorla &

FIGURE 8-4.

Mean responses per minute as a function of successive 5-minute periods (CS presentation labelled as "CS") for subjects who had received excitatory (CS+), inhibitory (CS-), or random pairings.

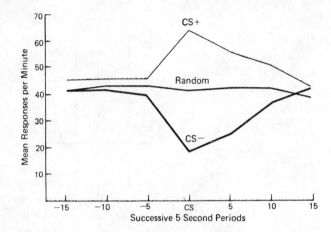

LoLordo, 1965; Weisman & Litner, 1969 a,b). In the Weisman and Litner (1969a) study, for example, rats first were trained to turn a small wheel to postpone shock. Once a stable rate of responding was achieved, they were given Pavlovian training. For one group, a tone CS always was followed by a shock US during these sessions; a second group received the reverse, that is, a CS— was established by presenting the shock prior to the CS. A third group received the CSs and USs but their presentation was randomized; thus, the CS should have failed to become either an exciter or an inhibitor for those subjects. On the test, all animals were given the 5-second tone CS and changes in the rate of responding (wheel turns per minute) as a function of time were recorded. As shown in Figure 8-4, the CS presentations had a pronounced effect on avoidance performance. In the subjects for whom the CS had signaled shock during the Pavlovian training, the avoidance rate was increased. This is the same outcome that we discussed previously in connection with the Martin and Riess study (1969; see Figure 8-3, cell 6). Conversely, the presentation of a Pavlovian aversive CS— caused a reduction in performance. Both these effects were in contrast to the unchanging performance of the random subjects for whom the CS had acquired no strong excitatory or inhibitory valence. The conclusion, of course, from this study as well as others is that an aversive inhibitory state, stemming from a CS— that elicits relief, counteracts fear motivation.

An aversive CS— also has been presented during instrumental appetitive behavior. It follows from the discussion above that performance should be improved: relief is, in essence, compatible with the "pleasurable" motivational state underlying appetitive responding. This prediction was confirmed by Hammond (1966) who found that the CS+ produced suppression of responding (the "standard" CER outcome, Figure 8-3, cell 6), whereas the aversive CS− (one never followed by shock) had the opposite effect, i.e., the response rate accelerated above the baseline levels during the CS− presentation.

The designs represented in the four upper cells of Figure 8-3 also have been investigated. These interaction experiments deal with the presentation of Pavlovian appetitive CSs (either excitatory or inhibitory) during instrumental conditioning. In one study by Bolles, Grossen, Hargrave, and Duncan (1970), rats were trained to traverse an alley to obtain food. After 30 trials, they were placed in another apparatus and given Pavlovian appetitive conditioning. For one group of subjects, the CS+ was followed by food; for a second group, the CS− signaled the absence of food for at least 30 seconds. A third group of subjects was given the tone CS and food randomly. Later, on the test session, the tone CS was sounded when the subjects were in the start box of the alley. The authors generally confirmed the predictions indicated in Figure 8-3 (cells 1 and 3). Although the CS presentations curiously did not affect rewarded performance in the alley, they significantly influenced speed of responding during extinction. Specifically, the CS+ presentations caused subjects to respond much faster in the alley, whereas the CS− produced a suppression of startbox speeds. Both these effects were relative to the unaffected behavior of the random subjects. In summary, the expectancy/emotion elicited by the appetitive CS+ augmented the expectancy/emotion on which the appetitive instrumental behavior was based, thus causing an increase in performance. Conversely, the CS− elicited disappointment, an emotion that was counteractive to the emotion on which the instrumental task was based.

Finally, with regard to the remaining two types of Pavlovian/instrumental interactions, a number of studies (e.g., Bull, 1970; Davis & Kreuter, 1972; Grossen et al., 1969) generally have confirmed the predictions indicated in cells 2 and 4 of Figure 8-3. For example, in the study by Grossen, Kostansek, and Bolles (1969), rats were trained to avoid shock by traversing back and forth in a shuttlebox; a response of moving to the opposite side of the box postponed shock for 30 seconds. In the second phase of the experiment, all the subjects were given classical appetitive training. For Group CS+, the 5-second tone was followed immediately by the food US. For Group CS−, the tone never was followed by food for at least 30 seconds; these subjects, however, did receive food after that time. Subjects in Group R were given both stimuli but in a random fashion; therefore, it was not expected that the CS would become either excitatory or inhibitory. In the third phase, all the animals were returned to the shuttlebox for four avoidance test sessions. Toward the end of these sessions, extinction trials (no shock) were given during which the Pavlovian appetitive CS was presented. The authors measured the effect of the CS on rate of avoidance responding. The specific measure of performance was the mean speed on the CS-added trials expressed as a percentage of the

FIGURE 8-5.

Mean percentage of baseline (no-CS trials) during the four test sessions for the CS+, CS-, and R (random) groups.

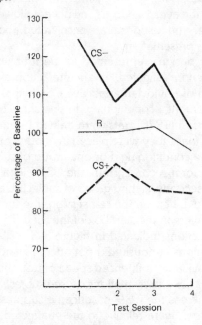

As shown in Figure 8-5, the addition of the CS+ retarded avoidance performance; speed on the tone trials, relative to the no-tone trials, was reduced indicating a conflict between the emotional state elicited by the appetitive CS+ and the state underlying the Sidman avoidance behavior. As predicted in cell 4 of Figure 8-3, the addition of a CS−, however, caused an increase in avoidance rate. Finally, superimposing the Pavlovian CS on the avoidance behavior did not affect the performance in Group R; here, the tone had not acquired either excitatory or inhibitory valence.

mean speed on the no-CS trials; if the tone had no effect on behavior, a score of 100 percent would be recorded.

As shown in Figure 8-5, the addition of the CS+ retarded avoidance performance; speed on the tone trials, relative to the no-tone trials, was reduced indicating a conflict between the emotional state elicited by the appetitive CS+ and the state underlying the Sidman avoidance behavior. As predicted in cell 4 of Figure 8-3, the addition of a CS−, however, caused an increase in avoidance rate. Finally, superimposing the Pavlovian CS on the avoidance behavior did not affect the performance in Group R; here, the tone had not acquired either excitatory or inhibitory valence.

In summary, all the predictions depicted in Figure 8-3 have been confirmed. Classically conditioned emotions (or expectancies) have a predictable effect on ongoing instrumental behavior. The type of change in the instrumental responding (i.e., facilitation or inhibition) indicates the general compatibility between the Pavlovian emotions (cognitions) and those on which the instrumental behavior is based. The interaction studies, therefore, provide indirect support for a general two-factor approach. The fact that a Pavlovian fear cue increases avoidance responding suggests that avoidance may be based on fear motivation. However, the "strong" version of Mowrer's theory almost certainly is not correct (see Chapter 4).

COMPOUND CONDITIONING

There is a second area of research for which the recent emphasis on cognitions and expectancies has been important. Here, the focus has been on *compound conditioning*, that is, the use of two CSs simultaneously presented during Pavlovian conditioning. Most of the studies in this area have tried to determine the exact conditions under which the cues (elements or components of the compound) acquire the same, or different, strength. Traditional Pavlovian theory (see Chapter 2) suggests that both cues in a compound would acquire the same strength. All that is needed for conditioning is the contiguous pairing of a CS and a US. The presence of additional cues does not affect the basic contiguity relationship of a given CS and the US and, thus, should not affect the ultimate strength of that CS. In short, the contiguity theory of classical conditioning emphasizes that CS-US contiguity is the single underlying principle of conditioning (although the strength of the CR may vary with the number of pairings, the intensity of the US, and so forth). Therefore, the various elements in a compound CS should acquire equal strength.

Blocking

Under normal circumstances, when all acquisition trials involve a compound CS, each element of the compound does indeed gain approximately equal strength. However, in other situations, elements in a compound do not necessarily acquire the same strength even though both are equally contiguous with the US. What has been demonstrated is that conditioning to one element may be blocked (prevented) if the other element in the compound happens already to be strongly excitatory.

One important series of studies by Kamin (1969) illustrated this point. Several groups of rats were trained to press a lever for food. Then, a typical CER procedure was used to assess CS strength during Pavlovian conditioning. For Group B, 16 noise-shock pairings were superimposed on the lever pressing behavior and the usual suppression of pressing was observed. In the next phase of the study, these animals were given eight trials comprised of a compound CS (light/noise) followed by shock. Finally, the subjects were tested with the light alone. A control Group G was given only the eight compound conditioning trials and the light test.

The results indicated almost complete suppression of lever pressing in the control subjects (a median CER ratio of .05, where zero is complete suppression). The light CS clearly had become a potent fear stimulus. In contrast, the experimental group that had received noise-US trials *prior to* their compound CS trials showed no evidence of conditioning to the light (median CER ratio was .45 where a score of .50 indicates no suppression whatsoever). The prior conditioning to the noise CS apparently blocked, or prevented, later conditioning to the light CS. In summary, each element

FIGURE 8-6.

Median CER ratio as a function of the sessions during phase 3 for Groups B (blocked) and C (control).

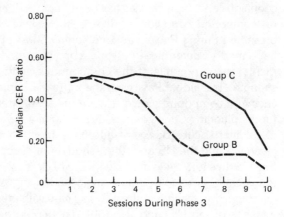

in a compound CS acquired comparable strength if acquisition involved only that compound. The elements, however, did not acquire equal strength if one of them was used in a prior conditioning phase. Specifically, the strengthening of the tone in the first phase precluded conditioning to the light in the second phase.

A variation of Kamin's blocking experiment was done by Suiter and LoLordo (1971). Their basic goal was to demonstrate that an inhibitory CS− also could be blocked by prior conditioning to another cue. All subjects were taught to press a lever for food as a preliminary to the CER procedure. Then, as in Kamin's study, Pavlovian conditioning was given in three phases. For Group B, a light CS was negatively correlated with shock during the first phase; that is, the light was presented after shock, and since it predicted the absence of shock (usually for about 15 minutes), it was considered to be an inhibitory CS−. The subjects in Group C, on the other hand, received only the shock presentations during phase 1; no prior inhibitory training to the light CS was given. In the second and third phases of the experiment, both groups received the same treatment. Specifically, phase 2 consisted of inhibitory conditioning to a compound (light/tone) CS. Here, the compound was negatively correlated with the shock delivery, i.e., predicted the absence of shock. Finally, phase 3 was a test of the inhibitory strength of the tone CS. This was accomplished by pairing the tone with shock and observing how quickly it acquired excitatory valence. If the cue were a strong conditioned inhibitor, then excitatory conditioning should be retarded. On the other hand, if inhibitory conditioning to the tone during phase 2 had been blocked by prior inhibitory conditioning to the light during phase 1, then the tone CS should acquire excitatory strength during phase 3 quite readily.

As shown in Figure 8-6, the results confirmed the predictions. The acquisition of excitatory strength to the tone occurred more rapidly in

Group B than in Group C; that is, after 5 or 6 sessions of excitatory tone-shock pairing, the tone itself suppressed lever pressing in Group B but not in Group C. The reason for this difference stemmed from the blocking of inhibition in Group B, that is, inhibitory conditioning to the tone had been blocked in those subjects (by prior inhibitory training to the light), and therefore, excitatory strength to the tone, the reverse of inhibition, was acquired readily. In contrast, the tone became a strong conditioned inhibitor in Group C during phase 2 (blocking procedures had not been used); therefore, in phase 3, it was far more difficult to achieve excitatory conditioning to the tone.

A number of studies have been done to explain the blocking effect. One hypothesis that Kamin (1969) considered involved *attention*. According to this position, the addition of a second element to the CS during phase 2 was not noticed, or attended to, by the subject. Certainly this seemed to be a viable explanation since the subjects later responded (on the test) as if the second element had never been presented. However, Kamin showed that this hypothesis was incorrect. In one study, for example, two groups of rats were conditioned to noise in stage 1; after 16 noise-shock pairings, suppression was nearly complete. Then, extinction procedures were initiated. One group continued to receive the noise only. The other group got a light/noise compound. If these rats failed to notice the second element, the light, then both groups should have extinguished at the same rate, that is, the light should have had no effect on the suppression ratio.

Contrary to the attention theory, the results suggested that the light *was* noticed. Even by the second extinction trial, the light/noise stimulus elicited less suppression than the noise CS alone. Since both groups had received identical training up to this point, the added light element must have caused the difference in responding inasmuch as it was the only methodological change that could have caused a difference in the behavior of the two groups.

The alternative explanation for blocking, favored by Kamin as well as by other investigators, draws on the notion of predictability or CS information value. The basic argument is that the added element in the CS compound, although noticed by the subject, fails to become conditioned because it is redundant. The US already is predicted by the first CS; the added element, therefore, provides no new information about the US presentation. As a result, subjects ignore the added element. In short, conditioning occurs only when the CS has predictive value. If, through prior conditioning, one cue adequately predicts the US presentation, an added, redundant, cue will not become conditioned. As you can see, this argument is nearly identical to the one discussed previously in connection with Egger and Miller's (1962) experiment.

The information theory of blocking has been supported in a number of experiments. Kamin (1969), for example, showed that blocking failed to occur if the US intensity was increased during stage 2 (when the compound CS first was presented). The reason for this finding was that the new element was not redundant; it predicted a "new" US, namely a shock of greater intensity than previously experienced (see also Mackintosh & Turner, 1971).

Wagner-Rescorla Model

A number of studies by Wagner and Rescorla have clarified and extended Kamin's blocking effect. In one experiment (reported by Rescorla & Wagner, 1972), rabbits were given eyelid conditioning. The CS was a light/noise compound and the US was a mild shock. Three groups of subjects were used. The control subjects received 200 compound-CS conditioning trials. The other two groups also received 200 trials with the compound CS, but, in addition, they received extra trials interspersed throughout training—the Excitatory group received additional light-shock pairings whereas the Inhibitory group got additional light-no shock trials. After training, all groups were given 16 test trials where the conditioned reaction to the tone was measured. In summary, the experiment focused on the effect of additional pairings (or nonpairings) of one cue on the strength of the other cue in the compound.

As predicted, the level of conditioning to the tone in the control subjects was substantial; however, the other two groups differed from that control level. Specifically, the Excitatory subjects (who had received extra excitatory training with the light CS) showed *less* response to the tone whereas the Inhibitory subjects (who had received extra inhibitory training with the light) showed a *greater* response to the tone. The former result, of course, is similar to Kamin's blocking effect although, here, blocking to the tone was achieved when the extra trials to the light were interspersed throughout training as opposed to being given before the compound trials. The effect shown in the Inhibitory subjects was the opposite to blocking: a reduction in strength of response to the light, through extra inhibitory CS-no US trials, increased the strength of the tone.

The general conclusion we can draw from this work is that the strength of one stimulus depends, in large part, on the associative strength of other stimuli in the compound. In fact, it appears that stimuli "compete" for strength; when one becomes stronger or more salient (through extra CS-US pairings) the other stimulus in the compound decreases in strength. Conversely, when one stimulus loses excitatory strength (through additional CS-no US trials) the other stimulus in the compound gains in strength. (See Rescorla & Wagner, 1972, for a discussion of a mathematical formulation that accommodates these and other findings remarkably well.)

In summary, the underlying dimension of CS strength is the information value of the cue. Additional excitatory trials for one stimulus makes that stimulus all the more important as a predictive cue. Consequently, the other, redundant cue is ignored by the subject. On the other hand, additional CS-only trials render a cue unreliable; the subjects, therefore, depend on the other cue for predicting the US.

EXPECTANCY THEORY

The basic concept or theme that underlies the research discussed in this chapter is *predictability*: stimuli acquire information value about the US occurrence (or nonoccurrence) and thus generate expectancies. As we suggested previously in the section on cognitive space (see Figure 8-2), a cognitive reaction on the part of the subject may also be accompanied by an emotional response. Regardless, conditioned stimuli do produce expectancies about the events with which they are correlated.

Although the concept of expectancy is not a new development in learning theory (see Tolman, 1932), it has become more prominent recently. One reason that is related to the material discussed in Chapter 7 is suggested in an important paper by Bolles (1972). Bolles notes that reinforcement procedures, unaccountably, do not seem to work in all cases; most organisms acquire prepared or contraprepared responses largely independent of the reinforcement contingency. According to Bolles, this common observation suggests that those responses (or perhaps all responses) are not simple arbitrary reactions that are strengthened through reinforcement. Rather, animals execute species-specific reactions (either defensive or appetitive) that are appropriate to the situation.

But how do the subjects learn what *is* appropriate? Bolles claims that they acquire expectancies which guide their natural, species-specific behavior. Stated in more formal terms: (1) animals are capable of performing naturalistic behaviors prior to the experiment; (2) once the subjects are involved in the experiment, they form expectancies based on the events they experience (i.e., the correlations between events); and (3) performance of the instinctive responses is guided by the expectancies. Bolles' justification for the concept of expectancy stems from the observation that reinforcing events don't necessarily strengthen arbitrary motor responses; rather, reinforcers create a cognitive framework, a network of expectancies, within which species-specific behaviors occur.

Bolles (1972) suggests that two types of expectancies may be learned in any given situation. First, a *stimulus expectancy* is acquired when a CS consistently signals an important outcome such as the presentation or omission of a US. Here, the CS gains predictive value because of the CS-outcome correlation—the procedures for creating a stimulus expectancy are those of Pavlovian conditioning. All the material in the previous sections of this chapter, of course, has referred to this type of expectancy.

According to Bolles, a second type of expectancy may also be acquired: a *response expectancy*. Subjects learn the predictive relationship between a particular response and its outcome. For example, subjects might learn in one situation that a lever press (R) is always followed by food (outcome); in another situation, they may learn to expect the omission of shock after a response. Therefore, what is acquired or strengthened by the reinforcer is not the motor response or S-R association but rather the expectancy that the reinforcer will follow the response. A subject may use its own behavior in addition to Pavlovian CSs as a source of information about an impending event if that behavior and event are correlated.

Helplessness

The sections above indicated that subjects may come to expect certain outcomes on the basis of their behavior. That is to say, they learn to expect their behavior to be effective in producing reward if the correlation between their behavior and reward is highly positive. In the sense that the behavior "works" in producing reward, the response expectancy stemming from the behavior could be characterized as reflecting a state of confidence.

However, what if the correlation between a response and reward were zero? Clearly, neither the expectancy that the reward would follow the response nor that no reward would follow the response would be learned. A different expectancy, however, would develop even under these conditions, namely, that the response is independent of the reward.

The expectancy that responding is independent of reward could be expressed in somewhat different terms: when the correlation between responding and reward is zero, the subjects learn that their behavior doesn't predict the reward or, more importantly, control the reward. This cognitive state, stemming from uncontrollability, is the basis for an important phenomenon in learning: learned helplessness (see Maier & Seligman, 1976; Maier et al., 1969; and Seligman, 1975, for reviews).

Learned helplessness occurs when a subject is unable to learn a simple response because of having received uncontrollable punishers in the past. One of the earliest demonstrations was done by Seligman and Maier (1967), using three groups of dogs as subjects. The animals in one group (Escape) were allowed to terminate a hindleg shock (while being restrained in a "hammock") by pressing a panel with their snouts. A second group was placed in the hammock and shocked whenever the first group was shocked. These animals were in essence "yoked" to those in the first group; they received identical treatment except for the single fact that any responses they made to the panel were not effective in controlling the shock. Finally, a third control group was placed in the hammock but given no shock.

In the second phase of the study, all the subjects were placed in a two-compartment shuttlebox and given escape/avoidance training. As shown in Figure 8-7, Seligman and Maier found that the Escape and No-shock groups learned easily; median latency in both cases decreased in a normal fashion over the course of escape/avoidance acquisition. In contrast, the Yoked subjects failed to learn; in fact, most of these dogs did not even terminate the shock once it came on.

FIGURE 8-7.

Median latency during phase 2 as a function of trials for the naive (no-shock), yoked, and escape subjects.

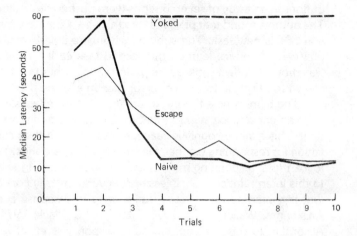

The failure to perform the escape/avoidance response by the Yoked subjects certainly could not have been due merely to the prior shock itself. Subjects in the Escape group, that is, those subjects who could terminate the shock in phase 1, received the *same* amount and pattern of shock as the Yoked subjects yet they did not fail to learn. However, the important difference between the two groups that could have accounted for these results was the fact that the Yoked subjects lacked control over the shock during phase 1 of the experiment. It is claimed that the Yoked animals, because of the random inescapable shock, developed the expectancy that their behavior was independent of reward. Indeed, the animals were helpless in this regard since shock offset was controlled not by themselves but by the subjects in the Escape group. According to the authors, then, a general state of helplessness developed during phase 1 and prevented subsequent learning; the expectancy in the Yoked subjects that behavior and reward were independent prevented them from acquiring a new, appropriate, and adaptive expectancy, namely that responding did, in fact predict (or control) reward in phase 2.

The concept of helplessness is an important one for theories of human depression (see Seligman, 1975). Presumably, humans may become depressed when they cannot control or predict the consequences of their behavior. A large number of studies have supported the notion that lack of control may be the basis for human depression by demonstrating the interference effect with human subjects (e.g., Hiroto & Seligman, 1975; Roth & Bootzin, 1974; Thornton & Jacobs, 1971; Thornton & Powell, 1974). In the Thornton and Jacobs (1971) study, for example, one group of individuals could avoid a mild finger shock by pressing the correct button when a light was turned on. A second group was yoked; that is, inescapable shock was delivered whenever the subjects in the first group received shock. In phase 2 of the study, all the subjects were required to learn a second task. Here, shock could be avoided if the correct two buttons in an array of seven buttons were pushed during the warning light. The authors found that prior inescapable shock interfered with the acquisition of this new task. The subjects who were able to avoid shock during phase 1, of course, learned the second task easily. Thus, lack of control was shown to affect subsequent performance in humans just as it has been shown to affect performance of subhuman species.

The helplessness theory for the interference effect states that subjects learn an expectancy, namely, that their behavior and reward are independent. This general cognitive reaction reduces both their subsequent motivation for responding (so they fail even to terminate shock) and their ability to learn that responding may, in fact, control reward. However, in contrast to this interpretation of helplessness, several investigators have suggested that the interference effect is due merely to response competition (e.g., Anisman & Waller, 1972, 1973; Bracewell & Black, 1974; Levis, 1976). According to this position, since no response is effective in terminating shock during phase 1, freezing develops; freezing, of course, is one of the rats' species-specific defense reactions to shock which is executed after other SSDRs, such as running or jumping, have been suppressed. The competing response theory then postulates that in phase 2 of the typical helplessness study, the freezing behavior that was covertly conditioned during phase 1 competes with the task required in phase 2. In summary, the interference effect, that is, the inability (or unwillingness) to perform an escape response following inescapable shock, may not be due to a general, debilitating expectancy of helplessness; rather, the subjects may learn a particular response during inescapable shock (namely, freezing) which later hinders their performance during phase 2.

The evidence favoring the response competition theory generally shows that the interference effect is decreased when precautions are taken to reduce the amount of freezing; conversely, the interference effect is increased when procedures are followed that increase the amount of freezing. For example, Anisman and Waller (1971) administered methamphetamine to some of their subjects as well as inescapable shock. One usual consequence of this drug is an increase in activity. The authors found that during phase 2, the one-way avoidance learning was better in those subjects that had received the drug.

Although the response competition theory has posed a significant challenge to the cognitive explanation for the interference effect (see especially Glazer & Weiss, 1976 a,b; and Levis, 1976), most of the evidence appears to favor the learned helplessness interpretation. First, several studies (e.g., Overmier & Seligman, 1967) have shown that helplessness occurred even when subjects who were curarized were given the inescapable shock. (As we have said earlier, curare paralyzes the muscles; animals are fully awake and sensitive to sensory input but they cannot move.) Later, learning did not occur in these subjects. The reason this finding does not favor the competing response theory is that since no responding what-soever was possible during phase 1, no particular response such as freezing could become dominant and later compete with responding in phase 2.

A second argument favoring the helplessness theory is that subjects can be immunized against the effects of inescapable shock (e.g., Seligman & Maier, 1967; Seligman et al., 1975). Seligman, Rosellini, and Kozak (1975), for example, gave inescapable shock to two groups of rats and then tested them for helplessness (the learning task during phase 2 was a lever press which terminated shock). One group, however, had been given escapable shock before the inescapable shock phase in which they were permitted to jump onto a platform to escape. The authors found that these rats did not show helplessness; the prior exposure to escapable shock had immunized them against the effects of inescapable shock.

According to the competing response theory, all the subjects should have developed a freezing posture since both groups eventually got ines-capable shock and therefore should have shown helplessness during phase 2. However, the immunized group did not have difficulty learning the new escape response relative to a third control group. Presumably, the original expectancy of these subjects that their responding did indeed control shock offset protected them from acquiring helplessness.

Finally, an important study by Maier (1970) confirmed the cognitive explanation as opposed to the competing response theory. One group of dogs was trained to escape shock by remaining immobile. These animals could terminate shock by *not* touching two panels that were located one-quarter inch on either side of their heads. A yoked group also was used; these subjects received the same shock but they could not control its offset. In a second phase of the study, all the animals were given escape training in a shuttlebox.

The competing response theory predicts that the first group would show greater interference during phase 2: those animals *explicitly* were taught to freeze during phase 1. In contrast, the helplessness theory pre-dicts the opposite. The subjects who were taught to remain immobile were able to control shock offset whereas the expectancy that behavior and reward are independent (helplessness) should have formed in the yoked subjects.

The results favored the cognitive interpretation: although the yoked subjects generally failed to escape shock during phase 2, the ones who were previously trained to escape by remaining motionless learned the next task without difficulty. In other words, interference during phase 2 was highly related to the degree of uncontrollability during phase 1 and not to the strength of an explicit competing behavior.

The helplessness phenomenon highlights the increasing role that cog-nitive language and concepts are assuming in basic learning theory. Be-havior, even in most subhuman organisms, cannot be described in purely mechanistic terms. The notion that organisms do (or do not) expect certain consequences on the basis of external signals or their behavior certainly has become an important explanatory concept.

SUMMARY

Many psychologists in learning research have had a renewed interest in using cognitive terminology to explain animal behavior. They claim that animals can be said to expect certain outcomes based on the correlation between CSs and those outcomes. Pavlovian conditioning, then, is viewed as a process by which expectancies are acquired in addition to behavioral reflexes. Indeed, a large number of studies have shown that the "power" of a Pavlovian CS is related to its information value, the degree to which it reliably signals an important outcome.

In this chapter we noted also that another type of covert CR may be learned during classical conditioning: acquired emotion. The type of emotion depends on the type of outcome that the CS predicts: aversive consequences lead to fear or disappointment while positive consequences, such as the cessation of shock or the presentation of food, generate hope or relief. We argued that all CSs potentially elicit both types of covert reactions; that is, they may signal the occurrence or nonoccurrence of a subsequent event (elicit an expectancy) while at the same time they may arouse an emotion regarding that event.

The concept of conditioned expectancies/emotion has been employed in the context of the two-factor theory which claims that certain emotions are critical to certain instrumental behaviors (e.g., fear underlies avoidance responding). If, say, avoidance were indeed based on fear, and if we presented a known fear cue during avoidance performance, then we would expect the overall fear level to rise and, accordingly, the rate of behavior to improve. This is what is found in such interaction studies. Moreover, other types of emotional cues have been used and the predictable interactions, between the known Pavlovian state and the "still-to-be-determined" state that is said to underlie the instrumental behavior, have been confirmed. When the Pavlovian emotion and the "unknown" state are compatible, behavior improves; when incompatible, behavior declines.

Another important area of study has been on compound conditioning—the use of two or more CSs simultaneously. These results are also in accord with an information or expectancy viewpoint. If, for example, one element is strong, the other element fails to become conditioned. However, if the first element is weakened through extinction, the other element in the compound is strengthened. Conditioning, therefore, does not depend merely on CS-US contiguity but on the predictive value of the cue.

Finally, we discussed Bolles' theory which claims that since responses may also be correlated to certain outcomes, animals come to expect those outcomes; that is, response as well as stimuli can elicit expectancies. If, however, response and reward are independent, subjects may develop a state of helplessness, in which case later learning is retarded.

9/ Basic Verbal Learning

Preview

This chapter investigates how human beings acquire, retain, and retrieve verbal material. *Acquisition* refers to the process by which information is encoded or incorporated in memory. *Retention* refers to the way information is retained or forgotten over time in memory. *Retrieval* refers to the process by which humans remember the information they have acquired. In this chapter, we'll look first at the three major characteristics of the acquisition process: stimuli that are high in meaningfulness are more easily learned and remembered than those low in meaningfulness; items from the beginning and the end of a list are better learned and remembered than those in the middle; and spaced practice often results in better learning than massed practice. Then we shall deal with the problem of transfer of training, that is, how does previous learning influence new learning? Finally, we'll consider several theories of remembering and forgetting. Our general approach is to use very simple, standard experimental procedures as a basis to study very complex cognitive processes. Our fundamental question is: What variables affect how much is learned and remembered and in what ways? The closely related question of how knowledge is organized and structured in memory will be explored in Chapter 12.

INTRODUCTION

The study of verbal learning involves trying to understand the very complex cognitive processes of how knowledge is acquired, retained, and retrieved. However, the methods used to study these complex processes are often quite simple—some studies, for example, use nonsense syllables instead of words. Can such simple procedures help in developing theories of complex learning and memory? Let's start the answer to that question with an example of a typical procedure used in verbal learning experiments.

First, a subject might hear a list of words or nonsense syllables read aloud at a constant rate. The list might consist of: TOR, NIS, XAB, DIL, SEV, PAQ, CEW, BOF. Once the subject has heard the entire list, he or she is asked to try to state the first word,* is then told the correct one by the experimenter, tries then to recall the second word, receives feedback, and so on. This process continues until the subject can correctly anticipate each word in the list without error. Each time the subject goes through the list is called a *trial*; the German psychologist Hermann Ebbinghaus found it took him about five trials to learn a list like the one above.

This procedure is similar to that used by Ebbinghaus and described in his 1885 monograph, *Memory*.** That date, less than a century ago, marks the formal beginning of our attempt to apply the scientific method to the study of higher mental processes in humans. The monograph reported an extensive six-year series of experiments in which Ebbinghaus served as the experimenter, the sole subject, the inventor of the experimental design, and the theoretician for explaining the results.

THE EBBINGHAUS EXPERIMENT

Ebbinghaus's method was simple and has served as the prototype for subsequent work. First, he devised hundreds of lists of what he called *nonsense syllables*, consonant-vowel-consonant (CVC) combinations that were not words. He invented these three-letter nonsense syllables because he wanted to study "pure" learning uncontaminated by previous experience; however, as we will see in a later section of this chapter, not all nonsense syllables are equally meaningless. Second, he devised the method of *serial learning*. When he had made up all his lists, he chose one and memorized it. He then read the list over, one syllable at a time, at a constant rate. He continued this for a predetermined number of trials or until he

---

* "Word" will refer to all types of items including nonsense syllables.

** Actually, Ebbinghaus's method was to read each syllable in order, and then repeat the list until he was ready for a test. The method described above is a refinement of his technique sometimes called the "serial anticipation method."

FIGURE 9-1.

Sample learning and forgetting curves from Ebbinghaus's research.

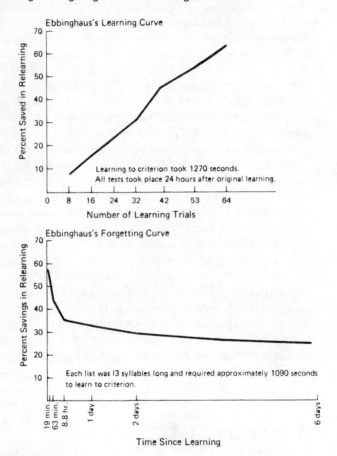

reached a predetermined criterion (e.g., being able to recall all the words without error). Third, he developed a measure of learning called *savings in relearning*. After some amount of time (i.e., some predetermined *retention interval*), Ebbinghaus tried to relearn the list. He counted the number of trials (or amount of time) it took him to learn to criterion on this second learning and compared that with the number of trials (or amount of time) required for original learning. The difference was the savings in relearning. Ebbinghaus divided this savings by the number of trials (or time) for original learning which yielded a percentage that indicated how much was remembered.

Two major findings of Ebbinghaus's many experiments were the learning curve and the forgetting curve. The learning curve is shown in the top portion of Figure 9-1: the more trials that Ebbinghaus devoted to a list, the easier it was to "relearn" it to criterion twenty-four hours later. One interesting aspect of his data is that each increase in practice had an equal increase in savings. However, there is some evidence that beyond a certain point, practice yielded diminishing returns. The forgetting curve is shown in the lower portion of Figure 9-1: the longer Ebbinghaus waited after learning a list to criterion, the longer it took him to relearn it. One interesting aspect of this forgetting curve is that most forgetting occurred very early; almost half of the list was forgotten within 20 minutes (58 percent savings) and even a month later, the savings had only decreased to 21 percent. Ebbinghaus performed many other manipulations, such as varying the length of the lists, varying the time between practice trials, and varying the order of items in a list. Most of his results, which have been replicated many times by psychologists who followed him, will be discussed later in this chapter.

Ebbinghaus developed several statistical techniques to help clarify his data (such as his percentage measure of savings in relearning as shown in Figure 9-1) and several theoretical ideas to explain his results. His main theoretical approach was a refinement of the older associationist philosophy (discussed in Chapter 1) which suggested that the learning process is basically the formation of associations from one syllable to another. Learning involved strengthening associations, and forgetting involved weakening associations or developing new associations that conflicted with the old ones.

Ebbinghaus deserves to be remembered as a founder of the experimental psychology of human learning because of the long list of contributions which he made, including: (1) the first demonstration that it is possible to study higher level cognitive processes using a rigorous experimental method, thus countering the dogma of the late nineteenth century that such study was not possible; (2) developing materials, such as nonsense syllables, and methods, such as serial learning, which are still in use today and which have helped to generate much useful research. By providing psychologists with a shared, agreed-upon set of methods, Ebbinghaus helped to foster an integrated and systematic study of verbal learning; (3) a number of major findings, such as the learning and forgetting curves, which are still considered fundamental principles of learning; and (4) helping to establish a tradition of rigorous, systematic experimentation and quantitative analysis that still characterize the psychology of verbal learning. The introduction to Ebbinghaus's monograph proclaims: "From the most ancient subject we shall produce the newest science." This hope and challenge is still shared by modern psychologists of verbal learning, and the remainder of this chapter will explore how far psychologists who work in the Ebbinghaus tradition have come in their study of one aspect of the human mind.

DEFINITION OF VERBAL LEARNING

The study of verbal learning has long occupied an important place in the psychology of learning. Ebbinghaus's work had a monumental influence on the theory and methodology in verbal learning studies. In recent years, the interest in human verbal learning has expanded so much that it became necessary in 1962 to establish the *Journal of Verbal Learning and Verbal Behavior*, a periodical devoted entirely to the study of "verbal learning, human memory, psycholinguistics, and other closely related verbal processes."

In one sense the study of verbal learning may be defined by the stimulus materials, which are verbal (usually nonsense syllables or words), and the research methods (usually a fundamental learning or transfer paradigm such as serial learning, free recall, or paired-associate learning). However, in a broader sense, verbal learning involves the acquisition, storage, and retrieval of verbal knowledge, including the comprehension and processing of natural language.

Cofer (1975) has suggested a fundamental distinction between two different traditions in verbal learning: the *Ebbinghaus tradition* and the *Bartlett tradition*. The Ebbinghaus tradition is based on the question of *how much*; typical studies concern the effect of variables on how much is learned, transferred, or forgotten. The central issues involve determining the characteristics of behavioral effects such as the fact that the rate of presentation influences the amount learned, or that the time elapsed since learning influences the amount forgotten. Typically, the stimulus materials are nonsense syllables or words, and the dependent variables are the number of items recalled or the number of items recognized.

The Bartlett tradition considers the question of *what kind*; typical research investigates the organization of memory or the different ways people relate new knowledge to old. The central issues here involve determining the cognitive structures (or *schemata*) which underlie learning and memory and how these structures are changed by learning and retrieval. Typically, the stimuli are sentences or passages (but may sometimes be words) and the dependent variable is some measure of the structure of the learning outcome rather than the amount learned.

These two traditions have recently begun to merge and we can hope the resulting approach will take the best features of each—the rigorous methods of the Ebbinghaus tradition and the interesting questions of the Bartlett tradition. This chapter will share Ebbinghaus's interest in explaining *how much* is learned, transferred, and forgotten, while Chapters 11 and 12 will explore *what processes* and *what cognitive structures* are used during learning and remembering. Thus, while this chapter will focus on the studies using nonsense syllables and word lists, Chapters 11 and 12 will focus on the Bartlett approach in the sense that learning of sentences and passages will be explored.

BASIC METHODS FOR VERBAL LEARNING RESEARCH

Since Ebbinghaus's time, many refinements of his methods and materials have developed. As we said in Chapter 1, the three main methods (or paradigms) used in verbal learning research are *serial learning*, *free recall learning*, and *paired-associate learning*. Each of these methods represents an attempt to simulate a common type of verbal learning that might occur in schools or in the real world.

In serial learning, a subject either listens to or reads a list of words (or other verbal material) which are presented one at a time. The list is repeated in the same order until some criterion is reached, such as until the subject has learned all the words and can recite them without error. Ebbinghaus used a *study-test* (or complete presentation) version of this method in which he studied each item in the list and then tried to recall them all in order; however, a more commonly used version for serial learning is *anticipation* in which after studying each word the subject tries to "guess" what the next one will be. In either case, the distinguishing characteristic of serial learning is that the subjects must learn a chain of verbal stimuli *in order*, as would be required in the example in the introduction. Each time the list is repeated, the items are given in the same order. Another example of serial learning could be memorizing the U.S. presidents in order, starting with Washington.

In free recall list learning, a subject either listens to or reads a list of words (or verbal items) which are presented one at a time, and then tries to recall them in *any* order. If more than one learning trial is used, the list is often given a different randomized order on each subsequent trial. For example, below is a list of words that might be used in a free recall task. Typical instructions would be: "Read the following list at a constant rate of one word every 2 seconds. Then try to write down all you can remember, in any order."

| valley | finding | accent | treason | office | walker |
| garden | issue | maxim | lagoon | barrack | jungle |

Note that free recall differs from serial learning because the order of recall is not important for the former. Another example of free recall list learning would be to memorize all the teams in the National League of Baseball in any order.

In paired-associate learning, the subject either listens to or reads *pairs* of words (or verbal items). The first member of each pair is the *stimulus term* and the second member is the *response term*. Typical instructions might be to read each word pair: TOR—valley, NIS—finding, XAB—accent, DUL—treason. Then the subject is asked to try to give the response term for each stimulus term: NIS—_____, DUL—_____, XAB—_____, and TOR—_____. On the next trial, the study pairs and test are generally given in random order and the experiment continues until the subject correctly answers all the test items. This version of paired-associate learning is called the study-test technique, since on each trial the subject sees each of the stimulus-response pairs and is then tested on each of the stimulus terms. However, another version is called the anticipation technique; for each trial, the subject is first given a stimulus term and asked to supply the response, then the stimulus-response pair is given, and so on for each pair. In this case, the sequence would be: NIS—_____, NIS—finding, DUL—_____, DUL—treason, XAB—_____, XAB—accent, TOR—_____, TOR—

valley. Note that the subject must guess or "anticipate" what the response term will be for each stimulus term. Although performance on the first trial will, of course, be very poor, after many trials the subject should learn to anticipate all responses correctly. For both versions, each time a trial is repeated the order of presentation of the pairs (and test items) is randomized. An example of paired-associate learning would be listing the state capitals for each state in the union.

With each of these methods, a *criterion of learning* must be used to determine how many *trials* are needed, that is, how many times the list will be given. There are two basic types of criteria for learning. One is the *performance criterion*, which means the list is repeated until the subject performs at some predefined level of competence such as one errorless trial or two errorless trials. When a performance criterion is used, then measures of the number of trials to criterion or amount of time to criterion may be used as quantitative measures of the difficulty or rate of learning. The second is the *trials or time criterion*, which means the list is repeated for a number of trials or amount of time predetermined by the experimenter, regardless of the subject's performance, such as 1 trial or a 5-minute limit.

The apparatus used to present verbal lists can be anything ranging from a set of index cards, to a slide projector, to a tape recorder, to a memory drum, or even a specially programmed computer-controlled TV screen. A typical memory drum is shown in Chapter 1. This device was developed to better control the rate of exposure for each verbal item. It consists of a metal plate with a window over a roller which pulls long sheets of paper by the window one line at a time. Typically, memory drums can be adjusted to present words at the rate of one per second, one per two seconds, one per four seconds, as well as other rates.

To obtain measures of how much is remembered, psychologists have developed three basic measures: recall, recognition, and relearning. In *recall*, subjects are asked to write or speak the to-be-remembered items. In *recognition*, an item (or group of items) is presented and the subject is asked to tell whether or not the item was in the original list. In *relearning*, subjects relearn the original list and the experimenter notes the number of trials or amount of time saved in the second learning as compared with the first. These three *R*'s of remembering—number (or percentage) of items correctly recalled, number (or percentage) of items correctly recognized, and savings in relearning—all measure *how much* is remembered, although recall and recognition are the most commonly used. Chapter 11 will explore measures which attempt to indicate not only how much is remembered but also what is lost from memory.

Most research on verbal learning has tried to explain one or more of the three following phenomena: (1) *acquisition*—how information is encoded into memory: (2) *transfer*—how old learning influences new learning; and (3) *forgetting*—how information is retrieved from memory. The following three sections will explore the basic findings with respect to acquisition (effects of meaningfulness, serial position effect, and practice effects) and the subsequent sections will deal with transfer and forgetting, respectively.

EFFECT OF MEANINGFULNESS ON VERBAL LEARNING

There has been a great deal of research on the variables that influence the learning of verbal materials. Among the many factors which have been shown to influence verbal learning are rate of presentation, directions to the learner, characteristics of the learner, meaningfulness of the stimuli, amount of practice, spacing of practice, order of presentation of the stimuli, and many others. In this and the two following sections, several of the more important factors or acquisition effects will be discussed. Although most of them have been replicated so often they are now accepted as facts, there is much less agreement on how to interpret them or relate them to a theory of human cognitive functioning.

One problem with nonsense syllables is that they are not equally meaningless.* In fact, it may not be possible to produce verbal materials which are perfectly "new" since human learners are quite proficient at inventing ways to relate nonsense syllables to their own experiences. For example, to remember VIK, a person may think of the Vikings, or a friend named Victor, or think of six thousand (VI = six, K = thousand), and so on.

Since all types of verbal stimuli may differ in meaningfulness, we need to define what is meant by "meaningful" and to develop scientific methods of quantitatively measuring the characteristics of stimuli. Several basic characteristics of stimuli that may be important for learning are discussed below.

Association Value

One of the first measures of verbal material to be developed was the *rating method* for association value (a-value). For example, Glaze (1928) provided norms for 2,000 nonsense syllables by asking fifteen subjects to state (yes or no) whether the syllables evoked an association within 2 or 3 seconds. The subjects did not have to produce the association, but rather to tell if there was one.

The resultant measure was simply the percentage of subjects who said "yes" for each CVC. More recently, Archer (1960) asked 319 subjects to rate 2,480 CVCs on whether each was a word, reminded them of a word, sounded like a word, and so on; again, association value was indicated by the proportion of subjects who answered "yes."

There is an alternative to the rating method used by Glaze, Archer, and others called the *production method*. Kent and Rosanoff (1910) developed a word-association test (WAT) in which subjects were asked to "give the first word that comes into your mind" for each of 100 common words. More recently, Palermo and Jenkins (1964) produced a more comprehensive set

*The reader should note that meaningfulness is not the same as meaning, e.g., nonsense syllables may have no meanings but may vary widely in meaningfulness.

FIGURE 9-2.

Percentage of correct responses on 12 learning trials as a function of the meaningfulness of materials.

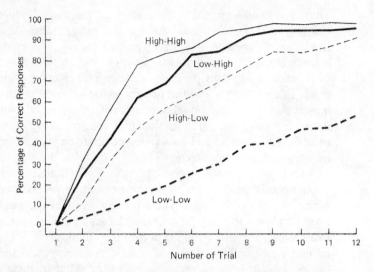

of norms by using the same method. In order to obtain a measure of the meaningfulness of a verbal unit, Noble (1952) asked 119 subjects to write as many free associations as they could think of in 60 seconds to 18 artificial and 96 real noun syllables. As a measure of meaningfulness, called m-value, Noble simply counted the average number of associations given each word within 60 seconds. For example, PERCEPT and ROSTRUM have low meaningfulness ratings (less than 3) while INSECT and KITCHEN have high ratings (over 8).

The rating method and the production method both attempt to measure the same dimension: how well associated a verbal unit is to other words. Noble (1963) has shown that the correlation between ratings and number of produced associations is quite high (e.g., correlation coefficients are usually greater than +.9 for nouns and greater than +.7 for nonsense syllables). Thus, both measures may be tapping the same variable.

How does meaningfulness (as measured by a-value or m-value) relate to learning? There have now been many replications of the fact that verbal materials that rank high in a-value or m-value are learned faster and remembered better than items low in a- or m-value. This appears to be the case regardless of whether serial learning, free recall, or paired-associate tasks are used (Cofer, 1971). For example, Underwood and Schultz (1960) varied a-value and m-value in serial learning and found that the items rated highest were learned up to three times faster than those rated lowest. Similarly, in a paired-associate study, Cieutat, Stockwell, and Noble (1958) varied the m-values of both the stimulus and the response words so that both were high, both were low, or one was high and the other was low. The results, shown in Figure 9-2, indicated that the high-high group learned fastest and the low-low group learned slowest. One explanation of such

FIGURE 9-3.

Average number of words recalled as a function of the frequency value.

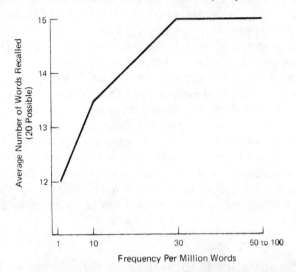

findings is that the high-meaningfulness words have more potential connections with a subject's existing knowledge (Underwood & Schultz, 1960).

Frequency

A second important characteristic of verbal items is how frequently they occur in everyday language. Thorndike and Lorge (1944) compiled a list of over 30,000 words and indicated how many times per million words each occurred in a standard selection of books, magazines, newspapers, and so on. There have, of course, been other, smaller-scale attempts to count how frequently certain words occur (French, Carter, & Koenig, 1930; Howes, 1966; Jones & Wepman, 1966; West, 1953; Miller, Newman, & Friedman, 1955; Mann, 1944), but the Thorndike and Lorge word count and the updated Kucera and Francis (1967) count are still used in verbal learning studies and are among the most common references in the field.

Results from a wide variety of studies, including serial, free recall, and paired associates have clearly indicated that, like m-value, word frequency influences the rate of learning (Cofer, 1971). For example, Hall (1954) and Deese (1959) found faster or more learning of high frequency lists than low frequency lists. In Hall's (1954) study, subjects listened to lists of 20 words, with all words in the list coming from the same frequency range. Figure 9-3 shows a clear relationship: more words are recalled from high frequency lists.

There are, however, several alternative explanations to account for the relationship of frequency and ease of learning (or remembering). For example, Deese (1959) attributes the finding to the fact that words in the high frequency lists are more associated with one another. Cofer (1971) suggests that another factor may be pronounceability, with high frequency words generally shorter and easier to pronounce. Unfortunately, there is no clear reconciliation of the problem of determining the best index of meaningfulness, that is, whether learning is more closely related to m-value, a-value, frequency, association of items in the list with one another, pronounceability, or other possible factors. Interest in this aspect of "meaningfulness" reached a peak with Underwood and Schultz's (1960) book *Meaningfulness and Verbal Learning*, and since then research on meaningfulness has taken on new forms (see Chapter 11). One reasonable conclusion is that each of these measures is correlated with learning and with each other; in any particular situation subjects may have available several ways to make words "meaningful" and may use the system that is most appropriate. Further research is needed to identify more accurately those situations in which one particular index of meaningfulness as opposed to another is related to learning.

Sequential Dependencies

Another way to assess the meaningfulness of verbal units is to determine the probability that one letter would follow another. The main concept here is that some letter sequences are more probable or frequent than others. A method devised by Underwood and Schultz (1960) was to take 150 typical 100-word passages from books and other sources and count how many times each trigram (three-letter combination), bigram (two-letter combination), and single letter occurred. For example, the word "frequency" would be broken down into *fre, req, equ,* and so on for the trigram count. This method produced a table of facts showing that *fre* occurred 18 times per 15,000, *fr* occurred 111 times per 15,000, and *f* occurred 1,494 per 15,000. This method, it can be noted, is similar to Thorndike and Lorge's word frequency count.

In another study similar to the production method, Underwood and Schultz (1960) gave their subjects a set of single letters and asked them to give the first letter that came to mind; then they gave the subjects all the two-letter combinations and asked for the next letter that came to mind. In this way, they could rate the trigrams on how likely the letters were to follow one another. For example, given an *S*, no subject responded with a *B*, but 110 out of 273 subjects gave an *O*; given *SB*, no one responded with *M*, but if *SO* was the cue, 50 subjects out of 273 gave *T*. Underwood and Schultz found they could predict that certain trigrams like *SBM* would be harder to learn than, say, *SOT*. To test these predictions based on sequential dependencies, they used trigrams as response terms in a paired-associate learning task and found that, as predicted, the trigrams with high sequential dependencies were easier to learn than the low. The correlation between letter transition probability and ease of learning was between .67 to .89 in a series of studies (Underwood & Schultz, 1960).

FIGURE 9-4.

Mean number of words recalled as a function of imagery value and association value. For List I, all lists are equivalent in association value; for List M, all lists are equivalent in imagery value.

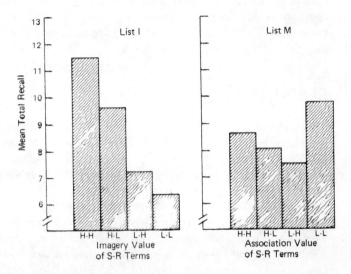

Imagery Value

Paivio (1971) has argued that another important determination of the meaningfulness of verbal material is *imagery value*: the tendency of the word to evoke a vivid image in the learner. Further, Paivio has proposed a "dual coding hypothesis" based on the idea that verbal stimuli may be encoded verbally or visually. For example, Paivio, Yuille, and Madigan (1968) asked subjects to rate 925 nouns for imagery, concreteness, and meaningfulness on a scale of 1 to 7. As might be expected, there were high intercorrelations among these three measures. For instance, the correlation between concreteness and imagery was .83. Typical high-imagery words were "elephant" and "beggar," while low-imagery words were "interim" and "context."

In a subsequent study (Paivio, Smythe, & Yuille, 1968), four types of paired associates were constructed. All were equal in meaningfulness but one set had high imagery stimulus and response words, one had low imagery stimulus and response words, and two were mixed high-low or low-high. The learning rates were fastest for the high-high group and slowest for the low-low group as shown in the left panel of Figure 9-4. In addition, Paivio, Smythe, and Yuille (1968) constructed four lists that were equivalent in imagery value but varied in meaningfulness (as measured by association value). The recall results, shown in the right side of Figure 9-4, failed to produce a positive relationship between meaningfulness and recall. Paivio et al. suggest that previous research produced a "meaningfulness effect" because high association value words also tend to be high imagery words;

when one controls for imagery value, the effect of association value on learning is eliminated.

Apparently, there are many ways to measure meaningfulness, and with each way we have discussed, there is a positive effect of meaningfulness on learning. What is lacking, of course, is a reconciliation that can account for these facts. The information processing approach discussed in Chapter 10 may ultimately provide such a theory.

SERIAL POSITION EFFECT

A second major acquisition factor that has received much research attention is the *serial position* of items on a list. Any item on a list of, say 20 items, has a serial position ranging from first to twentieth. Ebbinghaus, using a serial learning method, was the first to note that the first few words and the last few words of a list were learned faster than those in the middle. Similar results have also been obtained using the paired-associate method and the free recall method, that is, the probability of correct recall is better for the first few words and the last few words than for the middle items. Figure 9-5 shows the results of several studies using lists of unrelated words with varying list lengths and presentation rates (Murdock, 1962). Note that for each situation, the curve is U-shaped. These findings are called the *serial position effect* and involve the *primacy effect*, that words at the beginning of the list are more easily learned and remembered than those in the middle, and the *recency effect*, that words at the end of the list are more easily learned and remembered than those in the middle.

A related finding, first reported by von Restorff (1933), is that if any one word in the list is unusual or different from the other words, it will be more easily learned and remembered regardless of its serial position. For example, in a list of 20 nouns which are all names of animals, if word #12 is the name of a fruit (or a number or an obscene word), it will be better remembered even though it occurs in the middle of the list. This finding has been called the *von Restorff effect* or the *isolation effect*, and it suggests that the relative distinctiveness of each item must be taken into account when examining the shape of the jagged serial position curve.

There are several theoretical explanations for this curious empirical fact that we call the serial position effect, and four of them will be explored in this section. One reason for the interest in the theoretical mechanisms underlying this effect is that understanding the serial position effect might ultimately reveal something fundamental about how the human mind works. The four theories to be discussed are: *remote association* theory, *interference* theory, *cognitive landmark* theory, and *dual memory* theory.

FIGURE 9-5.

Proportion of material recalled as a function of serial position. The figure illustrates the serial position effect. Length of list (10, 15, 20, 30, 40 words) and presentation rate (1 or 2 seconds per word) were varied.

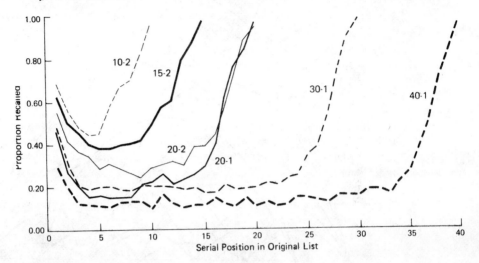

Remote Associations

In discussing his research, Ebbinghaus developed a straightforward theory of serial learning. He suggested that (1) each item in the list became associated, not only with the next adjacent item, but also with all other items farther down the list, and (2) the farther apart items were in the list, the weaker these remote associations would be. A pictorial representation of this theory is given in Figure 9-6. Note that items in the middle of the list have more remote associations crossing them than items at the ends.

Both Hull (1935) and Lepley (1934) employed the concept of remote associations to explain the serial position effect. Their basic argument was that the middle items have more associations going across them, and thus more interference. For example, in an 8-item list such as is shown in Figure 9-6, the first and last items have no remote associations crossing over them, the second and seventh have 6, the third and sixth have 10, and the fourth and fifth have 12; therefore, the middle items have more interfering associations than the ends.

One prediction of this theory is that the serial position effect should be perfectly symmetrical, with the recency effect and the primacy effect equal to one another. There is, however, much evidence that the curve is often asymmetrical; for example, the free recall data from Murdock (1962) shown in Figure 9-5 summarize the finding that the recency effect is often stronger than the primacy effect in free recall.

Another prediction of the Hullian theory is that a slower presentation rate or more time between trials should allow stronger forward associations

FIGURE 9-6.

Schematic diagram illustrating Hull's theory of remote associations.

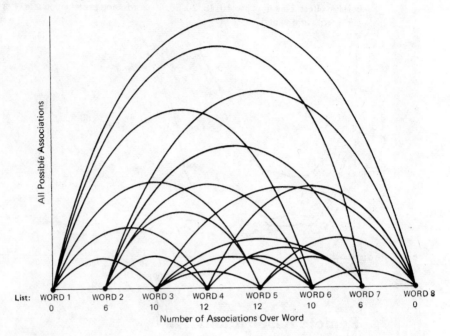

List:
WORD 1	WORD 2	WORD 3	WORD 4	WORD 5	WORD 6	WORD 7	WORD 8
0	6	10	12	12	10	6	0

Number of Associations Over Word

among adjacent items and thus lessen the serial position effect. In an early study, Hovland (1938) found that the serial position curve was much less bowed when the intertrial interval was 2 minutes rather than 6 seconds. However, fifteen years later, when Hullian theory was declining in popularity, McCrary and Hunter (1953) recalculated the Hovland data in a way that produced results contrary to predictions. Instead of plotting the serial position curves based on the number of errors (or number correct) they used percents of total errors; using this method, both intervals produced similar curves, again against the predictions of the remote associations theory. Apparently, the effect obtained by Hovland was due mainly to the fact that the longer interval allowed more learning overall.

Interference Theory

Another explanation for the serial position effect is that both previous words and subsequent words interfere with memory for words that occur in the middle of the list. Only one type of interference, however, is involved with memory for the first or last items (Foucault, 1928; Melton, 1963; Murdock, 1974). The interfering effects of previous words on later words is called *proactive interference*, while the interfering effects of later words on remembering earlier words is called *retroactive interference*. These processes are discussed more fully in the section on transfer. Thus the serial position effect can be conceived of as resulting from the additive effects of two separate memory interference processes. This view is a refinement of the remote association theory which is based solely on forward associations while the interference theory supposes both forward (proactive) and backward (retroactive) interference.

If both interference processes are equally strong, the interference theory would share the remote association theory's prediction of a symmetrical curve—a prediction that is generally not upheld. There are other problems with this theory as well. For example, Ebenholtz (1963, 1972) presented 10 paired associates with digits 1 through 10 as the stimulus terms; even though the pairs were presented in random order, recall was best for the responses to 1, 2, 9, and 10 regardless of their serial positions. These results are certainly inconsistent with both the remote association and the interference ideas, and suggest a third theory based on the concept of *cognitive landmarks* or *anchors*.

Cognitive Landmarks

In a review of the serial position literature, Ebenholtz (1972) concluded that the effect may be due to the distinctiveness of the beginning and ending of the lists as *cognitive anchors* or *landmarks* to which words could be attached. That this view is consistent with the von Restorff effect (which illustrates that distinctive items are better recalled regardless of serial position) has received some research support (Jensen, 1962; Glanzer & Dolinsky, 1965).

One line of research has involved making one item in the list "distinctive," for example, by printing it in red ink while the other words are printed in black. Typically, the distinctive item is learned more rapidly as compared to a nondistinctive item placed in the same serial position (Glanzer & Dolinsky, 1965; Goulet, Bone, & Barker, 1967; McLaughlin, 1966). In a more striking study, Coppage and Harcum (1967) produced a "closed cycle" list (i.e., there was no temporal break after the last word) and provided an "anchor" by having one of the words printed in red ink. Although the distinctive item appeared in different positions for different subjects, the serial position curve reflected a peak at that point with surrounding items also better recalled.

Dual Memory Theory

A fourth theory, the *dual memory* theory (Waugh & Norman, 1965) suggests that the cognitive anchor idea is only half the story. The dual memory theory involves an *information processing* approach to learning and memory (see Chapter 10) that assumes several stages. First, incoming information passes through a limited capacity short-term memory (STM) that fades if items are not rehearsed, and second, some of the rehearsed

FIGURE 9-7.

Proportion correct as a function of serial position. The top panel shows data from a free recall test given 0, 10, or 30 seconds after learning. The lower panel shows recall for immediate and delayed tests.

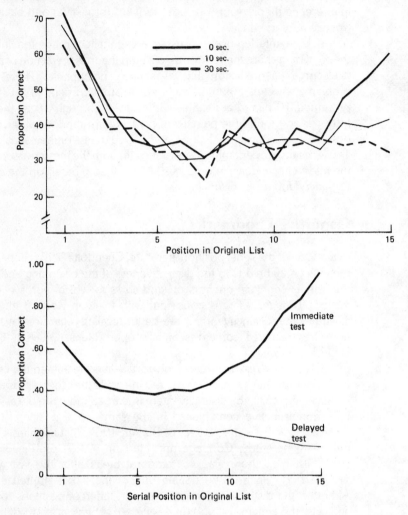

items enter long-term memory (LTM) which is organized (and presumably includes cognitive anchors).

According to this view, the recency effect results because the learner empties the items out of the STM at the start of the recall period. This idea is consistent with the often-cited finding that in free recall the subject gives the last few items first. The primacy effect results because early items have more time to be rehearsed in STM and thus have more chance of being transferred to the LTM. These items get more processing "attention" because they are put into an empty STM. (This is discussed more fully in Chapter 10.)

One further prediction of the dual memory theory is that delaying the retention interval while preventing rehearsal should eliminate the recency effect because STM will be erased but have no effect on primacy. This is so because the subject is recalling those last few items that are being actively rehearsed in short-term memory; when the recall test is delayed and subjects are not allowed to rehearse the material in STM, it will fade away so all that is left are the items that were encoded into LTM. This prediction has been upheld in several studies (Postman & Phillips, 1965; Glanzer & Cunitz, 1966; Tulving & Arbuckle, 1963). For example, the top panel of Figure 9-7 shows the recall by serial position in the Glanzer and Cunitz study for immediate and delayed recall groups. As can be noted, the two groups show nearly identical primacy effects but the upturn in the recency effect is eliminated for the delayed recall group. Apparently, the items in STM were no longer available to subjects in the delayed group.

In a related study, Craik (1970) presented ten lists, each with 15 words, and asked for recall immediately after each list. In addition, at the end of the experiment, there was a surprise: all the subjects were asked to recall as many of the 150 words as possible. The results, shown in the lower panel of Figure 9-7, indicate the typical recency effect for immediate recall but a negative recency effect for the surprise delayed test. Apparently, words that came at the end of the list were *less* likely to be selected for storage in long-term memory. One hypothesis (Craik & Lockhart, 1972) is that subjects do not try to encode the last few words into LTM because maintaining them in STM is all that is needed.

Another prediction of the dual storage theory is that decreasing the rate of presentation should allow more rehearsal time for each item and thus allow more early items to get into LTM (producing a stronger primacy effect). However, this procedure should have no effect on recency. Again, this prediction has been upheld in several experiments (Murdock, 1962; Glanzer & Cunitz, 1966).

Finally, another prediction can be made if we accept the idea that STM is based on the sound of words and LTM is based on the meanings of words (this distinction is discussed more fully in Chapter 10). We would then expect that presenting words by reading them aloud rather than visually would increase the recency effect (presumably due to the auditory nature of STM) but would not affect the primacy effect or the rest of the curve. This prediction has received support both in cases when serial recall was required (Madigan, 1971) and in free recall (Murdock & Walker, 1969; Watkins, 1972; Craik, 1969).

Although the findings cited above support the dual memory explanation of the serial position effect, there is also some evidence that the distinction between STM and LTM may not be quite as neat as originally supposed (Melton, 1963; Craik & Lockhart, 1972). These criticisms are discussed in Chapter 10.

EFFECT OF AMOUNT OF PRACTICE ON VERBAL LEARNING

One of the most obvious factors that influences learning is practice: the repetition of to-be-learned materials. Ebbinghaus was the first to note that more nonsense syllables were remembered as a function of the number of times the list was presented (see the learning curve in Figure 9-1). Such *repetition effects* have been a fundamental variable in learning experiments since then. Although the empirical fact that learning is a function of repetition is well established, there remains the problem of how to account for it.

Gradual versus All-or-None Theories

A fairly straightforward idea, proposed by Ebbinghaus (1885) and refined by Hull (1943), is that repetition acts to strengthen new associations gradually. This theory predicts that the shape of the learning curve should be generally smooth, showing a gradual increase in amount remembered as a function of the number of learning trials; this kind of curve is indeed frequently obtained.

An alternative theory is the all-or-none theory (Guthrie, 1935, 1952; Estes, 1950, 1964), which states that learning of individual associations is not gradual but rather occurs in all-or-none fashion: on each trial, the association is either completely learned (i.e., learned state) or remains completely unlearned (i.e., unlearned state). This theory predicts that the smooth shape of the learning curve occurs only because the investigator averages over many subjects and many associations. According to Estes, however, if we analyzed the performance of individual subjects on individual associations, the learning curves would be jagged, going from chance performance to 100 percent correct in one trial. When data have been analyzed in such a manner, the smooth, averaged curve did become a set of all-or-none curves, at least in some cases (Bjork, 1968). Again, as with explanations of the serial position effect, how data are analyzed is crucial.

Important evidence on this issue was shown in a classic study by Rock (1957) in which subjects learned a list of paired associates. For one group (control) the same list of paired associates was repeated until the subject could correctly recall all 12 responses. In contrast, for the experimental group, each time the subject made an error a new paired associate was substituted for the missed one in the next trial. This "drop-out" procedure assured that all responses would be learned in just *one* trial. The results were that the two groups did not differ in how many trials it took to reach criterion. Rock concluded that repetition was not necessary for learning.

Although Rock's study apparently provides support for the all-or-none theory, several other investigators (Postman, 1962; Underwood, Rehula, & Keppel, 1962) have pointed out fundamental flaws in the design. The crucial criticism is that, in Rock's study, the experimental group may have been "selecting" the easier paired-associate items since those that caused errors were replaced. Although easy items can be learned "all-or-none," perhaps the difficult ones cannot. These researchers replicated Rock's experiment but included a second control group that received the same lists as the final lists "selected" by the experimental subjects; this control group learned faster than the others, suggesting that the experimental subjects did receive easier lists.

A second major study investigating the all-or-none theory was conducted by Estes (1960; Estes, Hopkins, & Crothers, 1960) using a paired-associate task. The subjects first studied eight paired associates, with words as the stimulus terms and the digits 1 through 8 as the responses; they then took two successive tests. If we assume that no learning occurs between the first and second tests and that all items are equally difficult, then the all-or-none and gradual theories offer quite different predictions.

If learning were incremental, then each of the eight associations should have been learned slightly. Thus, the chances of being correct for each item on each test should be above 0 and below 100 percent and subjects should not perform extremely well or extremely poorly on both tests for any item. Since each item is only slightly learned, the gradual theory predicts that the subject typically might get an item right on one test but incorrect on the other. In contrast, if learning were all-or-none, then each association is either completely learned or completely unlearned. If it were completely learned, then the subject should be correct 100 percent on both tests, and if it were unlearned, then the subject has only one chance in eight of making a lucky guess on each test. Therefore, the all-or-none theory predicts a fairly high probability of getting an item correct on both tests or incorrect on both tests.* The obtained results closely matched the predictions of the all-or-none theory; for example, the probability of moving from an error on Test 1 to a correct response on Test 2 for any item was quite low (.09) but the probability of moving from a correct response on Test 1 to a correct response on Test 2 was quite high (.71).

The Estes experiment has been criticized on several grounds, including the argument that the premises are not met. For example, all items may not be equally difficult in which case the obtained results could be consistent with the gradual theory. That is, the easy items may have been strengthened greatly by one trial, thus producing a high probability of corrects on both tests, while the difficult items were not strengthened much at all, thus producing a low probability of an error followed by a correct.

In a replication of Estes' study, Postman (1963) found that the probabil-

---

* The actual calculations from the all-or-none model are as follows. If a subject is correct on Test 1, he or she has a 12.5 percent chance of still being in the unlearned state (and having made a lucky guess) and an 87.5 percent chance of having learned the association. If the subject is in the learned state, the probability of being correct on Test 2 is 100 percent, but if the subject is in the unlearned state, the probability of success on Test 2 is again only chance (one in eight). So the probability of being correct on Test 2, given that the subject was correct on Test 1, is: $.875 \times 100$ plus $.125 \times .125 = .89$. If the subject made an error on Test 1, then the subject is definitely in the unlearned state so the probability of making a correct response on Test 2 is simply the chance of a lucky guess: one in eight or .125. The method for determining these values is discussed in detail by Restle and Greeno (1972).

ity of being correct on trial $n + 1$, given an error on trial n, depended on the number of *prior* repetitions. In other words, if an error were made on trial 20, it was more likely that it would be followed by a correct answer than if it were made on trial 2, for example. This evidence, that the transition from wrong to correct is influenced by the amount of prior practice, is contrary to the all-or-none theory.

How can this apparent problem be reconciled? One reconciliation is that learning requires *many* small associations, each learned all-or-none, but which when viewed as a whole appear to be gradual. Another reconciliation is that two separate learning systems are available to adults: gradual learning, which is usually used for simple learning, and all-or-none learning, which is usually used for complex.

EFFECT OF SPACING OF PRACTICE ON VERBAL LEARNING

As part of his 1885 monograph, Ebbinghaus reported studies in which studying a list once a day for six days resulted in more learning than studying an equivalent list six times all in one day. This was the first demonstration that *spaced practice* (also called *distributed practice*) is more effective than *massed practice*. Others since Ebbinghaus's time have demonstrated similar results (Underwood, 1961; Underwood, Kapelak, & Malmi, 1976). In particular, increased learning due to spaced practice is most often reported for motor tasks, and for verbal tasks with long lists, fast presentation rates, or unfamiliar stimulus material (Underwood, 1961; Hovland, 1938, 1940). Findings such as these have lead to the hypothesis that learning involves a response learning stage (i.e., learning what all the words in the list are) and the association stage (i.e., learning to associate the words with one another); further, distributed practice seems to have its main influence on response learning.

Although the spacing effect is not found in all learning, there have been several attempts to account for this interesting phenomenon. Three such theories are discussed in the following sections.

Consolidation

Hebb (1949, 1958) proposed a consolidation theory that is couched in physiological terms but is also similar to the distinction the dual memory theory makes between STM and LTM. The consolidation theory proposes first that initial learning is maintained by electrical activity on the surface of the brain (i.e., neocortex). This is called *activity trace*. Within some amount of time, however, the activity traces are "consolidated"; there is a change in the structure of the neurons which is called the *structural trace*. Interference of learning during the activity trace can eliminate any chance of a permanent structural trace being formed. One example of this phenomenon may be retrograde amnesia, in which a person who is hit over the head or goes into shock usually has no memory of the events prior to the shock (up to 30 to 60 minutes before). Fcr example, people who suffer head injuries in automobile crashes often have no recollection of the minutes preceding the accident. Retrograde amnesia can also be simulated in the laboratory by applying electroconvulsive shock (ECS) after learning. In research on animals, ECS has the effect of diminishing memory for prior learning if the shock occurs within a critical time following the initial learning. This critical time may range from a few seconds up to over an hour, as shown by different studies (Baddeley, 1976). Apparently, the shock erases the "activity trace" so that there is nothing to consolidate.

The consolidation theory proposes that more is learned during spaced practice because it allows several separate encodings into structural traces while during massed practice, two or more activity traces are consolidated into one single structural encoding. A major problem with the consolidation theory, however, is to determine the time required for consolidation. Evidence such as retrograde amnesia suggests 30 to 60 minutes are required, and ECS research suggests time intervals from 15 seconds to over an hour, but learning studies show spacing effects for shorter time periods. In a survey of research on the spacing effect for a word in a word list, Hintzman (1974) concluded that the maximum spacing effect was achieved if a word was repeated approximately 15 seconds after its first presentation. Until the critical time period for consolidation can be established, this theory's usefulness will be limited.

Rehearsal

Another plausible theory, the *rehearsal theory*, was proposed by Rundus (1971) to account for a type of spacing effect called the *lag effect*. The lag effect is found when subjects learn word lists with the repeated words far apart from each other in the list (high lag) or next to each other (zero lag); generally, repeated words with high lag (many intervening words) are better remembered than words with zero lag (no intervening words). Of course, one possibility is that the serial position effect is playing a part, so lag-effect experiments must take special care to counterbalance for serial position. For example, in a list of twelve words, there are twelve positions: 1-2-3-4-5-6-7-8-9-10-11-12. One word might occur in place #4 and place #5; this is an example of a lag of 0 intervening words. If a word occurs in place #3 and place #9, there is a lag of 5 intervening words.

In this study, Rundus noted in observing the behavior of the subjects that when there was a high lag, the subjects rehearsed the word more than when there was zero lag. Since the amount of rehearsal aids in the transfer of information from short-term memory into long-term memory, the spacing effect may be accounted for by saying that it encourages more self-initiated rehearsal.

Encoding Variability

Although both the consolidation theory and the rehearsal theory provide plausible explanations of the spacing effect, there is now evidence for an alternative theory which we will call *encoding variability* (Martin, 1968, 1972; Melton, 1970). The basic idea here is that spacing allows the subjects to encode new material into several different *contexts*, thus providing more chances for retrieval. In this case, context refers to the concepts in memory to which the presented word is assimilated. In contrast, all items are more likely to be encoded within the same context during massed practice. For example, free recall of a 50-item list is better if the items are presented twice with 40 items intervening than twice with no intervening items (Underwood, 1970; Madigan, 1969). Further, in a continuous paired-associate task, the number of trials required to learn a response was less if the trials were separated by intervening items than if they were blocked together. These results are consistent with all three theories, but Melton (1970) has argued that the lag effect is due to availability of different encoding contexts. In other words, a word presented at time X will be encoded within the context of the subject's active ideas at that time. If it is repeated immediately, the context will be similar so the word will have just one *mental* context. However, if the word is instead repeated later in the list at a later time, then the learner will have a different context to encode it into.

For example, when the to-be-learned words are given distinct contexts (e.g., by providing an adjective for a to-be-learned noun), the effect of lag (spacing) is reduced; using the same context each time the word is presented reduces the effect of repetition (Madigan, 1969; Winograd & Raines, 1972). Similarly, Glanzer and Duarte (1971), using bilingual subjects, found that repeating a word in the same language reduced the lag effect as compared with repeating it in different languages. Bjork and Allen (1970) found that varying the difficulty of an intervening task did not hurt the spacing effect, thus conflicting with the rehearsal theory.

A striking result was obtained in a series of interesting experiments by Glenberg (1976). Subjects learned word lists in which words were repeated at lags of 0, 1, 4, 8, 20, and 40 intervening words. If the recall test followed a long interval after the second presentation of the repeated word (e.g., retention intervals of 32 or 64 intervening words), then the typical, increasing lag effect was found: the farther apart the original and the repetition of the word were in the list, the more likely it was to be recalled. However, if the recall test came shortly after the second presentation of the word (retention interval of 2 intervening words), the typical lag effect was disrupted: highest recall performance occurred for a lag of 4 and performance *fell* for larger lags. Glenberg attempted to relate his findings to a context theory (p. 13): "For the present, the most satisfactory explanation of these results is a variant of encoding variability theory. The major assumptions are as follows. Over time the context changes. . . . The context at time $n + 2$ is more similar to the context at time $n + 1$ than to the context at time n. In other words,

FIGURE 9-8.

Basic method for transfer experiments.

Group	Task 1	Task 2
Experimental	Learn A	Learn B
Control 1	Irrelevant Activity	Learn B
Control 2	(Nothing)	Learn B

what a person is thinking and feeling at time $n + 2$ is more closely associated with whatever [the individual] was thinking and feeling at time $n + 1$ than time n. The encoding of stimuli and their resultant functional stimuli are *determined by the nominal stimulus and the context*" (italics added). Thus, at longer retention intervals, longer lags are helpful because they are more likely to provide two separate encodings, or two chances of retrieving the target word; but at short retention intervals, the context is still quite similar at test time to that at the second encoding.

TRANSFER OF LEARNING

Basic Methods

One of the most important tasks in verbal learning research has been to determine how previous learning influences the learning of new material. For example, an important methodological problem in Ebbinghaus's study was that after he memorized one set of nonsense syllables, learning another (supposedly equivalent) list was affected. Of course, the practical implications for education are enormous; essentially we are asking how does prior learning affect new learning. If we can understand this process, perhaps valuable improvements in education can be devised.

This process is called *transfer*: the effect of previous learning on the acquisition of new material. A typical transfer paradigm is shown in Figure 9-8. The experimental group learns some information, such as a verbal list, and then learns a new list. The performance of the experimental group on learning the transfer list is compared to a control group. Two types of control groups are typical. In one case (control condition 1), the subjects first learn an unrelated task, then perform the transfer task. The second control group (condition 2) does nothing and then learns the "transfer" list. The first control condition usually is preferred in transfer studies because it assures that both groups are equally familiar with the general learning task.

The main question posed in transfer studies of this sort concerns the effect of learning A on the acquisition of B (as compared to having learned something else, X, or nothing else). There are several possible answers.

First, there might be *positive transfer*. If the experimental group learns B faster (or with fewer errors or less trials) than the control group, this is an example of positive transfer. Previous learning aids in the acquisition of new material. A typical example of positive transfer might be that taking the course Introductory Psychology will help students to learn material for the course Psychology of Learning more than taking Introductory Basket Weaving will help them.

Second, there might be *negative transfer*. If the experimental group learns B more slowly (or with more errors or more trials) than the control group, this is an example of negative transfer. Previous learning hurts in the acquisition of new material. A typical example of negative transfer might be that learning to drive on the right side of the road in the U.S. makes it harder to learn to drive on the left side in England.

Finally, there might be *zero transfer*. If the experimental group learns at the same rate as the control group, this is an example of zero transfer. Previous learning has no effect on new learning.

A second kind of distinction that is made in research on transfer concerns what is transferred from learning A to learning B. *Specific transfer* occurs when specific parts of A are also identical to parts of B. For example, suppose a student learned the definitions for conditioned stimulus, unconditioned stimulus, conditioned response, and unconditioned response in an introductory psychology course and was then given the same terms to learn in a learning course. Here, we would expect specific, positive transfer. Suppose, on the other hand, that the definitions of these terms were completely different in the two courses; here we might expect specific negative transfer in learning for the learning course.

General transfer refers to transfer which cannot be attributed to specific elements in A and B. For example, a "skill" that might be gained from an introductory psychology course is an ability to examine experimental work critically; if this ability transfers to the new course, even on material that is completely different, this would be an example of general positive transfer. If, on the other hand, the general strategies developed for learning in introductory psychology are too simplistic for an advanced course, this might produce an example of general, negative transfer.

Many of the research studies on transfer of verbal learning have used a paired-associate method. Several different transfer procedures for two paired-associate lists are given in Figure 9-9. The procedures involve varying the similarity of the stimulus terms (S), the response terms (R), and the S-R associations between List 1 and List 2. For example, if List 1 contained ten pairs of words, such as HAT-RACK, HOT-DOG, and so on, it could be symbolized as the A-B list. "A" refers to the stimulus terms—HAT and HOT—while "B" refers to the response terms—RACK and DOG. If List 2 used the same stimulus terms (e.g., HAT and HOT) but different response terms (e.g., DANCE and ROD), it would be called an A-C list. The A indicates that the stimulus words are the same while the C refers to the fact that List 2 has different response terms than List 1. Other examples of this shorthand are given in Figure 9-9. Several of the most common procedures

FIGURE 9-9.

Transfer paradigms.

First List

A-B
Lake—Boy
Fast—Sickness
Name—Quiet

Second List

A-C	C-B	A-B′	A-B$_r$	C-D
Lake—North	North—Boy	Lake—Lad	Lake—Sickness	North—King
Fast—Book	Book—Sickness	Fast—Disease	Fast—Quiet	Book—Soft
Name—Hand	Hand—Quiet	Name—Silence	Name—Boy	Hand—Anger

are: A-B, A-C, in which the same stimulus terms are used in both lists but the response words differ; A-B, C-B, in which the same response terms are used in Lists 1 and 2 but the stimulus terms are different; A-B, A-B′, in which the stimulus terms are the same in both lists and the responses are similar; A-B, A-B$_r$, in which the same stimulus terms and response terms occur in both lists but they are paired differently; and A-B, C-D, in which two distinctly different lists are used.

A transfer score can be computed by noting the trials to criterion (or errors or time) in learning the transfer task for the control group (C) and for the experimental group (E). In general, the A-B, C-D procedure is used as a control because this allows subjects to have general practice on verbal paired-associate tasks without any specific practice on the to-be-learned task. One way to compute a score is expressed in the formula:

$$\text{transfer score} = \frac{E\text{-}C}{C} \times 100.$$

For example, if both groups practice equally on A-B, then the control group takes 10 trials to learn C-D but the experimental group takes 20 trials to learn A-B$_r$ the score is:

$$\frac{10\text{-}20}{20} \times 100 = -100\%.$$

In this case, prior learning results in strong negative transfer (that is also specific).

Transfer Surface

In an attempt to summarize the findings concerning transfer, Osgood (1949) proposed the idea of *transfer surface* (see Figure 9-10). The surface is based on two dimensions: how similar the stimulus terms are between lists 1 and 2 and how similar the response terms are between the two lists. Using the surface, Osgood predicted the amount and direction of transfer for all possible combinations. When the stimulus terms are identical in the two lists, the transfer surface shows best transfer performance when the responses are also identical (A-B, A-B), less when they are similar (A-B, A-B′), and worst

FIGURE 9-10.

Osgood's transfer surface.

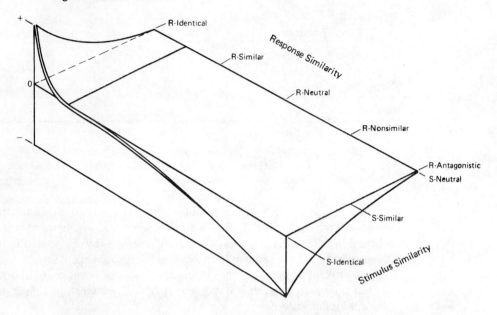

transfer when they are quite different (A-B, A-C) (Bruce, 1933; Underwood, 1951). When the response terms are identical in both lists, the transfer surface shows the best transfer when the stimulus terms are also identical, with increasingly poorer performance as the stimulus terms become more different, such as A-B, C-B (Yum, 1931; Hamilton, 1943). When the response terms are different, increasing the stimulus similarity results in poorer transfer, such as A-B, A-D resulting in better performance than A-B, C-D (Gibson, 1940).

The relative predictions of the transfer surface have been partially upheld, but the differences from control performance have not always reached statistically significant levels (Dallett, 1962; Wimer, 1964). In addition, Osgood's surface fails to account for results using other paradigms or using low meaningful material. For example, generally there is poorer transfer for A-B, A-B$_r$ than for control subjects (A-B, C-D), even though in the former case the stimulus terms and response terms are identical (Martin, 1968). Such findings suggest that the transfer surface (which does not even have a place for the A-B, A-B$_r$ procedure) must be modified. Modification is necessary to account for both forward S-R associations, that is, learning to give the response when presented with the stimulus word, and backward R-S associations, that is, learning to give the stimulus word when presented with the response word.

FIGURE 9-11.

Component analysis of paired-associate learning.

Paradigm	Learning to Learn	Stimulus Similarity	Response Similarity	Forward Associations	Backward Associations
A-B, C-D	+	0	0	0	0
A-B, A-B'	+	+	partial +	partial +	partial +
A-B, A-C	+	+	0	−	0
A-B, C-B	+	0	+	0	−
A-B, A-B$_r$	+	+	+	−	−

+ indicates positive transfer   − indicates negative transfer   0 indicates no transfer

Component Analysis

Another theoretical approach to transfer is component analysis. A component analysis of transfer has produced four specific and separate aspects of learning paired associates: (1) *stimulus differentiation*, in which each stimulus is encoded as an entity separate from each other, (2) *response learning*, in which the responses are integrated and learned, (3) *forward association*, in which the subject associates a resonse with a given stimulus, and (4) *backward association*, in which the subject associates a stimulus with a given response term.

Figure 9-11 gives the transfer predicted for each component for various paradigms. For example, in the A-B, A-C paradigm, there is positive transfer for stimulus learning because the stimulus terms are the same in List 1 and List 2. Also, since the response terms differ, there is zero transfer for response learning. There is negative transfer for forward associations since the subject must learn to forget the old response when given A and instead learn to give the response terms from List 2. However, since the response terms are new and the backward associations are new, they produce zero transfer.

The component analysis theory suggests several testable predictions. For example, when low-meaningful stimulus terms are used, subjects must first go through the stimulus learning phase, then form associations. However, if high-meaningful stimulus terms are used, the subjects will need only a very short stimulus differentiation phase and will move quickly to forming strong associations. Thus we can predict that more negative transfer will occur for A-B, A-C or for A-B, A-B$_r$ when the stimulus terms (i.e., As) are meaningful or familiar. This is so because the low-meaningful stimulus terms are learned during study of List 1 and can be positively transferred, while for high-meaningful stimulus terms, subjects will move promptly to forming forward and backward associations which will produce negative transfer. Results have supported this prediction in that massive negative transfer is found for high-meaningful stimulus terms but less, or in some cases positive transfer, is found for low-meaningful terms (Jung, 1963; Merike & Battig, 1963; Richardson & Brown, 1966). For example, Martin (1968) presented lists of six paired associates with the stimulus terms being low- or high-meaningful nonsense syllables and the responses being digits; in this case,

FIGURE 9-12.

Amount of transfer after varying amounts of practice on List 1 for various transfer paradigms. The amount of transfer equals the number of correct responses for the first 10 trials minus the number of correct responses for the first 10 trials of the control group.

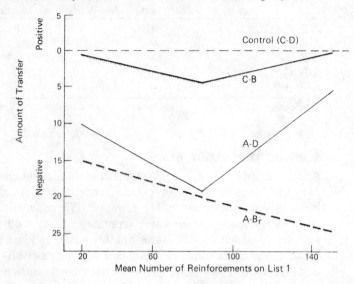

A-B, A-B$_r$ transfer was *very* difficult for the high-meaningful syllable group but not for the low. A similar prediction regarding A-C, C-B transfer is that high-meaningful terms should result in more negative transfer than low, a finding that is also generally upheld (Martin, 1968; Twedt & Underwood, 1969).

Another prediction of this theory is that the amount of practice on List 1 should have different effects for different transfer paradigms. For example, in an A-B, A-D situation, overlearning of A-B could aid in transfer because stimulus terms and response terms will be well learned; in learning the transfer list A-D, the subject has the advantage of knowing the stimulus terms and also of knowing a set of response terms that definitely cannot be used. In general, overlearning does reduce negative transfer for A-B, A-D as compared to a control A-B, C-D condition (Jung, 1962; Postman, 1962).

In a classic study, Postman (1962) allowed subjects to practice on List 1 (A-B) for 20 (low), 70 (medium), or 140 (overlearning) trials, and then measured their difficulty in learning List 2 (which was either C-B, A-D, or A-B$_r$ as compared to C-D). The results are summarized in Figure 9-12. For the A-B, C-B group, amount of learning of A-B had no effect on learning C-B, that is, this group performed like the control group. For the A-B, A-B$_r$ group, increasing practice on List 1 resulted in increasing negative transfer for List 2, presumably because the strong forward and backward associations had to be unlearned in order for List 2 to be learned. For A-B, A-D learning, practice first increased negative transfer (because forward associations were being strengthened), but then decreased negative transfer (because the subjects learned the response set well enough to discriminate these items from those used in List 2).

Encoding Variability

The results concerning meaningfulness and overlearning seem to be consistent with the component analysis approach to paired-associate transfer. However, there are more sophisticated theories which also complement it, such as Martin's (1968) encoding variability hypothesis. For example, the encoding variability hypothesis explains the effect of low meaningfulness in the A-B, A-C condition as follows: if the A terms are low in meaningfulness, they are subject to many different encodings so that they can be encoded in one way (e.g., using only the first letter) for List 1 and another way (e.g., last letter) in List 2; since high-meaningful words evoke a strong, consistent reaction, it is harder to develop two different ways of encoding it and thus, the list associations must be unlearned.

Suppose List 1 consisted of pairs like BOJ-tiger or VIH-airplane while the transfer list had pairs like BOJ-ruby or VIH-carrot. Subjects could use one letter of the stimulus terms for one list and another letter for the transfer task; for example, B-tiger (big tiger) and V-airplane (victory airplane) for List 1 and J-ruby (jewel ruby) and H-carrot (hare carrot) on the transfer list. However, for meaningful stimulus terms, the same encoding of the stimulus is used for both lists: for example, SIT-tiger or FIX-airplane must be relearned on the transfer list as SIT-ruby or FIX-carrot. Since the low-meaningful terms are more variable, they may result in less negative transfer in an A-B, A-C paradigm.

General Transfer

The previous section shows how the specific characteristic of meaningfulness in List 1 can affect the learning of List 2; however, a more subtle transfer process is general transfer in which something nonspecific is transferred from List 1 to the learning of List 2. This topic is introduced in Chapter 6. For example, Bastian (1961) used an A-B, A-B' paradigm in which the response words for List 2 had a related meaning (but were different words) as compared to their counterparts in List 1. In this case, learning of List 2 was quite fast, that is, strong positive transfer was shown. Similarly, an A-B, A-B' paradigm involving positive general transfer would be expected when the response terms in the two lists both came from the same categories. In these cases, apparently, something general as well as specific is transferred from List 1 to List 2.

Practice on similar tasks prior to learning a transfer task also generally improves performance. Thune (1951) has separated out two aspects of this effect. One of these aspects is *warm-up*, a short-term increase in performance within an experimental session. The other is *learning-to-learn*, a

FIGURE 9-13.

Mean number of correct responses as a function of trials and sessions. Results show warm-up and learning-to-learn.

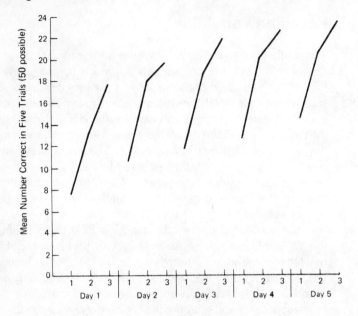

long-term development of a strategy for performance. Thune gave three paired-associate lists (10 pairs) per day for five days with all 15 lists different but equal in difficulty. Results, shown in Figure 9-13, showed an improvement within each day from List 1 to 3 (warm-up) and a general increase across days from day 1 to 5 (learning-to-learn). Harlow's work on learning sets, discussed in Chapter 6, provides another example of learning to learn. Although general transfer may be a more important objective of education, much less is known about it than specific transfer, and future work must incorporate the phenomena of general transfer.

REMEMBERING AND FORGETTING

Previous sections of this chapter have dealt with how humans learn and transfer what they have learned to new situations. Another approach to the problem of human verbal learning is to ask, "How do humans retain and remember what they learn?" Although we can separate encoding, storage, and retrieval, they are interrelated processes. For example, if a subject fails to remember, the reason could be that the material was never learned (encoding), that it was forgotten (storage), or that it was learned and retained but cannot be found (retrieval). The focus of this section will be on the process of storage and retrieval, but as you will see, we cannot give a complete account of one without talking about the others.

FIGURE 9-14.

Median percent of correct recognitions of previously presented pictures as a function of retention interval.

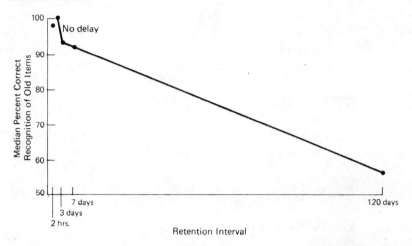

Human beings are capable of remembering great amounts of information over long periods of time (although we also are capable of forgetting great amounts of material). For example, Burt (1932) read passages from Sophocles, in the original Greek, to his 3-month-old son every day until the child was 3 years old; Burt read each passage for three months before switching to a new one. When his son was 8 years old, Burt, without explanation, asked the boy to memorize some of the old passages as well as some equally difficult passages that he had never heard. It took his son 435 repetitions to learn the new passages but only 317 to learn the old—a savings of 27 percent. Several years later, when the boy was 14, there was still evidence of savings, although it had fallen to 9 percent. Burt concluded that memory persists, albeit in diminished strength, for long periods of time even when the material is totally meaningless.

Another demonstration of the power of memory (in this case, the accuracy rather than the persistence) comes from Shepard (1967). Shepard presented his subjects with 612 colored pictures; in a forced choice recognition test, subjects picked the correct picture 97 percent of the time. Shepard's results are given in Figure 9-14. Performance remained high for retention intervals up to 7 days but eventually fell slowly to lower levels by 120 days. In similar experiments using 612 sentences or 540 words, Shepard found that subjects correctly recognized 89 percent of the sentences and 88 percent of the words on an immediate test. One conclusion is that humans can store large quantitites of information.

FIGURE 9-15.

Interference paradigms.

PROACTION

Group	Task 1	Task 2	Task 3
Experimental Group	Learn A	Learn B	Test for B
Control Group	(Irrelevant Activity)	Learn B	Test for B

RETROACTION

Group	Task 1	Task 2	Task 3
Experimental Group	Learn A	Learn B	Test for A
Control Group	Learn A	(Irrelevant Activity)	Test for A

Basic Methods

These demonstrations of retention lead to the obvious question, "How do we remember?" Another, perhaps more pessimistic formulation of the question could be, "Why do we forget?" Two experimental paradigms which have been developed to study this issue are summarized in Figure 9-15.

In the *proactive paradigm*, prior learning influences the remembering of subsequently learned material. For example, the experimental group learns some material (A), then learns other material (B), and then is tested on memory for B. The control group performs some irrelevant activity, learns B, and then is tested on memory for B. If the experimental group remembers more than the control group, this is an example of *proactive facilitation*: prior learning "comes forward" to aid the memory for subsequent material. If the experimental group performs worse than the controls, this is an example of *proactive interference* (PI): prior learning interferes with the memory for new material. An example of proaction could involve studying for an accounting exam (A), then studying for a biology exam (B), and then taking the biology exam. If performance on the exam is better than that of a control group (e.g., view TV, study biology, take biology exam), this is an example of proactive facilitation; but if performance on the exam is better in the control group, this is an example of proactive interference (PI).

In the *retroactive paradigm*, learning subsequent to the original learning affects remembering of the original material. In this case, the experimental group learns some material (A), then learns other material (B), and then is tested on the original material (A): the control group learns A, performs some irrelevant activity, and then tries to remember A. If the experimental group performs better than the controls on remembering A, this is an example of *retroactive facilitation*: subsequent learning "works backwards" to aid in remembering original learning. If the experimental

FIGURE 9-16.

Percent of words recalled as a function of the number of previous lists. Results show proactive interference.

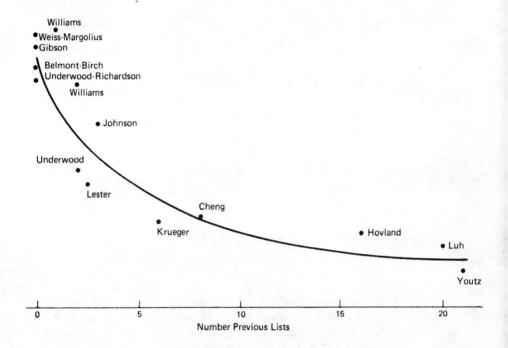

group performs worse than the control, this is an example of *retroactive interference* (RI): subsequent learning hurts memory for original learning. As suggested in Figure 9-15, an example of retroaction could involve the sequence of studying accounting (A), then studying biology (B), and then taking the accounting exam; a control situation would be studying accounting, watching television, then taking the accounting exam. If studying biology aids performance of the accounting exam relative to the control situation, this is an example of retroactive facilitation; however, if studying biology tends to hurt performance, this is an example of retroactive interference (RI).

There are many experimental examples of PI and RI, and much work has been directed at determining the factors that influence the rate and strength of interference. A classic summary of PI research is shown in Figure 9-16 from a paper by Underwood (1957). Each dot represents the percentage of word items recalled after a 24-hour retention interval, as a function of how many similar lists were previously learned. With no prior lists, recall is in the 70 to 80 percent range, but the rate falls to 25 percent for 6 or 8 prior lists.

Another important study of RI was conducted by Melton and Irwin (1940) and is summarized in Figure 9-17. Subjects learned a list to the criterion of one perfect trial, then learned a second list for 5, 10, 20, or 40

FIGURE 9-17.

Absolute retention interval as a function of trials on interpolated list; Melton and Irwin's two-factor theory of interference.

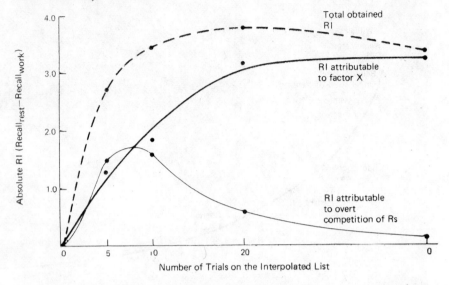

trials, and then relearned the original list. The top line in the figure shows that the greater the number of trials spent on the second task, the more difficult it was to relearn the original list (i.e., more RI), but that RI seems to level off at 20 trials of the interfering task.

Decay Theory

One of the first and most straightforward theories to account for forgetting was the *decay* (or disuse) theory, that is, the idea that memories fade merely with the passing of time. The decay theory is consistent with results, such as Ebbinghaus's forgetting curve, that less is remembered as more time passes since original learning. Further, decay theory predicts that faster presentation rates should result in better recall since there is a shorter retention interval. There is some support for this prediction but only when subjects are not allowed to *rehearse* during the retention interval (Hockey, 1973; Peterson & Peterson, 1959; Brown, 1958). Since decay may be more important for some kinds of memories, it will be discussed more fully in Chapter 10, especially with respect to short-term sensory store and short-term memory.

Interference Theory

The decay theory, however, has not stood up well to challenges from the *interference theory*, largely because of the work discussed above on retroactive and proactive interference. The interference theory states that forgetting appears to occur over time only because new, conflicting information enters memory and interferes with original learning; forgetting depends on the amount of interfering information, not on time. A classic comparison of the decay versus interference theories was performed by Jenkins and Dallenbach (1924). Subjects learned a list of 10 nonsense syllables and then were tested after 1, 2, 4, or 8 hours during which they were either sleeping or awake (i.e., performing their normal daily activities). The decay theory predicts no difference in amount recalled between the sleeping versus the awake subjects since the retention interval is the same (e.g., 8 hours); however, the interference theory predicts that more will be forgotten over 8 waking hours of active behavior than 8 hours of sleep since during wakeful activity, competing memories would be generated. The results clearly supported the interference theory; after 8 hours, the sleeping subjects remember 6 of the 10 syllables but the active subjects remembered 1 out of 10. Experiments of this sort can be criticized if they are not counterbalanced for time of day, but this finding has been replicated under better controlled situations (McGeoch & McDonald, 1931).

Melton and Irwin (1940) proposed a two-factor theory of RI based partly on the experiment discussed earlier and summarized in Figure 9-17. They noted the number of times errors in relearning List 1 occurred due to intrusion from List 2, and summarized these findings in Figure 9-17 as the line labeled "RI attributable to overt competition of Rs." As can be seen, the number of intrusions increased with increasing practice on the interfering list (List 2) up to 5 – 10 trials, but fell sharply with more practice on the interfering list. Apparently, practice on List 2 beyond 10 trials provided a way for the subject to differentiate which items belonged there and which did not. Thus, intrusions could be minimized. Melton and Irwin then subtracted the "competition" line from the "total" RI line to produce a line that represented a second factor which they called "factor X," and which more recently has been called *unlearning*. This analysis led to the conclusion that RI is due to at least two factors: (1) specific responses from List 2 compete with those in List 1; and (2) general unlearning of the unreinforced responses of List 1 occurs.

There has been some evidence to support the unlearning idea proposed by Melton and Irwin. For example, Briggs (1954) used an A-B, A-C paradigm, but after the subjects had learned the second list, they were presented with each stimulus term (A) and asked to give their strongest response, that is, the first word that came to mind (either B or C). This procedure is called *modified free recall* (MFR). The results showed that as the subjects learned the second list, they tended to give the responses from that list (C) more frequently than those for the first list (B). Furthermore, after a 4-minute retention interval, the subjects tended to give the re-

FIGURE 9-18.

Mean number of competing responses recalled as a function of practice on List 2.

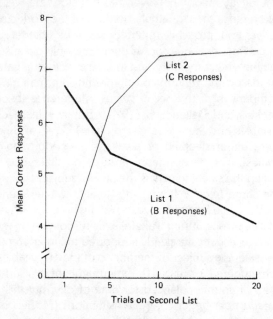

sponses for the second list more frequently than for the first, but as the retention interval increased, more List 1 responses were given until, after 72 hours, more List 1 words were given than List 2. This phenomenon of List 1 responses disappearing is similar to the process of extinction and spontaneous recovery discussed in Chapters 2 and 5.

One problem with the MFR method is that it does not allow us to conclude that List 1 responses are actually "unlearned" or "extinguished" during learning of List 2 since subjects may know *both* responses. To overcome this problem, Barnes and Underwood (1959) developed a modified version of MFR known as MMFR, in which the subjects learned the first paired-associate list (A-B) to criterion, and then learned the second list (A-C) for 1, 5, 10, or 20 trials. They then took a test which required them to give *both* the List 1 and List 2 responses for each stimulus term. Figure 9-18 shows that with increased practice on List 2, more responses from List 2 (C) were recalled and fewer from List 1 (B). Moreover, this procedure has provided only weak evidence for spontaneous recovery of B responses over longer retention intervals (Koppenaal, 1963; Houston, 1966; Ceraso & Henderson, 1965; Postman, Stark, & Henschel, 1969).

The MMFR results are consistent with the unlearning idea that new learning requires extinguishing old conflicting knowledge. However, there is other evidence against one of the predictions of the unlearning hypothesis, namely, that learning a particular new association requires the unlearning of the corresponding old one (Martin, 1971; Greeno, James, & DaPolito, 1971). In a closer analysis of responses in the MMFR task, evidence was found that the probability of unlearning the B response was independent of learning a C response. This *independent retrieval phenomenon* is not consistent with one of the predictions of the unlearning idea, according to Martin (1971, p. 316): "If learning an A-C association entails unlearning the corresponding A-B association, and if the likelihood of recalling C indexes the A-C association strength, then we must expect . . . that recall of B is less likely when C is recalled than when C is not recalled." However, the evidence fails to substantiate this prediction (Martin, 1971; Greeno, James & DaPolito, 1971). A recent review of the two-factor theory of forgetting (Postman & Underwood, 1973) has attempted to reconcile this finding, that better performance on A-C does not correlate with poorer performance on A-B and argues that after over 35 years, the interference theory is still strong.

Context Theory

Several important alternatives or elaborations to the interference theory have emerged since 1940 and one of them involves the idea of *context*. According to this view, RI (or PI) occurs because new learning (List 2) is assimilated into the same cognitive context as the previous list (List 1). Thus, when subjects go to retrieve the information, they have no way to separate the lists. As you may note, this idea is an application of the encoding variability hypothesis to the problem of memory and has some support from studies of the lag effect we discussed earlier.

One typical experiment that provided some information concerning the context theory was performed by Bilodeau and Schlosberg (1951) using an RI paradigm. Subjects learned two lists of words under either identical conditions or different conditions, such as standing for one list versus sitting for the other, learning the lists in different rooms, and so on. More RI was obtained in tests for List 1 with the subjects who learned under identical conditions.

A more compelling series of twenty experiments was summarized by Wickens (1970, 1972) using a "release from PI" technique. On each trial, the procedure was to present three words on a screen, such as, say, SIX, TWO, and NINE, wait 20 seconds, during which time the subjects performed a distractor task to prevent rehearsal, and then ask the subjects to recall the three words. This task was repeated for a total of four trials. For trials 1 through 3, the words were taken from the same category (e.g., numbers), but on trial 4, some subjects were given words in the same category while others were given words in a new category (e.g., BOOK, CHAIR, DOCTOR). As Figure 9-19 shows, recall performance fell across the first three trials, presumably due to the build up of PI. However, on the fourth trial, the control subjects were given a triad from the same category but the experimental subjects were given a triad from a new category. Figure 9-19 shows that the control subjects continued to suffer from a build up of PI but the performance of the experimental subjects zoomed up as if they had been "released from PI." These results were obtained when the

FIGURE 9-19.

Percent correct recall on 4 trials for control and shifted groups. Results show release from proactive interference.

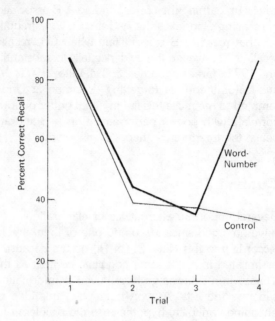

subjects were switched between number-word, taxonomic category, different sense impressions, different connotations, masculine-feminine, different languages (for bilinguals), and many other categories. These results are consistent with the idea that interference can be reduced by encoding within different cognitive contexts.

Retrieval Theory

Another alternative or extension of the interference theory is the idea of retrieval failure, that is, apparent forgetting occurs not because items are no longer stored in memory but rather because the retrieval route to them has been blocked or lost. A common piece of supporting evidence is that recognition performance is generally far better than recall performance. For example, Postman and Stark (1969) replicated the Barnes and Underwood experiment using a recognition test as well as recall. The results were that subjects correctly recognized almost 100 percent of the A-B associations even though they could not recall them. In another study, Tulving and Pearlstone (1966) asked their subjects to memorize lists with four categories totaling 12, 24, or 48 items in each list; recall was better if the category names (e.g., animals, parts of body) were presented during free recall, especially for long lists (see Figure 9-20).

FIGURE 9-20.

Average number of words recalled as a function of list length, with and without cueing.

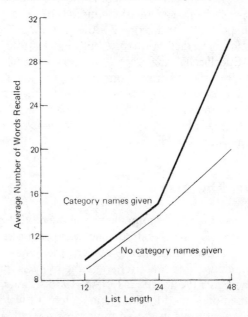

A more striking study of the retrieval process for memorized word lists is provided by Tulving and his associates (Tulving & Thomson, 1973; Tulving & Thomson, 1970; Tulving & Watkins, 1975; Watkins & Tulving, 1975). In a typical experiment, the subjects are instructed to learn a list of 24 target words printed in capital letters. Each target word is preceded by another word printed in lower case letters (e.g., ground COLD; head LIGHT). After learning the list, the subjects are given a free association test with stimulus words that differ from the lower case words in the original list but which often evoke the target words (e.g., hot, dark). The subjects are asked to write as many free associates as they can think of, up to six per word, within 12 minutes; they are then asked to circle any recalled words which were target words from the original list. On the average, the free associations included 17.7 of the 24 target words but only 4.2 or 24 percent were recognized as being on the original list. In a subsequent cued recall test, the subjects were given the 24 lower case words from the original (e.g., ground, head) and asked to write as many of the original 24 target words as they could. On this test, the subjects recalled 15.2 or 63 percent of the original words. Tulving and Thomson (1973, p. 364) concluded that people could recall more words than they could recognize, and thus there was "recognition failure of recallable words."

These results are both puzzling and important because they contradict a more straightforward theory of retrieval, namely, the idea that subjects first generate the to-be-remembered word and then perform a recognition test on it (see Anderson & Bower, 1972). According to this generation-recognition theory of memory retrieval, recall involves recognition *plus* something more. Recall therefore should always result in poorer performance than recognition. There is much evidence for this finding and it is incorporated into several of the models of semantic memory we discussed in Chapter 11 (Anderson & Bower, 1972). Certainly, Tulving's results seem to contradict the theory, but Martin (1975) has suggested a resolution. Specifically, the "light" a subject recalls for "head LIGHT" is psychologically different from the "light" in "dark LIGHT"; since they were encoded within different contexts, they have different meanings. Therefore, although a subject may give "light" as a free association to "head," the subject may not recognize it as belonging to another context such as "dark LIGHT."

Other Theories

Two other theories of forgetting are *motivated forgetting* and *trace change*. The idea of motivated forgetting was proposed by Freud (1914; Sears, 1936) and states that anxiety-evoking memories may be repressed into the unconscious. The trace change theory was proposed by the Gestalt psychologists (Wulf 1922; Koffka, 1935; Kohler, 1929, 1940) and states that memories tend to change in systematic ways, that is, they change in structure, not just in the amount remembered, and they change to fit in with the individual's existing preconceptions. The Freudian notion is an interesting and important one, but it has, unfortunately, not generally led to many testable studies. The Gestalt notion is closely related to the context theory (except that the strict Gestaltists originally held that traces changed towards innately "good" structures); however, research in this area has been subject to flaws and theoretical predictions have been unclear (Baddeley, 1976).

EVALUATION

The study of verbal learning has brought experimental rigor and an agreed-upon set of experimental procedures to the laboratory study of human learning. Within psychology, verbal learning offers one of the strongest and most well-developed set of experimental procedures, and other areas of psychology have borrowed from these basic methods. Thus, the verbal learning area has made a large contribution to the scientific maturity of psychology.

The tradition of the verbal learning approach has been to begin with a set of methods and empirical facts rather than a specific theory; however, this approach has allowed for the testing of many theoretical notions, among them, interference theory, context theory, and others. Chapters 10 and 11 offer further theories of learning and memory.

The major criticism of the verbal learning area has been that it is engaged in studying learning situations which are sterile and trivial, and too distant from actual human learning. In a moment of perhaps overly critical depression, Tulving and Madigan (1970) summarized nearly one hundred years of work on verbal learning as follows: "Tireless investigators compiled endless measures of performance in laboratory tasks which bear little or no relation to the complexities and subtleties of human memory" (as summarized by Postman, 1975, p. 291). In their review of hundreds of papers on verbal learning, Tulving and Madigan rated only 10 percent as "worthwhile" in the sense that they provided useful information about human learning or memory.

The area of verbal learning, however, has experienced a nearly incredible broadening both in its methods and its content. In a much more positive review of the recent history of verbal learning, Postman (1975, p. 294) points out that the "methodological constraints of behaviorism and the frugal tenets of functionalism were eagerly put aside" and that "concepts that had lain dormant because they appeared to lack complete scientific respectability made a spectacular comeback—organization, imagery, attention, consciousness. . . ." Many of these new developments are continued in Chapters 10 and 11 and build on the solid groundwork discussed in this chapter.

SUMMARY

This chapter was concerned with how humans acquire, store, and retrieve verbal information. Several major phenomena were presented, including the various effects of meaningfulness, serial position, spacing, transfer, and forgetting. We explored the basic theories which have been developed to account for each of these phenomena and cited many of the experiments that have been performed to test them. Although there are still many unresolved issues in the study of verbal learning, the work presented in this chapter does show how experimental data can be related to theories.

We began with an example of a typical learning task and then paid tribute to the many contributions made by Ebbinghaus toward establishing the field of verbal learning. We specified how the area of verbal learning may be defined by its use of a standard paradigm (serial, paired-associate, or free recall learning) and of stimuli that are words or nonsense syllables.

In serial learning, the subject is presented with a list of words and asked to recite them in order. In paired-associate learning, the subject is shown pairs of words and asked to recite the correct second word in response to each first (stimulus) word. In free recall learning, the subject is presented with a list of words and asked to recall them in any order.

One of the most important of the variables that affect ease of learning and retention is how meaningful the words are. This has been called the meaningfulness effect. There are several ways to measure (and explain) this effect; among them are: association value, frequency, sequential dependencies, and imagery. Although all are related, there is some current work which suggests that imagery might be the most crucial effect, as suggested by Paivio's dual encoding hypothesis.

Another major finding is the serial position effect—the tendency for words from the beginning and the end of a list to be learned more easily and recalled better than words from the middle. Several theories to account for the phenomenon of the serial position effect include: remote associations, interference, cognitive landmarks, and dual memory. The latter two theories are not mutually exclusive and there is some evidence to support each. The dual memory theory is the basis for the information processing approach to learning and memory we shall discuss in the following chapter.

Another variable that affects learning and retention is practice. An obvious fact is that more is remembered when there is more practice (although there are limits to this). A second, less obvious fact is that spaced practice is sometimes more effective than massed practice in facilitating learning and memory. Three theories to account for this are consolidation, rehearsal, and encoding variability. Since the theories are not mutually exclusive, any ultimate theory might include all three.

This chapter also investigated the phenomenon of transfer: the influence of past learning on new learning. We looked at several transfer paradigms based on learning two different paired-associate lists. Osgood's transfer surface was one early attempt to account for the various transfer effects; two more recent theories are component analysis and encoding variability. Each approach successfully accounts for some of the findings. In addition, we drew distinctions between general and specific transfer, positive and negative transfer, and between warm-up and learning-to-learn.

Finally, we examined forgetting. Theories to account for forgetting include: decay, interference, encoding variability, retrieval, motivated forgetting, and trace change. Retrieval theory, interference, and encoding variability are the theories which seemed to be the most popular explanations and the most consistent with current research findings.

10/ Human Information Processing: General Model

Preview

The information processing approach to human learning and memory
offers a unified framework for discussing complex cognitive processes.
Basically, the idea is that human beings may be thought of as complex
computers and that learning and remembering can thus be thought of as
the processing of information. In this chapter, we can begin with a model
that divides memory into three distinct and different memory stores
(short-term sensory store, short-term memory, and long-term memory),
and several different control processes for transferring information from one
store to the next (attention, rehearsal, encoding). We will explore the
research aimed at understanding how this information processing system
operates. Our strategy here differs from that of the verbal learning chapter
(Chapter 9), which focuses on an agreed-upon set of methodological
paradigms, and from the chapter on concept learning (Chapter 13), which
focuses on an intensive study of one agreed-upon task. The information
processing idea is based on a shared, theoretical framework that may
eventually include all of psychology (Lindsay & Norman, 1977).

INTRODUCTION

Figure 10-1 shows a detailed picture from *Alice in Wonderland* in which Alice is looking up at a grinning Cheshire cat. Haber and Haber (1964; Haber, 1969) asked their subjects, 150 schoolchildren from New Haven, to look at the picture for 30 seconds. The youngsters were instructed to move their eyes all around the picture in order to take in the details, and after the picture was removed, they were asked to continue moving their eyes over the place where the picture had been. Although the task of looking at pictures that are no longer present may sound a bit strange, Haber reported that a small but significant number of children were able to describe the picture in almost perfect detail by referring to an *image* of the picture that persisted for up to 4 minutes. In Haber's study, approximately 8 percent of the children possessed this ability, called *eidetic imagery,** although few adults seem to have it. One explanation (Doob, 1964) is that society requires us to encode information verbally rather than visually, and, as the ability to read and write increases, the use of imagery falls.

Although there is little agreement on what causes eidetic imagery (EI), or even if it really exists, demonstrations like this offer the intriguing idea that other memory systems are possible in contrast to those we suppose to operate in adults. Consider, for a moment, what human learning and memory would be like if it were based entirely on vivid, detailed images—images that do not fade as those of eidetic children do, but rather last indefinitely. One might even consider that such a system could have been operating in preverbal, prehistoric mankind, for example.

The Russian psychologist Luria (1968) provided just such a case study in his little book, *The Mind of a Mnemonist*. The subject is a man called S who had a very peculiar memory system:

> The actual beginning of this account dates back to the 1920s, when I had only recently begun to do work in psychology. It was then that a man came to my laboratory who asked me to test his memory. . . . I gave S a series of words, then numbers, then letters, reading them to him slowly or presenting them in written form. He read or listened attentively and then repeated the material exactly as it was presented. I increased the number of elements in each series giving him as many as 30, 50 or even 70 words or numbers but this too presented no problem for him. . . . He could reproduce a series in reverse order—from end to beginning—just as easily as from start to finish; he could readily tell me which word followed another in the series, or reproduce the word which happened to precede one I'd name. . . . I simply had to admit that the capacity of his memory *had no distinct limits*. . . . He had no difficulty reproducing any lengthy series of words whatever, even though these had originally been presented to him a week, a month, a year or even many years earlier . . . (pp. 7–12).

* Eidetic imagery is different from afterimages: for example, afterimages occur only when one stares at a particular point of a stimulus field and then stares at a particular point in a contrasting field, while EI involves active eye movement; afterimages persist for only a few seconds while EI lasts for up to a few minutes. EI also differs from so-called "photographic memory" in that EI eventually fades; some of the feats of photographic memory are actually due to mnemonic techniques discussed in this chapter.

FIGURE 10-1.

Eidetic imagery.

Experimenter: Do you see something there?

Subject: I see the tree, gray tree with three limbs. I see the cat with stripes around its tail.

E: Can you count those stripes?

S: Yes *(pause)*. There's about 16.

E: You're counting what? Black, white or both?

S: Both.

E: Tell me what else you see.

S: And I can see the flowers on the bottom. There's about three stems, but you can see two pairs of flowers. One on the right has green leaves, red flower on bottom with yellow on top. And I can see the girl with a green dress. She's got blonde hair and a red hair band and there are some leaves in the upper left-hand corner where the tree is.

E: Can you tell me about the roots of the tree?

S: Well, there's two of them going down here *(points)* and there's one that cuts off on the left-hand side of the picture.

E: What is the cat doing with its paws?

S: Well, one of them he's holding out and the other one is on the left.

E: What color is the sky?

S: Can't tell.

E: Can't tell at all?

S: No. I can see the yellowish ground, though.

E: Tell me if any of the parts go away or change at all as I'm talking to you. What color is the girl's dress?

S: Green. It has some white on it.

E: How about her legs and feet?

(The subject looks away from the easel and then back again.)

E: Is the image gone?

S: Yes, except for the tree.

E: Tell me when it goes away.

S: *(pause)* It went away.

S also performed perfectly on many other tasks and seemed to do so by forming an image that was apparently indestructible.

Lest the reader overly admire S's memory, consider also the drawbacks of S's system. Since all new learning evoked clear, detailed, literal images, S had much trouble in reading and found the metaphors of poetry incomprehensible:

If a story was read at a fairly rapid pace, S's face would register confusion and finally utter bewilderment. "No," he would say. "This is too much. Each word calls up images; they collide with one another, and the result is chaos. I can't make anything out of this" (p. 65).

S's memory was also quite specific and apparently did not allow him to categorize or lump things together very well:

S had often complained that he had a poor memory for faces: "They're so changeable," he would say (p. 64).

Finally, S didn't have good control over retrieval of his memory images:

Inasmuch as S's images were particularly vivid and stable, and recurred thousands of times, they soon became the dominant elements in his awareness, uncontrollably coming to the surface whenever he touched upon something that was linked to them in even the most general way (p. 114).

This chapter will explore the way in which incoming information, particularly verbal information, is stored and manipulated by humans. Mr. S and the 150 New Haven schoolchildren suggest some of the unfinished business concerning our understanding of visual memory. Unfortunately, this chapter will not shed much light on these peculiar phenomena, but they are interesting preludes because we will explore the idea that incoming information is held in an exact, short-term sensory store that has some of characteristics of eidetic imagery or of Mr. S's system. Although such phenomena are extreme cases, they may eventually fit into the puzzle of human information processing; certainly they seem curiously relevant to the current contention that the first major step in learning and perception is a short-term sensory store in which information is held in exact and complete form.

INFORMATION PROCESSING FRAMEWORK

The information processing approach to human learning, memory, and cognitive functioning is a relatively new approach—emerging during the 1960s—that is based on the idea that *humans are processors of information*. According to this view, the goal of learning and memory psychologists is to determine the *series of states* that information goes through as it progresses through the information processing system. Another way to express this idea is to say that our goal is to determine the *series of operations* that is performed on information as it progresses through the information processing system.

The information processing approach is based on a human/machine analogy: both humans and computers can learn, remember, and solve problems; the computer accomplishes these feats by performing a series of operations on information that is input; therefore, an analysis of human intellectual performance can also be based on determining the relevant series of information processing operations. In his famous paper, "What

Kind of Computer Is Man?" Hunt (1971) attempted to show the similarities between humans and machines (both have memories, process information, and so on). However, it is also clear that the human/machine analogy is not perfect; for example, humans are alive, they have emotions and motivations, and perhaps are qualitatively different than machines. To the extent that humans are not *solely* processors of information, the information processing approach is limited.

The information processing approach, however, offers a way of providing precision and analysis for speculation about human learning and memory. *Precision* is afforded by developing models (e.g., flow charts, computer programs, knowledge structures) which allow clear predictions: *analysis* is afforded by investigating the (cognitive) locus of various effects (e.g., which components in the model are influenced by which variables). Although the information processing approach is a recent development, it has gained much prominence in the field of human learning and memory. There is no actual date one can cite as the official beginning, but by 1967 there was enough literature for Ulric Neisser to publish his now classic book, *Cognitive Psychology*, and by 1970 there was a need for a journal of the same name.

Although it is still too early to determine the overall effect of the information processing revolution on psychology, two important contributions will be explored in this chapter. The first is the distinction among short-term sensory store, short-term memory, and long-term memory. The second is the distinction between memory structures and memory processes.

This chapter will focus particularly on the first contribution—the general framework of information processing that divides the cognitive system into a series of memory stores, each with specific characteristics and each with its own control processes.

Figure 10-2 shows a typical representation of the general information processing model. The model contains three separate *memory stores*, each with different characteristics. Information from sense receptors is first stored in a sensory memory which can be called *short-term sensory store*, or STSS. STSS has infinite capacity, represents visually presented information as an exact visual image, and loses information by having it decay very rapidly. The next memory store is *short-term memory*, or STM. STM is a limited capacity store, represents information as an auditory echo, and loses information by having it displaced by something else. The last memory store is called *long-term memory*, or LTM. It is like STSS in that its capacity is technically infinite but it is different from the other stores in that information is represented in a meaningful, organized, abstract way, and information is lost because of interference or retrieval failure.

There are also several *control processes* which determine how information flows from one memory store to the next. *Attention* is a control process that determines whether information will be transferred from STSS to STM: if information in the image of STSS is attended to before the image fades away, then some of it can be transferred to STM. Two of the

FIGURE 10-2.

Schematic diagram showing basic information processing system.

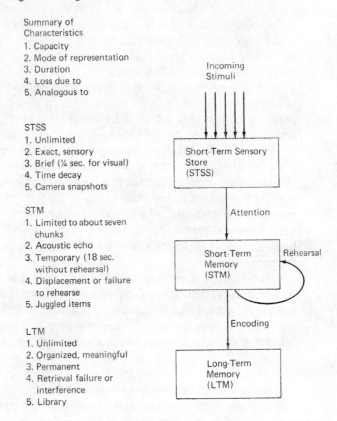

Summary of
Characteristics
1. Capacity
2. Mode of representation
3. Duration
4. Loss due to
5. Analogous to

STSS
1. Unlimited
2. Exact, sensory
3. Brief (¼ sec. for visual)
4. Time decay
5. Camera snapshots

STM
1. Limited to about seven
   chunks
2. Acoustic echo
3. Temporary (18 sec.
   without rehearsal)
4. Displacement or failure
   to rehearse
5. Juggled items

LTM
1. Unlimited
2. Organized, meaningful
3. Permanent
4. Retrieval failure or
   interference
5. Library

basic control processes that operate on information in STM are *rehearsal* and *encoding*. Rehearsal of information in STM keeps the rehearsed items "alive" in STM: however, only a limited number of items can be rehearsed during any time period. Although the nature of the rehearsal process is not well understood, there is some evidence that it resembles an acoustic echo. Encoding items in STM involves trying to integrate them into the existing structures in LTM so they can be retained permanently. Thus, encoding involves transfer of information from STM to LTM while rehearsal involves maintenance of information in STM.

Each of the memory stores, along with its control processes, can be thought of in its own way. For example, STSS can be thought of as a camera which takes exact pictures of the world every .50 second or so, with each new picture completely wiping out previous ones. Information that is attended to gets transferred into STM. Short-term memory can be thought of as a sort of juggling act: only a limited number of items can be juggled in the air at any one time (e.g., about seven). As a new item enters STM from STSS, it may also be tossed up in the air with the other juggled items, thus resulting in the failure to keep one of the other items in the air.

To imagine rehearsal, think of the juggler continuously tossing items in the air at the rate of about seven at a time; if an item is not tossed up (rehearsed) regularly, it will fall out of STM and be lost. Finally, some of the items in STM are selected for integration into LTM. For LTM, think of a giant library with ideas stored on shelves with similar ideas, and referenced in a catalog on the main floor. Loss of information can occur because catalog cards are misplaced, or because ideas on the same shelf combine with one another. One interesting point in this system is that while STSS and LTM are infinitely large (e.g., any amount of information can go into the camera picture or the library), STM is limited (e.g., the juggler can only toss a few items at a time) so that STM is a sort of logjam in the system.

SHORT-TERM SENSORY STORE

One of the earliest theories of human perception and memory was the "copy theory"—the idea dating back to ancient Greek philosophers that exact duplicates of a perceived object are received and imprinted on the mind. This idea had been long since rejected, except for rare cases such as Luria's study or reports of eidetic imagery; however, with the advent of new research instruments and methods, there is now modern evidence that the copy theory might not be *all* wrong after all. During the 1960s, several experiments were performed which indicated that humans possess an exact sensory memory of presented stimuli that acts very much like that supposed by the copy theory; however, unlike the copy theory, the short-term sensory store (or STSS) apparently lasts for quite brief durations, probably less than .5 second for visual material.

One hint of the existence of a sort of "snapshot" mechanism in the acquisition of visual information comes from observations of eye movements during reading (e.g., Kavanagh & Mattingly, 1972). Typically, reading or any visual search involves *fixation* periods, up to 300 msec in duration, when the eyes are still; and *saccades*, when the eyes quickly jerk or jump, lasting approximately 30 msec. The fact that saccades occur roughly three times per second is consistent with the idea of a short-term sensory store (i.e., the idea that we are taking visual snapshots every one-third or one-half second), but certainly more direct testing is required.

Brief and Exact

How can we be certain that humans possess an exact image of incoming visual information, but that the image fades in less than .5 second? One important piece of evidence comes from a classic and ingenious experiment by Sperling (1960). Sperling presented an array of 3 rows of 4 letters each for 50 msec* using a tachistoscope (as shown in Figure 10-3). Then the screen went blank for some retention period ranging from 0 to 1

---

*Msec means millisecond or 1/1000 of a second; 50 msec = 50/1000 or 1/20 sec

FIGURE 10-3.

Schematic diagram showing standard three-channel tachistoscope. Three stimuli fields (A, B, C) may be presented to the subject. Each channel can be precisely controlled for length of presentation.

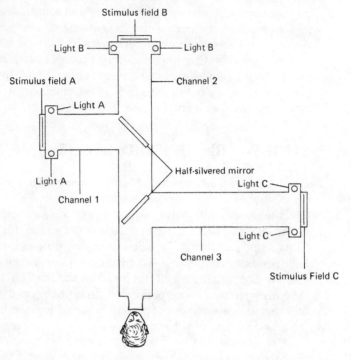

second. If the subjects were then asked to recall the 12 letters, they averaged 4.5 letters correct. The retention period had no apparent effect: 4.5 letters were recalled if there was no delay or 1 second or any delay in between. The number of presented letters had no apparent effect either: if 3 or 4 letters were presented, the subjects remembered all of them, but for 5 or more presented letters, the subjects recalled only about 4.5. This finding was not new and there is much replicatory support for the idea that "memory span" is limited to about 5 or 6 or 7 units, depending on the material (Miller, 1956).

Sperling, however, decided to go beyond this finding and ask whether there is any point during the processing of incoming information at which the subject has a total, exact memory representation for the presented information. In order to help provide some information on this question, he used a "partial report procedure" instead of the "whole report procedure" described above. In the partial report procedure, the subjects see the array for 50 msec, wait a particular retention interval, and then a tone is sounded to indicate which of the three rows should be recalled. It is important to note that the subjects do not know in advance which row they will be asked to recall. The results are given in Figure 10-4. The subjects performed quite well on tests when there was no retention interval, indicat-

FIGURE 10-4.

Sperling's experiments on memory for briefly presented alpha-numeric arrays. Top: Average number of items recalled for various array sizes (0 retention interval). Bottom: Proportion recalled for various retention intervals (3 × 4 array) under whole and partial report conditions.

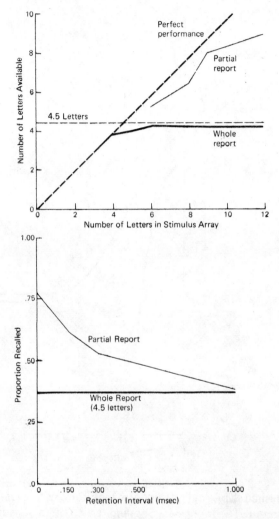

ing they must have known far more than just 4.5 letters; however, when the interval was extended beyond about .25 to .50 second, performance leveled off at about 1.5 per row (or 4.5 out of 12) as with the whole report procedure.

These results were surprising because they suggested that a human subject has available in memory an exact copy of the array that fades within .25 to .50 second. If the subject is asked to search the copy before it fades, memory is quite good; but if the retention interval is long or if the subject is asked to recall all the letters, the image fades before the subject is

FIGURE 10-5.

Proportion correct on recall test for varying retention intervals (2 × 8 array).

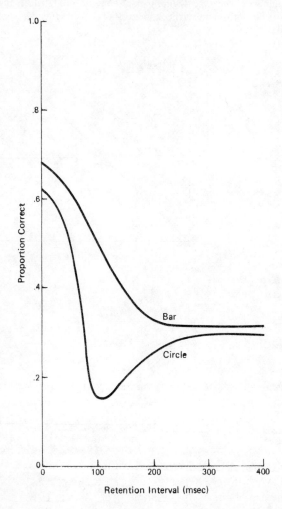

Retention Interval (msec)

finished. This finding suggests that humans possess a short-term sensory store (STSS)—or, as Sperling called it, a "visual information store" (VIS)—that contains an exact but rapidly fading copy.

In a similar study, Averbach and Coriell (1961) presented an 8 × 2 array of letters for 50 msec, followed by a white field (for 0 to .5 second), then a marker for 50 msec indicating the position of the to-be-recalled letter. The marker was either a circle around the position that the letter had occupied or a bar over the position of the letter. The results are shown in Figure 10-5. For the circle and the bar, performance was high for immediate recall, but for retention intervals longer than .25 second, performance leveled off to about an average of 4.5 to 5 correct (out of 16) as in Sperling's study. A new piece of information was that for intermediate

FIGURE 10-6.

Neisser's visual search task.

Find the letter Z in this list.	Find the letter Z in this list.
ODUGQR	IVMXEW
QCDUGO	EWVMIX
CQOGRD	EXWMVI
QUGCDR	IXEMWV
URDGQO	VXWEMI
GRUQDO	MXVEWI
DUZGRO	XVWMEI
UCGROD	MWXVIE
DQRCGU	VIMEXW
QDOCGU	EXVWIM
CGUROQ	VWMIEX
OCDURQ	VMWIEX
UOCGQD	XVWMEI
RGQCOU	WXVEMI
GRUDQO	XMEWIV
GODUCQ	MXIVEW
QCURDO	VEWMIX
DUCOQG	EMVXWI
CGRDQU	IVWMEX
UDRCOQ	IEVMWX
GQCORU	WVZMXE
GOQUCD	XEMIWV
GDQUOC	WXIMEV
URDCGO	EMWIVX
GODRQC	IVEMXW

retention intervals (e.g., .1 second), the circle marker resulted in very low recall performance while the bar marker did not. One explanation is that the circle "masked" the to-be-remembered letter by essentially erasing it and taking its place; the process is called *backward masking* because the circle followed the letter. The bar, apparently, was far enough away from the location of the letters that it did not serve as a mask. These results suggest that if the marker comes immediately, it is integrated into the image, but if it comes in between it can serve as a mask (for a review of masking literature, see Breitmeyer & Ganz, 1976). Masking, then, may be another source of loss of information from STSS.

There have been many further replications of Sperling's finding since 1960 (e.g., see Haber, 1968, 1969; Neisser, 1967). Most of the work has continued to use visual stimuli, although there is now an increasing literature on "auditory short-term sensory store" which may persist up to 4 seconds (Darwin, Turvey, & Crowder, 1972). A very simplified way of thinking about visual short-term sensory store, as we said earlier, is to think of a camera which takes snapshots of the world every .50 second, with each new snapshot erasing the preceding one. If the subject does not pay attention to some of the information in the snapshot, it is forever lost (unless it is reentered into STSS); if attention is paid to some of the information, that information is transferred to the next memory store— short-term memory (STM).

Physical

This view suggests that STSS contains only raw, unanalyzed images devoid of any meaning or relation to past experience. If STSS is based entirely on raw physical characteristics, then the subjects should be unable to pick out specific letters, or types of letters, without having to closely inspect each character in the image. Sperling (1960) tested this idea by presenting a 2 × 4 array containing four letters and four digits such as:

F 6 Y 9
7 G L 4

The whole report procedure and two partial report procedures were used. One partial report procedure simply asked the subject to recite either the first or second row; the other partial report procedure asked the subjects to recite either the digits or the letters. Results indicated that the "digit-letter" partial report group performed no better than the whole report group although the "row" partial report group showed the usual advantage, that is, they performed better than the "whole report group." Apparently, search for letters or digits in STSS required subjects to investigate each character individually as would be expected if STSS contained only unanalyzed, raw stimuli. If STSS contained organized, analyzed information, then the subjects should be able to quickly pick out digits versus letters.

PROCESSING IN STSS

Visual Scanning

Sperling's experiments lead to a slightly different question, namely, how is information searched and processed in STSS? Some information on this question was provided by a series of "visual scanning" experiments by Neisser (1963, 1964, 1967) and summarized by Egeth (1967). In a typical experiment, subjects were given an array of letters, usually printed on a sheet of paper, and asked to find a specific target letter. For example, in Figure 10-6, the task is to find the letter Z in each array. One important finding was that subjects could find the letter Z faster if it was embedded in an array of curved letters, as on the left, than if it was embedded in an array of straight letters, as on the right. Similarly, curved letters, like C, were easier to find if they were in an array of straight letters.

There are two basic theories to account for these "pattern recognitions." *Template matching* is the idea that subjects compare a mental template for the target letter against each letter in the array until there is a direct match. The other theory, *feature detection*, is the idea that subjects detect features, one at a time, from each letter in the array and if any feature is inconsistent with the target letter, that letter is rejected without further analysis.

The results of Neisser's experiments more clearly favor the feature detection theory. For example, the results are inconsistent with a prediction

FIGURE 10-7.

A flowchart showing a feature detection process for finding the letter Z.

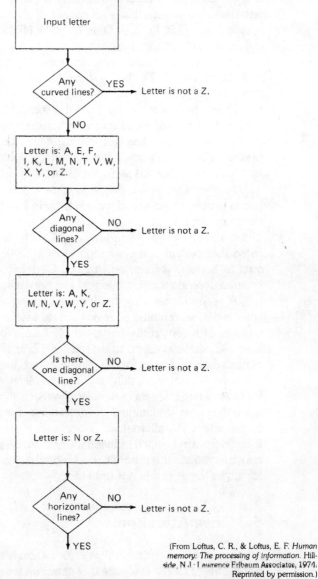

```
        ┌─────────────────┐
        │   Input letter  │
        └─────────────────┘
                 │
                 ▼
              ╱Any╲          YES
            ╱curved╲ ──────────────► Letter is not a Z.
            ╲lines?╱
              ╲  ╱
              │ NO
              ▼
        ┌─────────────────┐
        │ Letter is: A, E, F, │
        │ I, K, L, M, N, T, V, W, │
        │ X, Y, or Z.     │
        └─────────────────┘
                 │
                 ▼
              ╱Any╲          NO
          ╱diagonal╲ ──────────────► Letter is not a Z.
           ╲lines? ╱
              ╲  ╱
              │ YES
              ▼
        ┌─────────────────┐
        │ Letter is: A, K, │
        │ M, N, V, W, Y, or Z. │
        └─────────────────┘
                 │
                 ▼
            ╱Is there╲       NO
         ╱one diagonal╲ ─────────────► Letter is not a Z.
           ╲  line? ╱
              ╲  ╱
              │ YES
              ▼
        ┌─────────────────┐
        │ Letter is: N or Z. │
        └─────────────────┘
                 │
                 ▼
              ╱Any╲          NO
         ╱horizontal╲ ──────────────► Letter is not a Z.
           ╲lines? ╱
              ╲  ╱
              │ YES
```

(From Loftus, C. R., & Loftus, E. F. *Human memory: The processing of information.* Hillside, N.J.: Lawrence Erlbaum Associates, 1974. Reprinted by permission.)

of the template theory that overall time-to-find-the-target should depend on the number of letters in the array regardless of their particular characteristics. However, the results are consistent with a prediction of the feature detection theory that less time should be required if array letters can be rejected on the basis of processing only one feature rather than many.

An example of a feature detection process* for the letter Z is given in

*Boxes represent processes (things to do) and diamonds represent decisions.

Figure 10-7 (Loftus & Loftus, 1976), although there are other more general models (Selfridge, 1959). In the Loftus and Loftus system, if a subject is given an array of letters and asked to circle the Zs, the first step for any letter is to make sure it has no curves. If all the non-Zs in the array have curves (e.g., C, B, D, G, J, O, P, Q, R, S, U) then the subject needs to use only one decision step for each letter: Is it curved or not? However, if the array contains some non-Zs that are curved and some that are straight (e.g., E, F, B, H, I, L, J, T), then the subject must apply two decisions to each letter: Is it a curved letter? And does it have a diagonal line? If all the 25 non-Zs are part of the array, then the subject has to process even deeper for many of the letters, asking whether each is curvy, has diagonals, how many diagonals, or has horizontals. Thus, according to this view, supported by Neisser's work, letter scanning involves a series of feature detection tests, with subjects stopping as soon as they can make a decision.

Further support for the feature detection theory comes from experiments which recorded electrical activity in individual neurons in the visual cortex of cats and frogs as visual patterns were presented (Hubel & Weisel, 1959, 1962; Lettvin, Maturana, McCulloch, & Pitts, 1959). Results indicated that certain neurons respond *only* to vertical lines, some respond *only* to horizontal lines, and so on. Certainly, more work is required in order to describe the physiological location of the feature detection system.

A second interesting finding concerning visual scanning for a target letter is that search time does not increase when there is an increase in the number of letters in the target set (Neisser, Novick, & Lazar, 1963). For example, subjects asked to search for "Z or K" found this task no more difficult than searching for "Z" alone; in fact, increasing the target set up to 10 letters did not affect difficulty. This result suggests that subjects can look for several target letters in *parallel*; that is, as they inspect each letter in the array they can simultaneously determine if it fits the criteria for several target letters. An alternative theory is that processing is *serial* with each letter in the array tested individually and successively against each possible target; however, this theory's prediction that longer search time is required for larger target sets is not upheld.

Selective Attention

Another question concerns how information is transferred from STSS into STM. There is some evidence that *attention* is essential for this transfer. For example, Cherry (1953) used a *dichotic listening* experiment in which subjects wore earphones and received different messages in each ear. They were asked to pay attention to only one channel, e.g., the right ear, and to *shadow* that message—that is, to repeat it aloud as it was received. One important result was that the subjects had almost no memory for what had happened in the unattended channel; they were aware of only the grossest physical characteristics of the unattended message, such as whether it was a human voice or a machine sound, and whether it changed from male to female voice, but they knew nothing about what the message said, or even whether or not it was in a foreign language. This result also is consistent with the idea that STSS, even for auditory information, is based on raw, unanalyzed stimuli. In a similar experiment, Moray (1959) asked subjects to shadow a message in one channel while a short word list was repeated over and over in the unattended channel. Again, subjects had no memory for the unattended channel and were unable to recognize a word that had been constantly repeated to the unattended ear.

Findings such as these have been called the *cocktail party phenomenon*—the ability to follow one message and ignore the others. One of the first theories to explain this phenomenon was Broadbent's (1958) "filter model." Basically, the idea is that irrelevant incoming perceptual information is filtered out at the sensory level before it is ever analyzed for meaning; the information processing system is presumed to involve a single channel, limited-capacity receiver so that one attended message may be processed at a time with all others receiving almost no processing. Information that gets through the filter goes from STSS to STM; otherwise it is lost. This model is consistent with some of the results of Cherry and Moray, but it is clearly at loss to explain a related "cocktail party phenomenon"—the fact that subjects *do notice* important words (such as their own names) from the "unattended channel" (Treisman, 1961). Broadbent's "filter model" has another important flaw: How can subjects reject the "irrelevant" information without first subjecting it to some analysis? For example, if a selected message shifts from ear to ear with the unselected message simultaneously shifting to the complementary ear, the subject can follow the message; this suggests that the subject must be analyzing to some extent the "meaning" of information coming in over the unselected channel (Gray & Wedderburn, 1960).

Apparently, attentional processes must rely partly on past experience stored in long-term memory. There are two major theories which add deeper analyses to Broadbent's theory. Treisman's (1960, 1964, 1969) *"early" selection model* is based on the idea that a series of analyses are performed going on as far down as needed, beginning with low level sensory analysis (as suggested by Broadbent), then an analysis of syllable patterns and sounds, then words, then grammar and meaning. Deutsch and Deutsch's (1963) *"late" selection model* is based on the idea that all sensory inputs excite their representations in long-term memory and that analyses of prior items establishes a set of pertinent items; new sensory items that are also pertinent are selected for further analysis.

Both Treisman's theory and the Deutschs' theory allow for much more processing at the "attention" level but they differ in certain predictions. For example, Treisman's theory predicts that the more similar the information in the unattended channel is to the selected messages, the more difficult it will be to attend to the selected channel. This is so because the subject must pay more attention, that is, go through more levels of analysis to the nonselected message in order to distinguish it from the selected message if the two messages are more similar. The results support this prediction: making the unselected message similar to the selected message in terms of voice (male or female), language, and the nature of the material all increased the difficulty of shadowing the selected message (Treisman, 1964).

Another positive test of Treisman's theory comes from a study in which subjects were asked to shadow a message in a dichotic listening situation, but also to press a button whenever they heard certain "target" words. According to Treisman, the difficulty should be higher if the target word occurs in the unattended channel since it will not be processed in as much depth. Again, the results supported this prediction (Treisman & Geffen, 1967).

However, there is also evidence more consistent with the Deutschs' theory that all inputs receive some processing on the "memory representation" level before decisions are made about what to attend to. For example, Von Wright, Anderson, and Stenman (1975) conditioned subjects to make an emotional reaction as measured by galvanic skin resistance (GSR) changes to certain words by shocking them immediately after such words were presented. Later, in a dichotic listening experiment in which no shocks were ever administered, subjects exhibited higher GSRs for "fear" words and to a lesser extent for their synonyms, even when these words occurred in the nonattended channel. Apparently, the meaning of these words was being analyzed at some level.

These conflicting results are typical of the problems psychologists have experienced in trying to understand the control process that has been called "attention." In addition, Moray (1970) presented data that are clearly inconsistent with both theories! The dilemma is something like this: to decide on whether to reject or select incoming information for further analysis, humans must analyze the information fairly deeply, but the whole purpose of attention is to limit the need for analyses and to use the very limited processing capacity to full advantage. In summarizing this line of research, Norman (1976, p. 37) suggested that although "attention is at the heart of the organism's activity in interpreting, understanding, and reacting to information," it may be more advantageous for psychology to "postpone the final description of the attention mechanism" until there is a better understanding of the other components in the information processing system (e.g., short-term memory and long-term memory).

SHORT-TERM MEMORY

Unlike Luria's Mr. S, or even the eidetic imagery of some children, adults normally do not seem to have access to a long-term sensory store. What happens to information that enters the cognitive system through STSS and is transferred to the next store (STM)? There is some evidence that the information is changed in several ways. First, information may be changed to *auditory modality*: letters or words presented visually may be stored by sound rather than image in STM. Second, information may be *recoded* slightly but still retain its basically nonmeaningful form (e.g., C A T D O G may be stored as "CAT," "DOG"). There are also two apparent peculiarities of the STM. The memory store is *limited in capacity*: only a limited number of pieces of information can be stored at any one time in STM. The memory store requires *rehearsal*: items in STM must be periodically rehearsed or they will fade away.

Limited Capacity

The evidence for a limited capacity STM is now quite large, but some of the most important studies will be pointed out in this section. In 1956, Miller published a now classic paper entitled, "The Magic Number Seven Plus or Minus Two: Some Limits on Our Capacity for Processing Information." In this paper, Miller convincingly summarized data that show that humans can actively (consciously) "think about" approximately only seven things at a time. For example, consider some of the pieces of evidence that Miller cited to suggest that human consciousness is of limited capacity. Listeners can easily learn to label two or three or four tones (or levels of loudness), but make many confusions with five or more (Pollack, 1952; Garner, 1953); this is called *span of absolute judgment*. Viewers can accurately tell how many dots are flashed for .2 second up to five or six dots, but must use a process of "estimating" for dot patterns of more than six (Kaufman, Lord, Reese, & Volkman, 1949); this is called *span of attention*. Finally, listeners can recall about six or seven items from a list of words, letters, or digits that is read at a fast, constant rate (Hayes, 1952; Pollack, 1953; Cavanagh, 1972); this is called the *span of immediate memory*.

Miller suggested that humans can actively think about seven *chunks* of information at any one time. Memory is not limited to only seven words or letters, however, because humans can learn to *recode* smaller units into larger chunks. Theoretically, there is no limit to the size of a chunk although for most unpracticed subjects, a word or single letter may serve as one chunk. Figure 10-8 shows how a string of digits or letters can be recoded into a smaller set of chunks. The chunking process in STM can be seen as a technological advance that allows humans to handle more information at one time. Apparently, to some extent, improvements in chunking can be taught.

Rehearsal

Miller's paper provided evidence that STM is limited. What evidence is there that it fades without rehearsal? Two experiments provided striking information on this question. First, Brown (1958) found that a pair of

FIGURE 10-8.

System for recoding into larger chunks.

A Binary Sequence

Original Sequence	1 0 1 0 0 0 1 0 0 1 1 1 0 0 1 1 1 0 0 1

Chunking by Twos	(10)	(10)	(00)	(10)	(01)	(11)	(00)	(11)	(10)	(01)
New, Recoded Sequence	2	2	0	2	1	3	0	3	2	1

Chunking by Fours	(1010)	(0010)	(0111)	(0011)	(1001)
New, Recoded Sequence	10	2	7	3	9

A Letter Sequence

Original Sequence	D E P W E L B O T R O G D A R T E R

Chunking by Threes	DEP	WEL	BOT	ROG	DAR	TER
New, Recoded Sequence	DEeP	WELl	BOTtom	fROG	DARk	waTER

Chunking by Sixes	DEPWEL	BOTROG	DARTER
New Recoded Sequence	It was a deep well.	At the bottom lived a frog.	It was dark and full of water.

consonants was poorly recalled after a 5-second interval if no rehearsal was allowed. In a larger study, Peterson and Peterson (1959) read a three-letter trigram (such as CHJ), followed by a retention interval ranging from 0 to 18 seconds, and then asked the subject to recall the trigram. To prevent rehearsal during the retention interval, Peterson and Peterson asked their subjects to count backwards by threes from some large number that was given with the trigram. For example, a subject who was given "CHJ 412" would immediately count, "412, 409, 406, 403, 400, 397 . . . " until asked to recall the trigram. Results, as shown in Figure 10-9, indicate that recall was nearly 100 percent correct for immediate tests but fell to below 20 percent correct after only 18 seconds!

Similar results, also shown in Figure 10-9, were obtained by Murdock (1961) using three words instead of three letters. These results were taken as evidence that material in STM must be actively rehearsed on a regular basis or it will fade; apparently, the limited capacity of STM is observed because the *rehearsal* process is limited.

This interpretation of the results of Peterson and Peterson, and of Brown, have not gone unchallenged. One particularly interesting piece of evidence is that if just *one* word or one letter is presented, it is still recalled quite well after 18 seconds (Murdock, 1961). It has been suggested that a

FIGURE 10-9.

Proportion correct recall when rehearsal is prevented for various retention intervals and types of stimuli.

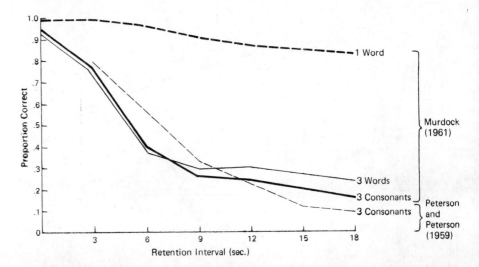

single letter or word is remembered, perhaps, because it can be transferred immediately into LTM.

A more serious problem for the "spare-the-rehearsal-and-lose-the-memory" idea comes from a replication study by Keppel and Underwood (1962) which used a method nearly identical to that of the Petersons. The overall data appeared to be similar to that obtained by the Petersons; however, when the data are plotted by trial, the curves look very different (see Figure 10-10). For example, on the first trial there is good recall at each retention interval; for the second trial trigrams, the recall is still fair even at 18 seconds; for trials beyond the third, however, the performance is similar to that obtained by Peterson and Peterson. Apparently, proactive interference (as discussed in Chapter 9) has some influence on what happens in STM. Similarly, Wickens' evidence for "release from proactive interference" described in Chapter 9 provides further evidence that something more than STM is involved. In his study, semantic categories (presumably stored in LTM) affected performance on an STM task. One hypothesis is that LTM and STM are not as neatly separable as indicated in the general model (Figure 10-2) but rather LTM sometimes affects the processes that occur in STM.

Acoustic

Miller suggested that STM is limited; the Petersons suggested that STM requires rehearsal; there is also evidence for the idea that STM involves a translation into acoustic (or auditory) storage modes. For example, Conrad

FIGURE 10-10.

Proportion correct responses as a function of retention intervals for the first, second, and third trials.

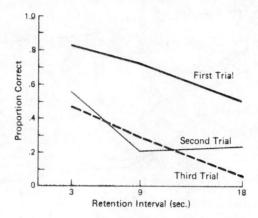

(1964) presented a set of letters visually to subjects and asked for total recall. An analysis of the resulting errors revealed that the subjects tended to make errors based on the sounds of the letters rather than on their physical appearance, that is, the subjects might recall V when T was the presented letter, or S instead of X. Apparently, although STSS may be a visual image for visually presented letters, STM can also be thought of as an auditory echo that acoustically rehearses the letters until they are selected for storage in LTM or replaced by new incoming letters attended to from STSS.

PROCESSING INFORMATION IN SHORT-TERM MEMORY AND LONG-TERM MEMORY

How is information searched in short-term memory? In order to help provide information on this question, Sternberg (1966, 1969, 1975) presented a target set of digits visually to subjects, then presented one digit as a probe. The subjects were asked to press a button labeled Yes if the probe matched one of the digits in the target and one marked No if it did not. Sternberg varied the size of the memory set from 1 to 6 digits. Longer reaction time (RT) would indicate that more cognitive processing by subjects is required to answer questions. Figure 10-11 shows that response time increased directly with set size. In fact, the data were so consistent and predictable it could be seen that adding one digit to the memory set added a constant 38 msec to RT. This finding indicated that memory search in STM is *serial*, where each letter is inspected individually, rather than *parallel*, where all the letters are inspected simultaneously. Another interesting

FIGURE 10-11.

Reaction times for various memory set sizes in Sternberg's memory search task.

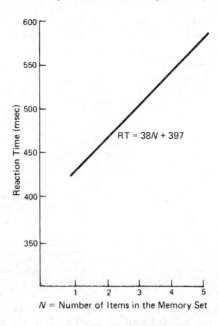

N = Number of Items in the Memory Set

result was that for each set size, RT to answer Yes when the answer was yes was the same as RT to answer No when the answer was no. In other words, it appeared that the subjects searched all the letters in the target set regardless of whether they had already found a match. This finding suggests that the subject inspects all the letters in the memory set before making a decision (this is called an *exhaustive search*) rather than stopping the search as soon as the match is found (called *self-terminating search*).

Cavanagh (1972, p. 526) has summarized data from forty-five studies on two topics: (1) "processing rate," as in Sternberg's study, in which a target set of items is given and the subject must then tell whether one of them matches a probe, and (2) "memory span," as it is discussed by Miller, in which the span is measured as the number of items in the longest list a subject can recall in order without error immediately after presentation. Figure 10-12 shows the average processing time per item and the average memory span for digits, letters, words, nonsense syllables, and other stimuli. As the figure shows, in a Sternberg task digits can be processed faster than letters, letters faster than words, and words faster than nonsense syllables; similarly, the greatest memory span is for digits, then letters, then words, and the shortest is for nonsense syllables. One explanation for the differences among different types of stimuli is that digits and letters can be *chunked* more easily than nonsense syllables. A striking finding is that memory span—which hovers around Miller's magic number seven plus or minus two—seems to be equal to how many items can be processed in .25

FIGURE 10-12.

Processing time as a function of memory span for various types of stimuli.

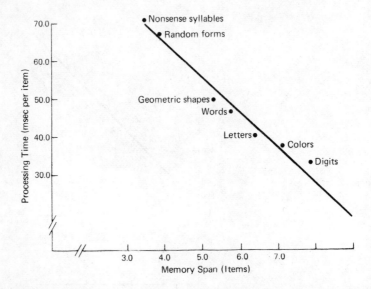

second. For example, at a rate of 33.4 msec per item, it requires 257 msec to process 7.7 digits; at a rate of 73.0 msec per item, it would require 248 msec to process 3.4 nonsense syllables. Thus an important hypothesis for future work is that the breadth of STM depends on how many items can be processed (or rehearsed) in 250 msec.

Shulman (1971) presented a target set of 10 words, then a signal similar to Sternberg's, and then a probe word. The signal called for the subject to respond Yes for either an identical probe, a probe with the same sound, or a probe with the same meaning. The presented probe words were either identical, synonymous, homophonous, or unrelated to one of the targets. The RT to answer correctly were as follows: to judge if a probe was identical to a target—472 msec; to judge if a probe was a homophone for a target—617 msec; to judge if a probe was a synonym for a target— 905 msec. In other words, the more similar the probe and target were, the faster the RT. Apparently, there are various depths of processing in STM, and it seems that information from LTM (such as meanings) can be readily used to process in STM.

Posner and his associates (Posner, 1969; Posner & Mitchell, 1967; Posner, 1970; Posner & Boies, 1971) have conducted a number of studies of levels of processing for letter pairs. For example, subjects were given letter pairs such as AA or Aa or AB and asked to respond "same" or "different" by pressing appropriate keys. When the subjects were told to base their judgments on physical characteristics alone (e.g., AA = yes; Aa = no), the RTs were faster than when they were told to base their judgment on names (e.g., AA = yes; Aa = yes; AB = no). RTs to judge if the letter pairs were both vowels or both consonants were longest of all. Typical RT results reported by Posner and Mitchell, on immediate tests, were: to say "same" for physical matches, approximately 525 msec; for "name" matches, approximately 575 msec; and for vowel-consonant matches, approximately 675 msec. Again, apparently subjects can deal with different "levels of processing" even when some information from LTM seems to be required (Craik & Lockhart, 1972).

The kind of work cited in this section, as well as work in problem solving, has moved some researchers to propose a fourth memory store—"working memory" or WM (Feigenbaum, 1970; Greeno, 1974). Working memory is a sort of "scratch pad" storage, sharing with STM the characteristic of limited capacity and in which information from STM and LTM is combined and manipulated; information may be transferred to and from it and STM or LTM. The processing required to make the judgments discussed in the tasks in this section occur in WM since both STM and LTM are involved. Although WM is not shown in Figure 10-2, it is an important concept in theories of human problem solving and complex human learning.

LONG-TERM MEMORY

According to the general model summarized in Figure 10-2, LTM is the permanent repository for newly acquired knowledge. Determining the characteristics of LTM, including how information is acquired, stored, and forgotten, was a major goal of the verbal learning literature briefly outlined in the previous chapter. In the information processing context, the characteristics of LTM are quite different from either STSS or STM: information in LTM is *organized* rather than kept in its original form, it is represented by *meaning* rather than physical or acoustic characteristics, it is *assimilated* to existing knowledge rather than stored individually, and information is "lost" due to *retrieval failure* rather than decay or limited capacity. Let us consider some of the evidence for each of these claims; the evidence cited below will come mainly from studies involving learning and memory of words while evidence from work involving sentences and whole passages will be presented in the following chapters.

Organization

One of the most cited series of investigations concerning the organization of LTM was conducted by Bousfield and his associates (Bousfield, 1953; Bousfield & Cohen, 1953; Bousfield, Cohen, & Whitmarsh, 1956). In a typical experiment, Bousfield read a list of 60 nouns to subjects at a constant rate, and then asked for free recall of the list. The list contained 15 words from each of four categories, e.g., animals, names, professions, vegetables. The presented list was scrambled: baker, wildcat, Howard, radish, Otto, chipmunk, and so on. The free recall performance of subjects, however, indicated a tendency to organize the lists by categories; for example, the subject might recite several of the animal words, then several

FIGURE 10-13.

Logical and random hierarchies for word lists.

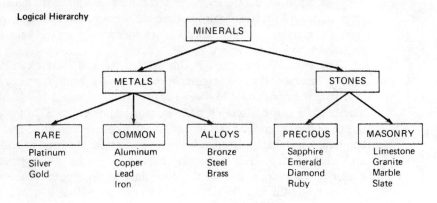

Logical Hierarchy

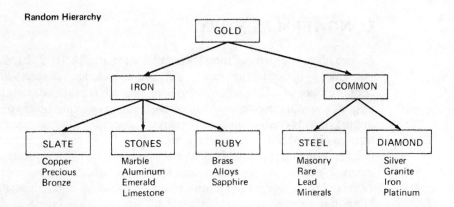

Random Hierarchy

vegetable words, and so on. Bousfield called this phenomenon "cluster-ing" in free recall—the tendency of subjects to output words by category even though the input order was scrambled. Clustering suggests that memory—at least LTM—is organized, and that as information is entered into LTM, storage is based on meaning.

Bousfield's experiments have been criticized on the grounds that the organization was artificially determined by the experimenter rather than by the subject. To help overcome this criticism, Tulving (1962) used a "multiple-trial free-recall procedure." A list of 16 *unrelated* words was presented at a rate of one word per second with a 90-second free recall period; this procedure was continued for a total of 16 trials with the same words presented in a different order on each trial. Tulving measured the organization of the output words that subjects gave on each trial and noted that although the input order was varied on each trial, the output order tended to be similar from trial to trial. For example, the subjects tended to produce the same clusters of words together on each trial. Tulving referred to this phenomenon as "subjective organization," since each subject clustered in his or her own, consistent way.

The clustering and subjective organization experiments suggest that recall is organized, and there is complementary evidence that learning is also influenced by organization. For example, Bower, Clark, Lesgold, and Winzenz (1969) asked their subjects to learn 26 words that were grouped meaningfully into a hierarchy (as in Figure 10-13) or grouped randomly into the positions in the same hierarchy. Following learning, the subjects were given a recognition test. The results indicated that the meaningful hierarchy group correctly recognized 84 percent of the original words versus only 60 percent for the subjects given the nonsense hierarchy; further, there was no difference between the groups in frequency of falsely "recognizing" a word that had not been on the list. Bower et al. concluded that organization had its main effect on how many words were learned rather than on retrieving words from memory.

In an often-cited series of studies, Mandler (1967, 1968; Mandler & Pearlstone, 1966) asked subjects to sort 52 to 100 unrelated words into from two to seven categories in any way they chose. When the subjects were later asked to recall the words, more words were remembered by subjects who had used many categories, at the rate of approximately five words per category, as opposed to those who used only a few categories. Dallett (1964) obtained similar increases in recall performance by increasing the number of categories in word lists up to six categories; however, adding more than six categories decreased performance. Similarly, Tulving and Pearlstone (1966) found that subjects tended to recall only about six or seven categories. Thus, increasing the number of categories beyond six or seven would tend to lower performance. Apparently, as suggested by Miller's magic number seven plus or minus two, having about six or seven separate categories helps subjects store more words; however, when more than six or seven categories are involved, a hierarchy might be more useful.

Using less meaningful material, Johnson (1970) also investigated the effects of organization on learning. Johnson asked subjects to learn paired-associate lists that contained a digit as the stimulus term and a set of seven letters as the response. The letters were grouped in different ways for different subjects; for example, 1 - SBJ FQLZ, or 1 - SB JFQ LZ. In recall tests, the subjects tended to make errors at transition points between letter groupings; in other words, errors occurred most often for the first letter of a chunk, but if the first letter was correctly recalled, the other letters in the chunk were also likely to be recalled. Apparently, the organization of the presented material heavily influences the structure of long-term memory when information is not meaningful.

There has been a great deal of other work on the organization of memory (see Tulving & Donaldson, 1972; Cofer, 1976; Bower, 1970); this work indicates that a major emerging theme in the field of human learning is a precise model of the structure of human memory. This direction is dealt with in Chapter 11.

Meaning

There is also a large literature dedicated to uncovering how meaning is abstracted from information stored in memory. (Some of this work will also be discussed in the next chapter on linguistic structures and semantic memory.)

As an example of the idea that LTM is based on meaning rather than physical or acoustic characteristics, let's consider an experiment by Underwood (1965). In a "continuous" recognition task, subjects were presented with a list of words; for each word the subject was asked to answer Yes if the word had occurred earlier on the list and No if it had not. An analysis of errors committed by subjects revealed that they tended to make "false positives" (i.e., to say Yes when the correct answer was No) for words that had the same *meaning* as an earlier word. For example, word #5 might be "happy," and word #15 might be "glad"; the subject might say that "glad" had already appeared in the list even though it had not. Unlike Conrad's (1964) experiments on STM, errors rarely occurred for acoustically similar words; "loan," for example, was not confused with "lone."

Assimilation

The work on organization and meaning for words suggests that subjects "assimilate" new words to their own existing system of categories and meanings. A study of the idiosyncratic nature of this assimilation process was conducted by Bower and Clark (1969). Subjects were given 12 successive serial lists of 10 concrete nouns per list. One group was instructed to make up a running story based on the words while a control group received the usual instructions. Performance on immediate recall was high for both groups, but on a delayed recall test, the narrative group averaged 93 percent compared to 13 percent recalled for the control group. Apparently, long-term retention requires that new material be actively integrated with existing knowledge in a "meaningful" way.

Retrieval Failure

Another possible characteristic of LTM is that information is lost due to retrieval failure, a failure to "find" knowledge that is somewhere in LTM. An important piece of evidence for this idea comes from an experiment by Tulving and Pearlstone (1966). Subjects were given lists of 12, 24, or 48 words; the words were organized by category, with the category name given and either 1, 2, or 4 words per category. Recall performance was better when category names were provided (cued recall) than not (uncued recall), especially when there were many items per category. The superior recall was mainly due to subjects recalling more categories rather than more words per category.

In a related study, Slamecka (1968) presented a 30-word list made up of five categories with 6 words per category. During recall, subjects were given either 1, 3, or 5 of the words in a category and were asked to produce the others; giving them more cue words, however, did not increase recall performance for the remaining words. Apparently, cueing serves to aid in locating categories; in Slamecka's study, the subjects could easily remember the five categories without cues. These results suggest that a major problem in locating information in LTM is to find the general "category" or "cluster" in which the desired information is stored.

Finally, the study by Tulving and Thomson (1973) discussed in Chapter 9 suggests that recall depends on finding the appropriate retrieval route.

LEVELS OF PROCESSING

Control Processes

One of the major concepts in the information processing framework discussed in this chapter up to this point is the idea of *multistage storage*—the distinction among STSS, STM, and LTM as separate entities. However, even this central idea has frequently been criticized (Melton, 1963; Atkinson & Shiffrin, 1968) and recently the criticism has intensified (Craik & Lockhart, 1972). There are alternative frameworks to the concept of multistage storage, and particularly to the *duplex theory* which distinguishes STM from LTM. One major alternative is to assume that memory is a unitary continuum with differences in learning and memory due to differences in the type of rehearsal and coding processes used; this alternative shifts the focus from the distinction among memory stores to the role of controlling processes like attention, rehearsal, and encoding.

For example, Melton's (1963) paper, "Implications of Short-Term Memory for a General Theory of Memory," suggested that it is possible to consider STM and LTM as part of a memory continuum rather than neatly separable entities. As an example of the blurring of STM and LTM, consider an experiment by Hebb (1961). On each trial, subjects were presented with 9 digits at a rate of one per second and asked to recall them in order; the experiment continued for 24 trials, but on every third trial an identical 9-digit string was repeated. Although the subjects were not aware that the string was being repeated, and although they were asked only to keep the strings active in STM, the results indicated that performance increased for the repeated string but not for the new strings. These results are summarized in Figure 10-14. Apparently, the recall task involves more than STM; there is evidence of a buildup or strengthening of the repeated digits, thus suggesting a blurring of STM and LTM. Melton and Martin (1972) suggested that psychologists, instead of emphasizing memory structures (e.g., STM and LTM), should focus on the *coding process*—how individuals respond to incoming information. "The critical determinates of

FIGURE 10-14.

Percent correct recall as a function of ordinal number of 9-digit series for repeated and nonrepeated digit strings.

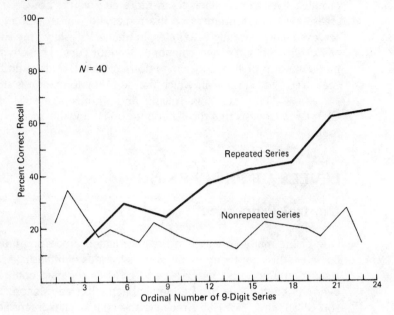

learning and memory are to be found in the coding responses to an experienced event. . . . This turn to questions about coding and coding processes exemplifies the new paradigm of the science of human learning and memory" (p. xii). Several important investigations of the role of coding processes in learning and memory are included in their edited volume, *Coding Processes in Human Memory* (1972).

Another landmark that emphasized the role of control processes was the influential paper by Atkinson and Shiffrin (1968) entitled "Human Memory: A Proposed System and Its Control Processes." In their paper, Atkinson and Shiffrin argued for a distinction between *memory structures*, such as STM and LTM, which are assumed to be fixed features of memory, and *control processes* which are flexible features of memory processing that are under the control of the subject. Atkinson and Shiffrin suggested that an analysis of learning and memory in terms of control processes rather than sole reliance on the model of memory structure will help to clarify and unify the field of human memory.

How does the control processes approach differ from, or add to, the multistage model in the explanation of interesting phenomena? Consider the serial position effect discussed in Chapter 9: in free recall of a word list, subjects tended to better remember the first few words (primacy effect) and the last few words (recency effect) than the middle words. The multistage model (or "duplex theory") explained that the primacy effect was due to long-term memory because more rehearsal of the early items allowed for higher probability of entry into LTM, whereas the recency effect was due to an unloading of the short-term memory. The control processes framework suggests that the primacy effect results from the subject's use of a deeper coding or rehearsal strategy for the first few words, and the recency effect results from a sort of low-level maintenance rehearsal that keeps the last few items given to the subject actively in consciousness. In other words, the serial position effect could be explained as the result of two different types of rehearsal/coding processes that the subject chooses to use rather than a multistage analysis of memory. There is, of course, some question as to how different these two explanations really are. Are they simply using different words to say the same thing? Are they really two compatible theories? These questions must eventually be answered.

In a classic paper titled, "Levels of Processing: A Framework for Memory Research," Craik and Lockhart (1972) presented rationale and evidence for an alternative to multistage theories of memory. Their central theme was that the processing of incoming perceptual stimuli may occur on several levels, ranging from a low-level "sensory" analysis to a deep-level "semantic" analysis. This idea of a hierarchy of processing stages was not new, of course, and the similarity to Treisman's (1960, 1969) theory of attention discussed earlier in this chapter was acknowledged by Craik and Lockhart. Similarly, Posner's (1969) work on yes/no judgments for letter and word pairs provided another example of "levels of processing" involved in making decisions. The basic new idea presented by Craik and Lockhart is that retention, measured by the amount recalled, is a function of the depth of processing: the more deeply an input stimulus is analyzed, the higher the probability that it will be learned and recalled in a later test.

For example, Craik and Lockhart (1972, p. 675) stated: " . . . trace persistence is a function of depth of analysis, with deeper levels of analysis associated with more elaborated, longer lasting, and stronger traces." The levels of processing do not necessarily have to occur in order, however. " . . . we can perceive at meaningful, deeper levels before we perceive the results of logically prior analyses" (p. 676). Since familiar or meaningful items are subject to instant deep analysis, "speed of analysis does not necessarily predict retention" (p. 676). Instead, retention is related to the "degree of stimulus elaboration" (p. 677), that is, how deeply the stimulus is analyzed.

Although Craik and Lockhart did not clearly specify what the levels of processing are, they did make a distinction between two extreme *levels of rehearsal* processes. One is *sensory analysis*, a low-level analysis of the phonemic or physical characteristic of the stimulus; the other is *semantic analysis*, a deep-level analysis in which the meaningful memory representation of the stimulus is activated and the stimulus is "elaborated" in a meaningful way. A second major distinction is between *type 1 rehearsal processing*, which occurs on only one level and actively maintains the trace in consciousness but does not elaborate on it in a way to aid retention, and *type 2 rehearsal processing*, which involves deeper analysis and elaboration and thus aids retention.

Levels of Rehearsal

Although Craik and Lockhart offer a general framework rather than a specific theory, they do suggest several basic predictions. For example, information that is subjected to semantic analysis should be better retained than information that is subjected only to sensory analysis. There is abundant support for this prediction. Tresselt and Mayzner (1960) presented word lists to three groups of subjects with different instructions. One group was asked to cross out the vowels in the list, the second to copy the words, and the third to judge whether each word was an instance of the concept "economic." As predicted, the latter group, which performed the semantic analysis of each word, recalled four times as many words as the other two groups in a surprise free-recall test.

More recently, Jenkins and his associates (Jenkins, 1974; Hyde & Jenkins, 1969, 1973; Till & Jenkins, 1973; Walsh & Jenkins, 1973) have shown that orienting tasks that required semantic analysis of word lists resulted in superior recall performance for intentional learning tasks as well as incidental learning tasks. In another study, Mandler (1967) found that subjects who were asked to work words into meaningful categories performed as well on a surprise free-recall test as subjects who sorted and were expecting the test. One criticism of these lines of research is that they can be explained by a simpler idea such as practice: subjects given "semantic" practice are better on tests of the "semantic" features of words (e.g., recall). An important additional question is whether subjects given lower-level types of practice retain more information about these lower-level characteristics. In other words, the present results have tested the idea that deeper processing leads to a *higher amount* of retention of the semantic features of words; a new question that requires further research is whether different levels of rehearsal lead to *different types* of information stored in memory.

Complementary results have been obtained when subjects were presented with meaningful passages rather than word lists. Low-level orienting tasks, such as circling every letter "e," resulted in lower recall of the passage than sorting the sentences or outlining them (Arkes, Schumacher, & Gardner, 1976). However, when the subjects were asked to simply copy the passage or read it carefully, they performed as well or better in recall as compared with the "deeper" analyses of copying or outlining. Apparently, further research is needed to determine what orienting variables encourage deeper processing of meaningful prose passages.

One type of orienting task—or what Rothkopf (1970) called "mathemagenic activity"—is the placement and type of adjunct questions that are attached to text. For example, Watts and Anderson (1971) asked high-school seniors to read five 450-word passages explaining a psychological principle and to answer inserted questions after each passage. On a comprehensive posttest given at the end, subjects who were asked to find applications of principles during learning performed best overall and showed a different pattern of performance from subjects asked only to identify examples repeated from the text or to associate a name with a principle. Similarly, Mayer (1975) found that subjects reading a mathematics lesson performed best on calculating answers to test problems if that was the type of question they had received on prior lessons, best on reciting definitions if that was the type of question they had received on prior lessons, and well on all types of problems if they had been asked to find applications of principles on earlier lessons. These results suggest that different types of adjunct questions may lead to different types of learning outcomes.

Types of Rehearsal

Is there any evidence to support Craik and Lockhart's suggestion that there are two types of rehearsal processes—those which serve only to maintain a stimulus in active consciousness (type 1), and those which serve to elaborate a stimulus and aid in its retention (type 2)? One way to test this concept of dual rehearsal is to explore more closely the *total time hypothesis* first noted in Ebbinghaus's data that there is a simple linear relationship between the amount of study time (rehearsal) and the amount of material retained.

There has been much support for the total time hypothesis. For example, as long as total study time is the same, the amount retained in paired-associate learning is the same for many trials at a fast presentation rate or few trials at a slow presentation rate (Bugelski, 1962), for several short lists or one long list (Postman & Goggin, 1964, 1966), and for cumulative presentation or presentation of words all at once (Jung, 1964). Craik and Lockhart predicted, however, that the total time hypothesis should hold only for type 2 processing, and in a review of literature on the total time hypothesis, Baddeley (1976) concluded that the nature of material and the type of coding process heavily limit the effect.

In a recent experiment, Craik and Watkins (1973) attempted to encourage type 1 processing of words for varying amounts of time. For example, subjects were given 21-word lists and asked to recall the last word mentioned in the list that began with a certain letter (e.g., G). Once a subject saw a "G" word, that word had to be held in memory until a new "G" was given later in the list; at that point the old "G" word could be forgotten and the new one had to be held in memory. A typical experimental sequence could be: (Instructions: "Remember the latest word that begins with 'G.'"

> DAUGHTER, OIL, RIFLE, GARDEN, GRAIN,
> TABLE, FOOTBALL, ANCHOR, GIRAFFE

Note that the subject had to hold GARDEN in memory for only a short time (zero intervening words) but GRAIN had to be held a bit longer (three intervening words). Craik and Watkins varied the retention interval from 0 to 12 words, and later tested for recall. The results were clear: the ability to recall a word was independent of the number of trials on which it had to be rehearsed. For example, subjects remembered 17 percent of the words with short retention intervals (0, 1, or 2 intervening words), 20 percent of the medium retention interval words (3, 4, or 5 intervening words), and 18 percent with long intervals (6, 8, or 12 intervening words). Craik and Watkins suggested that there is a distinction between maintenance rehearsal (in type 1) and elaborative rehearsal (in type 2). Furthermore, when the subjects were using maintenance rehearsal, the amount of rehearsal had no straightforward effect on retention. Additional supporting evidence was obtained in a follow-up study by Craik and Tulving (1975).

An important related line of research involves "directed forgetting," in which subjects are asked to hold information in memory for some time, then they are tested, and then they are told to "forget" the information (Bjork, 1972, 1975; Geiselman, 1975; Reitman, Malin, Bjork, & Higman, 1973). In a typical experiment, Bjork and Jongeward (reported in Bjork, 1975) gave subjects sequences of six words to rehearse for 20 seconds. For each set of six words, the subjects were asked either to rehearse so as to remember the words or to rehearse to keep the words actively in consciousness (i.e., forget them after the immediate test). The subjects performed almost identically on an immediate recall test after each trial, but on a surprise delayed test, words from elaboration rehearsal trials were recalled much better than words from maintenance rehearsal trials.

In a related study, Woodward, Bjork, and Jongeward (1973) presented their subjects with a list of words. Each word was presented for 1 second, followed by a retention interval of 0 to 12 seconds, and then a recall test for that word. The subjects were instructed to forget the word after the trial and thus use only a type 1 or maintenance rehearsal. The results again clearly contradicted the total time hypothesis—the amount recalled on a surprise delayed test was independent of the length of rehearsal interval. Apparently, there are several types of rehearsal processes and subjects are capable of exercising some control over them.

Although the new interest in rehearsal and coding processes has produced an interesting complement to the multistage model, it is still too early to gauge the impact. One major question is whether the "levels of processing" approach is simply a new framework for expressing the same ideas as the multistage model, or whether it will actually lead to testable theories that are more useful than the multistage model.

MNEMONICS

This chapter has focused on what happens to visually presented words or letters as they pass through the information processing system. The development of this chapter and the previous one have led us to the investigation of the nature of long-term memory. There is some evidence that long-term memory is organized and meaningful, based on logical subdivisions, and that much human learning involves integrating new words into existing structures. As modern and new as all that sounds, it is interesting to note that most of these ideas were part of the field of *mnemonics* that has existed for centuries. Mnemonics or mnemonic techniques are simply mental devices (some might call them "tricks") to help improve one's memory, mainly one's long-term retention. In this section we will consider four popular techniques: *method of loci, pegword, chunking,* and *recitation.*

Loci

Cicero (in *De Oratore*) described the invention of one of the earliest mnemonic devices, the method of loci, by the Greek poet Simonides. According to the story (see Yates, 1966), Simonides had been reciting poetry at a banquet when he was abruptly called away; while he was outside the banquet hall the roof caved in, crushing all the guests to death. Because the disaster had mutilated the bodies beyond recognition, the relatives desperately needed a way of identifying their loved ones. Simonides was able to walk through the rubble pointing out the exact place where each person had been sitting and thus identify the bodies. This amazing ability to remember locations and assign "faces" to each led Simonides to the invention of a new mental tool for remembering long strings of words—each word could be assigned to a spot in the room with each spot logically related to the next, and every fifth spot (or tenth) distinguished as a marker. By systematically looking from spot to spot, the entire string of words (e.g., poem) could come "bouncing" back to him. This became known as the method of loci (or places).

Pegword

Another traditional method of memorizing a list of words is to peg each word not to a location in a room, as in the method of loci, but rather to an existing chain in an already-known series. For example, Miller, Galanter, and Pribram (1960) suggested the standard rhyming pegword list:
  one is a bun
  two is a shoe
  three is a tree
  four is a door
  five is a hive
  six are sticks
  seven is heaven
  eight is a gate
  nine is a line
  ten is a hen
If a list of words must be learned such as:
  1. ashtray
  2. firewood
  3. picture

4. cigarette
5. table
6. matchbook
7. glass
8. lamp
9. shoe
10. phonograph

Miller, Galanter, and Pribram argued that memory would be aided by attaching each new word to its respective position in the one-is-bun chain, as, for example, one-bun-ashtray, two-shoe-firewood, and so on.

Paivio (1968) tested this idea in an experiment in which all the subjects first learned a list of 10 nouns presented one at a time and then were tested for recall. Then, for a second list, the subjects were instructed to use either the one-is-a-bun list as a peg list or an abstract list such as:

one is fun
two is true
three is free
four is bore
five is live
six is tricks
seven is given
eight is fate
nine is time
ten is sin

Half the subjects were told to form images connecting each pegword with its companion from the new list of 10 words, and the other half were told to simply repeat the number, pegword, and new word over and over again. The results indicated that more words in the second list were recalled when a peg list was given (both peg lists worked the same) as compared to a control group given no peg list. In addition, the subjects who were instructed to form images improved their performance much more than those who were not. Apparently, pegwords help by providing a sort of internal imagery while loci provide a sort of external imagery.

Chunking

Miller's (1956) paper suggested that material can be recoded into chunks in STM and subsequent work suggested that LTM is also made more efficient by the organization of items into logically related groups. Musicians may be familiar with the chunking mnemonic for reading sheet music, "Every Good Boy Does Fine," which translates into EGBDF; or space travelers may use the handy sentence, "Men Very Easily Make All Jobs Serve Useful Needs Promptly," which translates into Mercury, Venus, Earth, Mars, Asteroids, Jupiter, Saturn, Uranus, Neptune, Pluto. An experiment by Bower (1972) points to the potential usefulness of integrated images, as well as "sentences," in the recoding process. Bower gave paired-associate lists to his subjects and asked some of them to form images connecting the pairs. For instance, for the pair DOG-BICYCLE, one might think of a DOG peddling away on a big BICYCLE. The other subjects were given standard instructions for learning the lists. The images, which unified the word pairs, resulted in much better long-term recall on the part of the experimental subjects than the controls. Relating seemingly arbitrary words together into a meaningful chunk, such as a sentence or an image, is thus a learning technique of both practical and theoretical interest.

Recitation

Another technique for improving memory is self-recitation, rehearsing a list of words by oneself rather than simply repeating it over and over again. For example, Woodworth and Schlosberg (1954) discussed an experiment by Gates (1917) in which 16 nonsense syllables were given to subjects for study; some of the subjects were asked to read the list over and over while others were asked to read it for part of the time and try to recite the words to themselves without referring to the list for part of the time. The results indicated that subjects retained more than twice as much when they recited for 80 percent of the time as compared to a group that simply read the list over and over. Apparently, self-recitation helps subjects to organize and assimilate the material into existing cognitive structures.

Honeck (1973) provided a study which suggested that an important aspect of self-recitation is the restating of new material in a way consistent with general past experience. For example, Honeck read proverbs aloud to college subjects, such as, "Great weights hang on small wires." After each proverb, the subject heard either a repetition of the same proverb or a meaningful paraphrase like, "Many important things are dependent for their outcome on details, small wires that is." Memory for the proverbs was better in this paraphrase condition even though subjects heard each proverb only once rather than twice. Apparently, memory devices which help a learner connect new, unfamiliar words with some existing, meaningful knowledge are quite helpful.

Finally, a study by Mayer (1976) suggested that recitation has different effects when a clear organizing context is available. Subjects were asked to memorize a set of interlocking paired-associates such as: 1. C to N; 2. H to L; 3. S to C; 4. N to M; 5. H to C; 6. L to S; 7. M to H; 8. L to C; 9. H to N. Some subjects were told *before* memorizing that the paths represented airline flights between Chicago, Houston, New York, Miami, Los Angeles, and Seattle, while other subjects were given the same information *after* memorizing the nine paths. On tests that required subjects to integrate long chains of paths, e.g., "How many legs from S to L?" (Answer: 5), the Before group performed much faster than the After group. Apparently, good integration of recited information into LTM requires that existing assimilatory sets exist in LTM at the time of memorizing.

SUMMARY

The information processing approach to human learning and memory offers an agreed-upon framework for discussing complex cognitive processes. As an introduction to the idea that human beings may possess several types of memory stores, we looked at two different examples: eidetic imagery and the recall of Luria's mnemonist. These examples suggest that we humans may have a visual memory that differs from long-term memory.

The information processing approach is based on the idea that there are several memory stores, such as short-term sensory store, short-term memory, and long-term memory. Each store has a different capacity, a different mode of representation, and a different way of losing information. There are also three control processes: attention, which is involved in transferring information from STSS to STM, rehearsal, which keeps information alive in STM, and encoding, which acts to transfer information from STM to LTM.

In addition, there is evidence for the idea that STSS is exact and brief, and represents information in the physical mode. In this connection, we discussed the process of visual scanning and pattern recognition and the concept of selective attention, including a discussion of dichotic listening experiments and how they relate to the theories of selective attention.

There is evidence too of the limited capacity of STM and for the role of rehearsal and an acoustic mode of representation in STM. Information processing in STM and LTM was investigated by exploring the ideas of processing rate and levels of processing.

In the section on long-term memory, we looked at the evidence that permanent memory is organized, meaningful, assimilatory, and that information is lost as a result of retrieval failure.

A major alternative to the emphasis on memory stores (i.e., multistage storage) is the concept of levels of processing or control processes. This approach suggests that different types of rehearsal strategies (e.g., maintenance versus elaborative) will result in different amounts of learning.

The chapter closed with a section on memory mnemonics, including the method of loci, the pegword procedure, chunking, and recitation.

As Blumenthal (1977) noted in a recent survey, the unifying theme of the information processing approach concerns "active internal processes." These processes interact with the flood of incoming stimulation to produce a coherent flow of immediate experience. One advantage of the information processing approach is that it allows for the integration of all cognitive functioning, ranging from perception to learning to thinking. It also suggests new experiments and new interpretations for many of the perplexing problems raised by other approaches.

However, there is a price paid for the strategy of relying on just one point of view—whether it is the modern information processing approach or the overemphasis during the 1930s and 1940s of Hull's (1943) associationist framework of learning. Divergent points of view which are not readily assimilated to the information processing framework are likely to be ignored. The psychology of learning would suffer if it became a prerequisite that all theories of learning and memory must be stated in information processing terms. Further, to the extent that humans are not *entirely* information processing systems, the approach is limited; presently, it has no obvious place for affect, emotion, motivation, social interaction, or personality.

The information processing approach is fairly young, but even in its short lifespan it has shown remarkable resilience. For example, the current shift of interest from multistage storage to the focus on control processes such as rehearsal and encoding indicates that it is not a stagnant, unchangeable approach. The following two chapters will explore two fundamental issues raised by the information processing approach: how knowledge is represented in memory (Chapter 11), and how knowledge that is in memory is processed and manipulated to answer questions (Chapter 12).

11/ Memory for Meaning

INTRODUCTION

THE BARTLETT EXPERIMENT

PSYCHOLINGUISTICS

MEMORY REPRESENTATION OF SENTENCES

MEMORY REPRESENTATION OF TEXT
   PASSAGES

SEMANTIC MEMORY

SUMMARY

Preview

Chapter 9 (Verbal Learning) focused on how stimulus variables such as the order of presentation and type of practice influence response variables. The focus of this chapter is on the more complex cognitive question of how meaningful information is acquired from textual material, how it is structured and represented in memory, and how that memory representation is used for retrieval. The research we'll look at here uses sentences and passages of prose rather than the simple laboratory stimuli (e.g., nonsense syllables) and procedures (e.g., paired-associate learning) described in Chapter 9. Thus, both the materials used and the research questions asked in this chapter are more complex than what we have discussed previously. We shall examine several theories which try to explain how meaningful information is represented in long-term memory; however, it will soon become apparent that this is a new and emerging area of study in psychology with—as yet—few well-defined "laws."

INTRODUCTION

When a person reads a text or listens to another person talking, he or she will remember some elements of the presented material but not others. Furthermore, some things that were not in fact presented are "remembered," and some of the material that actually was presented may be changed in memory. These common and well-known events have led to an important set of questions for learning psychologists: What is learned from a prose passage? How is complex verbal information represented in memory, and how is it used to answer questions?

One way to provide some answers to these questions is to ask subjects to read a passage, such as the one given below, and then reproduce it in writing as well as they can.

The War of the Ghosts

One night two young men from Egulac went down to the river to hunt seals, and while they were there it became foggy and calm. Then they heard war-cries, and they thought: "Maybe this is a war-party." They escaped to the shore, and hid behind a log. Now canoes came up, and they heard the noise of paddles, and saw one canoe coming up to them. There were five men in the canoe, and they said:

"What do you think? We wish to take you along. We are going up the river to make war on the people."

One of the young men said: "I have no arrows."

"Arrows are in the canoe," they said.

"I will not go along. I might be killed. My relatives do not know where I have gone. But you," he said, turning to the other, "may go with them."

So one of the young men went, but the other returned home.

And the warriors went on up the river to a town on the other side of Kalama. The people came down to the water, and they began to fight, and many were killed. But presently the young man heard one of the warriors say: "Quick, let us go home: that Indian has been hit." Now he thought: "Oh, they are ghosts." He did not feel sick, but they said he had been shot.

So the canoes went back to Egulac, and the young man went ashore to his house, and made a fire. And he told everybody and said: "Behold I accompanied the ghosts, and we went to fight. Many of our fellows were killed, and many of those who attacked us were killed. They said I was hit, and I did not feel sick."

He told it all, and then he became quiet. When the sun rose he fell down. Something black came out of his mouth. His face became contorted. The people jumped up and cried.

He was dead.

THE BARTLETT EXPERIMENT

This passage comes from the pioneering work of Bartlett and is summarized in his monograph *Remembering* (1932). In his experiments, Bartlett used a version of the child's game of "telephone" in which a message is passed along a chain of people, changing a bit with each retelling. Bartlett called his procedure the "method of serial reproduction," and employed it as follows: he presented native folk stories (or pictures) from unfamiliar cultures to British college students, asking Subject #1 to read the story, put it aside, reproduce it from memory and pass his reproduction on to Subject #2, who would read the reproduced version, put it aside, reproduce his own version and pass it on to Subject #3, and so on.

Something quite curious happened in Bartlett's studies. The stories (and pictures) changed as they were passed along but they changed in systematic ways. For example, the reproduced version of the story for Subject #10 is given below:

The War of the Ghosts

Two Indians were out fishing for seals in the Bay of Manpapan, when along came five other Indians in a war-canoe. They were going fighting.

"Come with us," said the five to the two, "and fight."

"I cannot come," was the answer of the one, "for I have an old mother at home who is dependent upon me." The other also said he could not come, because he had no arms. "That is no difficulty," the others replied, "for we have plenty in the canoe with us"; so he got into the canoe and went with them.

In a fight soon afterwards this Indian received a mortal wound. Finding that his hour was coming, he cried out that he was about to die. "Nonsense," said one of the others, "you will not die." But he did.

Based on this and other examples, Bartlett noted several ways the students' versions tended to change. One kind of change he observed was *flattening*: most of the details, such as the proper names (Egulac, Kalama), titles (The War of the Ghosts), and the individual style of writing tended to fall out of the passage. Bartlett attributed this loss to the fact that British college students had had little prior experience with folk tales native to other cultures, or to spirits and ghosts; thus, since learning required assimilating the new material to existing concepts, the students were at a loss. According to Bartlett (1932, p. 172): "Without some general setting or label as we have repeatedly seen, no material can be assimilated or remembered."

A second characteristic change was *sharpening*, in which certain details become exaggerated in memory. For example, the "relatives" became "an old mother at home who is dependent on me."

The third process of change he called *rationalization*. Passages tended to become more compact, more coherent, and more consistent with the readers' expectations. All the references to spirits and ghosts faded away

FIGURE 11-1.

Effects of verbal labels on memory for ambiguous figures.

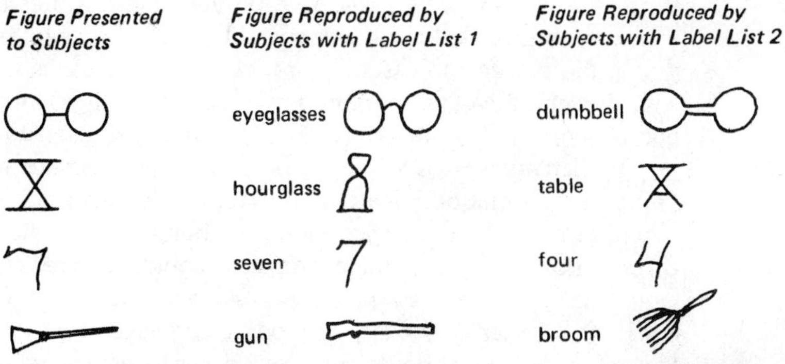

Figure Presented to Subjects	Figure Reproduced by Subjects with Label List 1		Figure Reproduced by Subjects with Label List 2	
O—O	eyeglasses	O—O	dumbbell	O=O
X	hourglass	�	table	X
7	seven	7	four	4
▷—	gun	▷═══	broom	🖌

and the story became one of a simple fishing trip and fight. Bartlett argued that the reader is actively engaged in "an effort after meaning"—an attempt to make the story fit his or her expectations. Since mystical concepts are not a major part of Western culture, the mystical aspects of the story were not well remembered; instead, many subjects tended to add on a "moral" which was a widely accepted practice in other stories they were more familiar with.

Although Bartlett's work lay dormant for many years as the behaviorist movement swept across American psychology, he is now recognized as one major forerunner of modern cognitive psychology because his work suggested two fundamental ideas about human mental processes. First, Bartlett argued that *learning* requires active comprehension. The act of learning and comprehending new material requires "an effort after meaning": in reading a complex text, or acquiring any new information, humans must assimilate the new material to existing concepts or schemata. The outcome of learning (i.e., what is stored in memory) is not an exact duplicate of what was presented but rather depends both on what was presented and the schema to which it is assimilated. Individuals change the new information to fit their existing concepts, and in the process, details fall out and the knowledge becomes more coherent. Second, the act of *remembering* requires an active "process of construction"; during recall, an existing schema is used to generate or construct details which are consistent with it. Memory is not detailed, but rather is schematic, that is, based on general impressions. Although recall produces specific details which seem to be correct, many of them are, in fact, incorrect.

Carmichael, Hogan, and Walter (1932) provided complementary evidence for Bartlett's theory by using pictorial figures and providing subjects with schema for how to interpret them. They showed their subjects a series of 12 figures like those in Figure 11-1 and gave each one a name. For example, before presenting shape 1 the experimenter might say, "This figure resembles eyeglasses," or "This figure resembles a dumbbell." For shape 4, the experimenter might suggest either a "gun" or a "broom." When the subjects were asked to reproduce these figures from memory, their drawings tended to be influenced by the labels they had been given during the presentation (see Figure 11-1). These results were consistent with Bartlett's idea that memory for figures or passages involves assimilation to schemata—in this case, the labels may have served as schemata.

Bartlett's work was tantalizing because it demonstrated that memory is "schematic"—that both learning and remembering are based on general schemata rather than specifics. However, Bartlett's work did not yield clear or powerful predictions; for example, it could not predict which details would "fall out" of a passage or how a subject would make a passage more coherent. In a sense, the task of modern cognitive psychologists has been to clarify exactly what Bartlett was saying and to test and refine his theories.

PSYCHOLINGUISTICS

When psychologists became interested in the study of complex verbal processes, a logical starting place seemed to be the field of linguistics. Linguistic theories were concerned with defining the characteristics of a given language such as its grammatical rules. Unfortunately, the field of linguistics is not directly concerned with psychological problems such as comprehension and encoding, and as Anderson and Bower (1973, p. 101) have pointed out, "little of the work occurring in linguistics has anything definitive to say about the problems of human memory."

Beginning in the 1950's, however, a new area of psychology called psycholinguistics was born (see Chapter 7 for some consideration of this topic). Psycholinguistics is a subfield of psychology that attempts to integrate useful linguistic theories into a testable, psychological account of human verbal learning and memory. Greene (1974) notes that the term was first used in the 1950s and that it most often referred to a structural analysis of language into units and rules for combining the units. Psycholinguistics, then, can be seen as an extension of verbal learning (discussed in Chapter 9); instead of studying basic learning of word lists, however, psycholinguistics involves the study of more complex verbal processes such as the comprehension and storage of entire sentences or passages.

It is customary in psycholinguistics to make distinctions among three aspects of language: (1) *basic structural units*, such as phonemes (sounds), or morphemes (meaning units such as words, "ed," "s," "er," "non"), or phrases; (2) *syntax*, the ordering of language units in an utterance as specified by grammatical rules; and (3) *semantics*, the rules for discovering the meaning or reference of an utterance. For example, the morpheme units of the sentence, "I stopped talking," are: I, stop, ed, talk, ing. Each represents a basic unit of language. The syntax of the sentence follows the pattern: subject + verb phrase. The meaning of the sentence depends on the comprehender's referents for "I," "stop," and "talk."

The history of psycholinguistics can be divided into three eras. At first, the behaviorist theories of language dominated psychology; these theories focused on "language behavior," such as the production of strings of morphemes. Then, the linguist Noam Chomsky introduced his *generative theory* in 1957 (and again in revised form in 1965); Chomsky's theory had implications for psychology because it focused on the syntactic rules underlying utterances. More recently, interest has turned to developing the semantic component of psycholinguistic theories; instead of focusing only on syntax, these theories focus on the semantic relations that underlie utterances. These three periods can be called "before Chomsky," "Chomsky," and "after Chomsky" respectively, and we will discuss each in turn.

Before Chomsky

Before Chomsky's "generative" theory burst onto the scene in 1957, both American linguistics and the subfield psycholinguistics were heavily influenced by behaviorism. For example, the prominent American linguist Leonard Bloomfield emphasized a pragmatic, empiricist approach to the study of language; he avoided nonbehavioral concepts such as "meaning" or "mental events" and called instead for the rigorous, scientific study of observable language behaviors. Anderson and Bower (1973) point out that this position in American linguistics was quite similar to that espoused by Watson for the field of psychology.

In psychology, the behaviorist position called for the study of *language behavior* rather than of mysterious underlying mental structures and processes which cannot be observed. Language behavior, like all behavior, can ultimately be described in terms of classical and operant conditioning, generalization and discrimination, and other fundamental learning principles. In other words, according to the behaviorist approach, language behavior is a learned behavior and is subject to the basic laws of learning (Skinner, 1957; Staats, 1964).

A landmark publication for the behaviorist approach to human language performance was Skinner's *Verbal Behavior* which appeared in 1957. Skinner's main points were (1) that verbal behavior (e.g., talking) is learned just like any other behavior; (2) that instrumental conditioning is the principal mechanism by which verbal learning takes place; and (3) that it is not necessary or appropriate to describe the internal, cognitive processes and structures that underlie language behavior because only observable behavior (i.e., utterances) can be measured and scientifically described. Thus the theme of Skinner's book was that *reinforcement* is the key to verbal learning.

For example, an infant lying in its crib may engage in occasional babbling; these vocalizations include many types of sounds. If a sound is not a common English one, it will likely be ignored (assuming the parents speak English), but if an occasional English-like phoneme is produced (e.g., "ma," "pa," "da"), the infant may be reinforced by a hug, kiss, and plenty of parental attention. In this Skinnerian scenario, reinforced sounds (i.e., English-like phonemes) will increase in frequency while nonreinforced babbling will extinguish.

Instrumental conditioning can also account for the production of words and sentences. Skinner distinguishes among several functions for sentence-like utterances. One concept is the *mand*. Mands are similar to "commands" or "demands" such as "Milk, please" which are reinforced by producing the desired reward. In other words, children learn to produce utterances like these because such utterances are instrumental in obtaining a reward rather than because they "understand" the meaning of the sentence. Another concept is the *tact*. Tacts require "contact" with the environment and result in a sort of classification learning as discussed in Chapter 13 or discrimination learning as discussed in Chapter 6. For example, the sequence "What's that? It's an orange. No, it's an apple" indicates that the child is reinforced for responding to an object depending on a particular feature of the object. The tact "apple" may be controlled by the color "red" in this case. Skinner's book contains many interesting anecdotes that support his theory. However, it does not contain convincing human experimental research that tests his theory; for all its emphasis on a scientific analysis of language, Skinner's book suffers from a lack of verification from actual scientific experiments. Skinner assumes that the learning processes he observed in pigeons and rats are essentially the same as those responsible for complex human verbal performance such as creative writing, producing and understanding a novel sentence, and so on; these novel productions are partially explained by the process of "generalization" (discussed in Chapter 6). These claims, coupled with the lack of experimental support, have not been well received by psycholinguists, and Skinner's theory has not yet had much impact (Hilgard & Bower, 1975). Certainly, some of Skinner's theory has great intuitive appeal and it remains for subsequent research to determine the limits of "instrumental conditioning" as an important aspect of human language behavior.

There has also been some theory and supporting research based on the idea that classical conditioning is involved in some verbal behavior, especially the learning of word meanings and connotations. For example, Osgood (1953) proposed that words can evoke internal responses, which he called *mediating responses*, and that these responses are subject to the laws of classical conditioning. To illustrate, the words "ice cream" may elicit no particularly strong emotional response in a young child at first; however, after many pairings of the words "ice cream" with the taste of ice cream, they may eventually evoke a conditioned response similar to that for ice cream itself—enjoyment, pleasure, and so on. In this case, as described in Chapter 2, the unconditioned stimulus is the actual taste of ice cream, the unconditioned response is the enjoyment of ice cream, the conditioned stimulus is the expression "ice cream," and the conditioned response is an enjoyment response to the words.

To assess the connotative reaction evoked by words, Osgood and his associates (Osgood, Suci, & Tannenbaum, 1957) developed a technique based on the *semantic differential*. Subjects were asked to rate words on bipolar scales, such as:

Rate the word, "psychology"
Good	1	2	3	4	5	6	7	Bad
Active	1	2	3	4	5	6	7	Passive
Strong	1	2	3	4	5	6	7	Weak

Many scales (i.e., pairs of words) were used in addition to the three presented above, but a statistical technique revealed that there were basically three main factors involved. The three main dimensions were: evaluation (e.g., good versus bad), activity (e.g., active versus passive), and potency (strong versus weak). In other words, most of the pairs fell into one of these three groups and evoked the same rating as other pairs in the same dimension; typical pairs for the evaluation dimension are good-bad, pleasant-unpleasant, valuable-worthless, positive-negative, and so on. The work of Osgood et al. provided a relatively stable measurement of word connotations different from the methods of measuring meaningfulness discussed in Chapter 9, and provided a useful instrument for subsequent research.

For example, one application of Osgood's idea that words evoke emotional responses is in the field of attitude change (Tannenbaum, 1968). If a neutral term like "Candidate X" is continually paired with one that tends to elicit a certain emotional response, such as "scandal" which has a low evaluative rating, or "great American" which has a high evaluative rating, then the originally neutral "Candidate X" will begin to take on the characteristics of the term it is paired with. Hence, a campaign aimed at increasing the voters' evaluative rating of a candidate might picture the candidate near an American flag (high evaluative rating), seated in an overstuffed chair next to a warm fireplace (high evaluative rating), with patriotic music playing in the background (high evaluative rating), and the caption superimposed on the picture: "Candidate X is a Great American" (high evaluative rating); the hope is, of course, that all the high evaluative ratings will become conditioned to the candidate. It is also possible for the reverse to occur. For example, if a positive word like "nurse" is combined with a negative word like "cruel," the pair, "cruel nurse," will elicit a more negative rating than "cruel" by itself (Tannenbaum, 1968).

The classical conditioning approach to word meaning has been summarized by Staats, Staats, and Crawford (1962, p. 159) as follows:

" . . . when a word is contiguously presented with a stimulus object, the conditionable components of the total response elicited by the object are conditioned to the word. A word thus comes to elicit part of the behavior elicited by the object it denotes."

In addition, Staats and Staats have shown that words with strong meanings (i.e., which elicit stable responses) may be paired with neutral words, and that the originally neutral words will also elicit some of the same response. The Staats have used this classical conditioning paradigm for nonsense syllables (Staats & Staats, 1957), national and proper names (Staats & Staats, 1958), and English words (Staats, Staats, & Biggs, 1958).

In one experiment described by Staats (1968), subjects were given a list of words such as "radio, chair, lake, box, large, five. . . ." The list was repeated many times, but on several trials the experimenter delivered either a loud noise or an electric shock immediately after one of the words. After the experiment, words that had been paired with the noxious stimuli tended to elicit an emotional CR as measured by galvanic skin response (GSR, a measure of "sweating") or as measured by rating the word on a semantic differential. In another experiment, students were asked to attend to paired-associates such as XEH-beauty, LAJ-thief, and so on. Nonsense syllables paired with positive words such as "beauty, win, gift, sweet, honest, smart" were later rated as more positive than nonsense syllables that had been associated with words like "thief, bitter, ugly, sad, worthless." The Staats' work indicates that some word meanings may be learned by classical conditioning, but it does not address the larger question of how humans come to produce and understand sentences and discourse.

Chomsky's Theory

The idea that all language behavior is learned simply through the laws of conditioning certainly had its shortcomings, and Chomsky pointed many of them out. For example, these theories have trouble explaining how humans can produce or understand a sentence that is completely novel, or how one sentence can have two different meanings. Chomsky suggested that memory structure (how sentences are stored) may not necessarily be the same as language behavior. For example, consider the sentence: They are eating apples. According to Chomsky, the meaning of this sentence depends on how one transfers it into a memory representation; if one assumes that "they" refers to people, then the meaning of the sentence is quite different than if "they" is interpreted as referring to the apples. A similar example of one sentence with two meanings was seen by one of the authors in a local laundromat: Not responsible for clothes you may have stolen. The importance of these examples is that they show that the same objective behavior (e.g., presenting a sentence) may lead to different cognitive interpretations; apparently, the study of language behavior alone (as proposed by Skinner) is not enough to explain how humans comprehend and produce utterances.

The modern rebirth of interest in psycholinguistics, and especially in the study of how sentences are comprehended and stored, was touched off by Chomsky's "generative theory" of language (Chomsky, 1957, 1965,

1968, 1969). Although the linguistic theory described in his two major books, *Syntactic Structures* (1957) and *Aspects of a Theory of Syntax* (1965), is quite complex, sometimes contradictory, and certainly not a psychological theory, some of the major points that have generated psychological research will be noted in this section.

Chomsky reemphasized a fundamental distinction between *competence* (what a person knows) and *performance* (what behavior a person displays). While the behaviorists focused on performance, Chomsky's theory attempts to determine the competence that underlies language behavior. Chomsky begins by defining language: " . . . utterances can be divided into two mutually exclusive classes: sentences (i.e., correct grammatical utterances) and nonsentences (i.e., ungrammatical utterances). A language will be defined as the set of all possible sentences and the grammar of a language as the rules which distinguish between sentences and nonsentences." (Greene, 1974, p. 25). Thus, the goal of linguistics is to determine a finite set of "rules" which can be used to generate all possible correct sentences but no incorrect sentences.

Chomsky developed four major types of rules to reach this goal:

(1) *Phonological rules* (or morphophonemical rules) are rules concerned with morphophonemic units of language, such as rules for combining sounds "legally" to form a word. Typical phonological rules might be:

cookie + plural = cookies

bake + past = baked

person + negation = nonperson

Chomsky's rules were similar to these, although he did not emphasize phonological rules. In the English language there are, of course, many exceptions to the basic rules (e.g., eat + past = ate).

(2) *Base rules* (or phrase structure rules) are rules concerned with syntactic units of language, such as rules for combining parts of speech to form a sentence. Typical base or phrase structure rules might be:

sentence = noun phrase + verb phrase

noun phrase = article + noun

noun phrase = noun

verb phrase = verb + noun phrase

verb phrase = verb

verb phrase = verb + adjective

A sentence like, "John understands the theory," could be generated by using the following rules:

sentence = noun phrase + verb phrase

noun phrase = noun

verb phrase = verb + noun phrase

noun phrase = article + noun

noun = John

verb = understands

article = the

noun = theory

FIGURE 11-2.

Phrase structure of a sentence.

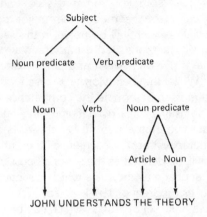

A diagrammatic representation of the phrase structure is shown in Figure 11-2. There are, of course, many sentences that could fit this structure, including "Mary understands the theory," "Pete hits the ball," "Sally likes the book."

(3) *Transformational rules* are also concerned with syntax, but describe how a sentence can be transformed to an equivalent form (for example, how to change from the passive to the active voice). A typical transformation might be:

noun phrase 1 + verb + noun phrase 2 =
noun phrase 2 + *is* + verb + past + *by* + noun phrase 1

This rule could be applied to some active-passive transformations. "John understands the theory," for example, could be transformed into "The theory is understood by John."

(4) *Projection rules* are rules for determining the meaning of words. Projection rules are a bit more difficult to specify, but they are based on the idea that a word may have several meanings. For example, Katz and Fodor (1963) point out that "bachelor" can mean an academic degree, an unmarried male, a young knight, or a male fur seal without a mate. A system is needed to select the appropriate meaning for the words, and much of the work described in the subsequent sections of this chapter will attempt to do this.

The first three types of rules were discussed in Chomsky's 1957 and 1965 books, but the projection rules dealing with semantics were not discussed until 1965.

In addition to the exciting idea that the production and comprehension of sentences involves a set of underlying rules, Chomsky has provided several major concepts which have interested psychologists. One of these concepts is the *distinction between surface structure and deep structure*. The surface structure of a sentence is the way it is written or spoken, but its deep structure is the way it is represented in memory. For example, the sentence, "The ball was hit by John" may be stored in memory as "John hit the ball." The deep structure representation of a sentence can be called the *kernel sentence*. A second concept suggested by Chomsky is that of *transformation rules*. Language consists of a set of rules, described above, for converting surface structure into deep structure (comprehension) and deep structure into surface structure (recall and communication). Finally, the concept of *universal grammar* holds that all humans are born with an innate set of rules common to all languages; it is argued that classical or operant learning of these rules is not possible because they are too complex.

Chomsky's cognitive approach to language came as an alternative to Skinner's book *Verbal Behavior* (1957), which viewed language as a learned behavior subject to the laws of conditioning. By introducing the idea of deep structure and transformation rules, Chomsky suggested that memory structure—how sentences are stored and used—is not necessarily the same as surface structure. Unfortunately, though, Chomsky's theory was not based on psychological study, but rather on logical arguments.

After Chomsky

Chomsky's theory was an advance over previous linguistic theories because it offered the idea that a finite set of rules which generate all the utterances of a language could be determined. However, Chomsky's rules were based largely on syntax—the parts of speech in a sentence for example—and did not deal much with meanings. When Chomsky did add a "semantic component" to his theory, it served only to interpret deep structure but had no role in the generation of deep structure or surface structure. Anderson and Bower (1973, p. 113) aptly point out that: " . . . as a psychological model of the causal sequence by which a sentence is generated, this scenario is utterly ridiculous. It would claim that we first decide what utterance we are going to say and then decide what meaning we want to convey. . . ."

For these reasons, attention has shifted to the "semantic" component of language use, and particularly to how meanings influence the generative process. One concept that has had a significant influence on psycholinguistics is the idea of *case grammar* (Fillmore, 1968, 1971). The basic idea in case grammar is that a sentence can be written as a verb and its arguments, and each argument holds a particular case relation (or *case category*) to the verb. Fillmore's main case categories or role relations, according to Kintsch (1972), are as follows:

(1) *agentive* (A): names the instigator of an action;

(2) *instrumental* (I): an inanimate object used by the agent to perform an action;

(3) *experiencer* (E): a person or an object on whom an action has an effect;

(4) *result* (R): the object or state that results from the action;

(5) *locative* (L): location or orientation of the action;

(6) *objective* (O): the object that is acted on by the verb.

For example, the sentence "John drives the truck in the road" could be represented as:

(DRIVE, O:TRUCK, A:JOHN, L:ROAD)

This means that DRIVE is the main action, TRUCK is the object, JOHN is the agent, and ROAD is the location (Kintsch, 1972). In addition, the proposition outlined above contains all of the following: John drives on the road, John drives the truck, The truck is driven on the road, John drives, The truck is driven by John.

There are, of course, several alternative systems for expressing possible case relations (Meyer, 1975; Grimes, 1972; Perfetti, 1972), but all are similar to that outlined above. The case grammar approach is exciting because it provides a means for analyzing text into units and also because it suggests a way that information might actually be stored in memory. Many of the implications of Chomsky's work and of the post-Chomsky work in psycholinguistics yield testable predictions concerning human language behavior and some of the tests will be explored in the following sections.

MEMORY REPRESENTATION OF SENTENCES

Although Chomsky's theory was not intended to be a psychological theory, it does provide certain predictions that have been tested in psychological laboratories. One important psychological implication of this theory involves "phrase structure" (or base) rules—the idea that sentences are stored in memory in terms of the grammatical relations among the words rather than simply as a sequence of individual words. Thus, one prediction is that sentences with straightforward syntactic relations will be easier to remember than the same set words in nongrammatical order.

Miller and Selfridge (1950) investigated this question by varying the "approximation to English" for strings of words. Word strings were constructed by taking a random sampling of words (Zero-Order Approximation), a random ordering of words all from the same passage (First-Order Approximation), an actual text in grammatical order lifted from a passage (Text), and several levels in between (Second-, Third-, Fourth-, Fifth-, and Seventh-Order Approximation). For example, the procedure for developing the Second-Order was to ask a subject to complete a sentence beginning with, for example, the word "he"; then the experimenter would take the first word the subject gave after "he," and give that word to the next subject, ask for a sentence completion, pass the subject's first response

FIGURE 11-3.

Percent of words correctly recalled as a function of order to approximation to English.

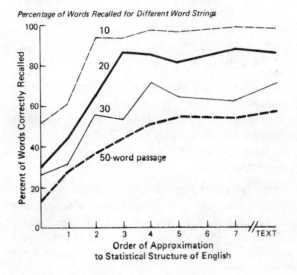

Word Strings (10-Words Lists)

0-order approximation: byway consequence handsomely financier flux cavalry swiftness weatherbeaten extent
1-order approximation: abilities with that beside I for waltz you the sewing
2-order approximation: was he went to the newspaper is in deep and
3-order approximation: tall and thin boy is a biped is the beat
4-order approximation: saw the football game will end at midnight on January
5-order approximation: they saw the play Saturday and sat down beside him
7-order approximation: recognize her abilities in music after he scolded him before
Text: the history of California is largely that of a railroad

Percentage of Words Recalled for Different Word Strings

word on to the next subject, and so on. The first words given by each successive subject were put together into a string called "Second-Order Approximation" to English; to obtain Third-Order, Miller and Selfridge took the first *two* words given by each subject, and so on. Examples are given in Figure 11-3.

Lists of 10, 20, 30, or 50 words were constructed using these methods; new subjects were asked to listen to the string and then recall it in order. The results, shown in Figure 11-3, indicate that as the word strings more closely approximated English word orders, more words were recalled. Miller and Selfridge concluded that in normal prose reading, subjects use their knowledge of syntax (grammatical rules for word order) as an aid to comprehension and remembering rather than simply storing and recalling each word individually.

More recently, there has been some evidence that the syntactic complexity of a passage influences the amount recalled and the reading time but not the time to answer questions about the material after reading

(Kintsch & Monk, 1972; Kintsch, 1974; King & Greeno, 1974). These results are consistent with the idea that syntactically complex passages must be translated by the reader into a more basic "phrase structure"; although the transformation takes time, once it is completed the underlying knowledge is apparently identical to that constructed for simpler syntax.

A more definitive test of Chomsky's theory was proposed by Miller (1962). He suggested that storing and recalling a sentence involves transforming it into a "kernel" sentence (K) plus a mental "footnote" describing the syntactic structure. The basic unit of knowledge in memory is the *kernel sentence*, a sentence in the active voice, affirmative mood, and declarative form. Surface structure sentences require certain *transformations* before they can be put into kernel form, and must be stored as kernel plus a mental note for the form of the sentence, such as the passive voice, negative mood, interrogative form, and so on. This theory predicts that a sentence such as "The boy hit the ball" would serve as the kernel (along with the appropriate footnote) for each of the following:

> Passive: The ball was hit by the boy. (Stored as: The boy hit the ball; *passive*.)
> Negative: The boy did not hit the ball. (Stored as: The boy hit the ball; *negative*.)
> Interrogative: Did the boy hit the ball? (Stored as: The boy hit the ball: *interrogative*.)

There also can be combinations of passive, negative, and interrogative which require even more transformations and more footnotes to be put into kernel form. One prediction of this interpretation of Chomsky's theory is that it should be easier for individuals to remember (and comprehend) sentences presented in kernel form as compared with sentences presented in other forms.

To study this prediction, Miller and McKean (1964) attempted to measure the time required to apply a transformation rule. They presented a sentence on a screen and asked the subject to convert it into the opposite voice (e.g., passive to active) or opposite sign (e.g., negative to positive); when the subject had completed the mental transformation, he or she pressed a button which was immediately followed by a test. To obtain a measure of "transformation time," Miller and McKean subtracted the time it took to read a sentence (in preparation for the test) from the time it took to transform a sentence; the average times to perform the transformation (corrected for reading time) were: .91 seconds for an active/passive transformation, .41 for a positive/negative transformation, and the longest time, 1.53 seconds, for a sentence that required both transformations.

One problem with the Miller and McKean study was that it did not provide a true *test* of Chomsky's theory; further, its procedure of requiring subjects to consciously apply the rules seems unrelated to the actual process of transformation that is required in real-life comprehension of sentences.

A different procedure was used by Savin and Perchonock (1965) in an attempt to test the idea that sentences are stored as kernels (plus footnotes). Subjects were asked to memorize a sentence followed by a string of unrelated words; they recalled more of the unrelated words with the target sentence when it was given in kernel form than when transformations were involved. One interpretation is that presenting the sentences in kernel form allowed more space for the extra words but the transformations required by nonkernel sentences reduced the extra memory space available.

In another promising study, Mehler (1963) presented lists of sentences in kernel form or transformed into passive, interrogative, negative, or all combinations of these. Recall was best for the lists of kernel sentences and worst for passive-interrogative, interrogative, and passive-interrogative-negative sentences. These results seemed consistent with Miller's and Chomsky's idea that sentences are converted into deeper structure as K sentences. However, when Martin and Roberts (1966) essentially replicated the Mehler study but controlled for sentence length, they obtained the opposite results and concluded that Mehler's findings could be explained by the fact that K sentences were shorter and thus easier to recall.

In addition, Greene (1974) has criticized "verbatim recall" studies such as these on the grounds that they do not provide information on the process of comprehension. A typical comprehension study aimed at testing the kernel sentence hypothesis might ask subjects to compare a sentence with a picture, answering Yes if they match and No if they don't (Slobin, 1966; Gough, 1966; Clark & Chase, 1972; Chase & Clark, 1972; Trabasso, 1972). The general results of "sentence-picture comparison" studies are consistent with the kernel sentence idea: sentences presented in kernel form require less reaction time than the same sentence-picture comparison for a transformed sentence. However, there are also several well-supported findings which are not readily explained by a neo-Chomsky theory: for example, it takes less time to answer Yes than No for positive sentences but longer to say Yes than No for negative sentences. Information processing models of the process of sentence comprehension that go beyond Chomsky's theory are discussed in the next chapter.

Based on a review of studies of sentence memory, Adams (1976, p. 355) concluded: "There is no evidence that Miller's hypothesis about sentences, derived from generative theory, is valid. . . . Generative theory may have a short theoretical life in psychology because it is not a psychological theory." In other words, Chomsky was useful to psychologists in popularizing the idea of deep structure; however, the particular theory that the kernel sentence represents the meaning of a sentence is based on a logical or linguistic analysis rather than on a psychological study. It is now the task of psychologists to determine how a sentence is represented in human memory through empirical study. In other words, the search continues for the "schema" of a sentence.

MEMORY REPRESENTATION OF TEXT PASSAGES

Abstraction of Linguistic Ideas

More recently, cognitive psychologists have attempted to study more care-fully Bartlett's idea that subjects *abstract* the general idea from prose as they read and *construct* their answers during recall. In an already classic study, Bransford and Franks (1971) read the sentences shown in the first part of Figure 11-4 to their subjects and then asked the recognition questions shown in the second part of the figure. (The reader may be interested in reading the list of sentences and taking the recognition test.) In the original study, the subjects were asked to rate on a 10-point scale how sure they were that the test sentence had been in the original list.

FIGURE 11-4.

The Bransford and Franks experiment: A typical set of sentences.

Sentence	*Question*
Acquisition sentences: Read each sentence, count to five, answer the question, go on to the next sentence.	
The girl broke the window on the porch.	Broke what?
The tree in the front yard shaded the man who was smoking his pipe.	Where?
The hill was steep.	What was?
The cat, running from the barking dog, jumped on the table.	From what?
The tree was tall.	Was what?
The old car climbed the hill.	What did?
The cat running from the dog jumped on the table.	Where?
The girl who lives next door broke the window on the porch.	Lives where?
The car pulled the trailer.	Did what?
The scared cat was running from the barking dog.	What was?
The girl lives next door.	Who does?
The tree shaded the man who was smoking his pipe.	What did?
The scared cat jumped on the table.	What did?
The girl who lives next door broke the large window.	Broke what?
The man was smoking his pipe.	Who was?
The old car climbed the steep hill.	The what?

The large window was on the porch.	Where?
The tall tree was in the front yard.	What was?
The car pulling the trailer climbed the steep hill.	Did what?
The cat jumped on the table.	Where?
The tall tree in the front yard shaded the man.	Did what?
The car pulling the trailer climbed the hill.	Which car?
The dog was barking.	Was what?
The window was large.	What was?

STOP—Cover the preceding sentences. Now read each sentence below and decide if it is a sentence from the list given above.

Test set. . . . How many are new?

The car climbed the hill.	(old___, new___)
The girl who lives next door broke the window.	(old___, new___)
The old man who was smoking his pipe climbed the steep hill.	(old___, new___)
The tree was in the front yard.	(old___, new___)
The scared cat, running from the barking dog, jumped on the table.	(old___, new___)
The window was on the porch.	(old___, new___)
The barking dog jumped on the old car in the front yard.	(old___, new___)
The cat was running from the dog.	(old___, new___)
The old car pulled the trailer.	(old___, new___)
The tall tree in the front yard shaded the old car.	(old___, new___)
The tall tree shaded the man who was smoking his pipe.	(old___, new___)
The scared cat was running from the dog.	(old___, new___)
The old car, pulling the trailer, climbed the hill.	(old___, new___)
The girl who lives next door broke the large window on the porch.	(old___, new___)
The tall tree shaded the man.	(old___, new___)
The cat was running from the barking dog.	(old___, new___)
The car was old.	(old___, new___)
The girl broke the large window.	(old___, new___)
The scared cat ran from the barking dog that jumped on the table.	(old___, new___)
The scared cat, running from the dog, jumped on the table.	(old___, new___)
The old car pulling the trailer climbed the steep hill.	(old___, new___)
The girl broke the large window on the porch.	(old___, new___)
The scared cat which broke the window on the porch climbed the tree.	(old___, new___)
The tree shaded the man.	(old___, new___)

The car climbed the steep hill.	(old___, new___)
The girl broke the window.	(old___, new___)
The man who lives next door broke the large window on the porch.	(old___, new___)
The tall tree in the front yard shaded the man who was smoking his pipe.	(old___, new___)
The cat was scared.	(old___, new___)

STOP. Count the number of sentences judged
"old." See text for answer.

In order to make up the sentences given in the first part of Figure 11-4, Bransford and Franks used the following four basic "idea sets":
"The scared cat running from the barking dog jumped on the table."
"The old car pulling the trailer climbed the steep hill."
"The tall tree in the front yard shaded the man who was smoking his pipe."
"The girl who lives next door broke the large window on the porch."
Each idea unit was broken down into four single ideas (called ONES), such as:
"The cat was scared."
"The dog was barking."
"The cat was running from the dog."
"The cat jumped on the table."
The ONES could be combined to form TWOS, such as:
"The scared cat jumped on the table."
The ONES could be combined to form THREES, such as,
"The scared cat was running from the barking dog."
Finally, the ONES could be combined to form an entire idea unit like the examples given above, and called a FOUR.

The subjects heard a long list of sentences consisting of some ONES, some TWOS, some THREES, but no FOURS from the idea sets, presented in random order. For example, all the sentences shown in the second section of Figure 11-4 are "new." Each sentence that was recognized as "old" was a "false recognition"—the subjects thought they saw it in the original list but it was not there. In a typical study, Bransford and Franks presented the same kind of study sentences, but this time the test consisted of some sentences that were in the original list (old) some that were not in the original list but could be inferred from one of the idea units (new), and some (called NONCASE) that were based on putting parts of different idea sets together.

The ratings of the subjects for the test sentences are given in Figure 11-5. It is clear that the subjects could not tell the difference between sentences which had actually appeared in the original list and those which were simply consistent with an idea set. In fact, they were most confident about having seen FOURS. Bransford and Franks concluded that during

FIGURE 11-5.

Recognition confidence for four types of old and new sentences.

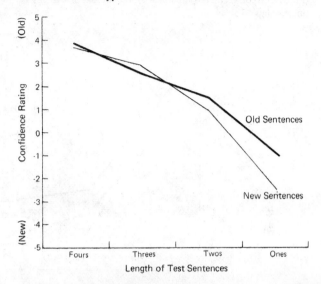

reading, the subjects abstracted the four general linguistic ideas; during recall, they used these general, abstract ideas but had no memory of the specific sentences from which they were abstracted.

Further evidence for "abstract" memory of prose was obtained by Sachs (1967). Her subjects heard the following passage about the invention of the telescope:

> There is an interesting story about the telescope. In Holland, a man named Lippershey was an eye-glass maker. One day his children were playing with some lenses. They discovered that things seemed very close if two lenses were about a foot apart. Lippershey began experiments and his "spyglass" attracted much attention. *He sent a letter about it to Galileo, the great Italian scientist.* (0 syllable test here.) Galileo at once realized the importance of the discovery and set out to build an instrument of his own. He used an old organ pipe with one lens curved out and the other curved in. On the first clear night he pointed the glass towards the sky. He was amazed to find the empty dark spaces filled with brightly gleaming stars! (80 syllable test here.) Night after night Galileo climbed to a high tower, sweeping the sky with his telescope. One night he saw Jupiter, and to his great surprise discovered with it three bright stars, two to the east and one to the west. On the next night, however, all were to the west. A few nights later there were four little stars. (160 syllable test here.)

Then she presented a test sentence and asked them to tell whether or not it had occurred verbatim in the passage. The test sentence was based on a sentence from the text, and the test was given either immediately after the subject had heard the sentence (0 syllables), 80 syllables beyond the sentence, or 160 syllables beyond the sentence. The test sentence con-

FIGURE 11-6.

Proportion correct on recognition test for four types of changes as a function of the number of intervening syllables.

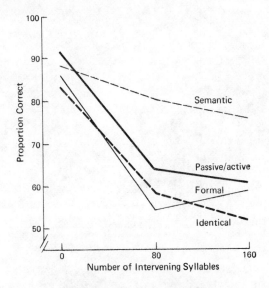

tained either a change in meaning (semantic change), a change in voice (active/passive change), a change in a minor detail that did not alter meaning (formal change), or no change (identical) from the text sentence. For example, the text sentence, "He sent a letter about it to Galileo, the great Italian scientist," was presented in the test in one of the following forms:

Semantic change: Galileo, the great Italian scientist, sent him a letter about it.
Active/Passive change: A letter about it was sent to Galileo, the great Italian scientist.
Formal change: He sent Galileo, the great Italian scientist, a letter about it.
Identical: same as above.

The results of the experiment are given in the bottom of Figure 11-6. If the subjects had just heard the sentence (0 interpolated syllables), they performed well in saying Yes to the identical sentence and No to each of the changed sentences. However, if the test came after the subject had heard 80 to 160 syllables beyond the target sentence, then performance fell sharply for detecting formal or voice changes but the subjects were still fairly accurate at noticing a change in meaning. In other words, once a sentence from prose had been "digested" by the subject, the individual retained very little information about the original grammatical form of the sentence but did retain the general meaning. Sachs' conclusion was that in the course of hearing a passage, a subject abstracted the general meaning but not the specific grammatical details.

Text Analysis

The results of Bransford and Franks, and of Sachs complement those of Bartlett and help to extend the idea that memory for prose is schematic. However, another important question is whether we can predict in advance what a person will remember about a passage. Johnson (1970) investigated this question by breaking a story down into "idea units" and asking a group of subjects to rate the idea units for their importance to the story. Then another group read the story and were asked to recall it. As predicted, the new subjects remembered more of the important units, even when the experimenter controlled study time for each with a slide projector.

Johnson's results are interesting because they imply that certain ideas in a passage are more important than others, and that it is possible to predict in advance what these well-remembered ideas will be. In addition, similar results have been obtained in some cases that used different material (Meyer & McKonkie, 1973). More recently, other researchers have attempted to devise methods of *text analysis*, procedures for analyzing a text into a hierarchical structure. Structural variables were discussed in the previous chapter as affecting memory for word lists. Those results suggest as a working hypothesis for the study of memory for passages that ideas high in the structural hierarchy are more likely to be remembered than ideas low in the hierarchy.

In a recent review of the advances in text analysis, Meyer (1975, p. 1) described the goal of her research as follows: "After reading a passage, people are unable to recall all the information that it contained. When a number of people read or hear the same passage, some ideas are recalled by almost everyone whereas other ideas are recalled by very few. The goal . . . is to determine whether certain variables can account for these differences in recall."

In an exploratory study, Meyer (1971) broke a 500-word prose passage from *Scientific American* into idea units and then arranged them into a hierarchical outline which she called a "tree structure" or "content structure." Independent judgments by one group of subjects produced almost identical tree structures from the same materials, thus indicating that objective text analysis may be possible. When new subjects were asked to read and recall the passage, there was a clear relationship between the "height" of an idea in the structure and the likelihood of its being recalled—ideas high in the structure were recalled better than those low in the structure. Apparently, findings based on subjective ratings of "importance," such as those used by Johnson, may be accounted for by Meyer's concept of "height" in a content structure. Unfortunately, one problem with interpreting the results of Meyer's study is that the "height" of an idea in the structure is often closely related (or confounded) with its serial order; high, important ideas more often come first, and verbal learning research on the serial position effect (see Chapter 9) indicates that subjects are more likely to recall the first few items in a list.

Meyer (1975) attempted to overcome this problem in a subsequent study that used three passages of approximately 575 words each. The passages dealt with topics such as "breeder reactors," "schizophrenia," and "parakeets." A target paragraph was selected from each passage, and two similar versions of each passage were constructed; the same target was inserted in the same place in both versions, but in one version the ideas in the target paragraph were high on the content structure, that is, important to the theme and to other ideas presented in the passage, but for the other passage they were low. Subjects recalled much more about the target paragraph if it was high in the structure than if it was low. One important problem in interpreting these results is that the "high" and "low" passages might not have been equally difficult; this problem was mitigated partially by the fact that Meyer did make sure they were similar in number of words, number of idea units, and number of levels in the content structure.

Kintsch (1974, 1976) has developed a method for dividing a text into a hierarchy of propositions called the *text base*. The system is similar to that used by Meyer to generate *content structure* and is inspired by the case grammars we discussed earlier in this chapter. Each proposition consists of two or more words that are related to one another; the propositions generally consist of verbs and arguments that relate to the verb. For example, consider the text:

TURBULENCE FORMS AT THE EDGE OF A WING AND GROWS IN STRENGTH OVER ITS SURFACE, CONTRIBUTING TO THE LIFT OF A SUPERSONIC AIRCRAFT.

This text can be analyzed into a text base as follows:

1.	TURBULENCE FORMS	(Verb Frame)
2.	AT THE EDGE	(Location)
3.	OF A WING	(Part of)
4.	TURBULENCE GROWS IN STRENGTH	(Verb Frame)
5.	OVER THE SURFACE	(Location)
6.	OF A WING	(Part of)
7.	TURBULENCE CONTRIBUTES TO THE LIFT OF AN AIRCRAFT	(Verb Frame)
8.	THE AIRCRAFT IS SUPERSONIC	(Characteristic)

Note that the system for building a text base is based on finding the main verbs and using them as basic frames around which to place the arguments such as location, part of, characteristic, and others. Each indentation represents a lower *level* in the text base, so that proposition 1 is at level 1, propositions 2, 4, and 7 are at level 2, propositions 2, 5, and 7 are at level 3, and proposition 6 is at level 4. When the arguments are read, they can be added after the proposition at the above level; for example, Proposition 1 is "TURBULENCE FORMS," Proposition 2 involves "TURBULENCE FORMS AT THE EDGE," and Proposition 3 involves "TURBULENCE FORMS AT THE EDGE OF A WING."

Kintsch's notation is different from that given above but is based on the same principles. A proposition is represented within a set of par-

FIGURE 11-7.

Relationship between reading time and number of propositions recalled.

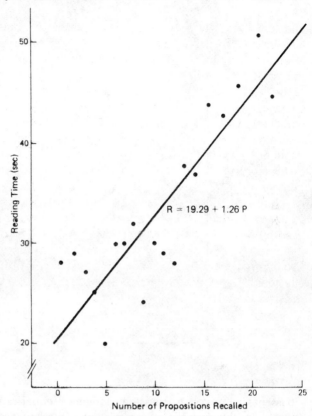

entheses, and the first word gives the verb or the relation involved. For example, in Kintsch's notation, the text base is:

1. (FORM, TURBULENCE)
2.   (LOC: AT, 1, EDGE)
3.   (PART OF, WING, EDGE)
4.   (GROW, TURBULENCE, STRENGTH)
5.   (LOC: OVER, 4, SURFACE)
6.   (PART OF, WING, SURFACE)
7.   (CONTRIBUTE, TURBULENCE, LIFT, AIRCRAFT)
8.   (SUPERSONIC, AIRCRAFT)

The numbers refer to the propositions.

Kintsch's system for analyzing text yields several interesting predictions if one assumes, as Kintsch does, that the text base for a passage is an indication of how the information is represented in a subject's memory. For example, one prediction is that if propositions—as defined by Kintsch's system—are the basic units of comprehension and memory, then reading time ought to depend on the number of propositions. To test this idea,

FIGURE 11-8.

Percent recall of propositions as a function of different levels in the text base hierarchy.

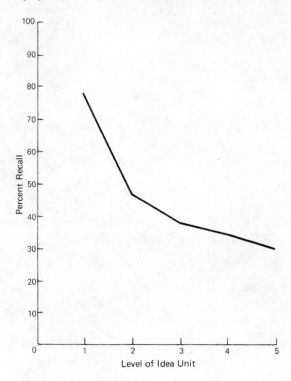

passages were constructed that contained equal numbers of words but varied in the number of propositions; reading time increased as the number of propositions increased even though the same number and kind of words were processed (Kintsch, 1976).

In a related study, subjects were asked to read and recall a passage from *Scientific American* that contained 70 words and 25 propositions; time required to read the passage was a direct linear function of the number of propositions which were recalled. These results, summarized in Figure 11-7, indicate that each proposition that was recalled added 1.26 seconds to the reading time on the average.

In a more striking test of the idea that certain propositions are more central than others, Kintsch (1976) measured the percentage of propositions recalled at each level in the text base. Figure 11-8 shows that subjects recalled about 80 percent of the level 1 propositions and that lower level propositions were less likely to be recalled. Similar procedures for organizing folk stories have been proposed, and there is some evidence that higher level features of the story are best rememberd (Rumelhart, 1975). These findings add support to Meyer's findings and reveal an advance in our attempt to extend Bartlett's original work.

Inferences

Another aspect of what-is-remembered from prose passages is that human often "remember" things that are not presented. Schank (1972) argues that subjects must make inferences and that they use their past experience to comprehend prose. For example, the following passage requires that the reader make certain inferences about the intention of John (Schank, 1972, p. 611).

Fred: Hi.

John: What are you doing with that knife?

Fred: Thought I'd teach the kids to play mumbletypeg.

John: I could use a knife right now. (agitated tone)

Fred: What's the matter?

John: Damn Mary, always on my back. She'll be sorry.

Fred: I don't think a knife will help you.

John: You're just on her side. I think I ought to. . . .

In a recent summary, Schank (1976, p. 167) points out that: "human communication is based largely on what is left out of discourse."

If people use ideas that are *not* presented to comprehend and re- member prose, then a theory based solely on trying to structure what *is* presented will not be adequate. Kintsch (1974) has used the term *inferred proposition* to characterize the need of subjects to make inferences, and linguists have used the term *presupposition* to refer to the aspects of a passage which must be assumed. For example, if someone says: "I hit the nail," a natural assumption to make is that a hammer was used—one would presuppose that the agent of the action was a hammer.

Kintsch (1976) asked subjects to read an explicit version of a story such as, "A carelessly discarded burning cigarette started a fire. The fire destroyed many acres of virgin forest," or an implicit version such as, "A burning cigarette was carelessly discarded. The fire destroyed many acres of virgin forest." The implicit version does not tell how the fire started. Subjects took a true-false test either immediately after reading or 15 min- utes later, with statements such as, "A discarded cigarette started a fire." On the immediate test, the implicit group took longer to verify the target sentence than did the explicit group, but both groups performed at the same level on the delayed test. These results suggest that, by the time of the delayed test, both groups had the same type of memory trace available to them—somehow the implicit group had included an "implicit proposi- tion" along with the actual material presented.

In a different type of study, Frederiksen (1975) attempted to manipu- late the number of inferences a subject would make while listening to a 500-word story about the problems of a mythical "Circle Island." One group of subjects was asked to listen and be ready for a written test; another group was told they would be asked to use the information to solve the socioeconomic problems of the island. In a recall test, both groups recalled the same amount of basic facts that were part of the passage, but the "problem solving" group included significantly more inferences in their recall. Apparently, the subjects had some control over the inference process.

SEMANTIC MEMORY

Question Answering

The previous sections investigated recall of newly learned sentences and prose; the present section focuses on recall of one's existing general knowledge. For example, consider the following question and try to describe how one might go about answering it:

Query: In the house you lived in three houses ago, how many windows were there on the north side?

Rumelhart, Lindsay, and Norman (1972) found that most people can solve this problem; they do so by visualizing their current dwellings, then moving back in time to visualize their previous homes, determining the north wall, and counting the windows.

Although this example may tap a trivial piece of information, it does point to the amazing ability we have to use our memories to answer questions. Lindsay and Norman (Lindsay & Norman, 1972, p. 379) have suggested how an individual's memory may work in recall in a hypothetical set of responses to the query: What were you doing on Monday afternoon on the third week of September two years ago?

1. Come on. How should I know? (Experimenter: Just try it anyhow.)
2. O.K. Let's see. Two years ago . . .
3. I would be in high school in Pittsburgh . . .
4. That would be my senior year.
5. Third week in September—that's just after summer—that would be the fall term . . .
6. Let me see. I think I had chemistry lab on Mondays.
7. I don't know. I was probably in the chemistry lab . . .
8. Wait a minute—that would be the second week of school. I remember he started off with the atomic table—a big fancy chart. I thought he was crazy, trying to make us memorize that thing.
9. You know, I think I can remember sitting . . .

The interesting aspect of such examples is that humans are capable of answering a wide variety of complex questions and that we do so, not always by direct recall, but by working on a series of subquestions that get us progressively closer to the answer. In observing the process of question answering, Lindsay and Norman were struck by the observation that their subjects engaged in productive thinking; retrieval is a process that requires several levels of memory.

Another example is to consider the following dictionary definition and try to think of the word it defines:

"A navigational instrument used in measuring angular distances, especially the altitude of the sun, moon, and the stars at sea."

If the answer does not immediately come, try to answer the following questions: What is the first letter of the word? How many syllables does the word have?

The answer the dictionary gives is: SEXTANT.

Brown and McNeil (1966) gave a series of these problems to subjects in a laboratory setting and found that sometimes the answer came right away, sometimes the subjects had no idea what to say, and in a number of cases the subjects were "seized by a tip-of-the-tongue (TOT) state." In this state, the subjects felt that they were on the verge of finding the answer but had not yet found it; they were in a "mild torment, something like the brink of a sneeze." Brown and McNeil were particularly interested in these cases of TOT, and in fact, were trying to induce them as a way of studying the structure of human memory and the process of answering questions. The subjects were asked to describe their thought process aloud; in addition, they were asked the same questions given above while they were in the TOT state: What is the first letter of the word? How many syllables does it have?

In a typical study, 57 instances of the TOT state were induced, and while the subjects could not state the specific word, they were amazingly accurate at "guessing" the first letter (51 percent correct) and guessing the number of syllables (47 percent correct). Brown and McNeil concluded that in the course of searching one's memory for a piece of information, *generic* recall (or a general memory) may precede the *specific* recall of a word, especially when specific recall is felt to be imminent.

Since Brown and McNeil's tantalizing study, psychologists have proposed very detailed and precise theories of how humans organize particular sets of knowledge about the world. These theories have been called "models of semantic memory" because they attempt to represent how meaningful (i.e., semantic) knowledge is stored and used. The two basic models of semantic memory are called *network models* and *set models*, and we shall discuss them in the next two sections of this chapter.

The method used to test these theories is called the reaction time method: subjects are asked to press a Yes or No button in response to questions about their general knowledge base (e.g., Is a collie a dog?). The time to respond is measured in milliseconds and the results are interpreted on the basis of the simple idea that more time means more processes were performed.

Network Models of Semantic Memory

Network models are based on the idea that memory is made up of elements and the associations among them; this view goes beyond the early associationist ideas because (1) the relations may be of many types; (2) the units are meaningful concepts; and (3) the theories can be tested.

FIGURE 11-9.

Hypothetical adult's knowledge structure about animals: Collins and Quillian's network hierarchy.

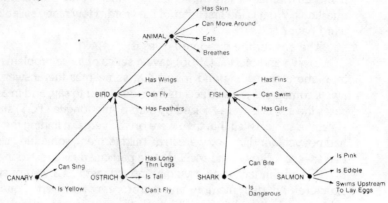

One of the first popular network models was called the *teachable language comprehender* or TLC (Collins & Quillian, 1969; 1972). Although they have revised and amended the specifics of their original model, the goal of Collins and Quillian was to develop a computer program to simulate how humans answer factual questions. According to one version of TLC, the structure of semantic memory is based on (1) *units*— words which represent one thing or subject; (2) *properties*—words which represent characteristics of the unit; and (3) *pointers*—associations of various types among units and properties. An example of a hypothetical adult's knowledge about certain animals is given in Figure 11-9. In this case, words such as *animal, bird,* and *canary* represent units, words such as *is yellow, has wings,* and *has skin* represent properties, and the arrows represent pointers. According to this hierarchical structure, the characteristics or properties of a unit at any one level apply to units connected by pointers at lower levels. In other words, a bird has wings and so does a canary, but the property of having wings is stored only with the higher unit, bird; it cannot be stored with animals because some animals do not have wings.

According to TLC, the process a hypothetical human uses to respond Yes or No to a statement such as "A canary has skin" is a search process as follows:

1. Find the unit for the target word, *canary.*
2. Check to see if the property, *has skin,* is stored with that unit; if not, follow the pointer to the next higher level on the hierarchy, *bird,* and continue as needed to *animal.*
3. When the pointers lead to a unit that has that target property, respond Yes.

It is a bit more difficult to describe how subjects can figure how to respond No to a statement such as "A canary has fins," but one idea is that

FIGURE 11-10.

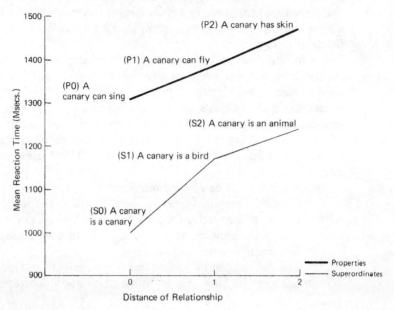

Mean reaction times for answering questions about animals.

the subjects terminate their search and answer No if they fail to reach the unit with the target property within a certain time period.

Formal models like these are elegant and plausible but in order to be useful they must also be testable. Fortunately, this model does offer certain predictions; for example, sentences which require working on just one level of the hierarchy (a canary can sing) should need less processing time than two-level problems (a canary can fly), and a three-level problem (a canary has skin) should take the most time to process. To test these predictions, Collins and Quillian asked their subjects to press a button labeled True or one labeled False in response to questions based on the hierarchies shown in Figure 11-10. Both true and false items were presented, but Collins and Quillian were primarily interested in the time it took their subjects to respond to various true statements, as shown in the figure. It is clear that the more levels there were, the longer the response time, and it took a particularly long time to answer False.

These results are clearly consistent with the predictions; however, to the nonpsychologist they may seem to be not very startling. In addition, the Collins and Quillian model is not the only explanation for such findings. For example, Landauer and Meyer (1972) were able to replicate the basic results of Collins and Quillian but they argued that the results could be explained by supposing that it takes longer to retrieve information from a large category (e.g., animals) than from a smaller category (e.g., birds). In other words, a less complex idea than Collins and Quillian's hierarchy is that subjects have lists of characteristics for various concepts and that it takes longer to answer questions about a long list (animals) than a shorter list (birds). One piece of evidence that seems to support the simpler view is that more time is required to answer false to false statements if they involve a large category (A cliff is an animal) than if they involve a small category (A cliff is a dog).

A second example of a network model of semantic memory has been proposed by Anderson and Bower (1973) in their detailed monograph, *Human Associative Memory*. The HAM (for Human Associative Memory) model, like that of Collins and Quillian, can be expressed as a computer program; however, HAM is based on a series of rules for transforming (or "parsing") incoming information into a deeper memory structure. For example, a proposition can be processed by HAM using the following rules:

1. A proposition can be broken down into its context (C) and its fact (F). For example, the proposition, "In the park the hippie said the debutante needed a deodorant" can be broken down into its context (in the park, in the past) and its fact (the hippie saying that the debutante needed a deodorant).
2. The context can be broken down into time (T) and location (L). In this example, the time is "in the past" and the location is "in the park."
3. The fact can be broken down into the subject (S) and the predicate (P). Here the subject is "the hippie" and the predicate is "saying "that the debutante needed a deodorant."
4. The predicate can be broken down into relation (R) and object (O). The relation in this proposition is "saying" and the object is "that the debutante needed a deodorant."
5. The subject or the object can be broken down into subject (S) and predicate (P) or into context (C) and fact (F). The object "that the debutante needed a deodorant" can be divided into subject ("debutante") and predicate ("needed a deodorant").

To represent a proposition such as the one given above, HAM constructs a "tree diagram" based on three components: (1) *propositions*— the overall proposition for which the tree is constructed; (2) *locations*— places in the tree for various applications of the above rules; and (3) *associations*—relations, including several different types, among locations in the tree.

Figure 11-11 gives the tree diagram and terminal nodes (given at the bottom of the tree) for the proposition about the hippie and the debutante. These nodes represent the meaning of the words. The process of answering a question that involves semantic knowledge is a matching process; for example to answer, "Where did the hippie say that the debutante needed a deodorant?" HAM would first translate the input question into a tree diagram, leaving a "?" for the location. Then the terminal nodes of the question (i.e., the nodes at the bottom) are matched with the corresponding locations in the existing memory. HAM would then continue along the paths until the same relation (in this case, the L relation) is found.

FIGURE 11-11.

Hypothetical adult's knowledge about a proposition: Anderson and Bower's tree diagram.

Proposition: In the park the hippie said the debutante needed a deodorant.

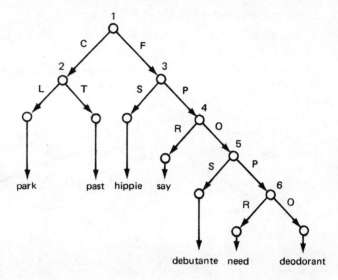

The HAM model has been subjected to various tests with human subjects; the model is clearly consistent with the research discussed in the previous section which indicates that subjects remember the gist (terminal nodes) of sentences rather than the specifics, and it is a concrete model that partly uses Chomsky's distinction between surface and deep structure. However, in summarizing their five hundred pages of research and theory, Anderson and Bower admit that they have failed to "produce decisive evidence" that their particular way of parsing propositions is the one most humans use.

A third network model of semantic memory has been proposed by Rumelhart, Lindsay, and Norman (1972). Their model is based on two structural components: *nodes*, words which stand for concepts or events; and *relations*, lines among nodes which are directed (go from one to another) and labeled (are of different types). Instead of using a hierarchy like Collins and Quillian's or a tree diagram like Anderson and Bower's, this group used the graph representation shown in Figure 11-12. As can be seen, a sentence or set of sentences can be converted into a graph with nodes and relations. To answer a question, the process is to go to the nodes that are mentioned in the question and take paths outward from there.

Unfortunately, there has been much more work in developing the Rumelhart, Lindsay, and Norman model than in testing it. Hulse, Deese, and Egeth (1975) suggested that one implication of the model is that verbs are crucial in remembering since the arrows center on verbs; however, they cited a study by Yates and Caramazza in which recall of learned sentences

FIGURE 11-12.

Hypothetical adult's knowledge about an event: Rumelhart, Lindsay, and Norman's directed graph.

Event: John murders Mary at Luigi's

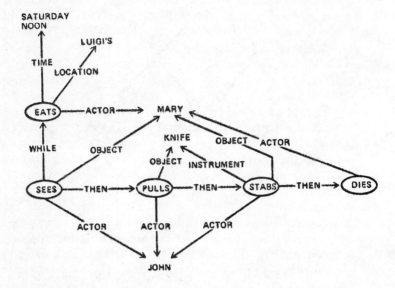

was not better when the cue was a verb from the sentence than when it was a noun.

Set Models of Semantic Memory

Although network models are currently the most numerous, there are other ways to represent semantic memory. For example, Meyer (1970) has proposed a model of how subjects answer questions about semantic memory that is based on the idea that memory is made up of features which belong to sets and sets which belong to larger or supersets and so on; Meyer assumed that each concept is stored in memory as a list of subsets (or features). When subjects were asked to respond to such statements as "All females are writers" or "Some females are writers," they seemed to go through two stages. First, they determined all the subsets of "writer" (including male and female) and all the subsets of "female" to see if there were any overlap, that is, if there were any subsets in common. If there were no common features (as in a sentence like "Some typhoons are wheat"), they answered False; if there were some common features (e.g., writers and females), they would answer True if the statement involved "some" and go on to the second stage if it involved "all." At the second stage, the task was to determine if each subset of "female" was also a subset of "writer"; if yes, the answer was True, if no, it was False.

Meyer's theory predicted that it should take longer to answer questions of the form "All S are P" than "Some S are P" because two stages were required for the first question and only one stage for the latter. Therefore, Meyer was able to predict that response time should increase if the size of category P was increased because the list of subsets was now longer. Meyer used experiments similar to those of Collins and Quillian and obtained results consistent with his (as well as Collins and Quillian's) model. However, while the Meyer model on sets may be just as powerful as Collins and Quillian's network model, neither model can explain results such as why it would take longer or about the same to answer Dog-Mammal than Dog-Animal.

Rips, Shoben, and Smith (1973; Smith, Shoben, & Rips, 1974) have developed a set model of semantic memory that can account for such findings. The main new ingredient in their model is based on a skepticism of Collins and Quillian's assumption that "memory structure mirrors logical structure." In one study, Rips, Shoben, and Smith asked a group of subjects to rate pairs of words in terms of how closely related they were to one another, in order to derive a measure of "semantic distance." For example, they asked the subjects to rate how closely related various kinds of birds were to each other, to the category "bird," and to the category "animal"; or how closely related various mammals were to each other, to the category "mammal," and to the category "animal." The two-dimensional chart that is shown in Figure 11-13 was derived from these ratings; note that high relatedness is represented by short distance.

This method of representing semantic memory predicts that reaction time judgments like those used by Collins and Quillian should be related to semantic distance, and these predictions have been upheld. In other words, according to the semantic distance idea, the reason its takes longer to press the True button for Robin-Animal than Robin-Bird, or longer for Dog-Mammal than Dog-Animal is that the actual semantic distance is greater from Dog to Mammal than Dog to Animal (regardless of logical structure) or from Robin to Animal than Robin to Bird. These authors have further argued that semantic distance is basically a function of how many semantic features the two concepts have in common; in other words, of how much overlap there is between the lists of features that make up the sets.

SUMMARY

This chapter was concerned with the question of "what is learned" by a person who is presented with prose material. Most of the work we have discussed has attempted to extend the early work of Bartlett and to clarify his ideas that memory involves an "effort after meaning" and that recall involves a "construction."

Psychological theories of language comprehension and memory have been heavily influenced by developments in linguistics. In particular, this chapter described behaviorist theories of language, Chomsky's "generative

FIGURE 11-13.

A semantic distance chart showing subjects' ratings of how "related" pairs of words were. Short distances represent high relatedness.

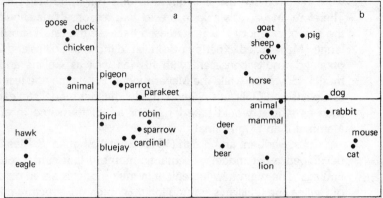

grammar," and more recently developed theories of "case grammar." Chomsky's theory has been interpreted to mean that sentences are stored as "kernel plus correction" or, stated differently, sentence comprehension requires the application of specific transformations.

When the implications of Chomsky's theory were tested in psychological experiments, the results of many of the experiments failed to uphold the theory. Certainly, the idea of transformations is an important one but this approach apparently needs to be modified to fit the reality of existing data.

This chapter also summarizes work on memory for prose passages. The results of Sachs, and Bransford and Franks and others have encouraged the belief that memory is constructive, abstract, and based on meaning rather than on specifics. Their results have also encouraged the development of text analysis systems—ways of representing the information in a text passage that may approximate the processing system used by humans. Although the various theories presented by Johnson, Kintsch, Meyer, Fredericksen and others differ, they are all based on the idea that there are specific sets of "case relations" underlying the meaning of sentences. The fact that these theories can, to varying degrees, predict what will be remembered from a text passage suggests that some progress has been made on the road to determining how knowledge is represented in memory.

Finally, we examined several models of semantic memory. The three network models, Collins and Quillian's TLC, Anderson and Bower's HAM, and Lindsay and Norman's graph theory, plus the two set theories, Meyer's two-stage model and the "semantic distance" model of Rips et al., represent five popular attempts to describe specifically how people structure knowledge and answer questions. These models try to represent what individuals "already" know, while the text analysis systems try to predict what people will learn from acquiring new information.

12/ Memory Processes

Preview

Memory theorists have made a major distinction between memory
structures (the knowledge in memory) and memory processes (the
operations performed on that knowledge). In Chapter 11, we focused
on memory structures, such as the semantic memory models; in this
chapter, we focus on memory processes. Where the previous chapter
took a "Bartlett" approach to human memory by asking "What is
learned from text?" this one follows from the classic work of Donders by
asking "What are the basic cognitive processes that underlie
performance on a particular task?" The goal of this approach is to
determine the internal stages involved in performing an intellectual task.
Among the problems explored in this chapter are: syllogistic and linear
inferences, sentence-picture verification, arithmetic, and computer
simulation of problem solving. Each task is analyzed by breaking the
problem down into the internal stages the subject must go through to
solve it, and the resultant model is then tested against the obtained data.

INTRODUCTION

Suppose a person is seated in front of a panel that has on it a light bulb and a response button. When the light comes on, the subject is required to press the button as quickly as possible. This simple task is called a *simple reaction time* task; it normally requires about .050 to .250 seconds to complete, depending on task characteristics, such as the intensity of the bulb, and on subject characteristics, such as attentiveness, eyesight, and so on.

The situation could be made a little more complicated. Suppose the subject is seated in front of a panel with five light bulbs and one response button. When the target light comes on (e.g., the one designated as "correct"), the subject should press the button, but should not when any of the other bulbs light up. This task is called a *discrimination reaction time* task because the subject must pay attention to (discriminate) *which* particular light comes on. This task normally requires more time than simple reaction time tasks when all the other variables are constant.

Finally, we could complicate the task even further by setting the subject in front of five light bulbs, each of which has its own response button. In this case, the subject must press the button corresponding to which light comes on. This is called a *choice reaction time* task because the subject must not only discriminate between stimuli but must also choose the the appropriate response. All other factors being equal, this task normally takes even longer than the other two.

THE DONDERS EXPERIMENT

Donders performed experiments using these types of tasks in 1868. His work represents the first attempt to analyze quantitatively the components of a very simple task. Donders' reasoning was that different stages of cognitive processing were required for each of the three tasks. As shown in Figure 12-1, a simple reaction task required perception and motor stages (i.e., time to perceive the stimulus and execute the response). In contrast, a discrimination reaction task required perception and motor stages plus a discrimination stage (i.e., time to distinguish which light was on). Finally, choice reaction tasks required perception, motor, and discrimination stages plus a fourth choice stage (time to decide which response to perform). As expected, choice tasks required the most time and simple tasks required the least. Based on these findings, it was possible to calculate the time required for each stage:

perception and motor time = time required for simple task;

discrimination time = time for discrimination task minus time for simple task; and

choice time = time for choice task minus time for discrimination task.

Donders' reasoning was simple and straightforward—more stages should

FIGURE 12-1.

Diagram illustrating components of reaction time.

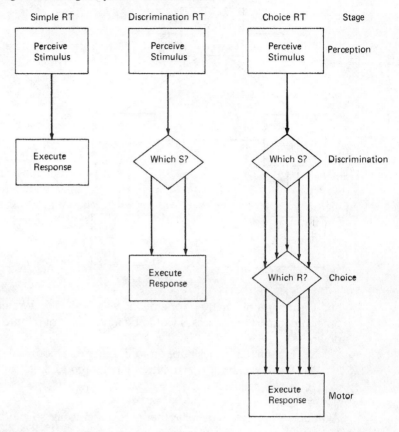

require more time—and his method of analyzing the cognitive components of his task is similar to those used more recently for more complex tasks.

PLANS AND BEHAVIOR

Donders' work is interesting because it offers a means of describing what is going on "inside the black box" by analyzing cognitive activity into separate stages. However, strong interest in subjecting complex intellectual tasks to such an analysis has often not existed and has only rematerialized during the last ten to fifteen years. The rebirth of interest in developing cognitive models of the processes involved in performing tasks can be marked by the appearance in 1960 of a remarkable book by Miller, Galanter, and Pribram called *Plans and the Structure of Behavior*. Figure 12-2 indicates a way of describing the processes involved in the task of hammering a nail. The plan shown is called a TOTE, for Test-Operate-Test-Exit,

FIGURE 12-2.

A hierarchical plan for hammering nails.

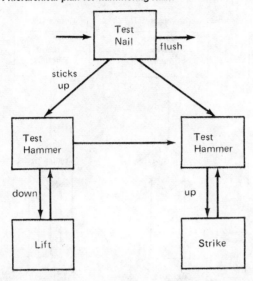

and is simply a hierarchy of operations with feedback. Written as a computer program, the processes would be in the form of a list to be read top down:

1. Test nail. If it sticks up, go to 2; otherwise stop.
2. Test hammer. If down, lift; otherwise, go to 3.
3. Strike nail.
4. Go to 1.

Although it may seem peculiar that psychologists are so interested in how to hammer a nail, such techniques as flowcharts and programs are important because they allow psychologists to specify with precision their theory of the cognitive processes for a certain intellectual task.

Unfortunately, these kinds of representations make no major distinctions between human and nonhuman thought processes. For example, Figure 12-3 shows the "thought processes" of a thermostat. The flowchart could also be represented as a program:

1. Test temperature. If under 70°, go to 2; if over 72°, go to 5; otherwise go to 1.
2. Test furnace. If on, go to 1; otherwise go to 3.
3. Turn furnace on.
4. Go to 1.
5. Test furnace. If off, go to 1; otherwise, go to 6.
6. Turn furnace off.
7. Go to 1.

The development of such ways of describing internal cognitive processes is obviously heavily influenced by the computer analogy—the idea that human thinking processes may be viewed as computer programs or flow-

FIGURE 12-3.

A plan for regulating temperature.

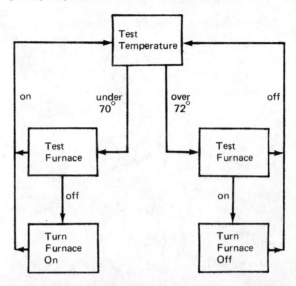

charts, and that humans may be viewed as complex computers. Certainly, the computer analogy is not perfect, but this chapter will explore the efforts to use it to describe in detail the memory processes involved in using learned information.

SYLLOGISMS

Humans are apparently capable of encoding sentences (propositions) and using the encoded information to produce a new, inferenced piece of information. A well-studied example of this ability is represented by syllogistic or logical reasoning tasks. In this section, we will explore the way logically related propositions are encoded in memory and what processes are used to answer questions which require combing the learned information.

Formal Logic

Before we look at the psychological research, it is useful to point out the basic definitions that evolved over centuries of philosophical interest in logical reasoning (Cohen & Nagel, 1962). Propositions that concern set-subset relations can be of four main types:

Universal Affirmative (UA): All A are B.
Universal Negative (UN): No A are B.

FIGURE 12-4.

Possible Venn diagrams for four types of propositions.

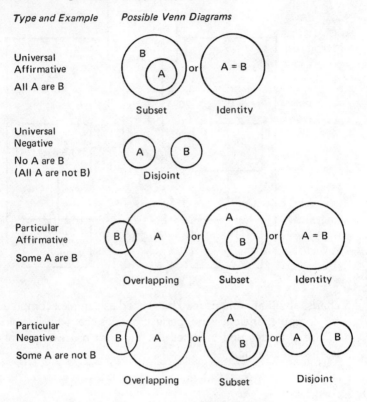

Particular Affirmative (PA): Some A are B.

Particular Negative (PN): Some A are not B.

Venn diagrams* of these four basic "categorical propositions" are given in Figure 12-4. Note that only the UN proposition is unambiguous, while all the others are subject to several interpretations. For example, UA propositions may be interpreted as Set A and Set B being identical, or as Set A being a subset of B. Thus, "All A are B" does not necessarily imply that "All B are A" but it does not rule it out either.

A syllogism consists of two premises and a conclusion with each being any one of the four types of categorical propositions. For example, the famous syllogism,

All men are mortal

Socrates is a man

Therefore, Socrates is mortal

consists of two premises, a UA and a PA, and a conclusion that is also a PA.

*A Venn diagram is a set of circles representing a class of objects or things. The circles can be disjoint (i.e., have nothing in common), identical (i.e., have all points in common), show an overlap relation (i.e., in which both circles have some common and some unique portions), or show a set-inclusion relation (i.e., with one circle entirely inside another).

Content Errors

Content errors occur when the truth or desirability of the premises or conclusion influence the subject's deductions regardless of the logic involved. For example, the following syllogism from McGuire (1960) has a conclusion that logically follows the premises but is undesirable, so that people might find it difficult to accept.

> Any form of recreation that constitutes a serious health menace will be outlawed by the City Health Authority. The increasing water pollution in this area will make swimming at local beaches a serious health menace. Swimming at local beaches will be outlawed by the City Health Authority.

In order to study content errors, Janis and Frick (1943) presented syllogisms as short paragraphs and asked subjects to rate whether they agreed or disagreed with the conclusion and whether or not the conclusion was valid based on the premises. As expected, a high number of errors were obtained, showing a strong tendency for subjects to judge the conclusions they agreed with as valid and the conclusions they disagreed with as invalid. One explanation for these content errors is that the memory processes involved do not occur in a vacuum, but rather the information in the syllogisms is assimilated or fitted into the general past experience of the subject. *Cognitive consistency*—the tendency for information in a person's mind to be internally consistent—may play a role in logical memory processes.

Lefford (1946), using syllogisms like the following, found similar results: there were more errors for conclusions with high emotional content (e.g., #1 and #2) than for less important ones (e.g., #3 and #4), even though the logical form was identical.

1. War times are prosperous times, and prosperity is highly desirable; therefore, wars are much to be desired.
2. All communists have radical ideas, and all CIO leaders have radical ideas; therefore, all CIO leaders are agents for communism.
3. Philosophers are all human, and all human beings are fallible; therefore, philosophers are fallible too.
4. All whales live in water, and all fish live in water too; therefore all fish must be whales.

Parrott (1969; cited in Johnson, 1972) presented three types of syllogisms that were identical in form but constructed with the symbols X, Y, and Z with actual sentences that were true (consistent with the subject's past experience) or with sentences that were false (not consistent with the subject's past experience). Although the instruction made it clear that the subjects were to judge the validity of the conclusion *assuming* the premises were true, there were large differences in performance. The time to produce an answer, in seconds, was 21.9 for symbols, 24.2 for true-premise, and 29.4 for false-premise. Apparently, the content-free syllogisms allowed the subjects to process the information as an independent syllogism and to be less influenced by the need for consistency with other information in their memories.

In a classic experiment on content effect, McGuire (1960) asked a group of subjects to rate a list of propositions for probability of occurrence and for desirability. Nested within the list were the components of several syllogisms with premises and conclusions separated by other propositions. If the subjects were entirely rational (thinking logically), the probability of a conclusion should equal the probability of premise 1 times premise 2. If the subjects were entirely irrational (indulging in wishful thinking), there should be a high correlation between desirability and probability, that is, the subjects should rate highly desirable conclusions as highly probable regardless of the premises. As might be expected, McGuire found evidence for both logical and wishful thinking with a moderately strong positive correlation of .48 between the judged probabilities of the conclusions and the products of the probabilities of the premises, and a correlation of .40 between the rated desirabilities of events and the rated probabilities of occurrence. These results seem to indicate that deductive reasoning involves more than the three propositions in the syllogism, and that subjects try to fit the propositions within their existing cognitive structure or knowledge. Inconsistent or undesirable premises and/or conclusions may be dealt with in a way which violates the rules of logic for a particular syllogism in exchange for preserving the cognitive consistency of the great mass of existing knowledge and beliefs. The important role of propositions and how they are encoded will be explored in more detail in our discussion of form errors.

Form Errors

There are two important categories of errors due to logical form. One is called the *fallacy of the undistributed middle term*; Wilkins (1928) gave the following example:

Wallonians dance the polka. My worthy opponent dances the polka.

Therefore, it is obvious that my worthy opponent is a Wallonian.

The form of the logic is: All A are B; All C are B; therefore, All C are A. The conclusion does not necessarily follow but it is often accepted as true.

The second typical form error is the *particular premises error*, of which Wilkins (1928) cited the following example:

Some Republicans have inherited oil wells. Some Wallonians are Republicans. Hence we know that some Wallonians have inherited oil wells.

The form of the logic is: Some A are B; Some C are A; therefore, Some C are B. Again, subjects often agree with this conclusion although it does not necessarily follow.

The two kinds of errors have also been explained in terms of underlying psychological mechanisms. Woodworth and Sells (1935) and Sells

FIGURE 12-5.

Proportion of subjects choosing each of five possible conclusions.

| Premises | Proportion of Subjects' Conclusions | | | | |
	All S are P.	Some S are P.	All S are not P.	Some S are not P.	None of these.
All P are M, All S are M.	.81	.04	.05	.01	.09
All M are P, No S are M.	.02	.03	.82	.05	.08
All P are M, Some M are S.	.06	.77	.02	.06	.07
Some M are P, All S are not M.	.01	.06	.62	.13	.18
Some M are not P, All M are not S.	.03	.07	.41	.19	.30
All M are not P, Some S are M.	.03	.10	.24	.32	.32

(1936) suggested that these errors resulted from an *atmosphere effect* in which the form of the two premises set an atmosphere favorable to accepting conclusions of certain forms. For example, two UA premises create an atmosphere for the acceptance of a UA conclusion, two UN premises for a UN conclusions, two PA premises for a PA conclusion, and two PN premises for a PN conclusion; in addition, any one negative premise creates a negative atmosphere and any one particular premise creates a particular atmosphere. Subjects were supposed to operate under the rules of logic for many syllogisms, but when they made an error it could be accounted for by the atmosphere effect. Predictions based on this theory have been fairly accurate (Sells, 1936; Morgan & Morton, 1944).

A related psychological explanation of logical errors is *invalid conversion*—the tendency to assume that if "All A are B" then "All B are A," or if "Some A are not B" then "Some B are not A." Note that conversion of the UA and PN propositions above is not valid while conversion of the UN and PA propositions is valid. Thus the invalid conversion theory suggests that errors are due to improper encoding of the premises rather than not following the rules of logic. Chapman and Chapman (1959) gave two premises, in letter form, and asked their subjects to choose the correct conclusion (i.e., the conclusion they could be sure of). An example is:

Some P are S.
Some S are M.
Therefore,
1. All M are P.
2. Some M are P.
3. All M are not P.

FIGURE 12-6.

A flowchart illustrating a model for the atmosphere effect.

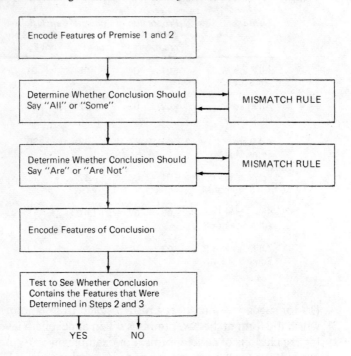

4. Some M are not P.
5. None of these.

Although the correct answer was always "none of these" for each of 42 experimental syllogisms, the subjects chose other conclusions over 80 percent of the time. Some typical responses are shown in Figure 12-5. As you can see, many of the responses like the first three in the figure fit both the atmosphere effect explanation and the invalid conversion explanation; however, the atmosphere effect would predict that the main error for the latter three syllogisms should be "Some S are not P" while the more preferred response was often "All S are not P," a response that could be derived if the subjects made invalid conversions. Thus, the results indicated that invalid conversion could account for a large proportion of errors, including some that could not be accounted for by the atmosphere effect.

Apparently, some errors may be explained by atmosphere and some by conversion, but while the former is a superficial attempt on the part of the thinker to be consistent, the latter reflects an attempt to be logical by using an encoding of the premises that is not quite right. Although conversions may be formally illogical, Chapman and Chapman (1959, p. 224) pointed out that they may be based on consistency with practical past experience: " . . . logically invalid [conversions] often correspond to our experience of reality, and being guided by experience are usually regarded as justifiable procedures. One may realistically accept the converse of

FIGURE 12-7.

A flowchart illustrating a model for the conversion theory.

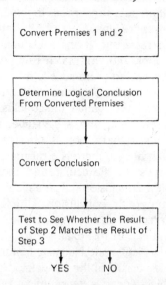

many, perhaps most PN propositions about qualities of objects; e.g., some plants are not green and some greens are not plants. The acceptance of the converse of UA propositions is also often appropriate, e.g., all right angles are 90 degrees and also all 90 degree angles are right angles."

Models for Syllogistic Reasoning

More recently, Erickson (1974) has shown that the way a subject encodes the premises will determine the conclusion that is accepted. For example, a UA proposition may be interpreted as an identity or a subset relation (see Figure 12-4). Erickson has developed norms for the probability that a given premise will lead to a given Venn diagram by asking subjects to draw diagrams for each type of premise. Based on the norms, Erickson can predict with some success the probability of a subject's accepting each possible conclusion. These findings suggest that subjects correctly apply the rules of logic but that they use encodings of the propositions that may not be complete.

Revlis (1975, 1977) has developed specific flowchart models of the atmosphere effect and of conversion; because the models are precise they generate quite specific predictions. Figure12-6 shows a simple flow diagram of the stages involved in syllogistic reasoning according to (one version of) the atmosphere effect. In the first stage, the two premises are "encoded"; for each premise all the subject does is note whether it says "All" or "Some" (i.e., universal or particular) and whether it is positive or negative. For example, the premises "All A are B" and "Some B are not C" would be encoded as Universal/Positive and Particular/Negative. The reasoner must then put the premises together. First the reasoner checks to see if both premises are Universal or both Particular; if so, the conclusion must share that characteristic. If one is Universal and one is Particular, the reasoner must apply the "mismatch rule" which says that if there is a mismatch, the prevailing characteristic must be Particular. Then the reasoner checks the only other "important" feature of the premises: if both are Positive or both are Negative, the conclusion must share this characteristic. If one is Positive and one is Negative, another mismatch rule must be applied which says that if there is a mismatch the winner is Negative. In the example given above, there is a mismatch for Universal/Particular so the conclusion must be Particular and there is a mismatch for Positive/ Negative so the conclusion must be Negative. The fourth step is to encode the two features of the conclusion; if the features match those generated (in this case, Particular and Negative), the reasoner answers Yes, otherwise the answer is No. In this example, the conclusion "Some A are not C" would yield Particular and Negative features and thus evoke a Yes answer.

A simple version of the conversion model is shown in Figure 12-7 . First the subject encodes the premises by translating them into their converted forms. For example, the premises "All A are B" and "Some B are not C" would be encoded as "All B are A" and "Some C are not B." Next the subject puts these two converted premises together to derive the logical conclusion "Some C are not A." The third step is to encode the given conclusion by converting it; if the given conclusion is "Some A are not C," the converted form would be "Some C are not A." The last step is to see if the given conclusion (as encoded into its converted form) matches the conclusion which the reasoner has derived in step 3. If so, as is the case in this example, the subject answers Yes, but if they do not match, the answer is No.

Both these models can account for many of the errors that humans make when judging syllogisms. However, Revlis, using models similar to these, has shown that neither model can explain all the errors. The search is continuing for a more precise model that can account for 100 percent of the data.

LINEAR ORDERINGS

Another type of problem similar to the syllogisms discussed above that has been carefully investigated is reasoning about information presented in linear fashion. For example, A is better than B; B is better than C; Is A better than C? Two important concerns are how the presented information is stored in memory and how it is manipulated to generate inferences needed to answer the question.

FIGURE 12-8.

Proportion correct responses for eight deduction problems.

Premises	Proportion Correct Response	Form of Premises	
		Within Premises	Between Premises
1. A is better than B B is better than C	.61	better-to-worse	better-to-worse
2. B is better than C A is better than B	.53	better-to-worse	worse-to-better
3. B is worse than A C is worse than B	.50	worse-to-better	better-to-worse
4. C is worse than B B is worse than A	.43	worse-to-better	worse-to-better
5. A is better than B C is worse than B	.62	ends-to-middle	better-to-worse
6. C is worse than B A is better than B	.57	ends-to-middle	worse-to-better
7. B is worse than A B is better than C	.41	middle-to-ends	better-to-worse
8. B is better than C B is worse than A	.38	middle-to-ends	worse-to-better

The question for the subjects was stated in each of four ways:
Is A better than C? Is C better than A? Is A worse than C?
Is C worse than A?

Spatial Paralogic

In an early study, DeSoto, London, and Handel (1965) allowed subjects 10 seconds to respond Yes or No to questions such as are given in Figure 12-8. According to the traditional view of logical reasoning, problems 1 and 4 ought to be the easiest since they proceed from one extreme to the middle to the other extreme in presenting the three terms, A, B, and C. However, the results indicated that problem 4 was one of the most difficult and problems 5 and 6, which should be difficult, were among the easiest.

The authors concluded that formal logic is not necessarily used in the way that subjects encode the premises nor how they manipulate them in memory: "Clearly, an altogether different paralogic is required to account for the findings. We would like to propose two paralogic principles . . . that people learn orderings better in one direction than the other . . . [and] that people end-anchor orderings" (p. 515). In other words, subjects try to organize the terms in order from highest to lowest based on the premise sentences and focus on the end terms (the highest and lowest) in the ordering. The first principle is demonstrated by the fact that subjects perform better on an ordering when the terms are presented better-to-worse (such as problem 1) than a mixed order (such as problem 2 and 3) and worst when presented worse-to-better (such as problem 4). The second principle is indicated by the fact that subjects perform better with propositions that give an extreme term first (e.g., the best or worst) followed by the middle term than with propositions that state the middle term followed by an end term; for example, problems 5 and 6 have two propositions that go from ends-to-middle, and are much easier than problems 7 and 8 which have two propositions that each go from middle-to-ends.

DeSoto et al. describe the structure that is required in this task as involving "spatial paralogic" in which an up-down or right-left series of spaces is imagined and the terms of the ordering (i.e., A, B, C) are placed in the spaces. Similar results were obtained using "better-worse," "above-below," "lighter-darker," and "left-right," although performance was generally poorer for left-right possibly because it is harder to imagine horizontal than vertical orderings. Performance was poorer with "worse" than "better," with "below" than "above," and with "right of" than "left of," suggesting that the direction of filling the spatial ordering is important.

Huttenlocher (1968) has summarized a series of experiments which replicated the DeSoto findings but used orderings of the form, "Tom is shorter than Sam. Sam is shorter than Pete. Who is tallest?" Huttenlocher noted that the first premise set up a relationship between two terms (e.g., X taller than Y) and the second premise told the subject where to place the third term (e.g., Z), either "above" or "below" the other two terms. If the subject of the second premise was the third term (such as: Tom is taller than John, Sam is shorter than John; or, Tom is taller than John, Sam is taller than Tom) the error rates and response times to answer "Who is tallest?" or "Who is shortest?" were lower than if the third term was the object of the second premise (such as: Tom is taller than John, John is taller than Sam; or, Tom is taller than John, John is shorter than Sam). Even when the premises were given in the passive voice, performance was better when the third (or mobile) term was the logical subject and grammatical object of the second premise. For example, "Tom is leading John, Tom is led by Sam" was easier than "Tom is leading John, Sam is led by John." Apparently the ability to process the second proposition depends on how it fits into the fixed relation established by the first premise.

Huttenlocher's emphasis on the subject-object grammar of the mobile third term in the second premise adds a new perspective to DeSoto's principle of "end-anchoring." In a clever set of experiments, Huttenlocher found that children could more easily place a block into a concrete ladder or array, as shown in Figure 12-9, if the subject of the instruction sentence was the to-be-placed block. For example, if the ladder had a red block above a yellow block, the children could more easily place a third block (green) in the ladder when they were given sentences in which the green block was the subject, as in "put green over red" or "put green under yellow," than when the mobile block was the object of the sentence as "put red under green" or "put yellow over green." The representation of the premises by adults in linear ordering problems may be similar to placing

FIGURE 12-9.

Huttenlocher's block problem.

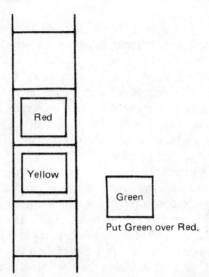

Put Green over Red.

objects into an imaginary array, with the first proposition setting the fixed relation between two terms and the second proposition telling the subject where in the array to place the third term. Answering questions about who is tallest or shortest involves referring to the constructed mental array. Thus, while Huttenlocher retained the idea that humans construct a spatial linear ordering from the premises, she suggested that the difficulty in placing items into the imaginary array was influenced by the grammar of the second premise or what DeSoto called "ends-to-middle" end-anchoring.

Linguistic Approach

While DeSoto and Huttenlocher described the process of representing premises as constructing a spatial image, using principles such as end-anchoring, Clark (1969) attempted to show that deductive reasoning can better be described in terms of (nonspatial) linguistic processes and structures. Clark asked his subjects to respond to questions such as: "If John isn't as good as Peter, and Dick isn't as good as John, then who is the best?" The performance of his subjects on some of the problems seems to fit nicely with the results of DeSoto and Huttenlocher. For example, performance was better on problems in which the propositions went from better-to-worse (A is better than B, B is better than C) than on problems in which the propositions went from worse to better (C is worse than B, B is worse than A). Performance was also better when the third term was the subject of the second proposition (B is better than C, A is better than B) than when it was the object (B is better than C, B is worse than A).

However, based on new information provided by problems using negatives, Clark proposed three principles to describe the encoding in terms of linguistic processes.

The first is the *primacy of functional relations.* Clark argued that it is the logical (or functional) relations in a sentence that are stored rather than the grammatical relations of voice and negation. For example, a sentence like "C is not as good as B" is stored as "B is better than C." According to this principle, sentences with negatives require a translation step which takes more processing time than sentences without negatives. Clark's results generally support this prediction. This idea is closely related to Chomsky's transformational rules discussed in Chapter 11.

The second principle is *lexical markings.* The idea here is that marked adjectives such as "bad" or "short" require more effort to encode than unmarked adjectives such as "good" or "tall." (To test whether an adjective is marked, one might ask whether there is a difference between "How tall is X?" versus "How short is X?" The marked adjective carries the implication that X is short.) According to this view, propositions with simpler lexicons, such as "A is better than B," should be easier to store and process than "B is worse than A." This prediction is also upheld in the results.

The third encoding principle is *congruence.* Performance should be faster if the question is in the same form as the premises. For example, "A is better than B, B is better than C, who is best?" should be easier to answer than "A is better than B, B is better than C, who is worst?" This prediction is also generally upheld.

Most of Clark's results are consistent with Huttenlocher's and with DeSoto's findings, and his linguistic interpretation provides a different—albeit not necessarily contradictory—analysis of how propositions are represented. One fact that Clark's system does not handle well is that reversing the order of the two premises (e.g., from B is worse than A, C is worse than B; to C is worse than B, B is worse than A) increases the difficulty of problems. This finding seems most consistent with the idea of end-anchoring. For example, the first problem in the parentheses above presents items in the order B-A-C so that the end term, C, is anchored into the A-B relation; while the second problem presents items in the order C-B-B so that first the B-C relation is established but the end term, A, is not mentioned next.

Model for Linear Orderings

More recently, Potts (1972, 1974) has focused on the cognitive processes a subject goes through to answer a question about linear orderings. Potts had subjects read a paragraph about a four-term linear ordering which presented the terms in the form, A>B, B>C, C>D, as shown below.

> In a small forest just south of nowhere, a deer, a bear, a wolf, and a hawk were battling for dominion over the land. It boiled down to a battle of wits so

intelligence was the crucial factor. The bear was smarter than the hawk, the hawk was smarter than the wolf, and the wolf was smarter than the deer . . . In the end, each of the battles was decided in its own way and tranquility returned to the area.

One striking finding was that the subjects were faster (or more accurate) in answering questions about remote pairs of terms that were not even presented such as A>C, B>D, or A>D than in answering questions about the adjacent pairs that were actually given such as A>B, B>C, C>D. For example, one of the slowest response times occurred for "Is the hawk smarter than the wolf?" (2.1 seconds) while the fastest time was for a question that required several apparent inferences, "Is the bear smarter than the deer?" (1.0 seconds). Potts called this finding a *distance effect* because the items that were further apart in the ordering were easier to distinguish or "see" as apart than those close to one another. Apparently, subjects do not simply copy the list of three propositions into their memories as separate facts; rather, this finding is more consistent with the idea that they form cognitive representations that are more integrated than the original material such as lists with the items labeled first, second, third, fourth, or even spatial lists as discussed by De Soto.

Potts also provides a detailed model, shown in Figure 12-10, of the processing stages a subject uses to check his or her memory representation in order to answer questions. The stages can be represented in a flow diagram, with the idea that each step adds more time and more chance for error. When a subject has learned an ordering such as, "bear smarter than hawk smarter than wolf smarter than deer," and is given a question like, "Is the hawk smarter than the wolf?" the model suggests several stages. In stage 1, the question is input. Then, in stage 2, the first item in the test question (hawk) is checked to see whether it is the first item in the ordering (if so, the subject can stop and answer True) or, in stage 3, the first item in the test question is checked to see if it is the last item in the ordering (if so, the subject answers False). Otherwise the subject must continue to stage 4 by focusing now on the second item in the test question (wolf) to see whether in stage 5 it is the first item in the ordering (if so, the answer is False) or, in stage 6, the last item in the ordering (if so, the answer is True). If none of these four tests produces a response, the subject performs one final operation by checking to see if the second item in the question is the third item in the ordering; if so, the subject can stop and answer True and if not the answer is False. The model is interesting because it provides specific predictions which can be tested; for example, questions with A (bear) or D (deer) as the first item should be answered most quickly since they require only one or two stages; questions with A or D as the second term should be a little slower because they require three or four stages, and questions with B and C as the items in the question should take the longest. Potts' model is a partial reformulation of the end-anchoring idea because subjects are supposed to pay attention to items on the ends of the ordering; however, it provides a new and testable way of presenting the idea.

FIGURE 12-10.

A flowchart illustrating an information processing model of reasoning with a four-term linear ordering.

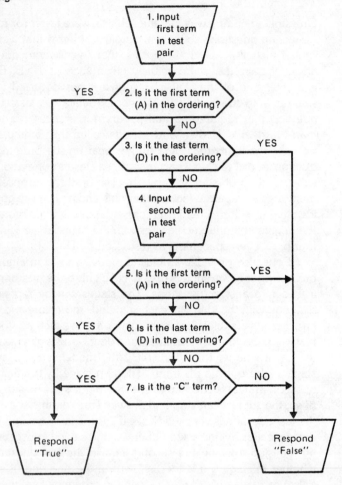

Potts' results deal with learned linear orderings based on information that was newly presented to the subject. Other researchers have obtained similar results in testing linear orderings that are already known to the subject. For example, Moyer and Landauer (1972) presented two digits such as 2 and 5, and asked their subjects to press the button which corresponded to the larger of the two. Reaction time decreased as the distance between the two numbers on the number line increased; (for example, 2−5 was easier than 2−3 and harder than 2−9). In another experiment, Moyer (1973) presented pairs of animal names and asked subjects to judge which animal was larger; again, reaction times were faster for larger differences in size (e.g., mouse-elephant versus mouse-rat). Moyer (1973) attributed his findings to what he called an "internal psychophysics" in which subjects had a spatial image and "perceptually" compared items along the dimensions; items farther apart were easier to discriminate. Holyoak and Walker (1976) provided additional support by testing for judgments concerning dimensions such as temperature, time, and quality; their results supported Moyer's idea in that reaction times were faster when there were greater differences between the items (e.g., ice cube and steam, which is colder?). More recently, Banks, Fujii, and Kayra-Stuart (1976) have proposed a model that assumes that subjects store semantic features rather than a visual image, and there is some preliminary support for their idea. With linear order processing, as with syllogisms, the search continues for a model that can account for all situations.

SENTENCE-PICTURE VERIFICATION

Another important question that has generated considerable research concerns the information processing stages involved in the comprehension of a sentence. In the previous chapter we looked at some of the ways psychologists have tried, with partial success, to represent a sentence in memory, as a kernel sentence or as a predicate and its arguments. In this section, we will explore the closely related question of how a subject comprehends a sentence. One basic experimental method has been to record the response time (RT) it takes a subject to respond True or False to a sentence as compared with a picture.

Clark and Chase (1972; Chase & Clark, 1972) presented sentences, such as, "star is above plus," simultaneously with pictures, such as $\ast$: The subjects were asked to press a True button if the sentence matched the picture, as it does in the example, or a False button if it did not. Four types of questions were asked:

true-affirmative (TA):	star is above plus $\ast$;
false-affirmative (FA):	plus is above star $\ast$;
false-negative (FN):	star isn't above plus $\ast$;
true-negative (TN):	plus isn't above star $\ast$.

Note that true items should be answered True but for false items, the sentence and picture do not match; negative sentences contain "isn't" and affirmative sentences contain "is." Typical results were: it took the subjects longer to respond to negative sentences than affirmatives; with affirmative sentences, the time to answer True was faster than to answer False, but for negatives, the trend was reversed, with time for True longer than that for False. Similar results were obtained for sentences like "star is below plus."

Just and Carpenter (1971) used sentences that involved the color of dots (which were presented as such):

true-affirmative:	dots are red (red dots);
false-affirmative:	dots are black (red dots);
false-negative:	dots aren't red (red dots);
true-negative	dots aren't black (red dots).

In a review of sentence-picture verification studies, Just and Carpenter

FIGURE 12-11.

A flowchart illustrating a linguistic model for sentence-picture verification tasks.

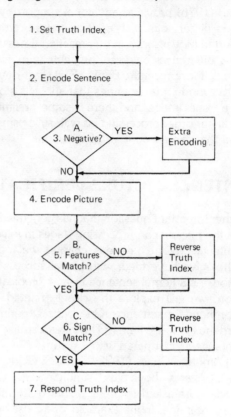

(1975) listed 10 experiments which obtained similar results and none that did not. In all cases, the response time increased from lowest to highest in order: TA, FA, FN, TN.

Do these apparently consistent findings tell us anything about human comprehension of sentences? A major task of researchers who obtained these findings has been to develop a model to account for the results: assuming that longer RTs mean that more cognitive stages are involved, what are the steps involved in simple sentence-picture verification?

First, the sentence and the picture must be encoded; one way to represent the encoding that is consistent with the methods used in the previous chapter is to break each sentence or picture down into its features (in parentheses) and its sign (in front of the parentheses). For example, the sentence, "the star is above plus" would be represented as AFF(star above plus), or "the dots are not red" would be represented as NEG(dots are red), where AFF means "affirmative" and NEG means "negative." Actually, one can assume that AFF strings do not need to be marked by the AFF sign, but negatives must be marked.

Four basic stages that may be involved in comparing sentences with pictures are: (1) *reading and response time*—time to read and encode each picture of a sentence and to execute a response; (2) *negation time*—extra time needed to encode or to process a sentence with a negative in it (e.g., "isn't" or "aren't"); (3) *features mismatch time*—extra time required when the features of two encoded strings do not match (e.g., the sentence may say "red dots" but the picture is of black dots); and (4) *signs mismatch time*—extra time required when the signs of two encoded strings do not match (e.g., the sentence is negative but the picture is affirmative). A model has been suggested by Clark and Chase (1972; Chase & Clark, 1972) based on these stages in which sentences and pictures are encoded and then their features and signs are compared.

Figure 12-11 gives a flow chart based on these stages that can account for the order of results (TA, FA, FN, TN) cited above. The first step is to set the "truth index" to "true" which means that if there are no mismatches the subject will answer "true." Then, in stages 2 and 4, the presented items must be encoded into strings of the form Sign(Features) for the sentence and Sign(Features) for the picture. If no negatives are involved, there is no need to include a sign since AFF is understood, but if the sentence contains a negative, then extra time is required to include the NEG sign in the representation (stage 3). The next decision (stage 5) involves the features of the two strings: if they match, the subject goes on to the next stage without delay, but if they do not, the subject must change the truth index, which takes additional processing time. The final decision (stage 6) involves comparing the signs of the two signs: if they match, the subject goes on to the final stage of response execution but if they do not, the subject must first change the truth index. Thus there are three stages that can add extra time: if the sentence contains a negative that must be encoded (stage 3), if the features do not match (stage 5), or if the signs do not match (stage 6).

This model predicts that true-affirmative sentences will require time only for stage A since there are no negatives or mismatches; false-affirmative sentences require stage A plus stage C (features mismatch) and so should take longer than TA items. False-negatives require stage A plus stage B (because of the negative) and stage D (a mismatch for sign); true-negatives require stage A plus stage B (due to the negative) plus stage C (features mismatch) plus stage D (signs mismatch). Thus TA requires only A processing time, FA requires A plus 1 more stage, FN requires A plus 2 more stages, TN requires A plus 3 more stages. This model, then, correctly predicts the order of RT for the types of sentences with TA fastest, then FA, then FN, and TN taking the longest.

The processing stages and typical RTs for each type of comparison are summarized in Figure 12-12. As both graphs show, the time to respond (RT) increases for questions which require more internal processing stages; for example, FA (2 stages) questions take longer than TA (1 stage), or TN (4 stages) take longer than FN (3 stages). Although the results follow the order predicted by the model, Just and Carpenter (1975) have developed

FIGURE 12-12.

Reaction times for four types of sentence-picture verification questions.

Type of Question	Components	Number of Steps
TA	A	K
FA	A + C	K + 1
FN	A + B + D	K + 4
TN	A + B + C + D	K + 5

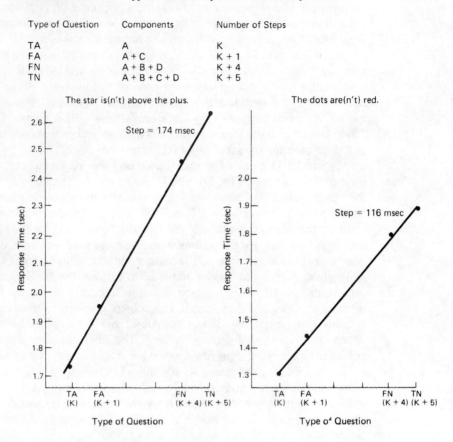

a more basic flowchart model that gives even more specific predictions. Just and Carpenter's model is based on the same idea as Clark and Chase's model, i. e., that subjects encode and then compare the details of the encodings; however, Just and Carpenter add an extra penalty for a mismatch that makes the whole process start over again. In the examples given in Figure 12-12, Just and Carpenter would predict that features mismatch time (C) and signs mismatch time (D) ought to be equal and that negation time should be four times greater than either of them. This prediction accounts for the specific RTs obtained almost perfectly, and indicates that sentence comprehension can be analyzed into a series of flowchart components.

In a clever set of experiments, Just and Carpenter (1976) examined the sentence-picture verification task by recording the eye fixations of subjects as they answered four types of question (TA, FA, FN, TN). Figure

FIGURE 12-13.

Duration of eye fixations for four types of sentence-picture verification questions.

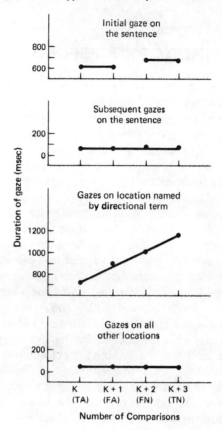

12-13 shows a typical question (in this case, TA) that was presented by tachistoscope; Just and Carpenter measured the length of the initial gaze at the sentence in the middle (perhaps a measure of encoding time), subsequent gazes at the sentence, gazes on the location that was named by the sentence, such as "North" (perhaps a measure of processing time), and gazes at all other locations. The graph labeled "Initial gaze on the sentence" in Figure 12-13 shows that an average of 57 milliseconds more was spent gazing at a negative sentence (e.g., "isn't North") than an affirmative sentence (e.g., "is North"), perhaps indicating added encoding time for negatives. Also, length of gaze at the indicated location (see the graph labeled "Gazes on location named by directional term") increased from TA to FA to FN to TN, perhaps indicating that additional comparisons were performed at the rate of 135 milliseconds per comparison. Thus length of initial gaze at the sentence seems to be correlated with encoding time, and length of gaze at the indicated position is related to match-mismatch processing, while the other two measures indicate random activity that is constant for all questions. These results are encouraging because they provide support for the model by using an entirely different experimental procedure.

ARITHMETIC PROCESSING

Another cognitive task that has received research attention is the problem of how children and adults solve simple arithmetic problems such as addition or subtraction. Since arithmetic behavior is certainly a learned behavior, this work is aimed at determining "what is learned"—e.g., what solution algorithm is used and whether it can be taught more effectively.

Groen and Parkman (1972) reviewed a series of experiments in which subjects were asked to answer problems in the form M + N = _____, where M and N were digits ranging from 0 to 9, and the total was always a single digit number (0 to 9). In a typical experiment (Suppes & Groen, 1967), the problems were presented by a slide projector and the subjects responded by pressing one of ten buttons labeled 0 through 9.

Groen and Parkman suggest five different "models" or information processing procedures that subjects might use in solving these simple addition problems. The one that most closely matched the data of most first graders is the "minimum model" shown in Figure 12-14. According to this procedure, the subject sets a counter to M or N (whichever is larger) and then increments the counter by the smaller of the two numbers. For example, for 4 + 2 = _____, the subject would start with 4, increment once to 5, once more to 6, and answer "6." This procedure predicts that the number of increments should always be equal to the smaller of the two numbers. The bottom of Figure 12-14 shows the mean reaction time for problems that have "smaller" numbers of 0, 1, 2, 3, or 4. As can be seen, the response time increases (on the average) as the size of the smaller number increases. The dashed line is a regression line which indicates the predicted performance if behavior was completely determined by the minimum model. In this case, the intercept averages 2.53 seconds, thus indicating that the average time to simply read and answer a problem is 2.53 seconds, and the slope is .34 seconds, indicating that each time a subject mentally increments the "counter," about one-third of a second is required. There were, of course, wide individual differences with slopes ranging from .12 to .73 seconds for different subjects. These results were very close to those obtained by Suppes and Groen (1967) and also fit nicely with the results of experiments on mental estimation and counting (Beckwith & Restle, 1966). Although the results in Figure 12-14 come from part of a sample of first graders, similar results have been obtained with adults; Parkman and Groen (1971) found that adults tend to use a minimum model but perform the internal counting much faster than children.

More recently, Woods, Resnick, and Groen (1975) have investigated five models of subtraction. In a typical experiment, subjects were given

FIGURE 12-14.

Top: Flowchart illustrating the minimum procedure for simple addition. Bottom: Results that were predicted and obtained.

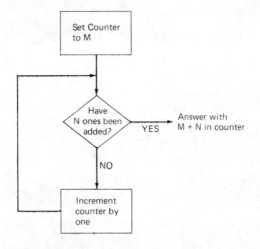

Results for selected first graders were as follows:

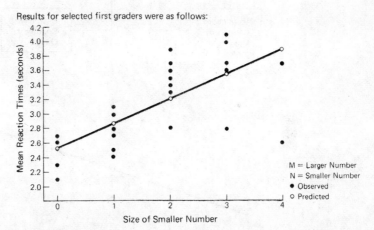

problems in the form M − N = _____, where M and N were digits from 0 to 9 and the answer was also a digit from 0 to 9. For some second graders, a "decrementing model" seemed to best fit their performance. The procedure is to set the counter to M (the higher number) and decrease it N times. This model would predict that reaction time should be related to the smaller number, N, because it determines the number of times a subject must count. The results showed that for these second graders, reaction time increased as the smaller number, N, increased.

For some second graders and all fourth graders, behavior could be best accounted for by a "choice" model shown in Figure 12-15. In this case, the subject either uses the decrementing procedure or sets the counter to N (the smaller number) and increments it until M is reached.

FIGURE 12-15.

Top: Flowchart illustrating the choice procedure for simple subtraction. Bottom: Results that were predicted and obtained.

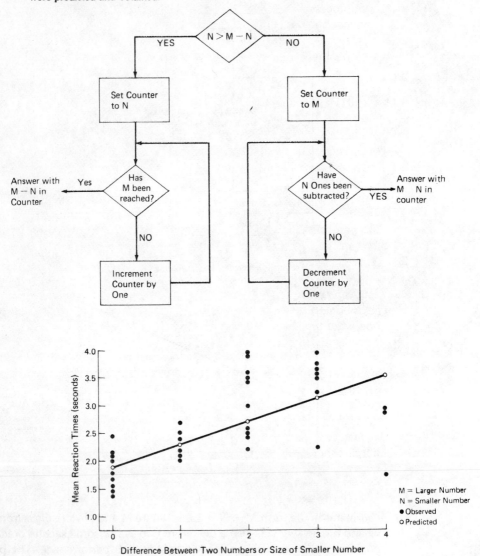

This model predicts reaction time should depend on the smaller of N or M−N and the results are given in the bottom section of Figure 12-15. Reaction times increase for problems requiring more decrements (larger N) or more increments (larger values of M−N).

Resnick (1976) has suggested that learning to subtract might involve building on "partial" knowledge such as the decrementing procedure; in other words, older subjects presumably add on new features such as the "increment" option to the decrementing model to produce the choice model. Further, if complex mathematical tasks can be analyzed into components as has been done for simple addition and subtraction, the component processes may be taught to children in logical ways, or errors can be diagnosed more effectively. Resnick, Wang, and Kaplan (1973), for example, have produced a task analysis of a mathematics curriculum that presents the to-be-learned algorithms as a hierarchy of behaviors.

COMPUTER SIMULATION

Models attempt to represent the stages that humans go through during the encoding and manipulation of new information; if they are precise enough they can be written as computer programs. Why would anyone want to spend the time to program a computer to perform some intellectual task? The motives probably vary, but the reason given for many early attempts was to see if machines could think. The attempt to develop computer programs that display intelligence, that is, can understand natural language or learn to play chess for example, is generally referred to as the field of *artificial intelligence*. A subfield of particular interest to cognitive psychologists is the development of computer systems that display the same problem-solving behavior as humans—i.e., behavior which simulates human behavior. This field is referred to as *computer simulation*. If one were interested in building a machine that could serve as an encyclopedia and answer any spoken question, such as HAL in *2001* or COMPUTER in *Star Trek*, it probably would not matter if its memory storage system and language perception system were not the same as in humans as long as it "worked"—hence, that would be a problem in artificial intelligence. However, if one had a particular theory of how humans solved a problem (not necessarily the best or most logical method), computer simulation could be used to test the theory. The logic of computer simulation is simple: if a computer program produces the same problem-solving behavior as a human, then those series of operations are an accurate representation of the human thought processes.

The experimental method used with computer simulation generally involves asking subjects to solve problems aloud while giving a running description of their thought processes and behavior. Based on careful analyses of the obtained *protocols* (the transcript of all the subject's comments), the experimenter may derive a description of the mental processes a subject used to solve the problem. By specifying these as a computer program, the experimenter has a precise description that can be tested by feeding it to a computer and observing how closely the computer's protocol matches the subject's. If the match is close, the experimenter may conclude that the description of the processes a subject is using to solve a particular problem is accurate; if not, it is necessary to make up a new program and try again.

Although computer simulation offers a new tool for generating and testing theories of human thinking, much popular attention has been directed towards a complementary issue: how can we know whether a machine thinks? Years before the technology for computer simulation existed, the mathematician Turing (1950) wrote an article entitled "Can Machines Think?" in which he proposed the following test—now called the Turing Test: put two teletypwriters in a room with a person to serve as a judge. The judge may ask any questions he or she likes by typing. One teletype is connected to a person in another room who communicates by typing the answers and the other is connected to a computer which also types out its answers. If the human judge cannot tell which teletype is connected to the machine and which is connected to the human, then the computer is thinking.

There is, of course, an interesting flaw in the "logic" of computer simulation. Just because a computer and a human give the same behavioral output, does that really mean they are using the same cognitive processes? In addition, protocol states may not accurately reflect internal states. The idea seems particularly absurd in light of the fact that computers use entirely different components than the human brain; yet, a computer program is a very precise and testable way to state a theory of human memory and thinking and as such offers an opportunity to go beyond earlier vague theories. Talking about programs and states may be no more absurd than talking about thoughts or ideas—all are abstractions which must ultimately be described in a way that provides clear tests.

Problem Space

Ernst and Newell (1969) suggested four major components in describing problem solving by computer simulation. First, the initial state is the point at which the given or starting conditions are represented. The goal state is the point where the final or goal situation is represented. Third are operators, which list all the allowable manipulations or moves which may be performed on any one state to change it into another state. Finally, the fourth component is the problem states, intermediate states that result from the application of an operator to a given state. The *problem space* or the *state-action tree* is the set of all possible *problem states* resulting from all possible sequences of the application of operators.

Thomas (1974) used an example of problem space in the problem of the Hobbits and the Orcs shown in Figure 12-16. Three Hobbits and three Orcs are on one side of a river and they all need to get to the other side. They must use a boat that can carry one or two riders, but at no time may the Orcs outnumber the Hobbits on either side of the river. Here the initial state is: Left = 3H, 3O, BOAT; Right = EMPTY. The goal state is: Left = EMPTY; Right = 3H, 3O, BOAT. The operations are to move a 1H, 2H, 1O, 2O, or 1H and 1O from the side with BOAT to the other side as long as H's are never outnumbered.

Solving a problem can thus be viewed as finding the correct path or

FIGURE 12-16.

Problem space for the Hobbits and Orcs problem. Each state is specified by a three-digit code: (1) the number of hobbits on the starting side, (2) the number of orcs on the starting side; (3) the location of the boat—1 if it is on the starting side and 0 if it is on the opposite side.

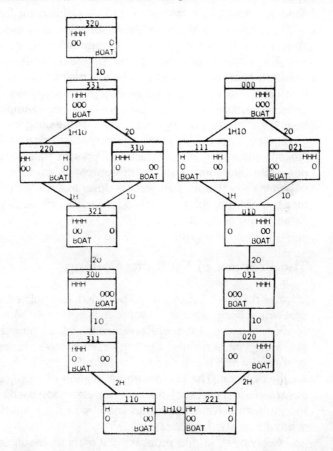

route through a problem space. As Wickelgren (1974) pointed out, it is often possible to "prune the tree." For example, the space can be reduced by thinking in terms of "macroactions" in which different sequences of actions often result in the same problem state. Alternately, the space can be reduced by working both forward (from the given state) and backward (from the goal state). Finally, the problem space can be broken down into smaller *subgoals*.

Past Experience

In solving problems, that is, in moving through a problem space, a subject must also rely on past experience. Lindsay and Norman (1972) have distinguished among several types of relevant past experience used in problem solving, including *facts*, which are immediately available to the subject; *algorithms*, which are sets of rules that automatically generate the correct answers; and *heuristics*, which are rules of thumb or general plans of action. For example, generating a solution to the question "What is 8 times 4?" involves a fact; generating a solution for "What is 262 times 127?" involves an algorithm or set of rules; and estimating the correct answer by rounding to manageable numbers may involve a heuristic.

Algorithms guarantee correct problem solutions since all that is needed is to apply a past set of rules to a new situation. The set of rules can be stored as a *subroutine*, thus saving memory load. Heuristics, on the other hand, may not solve the problem. For example, the heuristic of finding a related or analogous problem or breaking the problem into subgoals may help but does not guarantee solution. A major heuristic is "means-ends analysis" in which the present state is compared with the new state that could result from application of an operator in order to determine whether the new state is closer to the goal. If it is, the "move" is made; if not, the solver searches for another move that produces a state closer to the goal state.

The Process of Problem Solving

Ernst and Newell (1969) have provided a simplified description of the problem solving process. The *Input* is acted on by a *Translator* which converts it into an *Internal Representation* (including the initial state, the goal state, and a means of telling which problem states are closer to the goal state) which is acted on by *Problem Solving Techniques* which generate the *Solution*. The internal representation of a problem can take many forms including the problem space representation we discussed earlier, and the problem solving techniques may be represented as operators, facts, subroutines, and heuristics.

Greeno (1973) has proposed the memory model for problem solving shown in Figure 12-17. The three main components of interest in describing problem solving are: short-term memory, through which the external description of the problem is input; long-term memory (semantic and factual memory), which stores past experiences with solving problems such as facts, algorithms, heuristics, related problems, et cetera; and working memory, in which the information from STM and LTM interact and the solution route is generated and tested.

A description of the problem, including the initial state, the goal state, and the legal operators, comes into working memory by way of short-term memory as represented by arrows from STM to WM; and past experience about how to solve the problem enters working memory from LTM, as represented by the arrow from LTM to WM. The arrows from WM to STM and LTM to STM suggest that more information from the outside world may be required as problem solving progresses (i.e., the solver may pay attention to different aspects of the presented information) and the arrow

FIGURE 12-17.

Schematic diagram showing components of memory.

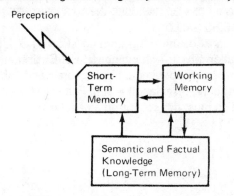

from WM to LTM suggests that the generation of new problem states in WM may require more old information from past experience. The concept of working memory, first introduced by Feigenbaum (1970), has special importance in Greeno's model: the internal representation of the problem occurs there, the construction of links between givens and unknowns occurs there, and relevant past experience is used to modify the structures held in WM.

For example, Bobrow (1964) developed a program called STUDENT to attempt to solve algebra story problems. Here is a typical problem:

The gas consumption of my car is 15 miles per gallon. The distance between Boston and New York is 250 miles. What is the number of gallons of gas used on the trip between New York and Boston?

The first step is translation from the external representation to an internal representation of the problem. The program derived the following equations from the statement of the problem:

(Distance between Boston and New York) = ([250] miles)

(X1) = (Number of gallons of gas used on trip between New York and Boston)

(Gas consumption of my car) = ([15 miles]/1[gallon])

An additional piece of information added to the internal representation comes from existing knowledge (or LTM):

(Distance) = (Gas consumption) × (Number of gallons of gas used)

Thus, with the preceding information entered into WM—the first three from STM and the latter one from LTM—the program is ready to start manipulating the information in WM. In order to work successfully on this information, several assumptions must be made:

Gas consumption = Gas consumption of my car

Distance = Distance between Boston and New York

Number of gallons of gas used = Number of gallons of gas used on a trip between New York and Boston

The problem-solving techniques, consisting of algebraic and computational algorithms, may now be applied, with the result being that the computer prints out:

> THE NUMBER OF GALLONS OF GAS USED ON A TRIP BETWEEN NEW YORK AND BOSTON IS 16.66 GALLONS.

As can be seen, most of the programming effort of STUDENT was devoted to the translation phase—changing natural English into an internal representation that can be operated on by algebraic and computational subroutines. The internal representation is simply a set of algebraic equations with phrases which must be recognized as equivalent to terms stored in memory.

GPS

One of the best-known and most general programs is known as General Problem Solver or GPS (Ernst & Newell, 1969). GPS was intended as a demonstration that certain general problem-solving techniques are involved in a wide spectrum of problems, and that it is possible to state explicitly what these general procedures are in a computer program that will be able to solve a wide variety of different types of problems.

GPS, like other programs, begins by translating a statement of the problem into an internal representation of the initial state, goal state, and set of operators. In addition, GPS has stored in its memory a "Table of Connections" for each problem it will solve; the table of connections contains all possible problem states for that problem with a listing of how far apart any two states are from one another. Problem solving involves *breaking a problem down into subgoals* and achieving each subgoal by *applying various problem-solving techniques*, each of which changes the problem state in the direction of the subgoal. For example, the program can try a technique and then test whether it changes the problem state to one that is closer to the subgoal by checking the difference on the table of connections; if the technique succeeds, the program uses that technique and the process starts over, but if it fails, the program tries another technique. Thus, when GPS solves a problem it performs the following steps: (1) translates the problem into initial state, goal state, and legal operators; (2) has the appropriate table of connections in memory in order to tell the difference between the states; (3) breaks the problem down into a hierarchy of goals and subgoals, each of which brings the problem closer to solution; (4) applies problem-solving techniques based on the principle of means-ends analysis (reducing the difference between the present state and the desired subgoal state); and (5) when one subgoal is achieved, moves on to the next one until the problem is solved. The entire process is presided over by the "problem-solving executive" which determines the order in which operators will be applied, attempts to achieve subgoals by using means-ends analysis, and develops a new subgoal structure if one does not work.

An example of one problem GPS can solve is the three-coin problem:

FIGURE 12-18.

Solution tree for the three-coin problem.

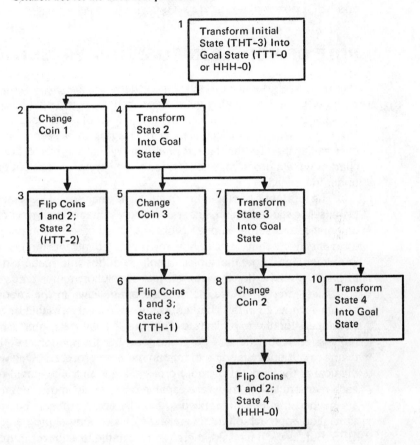

there are three coins on a table with the first and third coin showing tails and the second coin showing heads (i.e., THT). The problem is to make all three coins show the same—either heads or tails—in exactly three moves with each move consisting of flipping any two coins. The initial state is: THT-3 and the goal state is either TTT-0 or HHH-0 where T refers to tails, H to heads, and 3 to the number of moves remaining.

The problem requires ten goals, attempted in the order shown in Figure 12-18. The changes in the problem state progress from THT-3 to HTT-2 to TTH-1 to HHH-0. First, step 1 states the goal of getting from the initial state to the goal state. To accomplish this, GPS tries the move in step 2 and this results in a new problem state (step 3). Now the goal of GPS is to get from this new state to the goal state (step 4), so it tries the move in step 5 and produces a new problem state (step 6). This time the goal is to get from the new state to the goal state (step 7); in step 8, a move is made which produces a new state (step 9), and in step 10, GPS notes that the goal state has been achieved!

GPS can also solve variations of the Hobbits and Orcs problems, water jar problems, letter series completion problems, calculus problems, and half a dozen other different tasks.

ROLE OF MODELS IN COGNITIVE PSYCHOLOGY

Precise models such as detailed flowcharts or computer programs are useful ways of representing the memory processes involved in intellectual tasks because they provide a clearly testable set of predictions. The recent interest in analyzing intellectual tasks into stages can be seen as an advance over earlier theories that lacked precision. When one has to draw a flowchart or write a program, one is forced to be very precise about the theory under investigation.

The present chapter introduced stage analyses of several types of tasks: syllogistic reasoning, linear orderings, sentence-picture verifications, arithmetic, and some "move" problems. In all cases, two important features affecting behavior were how the presented information was encoded in memory, and how the subject manipulated the information in memory to produce a new (for the learner) fact or solution.

There are, of course, several important flaws in the modeling approach introduced in this chapter. As the number of tasks that have models developed for them proliferates, we are left with an impressive set of models, each specific to a particular task, but there is no overall general theme to our understanding of human memory processes. One wonders if the goal of the study of memory processes is to produce a mini-model for each memory task humans are capable of; certainly, more general models are needed that can be applied to a wider array of tasks. The computer simulation approach offers several examples of general programs, such as GPS. But, as we have said, there is a flaw in the logic of computer simulation: just because a computer program produces behavior similar to human behavior, this does not mean that the program represented the thought processes of the person.

In conclusion, the capacity for complex cognitive processing remains an exciting frontier of experimental work. With the aid of newly developed techniques for providing precise models, the work is continuing to bring us closer to a satisfactory theory of "how the human mind works."

SUMMARY

In this chapter we have explored how recent advances in cognitive psychology have allowed the development of precise models of the internal, cognitive stages that comprise various intellectual tasks. We began with a discussion of Donders' classic experiments on reaction time and his "subtraction" system for analyzing out the internal stages that mediated between stimulus and response.

Although Donders' interest in analyzing the internal, cognitive stages for intellectual tasks was largely ignored by the learning theorists who followed him, his approach has been revived during the 1960s and '70s. The revival was signaled by a book by Miller, Galanter, and Pribram called *Plans and the Structure of Behavior* in which the authors argued that individual cognitive processes, or plans, underlie behavior and that these plans can be analyzed.

One important task that has been much studied is syllogistic reasoning. Several theories to explain why subjects make logical errors were presented, including the notions of atmosphere effect and invalid conversion, and two of them were formulated as flowcharts. Although no theories as yet can predict 100 percent of performance in judging syllogisms, progress is being made toward developing a more precise model.

Another task involves drawing inferences from linear orderings of words. Again, we discussed several theories, including spatial paralogic and linguistic analysis. Finally, Potts' process model was presented as a means to account for the finding that subjects perform better on problems that require inferences than on problems that require simple recall.

A third task that has been analyzed into stages is sentence-picture verification. Several process models were presented, each of which closely predicts the data from experimental studies.

Arithmetic behavior has also been successfully modeled. Parkman and Groen provided a simple model for addition and Resnick provided one for subtraction. Both fit the obtained data fairly well.

The computer simulation approach is another way to define precisely the steps that are thought to be necessary to solve a given problem. An example from GPS was given to show how a task can be modeled.

Finally, we discussed the role and importance of precise models of cognitive processes, including their possible flaws and shortcomings.

13/ Concept Learning

Preview

The concept learning task involves an agreed-upon paradigm (or method) for studying a basic type of human learning. Although all the experiments in this section are concerned with how humans form concepts, and although most of the experiments share a common paradigm, a wide variety of theoretical issues are involved. Some of the questions that have been investigated in concept learning research are: Is learning a gradual or an all-or-none process? Which cues will the subject pay attention to in learning? How do imagery and language influence concept learning? Are there universal categories or classification systems all humans use in thinking? What mental strategies do subjects use? We shall look at how these questions can be answered by studying how humans behave in rule learning and concept learning tasks.

INTRODUCTION

In a typical concept-learning experiment, the investigator presents the subject with a pile of cards that contain pictures of different colors, shapes, sizes, and number of objects. For example, the colors could be RED or GREEN; the shapes CIRCLE or SQUARE; the sizes SMALL or LARGE; and the number of objects ONE or TWO. The experimenter picks one out, asks the subject to "guess" whether it is a Yes or a No, and then places it in either a Yes or a No box.

The first few instances could be: 1 red large square, No; 1 green large square, No; 2 red small squares, Yes; 2 red large circles, No; 1 green large circle, No; 1 red small circle, Yes; 1 green small square, Yes; 1 red small square, Yes. The subject must produce the same response for a different set of stimuli, that is, in this case, the subject must say Yes for 2 red small squares, 1 red small circle, 1 green small square, and so on. Furthermore, the subject must make different responses to a different set of instances based on some rule, as, for example, small is Yes, large is No.

The behaviors involved in concept learning may be seen as extensions of the discrimination and generalization learning we discussed in Chapter 6. However, in discrimination learning, the subject is repeatedly presented with the same stimuli (e.g., a black card is Yes and a white card is No), while in concept learning, the stimuli differ from trial to trial (e.g., 1 small red circle, 2 large green circles, and so on). The subject must *generalize* by putting all the different Yes instances together and all the No instances into another category; the subject must *discriminate* by responding Yes to some instances and No to others.

There are, of course, other possible categories and category names. For example, a child might form the concept of DOG by being presented with a poodle, a terrier, and a collie and being told that each was a dog. One problem with learning the concept this way—that is, from many positive instances but no negatives—is that the child may form a concept that is too broad: when presented with a cat or a rabbit, the child might also call it "Dog." Both the learning tasks cited above are examples of *concept learning*, which is also called *concept formation* or *concept identification*. In concept learning, a subject learns a rule for classifying a series of objects into mutually exclusive categories based on one or more dimensions of the stimuli. When the basic stimulus dimensions are given in advance (as in the first example), this kind of learning is sometimes called "concept identification"; when the subject is not told the basic set of potentially important stimulus dimensions, the task is sometimes called "concept formation." Note that when humans try to solve problems like these, they sometimes begin by forming rules or hypotheses that are based on the wrong or too few dimensions. However, as more experience with the various dimensions is acquired, correct performance increases. The remainder of this chapter will investigate the process underlying this improvement.

FIGURE 13-1.

Matrix illustrating the continuity theory of concept learning.

			Number		Color		Size		Shape	
			Habit Increment for Each Dimension							
Trials	Stimulus	Answer	1	2	R	G	L	S	C	S
1	1 red large square	No	−	+	−	+	−	+	+	−
2	1 green large square	No	−	+	+	−	−	+	+	−
3	2 red small squares	Yes	−	+	+	−	−	+	−	+
4	2 red large circles	No	+	−	−	+	−	+	−	+
5	1 green large circle	No	−	+	+	−	−	+	−	+
6	1 red small circle	Yes	+	−	+	−	−	+	+	−

THEORIES OF CONCEPT LEARNING

Concept learning is similar to but more complex than the discrimination process we discussed in Chapter 6; as a result, it provides a basis for theories of learning and cognition that go well beyond the conditioning theories described in earlier chapters. The process required in concept learning has been characterized in several ways, including the *continuity theory*, which views concept learning as a direct extension of the S-R associationist model (see Chapter 6), and the *noncontinuity theory*, which views concept learning as a process in which rules (or hypotheses) are induced and then tested. Since the continuity and the noncontinuity theories of learning yield different predictions about behavior, the following two subsections will investigate them in more detail.

Continuity Theory

The most obvious and straightforward theory of concept learning involves a simple extension of habit acquisition. During concept learning, the subject forms a response hierarchy for each attribute in the problem by tallying the number of times each category has been or has not been associated with a given attribute. When a new example is given, the subject simply "adds up" the response strengths for all attributes present in the new example. Eventually, after many examples or instances have been given, the critical dimension-value becomes the strongest. Learning and thinking in the continuity view then, are simply the building of response hierarchies.

For example, consider the first task described in the introduction of this chapter, in which subjects are shown cards with drawings that are either RED or GREEN in color, LARGE or SMALL in size, CIRCLE or SQUARE in shape, and ONE or TWO in number. The continuity theory assumes that each type or color, size, number, and shape builds its own response hierarchy (with the associated responses either Yes or No) based on past experience, as shown in Figure 13-1.

Suppose the subject has seen the following six instances: 1 red large square is No, 1 green large square is No, 2 red small squares is Yes, 2 red

FIGURE 13-2.

Stimuli used in Hull's concept learning experiment. Characters with the same radical had the same names.

Word	Concept	Pack I	Pack II	Pack III	Pack IV	Pack V	Pack VI
oo							
yer							
li							
ta							
deg							
ling							

large circles is No, 1 green large circle is No, and 1 red small circle is Yes. How do the subjects learn? The continuity theory suggests that they keep a mental tally of how many times each attribute-value (e.g., red, green, etc.) has been associated or not associated with a Yes or a No. The tallies for the first six instances are shown in Figure 13-1. For example, 1 red large square is No means 1 gets one minus (−), 2 gets a plus (+), red gets a minus, green gets a plus, and so on. In the system shown in Figure 13-1, minus means the attribute-value was part of an object put into Group No or not part of an object put into group Yes; plus means that the attribute-value was part of an object put into Group Yes or not part of an object put into Group No. There are alternative ways of specifying the tally system for the continuity theory, but all are similar to the one described above.

Now suppose the subject is given "1 green small square" and must predict whether it is a Yes or a No. In order to answer, the subject must "add" the tendencies to say Yes or No for each attribute-value based on past experience. For example, after six instances, the totals are as follows:

one: 2 Yes and 4 No
green: 2 Yes and 4 No
small: 6 Yes and 0 No
square: 3 Yes and 3 No

The totals for "1 green small square" are 13 Yes and 11 No, so the response may be a weak Yes. If "1 green small square" turns out to be in fact a Yes, the response strength for Yes after the attribute value would be modified, and so on. As practice continues, the difference between Yes and No response strengths will become closer to zero for all nonsize attributes and the differences for size will continue to grow.

Hull (1920) was the first to investigate this abstraction process in concept learning experimentally. Subjects learned to give one of 12 responses to 12 Chinese characters (shown in Figure 13-2). First the character was shown and the subject gave a response such as "oo," "li," "ta," and then the correct response was given to the subject. Once a subject had learned the correct name for all 12 characters, a second pack of 12 new characters was shown, but the same 12 responses were associated with each character as with the first group. This process continued with several different packs. Chinese characters are made up of certain basic features called "radicals," and in the experiment, the same radical was always associated with the same response. In the figure, the concept and the radical are shown on the left.

Subjects showed much improvement on later packs of characters and were often able to "guess" the correct response for characters they had never seen before. Hull concluded that the subjects had abstracted the basic radicals and had developed strong tendencies to respond to them as described by the continuity theory. That is, the relevant attributes—the radicals—strongly evoked the current responses because they were reinforced; the irrelevant features, however, tended to become neutral because they were not reinforced consistently. The process could be speeded up by coloring the radicals red, thus drawing the subject's attention to the relevant dimension. (This speed-up is an example of "cue salience" described in a later section of this chapter.)

Noncontinuity Theory

Can concept learning be explained by this relatively simple, straightforward view of the thinker as passively and gradually tallying past experience into multiple response hierarchies? The noncontinuity view is that concept learning is not a process of gradually strengthening associations at all but is rather a noncontinuous or discontinuous process of constructing and testing hypotheses (i.e., classification rules) until one works. According to the hypotheses-testing view, humans actively try to formulate rules and they stick with their rule until it fails—this has been called the "win-stay, lose-switch" strategy. (This idea is also discussed in the section on learning set formation in Chapter 6.)

For example, in the task discussed previously (see Figure 13-1), a subject who is first told that one-red-large-circle is No might hypothesize that "Red is No, Green is Yes." Then, on the next trial, when the subject sees one-green-large-square, the answer will be Yes. Since that is a wrong guess, the subject will make up a new hypothesis, such as "One is No, Two is Yes" which works for two-red-small-squares; but when this fails again on two-red-large-circles, the hypothesis may be changed to "Small is Yes,

FIGURE 13-3.

Schematic diagram illustrating reversal and nonreversal shifts.

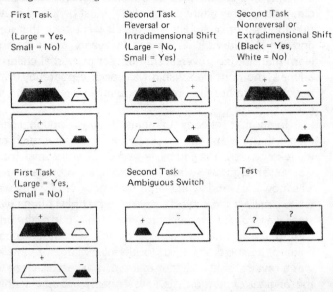

Large is No," and from then on out the subject will make no more errors. In this noncontinuity view, concept learning involves making up a hypothesis and keeping it until it is disconfirmed, rather than gradually learning associations. Finding the correct solution is an "all-or-none" process.

The Kendlers (Kendler & D'Amato, 1955; Kendler & Kendler, 1959; Kendler & Kendler, 1962; Kendler & Kendler, 1975) attempted to investigate which of the two theories of concept learning (continuity versus noncontinuity) best described behavior in a series of experiments involving "shifts" in the rules. For example, suppose on task 1 a subject learns the set of responses given in Figure 13-3: Yes for black-large and white-large and No for black-small and white-small. The dimension the subject must respond to is size; for a Yes response it is "large," for a No response it is "small." Then on a second task, the rule can be switched in two ways: to a *reversal shift* (also called intradimensional shift), in which the two larges become No and the two smalls become Yes (same dimension), or to a *nonreversal shift* (also called extradimensional shift), in which a new dimension is used, such as labeling black Yes and white No. If concept learning involves strengthening single S-R associations (continuity theory), then the reversal shift should be more difficult to learn since it requires changing *four* associations (e.g., change black-large, white-large, black-small, white-small), while nonreversal requires changing only two links (e.g., change black-small, white-large; keep black-large, white-small). However, if concept learning involves forming a rule which *mediates* between the stimulus and the response (noncontinuity theory), then in a reversal shift the same dimension mediates (e.g., "pay attention to size") and only new labels need be added, while in the nonreversal shift a new dimension ("pay attention to color") must be found as well as new labels. In a long series of studies, the results were clear that for college students and verbal children (children over five years) the reversal shift was easier to learn than the nonreversal shift but for preverbal children and laboratory animals, the nonreversal shift was easier. Apparently, the tendency to use hypotheses rather than rote associations increases with age and language use.

In another set of experiments using an "optional shift," subjects were taught that the appropriate responses for figures such as black-large and white-large were Yes and black-small and white-small were No. Then there was an ambiguous switch—for example, subjects were told black-small was now Yes and white-large was now No. What was black-large or white-small? If the subject responded that black-large was Yes and white-small was No, that was a nonreversal shift—two of the original associations were retained and the classification rule was based on a new dimension, color. If the subject said Yes for the black-large or white-small object, that was a reversal shift—all four of the original associations were changed but the original dimension, size, was retained. Since a nonreversal shift required making fewer new associations, it could be predicted by the continuity view; the noncontinuity theory would predict that since thinking is based on rules instead of individual associations, a reversal shift was more likely. Typical results were that younger children preferred nonreversal but older children and adults tended to prefer reversal shifts; for example, the percentage of reversal shifts was 37 percent for three-year-olds, 50 percent for five-year-olds, and 62 percent for ten-year-olds.

Kendler and Kendler concluded that adult thinking in the concept learning situation is *mediated* by a general rule (such as "Pick the large one") rather than by individual associations. A similar idea is discussed in Chapter 6 under the name of "attention theory."

Another test of the continuity-noncontinuity argument was conducted by Bower and Trabasso (1963; Trabasso & Bower, 1964, 1968). For example, college student subjects were given a concept learning task similar to the one shown in the introduction to this chapter; there were six dimensions with two attributes on each, such as color (red or blue), size (large or small), shape (square or hexagon), number (three or four), position (right or left), shaded area (upper right and lower left or upper left and lower right). The stimuli were presented one at a time; the subject was asked to anticipate which of two classes (such as Group 1 versus Group 2) each stimulus belonged to, the experimenter then gave the correct answer, and so on. Bower and Trabasso noted that for a long time the pattern of performance remained at chance level, then jumped suddenly to 100 percent correct. This observation seemed consistent with the noncontinuity theory but in order to test the theory more closely, in another experiment they changed the solution rule while the subjects were still responding at chance level. That is, before they had learned that Red = 1, Blue = 2, the rule was changed to Red = 2, Blue = 1. The continuity theory predicts that such a switch would seriously hurt learning since associative strengths have been slowly getting stronger for the relevant cues; the noncontinuity theory, however, predicts that the switch will not make any difference since the problem solver has not yet induced the correct classification rule. The results clearly supported the noncontinuity view—changing the solution rule prior to learning did not slow learning as compared to a group that retained the same rule throughout learning. Apparently, the subjects formed a hypothesis, tested it on new stimuli, and changed it based on negative feedback, without any need to tally up past experience with particular attributes. In fact, the Bower and Trabasso results seem to indicate that when subjects pick a new hypothesis they do not benefit at all from a long chain of past experience; each new selection of a hypothesis may be made independently of previous hypotheses. Mathematical models based on this idea are discussed by Restle and Greeno (1970).

Based on these and related findings, Levine (1975) has concluded that noncontinuity theory seems best to describe the thinking strategies of adults and some verbal children. Osler and Fivel (1961) investigated the pattern of choices prior to final solution on a concept identification task with high-school students. Among students with IQs over 110 they observed the same "sudden" learning noted by Bower and Trabasso—a period of chance performance (presumably while incorrect hypotheses were being selected) followed by 100 percent correct performance (when the correct hypothesis was finally chosen). However, students of average and below average intelligence displayed a pattern in which the rate of correct response increased gradually for each individual. One interpretation of these findings is that the strategy of the bright students was to make successive hypotheses while that of the others was to use association learning. Apparently, adults have both a continuity and a noncontinuity "system" and can use either one.

DOMINANCE OF CUES

Dominance Hierarchy

When humans form hypotheses for rule classification, they may not choose which features they attend to at random; certain features of the stimuli may attract their attention more readily than others. In a famous set of concept learning experiments, Heidbreder (1946, 1947) investigated this question. As in the earlier experiment done by Hull, the subjects were shown a series of pictures like those shown in Figure 13-4 one at a time and asked to anticipate the name (nonsense word) associated with it. The subject was then told the correct response word. After going through one set of pictures, Heidbreder repeated this procedure with a second set, and so on. The subjects did not see the same picture-name pair more than

FIGURE 13-4.

Stimuli used in Heidbreder's concept learning experiments.

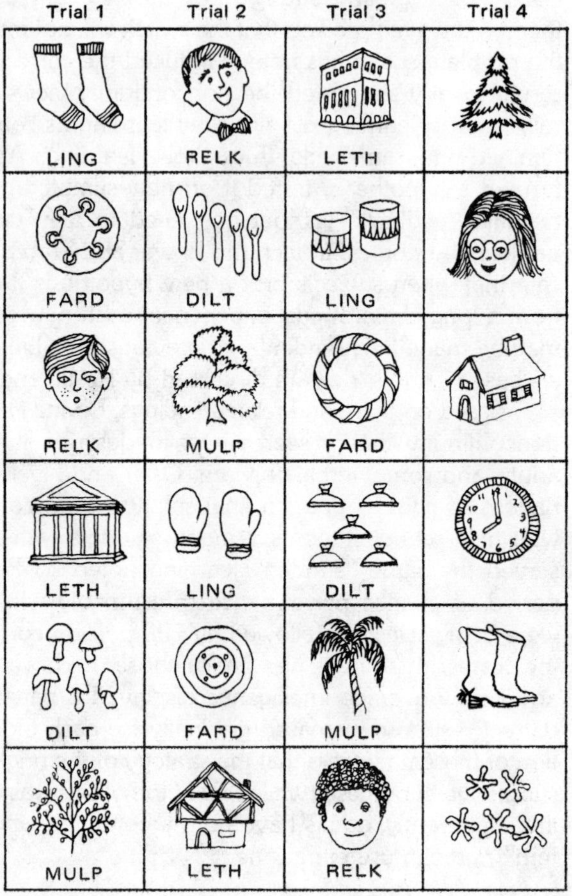

Trial 1	Trial 2	Trial 3	Trial 4
LING	RELK	LETH	(tree)
FARD	DILT	LING	(face)
RELK	MULP	FARD	(house)
LETH	LING	DILT	(clock)
DILT	FARD	MULP	(boots)
MULP	LETH	RELK	(snowflakes)

once, but the same response words were always associated with the same kind of picture. For each set of pictures, there were three concepts from each of three types of concepts: concrete objects, such as *relk* for face, *leth* for building, and *mulp* for tree; forms, such as *fard* for circle, *pran* for double cross, and *stod* for a triple cross form; and numbers, such as *ling* for two, *mank* for six, and *dilt* for five. Figure 13-4 shows some selected instances for some of these concepts.

Although the subjects could only "guess" on trial 1, of course, as they continued through more trials they eventually began to anticipate the names of the pictures correctly. Thus, like Hull's subjects, the subjects in Heidbreder's studies were able to abstract the appropriate feature of each picture and respond to it. What interested Heidbreder particularly was that certain pictures seemed to be easier to learn than others. For example, it was generally easier for the subjects to discover the concrete characteristics of buildings, faces, or trees than the concept of shapes, such as crosses or circles; and very abstract concepts, like the numbers two and five, were the hardest of all to identify.

Although other researchers have observed different patterns in their subjects (Dattman & Israel, 1951; Baum, 1954), such work does seem to indicate that individuals may enter the experimental situation with a certain set of preferences for which features of the situation they will notice or attend to. Heidbreder referred to these preferences as a "hierarchy of dominance"; that is, subjects may have a tendency to attend first to concrete objects, and when they have learned these, to shapes, and then to more abstract concepts like numbers. Dattman and Israel, and Baum found that a factor which influenced this hierarchy of attention was the number of interfering, similar concepts in the problem. For example, the subjects often made errors with the number concepts by giving the word that meant sixness when the picture was a twoness; when only one number concept was used, it was learned much faster. In other words, when several number concepts were used, they may have been interpreted first as "number," and only later classified as particular numbers two or six, etc., whereas trees, faces, and buildings were initially classified as such by the subjects.

Dominance Level

Underwood and Richardson (1956) developed the concept of *dominance level* to indicate the probability that certain stimuli will elicit a certain sensory reaction as a response (e.g., as in free association). For example, the term *white* has a high dominance level for the words milk, chalk, or snow because people generally think of them as white, but a low dominance level for words such as baseball, fang, and sugar because these terms rarely elicit the idea of white as a first response. In concept learning experiments like Heidbreder's, words that all shared the same high dominance level for a particular sensory impression were much easier to learn than words that shared low dominance level. Thus, instead of Heidbreder's idea that certain attributes are just more obvious than others, the "dominance level" theory supposes that when a stimulus is presented, it elicits a certain associated response. The subject will more quickly learn to classify stimuli according to a category if all instances of a category elicit the same associated response.

Cue Salience

Trabasso (1963) investigated concept learning using flower designs that varied in the number and shape of the leaves, angle of the branches, color, and so on. Trabasso found that certain cues were more meaningful or *salient* than others. For example, in one experiment in which the classifica-

FIGURE 13-5.

Stimuli used in Bruner, Goodnow, and Austin's concept learning experiment.

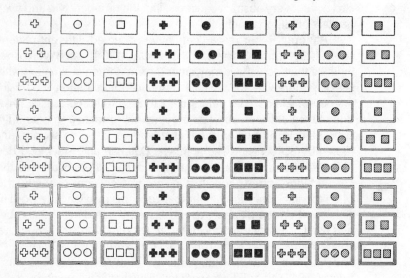

tion rule was based on color (angle fixed), errors averaged 4.05, but when the relevant dimension was angle (color fixed), errors averaged 19.50. Using these results, Trabasso was able to assign salience weights to the factors in his flower designs that indicated the tendency of the subjects to base their hypotheses on each cue. One interesting finding was that the weightings of cue saliences were cumulative; for example, if angle was the relevant dimension but color was always correlated with angle size, learning was much faster than when angle was relevant but the color was not.

These studies seem to indicate that in a given concept learning situation, hypotheses are more likely to be formed on the basis of certain "dominant" or "salient" dimensions, and that only if those hypotheses fail is the subject likely to develop new hypotheses on the basis of less salient dimensions. As you may have noticed, these ideas are closely related to the concept of "habit family hierarchy" discussed in Chapter 3.

STRATEGIES

Another important issue concerns the "strategies" that subjects use in concept-learning tasks. Probably the best known and most often-cited concept-learning experiment was conducted by Bruner, Goodnow, and Austin (1956) and published in their classic monograph, *A Study of Thinking*. Bruner et al. used a set of 81 stimuli, shown in Figure 13-5, which consisted of four *dimensions* with three *values* (or attributes) per dimension: *shape*—circle, square, cross; *color*—red, green, black; *number of borders*—1, 2, or 3; *number of objects*—1, 2, or 3.

Classification rules could be made in several ways, but Bruner et al. used three basic divisions. One group included *single-valued concepts*, in which the concept was defined as having one particular value on one particular dimension, ignoring all other dimensions (e.g., red). Another division included *conjunctive concepts*, in which the concept was defined as having one value on one dimension *and* another value on another dimension (e.g., red crosses). The third class of rules were *disjunctive concepts*, in which the concept was defined as having one value on one dimension *or* another value on a different dimension (e.g., red or cross).

Once a classification rule was selected by Bruner et al., a method of presenting the positive instances (or exemplars) of the concept and the negative instances (or nonexemplars) to the subject was needed. Two presentation methods were used. One was the *reception method*, in which the experimenter picked the stimulus cards one at a time, the subject said whether he or she thought it was a positive or negative instance of the rule, and the experimenter indicated whether or not the answer was correct. The other presentation system was the *selection method*, in which the entire board of 81 stimuli was given to the subject at once. The subject picked the cards one at a time and said for each whether he or she thought it was a positive or a negative instance; the experimenter then said whether the answer was correct or not.

In observing the subjects solve concept learning problems under these conditions, Bruner et al. noted that they seemed to use certain strategies. With the reception method, for example, two distinct "reception strategies" were noted. One was the *wholist strategy* which required the subject to remember all the attributes common to those instances where the response was correct and ignore everything else, thus eliminating any attribute that was not part of a positive instance. The other was the *partist strategy*, in which the subject focused on one hypothesis at a time (for example, color green = Yes), kept the hypothesis if it correctly predicted the membership of a stimulus card and formed a completely new one based on all past experiences if it did not. The strategies are specified in Figure 13-6. In general, Bruner et al. found that wholist strategy resulted in better performance especially when the subjects were under time pressure. Partist strategy requires the subject to retain all prior information and select a hypothesis consistent with it while wholist strategy incorporates a record of all past instances within the current hypothesis. This is because the subject using a wholist strategy remembers all the values of the first correct response or positive instance and gradually eliminates those that fail to appear on subsequent positive instances. Although negative instances have not been an important part of our discussion of Bruner's theory, other researchers have found that subjects can learn just as well with negative instances as with positive (Freibergs & Tulving, 1961).

With the selection method of presentation, Bruner et al. noted several similar selection strategies. One was *simultaneous scanning*, in which the subject began with all possible hypotheses and eliminated the untenable hypotheses after each instance. A second strategy was *successive scan-*

FIGURE 13-6.

Strategies in concept learning.

Wholist Strategy
Take the first positive instance and retain all the positive attributes as the initial hypothesis. Then, as more instances are presented, eliminate any attribute in this set which does not occur with a positive instance.

	Positive Instance	Negative Instance
Confirming	Maintain the hypothesis now in force	Maintain the hypothesis now in force
Infirming	Take as the next hypothesis what the old hypothesis and the present instance have in common	Impossible unless one has misreckoned. If one has misreckoned, correct from memory of past instances and present hypothesis

Partist Strategy
Begin with part of the first positive instance as an hypothesis (e.g., choose just one attribute). Then retain or change it in the following way.

	Positive Instance	Negative Instance
Confirming	Maintain hypothesis now in force	Maintain hypothesis now in force
Infirming	Change hypothesis to make it consistent with past instances: i.e., choose an hypothesis not previously infirmed	Change hypothesis to make it consistent with past instances; i.e., choose hypothesis not previously infirmed

ning, in which the subject began with one hypothesis, kept it if it correctly predicted class membership, and changed it to another based on all past experience if it did not. The third selection strategy was *conservative focusing*, in which the subject picked one positive instance and selected subsequent cards which changed one attribute value at a time. Finally, Bruner et al. identified the strategy of *focus gambling*, in which the subject picked one positive instance and selected subsequent cards which changed several attribute values at a time. The scanning strategies are similar to the partist strategies and the focusing strategies are similar to the wholist. Again, focusing is usually far more efficient because it does not require as much memory load. The main contribution of Bruner et al. is the discovery that subjects can use different strategies for different learning situations. More recently, Laughlin (1973) has proposed more precise descriptions of these strategies.

MODELS OF HYPOTHESIS TESTING

Many of the strategies suggested by Bruner et al. involved the idea that subjects create and test hypotheses based on all relevant past instances. However, Restle (1962) and Bower and Trabasso (1964; Trabasso &

FIGURE 13-7.

Hypothesis sampling models.

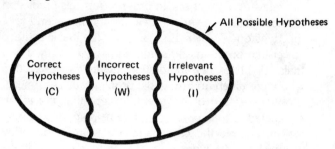

Bower, 1968) have proposed a basic model to account for the hypothesis testing process in which the subject samples a hypothesis or set of hypotheses from a pool of all possible hypotheses that can be either correct, incorrect, or irrelevant. If the hypothesis results in correct classification of an instance, it is retained; otherwise it is replaced in the pool and a new hypothesis (or set of hypotheses) is selected. This model is represented in Figure 13-7.

To test this kind of model, Levine (1966, 1975) used a new approach to determine which strategy a subject was using in concept learning. In Levine's experiments, the subjects had to choose between two letters (an X and a T) on a stimulus card. The letters differed in color (black or white), position (left or right), size (large or small), and form (X or T). The subjects were told they could choose from only eight possible hypotheses (e.g., right, left, large, small, black, white, T, or X) and were given four trials without being told if their answers were correct or not, followed by a fifth trial in which the experimenter randomly said either "Correct" or "Wrong." Levine noted that subjects clearly used hypotheses since their responses on any set of four nonfeedback trials were consistent with one of the eight hypotheses over 92 percent of the time and based on the prior four responses, their selections on the fifth trial could be correctly predicted 97 percent of time. Furthermore, they tended to choose a new hypothesis if given negative feedback on the fifth trial (98 percent of the time). Levine's experiment is consistent with the idea that subjects use strategies, that they sample hypotheses one at a time, and that they use the win-stay, lose-switch policy. However, it does not support the no-memory assumption of the model. For example, if the subjects sampled with replacement, they had a 12.5 percent (1 in 8) chance of picking the same hypothesis after an "error"; yet the retention rate was only 2 percent. Levine's results indicate that the subjects used some of their past experience but certainly not all of it.

Another test of the hypothesis-testing model is provided by Levine's (1971, 1975) idea that subjects who fail to solve a concept learning task should perform in the same way as subjects who are given corresponding problems that are insolvable. This is so because, according to the hypothesis-testing model, both the "unsolved" and the "insolvable" subjects would be sampling hypotheses from the irrelevant set—never from the relevant, correct set. In order to test this prediction, Levine presented stimulus pairs that varied in eight dimensions and asked subjects to "pick the right one." After 12 trials with feedback some of the subjects had solved the problem and some had not (i. e., they had made an error on trials 10, 11, or 12). In addition, Levine devised a third group of subjects who were given an insolvable problem; these subjects received the same problems as the other groups except that the relevant dimension was eliminated so that, based on the remaining seven dimensions, there was no way to sample the correct, relevant dimension. Although the "solved" group showed a jump from chance to 100 percent correct during the 12 trials, the "unsolved" and "insolvable" groups showed indistinguishable patterns of performance that hovered at or below the chance level. Apparently, both groups were sampling from the empty set—the relevant hypothesis was not in the set from which these subjects were sampling.

In a further experiment, Wicken and Millward (1971) gave their subjects large amounts of practice and tried to describe their performance in terms of a hypothesis-sampling model. The results were consistent with the idea that subjects tended to consider a small number of dimensions simultaneously; when a value was paired inconsistently with the correct response, that dimension was eliminated, and when all dimensions in a set were eliminated, the subject sampled a new set. Subjects apparently retained some information about previous dimensions which had been tested but there were large individual differences in how many prior hypotheses could be remembered. It was always more than zero—indicating some memory load—but it was definitely limited.

FACTORS THAT INFLUENCE DIFFICULTY

There have been many studies similar to the ones we have been discussing that have investigated which factors make concept problems more or less difficult. One question concerns the role of positive and negative instances. In general, when subjects have developed a hypothesis, they tend to pick test cards which confirm it—that is, they tend to rely on positive instances to test their hypotheses and may be less able to use the information they receive from correctly predicted negative instances. In a typical experiment, Freibergs and Tulving (1961) gave 20 different concept learning problems to a group of subjects. For each problem, the subjects were given either all positive or all negative instances of the to-be-learned concept. For the first few problems, the subjects solved much faster with all positive instances (median solution time 50 to 140 seconds) than with all negative (median solution time 210 seconds). However, after about 15 problems there was no difference between the groups. Apparently, the subjects had a preference for using information in positive instances but could learn, in a relatively short time, to effectively use the information in negative instances as well.

Another important factor is the complexity of the stimuli that are used. For example, several experiments have shown that increasing the number of relevant dimensions tends to decrease solution time since a subject can use any dimension to solve the problem while increasing the number of irrelevant dimensions makes the problem more difficult because it allows the subject more chances to pick a useless hypothesis (Bourne, 1966; Bourne, Ekstrand & Dominowski, 1971; Bourne & Haygood, 1959, 1960; Walker & Bourne, 1961). In addition, solution performance was made more difficult under some conditions* by increasing the number of values per dimension (Battig & Bourne, 1961; Bourne, 1966).

A third finding that has received more attention is that certain types of rules are more difficult to learn than others. For example, a problem can be made more difficult by using disjunctive rather than conjunctive rules (Bourne, 1966; Haygood & Stevenson, 1967). Bourne (1970) has proposed an important distinction between two components that may be involved in concept learning for a two-dimensional concept, such as "red circles." In *attribute learning*, the subject must learn to attend to the relevant attributes, in this instance, "red" and "circle," rather than to others. In *rule learning*, the subject must learn the appropriate rule which unites the relevant attributes, such as "and."

If a concept involves two attributes, there are several different types of rules which can connect them into a concept: the *conjunctive rule*—"all patterns which are red and circles are examples of the concept"; the *disjunctive rule*—"all patterns which are red or circles or both are examples of the concept"; the *conditional rule*—"if a pattern is red, then it must be a circle to be an example of the concept"; and the *biconditional rule*—"red patterns are examples if and only if they are circles."

In order to determine the relative difficulty of these four types of rules, Bourne (1970) asked four groups of subjects to solve nine concept-learning tasks with each group receiving only one type of rule for all nine problems. The stimuli were geometric diagrams that varied in color, form, number, and size; however, all the subjects were told what the relevant dimensions were so that a clearer measure of the rule learning phase of concept learning could be studied. The results are summarized in Figure 13-8. The easiest rule to learn was conjunctive, followed in difficulty by disjunctive, conditional, and biconditional in that order. The figure also shows that the mean trials to solution fell to a very low level after only a few problems, thus indicating that subjects learn to learn particular types of rules.

Bourne (1974) has suggested a "truth table" theory to account for

*Haygood, Harbert, & Omlor (1970) have defined the limited conditions under which increasing the number of values per dimension increases problem difficulty.

FIGURE 13-8.

Mean trials to solution as a function of successive learning rates for different types of classification rules.

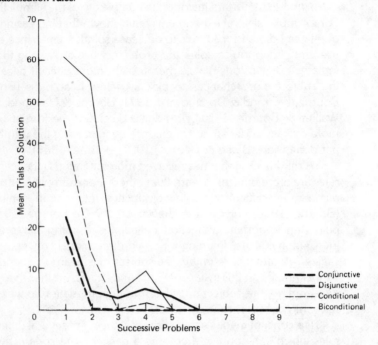

the differences in the difficulties of the four types of solution rules. For example, consider a simple task in which subjects learn to classify objects that vary in size and color. For each stimulus, the subject notes whether the relevant size feature (e.g., large) is present (T) or absent (F) and whether the relevant color feature (e.g., red) is present (T) or absent (F). Thus each stimulus can be classified as TT (large, red), FF (not large, not red), TF (large, not red), or FT (not large, red). Bourne's theory claims that the subjects make the following assumptions as they start out in learning: (1) TT stimuli are positive; (2) TT and FF stimuli belong to different categories; (3) FF is negative; and (4) TF and FT are the same as FF (therefore TF and FT are negative). Thus the subjects start out expecting a conjunctive rule (such as anything that is both red and large is positive but everything else is negative) that separates the truth table as TT versus FF, TF, FT. However, other rules violate some of these assumptions; for example, if the rule is disjunctive (such as red *or* large is positive), then the subjects must alter the second assumption. More complex rules such as conditional and biconditional require that even more assumptions be altered. Thus, according to this theory, subjects start out with a simple set of assumptions and change them one at a time if they fail to produce correct answers; since more complex rules require more assumption changes, they require longer solution times. In an interesting set of experiments, Bourne (1974) was able to

FIGURE 13-9.

A sequential decision tree.

Concept: Large and either red or circular

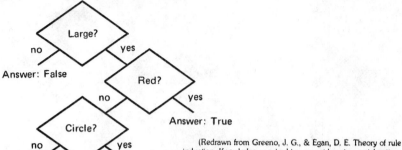

(Redrawn from Greeno, J. G., & Egan, D. E. Theory of rule induction: Knowledge acquired in concept learning, serial pattern learning, and problem solving. In L. W. Gregg (Ed.), *Knowledge and cognition.* Hillside, N.J.: Lawrence Erlbaum Associates, 1974. Reprinted by permission.)

show that trials to solution is a linear function of the predicted difficulty when predicted difficulty was based on the number of changed assumptions and reclassified stimuli.

Another way to measure the difficulty of a solution rule is to determine the number of decisions a subject must make before arriving at a solution. Hunt, Marin, and Stone (1966) have represented classification rules as sequential decision trees like the one shown in Figure 13-9. Since decisions about new instances are based on a series of tests going down the tree, more complex trees should be harder to learn. Evidence to support this idea came from a study by Trabasso, Rollins, and Shaughnessy (1971) in which subjects read statements like, "Large triangle and red circle," and were shown a triangle and circle on a slide. The task was to verify the statement by responding either Yes or No to the slide. Reading times were longer for complex trees than for simple ones, and decision times were also longer. Apparently, the classification can be represented as a sequential decision tree, and as more decisions are needed the problem becomes more difficult.

ABSTRACTION OF VISUAL PROTOTYPES

An alternative, or refinement, to the hypothesis testing models of concept learning comes from a series of studies on learning to classify visual patterns. In previous sections, concept learning was broken down into two phases—learning to attend to the relevant attributes and learning the rule that should be applied to the attributes. However, another way of characterizing this initial process involves "averaging" all the instances of each category into a schematic or prototypical instance. For example, consider how someone learns to classify cars into categories such as "Chevrolet," "Ford," "Dodge," regardless of year or model, or how we learn to sort

FIGURE 13-10.

Prototype pattern of dots and various degrees of distortion.

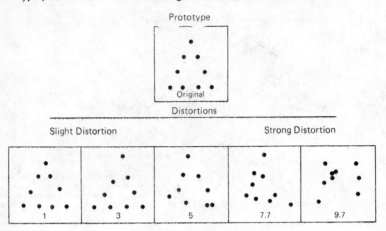

Note: Higher numbers indicate higher amount of distortion.

pocket change into "pennies," "nickels," "dimes," and so on, regardless of mint year or amount of wear. There are several alternative theories to explain this, one of which is the *abstraction of prototype*. In the automobile example, an individual might have a mental image of a "typical" Chevy or Ford and compare any car against this ideal image. Another classification theory is *feature differentiation*. Here the subject learns to attend to particularly distinguishing cues, such as, say, the square headlights of Chevrolets versus the round headlights of Fords. Although the feature-differentiation view was discussed in Chapter 6 as an aspect of discrimination learning, and although it is an implicit part of several models of concept learning, there is evidence that some subjects may use the prototype strategy in certain types of concept learning tasks. Eventually, these two approaches must be reconciled to a theory of concept learning.

In a classic set of studies, Posner and Keele (1968, 1970) presented dot patterns like those shown in Figure 13-10. Each pattern was constructed by distorting a nine-dot prototype; for example, to create a distortion, several of the dots, randomly selected, would be moved on the prototype either to the right or left or up or down. In a typical experiment, subjects were shown four different distortions of three separate prototypes and asked to classify each of these twelve-dot patterns into one of three categories. Although the subjects never saw the actual prototypes, they were able to learn to classify their exemplars. More importantly, once the subjects had learned to classify the initial set of distorted patterns, they were given a test that consisted of classifying "new" distorted patterns made in the same way as the original ones, "old" distorted patterns which were identical to those already learned, and the actual prototypes which had never been presented. The results were that the "old" patterns were

FIGURE 13-11.

Geometric figures used by Franks and Bransford.

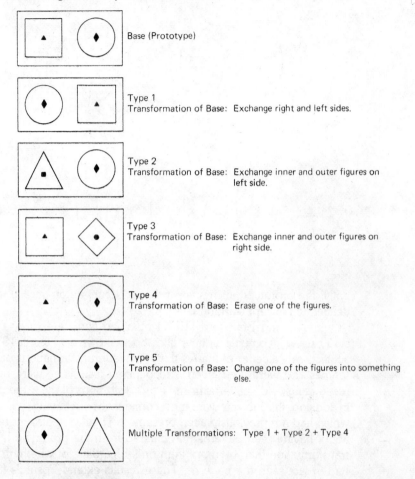

Base (Prototype)

Type 1
Transformation of Base: Exchange right and left sides.

Type 2
Transformation of Base: Exchange inner and outer figures on left side.

Type 3
Transformation of Base: Exchange inner and outer figures on right side.

Type 4
Transformation of Base: Erase one of the figures.

Type 5
Transformation of Base: Change one of the figures into something else.

Multiple Transformations: Type 1 + Type 2 + Type 4

classified quite well (about 87 percent correct) and the "new" patterns were a bit more difficult (about 75 percent correct); however, the most striking finding was that the prototypes were classified correctly just as well as the old patterns, that is, the subjects behaved as if the prototypes were "old" patterns even though they had never been presented before! These results are consistent with the conclusion that the subjects *abstracted* the general prototype of the categories by "averaging" the characteristics of the distortions they saw and that they created the prototypes in their own memories.

Additional support for the "prototype abstraction" idea comes from a similar study by Posner (1969) in which the subjects looked at a set of dot patterns that were distortions of a prototype. On a subsequent recognition test, they showed strong tendencies to classify the prototype as having been in the initial set although it had not been presented before. Appar-

FIGURE 13-12.

Two categories of faces.

Category 1

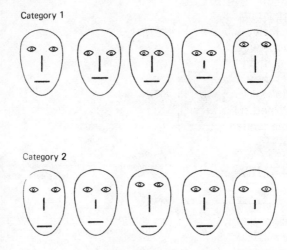

Category 2

ently, the prototype abstraction process occurs automatically even when deliberate concept learning is not called for.

Franks and Bransford (1971) obtained complementary results in a study using geometric figures like those shown in Figure 13-11. Their subjects saw a series of figures that involved transformations of basic prototypes and were then given a recognition test. They were no better at recognizing "old" patterns from "new" distortions of the same prototypes; in addition, the subjects were most confident about having seen prototypes which had not previously been presented. They were also more confident about having seen patterns that differed from the prototype by only one transformation than by more than one, regardless of whether or not they had in fact seen the patterns. These results extend Posner's finding that what the subjects learned about the initial set of stimuli was an *abstraction*, that is, the prototype.

Reed (1972) obtained similar results using a different kind of visual pattern. College students learned to classify drawings of faces like those shown in Figure 13-12 into two categories and were asked to report what strategy they used. The predominant strategy used by the students was to abstract a prototype and to compare the "distance" between the prototype and each new face pattern. This strategy is summarized as follows: "I formed an abstract image of what a face in category two should look like. Then I compared the projected face with the two abstract images and chose the category which gave the closest match" (p. 393). Other subjects, however, attended to certain disginguishing cues: "I looked at each feature on the projected face and compared how many times it exactly matched a feature in each of the two categories. I then chose the category which gave the highest number of matches" (p. 393).

Both types of strategies—prototype abstraction and feature differentiation—were also found in a study by Hyman and Frost (1974). Dot patterns were distorted by stretching them vertically (tall category) or horizontally (wide category). Hyman and Frost reasoned that if the subjects abstracted schematic prototypes, then the *averages* of the tall and the wide groups would be most easily classified; however, if they attended to features, then the *tallest* of the tall category and the *widest* of the wide category should be easiest to classify. They measured the speed and accuracy with which the subjects classified the various patterns, and like Reed, obtained mixed results: some subjects tended to rely on prototypes and some tended to rely on distinctive features.

NATURAL CATEGORIES

The work of the Kendlers and others indicates that the learning of category concepts may be influenced by internal mediators; in humans, the availability of internal language mediators may be particularly important for concept learning. When we consider how we learn to categorize our natural environments, an important consideration is how language influences this "natural" concept learning task. Although psychologists have not provided much data on this question, linguists and anthropologists have proposed the concept of "linguistic relativity"—the idea that the language one speaks influences the way one learns and thinks about the world (Sapir, 1960; Whorf, 1956). For example, based on an anthropological study of the language and culture of non-Western language speakers (e.g., the Hopi Indians of the southwestern U.S.), Whorf proclaimed the doctrine of linguistic relativity: "Every language and every well-knit technical sublanguage incorporates certain points of view and certain patterns resistant to widely divergent points of view" (p. 247). Further, the concepts and categories that we learn and use are also supposed to be influenced and limited by our native tongue: "We cut up and organize the spread and flow of events as we do, largely because, through our mother tongue we are parties to an agreement to do so and not because nature itself is segmented in exactly that way for all to see" (p. 240).

These ideas have, of course, profound implications for the study of human learning and cognition. One of the first experimental studies of the Whorfian hypothesis was conducted by Brown and Lenneberg (1954) and reported in their now famous paper, "A Study of Language and Cognition." Brown and Lenneberg began by selecting 240 color chips from the *Munsell Book of Color*, a catalog similar to the color charts for house paint colors. Then they asked five judges to pick the *best* examples of red, orange, yellow, green, blue, purple, pink, and brown from the set of 240 colors. There was high agreement among the judges. Brown (1976, p. 131), reminiscing about the experiment, reports that the colors looked quite familiar: "I remember thinking that there was something uncanny

FIGURE 13-13.

Frequency of names given by English speakers to various color chips.

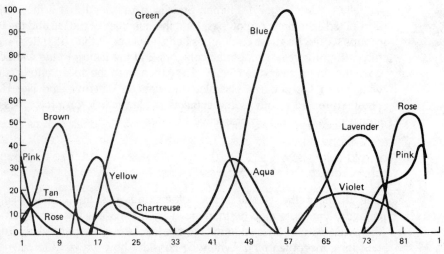

Stimulus Continuum (Farnsworth-Munsell Numbers)

about the eight best instances, and indeed, about the chips in the immediate neighborhood of each. I can see them still, that good Gulf orange, that Ticonderoga pencil yellow, that blood red; they all of them shine through the years like so many jewels." To these colors, Brown and Lenneberg added sixteen "filler" color chips which were spaced as evenly as possible within the other eight. Of these filler colors, however, Brown reports that he has no vivid visual memory.

Armed with the full array of 24 colors (8 distinctive and 16 filler), Brown and Lenneberg presented them to college subjects and asked them to name the colors. For each of the eight basic colors, the subjects tended to use a single word and they tended to agree on the word; for the other colors, they used longer phrases, such as "light green," and there was much less agreement between them. Codability scores were determined for each color and then new, different subjects were given a recognition task; they were shown a color chip (or a set of them) for a few seconds, then after some delay, were asked to point out the color from an array of 120 colors. The results indicated a moderately high correlation between codability and recognition: the colors that could be easily named were also easier to remember.

These results seemed to support the Whorfian notion of linguistic relativity because the availability of names for colors apparently influenced a cognitive task such as remembering stimuli. The colors used in the experiment formed a natural continuum based on wavelength, but language artificially "cut up" the colors into categories like those shown in Figure 13-13 (Lenneberg, 1957).

In an attempt to further explore the Whorfian hypothesis, Heider

FIGURE 13-14.

Universal order of evolution of color terms in 98 languages.

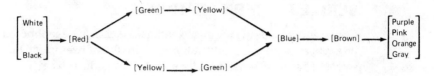

(1970, 1972; Heider & Oliver, 1972) investigated the color memory task in different cultures. For example, the Dani tribe of Indonesian New Guinea are a Stone Age people with only two basic color words—"mili" for dark or cold colors and "mola" for bright and warm colors. The Dani people can, of course, talk about other colors, but they must use longer descriptive phrases. According to the Whorfian idea, two colors that happen to fall in different categories in English should be easier for the Dani to remember if they also fall in the two separate Dani categories rather than in the same category; results, however, indicated no difference. A more striking discon-firmation of the Whorfian hypothesis comes from a study of several non-European languages. Colors that were easy to name in English were easier to remember for English speakers (as Brown and Lenneberg had found) but they were also easier to remember for speakers of every other lan-guage, including languages like Dani, even though no specific words for the colors existed.

The chart in Figure 13-14 gives a list of the order in which color names appear in languages based on a study of 98 different languages (Berlin & Kay, 1969). The figure shows that although languages differ in how many basic color terms are provided (ranging from two to twelve), there is a universal pattern: if two words are used, they signify black and white; if three are used, red is added; if five are used, green and yellow are added, and so on, up to twelve basic color words used frequently in English. These twelve are called "focal" colors and Heider's (now called Rosch's) results show that focal colors are remembered better than others regardless of whether the learner's language has specific names for them. As Brown (1976) pointed out in a recent review of this work, the Whorfian hypothesis has been turned inside-out—apparently, at least for colors, there are "natural categories that are shared by all humans with normal color vision. Languages apparently reflect these categories in that they all divide up the world of color in the same way, with some languages going into more detail.

Although the current state of our understanding casts doubt on the Whorfian hypothesis, there is certainly much more to language than "color names." At least one research study (Carmichael, Hogan, & Walter, 1932) has shown that "labeling" a picture does influence indeed how it is remembered. What is particularly important and to some extent unique about the study of color categories is this: it demonstrates that cross-cultural differences in cognition can be studied experimentally and that such investigations promise to increase our understanding of our common human capacity to think and to learn.

SERIAL PATTERN LEARNING

Consider the following problems: atbataatbat_____; aaabbbcccdd_____; wxaxybyzczadab_____; urtustuttu_____. In these examples, the problem solver is given a series of letters and must induce what the next letter should be. Simon and Kotovsky (1963) found that the rule the subject must learn consists of four main parts. First, the subject must determine the number of letters that constitute one cycle. In each of the problems cited here, for example, the cycle is three: atb/ata/atb/at_____; aaa/bbb/ccc/dd_____; wxa/xyb/yzc/zad/ab_____; urt/ust/utt/u_____. Second, the subject must note each of the letters in the initial cycle. In the first problem, for example, letter 1 is a, 2 is t, and 3 is b. The subject then must determine what are the possible letters that could occur for each letter space in the cycle: again in problem 1, the first two spaces of each cycle are fixed and the third is either a or b; however, in problem 4, the first and third positions are fixed but the second position may be any letter in the alphabet. Finally, the subject must determine what operation is performed on each letter when a new cycle occurs: in problem 1, letters 1 and 2 remained the same but letter 3 has changed to the next letter in the alphabet (the alphabet is limited to a and b in this problem, so letter 3 goes from a to b, back to a, and so on).

It is possible to represent the rules for each sequence as a program of things to do. In the fourth problem, for instance, the sequence can be listed as:

Write the letter L1.
Write the letter L2.
Add one letter to L2.
Write L3.
Go back to the first step.

All the subject needs to know is that the system begins with L1 = u, L2 = r, and L3 = t.

Simon and Kotovsky found that rules which required long descriptions (e.g., long computer programs) were more difficult both for humans and computers, and especially difficult were rules which placed large demands on immediate memory, such as urt/ust/utt/u_____.

How do subjects select rules to try in such complex situations? There is some evidence that when individuals are confronted with a serial pattern problem, they tend to rely on the most obvious or simplest rule based on their past experience and do not change that rule to a more complex one unless it fails. For example, Pollio and Reinhart (1970) presented number cards one at a time and asked their subjects to anticipate what numbers would be on the card. The cards were ordered by base 2, base 3, or base 4, such as 0, 1, 10, 11, 100, 101, 111, 1,000, et cetera (base 2).* The

_____
*The first few numbers for base 3 were 0, 1, 2, 10, 11, 12, 20, 21, 22, 100, and for base 4 were 0, 1, 2, 3, 10, 11, 12, 13, 100, etc.

results indicated that the subjects had the hardest time with base 2 (301 errors to learning), then base 3 (143 errors to learning), and the least with base 4 (91 errors). Most errors occurred at the point of shift to a higher base unit (for example, with base 2, the subject would say 3 instead of 10, or 12 instead of 100). At first, there was generally a long pause after each base change (e.g., 1 to 10, 11 to 100, 111 to 1,000), but *after* the subjects had had a little practice, there was a long pause *before* the change, suggesting that the subject was aware that something "different" happened at base changes. Pollio and Reinhart concluded that the subjects initially assumed that base 10 was being used (based on their successful past experience) but after they had made several errors, discovered the correct solution rule. The idea that the subjects learned a *rule* rather than a set of independent responses was suggested by the fact that they could add and subtract in base 2, base 3, and base 4 and could learn new base systems with relative ease.

This experiment uses just one type of rule; however, when subjects are given a series of symbols (e.g., a number sequence), more than one simple rule may be involved. Bjork (1968) constructed numerical sequences based on three separate rules. For example, the sequence 0421532643754 is based on the subrules "add 4," "subtract 2," and "subtract 1" for each set of three numbers. The subjects were given the numbers in order, one at a time, and were asked to anticipate the next number. First the subject sees 0, then a 4 (based on the rule "add 4"), then 2 (based on the rule "subtract 2"), then 1 (subtract 1), then 5 (add 4), 3 (subtract 2), and so on. The same sequence was continued until they correctly anticipated the numbers five times in a row up to a maximum total of 25 trials. The overall results were that the proportion correct gradually improved as subjects were given more trials; however, Bjork found that if he focused on just one rule at a time (e.g., "add 4"), learning was not gradual but jumped in an "all-or-none" fashion from a very low level on one trial to a very high level on the next and remained high. Thus, although the overall learning of sequence appears to be very complex, a more careful analysis by subrule indicates an orderly and "all-or-none" process.

Restle (1970) has further investigated how a complex set of rules is induced by subjects given serial pattern problems made up of numbers from 1 to 6. Restle designed serial patterns based on *structural trees* like the one in Figure 13-15. Structural trees represent a hierarchy of rules. For this diagram, the rules can be interpreted as *mirror* (M), *transpose* (T), and *repeat* (R). The mirror rule calls for the subtraction of each number in the preceding chunk from 7 (e.g., change 1234 to 6543). Transpose means to increment numbers in the preceding chunk by 1 (e.g., change 1234 to 2345). The repeat rule tells the problem solver to reproduce the numbers in the preceding chunk (e.g., 1234 becomes 1234). The subjects were

FIGURE 13-15.

Structural trees for serial pattern learning.

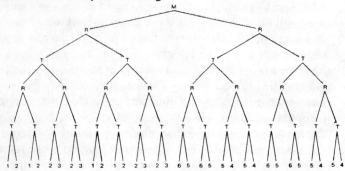

seated in front of a set of six lights with a response button under each light. First a light would go on, the subject had to predict the next light by pushing a button, then the next light would appear, and so on. Although sequences were based on a hierarchy of rules, the subjects were not told of any rules; they saw only a sequence of stimuli. In investigating the pattern of errors for the first 20 repetitions of the sequence, Restle found that subjects tended to learn the rules in order, starting with the lowest level and working up to the most complex. For example, the sequence 12122323121223236565545465644545 is made up of the hierarchy shown in Figure 13-15. The highest rule (M) says that the first 16 numbers are simply mirrored (that is, each one is subtracted from 7) to obtain the next 16; it is worth noting that most errors occur at position 17 where this high rule must be applied. The lowest rule (T) says that each even position is just one more than whatever number was in the previous odd position; here, the least number of errors occur in positions 2, 4, 6, and other positions where this rule must be applied. Analysis of the errors for the first twenty repetitions of the sequence revealed an average of 50 percent correct for the highest rule (M), 55 percent for the second highest (R), 65 percent for the third highest (T), 80 percent for the fourth highest (R), and 85 percent for the lowest (T). Other patterns based on a five-level hierarchy of rules produced similar results. Apparently, when many rules must be induced, subjects work on the lowest, most obvious level first and build up to more complex ones.

SUMMARY

In this chapter we have examined some of the research and theories of how humans learn to form concepts and rules.

The basic *concept learning paradigm* is to present subjects with a series of stimuli which include both *positive and negative instances* of a given category. For each instance the subject must tell which category it belongs to and the task continues until the subject can correctly predict category membership in advance.

There are two basic theories of the mechanisms which underlie concept learning performance. The continuity theory is an extension of S-R associationist theories and states that learning builds gradually. For each instance, subjects are thought to keep a tally of every feature (or cue) and to assign it a plus (+) if the instance is positive and a minus (−) if the instance is negative. The noncontinuity theory suggests that subjects test their hypotheses of the correct solution rule and that learning is all-or-none. It is believed that the subjects use a "win-stay, lose-switch" strategy.

An early experiment that was consistent with continuity theory was Hull's study showing that subjects gradually abstracted the underlying radical from Chinese characters.

Several more recent experiments give stronger support to the noncontinuity theory. Adults learn a reversal shift more easily than a nonreversal shift, although in the case of laboratory animals and preverbal children, the continuity theory better predicted the results. A switch in the solution rules before the subjects had learned a concept-learning task did not increase the difficulty of learning. Individual differences in concept-learning curves showed that high IQ students were more likely to produce "all-or-none" rather than gradual curves.

Subjects do not randomly attend to cues (or hypotheses) when they are trying to determine which cue in a given concept-learning task is critical. There appears to be a *dominance hierarchy* in which the subject first focuses on obvious concrete features and later on more abstract features. The concept of *dominance level* states that concept learning is easier when all the instances of a given category evoke the same strong associate. And finally, there are differences in *cue salience* for the features in a given concept learning task; some cues are consistently more meaningful or obvious to the subject than other cues.

Subjects have a number of strategies available to them in a concept-learning task. Bruner, Goodnow, and Austin found four distinct strategies: simultaneous scanning, successive scanning, conservative focusing, and focus gambling.

Several formal models of hypothesis testing have been developed in an attempt to describe the process of noncontinuous concept learning more precisely. The main assumptions of most models are that individuals select from a pool of correct, incorrect, and irrelevant hypotheses; and that they keep their hypothesis unless it produces an error.

Many factors which influence the difficulty in solving standard concept-learning tasks have been isolated. Among them are: the number of relevant dimensions, the number of irrelevant dimensions, the number of features per dimension, the complexity of the solution rule. Several experiments have shown that there are techniques to determine how many decisions are involved in a given rule and that problem solving is a function of the number of decisions required by the solution rule.

Another similar concept-learning task is one in which the categories are "prototype" visual patterns and the stimuli are distortions based on the prototypes. Subjects apparently tend to abstract internal representations of the prototypes even though they may never have seen them.

The role of language in concept formation has also been an important issue. Whorf argued that our language categories determine how we categorize the world. An early experiment that showed that subjects remembered easily-named colored chips more readily than hard-to-name colored chips tended to support this hypothesis. However, recent studies have shown that color categories are universal, that is, colors apparently are divided and "remembered" in the same way by adults in all cultures regardless of the divisions of their individual language.

Serial pattern learning is similar to the standard concept-learning task in that a subject must abstract a solution rule that will predict the nature of the next instance. This rule learning process may be all-or-none, and when a hierarchy of rules is involved, subjects tend to learn the lower rules faster than the higher-level rules.

The concept-learning and rule-induction task has been a major paradigm (or method) in the study of human thinking. One advantage of concentrating on an agreed-upon task and method is that researchers have amassed an impressive amount of detailed and thorough information about human thinking with respect to concept learning. A disadvantage, however, is that the concept-learning task is just one kind of problem-solving situation and it is not clear how far one can generalize from laboratory studies on concept learning to the full range of human thought. Along this line, Niemark and Santa (1975) have criticized research on concept learning for using artificial stimuli and have suggested that more attention be paid to "natural categories" such as faces or words. A second problem concerns the finding that subjects tend to use "rules" and "strategies" in problem solving; in the concept-learning task the rules and structure are built into the task by the experimenter (e.g., defining red as positive, or making a structural tree), and therefore it is not entirely surprising that the subjects display some effects of the experimenter's rules and structure. In problem-solving tasks that are less structured, an entirely different set of strategies may be observed. Finally, there is the problem of individual differences in which different people may show different reasoning processes in the concept-learning task. The Kendlers have demonstrated that preverbal children do not share the strategies of adult college students, but further research is needed to determine whether the performance of college students (who are the typical subjects in human learning research) is representative of all adult subjects.

Eventually there must be a reconciliation of our understanding of the discrimination learning discussed in Chapter 6 and based largely on nonhuman subjects and our understanding of concept learning based on human performance. One promising movement in that direction is a study by Herrnstein (1976), a prominent Skinnerian psychologist, who found that the discrimination learning even of pigeons could not be described by a simple continuity approach.

References

Abbott, D. W., & Price, L. E. Stimulus generalization of the conditioned eyelid response to structurally similar nonsense syllables. *Journal of Experimental Psychology*, 1964, *68*, 368–71.

Adams, J. *Learning and memory: An introduction.* Homewood, Illinois: Dorsey, 1976.

Adelman, H. M., & Maatsch, J. L. Resistance to extinction as a function of the type of response elicited by frustration. *Journal of Experimental Psychology*, 1955, *50*, 61–65.

Ader, R., Weijnen, J. A. W. M., & Moleman, P. Retention of a passive avoidance response as a function of the intensity and duration of electric shock. *Psychonomic Science*, 1972, *26*, 125–28.

Ahlers, R. H. & Best, P. J. Novelty vs. temporal contiguity in learned taste aversions. *Psychonomic Science*, 1971, *25*, 34–36.

Amsel, A. The role of frustrative nonreward in noncontinuous reward situations. *Psychological Bulletin*, 1958, *55*, 102–19.

Amsel, A. Frustrative nonreward in partial reinforcement and discrimination learning: Some recent history and a theoretical extension. *Psychological Review*, 1962, *69*, 306–28.

Amsel, A. Partial reinforcement effects on vigor and persistence: Advances in frustration theory derived from a variety of within-subjects experiments. In K. W. Spence & J. T. Spence (Eds.), *The psychology of learning and motivation* (Vol. 1). New York: Academic Press, 1967.

Amsel, A. Behavioral habituation, counterconditioning, and a general theory of persistence. In A. H. Black & W. F. Prokasy (Eds.), *Classical conditioning II: Current research and theory.* New York: Appleton-Century-Crofts, 1972.

Amsel, A., Hug, J. J., & Surridge, C. T. Number of food pellets, goal approaches, and the partial reinforcement effect after minimal acquisition. *Journal of Experimental Psychology*, 1968, *77*, 530–34.

Amsel, A., & Roussel, J. Motivational properties of frustration: I. Effect on a running response of the addition of frustration to the motivational complex. *Journal of Experimental Psychology*, 1952, *43*, 363–68.

Anderson, H. H. Comparison of different populations: Resistance to extinction and transfer. *Psychological Review*, 1963, *70*, 162–79.

Anderson, J. R., & Bower, G. H. Recognition and retrieval processes in free recall. *Psychological Review*, 1972, *79*, 97–123.

Anderson, J. R., & Bower, G. H. *Human associative memory.* New York: Wiley, 1973.

Andrews, E. A., & Braveman, N. S. The combined effects of dosage level and interstimulus interval on the formation of one-trial poison-based aversions in rats. *Animal Learning and Behavior*, 1975, *3*, 287–89.

Anisman, H., & Waller, T. G. Effects of methamphetamine and shock duration during inescapable shock exposure on subsequent active and passive avoidance. *Journal of Comparative and Physiological Psychology*, 1971, *77*, 143–51.

Anisman, H., & Waller, T. G. Facilitative and disruptive effects of prior exposure to shock on subsequent avoidance performance. *Journal of Comparative and Physiological Psychology*, 1972, *78*, 113–22.

Anisman, H., & Waller, T. G. Effects of inescapable shock on subsequent avoidance performance: Role of response repertoire changes. *Behavioral Biology*, 1973, *9*, 331–55.

Annau, Z., & Kamin, L. J. The conditioned emotional response as a function of intensity of the US. *Journal of Comparative and Physiological Psychology*, 1961, *54*, 428–32.

Archer, E. J. A re-evaluation of the meaningfulness of all possible CVC trigrams. *Psychological Monographs*, 1960, *74*, Whole No. 497.

Arkes, H. R., Schumacher, G. M., & Gardner, E. T. Effects of orienting tasks on the retention of prose material. *Journal of Educational Psychology*, 1976, *68*, 536–45.

Atkinson, R. C., & Shiffrin, R. M. Human memory: A proposed system and its control processes. In K. W. Spence & J. T. Spence (Eds.), *The psychology of learning and motivation* (Vol. 2). New York: Academic Press, 1968.

Averbach, E., & Coriell, A. S. Short-term memory in vision. *Bell System Technical Journal*, 1961, *40*, 309–28.

Averbach, E., & Sperling, G. Short-term storage of information in vision. In E. C. Cherry (Ed.), *Symposium on information theory.* London: Butterworth, 1961.

Ayllon, T., & Houghton, E. Control of the behavior of schizophrenics by food. *Journal of the Experimental Analysis of Behavior*, 1962, *5*, 343–52.

Azrin, N. H. Punishment of elicited aggression. *Journal of the Experimental Analysis of Behavior*, 1970, *14*, 7–10.

Azrin, N. H., & Holz, W. C. Punishment. In W.K. Honig (Ed.), *Operant behavior: Areas of research and application*. New York: Appleton-Century-Crofts, 1966.

Azrin, N. H., Holz, W. C., & Hake, D. F. Fixed-ratio punishment. *Journal of Experimental Analysis of Behavior*, 1963, *6*, 141–48.

Azrin, N. H., Hutchinson, R. R., & Hake, D. F. Pain-induced fighting in the squirrel monkey. *Journal of the Experimental Analysis of Behavior*, 1963, *6*, 620.

Azrin, N. H., Hutchinson, R. R., & Sallery, R. D. Pain-aggression toward inanimate objects. *Journal of the Experimental Analysis of Behavior*, 1964a, *7*, 223–28.

Azrin, N. H., Ulrich, R. E., Hutchinson, R. R., & Norman, D. G. Effect of shock duration on shock-induced fighting. *Journal of the Experimental Analysis of Behavior*, 1964b, *7*, 9–11.

Bacon, W. E. Partial-reinforcement extinction effect following different amounts of training. *Journal of Comparative and Physiological Psychology*, 1962, *55*, 998–1003.

Baddeley, A. D. *The psychology of memory*. New York: Basic Books, 1976.

Badia, P., & Defran, R. H. Orienting responses and GSR conditioning: A dilemma. *Psychological Review*. 1970, *77*, 171–81.

Baenninger, R., & Ulm, R. R. Overcoming the effects of prior punishment on interspecies aggression in the rat. *Journal of Comparative and Physiological Psychology*, 1969, *69*, 628–35.

Banks, R. K. Persistence to continuous punishment following intermittent punishment training. *Journal of Experimental Psychology*, 1966, *71*, 373–77.

Banks, W. P., Fujii, M., & Kayra-Stuart, F. Semantic congruity effects in comparative judgments of magnitude of digits. *Journal of Experimental Psychology: Human Perception and Performance*, 1976, *2*, 435–47.

Barnes, J. M., & Underwood, B. J. "Fate" of first-list associations in transfer theory. *Journal of Experimental Psychology*, 1959, *58*, 97–105.

Baron, A. Delayed punishment of a runway response. *Journal of Comparative and Physiological Psychology*, 1965, *60*, 131–34.

Baron, A., & Antonitis, J. J. Punishment and preshock as determinants of bar-pressing behavior. *Journal of Comparative and Physiological Psychology*, 1961, *54*, 716–20.

Baron, A., Kaufman, A., & Fazzini, D. Density and delay of punishment of free-operant avoidance.

Journal of the Experimental Analysis of Behavior, 1969, *12*, 1029–37.

Barrett, B. H. Reduction in rate of multiple tics by free operant conditioning methods. *Journal of Nervous and Mental Disease*, 1962, *135*, 187–95.

Bartlett, F. C. *Remembering: A study in experimental and social psychology*. London: Cambridge University Press, 1932.

Bastian, J. Associative factors in verbal transfer. *Journal of Experimental Psychology*, 1961, *62*, 70–79.

Battig, W. F., & Bourne, L. E., Jr. Concept indentification as a function of intra- and inter-dimension variability. *Journal of Experimental Psychology*, 1961, *61*, 329–33.

Battig, W. F., & Lawrence, P. S. The greater sensitivity of the serial recall than anticipation procedure to variations in serial order. *Journal of Experimental Psychology*, 1967, *73*, 172–78.

Bauer, R. H. The effects of CS and US intensity on shuttle box avoidance. *Psychonomic Science*, 1972, *27*, 266–68.

Baum, M. Extinction of an avoidance response following response prevention: Some parametric investigations. *Canadian Journal of Psychology*, 1969a, *23*, 1–10.

Baum, M. Extinction of an avoidance response motivated by intense fear: Social facilitation of the action of response prevention (flooding) in rats. *Behavior Research and Therapy*, 1969b, *7*, 57–62.

Baum, M. Extinction of avoidance responding through response prevention (flooding). *Psychological Bulletin* 1970, *74*, 276–84.

Baum, M., LeClerc, R., & St. Laurent, J. Rewarding vs. aversive intracranial stimulation administered during flooding (response prevention) in rats. *Psychological Reports*, 1973, *32*, 551–58.

Baum, M., & Myran, D. D. Response prevention (flooding) in rats: The effects of restricting exploration during flooding and of massed vs. distributed flooding. *Canadian Journal of Psychology*, 1971, *25*, 138–46.

Baum, M. H. Single concept learning as a function of intralist generalization. *Journal of Experimental Psychology*, 1954, *47*, 89–94.

Beck, S. B. Eyelid conditioning as a function of CS intensity, UCS intensity, and manifest anxiety scale score. *Journal of Experimental Psychology*, 1963, *66*, 429–38.

Beckwith, M., & Restle, F. Process of enumeration. *Psychological Review*, 1966, *73*, 437–44.

Beecroft, R. S. *Classical conditioning*. Goleta, Calif.: Psychonomic Press, 1966.

Beery, R. G. A negative contrast effect of reward delay in differential conditioning. *Journal of Experimental Psychology*, 1968, *77*, 429–34.

Behar, I., & LeBedda, J. M. Effects of differential pretraining on learning-set formation in rhesus monkeys. *Journal of Comparative and Physiological Psychology*, 1974, *87*, 277–83.

Benedict, J. O., & Ayres, J. J. B. Factors affecting conditioning in the truly random control procedure in the rat. *Journal of Comparative and Physiological Psychology*, 1972, *78*, 323–30.

Benson, H., Shapiro, D., Tursky, B., & Schwartz, G. E. Decreased systolic blood pressure through operant conditioning techniques in patients with essential hypertension. *Science*, 1971, *173*, 740–42.

Berlin, B., & Kay, P. *Basic color terms: Their universality and evolution*. Berkeley, Calif.: University of California Press, 1969.

Bersh, P. J., & Keltz, J. R. Pavlovian reconditioning and the recovery of avoidance behavior in rats after extinction with response prevention. *Journal of Comparative and Physiological Psychology*, 1971, *76*, 262–66.

Bersh, P. J., & Paynter, W. E. Pavlovian extinction in rats during avoidance response prevention. *Journal of Comparative and Physiological Psychology*, 1972, *78*, 255–59.

Bertsch, G. J. Punishment of consummatory and instrumental behavior: Effects on licking and bar pressing in rats. *Journal of Comparative and Physiological Psychology*, 1972, *78*, 478–84.

Bertsch, G. J. Punishment of consummatory and instrumental behavior: A review. *Psychological Record*, 1976, *26*, 13–31.

Best, M. R. Conditioned and latent inhibition in taste-aversion learning: Clarifying the role of learned safety. *Journal of Experimental Psychology: Animal Behavior Processes*, 1975, *1*, 97–113.

Best, P. J., Best, M. R., & Mickley, G. A. Conditioned aversion to distinct environmental stimuli resulting from gastrointestinal distress. *Journal of Comparative and Physiological Psychology*, 1973, *85*, 250–57.

Bilodeau, I. McD., & Schlosberg, H. Similarity in stimulating conditions as a variable in retroactive inhibition. *Journal of Experimental Psychology*, 1951, *41*, 199–204.

Bindra, I., & Palfai, T. Nature of positive and negative incentive motivational effects on general activity. *Journal of Comparative and Physiological Psychology*, 1967, *63*, 288–97.

Bintz, J. Effect of shock intensity on the retention of an avoidance response. *Psychonomic Science*, 1971, *22*, 17–18.

Bjork, R. A. All-or-none subprocesses in learning a complex sequence. *Journal of Mathematical Psychology*, 1968, *5*, 182–95.

Bjork, R. A. Theoretical implications of directed forgetting. In A. W. Melton & E. Martin (Eds.), *Coding processes in human memory*. Washington: Winston, 1972.

Bjork, R. A. Short-term storage: The ordered output of a central processor. In F. Restle, R. M. Shiffrin, N. J. Castellan, H. R. Lindman, & D. B. Pisoni (Eds.), *Cognitive theory* (Vol. 1). Hillsdale, N.J.: Erlbaum, 1975.

Bjork, R. A., & Allen, T. W. The spacing effect:

Consolidation or differential encoding? *Journal of Verbal Learning and Verbal Behavior*, 1970, *9*, 567–72.

Black, A. H. Autonomic aversive conditioning in infrahuman subjects. In F. R. Brush (Ed.), *Aversive conditioning and learning*. New York: Academic Press, 1971.

Black, A. H., Carlson, N. J., & Solomon, R. L. Exploratory studies of the conditioning of autonomic responses in curarized dogs. *Psychological Monographs*, 1962, *76*, Whole No. 548.

Black, A. H., & DeToledo, L. The relationship among classically conditioned responses: Heart rate and skeletal behavior. In A. H. Black & W. F. Prokasy (Eds.), *Classical conditioning II: Current research and theory*. New York: Appleton-Century-Crofts, 1972.

Black, R. W. Shifts in magnitude of reward and contrast effects in instrumental and selective learning. *Psychological Review*, 1968, *75*, 114–26.

Blanchard, E. B., & Young, L. D. Self-control of cardiac functioning: A promise as yet unfulfilled. *Psychological Bulletin*, 1973, *79*, 145–63.

Blanchard, R. J., & Blanchard, D. C. Crouching as an index of fear. *Journal of Comparative and Physiological Psychology*, 1969, *67*, 370–75.

Blanchard, R. J., & Blanchard, D. C. Defensive reactions in the albino rat. *Learning and Motivation*, 1971, *2*, 351–62.

Blumenthal, A. L. *The process of cognition*. Englewood Cliffs, N.J.: Prentice-Hall, 1977.

Bobrow, D. G. Natural language input for a computer problem solving system. In M. Minsky (Ed.), *Semantic information processing*. Cambridge, Mass.: M.I.T. Press, 1968, 135–215.

Boe, E. E. Variable punishment. *Journal of Comparative and Physiological Psychology*, 1971, *75*, 73–76.

Boe, E. E., & Church, R. M. Permanent effects of punishment during extinction. *Journal of Comparative and Physiological Psychology*, 1967, *63*, 486–92.

Bolles, R. C. *Theory of Motivation*. New York: Harper & Row, 1967.

Bolles, R. C. Species-specific defense reactions and avoidance learning. *Psychological Review*, 1970, *77*, 32–48.

Bolles, R. C. Reinforcement, expectancy, and learning. *Psychological Review*, 1972, *79*, 394–409.

Bolles, R. C., & Collier, A. C. The effect of predictive cues on freezing in rats. *Animal Learning and Behavior*, 1976, *4*, 6–8.

Bolles, R. C., & Grossen, N. E. Effects of an informational stimulus on the acquisition of avoidance behavior in rats. *Journal of Comparative and Physiological Psychology*, 1969, *68*, 90–99.

Bolles, R. C., Grossen, N.E., Hargrave, G.E., &

Duncan, P. M. Effects of conditioned appetitive stimuli on the acquisition and extinction of a runway response. *Journal of Experimental Psychology*, 1970, *85*, 138–40.

Bolles, R. C., & Moot, S. A. The rat's anticipation of two meals a day. *Journal of Comparative and Physiological Psychology*, 1973, *83*, 510–14.

Bolles, R.C., Moot, S. A., & Grossen, N.E. The extinction of shuttle box avoidance. *Learning and Motivation*, 1971, *2*, 324–33.

Bolles, R. C., Riley, A. L., Cantor, M. B., & Duncan, P. M. The rat's failure to anticipate regularly scheduled daily shock. *Behavioral Biology*, 1974, *11*, 365–72.

Bolles, R. C., & Seelbach, S. E. Punishing and reinforcing effects of noise onset and termination for different responses. *Journal of Comparative and Physiological Psychology*, 1964, *58*, 127–31.

Bolles, R. C., & Stokes, L. W. Rat's anticipation of diurnal and adiurnal feeding. *Journal of Comparative and Physiological Psychology*, 1965, *60*, 290–94.

Bolles, R.C., Stokes, L. W., & Younger, M. S. Does CS termination reinforce avoidance behavior? *Journal of Comparative and Physiological Psychology*, 1966, *62*, 201–7.

Bolles, R. C., Warren, J. A., & Ostrov, N. The role of the CS–US interval in bar press avoidance learning. *Psychonomic Science*, 1966, *6*, 113–14.

Boren, J. J., Sidman, M., & Herrnstein, R. J. Avoidance, escape, and extinction as functions of shock intensity. *Journal of Comparative and Physiological Psychology*, 1959, *52*, 420–25.

Boring, E. G. *A history of experimental psychology* (2nd ed.). New York: Appleton-Century-Crofts, 1957.

Bourne, L. E., Jr. *Human conceptual behavior.* Boston: Allyn & Bacon, 1966.

Bourne, L. E., Jr. Knowing and using concepts. *Psychological Review*, 1970, *77*, 546–56.

Bourne, L. E., Jr. An inference model for conceptual rule learning. In R. L. Solso (Ed.), *Theories in cognitive psychology: The Loyola symposium.* Potomac, Md.: Erlbaum, 1974.

Bourne, L. E., Jr., Ekstrand, B. R., & Dominowski, R. L. *The psychology of thinking.* Englewood Cliffs, N.J.: Prentice-Hall, 1971.

Bourne, L. E., & Haygood, R. C. The role of stimulus redundancy in concept identification. *Journal of Experimental Psychology*, 1959, *58*, 232–38.

Bousfield, W. A. The occurrence of clustering in the recall of randomly arranged associates. *Journal of General Psychology*, 1953, *49*, 229–40.

Bousfield, W. A., & Cohen, B. H. The effects of reinforcement on the occurrence of clustering in the recall of randomly arranged associates. *Journal of Psychology*, 1953, *36*, 67–81.

Bousfield, W. A., Cohen, B. H., & Whitmarsh, G. A. Associative clustering in the recall of words of different taxonomic frequencies of occurrence.

Psychological Reports, 1958, *4*, 39–44.

Bower, G. H. A contrast effect in differential conditioning. *Journal of Experimental Psychology*, 1961, *62*, **196**–99.

Bower, G. H. The influence of graded reductions in reward and prior frustrating events upon the magnitude of the frustration effect. *Journal of Comparative and Physiological Psychology*, 1962, *55*, 582–87.

Bower, G. H. Organizational factors in memory. *Cognitive Psychology*, 1970, *1*, 18–46.

Bower, G. H. Mental imagery in associative learning. In L. W. Gregg (Ed.), *Cognition in learning and memory.* New York: Wiley, 1972.

Bower, G. H., & Clark, M. C. Narrative stories as mediators for serial learning. *Psychonomic Science*, 1969, *14*, 181–82.

Bower, G. H., Clark, M. C., Lesgold, A. M., & Winzenz, D. Hierarchical retrieval schemes in recall of categorized word lists. *Journal of Verbal Learning and Verbal Behavior*, 1969, *8*, 323–43.

Bower, G. H., Fowler, H., & Trapold, M. A. Escape learning as a function of amount of shock reduction. *Journal of Experimental Psychology*, 1959, *58*, 482–84.

Bower, G. H., Starr, R., & Lazarovitz, L. Amount of response-produced change in the CS and avoidance learning. *Journal of Comparative and Physiological Psychology*, 1965, *59*, 13–17.

Bower, G. H., & Trabasso, T. R. Reversals prior to solution in concept identification. *Journal of Experimental Psychology*, 1963, *66*, 409–18.

Bower, G. H., & Trabasso, T. R. Concept identification. In R. C. Atkinson (Ed.), *Studies in mathematical psychology.* Stanford, Calif.: Stanford University Press, 1964, 32–94.

Bracewell, R. J., & Black, A. H. Effects of restraint and noncontingent preshock on subsequent escape learning in the rat. *Learning and Motivation*, 1974, *5*, 53—69.

Bransford, J. D., & Franks, J. J. The abstraction of linguistic ideas. *Cognitive Psychology*, 1971, *2*, 331–50.

Breitmeyer, B. G., & Ganz, L. Implications of sustained and transient channels for theories of visual pattern masking, saccadic suppression, and information processing. *Psychological Review*, 1976, *83*, 4–36.

Breland, K., & Breland, M. The misbehavior of organisms. *American Psychologist*, 1961, *16*, 681–84.

Brennan, J. F., & Riccio, D. C. Stimulus generalization of suppression in rats following aversively motivated instrumental or Pavlovian training. *Journal of Comparative and Physiological Pshchology*, 1975, *88*, 570–79.

Brener, J., & Goesling, W. J. Avoidance conditioning of activity and immobility in rats. *Journal of Comparative and Physiological Psychology*, 1970, *70*, 276–80.

Bridger, W. H., & Mandel, I. J. Abolition of the PRE by instructions in GSR conditioning. *Journal of*

Experimental Psychology, 1965, 69, 476–82.

Briggs, G. E. Acquisition, extinction and recovery functions in retroactive inhibition. Journal of Experimental Psychology, 1954, 47, 285–93.

Broadbent, D. E. Perception and communication. London: Pergamon Press, 1958.

Brogden, W. J. Sensory preconditioning. Journal of Experimental Psychology, 1939, 25, 323–32.

Brooks, C. I. Frustration to nonreward following limited reward experience. Journal of Experimental Psychology, 1969, 81, 403–5.

Brown, A. S. Catalogue of scaled verbal material. Memory & Cognition Supplement, 1976, 1–45.

Brown, B. L. Stimulus generalization in salivary conditioning. Journal of Comparative and Physiological Psychology, 1970, 71, 467–77.

Brown, J. A. Some tests of the decay theory of immediate memory. Quarterly Journal of Experimental Psychology, 1958, 10, 12–21.

Brown, J. S. Factors affecting self-punitive locomotor behavior. In B. A. Campbell & R. M. Church (Eds.), Punishment and aversive behavior. New York: Appleton-Century-Crofts, 1969.

Brown, J. S., Martin, R. C., & Morrow, M. W. Self-punitive behavior in the rat: Facilitative effects of punishment on resistance to extinction. Journal of Comparative and Physiological Psychology, 1964, 57, 127–33.

Brown, P. L., & Jenkins, H. M. Auto-shaping of the pigeon's keypeck. Journal of the Experimental Analysis of Behavior, 1968, 11, 1–8.

Brown, R. W. Reference in memorial tribute to Eric Lenneberg. Cognition, 1976, 4, 125–53.

Brown, R. W., & Lenneberg, E. H. A study of language and cognition. Journal of Abnormal and Social Psychology, 1954, 49, 454–62.

Brown, R. W., & McNeil, D. The "tip of the tongue" phenomenon. Journal of Verbal Learning and Verbal Behavior, 1966, 5, 325–37.

Bruce, R. W. Conditions of transfer of training. Journal of Experimental Psychology, 1933, 16, 343–61.

Bruner, J. S., Goodnow, J. J., & Austin, G. A. A study of thinking. New York: Wiley, 1956.

Bugelski, B. R. Presentation time, total time, and mediation in paired-associate learning. Journal of Experimental Psychology, 1962, 63, 409–12.

Bull, J. A. An interaction between appetitive Pavlovian CSs and instrumental avoidance responding. Learning and Motivation, 1970, 1, 18–26.

Burdick, C. K., & James, J. P. Spontaneous recovery of conditioned suppression of licking by rats. Journal of Comparative and Physiological Psychology, 1970, 72, 467–70.

Burr, D. E. S., & Thomas, D. R. Effect of proactive inhibition upon the post-discrimination generalization gradient. Journal of Comparative and Physiological Psychology, 1972, 81, 441–48.

Burt, H. E. An experimental study of early childhood memory. Journal of Genetic

Psychology, 1932, 40, 287–94.

Butler, R. A. Discrimination learning by rhesus monkeys to visual exploration motivation. Journal of Comparative and Physiological Psychology, 1953, 46, 95–98.

Camp, D. S., Raymond, G. A., & Church, R. M. Response suppression as a function of the schedule of punishment. Psychonomic Science, 1966, 5, 23–24.

Camp, D. S., Raymond, G. A., & Church, R. M. Temporal relationship between response and punishment. Journal of Experimental Psychology, 1967, 74, 114–23.

Campbell, B. A., & Kraeling, D. Reponse strength as a function of drive level and amount of drive reduction. Journal of Experimental Psychology, 1953, 45, 97–101.

Campbell, B. A., Smith, N. F., & Misanin, J. R., Effects of punishment on extinction of avoidance behavior: Avoidance-avoidance conflict or vicious circle behavior. Journal of Comparative and Physiological Psychology, 1966, 62, 495–98.

Campbell, P. E., Batsche, C. J., & Batsche, G. M. Spaced-trials reward magnitude effects in the rat: Single versus multiple food pellets. Journal of Comparative Physiological Psychology, 1972, 81, 360–64.

Capaldi, E. D. Simultaneous shifts in reward magnitude and level of food deprivation. Psychonomic Science, 1971, 23, 357–59.

Capaldi, E. D., & Hovancik, J. R. Effects of previous body weight level on rats' straight-alley performance. Journal of Experimental Psychology, 1973, 97, 93–97.

Capaldi, E. J. The effect of different amounts of training on the resistance to extinction of different patterns of partially reinforced responses. Journal of Comparative Physiological Psychology, 1958, 51, 367–71.

Capaldi, E. J. Effect of N-length, number of different N-lengths, and number of reinforcements on resistance to extinction. Journal of Experimental Psychology, 1964, 68, 230–39.

Capaldi, E. J. Partial reinforcement: A hypothesis of sequential effects. Psychological Review, 1966, 73, 459–77.

Capaldi, E. J. A sequential hypothesis of instrumental learning. In K. W. Spence & J. T. Spence (Eds.), The psychology of learning and motivation (Vol. 1). New York: Academic Press, 1967.

Capaldi, E. J. & Capaldi, E. D. Magnitude of partial reward, irregular reward schedules, and a 24-hour ITI: A test of several hypotheses. Journal of Comparative and Physiological Psychology, 1970, 72, 203–9.

Capaldi, E. J., & Deutsch, E. A. Effects of severely limited acquisition training and pretraining on the partial reinforcement effect. Psychonomic Science, 1967, 9, 171–72.

Capaldi, E. J., & Hart, D. Influence of a small number of partial reinforcement training trials on resistance to extinction. *Journal of Experimental Psychology*, 1962, *64*, 166–71.

Capaldi, E. J., Lanier, A. T., & Godbout, R. C. Reward schedule effects following severely limited acquisition training. *Journal of Experimental Psychology*, 1968, *78*, 521–24.

Capaldi, E. J., & Lynch, A. D. Magnitude of partial reward and resistance to extinction: Effect of N-R transitions. *Journal of Comparative and Physiological Psychology*, 1968, *65*, 179–81.

Capaldi, E. J., & Waters, R. W. Conditioning and nonconditioning interpretations of small-trial phenomena. *Journal of Experimental Psychology*, 1970, *84*, 518–22.

Cappell, H. D., LeBlanc, A. E., & Endrenyi, L. Aversive conditioning by psychoactive drugs: Effects of morphine, alcohol, and chlordiozepoxide. *Psychopharmacologia*, 1973, *29*, 239–46.

Carlson, J. G. Timeout punishment: Rate of reinforcement and delay of timeout. *Learning and Motivation*, 1972, *3*, 31–43.

Carlson, J. G., & Wielkiewicz, R. M. Delay of reinforcement in instrumental discrimination learning in rats. *Journal of Comparative and Physiological Psychology*, 1972, *81*, 365–70.

Carmichael, L. L., Hogan, H. P., & Walter, A. A. An experimental study of the effect of language on the reproduction of visually perceived form. *Journal of Experimental Psychology*, 1932, *15*, 73–86.

Carpenter, P. A., & Just, M. A. Sentence comprehension: A psycholinguistic processing model of verification. *Psychological Review*, 1975, *82*, 45–73.

Catania, A. C. Concurrent operants. In W. K. Honig (Ed.), *Operant behavior: Areas of research and application*. New York: Appleton-Century-Crofts, 1966.

Catania, A. C., & Reynolds, G. S. A quantitative analysis of the responding maintained by interval schedules of reinforcement. *Journal of the Experimental Analysis of Behavior*, 1968, *11*, 327–83.

Caul, W. F., Buchanan, D. C., & Hays, R. C. Effects of unpredictability of shock on incidence of gastric lesions and heart rate in immobilized rats. *Physiology and Behavior*, 1972, *8*, 669–72.

Cavanagh, J. P. Relation between the immediate memory span and the memory search rate. *Psychological Review*, 1972, *79*, 525–30.

Ceraso, J., & Henderson, A. Unavailability and associative loss in RI and PI: Second try. *Journal of Experimental Psychology*, 1966, *72*, 314–16.

Chapman, L. J., & Chapman, J. P. Atmosphere effect reexamined. *Journal of Experimental Psychology*, 1959, *58*, 220–26.

Chase, W. G., & Clark, H. H. Mental operations in the comparison of sentences and pictures. In L. W. Gregg (Ed.), *Cognition in learning and memory*. New York: Wiley, 1972, 205–32.

Cherry, E. C. Some experiments on the recognition of speech with one and two ears. *Journal of the Acoustical Society of America*, 1953, *25*, 975–79.

Chomsky, N. *Syntactic structures*, The Hague: Mouton, 1957.

Chomsky, N. Verbal behavior (a review by B. F. Skinner). *Language*, 1959, *35*, 26–58.

Chomsky, N. *Aspects of the theory of syntax*. Cambridge, Mass.: M.I.T. Press, 1965.

Chomsky, N. *Language and mind*. New York: Harcourt, Brace & World, 1968.

Church, R. M. The varied effects of punishment on behavior. *Psychological Review*, 1963, *70*, 369–402.

Church, R. M. Response suppression. In B. A. Campbell & R. M. Church (Eds.), *Punishment and aversive behavior*. New York: Appleton-Century-Crofts, 1969.

Church, R. M., Raymond, G. A., & Beauchamp, R. D. Response suppression as a function of intensity and duration of a punishment. *Journal of Comparative and Physiological Psychology*, 1967, *63*, 39–44.

Church, R. M., Wooten, C. L., & Matthews, T. J. Discriminative punishment and the conditioned emotional response. *Learning and Motivation*, 1970, *1*, 1–17.

Cicala, G. A., Masterson, F. A., & Kubitsky, G. Role of initial response rate in avoidance learning by rats. *Journal of Comparative and Physiological Psychology*, 1971, *75*, 226–30.

Cieutat, V. J., Stockwell, F. E., & Noble, C E. The interaction of ability and amount of practice with stimulus meaningfulness (m, m′) in paired-associate learning. *Journal of Experimental Psychology*, 1958, *56*, 193–202.

Clark, H. H. Linguistic processes in deductive reasoning. *Psychological Review*, 1969, *76*, 387–404.

Clark, H. H., & Chase, W. G. On the process of comparing sentences against pictures. *Cognitive Psychology*, 1972, *3*, 472–517.

Coate, W. B. Effect of deprivation on post discrimination stimulus generalization in the rat. *Journal of Comparative and Physiological Psychology*, 1964, *57*, 134–38.

Cofer, C. N. Properties of verbal materials and verbal learning. In J. W. Kling & L. A. Riggs (Eds.), *Woodworth and Schlosberg's experimental psychology*. New York: Holt, Rinehart, & Winston, 1971.

Cofer, C. (Ed.), *The structure of human memory*. San Francisco: Freeman, 1976.

Cohen, M. R., & Nagel, E. *An introduction to logic*. New York: Harcourt, Brace & World, 1962.

Coleman, S. R. Consequences of response-contingent change in unconditioned stimulus intensity upon the rabbit (*orycto Lagus cuniculus*) nictitating membrane response. *Journal of Comparative and Physiological Psychology*, 1975, *88*, 591–95.

Collins, A. M., & Quillian, M. R. Retrieval time from semantic memory. *Journal of Verbal Learning and Verbal Behavior*, 1969, *82*, 407–28.

Collins, A. M., & Quillian, M. R. How to make a language user. In E. Tulving & W. Donaldson (Eds.), *Organization and memory*. New York: Academic Press, 1972, 309–51.

Conrad, R. Acoustic confusions in immediate memory. *British Journal of Psychology*, 1964, 55, 75–84.

Coppage, E. W., & Harcum, E. R. Temporal vs. structural determinants of primacy in strategies of serial learning. *Journal of Verbal Learning and Verbal Behavior*, 1967, 6, 487–90.

Coppock, H. W., & Chambers, R. M. Reinforcement of position preference by automatic intravenous injections of glucose. *Journal of Comparative and Physiological Psychology*, 1954, 47, 355–57.

Coppock, W. J. Pre-extinction in sensory preconditioning. *Journal of Experimental Psychology*, 1958, 55, 213–19.

Corson, J. A. Observational learning of a lever pressing response. *Psychonomic Science*, 1967, 7, 197–98.

Coughlin, R. C. The frustration effect and resistance to extinction as a function of percentage of reinforcement. *Journal of Experimental Psychology*, 1970, 84, 113–17.

Coughlin, R. C. The aversive properties of withdrawing positive reinforcement: A review of the recent literature. *Psychological Record*, 1972, 22, 333–54.

Coulter, X., Riccio, D. C., & Page, H. A. Effects of blocking an instrumental avoidance response: Facilitated extinction but persistence of "fear." *Journal of Comparative and Physiological Psychology*, 1969, 68, 377–81.

Cousins, L. S., Zamble, E., Tait, R. W., & Subaski, M. D. Sensory preconditioning in curarized rats. *Journal of Comparative and Physiological Psychology*, 1971, 77, 152–54.

Craik, F. I. M. The fate of primary items in free recall. *Journal of Verbal Learning and Verbal Behavior*, 1970, 9, 143–48.

Craik, F. I. M., & Lockhart, R. S. Levels of processing: A framework for memory research. *Journal of Verbal Learning and Verbal Behavior*, 1972, 11, 671–84.

Craik, F. I. M., & Watkins, M. J. The role of rehearsal in short-term memory. *Journal of Verbal Learning and Verbal Behavior*, 1973, 12, 599–607.

Crespi, L. P. Quantitative variations of incentive and performance in the white rat. *American Journal of Psychology*, 1942, 55, 467–517.

Crider, A., Schwartz, G. E., & Shnidman, S. On the criteria for instrumental autonomic conditioning: A reply to Katkin and Murray. *Psychological Bulletin*, 1969, 71, 455–61.

Crider, A., Shapiro, D., & Tursky, B. Reinforcement of spontaneous electrodermal activity. *Journal of Comparative and Physiological Psychology*, 1966, 61, 20–27.

Culbertson, J. L. Effects of brief reinforcement delays on acquisition and extinction of brightness discriminations in rats. *Journal of Comparative and Physiological Psychology*, 1970, 70, 317–25.

Dallett, K. M. The transfer surface re-examined. *Journal of Verbal Learning and Verbal Behavior*, 1962, 1, 91–94.

Dallett, K. M. Number of categories and category information in free recall. *Journal of Experimental Psychology*, 1964, 68, 1–12.

Daly, H. B. Excitatory and inhibitory effects of complete and incomplete reward reduction in the double runway. *Journal of Experimental Psychology*, 1968, 76, 430–38.

D'Amato, M. R., & Fazzaro, J. Discriminated lever-press avoidance learning as a function of type and intensity of shock. *Journal of Comparative and Physiological Psychology*, 1966, 61, 313–15.

D'Amato, M. R., Fazzaro, J., & Etkin, M. Discriminated bar-press avoidance maintenance and extinction in rats as a function of shock intensity. *Journal of Comparative and Physiological Psychology*, 1967, 63, 351–54.

D'Amato, M. R., Fazzaro, J., & Etkin, M. Anticipatory responding and avoidance discrimination as factors in avoidance conditioning. *Journal of Experimental Psychology*, 1968, 77, 41–47.

D'Amato, M. R., & Schiff, D. Long-term discriminated avoidance performance in the rat. *Journal of Comparative and Physiological Psychology*, 1964, 57, 123–26.

D'Amato, M. R., & Schiff, D. Overlearning and brightness-discrimination reversal. *Journal of Experimental Psychology*, 1965, 69, 375–81.

Dattman, P. E., & Israel, H. The order of dominance among conceptual capacities: An experimental test of Heidbreder's hypothesis. *Journal of Psychology*, 1951, 31, 147–60.

Darwin, C. T., Turvey, M. T., & Crowder, R. G. An auditory analog of the Sperling partial report procedure: Evidence for brief auditory storage. *Cognitive Psychology*, 1972, 3, 255–67.

Davenport, J. W. Instrumental runway performance as a function of temporal distribution of reinforcement. *Journal of Comparative and Physiological Psychology*, 1964, 57, 205–10.

Davis, H., & Kreuter, C. Conditioned suppression of an avoidance response by a stimulus paired with food. *Journal of the Experimental Analysis of Behavior*, 1972, 17, 277–85.

Dawson, M. E., & Reardon, P. Effects of facilitory and inhibitory sets on GSR conditioning and extinction. *Journal of Experimental Psychology*, 1969, 82, 462–66.

Deane, G. E. Cardiac conditioning in the albino rabbit using three CS-UCS intervals. *Psychonomic Science*, 1965, 3, 119–20.

Deane, G. E., & Zeaman, D. Human heart rate during anxiety. *Perceptual and Motor Skills*, 1958, 8, 103–6.

Deese, J. Influence of inter-item associative strength

upon immediate free recall. *Psychological Reports*, 1959, *5*, 305–12.

Deese, J. *Psychology as science and art*. New York: Harcourt Brace Jovanovich, 1972.

Denny, M. R. Elicitation theory applied to an analysis of the overlearning reversal effect. In J. H. Reynierse (Ed.), *Current issues in animal learning*. Lincoln: University of Nebraska Press, 1970.

Der-Karabetian, A., & Gorry, T. Amount of different flavors consumed during the CS-US interval in taste aversion learning and interference. *Physiological Psychology*, 1974, *2*, 457–60.

Desiderato, O., Butler, B., & Meyer, C. Changes in fear generalization gradients as a function of delayed testing. *Journal of Experimental Psychology*, 1966, *72*, 678–82.

Desiderato, O., Foldes, J. M., & Gockley, J. S. Incubation of anxiety: Effect on temporal generalization. *Psychonomic Science*, 1966, *6*, 139–40.

Desiderato, O., MacKinnon, J. R., & Hissom, H. Development of gastric ulcers in rats following stress termination. *Journal of Comparative and Physiological Psychology*, 1974, *87*, 208–14.

DeSoto, C. B., London, M., & Handel, S. Social reasoning and spatial paralogic. *Journal of Personality and Social Psychology*, 1965, *2*, 513–21.

Deutsch, J. A., & Deutsch, D. Attention: Some theoretical considerations. *Psychological Review*, 1963, *70*, 80–90.

Devine, J. V. Stimulus attributes and training procedures in learning-set formation of rhesus and cebus monkeys. *Journal of Comparative and Physiological Psychology*, 1970, *73*, 62–67.

Dews, P. B. The effect of multiple SΔ periods on responding on a fixed-interval schedule. *Journal of the Experimental Analysis of Behavior*, 1962, *5*, 369–74.

Dews, P. B. Studies on responding under fixed-interval schedules of reinforcement: The effects on the pattern of responding of changes in requirement at reinforcement. *Journal of the Experimental Analysis of Behavior*, 1969, *12*, 191–99.

DiCara, L. V., & Miller, N. E. Instrumental learning of vasomotor responses by rats: Learning to respond differentially in the two ears. *Science*, 1968, *159*, 1485–86.

DiLollo, V. Runway performance in relation to runway-goal-box similarity and changes in incentive amount. *Journal of Comparative and Physiological Psychology*, 1964, *58*, 327–29.

Dinsmoor, J. A. Punishment: I. The avoidance hypothesis. *Psychological Review*, 1954, *61*, 34–46.

Dinsmoor, J. A. Punishment: II. An interpretation of empirical findings. *Psychological Review*, 1955, *62*, 96–105.

Domjan, M., & Bowman, T. G. Learned safety and the CS-US delay gradient in taste-aversion

learning. *Learning & Motivation*, 1974, *5*, 409–23.

Domjan, M., & Wilson, N. E. Specificity of cue to consequence in aversion learning in the rat. *Psychonomic Science*, 1972, *26*, 143–45.

Donders, F. C. Over de snelheid van psychische processen, *Ondersoekingen gedaan in het Psysiologisch Laboratium der Utrechtsche Hoogeschool*, 1868–1869, *2*, 92–120. Translated by W. G. Koster, *Acta Psychologica*, 1969, *30*, 412–31.

Doob, L. W. Eidetic images among the Ibo. *Ethnology*, 1964, *3*, 357–63.

Dreyer, P., & Renner, K. W. Self-punitive behavior—Masochism or confusion? *Psychological Review*, 1971, *78*, 333–37.

Dunham, P. J. Contrasted conditions of reinforcement: A selective critique. *Psychological Bulletin*, 1968, *69*, 295–315.

Dunham, P. J. Punishment: Method and theory. *Psychological Review*, 1971, *78*, 58–70.

Ebbinghaus, H. *Memory*. (Translated by H. A. Ruger & C. E. Bussenius.) New York: Teachers College, 1913; New York: Dover, 1964. (Originally published as *Uber das Gedachtnis*. Leipzig: Duncker & Humbolt, 1885.)

Ebenholtz, S. M. Position mediated transfer between serial learning and a spatial discrimination task. *Journal of Experimental Psychology*, 1963, *65*, 603–8.

Ebenholtz, S. M. Serial learning and dimensional organization. In G. N. Bower (Ed.), *The psychology of learning and motivation: Advances in research and theory* (Vol. 5). New York: Academic Press, 1972, 267–314.

Egeth, H. Selective attention. *Psychological Bulletin*, 1967, *67*, 41–57.

Egger, M. D., & Miller, N. E. Secondary reinforcement in rats as a function of information value and reliability of the stimulus. *Journal of Experimental Psychology*, 1962, *64*, 97–104.

Eisenberger, R. Explanation of rewards that do not reduce tissue needs. *Psychological Bulletin*, 1972, *77*, 319–39.

Eisenberger, R., Myers, A. K., & Kaplan, R. M. Persistent deprivation-shift effect opposite in direction to incentive contrast. *Journal of Experimental Psychology*, 1973, *99*, 400–404.

Ellis, W. R. Role of stimulus sequences in stimulus discrimination and stimulus generalization. *Journal of Experimental Psychology*, 1970, *83* 155–63.

Ellison, G. D. Differential salivary conditioning to traces. *Journal of Comparative and Physiological Psychology*, 1964, *57*, 373–80.

Erickson, J. R. A set analysis theory of behavior in formal syllogistic reasoning tasks. In R. L. Solso (Ed.), *Theories of cognitive psychology: The Loyola symposium*. Potomac, Maryland: Erlbaum, 1974, 305–30.

Erickson, J. R. Research on syllogistic reasoning. In

R. Revlin & R. E. Mayer (Eds.), *Human reasoning*. Washington: Winston, in press.

Ernst, G. W., & Newell, A. *GPS: A case study in generality and problem solving*. New York: Academic Press, 1969.

Essock, S. M., & Reese, E. P. Preference for and effects of variable- as opposed to fixed-reinforcer duration. *Journal of the Experimental Analysis of Behavior*, 1974, *21*, 89–97.

Estes, W. K. An experimental study of punishment. *Psychological Monographs*, 1944, *57* (Whole No. 263).

Estes, W. K. Toward a statistical theory of learning. *Psychological Review*, 1950, *57*, 94–107.

Estes, W. K. Learning theory and the new "mental chemistry." *Psychological Review*, 1960, *67*, 207–23.

Estes, W. K. All-or-none processes in learning and retention. *American Psychologist*, 1964, *19*, 16–25.

Estes, W. K., Hopkins, B. L., & Crothers, E. J. All-or-none and conservation effects in the learning and retention of paired associates. *Journal of Experimental Psychology*, 1960, *60*, 329–39.

Fehr, F. S., & Stern, J. A. Peripheral physiological variables and emotion: The James-Lange theory revisited. *Psychological Bulletin*, 1970, *74*, 411–24.

Feigenbaum, E. A. Information processing and memory. In D. A. Norman (Ed.), *Models of human memory*. New York: Academic Press, 1970.

Feinaigle, G. von *The new art of memory*. London: Sherwood, Neely & Jones, 1813.

Felton, M. & Lyon, D. O. The post-reinforcement pause. *Journal of the Experimental Analysis of Behavior*, 1966, *9*, 131–34.

Ferster, C. B., & Appel, J. B. Punishment of SΔ responding in matching to sample by time out from positive reinforcement. *Journal of Experimental Behavior*, 1961, *4*, 45–56.

Ferster, C. B., & Skinner, B. F. *Schedules of reinforcement*. New York: Appleton-Century-Crofts, 1957.

Filby, Y., & Appell, J. B. Variable-interval punishment during variable-interval reinforcement. *Journal of the Experimental Analysis of Behavior*, 1966, *9*, 521–27.

Fillmore, C. J. Some problems for case grammar. In R. J. O'Brien (Ed.), *Linguistics: Developments of the sixties—viewpoints for the seventies*. Monograph series on languages and linguistics, 1971, *24*, 35–56.

Fillmore, C. J. The case for case. In E. Bach & R. T. Harms (Eds.), *Universals of linguistic theory*. New York: Holt, Rinehart & Winston, 1968, 1–90.

Fischer, G., Viney, W., Knight, J., & Johnson, N. Response decrement as a function of effort. *Quarterly Journal of Experimental Psychology*, 1968, *20*, 301–4.

Fiske, D. W., & Maddi, S. R. *Functions of varied experience*. Homewood, Ill.: Dorsey, 1961.

Fitzgerald, R. D. Effects of partial reinforcement with acid on the classically conditioned salivary response in dogs. *Journal of Comparative and Physiological Psychology*, 1963, *56*, 1056–60.

Fitzgerald, R. D., & Martin, G. K. Heart-rate conditioning in rats as a function of interstimulus interval. *Psychological Reports*, 1971, *29*, 1103–10.

Fitzgerald, R. D., & Teyler, T. J. Trace and delayed heart-rate conditioning in rats as a function of US intensity. *Journal of Comparative and Physiological Psychology*, 1970, *70*, 242–53.

Flaherty, C. F., & Largen, J. Within-subjects positive and negative contrast effects in rats. *Journal of Comparative and Physiological Psychology*, 1975, *88*, 653–64.

Flanagan, B., Goldiamond, I., & Azrin, N. H. Operant stuttering: The control of stuttering behavior through response-contingent consequences. *Journal of the Experimental Analysis of Behavior*, 1958, *1*, 173–78.

Foucault, M. Les inhibitions internes de fixation. *Année Psychologique*, 1928, *29*, 92–112.

Fowler, H. Satiation and curiosity. In K. W. Spence & J. T. Spence (Eds.), *The psychology of learning and motivation* (Vol. 1). New York: Academic Press, 1967.

Fowler, H., Fago, G. C., Domber, E. A., & Mochhauser, M. Signaling and affective functions in Pavlovian conditioning. *Animal Learning and Behavior*, 1973, *1*, 81–89.

Fowler, H., & Miller, N. E. Facilitation and inhibition of runway performance by hind- and forepaw shock of various intensities. *Journal of Comparative and Physiological Psychology*, 1963, *56*, 801–5.

Fowler, H., & Trapold, M. A. Escape performance as a function of delay of reinforcement. *Journal of Experimental Psychology*, 1962, *63*, 464–67.

Fox, S. S. Self-maintained sensory input and sensory deprivation in monkeys. *Journal of Comparative and Physiological Psychology*, 1962, *55*, 438–44.

Franchina, J. J. Escape behavior and shock intensity: Within-subject versus between-groups comparisons. *Journal of Comparative and Physiological Psychology*, 1969, *69*, 241–45.

Franchina, J. J., Agee, C. M., & Hauser, P. J. Response prevention and extinction of escape behavior: Duration, frequency, similarity, and retraining variables in rats. *Journal of Comparative and Physiological Psychology*, 1974, *87*, 354–63.

Franchina, J. J., Bush, M. E., Kash, J. S., Troen, D. M., & Young, R. L. Similarity between shock and safe areas during acquisition, transfer, and extinction of escape behavior in rats. *Journal of Comparative and Physiological Psychology*, 1973, *84*, 216–24.

Franchina, J. J., & Schindele, T. E. Nonshock

confinement duration and shock- and safebox similarity during escape training in rats. *Animal Learning & Behavior,* 1975, *3,* 297–300.

Franks, C. M. *Behavior therapy: Appraisal and status.* New York: McGraw-Hill, 1969.

Franks, J. J., & Bransford, J. D. Abstraction of visual patterns. *Journal of Experimental Psychology,* 1971, *90,* 65–74.

Frederiksen, C. H. Effects of context-induced processing operations on semantic information acquired from discourse. *Cognitive Psychology,* 1975, *7,* 139–66.

Freedman, P. E., Hennessy, J. W., & Groner, D. Effects of varying active/passive shock levels in shuttle box avoidance in rats. *Journal of Comparative and Physiological Psychology,* 1974, *86,* 79–84.

French, N. R., Carter, C. W., & Koenig, W. The words and sounds of telephone conversations. *Bell System Technical Journal,* 1930, *9,* 290–324.

Freud, S. *Psychopathology of everyday life.* London: Fisher & Unwin, 1914.

Frey, P. W., & Butler, C. S. Rabbit eyelid conditioning as a function of unconditioned stimulus duration. *Journal of Comparative and Physiological Psychology,* 1973, *85,* 289–94.

Friebergs, V., & Tulving, E. The effect of practice on utilization of information from positive and negative instances in concept identification. *Canadian Journal of Psychology,* 1961, *15,* 101–6.

Friedman, H., & Guttman, N. Further analysis of the various effects of discrimination training upon stimulus generalization gradients. In D. I. Mostofsky (Ed.), *Stimulus generalization.* Stanford, Calif.: Stanford University Press, 1965.

Furedy, J. J. Explicitly-unpaired and truly-random CS-controls in human classical differential autonomic conditioning. *Psychophysiology,* 1971, *8,* 497–503.

Furedy, J. J., & Schiffmann, K. Concurrent measurement of autonomic and cognitive processes in a test of the traditional discriminative control procedure for Pavlovian electrodermal conditioning. *Journal of Experimental Psychology,* 1973, *100,* 210–17.

Galvani, P. F., Riddell, W. I., & Foster, K. M. Passive avoidance in rats and gerbils as a function of species-specific exploratory tendencies. *Behavioral Biology,* 1975, *13,* 277–90.

Gamzu, E., & Williams, D. R. The source of keypecking in autoshaping. *Animal Learning and Behavior,* 1975, *3,* 37–42.

Garcia, J., Ervin, F. R., & Koelling, R. A. Learning with prolonged delay of reinforcement. *Psychonomic Science,* 1966, *5,* 121–22.

Garcia, J., Ervin, F. R., Yorke, C. H., & Koelling, R. A. Conditioning with delayed vitamin injections. *Science,* 1967, *155,* 716–18.

Garcia, J., Hankins, W. G., & Rusiniak, K. W. Behavioral regulation of the *milieu interne* in man and rat. *Science,* 1974, *185,* 824–31.

Garcia, J., & Koelling, R. A. Relation of cue to consequence in avoidance learning. *Psychonomic Science,* 1966, *4,* 123–24.

Garcia, J., McGowan, B. K., Ervin, F. R., & Koelling, R. A. Cues: Their relative effectiveness as a function of the reinforcer. *Science,* 1968, *160,* 794–95.

Garcia, J., McGowan, B. K., & Green, K. F. Biological constraints on conditioning. In A. H. Black & W. F. Prokasy (Eds.), *Classical conditioning II: Current theory and research.* New York: Appleton-Century-Crofts, 1972.

Gardner, R. A., & Gardner, B. T. Teaching sign language to a chimpanzee. *Science,* 1969, *165,* 664–72.

Garner, W. R. An informational analysis of absolute judgments of loudness. *Journal of Experimental Psychology,* 1953, *46,* 373–80.

Gates, A. I. Recitation as a factor in memorizing. *Archives of Psychology of New York,* 1917, No. 40.

Geiselman, R. E. Semantic positive forgetting: Another cocktail party problem. *Journal of Verbal Learning and Verbal Behavior,* 1975, *14,* 73–81.

Gibson, E. J. A systematic application of the concepts of generalization and differentiation to verbal learning. *Psychological Review,* 1940, *47,* 196–229.

Gilbert, R. M., & Sutherland, N. S. *Animal discrimination learning.* New York: Academic Press, 1969.

Glanzer, M. Stimulus satiation: An explanation of spontaneous alternation and related phenomena. *Psychological Review,* 1953, *60,* 257–68.

Glanzer, M. Curiosity, exploratory drive, and stimulus satiation. *Psychological Bulletin,* 1958, *55,* 302–15.

Glanzer, M., & Cunitz, A. R. Two storage mechanisms in free recall. *Journal of Verbal Learning and Verbal Behavior,* 1966, *5,* 351–60.

Glanzer, M., & Dolinsky, R. The anchor for the serial position curve. *Journal of Verbal Learning and Verbal Behavior,* 1965, *4,* 267–73.

Glanzer, M., & Duarte, A. Repetition between and within languages in free recall. *Journal of Verbal Learning and Verbal Behavior,* 1971, *10,* 625–30.

Glaze, J. A. The association value of nonsense syllables. *Journal of Genetic Psychology,* 1928, *35,* 255–66.

Glazer, H. I., & Weiss, J. M. Long-term and transitory interference effects. *Journal of Experimental Psychology: Animal Behavior Processes,* 1976a, *2,* 191–201.

Glazer, H. I., & Weiss, J. M. Long-term interference effect: An alternative to "learned helplessness." *Journal of Experimental Psychology: Animal Behavior Processes,* 1976b, *2,* 202–13.

Glenberg, A. M. Monotonic and nonmonotonic lag effects in paired-associate and recognition memory paradigms. *Journal of Verbal Learning* and *Verbal Behavior*, 1976, *15*, 1–16.

Gliner, J. A. Predictable vs. unpredictable shock: Preference behavior and stomach ulceration. *Physiology & Behavior*, 1972, *9*, 693–98.

Gordon, A., & Baum, M. Increased efficacy of flooding (response prevention) in rats through positive intracranial stimulation. *Journal of Comparative and Physiological Psychology*, 1971, *75*, 68–72.

Gormezano, I. Yoked comparisons of classical and instrumental conditioning of the eyelid response; and an addendum on "voluntary responders." In W.F. Prokasy (Ed.), *Classical conditioning: A symposium*. New York: Appleton-Century-Crofts, 1965.

Gormezano, I. Investigations of defense and reward conditioning in the rabbit. In A. H. Black & W. F. Prokasy (Eds.), *Classical conditioning II: Current theory and research*. New York: Appleton-Century-Crofts, 1972.

Gormezano, I., & Coleman, S. R. The law of effect and CR contingent modification of the UCS. *Conditional Reflex*, 1973, *8*, 41–56.

Gormezano, I., & Moore, J. W. Effects of instructional set and UCS intensity on the latency, percentage, and form of the eyelid reponse. *Journal of Experimental Psychology*, 1962, *63*, 487–94.

Gormezano, I., & Moore, J. W. Classical conditioning. In M. H. Marx (Ed.), *Learning: Processes*. New York: Macmillan, 1969.

Gough, P. B. The verification of sentences: The effects of delay of evidence and sentence length. *Journal of Verbal Learning and Verbal Behavior*, 1966, *5*, 492–96.

Goulet, L. R., Bone, R. N., & Barker, D. D. Serial position, primacy, and the von Restorff isolation effect. *Psychonomic Science*, 1967, *9*, 529–30.

Gray, J. A. Stimulus intensity dynamism. *Psychological Bulletin*, 1965, *63*, 180–96.

Gray, J. A. Sodium amobarbital and effects of frustrative nonreward. *Journal of Comparative and Physiological Psychology*, 1969, *69*, 55–64.

Gray, J. A., & Wedderburn, A. A. Grouping strategies with simultaneous stimuli. *Quarterly Journal of Experimental Psychology*, 1960, *12*, 180–84.

Green, K. F., Holmstrom, L. S., & Wollman, M. A. Relation of cue to consequence in rats: Effect of recuperation from illness. *Behavioral Biology*, 1974, *10*, 491–503.

Green, L., Bouzas, A., & Rachlin, H. Test of an electric-shock analog to illness-induced aversion. *Behavioral Biology*, 1972, *7*, 513–18.

Greene, J. *Psycholinguistics: Chomsky and psychology*. Baltimore, Md.: Penguin, 1974.

Greeno, J. G. The structure of memory and the process of solving problems. In R. L. Solso (Ed.), *Contemporary issues in cognitive psychology: The Loyola symposium*. Washington, D.C.: Winston, 1973, 103–34.

Greeno, J. G., & Egan, D. E. Theory of rule induction: Knowledge acquired in concept learning, serial pattern learning, and problem solving. In L. W. Gregg (Ed.), *Knowledge and cognition*. Hillside, N.J.: Lawrence Erlbaum Associates, 1974.

Greeno, J. G., James C. T., & Da Polito, F. J. A cognitive interpretation of negative transfer and forgetting of paired-associates. *Journal of Verbal Learning and Verbal Behavior*, 1971, *10*, 331–45.

Greenspoon, J. The reinforcing effect of two spoken sounds on the frequency of two responses. *American Journal of Psychology*, 1955, *68*, 409–16.

Grice, G. R. The relation of secondary reinforcement to delayed reward in visual discrimination learning. *Journal of Experimental Psychology*, 1948, *38*, 1–16.

Grice, G. R. Stimulus intensity and response evocation. *Psychological Review*, 1968, *75*, 359–73.

Grice, G. R., & Davis, J. D. Mediated stimulus equivalence and distinctiveness in human conditioning. *Journal of Experimental Psychology*, 1958, *55*, 565–71.

Grice, G. R., & Davis, J. D. Effect of concurrent responses on the evocation and generalization of the conditioned eyeblink. *Journal of Experimental Psychology*, 1960, *59*, 391–95.

Grice, G. R., & Hunter, J. J. Stimulus intensity effects depend upon the type of experimental design. *Psychological Review*, 1964, *71*, 247–56.

Grimes, J. E. *The thread of discourse*. Ithaca, New York: Cornell University Press, 1972.

Groen, G. J., & Parkman, J. M. A chronometric analysis of simple addition. *Psychological Review*, 1972, *79*, 329–43.

Grossen, N. E., & Bolles, R. C. Effects of a classical conditioned "fear signal" and "safety signal" on nondiscriminated avoidance behavior. *Psychonomic Science*, 1968, *11*, 321–22.

Grossen, N. E., & Kelley, M. J. Species-specific behavior and acquisition of avoidance behavior in rats. *Journal of Comparative and Physiological Psychology*, 1972, *81*, 307–10.

Grossen, N. E., Kostansek, D. J., & Bolles, R. C. Effects of appetitive discriminative stimuli on avoidance behavior. *Journal of Experimental Psychology*, 1969, *81*, 340–43.

Gustavson, C. R., Garcia, J., Hankins, W. G., & Rusiniak, K. W. Coyote predation control by aversive conditioning. *Science*, 1974, *184*, 581–83.

Guthrie, E. R. Reward and punishment. *Psychological Review*, 1934, *41*, 450–60.

Guthrie, E. R. *The psychology of learning*. New York: Harper, 1935.

Guthrie, E. R. *The psychology of learning*. (Revised ed.) New York: Harper, 1952.

Guttman, N., & Kalish, H. I. Discriminability and stimulus generalization. *Journal of Experimental Psychology*, 1956, *51*, 79–88.

Gynther, M. D. Differential eyelid conditioning as a

function of stimulus similarity and strength of response to the CS. *Journal of Experimental Psychology*, 1957, *53*, 408–16.

Haber, R. Eidetic images. *Scientific American*, 1969, 36–44.

Haber, R. N. (Ed.) *Contemporary theory and research in visual perception*. New York: Holt, Rinehart, & Winston, 1968.

Haber, R. N. (Ed.) *Information processing approaches to visual perception*. New York: Holt, Rinehart & Winston, 1969.

Haber, R. N., & Haber, R. B. Eidetic imagery: I. Frequency. *Perceptual and Motor Skills*, 1964, *19*, 131–38.

Habley, P., Gipson, M., & Hause, J. Acquisition and extinction in the runway as a joint function of constant reward magnitude and constant reward delay. *Psychonomic Science*, 1972, *29*, 133–36.

Halgren, C. R. Latent inhibition in rats: Associative or nonassociative. *Journal of Comparative and Physiological Psychology*, 1974, *86*, 74–78.

Hall, G. Overtraining and reversal learning in the rat: Effects of stimulus salience and response strategies. *Journal of Comparative and Physiological Psychology*, 1973, *84*, 169–75.

Hall, J. F. Learning as a function of word frequency. *American Journal of Psychology*, 1954, *67*, 138–40.

Hamilton, R. J. Retroactive facilitation as a function of degree of generalization between tasks. *Journal of Experimental Psychology*, 1943, *32*, 363–76.

Hammond, L. J. Increased responding to CS in differential CER. *Psychonomic Science*, 1966, *5*, 337–38.

Hammond, L. J. A traditional demonstration of the active properties of Pavlovian inhibition using differential CER. *Psychonomic Science*, 1967, *9*, 65–66.

Hanson, H. M. Effects of discrimination training on stimulus generalization. *Journal of Experimental Psychology*, 1959, *58*, 321–34.

Hanson, H. M. Stimulus generalization following three-stimulus discrimination training. *Journal of Comparative and Physiological Psychology*, 1961, *54*, 181–85.

Harlow, H. F. The formation of learning sets. *Psychological Review*, 1949, *56*, 51–65.

Harlow, H. F. Learning sets and error-factor theory. In S. Koch (Ed.), *Psychology: A study of a science, Volume 2*. New York: McGraw-Hill, 1959.

Harvey, C. B., & Wickens, D. D. Effect of instructions on responsiveness to the CS and to the UCS in GSR conditioning. *Journal of Experimental Psychology*, 1971, *87*, 137–40.

Harvey, C. B., & Wickens, D. D. Effects of cognitive control processes on the classically conditioned galvanic skin response. *Journal of Experimental Psychology*, 1973, *101*, 278–82.

Hastings, S. E., & Obrist, P. A. Heart rate during conditioning in humans: Effect of varying interstimulus (CS-UCS) interval. *Journal of Experimental Psychology*, 1967, *74*, 431–42.

Haude, R. H., & Ray, O. S. Visual exploration in monkeys as a function of visual incentive duration and sensory deprivation. *Journal of Comparative and Physiological Psychology*, 1967, *64*, 332–36.

Hayes, J. R. M. Memory span for several vocabularies as a function of vocabulary size. In *Quarterly Progress Report*. Cambridge, Mass.: Acoustics Laboratory, Massachusetts Institute of Technology, 1952.

Haygood, R. C., Harbert, T. L., & Omlor, J. A. Intradimensional variability and concept learning. *Journal of Experimental Psychology*, 1970, *83*, 216–19.

Haygood, R. C., & Stevenson, M. Effects of number of irrelevant dimensions in nonconjunctive concept learning. *Journal of Experimental Psychology*, 1967, *74*, 302–4.

Hearst, E. Differential transfer of excitatory versus inhibitory pretraining to intradimensional discrimination learning in pigeons. *Journal of Comparative and Physiological Psychology*, 1971, *75*, 206–215.

Hearst, E., Besley, S., & Farthing, G. W. Inhibition and the stimulus control of operant behavior. *Journal of the Experimental Analysis of Behavior*, 1970, *14*, 373–409.

Hearst, E., & Koresko, M. B. Stimulus generalization and amount of prior training on variable-interval reinforcement. *Journal of Comparative and Physiological Psychology*, 1968, *66*, 133–38.

Hebb, D. O. *Organization of behavior*. New York: Wiley, 1949.

Hebb, D. O. *A textbook of psychology*. Philadelphia: Saunders, 1958.

Hebb, D. O. Distinctive features of learning in the higher animal. In J. F. Delafresnaye, A. Fessard, R. W. Gerard, & J. Konorski (Eds.), *Brain mechanisms and learning*. Oxford: Blackwell Scientific, 1961.

Heidbreder, E. The attainment of concepts: I. Terminology and methodology. *Journal of General Psychology*, 1946, *35*, 173–89.

Heidbreder, E. The attainment of concepts: III. The process. *Journal of General Psychology*, 1947, *24*, 93–108.

Heider, E. R. *The Dugum Dani: A Papuan culture in the highlands of West New Guinea*. Chicago: Aldine, 1970.

Heider, E. R. Universals in color naming and memory. *Journal of Experimental Psychology*, 1972, *93*, 10–20.

Heider, E. R., & Oliver, D. C. The structure of the color space in naming and memory for two languages. *Cognitive Psychology*, 1972, *3*, 337–354.

Herbert, M. J., & Harsh, C. M. Observational learning by cats. *Journal of Comparative and Physiological Psychology*, 1944, *37*, 81–95.

Herrnstein, R. J. Method and theory in the study of

avoidance. *Psychological Review*, 1969, *76*, 49 – 69.

Herrnstein, R. J., & Hineline, P. N. Negative reinforcement as shock-frequency reduction. *Journal of the Experimental Analysis of Behavior*, 1966, *9*, 421 – 30.

Herrnstein, R. J., Loveland, D. H., & Cable, C. Natural concepts in pigeons. *Journal of Experimental Psychology: Animal Behavior Processes*, 1976, *2*, 285 – 302.

Hilgard, E. R., & Bower, G. H. *Theories of learning.* (4th ed.) New York: Appleton-Century-Crofts, 1974.

Hilgard, E. R., & Marquis, D. G. *Conditioning and learning.* New York: Appleton-Century-Crofts, 1940.

Hill, W. F., & Spear, N. E. Extinction in a runway as a function of acquisition level and reinforcement percentage. *Journal of Experimental Psychology*, 1963, *65*, 495 – 500.

Hinde, R. A., & Stevenson-Hinde, J. *Constraints on learning: Limitations and predispositions.* New York: Academic Press, 1973.

Hintzman, D. L. Theoretical implications of the spacing effect. In R. L. Solso (Ed.), *Theories in cognitive psychology: The Loyola symposium.* Potomac, Md.: Erlbaum, 1974.

Hiroto, D. S., & Seligman, M. E. P. Generality of learned helplessness in man. *Journal of Personality and Social Psychology*, 1975, *31*, 311 – 27.

Hockey, R. Rate of presentation in running memory and direct manipulation of in-put processing strategies. *Quarterly Journal of Experimental Psychology*, 1973, *25*, 104 – 11.

Hoffman, H. S. Stimulus factors in conditioned suppression. In B. A. Campbell & R. M. Church (Eds.), *Punishment and aversive behavior.* New York: Appleton-Century-Crofts, 1969.

Holland, P. C., & Rescorla, R. A. Second-order conditioning with food unconditioned stimulus. *Journal of Comparative and Physiological Psychology*, 1975, *88*, 459 – 67.

Holyoak, K. J., & Walker, J. H. Representation of subjective magnitude information in semantic orderings. *Journal of Verbal Learning and Verbal Behavior*, 1976, *15*, 287 – 300.

Holz, W. C. & Azrin, N. H. Conditioning human verbal behavior. In W. K. Honig (Ed.), *Operant behavior: Areas of research and application.* New York: Appleton-Century-Crofts, 1966.

Honeck, R. P. Interpretive vs. structural effects on semantic memory. *Journal of Verbal Learning and Verbal Behavior*, 1973, *12*, 448 – 55.

Hooper, R. Variables controlling the overlearning reversal effect (ORE). *Journal of Experimental Psychology*, 1967, *73*, 612 – 19.

Houston, J. P. Stimulus recall and experimental paradigm. *Journal of Experimental Psychology*, 1966, *72*, 619 – 21.

Hovland, C. I. Experimental studies in rote-learning. II. Reminiscence with varying speeds of syllable presentation. *Journal of Experimental Psychology*, 1938, *22*, 338 – 53.

Hovland, C. I. Experimental studies in rote learning. III. Distribution of practice with varying speeds of syllable presentation. *Journal of Experimental Psychology*, 1938, *23*, 172 – 90.

Hovland, C. I. Experimental studies in rote learning theory. VI. Comparison of retention following learning to the same criterion by massed and distributed practice. *Journal of Experimental Psychology*, 1940, *26*, 568 – 87.

Howes, D. A word count of spoken English. *Journal of Verbal Learning and Verbal Behavior*, 1966, *5*, 572 – 604.

Hubel, D. H., & Wiesel, T. N. Receptive fields of single neurones in the cat's striate cortex. *Journal of Physiology*, 1959, *148*, 574 – 91.

Hubel, D. H., & Wiesel, T. N. Receptive fields, binocular interaction, and functional architecture in the cat's visual cortex. *Journal of Physiology*, 1962, *160*, 106 – 54.

Huff, D. *How to lie with statistics.* New York: Norton, 1954.

Hull, C. L. Quantitative aspects of the evolution of concepts. *Psychological Monographs*, 1920, *28*, No. 123.

Hull, C. L. The conflicting psychologies of learning—a way out. *Psychological Review*, 1935, *42*, 491 – 516.

Hull, C. L. *Principles of behavior.* New York: Appleton-Century-Crofts, 1943.

Hulse, S., Deese, J., & Egeth, H. *The psychology of learning.* New York: McGraw-Hill, 1975.

Humphreys, L. G. The effect of random alternation of reinforcement on the acquisition and extinction of conditioned eyelid reactions. *Journal of Experimental Psychology*, 1939, *25*, 141 – 58.

Hunt, E. What kind of computer is man? *Cognitive Psychology*, 1971, *2*, 57 – 98.

Hunt, E. B., Marin, J., & Stone, P. I. *Experiments in induction.* New York: Academic Press, 1966.

Huttenlocher, J. Constructing spatial images: A strategy in reasoning. *Psychological Review*, 1968, *75*, 550 – 60.

Hutton, R. A., Woods, S. C., & Makous, W. L. Conditioned hypoglycemia: Pseudoconditioning controls. *Journal of Comparative and Physiological Psychology*, 1970, *71*, 198 – 201.

Hyde, T. S., & Jenkins, J. J. Differential effects of incidental tasks on the organization of recall of a list of highly associated words. *Journal of Experimental Psychology*, 1969, *82*, 472 – 81.

Hyde, T. S., & Jenkins, J. J. Recall of words as a function of semantic, graphic, and syntactic orienting tasks. *Journal of Verbal Learning and Verbal Behavior*, 1973, *12*, 471 – 80.

Hyman, R., & Frost, N. Gradients and schema in pattern recognition. In P. M. A. Rabbitt (Ed.), *Attention and performance* (Vol. 5). New York: Academic Press, 1974.

Ison, J. R. Experimental extinction as a function of number of reinforcements. *Journal of Experimental Psychology*, 1962, *64*, 314 – 17.

Ison, J. R., & Cook, P. E. Extinction performance as a function of incentive magnitude and number of acquisition trials. *Psychonomic Science*, 1964, *1*, 245–46.

Ison, J. R., & Pennes, E. S. Interaction of amobarbital sodium and reinforcement schedule in determining resistance to extinction of an instrumental running response. *Journal of Comparative and Physiological Psychology*, 1969, *68*, 215–19.

James, J. P., Ossenkop, P., & Mostoway, W. W. Avoidance learning as a function of amount and direction of change in CS intensity without a constant background intensity. *Bulletin of the Psychonomic Society*, 1973, *2*, 18–20.

Janis, I. L., & Frick, F. The relationship between attitudes toward conclusions and errors in judging logical validity of syllogisms. *Journal of Experimental Psychology*, 1943, *33*, 73–77.

Jeffrey, W. E. The effects of verbal and nonverbal responses in mediating an instrumental act. *Journal of Experimental Psychology*, 1953, *45*, 327–33.

Jenkins, H. M., & Harrison, R. H. Effect of discrimination training on auditory generalization. *Journal of Experimental Psychology*, 1960, *59*, 246–53.

Jenkins, H. M., & Harrison, R. H. Generalization gradients of inhibition following auditory discrimination learning. *Journal of the Experimental Analysis of Behavior*, 1962, *5*, 435–41.

Jenkins, H. M., & Moore, B. A. The form of the auto-shaped response with food or water reinforcers. *Journal of the Experimental Analysis of Behavior*, 1973, *20*, 163–81.

Jenkins, J. G., & Dallenbach, K. M. Oblivescence during sleep and waking. *American Journal of Psychology*, 1924, *35*, 605–12.

Jenkins, J. J. Mediated associations: Paradigms and situations. In C. N. Cofer & B. S. Musgrave (Eds.), *Verbal behavior and learning: Problems and processes*. New York: McGraw-Hill, 1963.

Jenkins, J. J. Can we have a theory of meaningful memory? In R. L. Solso (Ed.), *Theories in cognitive psychology: The Loyola symposium*. Potomac, Md.: Erlbaum, 1974a.

Jenkins, J. J. Remember that old theory of memory? Well, forget it! *American Psychologist*, 1974b, *29*, 785–95.

Jensen, A. R. An empirical theory of the serial-position effect. *Journal of Psychology*, 1962, *53*, 127–42.

John, E. R., Chesler, P., Bartlett, F., & Victor, I. Observation learning in cats. *Science*, 1968, *159*, 1489–91.

Johnson, D. M. *A systematic introduction to the psychology of thinking*. New York: Harper & Row, 1972.

Johnson, N., & Viney, W. Resistance to extinction as a function of effort. *Journal of Comparative and Physiological Psychology*, 1970, *71*, 171–74.

Johnson, N. F. Organization and the concept of a memory code. In A. W. Melton & E. Martin (Eds.), *Coding processes in human memory*. Washington: Winston, 1972, 125–60.

Johnson, R. E. Recall of prose as a function of the structural importance of linguistic units. *Journal of Verbal Learning and Verbal Behavior*, 1970, *9*, 12–20.

Johnston, J. M. Punishment of human behavior. *American Psychologist*, 1972, *27*, 1033–54.

Jones, L. V., & Wepman, J. M. *A spoken word count*. Chicago: Language Research Associates, 1966.

Jung, J. Transfer of training as a function of first list learning. *Journal of Verbal Learning and Verbal Behavior*, 1962, *1*, 197–99.

Jung, J. Effects of response meaningfulness (m) on transfer of training under two different paradigms. *Journal of Experimental Psychology*, 1963, *65*, 377–84.

Jung, J. A cumulative method of paired-associate and serial learning. *Journal of Verbal Learning and Verbal Behavior*, 1964, *3*, 290–99.

Just, M. A., & Carpenter, P. A. Comprehension of negation with quantification. *Journal of Verbal Learning and Verbal Behavior*, 1971, *10*, 244–53.

Just, M. A., & Carpenter, P. A. Eye fixations and cognitive processes. *Cognitive Psychology*, 1976, *8*, 441–80.

Kalat, J. W., & Rozin, P. "Salience": A factor which can override temporal contiguity in taste-aversion learning. *Journal of Comparative and Physiological Psychology*, 1970, *71*, 192–97.

Kalat, J. W., & Rozin, P. Role of interference in taste-aversion learning. *Journal of Comparative and Physiological Psychology*, 1971, *77*, 53–58.

Kalat, J. W., & Rozin, P. "Learned safety" as a mechanism in long-delay taste-aversion learning in rats. *Journal of Comparative and Physiological Psychology*, 1973, *83*, 198–207.

Kalish, H. I. Strength of fear as a function of the number of acquisition and extinction trials. *Journal of Experimental Psychology*, 1954, *55*, 637–44.

Kalish, H. I. The relationship between discriminability and stimulus generalization: A reevaluation. *Journal of Experimental Psychology*, 1958, *55*, 637–44.

Kalish, H. I. Stimulus generalization. In M. H. Marx (Ed.), *Learning: Processes*. New York: Macmillan, 1969.

Kalish, H. I., & Haber, A. Generalization: I. Generalization gradients from single and multiple stimulus points. II. Generalization of inhibition. *Journal of Experimental Psychology*, 1963, *65*, 176–81.

Kalish, H. I., & Haber, A. Prediction of discrimination from generalization following variations in deprivation level. *Journal of Comparative and Physiological Psychology*, 1965, *60*, 125–28.

Kamil, A. C. The second-order conditio.1ing of fear in rats. *Psychonomic Science*, 1968, *10*, 99–100.

Kamil, A. C. Some parameters of the second-order conditioning of fear in rats. *Journal of Comparative and Physiological Psychology*, 1969, *67*, 364–69.

Kamin, L. J. Traumatic avoidance learning: The effects of CS-US interval with a trace conditioning procedure. *Journal of Comparative and Physiological Psychology*, 1954, *47*, 65–72.

Kamin, L. J. The effects of termination of the CS and avoidance of the US on avoidance learning. *Journal of Comparative and Physiological Psychology*, 1956, *49*, 420–24.

Kamin, L. J. The gradient of delay of secondary reward in avoidance learning. *Journal of Comparative and Physiological Psychology*, 1957a, *50*, 445–49.

Kamin, L. J. The gradient of delay of secondary reward in avoidance learning tested on avoidance trials only. *Journal of Comparative and Physiological Psychology*, 1957b, *50*, 450–56.

Kamin, L. J. The delay-of-punishment gradient. *Journal of Comparative and Physiological Psychology*, 1959, *52*, 434–37.

Kamin, L. J. Temporal and intensity characteristics of the conditioned stimulus. In *Classical conditioning: A symposium*. W. F. Prokasy (Ed.). New York: Appleton-Century-Crofts, 1965.

Kamin, L. J. Predictability, surprise, attention, and conditioning. In B. A. Campbell & R. M. Church (Eds.), *Punishment and aversive behavior*. New York: Appleton-Century-Crofts, 1969.

Kamin, L. J., & Schaub, R. E. Effects of conditioned stimulus intensity on the conditioned emotional response. *Journal of Comparative and Physiological Psychology*, 1963, *56*, 502–7.

Kandel, E., & Spencer, W. A. Cellular neurophysiological approaches in the study of learning. *Physiological Reviews*, 1968, *48*, 65–134.

Kaplan, M., Jackson, B., & Sparer, R. Escape behavior under continuous reinforcement as a function of aversive light intensity. *Journal of the Experimental Analysis of Behavior*, 1965, *8*, 321–23.

Karsh, E. B. Changes in intensity of punishment: Effect on running behavior of rats. *Science*, 1963, *140*, 1084–85.

Katkin, E. S., & Murray, E. N. Instrumental conditioning of autonomically mediated behavior: Theoretical and methodological issues. *Physiological Bulletin*, 1968, *70*, 52–68.

Katz, J. J., & Fodor, J. A. The structure of a semantic theory. *Language*, 1963, *39*, 170–210.

Kaufman, A., & Baron, A. Use of withdrawal of reinforcement within the escape-avoidance paradigm. *Psychological Reports*, 1966, *19*, 959–65.

Kaufman, A., & Baron, A. Suppression of behavior by timeout punishment when suppression results in loss of positive reinforcement. *Journal of the Experimental Analysis of Behavior*, 1968, *11*, 595–607.

Kaufman, E. L., Lord, M. W., Reese, T. W., & Volkmann, J. The discrimination of visual number. *American Journal of Psychology*, 1949, *62*, 498–525.

Kavanagh, J. F., & Mattingly, I. G. (Eds.). *Language by ear and by eye: The relationship between speech and reading*. Cambridge, Mass.: M.I.T. Press, 1972.

Keehn, J. D. On the nonclassical nature of avoidance behavior. *American Journal of Psychology*, 1959, *72*, 243–47.

Keller, F. S. "Goodbye, teacher. . . ." *Journal of Applied Behavior Analysis*, 1968, *1*, 79–89.

Kello, J. E. The reinforcement-omission effect on fixed-interval schedules: Frustration or inhibition? *Learning & Motivation*, 1972, *3*, 138–47.

Kendler, H. H., & D'Amato, M. F. A comparison of reversal and nonreversal shifts in human concept formation. *Journal of Experimental Psychology*, 1955, *49*, 165–74.

Kendler, H. H., & Kendler, T. S. Vertical and horizontal processes in problem solving. *Psychological Review*, 1962, *69*, 1–16.

Kendler, H. H., & Kendler, T. S. From discrimination learning to cognitive development: A neobehaviorist odyssey. In W. K. Estes (Ed.), *Handbook of learning and cognitive processes*, (Vol. 1). Hillsdale, N.J.: Erlbaum, 1975.

Kendler, T. S., & Kendler, H. H. Reversal and nonreversal shifts in kindergarten children. *Journal of Experimental Psychology*, 1959, *58*, 56–60.

Kent, G. H., & Rosanoff, A. J. A study of association in insanity. *American Journal of Insanity*, 1910, *67*, 37–96, 317–90.

Keppel, G., & Underwood, B. J. Proactive inhibition in short-term retention of single items. *Journal of Verbal Learning and Verbal Behavior*, 1962, *1*, 153–61.

Killeen, P. Reinforcement frequency and contingency as factors in fixed-ratio behavior. *Journal of the Experimental Analysis of Behavior*, 1969, *12*, 391–95.

Kimble, G. A. Shock intensity and avoidance learning. *Journal of Comparative and Physiological Psychology*, 1955, *48*, 281–84.

Kimble, G. A. *Hilgard and Marquis' conditioning and learning*. New York: Appleton-Century-Crofts, 1961.

Kimble, G. A., Mann, L. I., & Dufort, R. H. Classical and instrumental eyelid conditioning. *Journal of Experimental Psychology*, 1955, *49*, 407–17.

Kimmel, H. D. Instrumental inhibitory factors in classical conditioning. In W. F. Prokasy (Ed.), *Classical conditioning: A symposium*. New York: Appleton-Century-Crofts, 1965.

King, D. R. W., & Greeno, J. G. Invariance of inference times when information was presented in different linguistic formats. *Memory and Cognition*, 1974, *2*, 233–35.

Kintsch, W. Runway performance as a function of drive strength and magnitude of reinforcement. *Journal of Comparative and Physiological Psychology*, 1962, *55*, 882–87.

Kintsch, W. Notes on the structure of semantic memory. In E. Tulving & W. Donaldson (Eds.), *Organization of memory*. New York: Academic Press, 1972.

Kintsch, W. *The representation of meaning in memory*. Hillsdale, N.J.: Erlbaum, 1974.

Kintsch, W. Memory for prose. In C. N. Cofer (Ed.), *The structure of human memory*. San Francisco: Freeman, 1976, 90–113.

Kintsch, W., & Monk, D. Storage of complex information in memory: Some implications of the speed with which inferences can be made. *Journal of Experimental Psychology*, 1972, *94*, 25–32.

Kish, G. B. Learning when the onset of illumination is used as reinforcing stimulus. *Journal of Comparative and Physiological Psychology*, 1955, *48*, 261–64.

Klein, M., & Rilling, M. Effects of response-shock interval and shock intensity on free-operant avoidance responding in the pigeon. *Journal of the Experimental Analysis of Behavior*, 1972, *18*, 295–303.

Knouse, S. B., & Campbell, P. E. Partially delayed reward in the rat: A parametric study of delay duration. *Journal of Comparative and Physiological Psychology*, 1971, *75*, 116–19.

Koffka, K. *Principles of Gestalt psychology*. New York: Harcourt Brace, 1935.

Kohler, W. *Gestalt psychology*. New York: Liveright, 1929.

Kohler, W. *Dynamics in psychology*. New York: Liveright, 1940.

Kohn, B., & Dennis, M. Observation and discrimination learning in the rat: Specific and nonspecific effects. *Journal of Comparative and Physiological Psychology*, 1972, *78*, 292–96.

Koppenaal, R. J. Time changes in the strengths of A-B, A-C lists: Spontaneous recovery? *Journal of Verbal Learning and Verbal Behavior*, 1963, *2*, 310–19.

Koteskey, R. L. A stimulus-sampling model of the partial reinforcement effect. *Psychological Review*, 1972, *79*, 161–71.

Kraeling, D. Analysis of amount of reward as a variable in learning. *Journal of Comparative and Physiological Psychology*, 1961, *54*, 560–65.

Kramer, T. J., & Rilling, M. Differential reinforcement of low rates: A selective critique. *Psychological Review*, 1970, *74*, 225–54.

Krane, R. V., & Wagner, A. R. Taste aversion learning with a delayed shock US: Implications for the "generality of the laws of learning." *Journal of Comparative and Physiological Psychology*, 1975, *88*, 882–89.

Krasner, L. Studies of the conditioning of verbal behavior. *Psychological Bulletin*, 1958, *55*, 148–71.

Krasner, L., & Ullmann, L. P. (Eds.) *Research in behavior modification*. New York: Holt, Rinehart, & Winston, 1965.

Kremer, E. F. Truly random and traditional control procedures in CER conditioning in the rat. *Journal of Comparative and Physiological Psychology*, 1971, *76*, 441–48.

Kremer, E. F., & Kamin, L. J. The truly random procedure: Associative or nonassociative effects in rats. *Journal of Comparative and Physiological Psychology*, 1971, *74*, 203–10.

Kucera, H., & Francis, W. N. *Computational analysis of present-day American English*. Providence, R.I.: Brown University Press, 1967.

Kushner, M. Desensitization of a post-traumatic phobia. In L. P. Ullmann & L. Krasner (Eds.), *Case studies in behavior modification*. Holt, Rinehart & Winston, 1965.

Lacey, J. I., & Smith, R. L. Conditioning and generalization of unconscious anxiety. *Science*, 1954, *120*, 1045–52.

Lacey, J. I., Smith, R. L., & Green, A. Use of conditioned autonomic responses in the study of anxiety. *Psychosomatic Medicine*, 1955, *17*, 208–17.

Landauer, T. K., & Meyer, D. E. Category size and semantic memory retrieval. *Journal of Verbal Learning and Verbal Behavior*, 1972, *11*, 539–49.

Lane, H. L. Temporal and intensive properties of human vocal responding under a schedule of reinforcement. *Journal of the Experimental Analysis of Behavior*, 1960, *3*, 183–92.

Lane, H. L., & Shinkman, P. G. Methods and findings in an analysis of a vocal operant. *Journal of the Experimental Analysis of Behavior*, 1963, *6*, 179–88.

Lashley, K. S., & Wade, M. The Pavlovian theory of generalization. *Psychological Review*, 1946, *53*, 72–87.

Laties, V. C., Weiss, B., Clark, R. C., & Reynolds, M. D. Overt "mediating" behavior during temporally spaced responding. *Journal of the Experimental Analysis of Behavior*, 1965, *8*, 107–16.

Laties, V. C., Weiss, B., & Weiss, A. B. Further observations on overt "mediating" behavior and the discrimination of time. *Journal of the Experimental Analysis of Behavior*, 1969, *12*, 43–57.

Laughlin, P. R. Selection strategies in concept attainment. In R. L. Solso (Ed.), *Contemporary issues in cognitive psychology: The Loyola symposium*. Washington, D.C.: Winston, 1973.

Lawrence, D. H. The transfer of a discrimination along a continuum. *Journal of Comparative and Physiological Psychology*, 1952, *45*, 511–16.

Lawson, R. B., Goldstein, S. G., & Musty, R. E. *Principles and methods of psychology*. Cambridge: Oxford University Press, Inc., 1975.

Lazarus, A. A. *Behavior therapy and beyond*. New York: McGraw-Hill, 1971.

Leander, J. D. Shock intensity and duration interactions on free-operant avoidance behavior. *Journal of the Experimental Analysis of Behavior,* 1973, *19,* 481–90.

Lefford, A. The influence of emotional subject matter on logical reasoning. *Journal of General Psychology,* 1946, *34,* 127–51.

Leitenberg, H. Is time-out from positive reinforcement an aversive event? *Psychological Bulletin,* 1965, *64,* 428–41.

Lenderhendler, I., & Baum, M. Mechanical facilitation of the action of response prevention (flooding) in rats. *Behavior Research and Therapy,* 1970, *8,* 43–48.

Lenneberg, E. H. A probablistic approach to language learning. *Behavioral Science,* 1957, *2,* 1–12.

Lenneberg, E. H. *Biological foundations of language.* New York: Wiley, 1967.

Lenzer, I. I. Differences between behavior reinforced by electrical stimulation of the brain and conventionally reinforced behavior: An associative analysis. *Psychological Bulletin,* 1972, *78,* 103–18.

Leonard, D. W. Amount and sequence of reward in partial and continuous reinforcement. *Journal of Comparative and Physiological Psychology,* 1969, *67,* 204–11.

Leonard, D. W. Partial reinforcement effects in classical aversive conditioning in rabbits and human beings. *Journal of Comparative and Physiological Psychology,* 1975, *88,* 596–608.

Lepley, W. M. Serial reactions considered as conditioned reactions. *Psychological Monographs,* 1934, *46,* Whole No. 205.

Lettvin, J. Y., Matturana, H. R., McCulloch, W. S., & Pitts, W. H. What the frog's eye tells the frog's brain. *Proceedings of the IRE,* 1959, *47,* 539–49.

Levine, M. A model of hypothesis behavior in discrimination learning set. *Psychological Review,* 1959, *66,* 353–66.

Levine, M. Hypothesis behavior. In A. M. Schrier, H. F. Harlow, & F. Stollnitz (Eds.), *Behavior of nonhuman primates: Modern research trends.* New York: Academic Press, 1965.

Levine, M. Hypothesis behavior by humans during discrimination learning. *Journal of Experimental Psychology,* 1966, *71,* 331–38.

Levine, M. Hypothesis theory and nonlearning despite ideal S-R reinforcement contingencies. *Psychological Review,* 1971, *78,* 130–40.

Levine, M. *A cognitive theory of learning: Research on hypothesis testing.* Hillsdale, N.J.: Erlbaum, 1975.

Levine, S. UCS intensity and avoidance learning. *Journal of Experimental Psychology,* 1966, *71,* 163–64.

Levinthal, C. F. The CS-US interval function in rabbit nictitating membrane response conditioning: Single vs. multiple trials per conditioning session. *Learning and Motivation,* 1973, *4,* 259–67.

Levis, D. J. Learned helplessness: A reply and an alternative S-R interpretation. *Journal of Experimental Psychology: General,* 1976, *105,* 47–65.

Lewis, D. J. Partial reinforcement: A selective review of the literature since 1950. *Psychological Bulletin,* 1960, *57,* 1–28.

Lichtenstein, P. E. Studies of anxiety: I. The production of feeding inhibition in dogs. *Journal of Comparative and Physiological Psychology,* 1950, *43,* 16–29.

Lindsay, P. H., & Norman, D. A. *Human information processing: An introduction to psychology.* New York: Academic Press, 1972.

Linton, J., Riccio, D. C., Rohrbaugh, M., & Page, H. A The effects of blocking on instrumental avoidance response: Fear reduction or enhancement? *Behavior Research and Therapy,* 1970, *8,* 267–72.

Loftus, G. R., & Loftus, E. F. *Human memory: The processing of information.* Hillsdale, N.J.: Erlbaum, 1976.

Logan, F. A. A micromolar approach to behavior. *Psychological Review,* 1956, *63,* 63–73.

Lovejoy, E. Analysis of the overlearning reversal effect. *Psychological Review,* 1966, *73,* 87–103.

Low, L. A., & Low, H. I. Effects of CS-US interval length upon avoidance responding. *Journal of Comparative and Physiological Psychology,* 1962, *55,* 1059–61.

Lubow, R. E. Latent inhibition: Effects of frequency of nonreinforced preexposure of the CS. *Journal of Comparative and Physiological Psychology,* 1965, *60,* 454–57.

Lubow, R. E. Latent inhibition. *Psychological Bulletin,* 1973, *79,* 398–407.

Lubow, R. E., Rifkin, B., & Alek, M. The context effect: The relationship between stimulus preexposure and environmental preexposure determines subsequent learning. *Journal of Experimental Psychology: Animal Behavior Processes,* 1976, *2,* 38–47.

Lubow, R. E., Schnur, P., & Rifkin, B. Latent inhibition and conditioned attention theory. *Journal of Experimental Psychology: Animal Behavior Processes,* 1976, *2,* 163–74.

Luria, A. R. *The mind of a mnemonist: A little book about a vast memory.* Translated by L. Solotaroff. New York: Basic Books, 1968.

Lynch, J. J. Pavlovian inhibition of delay in cardiac and somatic responses in dogs: Schizokinesis. *Psychological Reports,* 1973, *32,* 1339–46.

Lyons, J., Klipec, W. D., & Steinsultz, G. The effect of chlorpromazine on discrimination performance and the peak shift. *Physiological Psychology,* 1973, *1,* 121–24.

MacKinnon, J. R. Competing responses in a differential magnitude of reward discrimination. *Psychonomic Science,* 1968, *12,* 333–34.

Mackintosh, N. J. Extinction of a discrimination habit as a function of overtraining, *Journal of*

Comparative and Physiological Psychology, 1963a, *56*, 842–47.

Mackintosh, N. J. The effect of irrelevant cues on reversal learning in the rat. *British Journal of Psychology*, 1963b, *54*, 127–34.

Mackintosh, N. J. Overtraining and transfer within and between dimensions in the rat. *Quarterly Journal of Experimental Psychology*, 1964, *16*, 250–56.

Mackintosh, N. J. Further analysis of the overtraining reversal effect. *Journal of Comparative and Physiological Psychology, Monograph Supplement*, 1969, *67*, part 2, 1–18.

Mackintosh, N. J., & Honig, W. K. Blocking and attentional enhancement in pigeons. *Journal of Comparative and Physiological Psychology*, 1970, *73*, 78–85.

Mackintosh, N. J., & Little, L. Intradimensional and extradimensional shift learning by pigeons. *Psychonomic Science*, 1969, *14*, 5–6.

Mackintosh, N. J., & Little, L. An analysis of transfer along a continuum. *Canadian Journal of Psychology*, 1970, *24*, 362–69.

Mackintosh, N. J., McGonigle, B., Holgate, V., & Vanderver, V. Factors underlying improvement in serial reversal learning. *Canadian Journal of Psychology*, 1968, *22*, 85–95.

Mackintosh, N. J., & Turner, C. Blocking as a function of novelty of CS and predictability of UCS. *Quarterly Journal of Experimental Psychology*, 1971, *23*, 359–66.

Madigan, S. A. Intraserial repetition and coding processes in free recall. *Journal of Verbal Learning and Verbal Behavior*, 1969, *8*, 828–35.

Madigan, S. A. Modality and recall order interactions in short-term memory for serial order. *Journal of Experimental Psychology*, 1971, *87*, 294–96.

Maier, N. R. F. *Frustration: The study of behavior without a goal*. New York: McGraw-Hill, 1949.

Maier, S. F. Failure to escape traumatic shock: Incompatible skeletal motor response or learned helplessness? *Learning and Motivation*, 1970, *1*, 157–70.

Maier, S. F., & Seligman, M. E. P. Learned helplessness: Theory and evidence. *Journal of Experimental Psychology: General*, 1976, *105*, 3–46.

Maier, S. F., Seligman, M. E. P., & Solomon, R. L. Pavlovian fear conditioning and learned helplessness: Effects on escape and avoidance behavior of (a) the CS-US contingency and (b) the independence of the US and voluntary responding. In B. A. Campbell & R. M. Church (Eds.), *Punishment and aversive behavior*. New York: Appleton-Century-Crofts, 1969.

Mandler, G. Organization and memory. In K. W. Spence & J. T. Spence (Eds.), *The psychology of learning and motivation: Advances in research and theory* (Vol. 1). New York: Academic Press, 1967, 328–72.

Mandler, G. Association and organization: Fact, fancies, and theories. In T. R. Dixon & D. L. Horton (Eds.), *Verbal behavior and general behavior theory*. Englewood Cliffs, N.J.: Prentice-Hall, 1968, 109–19.

Mandler, G., & Pearlstone, Z. Free and constrained concept learning and subsequent recall. *Journal of Verbal Learning and Verbal Behavior*, 1966, *5*, 126–31.

Mann, M. B. Studies in language behavior: The quantitative differentiation of samples of written language. *Psychological Monograph*, 1944, *56*, Whole No. 255, 41–74.

Manning, A. A., Schneiderman, N., & Lordahl, D. S. Delay vs. trace heart rate classical discrimination conditioning in rabbits as a function of ISI. *Journal of Experimental Psychology*, 1969, *80*, 225–30.

Marchant, H. G., & Moore, J. W. Blocking of the rabbit's conditioned nictitating membrane response in Kamin's two-stage paradigm. *Journal of Experimental Psychology*, 1973, *101*, 155–58.

Marchant, H. G., & Moore, J. W. Below zero conditioned inhibition of the rabbit's nictitating membrane response. *Journal of Experimental Psychology*, 1974, *102*, 350–52.

Marler, P. A comparative approach to vocal learning: Song development in white-crowned sparrows. *Journal of Comparative and Physiological Psychology Monograph*, 1970, *71*, No. 2, part 2, 1–25.

Marsh, G. An evaluation of three explanations for the transfer of discrimination effect. *Journal of Comparative and Physiological Psychology*, 1969, *68*, 268–75.

Marsh, G. Prediction of the peak shift in pigeons from gradients of excitation and inhibition. *Journal of Comparative and Physiological Psychology*, 1972, *81*, 262–66.

Martin, E. Stimulus meaningfulness and paired-associate transfer: An encoding variability hypothesis. *Psychological Review*, 1968, *75*, 421–41.

Martin, E. Verbal learning theory and independent retrieval phenomena. *Psychological Review*, 1971, *78*, 314–32.

Martin, E. Stimulus encoding in learning and transfer. In A. W. Melton & E. Martin (Eds.), *Coding processes in human memory*. Washington, D.C.: Winston, 1972, 59–84.

Martin, E. Generation-Recognition theory and the encoding specificity principle. *Psychological Review*, 1975, *82*, 150–53.

Martin, E., & Roberts, K. H. Grammatical factors in sentence retention. *Journal of Verbal Learning and Verbal Behavior*, 1966, *5*, 211–18.

Martin, L. K., & Riess, D. Effects of US intensity during previous discrete delay conditioning on conditioned acceleration during avoidance extinction. *Journal of Comparative and Physiological Psychology*, 1969, *69*, 196–200.

Marx, M. H. *Theories in contemporary psychology.* New York: Macmillan, 1963.

Marx, M. H. Positive contrast in instrumental learning from quantitative shift in incentive. *Psychonomic Science,* 1969, *16,* 254–55.

Marx, M. H., & Murphy, W. W. Resistance to extinction as a function of the presentation of a motivating cue in the start box. *Journal of Comparative and Physiological Psychology,* 1961, *54,* 207–10.

Masserman, J. H. *Behavior and neurosis.* Chicago: University of Chicago Press, 1943.

Masterson, F. A. Escape from noise. *Psychological Reports,* 1969, *24,* 484–86.

Mayer, R. E. Forward transfer of different reading strategies evoked by testlike events in mathematics text. *Journal of Educational Psychology,* 1975, *67,* 165–69.

Mayer, R. E. Integration of information during problem solving due to a meaningful context of learning. *Memory & Cognition,* 1976, *4,* 603–8.

McAllister, W. R., & McAllister, D. E. Increase over time in the stimulus generalization of acquired fear. *Journal of Experimental Psychology,* 1963, *65,* 576–82.

McAllister, W. R., McAllister, D. E., & Douglass, W. K. The inverse relationship between shock intensity and shuttle-box avoidance learning in rats: A reinforcement explanation. *Journal of Comparative and Physiological Psychology,* 1971, *74,* 426–33.

McCain, G. Partial reinforcement effects following a small number of acquisition trials. *Psychonomic Monograph Supplement,* 1966, *1,* 251–70.

McCrary, J. W., Jr., & Hunter, W. S. Serial position curves in verbal learning. *Science,* 1953, *117,* 131–34.

McDowell, A. A., Gaylord, H. A., & Brown, W. L. Learning set formation by naive rhesus monkeys. *Journal of Genetic Psychology,* 1965, *106,* 253–57.

McGeoch, J. A., & McDonald, W. T. Meaningful relation and retroactive inhibition. *American Journal of Psychology,* 1931, *43,* 579–88.

McGuire, W. J. A syllogistic analysis of cognitive relationships. In M. J. Rosenberg & C. I. Hovland (Eds.), *Attitude organization and change.* New Haven, Conn.: Yale University Press, 1960, 65–111.

McHose, J. H., & Tauber, L. Changes in delay of reinforcement in simple instrumental conditioning. *Psychonomic Science,* 1972, *27,* 291–92.

McLaughlin, J. P. The von Restorff effect in serial learning: Serial position of the isolate and length of list. *Journal of Experimental Psychology,* 1966, *72,* 603–9.

McMichael, J. S., & Corey, J. R. Contingency management in an introductory psychology course produces better learning. *Journal of Applied Behavioral Analysis,* 1969, *2,* 79–83.

McNeill, D. *The acquisition of language,* New York: Harper & Row, 1970.

Mehler, J. Some effects of grammatical transformations on the recall of English sentences. *Journal of Verbal Learning and Verbal Behavior,* 1963, *2,* 250–62.

Medin, D. L. Role of reinforcement in discrimination learning set in monkeys. *Psychological Bulletin,* 1972, *77,* 305–18.

Mednick, S. A., & Freedman, J. L. Stimulus generalization. *Psychological Bulletin,* 1960, *57,* 169–200.

Mellgren, R. L. Positive contrast in the rat as a function of number of preshift trials in the runway. *Journal of Comparative and Physiological Psychology,* 1971, *77,* 329–36.

Mellgren, R. L. Positive and negative contrast effects using delayed reinforcement. *Learning and Motivation,* 1972, *3,* 185–93.

Melton, A. W. Implications of short-term memory for a general theory of memory. *Journal of Verbal Learning and Verbal Behavior,* 1963, *2,* 1–21.

Melton, A. W. The situation with respect to the spacing and repetitions and memory. *Journal of Verbal Learning and Verbal Behavior,* 1970, *9,* 596–606.

Melton, A. W., & Irwin, J. M. The influence of degree of interpolated learning on retroactive inhibition and the overt transfer of specific responses. *American Journal of Psychology,* 1940, *53,* 173–203.

Melton, A. W., & Martin, E. (Eds.), *Coding processes in human memory.* Washington, D.C.: Winston, 1972.

Meltzer, D., & Brahlek, J. A. Quantity of reinforcement and fixed-interval performance. *Psychonomic Science,* 1968, *12,* 207–8.

Merike, P. M., & Battig, W. F. Transfer of training as a function of experimental paradigm and meaningfulness. *Journal of Verbal Learning and Verbal Behavior,* 1963, *2,* 485–88.

Meyer, B. J. F. *The organization of prose and its effects on memory.* Amsterdam: North-Holland, 1975.

Meyer, B. J. F., & McConkie, G. W. What is recalled after hearing a passage? *Journal of Educational Psychology,* 1973, *65,* 109–17.

Meyer, D. E. On the representation and retrieval of stored semantic information. *Cognitive Psychology.* 1970, *1,* 242–300.

Mikhail, A. A. Stress and ulceration in the glandular and nonglandular portions of the rat's stomach. *Journal of Comparative and Physiological Psychology,* 1973, *85,* 636–42.

Milby, J. B. Delay of shock-escape with and without stimulus change. *Psychological Reports,* 1971, *29,* 315–18.

Miles, R. C. Discrimination-learning sets. In A. M. Schrier, H. F. Harlow, & F. Stollnitz (Eds.), *Behavior of nonhuman primates: Modern research trends.* New York: Academic Press, 1965.

Miller, G. A. The magic number seven, plus or minus two: Some limits on our capacity to process information. *Psychological Review*, 1956, *63*, 81–97.

Miller, G. A. Some psychological studies of grammar. *American Psychologist*, 1962, *17*, 748–62.

Miller, G. A., Galanter, E., & Pribram, K. *Plans and the structure of behavior.* New York: Holt, Rinehart & Winston, 1960.

Miller, G. A., & McKean, K. O. A chronometric study of some relations between sentences. *Quarterly Journal of Experimental Psychology*, 1964, *16*, 297–308

Miller, G. A., Newman, E. B., & Friedman, E. A. Length-frequency statistics for written English. *Information and Control*, 1958, *1*, 370–89.

Miller, G. A., & Selfridge, J. A. Verbal context and the recall of meaningful material. *American Journal of Psychology*, 1950, *63*, 176–85.

Miller, N. E. Studies of fear as an acquirable drive: I. Fear as motivation and fear reduction as reinforcement in the learning of new responses. *Journal of Experimental Psychology*, 1948, *38*, 89–101.

Miller, N. E. Learnable drives and rewards. In S. S. Stevens (Ed.), *Handbook of experimental psychology.* New York: Wiley, 1951.

Miller, N. E. Learning resistance to pain and fear: Effects of overlearning, exposure, and rewarded exposure in context. *Journal of Experimental Psychology*, 1960, 137–45.

Miller, N. E. Learning of visceral and glandular responses. *Science*, 1969, *163*, 434–45.

Miller, N. E., & Dworkin, B. R. Visceral learning: Recent difficulties with curarized rats and significant problems for human research. In P. A. Obrist, A. H. Black, J. Brener, & L. V. DiCara (Eds.), *Cardiovascular psychophysiology: Current issues in response mechanisms, biofeedback, and methodology,* Chicago: Aldine, 1974.

Miller, N. E., & Kessen, M. L. Reward effects of food via stomach fistula compared with those via mouth. *Journal of Comparative and Physiological Psychology*, 1952, *45*, 555–64.

Miller, R. R., Daniel, D., & Berk, A. M. Successive reversals of a discriminated preference for signaled tailshock. *Animal Learning and Behavior*, 1974, *2*, 271–74.

Mink, W. D. Semantic generalization as related to word association. *Psychological Reports*, 1963, *12*, 59–67.

Misanin, J. R., Campbell, B. A., & Smith, N. F. Duration of punishment and the delay of punishment gradient. *Canadian Journal of Psychology*, 1966, *20*, 407–12.

Mitchell, D., Kirschbaum, E. H., & Perry, R. L. Effects of neophobia and habituation on the poison-induced avoidance of exteroceptive stimuli in the rat. *Journal of Experimental Psychology: Animal Behavior Processes*, 1975, *1*, 47–55.

Molliver, M. E. Operant control of vocal behavior in the cat. *Journal of the Experimental Analysis of Behavior*, 1963, *6*, 197–202.

Moltz, H. Latent extinction and the fractional anticipatory response mechanism. *Psychological Review*, 1957, *64*, 229–41.

Montgomery, K. C. The role of exploratory drive in learning. *Journal of Comparative and Physiological Psychology*, 1954, *47*, 60–64.

Moore, J. W. Differential eyelid conditioning as a function of the frequency and intensity of auditory CSs. *Journal of Experimental Psychology*, 1964, *68*, 250–59.

Moot, S. A., Cebulla, R. P., & Crabtree, J. M. Instrumental control **and** ulceration in rats. *Journal of Comparative and Physiological Psychology*, 1970, *71*, 405–10.

Moray, N. Attention in dichotic listening: Affective cues and the influence of instructions. *Quarterly Journal of Experimental Psychology*, 1959, *11*, 56–60.

Moray, N. *Attention: Selective processes in vision and hearing.* New York: Academic Press, 1970.

Morgan, J. J. B., & Morton, J. T. The distortion of syllogistic reasoning produced by personal convictions. *Journal of Social Psychology*, 1944, *20*, 39–59.

Morokoff, P. J., & Timberlake, W. Cue exposure and overt fear responses as determinants of extinction of avoidance in rats. *Journal of Comparative and Physiological Psychology*, 1971, *77*, 432–38.

Morse, W. H. Intermittent reinforcement. In W. K. Honig (Ed.), *Operant behavior: Areas of research and application.* New York: Appleton-Century-Crofts, 1966.

Mostofsky, D. *Stimulus generalization.* Stanford, Calif.: Stanford University Press, 1965.

Mountjoy, P. P., & Malott, M. K. Wave-length generalization curves for chickens reared in restricted portions of the spectrum. *Psychological Record*, 1968, *18*, 575–83.

Mowrer, O. H. On the dual nature of learning: A reinterpretation of "conditioning" and "problem-solving." *Harvard Educational Review*, 1947, *17*, 102–48.

Mowrer, O. H. *Learning theory and behavior.* New York: Wiley, 1960.

Moyer, K. E., & Korn, J. H. Effect of UCS intensity on the acquisition and extinction of an avoidance response. *Journal of Experimental Psychology*, 1964, *67*, 352–59.

Moyer, K. E., & Korn, J. H. Effect of UCS intensity on the acquisition and extinction of a one-way avoidance response. *Psychonomic Science*, 1966, *4*, 121–22.

Moyer, R. S. Comparing objects in memory: Evidence suggesting an internal psychophysics. *Perception and Psychophysics*, 1973, *13*, 180–84.

Moyer, R. S., & Landauer, T. K. Time required for judgments of numerical inequality. *Nature*, 1967, *215*, 1519–20.

Moyer, R. S., & Landauer, T. K. Determinants of reaction time for digit inequality tasks. *Bulletin of the Psychonomic Society*, 1973, *1*, 167–68.

Murdock, B. B., Jr. The retention of individual items. *Journal of Experimental Psychology*, 1961, *62*, 618–25.

Murdock, B. B., Jr. The serial position of free recall. *Journal of Experimental Psychology*, 1962, *64*, 482–88.

Murdock, B. B., Jr. *Human memory: Theory and data*. Potomac, Md.: Erlbaum, 1974.

Murdock, B. B., Jr., & Walker, K. D. Modality effects in free recall. *Journal of Verbal Learning and Verbal Behavior*, 1969, *8*, 665–76.

Myers, A. K. Effects of CS intensity and quality in avoidance conditioning. *Journal of Comparative and Physiological Psychology*, 1962, *55*, 57–61.

Myers, A. K., & Miller, N. E. Failure to find a learned drive based on hunger; Evidence for learning motivated by exploration. *Journal of Comparative and Physiological Psychology*, 1954, *47*, 428–36.

Nachman, M. Learned taste and temperature aversions due to lithium chloride sickness after temporal delays. *Journal of Comparative and Physiological Psychology*, 1970, *73*, 22–30.

Nachman, M., & Ashe, J. H. Learned taste aversions in rats as a function of dosage, concentration, and route of administration of LiCl. *Physiology and Behavior*, 1973, *10*, 73–78.

Nachman, M., & Jones, D. R. Learned taste aversions over long delays in rats: The role of learned safety. *Journal of Comparative and Physiological Psychology*, 1974, *86*, 949–56.

Nash, A. N., Muczyk, J. P., & Vettori, F. L. The relative practical effectiveness of programmed instruction. *Personnel Psychology*, 1971, *24*, 397–418.

Nation, J. R., Wrather, D. M., & Mellgren, R. L. Contrast effects in escape conditioning of rats. *Journal of Comparative and Physiological Psychology*, 1974, *86*, 69–73.

Neimark, E. D., & Santa, J. L. Thinking and concept attainment. In *Annual Review of Psychology* (Vol. 26). Palo Alto, Calif.: Annual Review, 1975, 173–205.

Neisser U. Decision time without reaction time: Experiments in visual scanning. *American Journal of Psychology*, 1963, *76*, 376–85.

Neisser, U. Visual search. *Scientific American*, 1964, *210* (June), 94–102.

Neisser, U. *Cognitive Psychology*. New York: Appleton-Century-Crofts, 1967.

Neisser, U., Novick, R., & Lazar, R. Searching for ten targets simultaneously. *Perceptual Motor Skills*, 1963, *17*, 955–61.

Neuringer, A. J., & Schneider, B. A. Separating the

effects of interreinforcement time and number of interreinforcement responses. *Journal of the Experimental Analysis of Behavior*, 1968, *11*, 661–67.

Newman, J. R., & Grice, G. R. Stimulus generalization as a function of drive level, and the relation between two measures of response strength. *Journal of Experimental Psychology*, 1965, *69*, 357–62.

Noble, C. E. An analysis of meaning. *Psychological Review*, 1952, *59*, 421–30.

Noble, C. E. Meaningfulness and familiarity. In C. N. Cofer & B. S. Musgrave (Eds.), *Verbal behavior and learning: Problems and processes*. New York: McGraw-Hill, 1963.

Norman, D. A. *Memory and attention: An introduction to human information processing*. (2nd ed.) New York: Wiley, 1976.

Norris, E. B., & Grant, D. A. Eyelid conditioning as affected by verbally induced inhibitory set and counter reinforcement. *American Journal of Psychology*, 1948, *61*, 37–49.

Notterman, J. M., Schoenfeld, W. N., & Bersh, P. J. A comparison of three extinction procedures following heart rate conditioning. *Journal of Abnormal and Social Psychology*, 1952a, *47*, 674–77.

Notterman, J. M., Schoenfeld, W. N., & Bersh, P. J. Conditioned heart rate responses in human beings during experimental anxiety. *Journal of Comparative and Physiological Psychology*, 1952b, *45*, 1–8.

Öhman, A., Eriksson, A., & Olofsson, C. One-trial learning and superior resistance to extinction of autonomic responses conditioned to potentially phobic stimuli. *Journal of Comparative and Physiological Psychology*, 1975, *88*, 619–27.

Olds, J. Satiation effects in self-stimulation of the brain. *Journal of Comparative and Physiological Psychology*, 1958, *51*, 675–78.

Olds, J. The central nervous system and the reinforcement of behavior. *American Psychologist*, 1969, *24*, 114–32.

Olds, J., & Milner, P. Positive reinforcement produced by electrical stimulation of septal area and other regions of rat brain. *Journal of Comparative and Physiological Psychology*, 1954, *47*, 419–27.

Olds, M. E., & Olds, J. Approach-avoidance analysis of rat diencephalon. *Journal of Comparative Neurology*, 1963, *120*, 259–95.

O'Leary, K. D., Becker, W. C., Evans, M. B., & Saudargas, R. A. A token reinforcement program in a public school: A replication and systematic analysis. *Journal of Applied Behavior Analysis*, 1969, *2*, 3–13.

O'Leary, K. D., & Drabman, R. Token reinforcement programs in the classroom: A review. *Psychological Bulletin*, 1971, *75*, 379–88.

Olton, D. S. Discrimination behavior in the rat:

Differential effects of reinforcement and nonreinforcement. *Journal of Comparative and Physiological Psychology*, 1972, 79, 284–90.

O'Neil, H. F., Skeen, L. C., & Ryan, F. J. Prevention of vicious circle behavior. *Journal of Comparative and Physiological Psychology*, 1970, 70, 281–85.

Osborne, F. H. Varied shock and simple escape. *Psychological Reports*, 1971, 29, 1231–36.

Osgood, C. E. The similarity paradox in human learning: A resolution. *Psychological Review*, 1949, 56, 132–43.

Osgood, C. E. *Method and theory in experimental psychology.* New York: Oxford University Press, 1953.

Osgood, C. E., Suci, G. J., & Tannenbaum, P. H. *The measurement of meaning.* Urbana: University of Illinois Press, 1957.

Osler, S. F., & Fivel, M. W. Concept attainment: I. The role of age and intelligence in concept attainment by induction. *Journal of Experimental Psychology*, 1961, 62, 1–8.

Ost, J. W. P., & Lauer, D. W. Some investigations of classical salivary conditioning in the dog. In W. F. Prokasy (Ed.), *Classical conditioning: A symposium.* New York: Appleton-Century-Crofts, 1965.

Overmier, J. B., Bull, J. A., & Pack, K. On instrumental response interaction as explaining the influences of Pavlovian CS+ upon avoidance behavior. *Learning and Motivation*, 1971, 2, 103–12.

Overmier, J. B., & Seligman, M. E. P. Effects of inescapable shock upon subsequent escape and avoidance responding. *Journal of Comparative and Physiological Psychology*, 1967, 63, 28–33.

Padilla, A. M. Analysis of incentive and behavioral contrast in the rat. *Journal of Comparative and Physiological Psychology*, 1971, 75, 464–70.

Paivio, A. Effects of imagery instructions and concreteness of memory pegs in a mnemonic system. *Proceedings of the 76th Annual Convention of the American Psychological Association*, 1969, 76, 3, 241–63.

Paivio, A. *Imagery and verbal processes.* New York: Holt, Rinehart, & Winston, 1971.

Paivio, A., Smythe, P. C., & Yuille, J. C. Imagery versus meaningfulness of nouns in paired-associate learning. *Canadian Journal of Psychology*, 1968, 22, 427–441.

Paivio, A., Yuille, J. C., & Madigan, S. Concreteness, imagery and meaningfulness values for 925 nouns. *Journal of Experimental Psychology Monograph Supplement*, 1968, 76, No. 1, Pt. 2.

Palermo, D. S., & Jenkins, J. J. *Word association norms: Grade school through college.* Minneapolis: University of Minnesota Press, 1964.

Paré, W. P. Gastric ulcers in the rat as a function of the temporal relationship between punishment and reward. *Psychosomatic Medicine*, 1972, 34, 9–18.

Parkman, J. M., & Groen, G. J. Temporal aspects of simple addition and comparison. *Journal of Experimental Psychology*, 1971, 89, 333–42.

Parrott, G. L. The effects of instructions, transfer, and content on reasoning time. Unpublished Ph.D. thesis, Michigan State University, 1969.

Pavlik, W. B., & Reynolds, W. F. Effects of deprivation schedule and reward magnitude on acquisition and extinction performance. *Journal of Comparative and Physiological Psychology*, 1963, 56, 452–55.

Pavlov, I. P. *Conditioned reflexes.* Translated by G. V. Amrep. London: Oxford University Press, 1927.

Peckham, R. H., & Amsel, A. The within-S demonstration of a relationship between frustration and magnitude of reward in a differential magnitude of reward discrimination. *Journal of Experimental Psychology*, 1967, 73, 187–95.

Perfetti, C. A. Psychosemantics: Some cognitive aspects of structural meaning. *Psychological Bulletin*, 1972, 78, 241–59.

Perin, C. T. A quantitative investigation of the delay-of-reinforcement gradient. *Journal of Experimental Psychology*, 1943, 32, 37–51.

Perkins, C. C. The relation between conditioned stimulus intensity and response strength. *Journal of Experimental Psychology*, 1953, 46, 225–31.

Perkins, C. C. An analysis of the concept of reinforcement. *Psychological Review*, 1968, 75, 155–72.

Perkins, C. C., & Weyant, R. G. The interval between training and test trials as a determiner of the slope of generalization gradients. *Journal of Comparative and Physiological Psychology*, 1958, 51, 596–600.

Petersen, M. R., & Lyon, D. O. An application of the species-specific defense reaction hypothesis. *The Psychological Record*, 1975, 25, 21–37.

Peterson, L. R. Paired-associate latencies after the last error. *Psychonomic Science*, 1965, 2, 167–68.

Peterson, L. R., & Peterson, M. J. Short-term retention of individual verbal items. *Journal of Experimental Psychology*, 1959, 58, 193–98.

Plotkin, R. C., & Oakley, P. A. Backward conditioning in the rabbit (*oryctolagus cuniculus*). *Journal of Comparative and Physiological Psychology*, 1975, 88, 586–90.

Pollack, I. The information in elementary auditory displays. *Journal of the Acoustical Society of America*, 1952, 24, 745–49.

Pollack, I. The information of elementary auditory displays. II. *Journal of the Acoustical Society of America*, 1953, 25, 765–69.

Pollio, H. R., & Reinhart, D. Rules and counting behavior. *Cognitive Psychology*, 1970, 1, 388–402.

Posner, M. I. Abstraction and the process of recognition. In G. H. Bower & J. T. Spence (Eds.), *The psychology of learning and motivation.* Volume 3. New York: Academic Press, 1969, 44–96.

Posner, M. I. On the relationship between letter names and superordinate categories. *Quarterly Journal of Experimental Psychology,* 1970, *22,* 279–87.

Posner, M. I., & Boies, S. J. Components of attention. *Psychological Review,* 1971, *78,* 391–408.

Posner, M. I., Goldsmith, R., & Welton, K. E., Jr. Perceived distance and the classification of distorted patterns. *Journal of Experimental Psychology,* 1967, *73,* 2–38.

Posner, M. I., & Keele, S. W. On the genesis of abstract ideas. *Journal of Experimental Psychology,* 1968, 77, 353–63.

Posner, M. I., & Keele, S. W. Retention of abstract ideas. *Journal of Experimental Psychology,* 1970, *83,* 304–8.

Posner, M. I., & Mitchell, R. F. Chronometric analysis of classifcation. *Psychological Review,* 1967, *74,* 392–409.

Postman, L. Transfer of training as a function of experimental paradigm and degree of first-list learning. *Journal of Verbal Learning and Verbal Behavior,* 1962, *1,* 109–18.

Postman, L. Repetition and paired-associate learning. *American Journal of Psychology,* 1962, *75,* 372–89.

Postman, L. One-trial learning. In C. N. Cofer & B. S. Musgrave (Eds.), *Verbal behavior and learning.* New York: McGraw-Hill, 1963, 295–321.

Postman, L. Verbal learning and memory. In *Annual Review of Psychology,* Volume 26. Palo Alto, California: Annual Review, 1975.

Postman, L., & Goggin, J. Whole versus part learning of serial lists as a function of meaningfulness and intralist similarity. *Journal of Experimental Psychology,* 1964, *68,* 140–50.

Postman, L., & Goggin, J. Whole versus part learning of paired-associate lists. *Journal of Experimental Psychology,* 1966, *71,* 867–77.

Postman, L., & Phillips, L. W. Short-term temporal changes in free recall. *Quarterly Journal of Experimental Psychology,* 1965, *17,* 132–38.

Postman, L., & Stark, K. Role of response availability in transfer and interference. *Journal of Experimental Psychology,* 1969, *79,* 168–77.

Postman, L., Stark, K., & Henschel, D. Conditions of recovery after unlearning. *Journal of Experimental Psychology Monograph,* 1969, *82,* (1, Pt. 2).

Postman, L., & Underwood, B. J. Critical issues in interference theory. *Memory & Cognition,* 1973, *1,* 19–40.

Potts, G. R. Information processing strategies used in the encoding of linear orderings. *Journal of Verbal Learning and Verbal Behavior,* 1972, *11,* 727–40.

Potts, G. R. Storing and retrieving information about ordered relationships. *Journal of Experimental Psychology,* 1974, *103,* 431–39.

Powell, R. W. The effect of punishment shock intensity upon responding under multiple schedules. *Journal of the Experimental Analysis of Behavior,* 1970, *14,* 201–11.

Prado-Alcala, R. A., Grinberg-Zylberbaum, J., Alvarez-Leefmans, J., & Brust-Carmona, H. Suppression of motor conditioning by the injection of 3 M KC1 in the caudate nuclei of cats. *Physiology and Behavior,* 1973, *10,* 59–64.

Premack, D. Toward empirical behavior laws: I. Positive reinforcement. *Psychological Review,* 1959, *66,* 219–33.

Premack, D. Reversibility of the reinforcement relation. *Science,* 1962, *136,* 255–57.

Premack, D. Predictions of the comparative reinforcement values of running and drinking. *Science,* 1963, *139,* 1062–63.

Premack, D. Reinforcement theory. In D. Levine (Ed.), *Nebraska Symposium on Motivation.* Lincoln: University of Nebraska Press, 1965.

Prewitt, E. P. Number of preconditioning trials in sensory preconditioning using CER training. *Journal of Comparative and Physiological Psychology,* 1967, *64,* 360–62.

Prokasy, W. F. Classical eyelid conditioning: Experimenter operations, task demands, and response shaping. In W. F. Prokasy (Ed.), *Classical conditioning: A symposium.* New York: Appleton-Century-Crofts, 1965.

Prokasy, W. F., & Hall, J. F. Primary stimulus generalization. *Psychological Review,* 1963, *70,* 310–22.

Prokasy, W. F., Hall, J. F., & Fawcett, J. T. Adaptation sensitization, forward and backward conditioning and pseudoconditioning of the GSR. *Psychological Reports,* 1962, *10,* 103–6.

Pubols, B. H. The facilitation of visual and spatial discrimination reversal by overlearning. *Journal of Comparative and Physiological Psychology,* 1956, *49,* 243–48.

Purtle, R. B. Peak shift: A review. *Psychological Bulletin,* 1973, *80,* 408–21.

Randall, P. K., & Riccio, D. C. Fear and punishment as determinants of passive-avoidance responding. *Journal of Comparative and Physiological Psychology,* 1969, *69,* 550–53.

Ratliff, R. G., & Ratliff, A. R. Runway acquisition and extinction as a joint function of magnitude of reward and percentage of rewarded acquisition trials. *Learning and Motivation,* 1971, *2,* 289–95.

Razran, G. H. S. A quantitative study of meaning by a conditioned salivary technique (semantic conditioning). *Science,* 1939, *90,* 89–90.

Razran, G. H. S. The observable unconscious and the inferable conscious in current Soviet psychophysiology: Interoceptive conditioning, semantic conditioning, and the orienting reflex. *Psychological Review,* 1961, *68,* 81–147.

Reed, S. K. Pattern recognition and categorization. *Cognitive Psychology,* 1972, *3,* 382–407.

Reid, L. S. The development of noncontinuity behavior through continuity learning. *Journal of*

Experimental Psychology, 1953, *46*, 107–12.

Reiss, S., & Wagner, A. R. CS habituation produces a "latent inhibition effect" but no active "conditioned inhibition." *Learning and Motivation*, 1972, *3*, 237–45.

Reitman, W. R., Malin, J. T., Bjork, R. A., & Higman, B. Strategy control and directed forgetting. *Journal of Verbal Learning and Verbal Behavior*, 1973, *12*, 140–49.

Renner, K. E. Delay of reinforcement: An historical review. *Psychological Bulletin*, 1964, *61*, 341–61.

Renner, K. E. Delay of reinforcement and resistance to extinction: A supplementary report. *Psychological Reports*, 1965, *16*, 197–98.

Rescorla, R. A. Inhibition of delay in Pavlovian fear conditioning. *Journal of Comparative and Physiological Psychology*, 1967a, *64*, 114–20.

Rescorla, R. A. Pavlovian conditioning and its proper control procedures. *Psychological Review*, 1967b, *74*, 71–80.

Rescorla, R. A. Probability of shock in the presence and absence of CS in fear conditioning. *Journal of Comparative and Physiological Psychology*, 1968, *66*, 1–5.

Rescorla, R. A. Pavlovian conditioned inhibition. *Psychological Bulletin*, 1969, *72*, 77–94.

Rescorla, R. A. Summation and retardation tests of latent inhibition. *Journal of Comparative and Physiological Psychology*, 1971, *75*, 77–81.

Rescorla, R. A. Effect of US habituation following conditioning. *Journal of Comparative and Physiological Psychology*, 1973a, *82*, 137–43.

Rescorla, R. A. Second-order conditioning: Implications for theories of learning. In F. J. McGurgan & D. B. Lumsden (Eds.), *Contemporary approaches to conditioning and learning*. Washington, D.C.: V. H. Winston & Sons, 1973b.

Rescorla, R. A. Effect of inflation of the unconditioned stimulus value following conditioning. *Journal of Comparative and Physiological Psychology*, 1974, *86*, 101–6.

Rescorla, R. A., & LoLordo, V. M. Inhibition of avoidance behavior. *Journal of Comparative and Physiological Psychology*, 1965, *59*, 406–12.

Rescorla, R. A., & Skucy, J. C. Effect of response-independent reinforcers during extinction. *Journal of Comparative and Physiological Psychology*, 1969, *67*, 381–89.

Rescorla, R. A., & Solomon, R. L. Two-process learning theory: Relationships between Pavlovian conditioning and instrumental learning. *Psychological Review*, 1967, *74*, 151–82.

Rescorla, R. A., & Wagner, A. R. A theory of Pavlovian conditioning: Variations in the effectiveness of reinforcement and nonreinforcement. In A. H. Black & W. F. Prokasy (Eds.), *Classical conditioning II: Current research and theory*. New York: Appleton-Century-Crofts, 1972.

Resnick, L. B. Task analysis in instructional design:
Some cases from mathematics. In D. Klahr (Ed.), *Cognition and instruction*, Hillsdale, N.J.: Erlbaum, 1976, 51–80.

Resnick, L. B., Wang, M. C., & Kaplan, J. Task analysis in curriculum design: A hierarchically sequenced introductory mathematics curriculum. *Journal of Applied Behavioral Analysis*, 1973, *6*, 679–710.

Restle, F. The selection of strategies in cue learning. *Psychological Review*, 1962, *69*, 329–43.

Restle, F. Speed of adding and comparing numbers. *Journal of Experimental Psychology*, 1970a, *83*, 274–78.

Restle, F. Theory of serial pattern learning: Structural trees. *Psychological Review*, 1970b, *77*, 481–95.

Restle, F., & Greeno, J. G. *Introduction to mathematical psychology*. Reading, Mass.: Addison-Wesley, 1970.

Restorff, V. H. Uber die wirkung von bereichsbildungen im spurenfeld. *Psychologie Forschung*, 1933, *18*, 299–342.

Revlis, R. Two models of syllogistic reasoning: Feature selection and conversion. *Journal of Verbal Learning and Verbal Behavior*, 1975, *14*, 180–95.

Revusky, S. H. The role of interference in association over a delay. In W. Honig & H. James (Eds.), *Animal memory*. New York: Academic Press, 1971.

Revusky, S. H., & Bedarf, E. W. Association of illness with prior ingestion of novel foods. *Science*, 1967, *155*, 219–20.

Revusky, S. H., & Garcia, J. Learned associations over long delays. In G. H. Bower & J. T. Spence (Eds.), *The psychology of learning and motivation* (Vol. 4). New York: Academic Press, 1970.

Revusky, S. H., & Parker, L. A. Aversions to unflavored water and cup drinking produced by delayed sickness. *Journal of Experimental Psychology: Animal Behavior Processes*, 1976, *2*, 342–53.

Reynierse, J. H., & Rizley, R. C. Stimulus and response contingencies in extinction of avoidance by rats. *Journal of Comparative and Physiological Psychology*, 1970, *73*, 86–92.

Reynolds, G. S. Behavioral contrast. *Journal of the Experimental Analysis of Behavior*, 1961, *4*, 57–71.

Reynolds, G. S., & Catania, A. C. Temporal discrimination in pigeons. *Science*, 1962, *135*, 314–15.

Richards, R. W. Stimulus generalization and delay of reinforcement during one component of a multiple schedule. *Journal of the Experimental Analysis of Behavior*, 1973, *19*, 303–9.

Richards, R. W. Inhibitory stimulus control and the magnitude of delayed reinforcement. *Journal of the Experimental Analysis of Behavior*, 1974, *21*, 501–9.

Richardson, J., & Brown, B. L. Mediated transfer in

paired-associate learning as a function of presentation rate and stimulus meaningfulness. *Journal of Experimental Psychology*, 1966, 72, 820–28.

Riess, B. F. Semantic conditioning involving the galvanic skin reflex. *Journal of Experimental Psychology*, 1940, 26, 238–40.

Riess, D. Sidman avoidance in rats as a function of shock intensity and duration. *Journal of Comparative and Physiological Psychology*, 1970, 73, 481–85.

Riess, D., & Farrar, C. H. Shock intensity, shock duration, Sidman avoidance acquisition, and the "all or nothing" principle in rats. *Journal of Comparative and Physiological Psychology*, 1972, 81, 347–55.

Riess, D., & Farrar, C. H. UCS duration and conditioned suppression: Acquisition and extinction between-groups and terminal performance within-subjects. *Learning and Motivation*, 1973, 4, 366–73.

Riley, A. L., & Baril, L. L. Conditioned taste aversions: A bibliography. *Animal Learning & Behavior Supplement.* 1976, 4, 1S–13S.

Riley, D. A., & Leuin, T. C. Stimulus-generalization gradients in chickens reared in monochromatic light and tested with a single wavelength value. *Journal of Comparative and Physiological Psychology*, 1971, 75, 399–402.

Rips, L. J., Shoben, E. J., & Smith, E. E. Semantic distance and the verification of semantic relations. *Journal of Verbal Learning and Verbal Behavior*, 1973, 12, 1–20.

Rizley, R. C., & Rescorla, R. A. Associations in second-order conditioning and sensory preconditioning. *Journal of Comparative and Physiological Psychology*, 1972, 81, 1–11.

Robbins, D. Partial reinforcement: A selective review of the alleyway literature since 1960. *Psychological Bulletin*, 1971, 76, 415–31.

Roberts, W. A. Resistance to extinction following partial and consistent reinforcement with varying magnitudes of reward. *Journal of Comparative and Physiological Psychology*, 1969, 67, 395–400.

Rock, I. The role of repetition in associative learning. *American Journal of Psychology*, 1957, 70, 186–93.

Ross, L. E., & Hartman, T. F. Human-eyelid conditioning: The recent experimental literature. *Genetic Psychology Monographs.* 1965, 71, 177–220.

Ross, S. M., & Ross, L. E. Comparison of trace and delay classical eyelid conditioning as a function of interstimulus interval. *Journal of Experimental Psychology*, 1971, 91, 165–67.

Roth, S., & Bootzin, R. R. Effects of experimentally induced expectancies of external control: An investigation of learned helplessness. *Journal of Personality and Social Psychology*, 1974, 29, 253–64.

Rothkopf, E. Z. The concept of mathemagenic activities. *Review of Educational Research*, 1970, 40, 325–36.

Rozin, P. Specific aversions as a component of specific hungers. *Journal of Comparative and Physiological Psychology*, 1967, 64, 237–42.

Rozin, P. Specific aversions and neophobia as a consequence of vitamin deficiency and/or poisoning in half-wild and domestic rats. *Journal of Comparative and Physiological Psychology*, 1968, 66, 82–88.

Rozin, P., & Kalat, J. W. Specific hungers and poison avoidance as adaptive specializations of learning. *Psychological Review*, 1971, 78, 459–86.

Rudolph, R. I., Honig, W. K., & Gerry, J. E. Effects of monochromatic rearing on the acquisition of stimulus control. *Journal of Comparative and Physiological Psychology*, 1969, 67, 50–57.

Rudy, J. W. Sequential variables as determiners of the rat's discrimination of reinforcement events: Effects on extinction performance. *Journal of Comparative and Physiological Psychology*, 1971, 77, 476–81.

Rumelhart, D. E. Notes on a schema for stories. In D. G. Bobrow & A. Collins (Eds.), *Representation and understanding.* New York: Academic Press, 1975, 211–36.

Rumelhart, D. E., Lindsay, P. H., & Norman, D. A. A process model for long-term memory. In E. Tulving & W. Donaldson (Eds.), *Organization of memory.* New York: Academic Press, 1972, 197–246.

Rundus, D. Analysis of rehearsal processes in free recall. *Journal of Experimental Psychology*, 1971, 89, 63–77.

Runquist, W. N., & Spence, K. W. Performance in eyelid conditioning as a function of UCS duration. *Journal of Experimental Psychology*, 1959, 57, 249–52.

Sachs, J. D. S. Recognition memory for syntactic and semantic aspects of connected discourse. *Perception and Psychophysics*, 1967, 2, 437–42.

Sadler, E. W. A within- and between-subjects comparison of partial reinforcement in classical salivary conditioning. *Journal of Comparative and Physiological Psychology*, 1968, 66, 695–98.

Sainsbury, R. S. Effect of proximity of elements on the feature positive effect. *Journal of the Experimental Analysis of Behavior*, 1971, 16, 315–25.

Sakitt, B. Iconic memory. *Psychological Review*, 1976, 83, 257–76.

Sapir, E. *Culture, language, and, personality.* Berkeley: University of California Press, 1960.

Savin, H. B., & Perchonock, E. Grammatical structure and the immediate recall of English sentences. *Journal of Verbal Learning and Verbal Behavior*, 1965, 4, 348–53.

Schank, R. C. Conceptual dependency: A theory of

natural language understanding. *Cognitive Psychology*, 1972, *3*, 552 – 631.

Schank, R. C. The role of memory in language processing. In C. N. Cofer (Ed.), *The structure of human memory*. San Francisco: Freeman, 1976, 162 – 89.

Scheuer, C., & Sutton, C. O. Discriminated vs. motivational interpretations of avoidance extinction: Extensions to learned helplessness. *Animal Learning & Behavior*, 1973, *1*, 193 – 97.

Schiff, R., Smith, N., & Prochaska, J. Extinction of avoidance in rats as a function of duration and number of blocked trials. *Journal of Comparative and Physiological Psychology*, 1972, *81*, 356 – 59.

Schneider, B. A. A two-state analysis of fixed-interval responding in the pigeon. *Journal of Experimental Analysis of Behavior*, 1969, *12*, 677 – 87.

Schneider, G. E., & Gross, C. G. Curiosity in the hamster. *Journal of Comparative and Physiological Psychology*, 1965, *59*, 150 – 52.

Schneiderman, N. Interstimulus interval function of the nictitating membrane response of the rabbit under delay versus trace conditioning. *Journal of Comparative and Physiological Psychology*, 1966, *62*, 397 – 402.

Schoenfeld, W. N. An experimental approach to anxiety, escape, and avoidance behavior. In P. H. Hock & J. Zubin (Eds.), *Anxiety*. New York: Grune & Stratton, 1950.

Schrier, A. M. Comparison of two methods of investigating the effect of amount of reward on performance. *Journal of Comparative and Physiological Psychology*, 1958, *51*, 725 – 31.

Schrier, A. M. Transfer between the repeated reversal and learning set tasks: A reexamination. *Journal of Comparative and Physiological Psychology*, 1974, *87*, 1004 – 10.

Schusterman, R. J. Successive discrimination-reversal training and multiple discrimination training in one-trial learning by chimpanzees. *Journal of Comparative and Physiological Psychology*, 1964, *58*, 153 – 56.

Schwartz, G. E. Biofeedback as therapy: Some theoretical and practical issues. *American Psychologist*, 1973, *28*, 666 – 73.

Schwartz, G. E. Biofeedback, selfregulation, and the patterning of physiological processes. *American Scientist*, 1975, *63*, 314 – 24.

Scobie, S. R. Interaction of an aversive Pavlovian conditional stimulus with aversively and appetitively motivated operants in rats. *Journal of Comparative and Physiological Psychology*, 1972, *79*, 171 – 88.

Scull, J. W. The Amsel frustration effect: Intepretations and research. *Psychological Bulletin*, 1973, *79*, 352 – 61.

Sears, R. P. Functional abnormalities of memory with special reference to amnesia. *Psychological Bulletin*, 1936, *33*, 229 – 74.

Seidel, R. J. A review of sensory preconditioning. *Psychological Bulletin*, 1959, *56*, 58 – 73.

Selfridge, O. G. Pandemonium: A paradigm for learning. In *The mechanization of thought processes*. London: H. M. Stationery Office, 1959.

Seligman, M. E. P. On the generality of the laws of learning. *Psychological Review*, 1970, *77*, 406 – 18.

Seligman, M. E. P. Phobias and preparedness. *Behavior Therapy*, 1971, *2*, 307 – 20.

Seligman, M. E. P. *Helplessness: On depression, development, and death*. San Francisco: W. H. Freeman Co., 1975.

Seligman, M. E. P., & Hager, J. *Biological boundaries of learning*. New York: Appleton-Century-Crofts, 1972.

Seligman, M. E. P., & Maier, S. F. Failure to escape traumatic shock. *Journal of Experimental Psychology*, 1967, *74*, 1 – 9.

Seligman, M. E. P., Rosellini, R. A., & Kozak, M. J. Learned helplessness in the rat: Time course, immunization, and reversibility. *Journal of Comparative and Physiological Psychology*, 1975, *88*, 542 – 47.

Sells, S. B. The atmosphere effect: An experimental study of reasoning. *Archives of Psychology*, 1936, No. 200.

Sgro, J. A. Complete removal and delay of sucrose reward in the double alleyway. *Journal of Comparative and Physiological Psychology*, 1969, *69*, 442 – 47.

Sgro, J. A., Dyal, J. A., & Anastasio, E. J. Effects of constant delay of reinforcement on acquisition asymptote and resistance to extinction. *Journal of Experimental Psychology*, 1967, *73*, 634 – 36.

Shanab, M. E., & Biller, J. D. Positive contrast in the runway obtained following a shift in both delay and magnitude of reward. *Learning & Motivation*, 1972, *3*, 179 – 84.

Shanab, M. E., Sanders, R., & Premack, D. Positive contrast in the runway obtained with delay of reward. *Science*, 1969, *164*, 724 – 25.

Sheafor, P. J., & Gormezano, I. Conditioning the rabbit's (*oryctolagus cuniculus*) jaw-movement response: US magnitude effects on URs, CRs, and pseudo-CRs. *Journal of Comparative and Physiological Psychology*, 1972, *81*, 449 – 56.

Sheffield, F. D. Relation between classical conditioning and instrumental learning. In W. F. Prokasy (Ed.), *Classical Conditioning: A symposium*. New York: Appleton-Century-Crofts, 1965.

Sheffield, F. D., & Roby, T. B. Reward value of a nonnutritive sweet taste. *Journal of Comparative and Physiological Psychology*, 1950, *43*, 471 – 81.

Shepard, R. N. Recognition memory for words sentences and pictures. *Journal of Verbal Learning and Verbal Behavior*, 1967, *6*, 156 – 63.

Shepp, B. E., & Eimas, P. D. Intradimensional and extradimensional shifts in the rat. *Journal of Comparative and Physiological Psychology*, 1964, *57*, 357 – 61.

Shepp, B. E., & Schrier, A. M. Consecutive

intradimensional and extradimensional shifts in monkeys. *Journal of Comparative and Physiological Psychology*, 1969, *67*, 199–203.

Shettleworth, S. J. Constraints on learning. In D. S. Lehrman, R. A. Hinde, & E. Shaw (Eds.), *Advances in the study of behavior* (Vol. 4). New York: Academic Press, 1972.

Shimp, C. P. The reinforcement of short interresponse times. *Journal of the Experimental Analysis of Behavior*, 1967, *10*, 425–34.

Shipley, R. H. Extinction of conditioned fear in rats as a function of several parameters of CS exposure. *Journal of Comparative and Physiological Psychology*, 1974, *87*, 699–707.

Shulman, H. G. Similarity effects in short-term memory. *Psychological Bulletin*, 1971, *75*, 399–415.

Sidman, M. Some properties of the warning stimulus in avoidance behavior. *Journal of Comparative and Physiological Psychology*, 1955, *48*, 444–50.

Sidman, M. Stimulus generalization in an avoidance situation. *Journal of the Experimental Analysis of Behavior*, 1961, *4*, 157–69.

Siegel, S. Latent inhibition and eyelid conditioning. In A. H. Black & W. F. Prokasy (Eds.), *Classical conditioning II: Current theory and research*. New York: Appleton-Century-Crofts, 1972.

Siegel, S. Flavor preexposure and "learned safety." *Journal of Comparative and Physiological Psychology*, 1974, *87*, 1073–82.

Simon, H. A., & Kotovsky, K. Human acquisition of concepts for sequential patterns. *Psychological Review*, 1963, *70*, 534–46.

Skinner, B. F. *Verbal behavior.* New York: Appleton-Century-Crofts, 1957.

Skinner, B. F. Teaching machines. *Science*, 1958, *128*, 969–77.

Skinner, B. F. Behaviorism at fifty. *Science*, 1963, *140*, 951–58.

Slamecka, N. J. An examination of trace storage in free recall. *Journal of Experimental Psychology*, 1968, *76*, 504–13.

Slobin, D. I. Grammatical transformations and sentence comprehension in childhood and adulthood. *Journal of Verbal Learning and Verbal Behavior*, 1966, *5*, 219–27.

Slotnick, B. M., & Katz, H. M. Olfactory learning-set formation in rats. *Science*, 1974, *185*, 796–98.

Smith, E. E., Shoben, E. J., & Rips, L. J. Structure and process in semantic memory: A featural model for semantic decisions. *Psychological Review*, 1974, *81*, 214–41.

Smith, M. C. CS-US interval and US intensity in classical conditioning of the rabbit's nictitating membrane reponses. *Journal of Comparative and Physiological Psychology*, 1968, *66*, 679–87.

Smith, M. C., Coleman, S. R., & Gormezano, I. Classical conditioning of the rabbit's nictitating membrane response at backward, simultaneous, and forward CS-US intervals. *Journal of Comparative and Physiological Psychology*, 1969, *69*, 226–31.

Smith, R. D., Dickson, A. L., & Sheppard, L. Review of flooding procedures (implosion) in animals and man. *Perceptual and Motor Skills*, 1973, *37*, 351–74.

Solomon, P. R., Brennan, G., & Moore, J. W. Latent inhibition of the rabbit's nictitating membrane response as a function of CS intensity. *Bulletin of the Psychonomic Society*, 1974, *4*, 445–48.

Solomon, P. R., Lohr, A. C., & Moore, J. W. Latent inhibition of the rabbit's nictitating membrane response: Summation tests for active inhibition as a function of number of CS preexposures. *Bulletin of the Psychonomic Society*. 1974, *4*, 557–59.

Solomon, R. L. Punishment. *American Psychologist*, 1964, *19*, 237–53.

Solomon, R. L., Kamin, L. J., & Wynne, L. C. Traumatic avoidance learning: The outcomes of several extinction procedures with dogs. *Journal of Abnormal and Social Psychology*, 1953, *48* 291–302.

Solomon, R. L., & Wynne, L. C. Traumatic avoidance learning: The principles of anxiety conservation and partial irreversibility. *Psychological Review*, 1954, *61*, 353–85.

Spear, N. E., & Spitzner, J. H. Simultaneous and successive contrast effects of reward magnitude in selective learning. *Psychological Monographs*, 1966, *80*, Whole No. 618.

Spence, K. W. The nature of discrimination learning in animals. *Psychological Review*, 1936, *43*, 427–49.

Spence, K. W. The differential response in animals to stimuli varying within a single dimension. *Psychological Review*, 1937, *44*, 430–44.

Spence, K. W. Cognitive and drive factors in the extinction of the conditioned eye blink in human subjects. *Psychological Review*, 1966, *73*, 445–58.

Spence, K. W., Homzie, M. J., & Rutledge, E. F. Extinction of the human eyelid CR as a function of the discriminability of the change from acquisition to extinction. *Journal of Experimental Psychology*, 1964, *68*, 545–52.

Spence, K. W., & Platt, J. R. UCS intensity and performance in eyelid conditioning. *Psychological Bulletin*, 1966, *65*, 1–10.

Spence, K. W., & Platt, J. R. Effects of partial reinforcement on acquisition and extinction of the conditioned eyeblink in a masking situation. *Journal of Experimental Psychology*, 1967, *74*, 259–63.

Sperling, G. The information available in brief visual presentations. *Psychological Monographs*, 1960, *74*, 1–29.

Sperling, S. E. Reversal learning and resistance to extinction: A review of the rat literature. *Psychological Bulletin*, 1965a, *63*, 281–97.

Sperling, S. E. Reversal learning and resistance to extinction: A supplementary report. *Psychological Bulletin*, 1965b, *64*, 310–12.

Spiker, C. C. An extension of Hull-Spence discrimination learning theory. *Psychological Review*, 1970, 77, 496–515.

Spooner, A., & Kellogg, W. N. The backward conditioning curve. *American Journal of Psychology*, 1947, 60, 321–34.

Staats, A. W. Conditioned stimuli, conditioned reinforcers and word meaning. In A. W. Staats (Ed.), *Human learning: Studies extending conditioning principles to complex behavior*. New York: Holt, Rinehart & Winston, 1964, 205–13.

Staats, A. W. & Staats. C. K. Attitudes established by classical conditioning. *Journal of Abnormal and Social Psychology*, 1958, 57, 37–40.

Staats, C. K., & Staats, A. W. Meaning established by classical conditioning. *Journal of Experimental Psychology*. 1957, 54, 74–80.

Staats, A. W., Staats, C. K., & Biggs, D. A. Meaning of verbal stimuli changed by conditioning. *American Journal of Psychology*, 1958, 71, 429–31.

Staats, A. W., Staats, C. K., & Crawford, H. L. First-order conditioning of meaning and the parallel conditioning of a GSR. *Journal of General Psychology*, 1962, 67, 159–67

Staveley, H. E. Effect of escape duration and shock intensity on the acquisition and extinction of an escape response. *Journal of Experimental Psychology*, 1966, 72, 698–703.

Stein, L. Chemistry of purposive behavior. In J. T. Tapp (Ed.), *Reinforcement and behavior*. New York: Academic Press, 1969.

Sternberg, S. High-speed scanning in human memory. *Science*, 1966, 153, 652–54.

Sternberg, S. The discovery of processing stages: Extensions of Donder's method. In W. G. Koster (Ed.), *Attention and performance*. (Vol. II). Amsterdam: North-Holland, 1969.

Sternberg, S. Memory scanning: New findings and current controversies. *Quarterly Journal of Experimental Psychology*, 1975, 27, 1–32.

Stimmel, D. T., & Adams, P. C. The magnitude of the frustration effect as a function of the number of previously reinforced trials. *Psychonomic Science*, 1969, 16, 31–32.

Suiter, R. D., & LoLordo, V. M. Blocking of inhibitory Pavlovian conditioning in the conditioned emotional response procedure. *Journal of Comparative and Physiological Psychology*, 1971, 76, 137–44.

Suppes, P., & Groen, G. J. Some counting models for first grade performances on simple addition facts. In *Research in mathematics education*. Washington, D.C.: National Council of Teachers of Mathematics, 1967.

Sutherland, N. S., & Mackintosh, N. J. *Mechanisms of animal discrimination learning*. New York: Academic Press, 1971.

Sytsma, D., & Dyal, J. A. Effects of varied reward schedules on generalized persistence of rats. *Journal of Comparative and Physiological Psychology*, 1973, 85, 179–85.

Tait, R. W., Marquis, H. A., Williams, R., Weinstein,

L., & Suboski, M. D. Extinction of sensory preconditioning using CER training. *Journal of Comparative and Physiological Psychology*, 1969, 69, 170–72.

Tait, R. W., Simon, E., & Suboski, M. D. "Partial reinforcement" in sensory preconditioning with rats. *Canadian Journal of Psychology*, 1971, 25, 427–35.

Tannenbaum, P. H. The congruity principle: Retrospective reflections and recent research. In R. P. Abelson, E. Aronson, W. J. McGuire, T. M. Newcomb, M. J. Rosenberg, P. H. Tannenbaum (Eds.), *Theories of cognitive consistency: A sourcebook*. Chicago: Rand-McNally, 1968, 52–72.

Tarpy, R. M. Reinforcement difference limen (RDL) for delay in shock escape. *Journal of Experimental Psychology*, 1969, 79, 116–21.

Tarpy, R. M., & Koster, E. D. Stimulus facilitation of delayed-reward learning in the rat. *Journal of Comparative and Physiological Psychology*, 1970, 71, 147–51.

Tarpy, R. M. & Sawabini, F. L. Reinforcement delay: A selective review of the last decade. *Psychological Bulletin*, 1974, 81, 984–97.

Terrace, H. S. Discrimination learning with and without "errors." *Journal of the Experimental Analysis of Behavior*, 1963, 6, 1–27.

Terrace, H. S. Behavioral contrast and the peak shift: Effects of extended discrimination training. *Journal of the Experimental Analysis of Behavior*, 1966, 9, 613–17.

Theios, J. The partial reinforcement sustained through blocks of continuous reinforcement. *Journal of Experimental Psychology*, 1962, 64, 1–6.

Theios, J., & Blosser, D. Overlearning reversal effect and magnitude of reward. *Journal of Comparative and Physiological Psychology*, 1965, 59, 252–57.

Theios, J., & Brelsford, J. Overlearning-extinction effect as an incentive phenomenon. *Journal of Experimental Psychology*, 1964, 67, 463–67.

Theios, J., Lynch, A. D., & Lowe, W. F. Differential effects of shock intensity on one-way and shuttle avoidance conditioning. *Journal of Experimental Psychology*, 1966, 72, 294–99.

Thistlethwaite, D. A critical review of latent learning and related experiments. *Psychological Bulletin*, 1951, 48, 97–129.

Thomas, D. R. The effects of drive and discrimination training on stimulus generalization. *Journal of Experimental Psychology*, 1962, 64, 24–28.

Thomas, D. R., & Lopez, L. J. The effects of delayed testing on generalization slope. *Journal of Comparative and Physiological Psychology*, 1962, 55, 541–44.

Thomas, D. R., & Mitchell, K. The role of instructions and stimulus categorizing in a measure of stimulus generalization. *Journal of the Experimental Analysis of Behavior*, 1962, 5, 375–81.

Thomas, E., & Wagner, A. R. Partial reinforcement of the classically conditioned eyelid response in the rabbit. *Journal of Comparative and Physiological Psychology*, 1964, *58*, 157–58.

Thomas, J. C. An analysis of behavior in the hobbits-orcs problem. *Cognitive Psychology*, 1974, *6*, 257–69.

Thomas, J. R. Fixed-ratio punishment by time-out of concurrent variable-interval behavior. *Journal of the Experimental Analysis of Behavior*, 1968, *11*, 609–16.

Thompson, R. F. Sensory preconditioning. In R. F. Thompson & J. S. Voss (Eds.), *Topics in learning and performance*. New York: Academic Press, 1972.

Thorndike, E. L. Animal intelligence. An experimental study of the associative process in animals. *Psychological Monographs*, 1898, *2*, No. 8.

Thorndike, E. L. *The fundamentals of learning*. New York: Teacher's College, 1932.

Thorndike, E. L., & Lorge, I. *The teacher's word book of 30,000 words*. New York: Columbia University Press, 1944.

Thornton, J. W., & Jacobs, P. D. Learned helplessness in human subjects. *Journal of Experimental Psychology*, 1971, *87*, 367–72.

Thornton, J. W., & Powell, G. D. Immunization to and alleviation of learned helplessness in man. *American Journal of Psychology*, 1974, *87*, 351–67.

Thune, L. E. Warm-up effect as a function of level of practice in verbal learning. *Journal of Experimental Psychology*, 1951, *42*, 250–56.

Till, R. E., & Jenkins, J. J. The effects of cued orienting tasks on the free recall of words. *Journal of Verbal Learning and Verbal Behavior*, 1973, *12*, 489–98.

Tinbergen, N. *The herring gull's world*. London: Collins, 1953.

Tolman, E. C. *Purposive behavior in animals and men*. New York: Appleton-Century-Crofts, 1932.

Tombaugh, J. W., & Tombaugh, T. N. Effects of delay of reinforcement and cues upon acquisition and extinction performance. *Psychological Reports*, 1969, *25*, 931–34.

Tombaugh, T. N. Resistance to extinction as a function of the interaction between training and extinction delays. *Psychological Reports*, 1966, *19*, 791–98.

Tombaugh, T. N. A comparison of the effects of immediate reinforcement, constant delay of reinforcement, and partial delay of reinforcement on performance. *Canadian Journal of Psychology*, 1970, *24*, 276–88.

Tombaugh, T. N., & Tombaugh, J. W. Effects on performance of placing a visual cue at different temporal locations within a constant delay interval. *Journal of Experimental Psychology*, 1971, *87*, 220–24.

Trabasso, T. R. Stimulus emphasis and all-or-none learning in concept identification. *Journal of Experimental Psychology*, 1963, *65*, 398–406.

Trabasso, T. R. Mental operations in language comprehension. In J. B. Carroll & R. O. Freedle (Eds.), *Language comprehension and the acquisition of knowledge*. Washington, D.C.: Winston, 1972.

Trabasso, T. R., & Bower, G. H. Presolution reversal and dimensional shifts in concept identification. *Journal of Experimental Psychology*, 1964, *67*, 398–99.

Trabasso, T. R., & Bower, G. H. *Attention in learning*. New York: Wiley, 1968.

Trabasso, T. R., Rollins, H., & Shaughnessy, E. Storage and verification stages in processing concepts. *Cognitive Psychology*, 1971, *2*, 239–89.

Tracy, W. K. Wavelength generalization and preference in monochromatically reared ducklings. *Journal of the Experimental Analysis of Behavior*, 1970, *13*, 163–78.

Trapold, M. A., & Fowler, H. Instrumental escape performance as a function of the intensity of noxious stimulation. *Journal of Experimental Psychology*, 1960, *60*, 323–26.

Traupmann, K. L. Drive, reward, and training parameters, and the overlearning-extinction effect (OEE). *Learning and Motivation*, 1972, *3*, 359–68.

Traupmann, K. L., Amsel, A., & Wong, P. T. P. Persistence early and late in extinction as a function of number of continuous reinforcements preceding partial reinforcement training. *Animal Learning and Behavior*, 1973, *1*, 219–22.

Treisman, A. M. Contextual cues in selective listening. *Quarterly Journal of Experimental Psychology*, 1960, *12*, 242–48.

Treisman, A. M. Verbal cues, language and meaning in selective attention. *American Journal of Psychology*, 1964, *77*, 206–19.

Treisman, A. M. Strategies and modes of selective attention. *Psychological Review*, 1969, *76*, 282–99.

Treisman, A. M., & Geffen, G. Selective attention: Perception or response? *Quarterly Journal of Experimental Psychology*, 1967, *19*, 1–17.

Tresselt, M. E., & Mayzner, M. S. A study of incidental learning. *Journal of Psychology*, 1960, *50*, 339–47.

Trowill, J. A., Panksepp, J., & Gandelman, R. An incentive model of rewarding brain stimulation. *Psychological Review*, 1969, *76*, 264–81.

Tulving, E. Subjective organization in free recall of "unrelated" words. *Psychological Review*, 1962, *69*, 344–54.

Tulving, E., & Arbuckle, T. Y. Sources of intratrial interference in immediate recall of paired associates. *Journal of Verbal Learning and Verbal Behavior*, 1963, *1*, 321–34.

Tulving, E., & Donaldson, W. (Eds.) *Organization of memory*. New York: Academic Press, 1972.

Tulving, E., & Madigan, S. Memory and verbal learning. In P. H. Mussen & M. R. Rosenzweig (Eds.), *Annual review of psychology*. Vol. 21. Palo Alto: Annual Review, 1970.

Tulving, E. & Pearlstone, Z. Availability versus accessibility of information in memory for words. *Journal of Verbal Learning and Verbal Behavior,* 1966, *5,* 381–91.

Tulving, E., & Thomson, D. M. Retrieval processes in recognition memory: Effect of associative context. *Journal of Experimental Psychology,* 1971, *87,* 116–24.

Tulving, E., & Thomson, D. M. Encoding specificity and retrieval processes in episodic memory. *Psychological Review,* 1973, *80,* 352–73.

Tulving, E., & Watkins, M. J. Structure of memory traces. *Psychological Review,* 1975, *84,* 261–75.

Turing, A. M. Computing machinery and intelligence. *Mind,* 1950, *59,* 433–50.

Turrisi, F. D., Shepp, B. E., & Eimas, P. D. Intra- and extra-dimensional shifts with constant- and variable-irrelevant dimensions in the rat. *Psychonomic Science,* 1969, *14,* 19–20.

Twedt, H. M., & Underwood, B. J. Mixed vs. unmixed lists in transfer studies. *Journal of Experimental Psychology,* 1959, *58,* 111–16.

Tyler D. W., Wortz, E. C., & Bitterman, M. E. The effect of random and alternating partial reinforcement on resistance to extinction in the rat. *American Journal of Psychology,* 1953, *66,* 57–65.

Uhl, C. N., & Garcia, E. E. Comparison of omission with extinction in response elimination in rats. *Journal of Comparative and Physiological Psychology,* 1969, *69,* 554–62.

Ulrich, R. E., & Azrin, N. H. Reflexive fighting in response to aversive stimulation. *Journal of the Experimental Analysis of Behavior,* 1962, *5,* 511–20.

Underwood, B. J. Associative transfer in verbal learning as a function of response similarity and degree of first-list learning. *Journal of Experimental Psychology,* 1951, *42,* 44–53.

Underwood, B. J. Interference and forgetting. *Psychological Review,* 1957, *64,* 49–60.

Underwood, B. J. Ten years of massed practice on distributed practice. *Psychological Review,* 1961, *68,* 229–47.

Underwood, B. J. False recognition produced by implicit verbal responses. *Journal of Experimental Psychology,* 1965, *70,* 122–29.

Underwood, B. J. A breakdown of the total-time law in free recall learning. *Journal of Verbal Learning and Verbal Behavior,* 1970, *9,* 573–80.

Underwood, B. J., Kapelak, S. M., & Malmi, R. A. The spacing effect: Additions to the theoretical and empirical puzzles. *Memory and Cognition,* 1976, *4,* 391–400.

Underwood, B. J., Rehula, R., & Keppel, G. Item selection in paired-associate learning. *American Journal of Psychology,* 1962, *75,* 353–71.

Underwood, B. J., & Richardson, J. Some verbal materials for the study of concept formation. *Psychological Bulletin,* 1956, *53,* 84–95.

Underwood, B. J., & Schultz, R. W. *Meaningfulness and verbal learning.* Philadelphia: Lippincott, 1960.

Vardaris, R. M. Partial reinforcement and extinction of heart rate deceleration in rats with the US interpolated on nonreinforced trials. *Learning and Motivation,* 1971, *2,* 280–88.

Vardaris, R. M., & Fitzgerald, R. R. Effects of partial reinforcement on a classically conditioned eyeblink response in dogs. *Journal of Comparative and Physiological Psychology,* 1969, *67,* 531–34.

Verplanck, W. S. Unaware of where's awareness: Some verbal operants—notates, moments, and notants. In C. W. Erikson, (Ed.), *Behavior and awareness.* Durham: Duke University Press, 1962.

Von Wright, J. M., Anderson, K., & Stenman, U. Generalization of conditioned GSRs in dichotic listening. In P. M. A. Rabbit & S. Dornic (Eds.), *Attention and performance,* (Vol. 5). London: Academic Press, 1975.

Wagner, A. R. Effects of amount and percentage of reinforcement and number of acquisition trials on conditioning and extinction. *Journal of Experimental Psychology,* 1961, *62,* 234–42.

Wagner, A. R. Frustrative nonreward: A variety of punishment? In B. A. Campbell & R. A. Church (Eds.), *Punishment and aversive behavior.* New York: Appleton-Century-Crofts, 1969

Wagner, A. R., Siegel, L. S., & Fein, G. G. Extinction of conditioned fear as a function of percentage of reinforcement. *Journal of Comparative and Physiological Psychology,* 1967, *63,* 160–64.

Wagner, A. R., Siegel, S., Thomas, E., & Ellison, G. D. Reinforcement history and the extinction of a conditioned salivary response. *Journal of Comparative and Physiological Psychology,* 1964, *58,* 354–58.

Walker, C. M., & Bourne, L. E., Jr. The identification of concepts as a function of amount of relevant and irrelevant information. *American Journal of Psychology,* 1961, *74,* 410–17.

Waller, T. G. Effect of consistency of reward during runway training on subsequent discrimination performance in rats. *Journal of Comparative and Physiological Psychology,* 1973, *83,* 120–23.

Walsh, D. A., & Jenkins, J. J. Effects of orienting tasks on free recall in incidental learning: "Difficulty," "Effort," and "Process" explanations. *Journal of Verbal Learning and Verbal Behavior,* 1973, *12 ,* 481–88.

Warren, J. M. Primate learning in comparative perspective. In A. M. Schrier, H. F. Harlow, & F. Stollnitz (Eds.), *Behavior of nonhuman primates: Modern research trends.* New York: Academic Press, 1965.

Wasserman, E. A. Pavlovian conditioning with heat reinforcement produces stimulus-directed pecking in chicks. *Science,* 1973, *181,* 875–77.

Wasserman, E. A., Franklin, S. R., & Hearst, E.

Pavlovian appetitive contingencies and approach versus withdrawal to conditioned stimuli in pigeons. *Journal of Comparative and Physiological Psychology,* 1974, *86,* 616–27.

Wasserman, E. A., Hunter, N. B., Gutowski, K. A., & Bader, S. A. Autoshaping chicks with heat reinforcement: The role of stimulus-reinforcer and response-reinforcer relations. *Journal of Experimental Psychology: Animal Behavior Processes,* 1975, *1,* 158–69.

Watkins, M. J. Locus of the modality effect in free recall. *Journal of Verbal Learning and Verbal Behavior,* 1972, *11,* 644–48.

Watkins, M. J., & Tulving, E. Episodic memory: When recognition fails. *Journal of Experimental Psychology: General,* 1975, *104,* 5–29.

Watson, J. B., & Raynor, R. Conditioned emotional reactions. *Journal of Experimental Psychology,* 1920, *3,* 1–14.

Watts, G. H., & Anderson, R. C. Effects of three types of inserted questions on learning from prose. *Journal of Educational Psychology,* 1971, *62,* 387–94.

Waugh, N. C., & Norman, D. A. Primary memory. *Psychological Review,* 1965, *72,* 89–104.

Weinberg, S. G. Some determinants of the peak shift in stimulus generalization. *Psychological Reports,* 1973, *32,* 47–58.

Weinstock, R. B. Maintenance schedules and hunger drive: An examination of the rat literature. *Psychological Bulletin,* 1972, *78,* 311–20.

Weinstock, S. Acquisition and extinction of a partially reinforced running response at a 24-hr. intertrial interval. *Journal of Experimental Psychology,* 1958, *56,* 151–59.

Weisman, R. G., & Litner, J. S. Positive conditioned reinforcement of Sidman avoidance behavior in rats. *Journal of Comparative and Physiological Psychology,* 1969a, *68,* 597–603.

Weisman, R. G., & Litner, J. S. The course of Pavlovian excitation and inhibition of fear in rats. *Journal of Comparative and Physiological Psychology,* 1969b, *69,* 667–72.

Weisman, R. G., & Palmer, J. A. Factors influencing inhibitory stimulus control: Discrimination training and prior nondifferential reinforcement. *Journal of the Experimental Analysis of Behavior,* 1969, *12,* 229–37.

Weiss, J. M. Effects of coping behavior in different warning signal conditions on stress pathology in rats. *Journal of Comparative and Physiological Psychology,* 1971a, *77,* 1–13.

Weiss, J. M. Effects of coping behavior with and without a feedback signal on stress pathology in rats. *Journal of Comparative and Physiological Psychology,* 1971b, *77,* 22–30.

Wenger, N., & Zeaman, D. Strength of cardiac conditioned responses with varying unconditioned stimulus durations. *Psychological Review,* 1958, *65,* 238–41.

Wertheimer, M. *A brief history of psychology.* New York: Holt, Rinehart & Winston, 1970.

West, M. *A general service list of English words, with semantic frequencies and a supplementary word-list for the writing of popular science and technology.* New York: Longmans Green & Co., 1953.

Westcott, M. R., & Huttenlocher, J. Cardiac conditioning: The effects and implications of controlled and uncontrolled respiration. *Journal of Experimental Psychology,* 1961, *61,* 353–59.

Whorf, B. L. *Language, thought and reality.* Cambridge, Massachusetts: M.I.T. Press, 1956. (Edited by J. B. Carroll).

Wickelgren, W. A. *How to solve problems: Elements of a theory of problems and problem solving.* San Francisco: Freeman, 1974.

Wicken, T. D., & Millward, R. B. Attribute elimination strategies for concept identification with practiced subjects. *Journal of Mathematical Psychology,* 1971, *8,* 453–80.

Wickens, D. D. Encoding categories of words: An empirical approach to meaning. *Psychological Review,* 1970, *77,* 1–15.

Wickens, D. D. Characteristics of word encoding. In A. W. Melton & E. Martin (Eds.), *Coding processes in human memory.* New York: Winston, 1972, 191–215.

Wickens, D. D., Nield, A. F., Tuber, D. S., & Wickens, C. Strength, latency, and form of conditioned skeletal and autonomic responses as functions of CS-UCS intervals. *Journal of Experimental Psychology,* 1969, *80,* 165–70.

Wike, E. L., & Atwood, M. E. The effects of sequences of reward magnitude, delay, and delay-box confinement upon runway performance. *Psychological Record,* 1970, *20,* 51–56.

Wike, E. L., & King, D. D. Sequences of reward magnitude and runway performance. *Animal Learning & Behavior,* 1973, *1,* 175–78.

Wike, E. L., & McWilliams, J. The effects of long-term training with delayed reinforcement and delay-box confinement on instrumental performance. *Psychonomic Science,* 1967, *9,* 389–90.

Wike, E. L., Mellgren, R. L., & Wike, S. S. Runway performance as a function of delayed reinforcement and delay-box confinement. *Psychological Record,* 1968, *18,* 9–18.

Wilcoxon, H. C., Dragoin, W. B., & Kral, P. A. Illness-induced aversions in rat and quail: Relative salience of visual and gustatory cues. *Science,* 1971, *171,* 826–28.

Wilkins, M. C. The effect of changed material on ability to do formal syllogistic reasoning. *Archives of Psychology,* 1928, No. 102.

Williams, D. R., & Williams, H. Auto-maintenance in the pigeon: Sustained pecking despite contingent nonreinforcement. *Journal of the Experimental Analysis of Behavior,* 1969, *12,* 511–20.

Williams, S. B. Resistance to extinction as a function of the number of reinforcements. *Journal of*

Experimental Psychology, 1938, *23*, 506–22.

Willis, R. D. The partial reinforcement of conditioned suppression. *Journal of Comparative and Physiological Psychology*, 1969, *68*, 289–95.

Wilson, G. T. Counter conditioning versus forced exposure in extinction of avoidance responding and conditioned fear in rats. *Journal of Comparative and Physiological Psychology*, 1973, *82*, 105–14.

Wilson, J. J. Level of training and goal-box movements as parameters of the partial reinforcement effect. *Journal of Comparative and Physiological Psychology*, 1964, *57*, 211–13.

Wilson, R. S. Cardiac response: Determinants of conditioning. *Journal of Comparative and Physiological Psychology Monograph*, 1969, *68*, (Pt. 2).

Wimer, R. Osgood's transfer surface: Extension and test. *Journal of Verbal Learning and Verbal Behavior*, 1964, *3*, 274–360.

Winograd, E., & Raines, S. R. Semantic and temporal variation in recognition memory. *Journal of Verbal Learning and Verbal Behavior*, 1972, *11*, 114–19.

Wolfe, J. B. The effect of delayed reward upon learning in the white rat. *Journal of Comparative Psychology*, 1934, *17*, 1–21.

Wood, D. M., & Obrist, P. A. Effects of controlled and uncontrolled respiration on the conditioned heart rate response in humans. *Journal of Experimental Psychology*, 1964, *68*, 221–29.

Woodard, W. T., Schoel, W. M., & Bitterman, M. E. Reversal learning with singly presented stimuli in pigeons and goldfish. *Journal of Comparative and Physiological Psychology*, 1971, *76*, 460–67.

Woods, P. J., Davidson, E. H., & Peters, R. J. Instrumental escape conditioning in a water tank: Effects of variations in drive stimulus intensity and reinforcement magnitude. *Journal of Comparative and Physiological Psychology*, 1964, *57*, 466–70.

Woods, S. S., Resnick, L. B., & Groen, G. J. An experimental test of five process models for subtraction. *Journal of Educational Psychology*, 1975, *67*, 17–21.

Woodward, A. E., Jr., Bjork, R. A., & Jongeward, R. H., Jr. Recall and recognition as a function of primary rehearsal. *Journal of Verbal Learning and Verbal Behavior*, 1973, *12*, 608–17.

Woodworth, R. S., & Sells, S. B. An atmosphere effect in formal syllogistic reasoning. *Journal of Experimental Psychology*, 1935, *18*, 451–60.

Woodworth, R. W., & Schlosberg, H. *Experimental psychology*. (Revised Ed.) New York: Holt, 1954.

Wulf, F. Uber die veranderung von vorstellungen (gedachtnis und gestalt). *Psychologie Forschung*, 1922, *1*, 333–73.

Yates, F. A. *The art of memory*. Chicago: University of Chicago Press, 1966.

Yelen, D. Magnitude of the frustration effect and number of training trials. *Psychonomic Science*, 1969, *15*, 137–38.

Young, F. A. Studies of pupillary conditioning. *Journal of Experimental Psychology*, 1958, *55*, 97–110.

Young, F. A. Classical conditioning of autonomic functions. In W. F. Prokasy (Ed.), *Classical conditioning: A symposium*. New York: Appleton-Century-Crofts, 1965.

Yum, K. S. An experimental test of the law of assimilation. *Journal of Experimental Psychology*, 1931, *14*, 68–82.

Zahorik, D. M., & Maier, S. F. Appetitive conditioning with recovery from thiamine deficiency as the unconditioned stimulus. *Psychonomic Science*, 1969, *17*, 309–10.

Zahorik, D. M., Maier, S. F., & Pies, R. W. Preferences for tastes paired with recovery from thiamine deficiency in rats: Appetitive conditioning or learned safety? *Journal of Comparative and Physiological Psychology*, 1974, *87*, 1083–91.

Zaretsky, H. H. Runway performance during extinction as a function of drive and incentive. *Journal of Comparative and Physiological Psychology*, 1965, *60*, 463–64.

Zeaman, D., Deane, G. E., & Wenger, N. Amplitude and latency characteristics of the conditioned heart response. *Journal of Psychology*, 1954, *38*, 235–50.

Zeaman, D., & Smith, R. W. Review of some recent findings in human cardiac conditioning. In W. F. Prokasy (Ed.), *Classical conditioning: A symposium*. New York: Appleton-Century-Crofts, 1965.

Zeaman, D. & Wenger, N. The role of drive reduction in the classical conditioning of an autonomically mediated response. *Journal of Experimental Psychology*, 1954, *48*, 349–54.

Zener, K. The significance of behavior accompanying conditioned salivary secretion for theories of the conditioned response. *American Journal of Psychology*, 1937, *50*, 384–403.

Ziff, D. R., & Capaldi, E. J. Amytol and the small trial partial reinforcement effect: Stimulus properties of early trial nonrewards. *Journal of Experimental Psychology*, 1971, *87*, 263–69.

Zimmer-Hart, C. L., & Rescorla, R. A. Extinction of Pavlovian conditioned inhibition. *Journal of Comparative and Physiological Psychology*, 1974, *86*, 837–45.

(Acknowledgments continued)

(4-1, left) From Bower, G. H., Fowler, H., & Trapold, M. A. Escape learning as a function of amount of shock reduction. *Journal of Experimental Psychology,* 1959, *58,* 482–84. Copyright ' 1959 by the American Psychological Association. Reprinted by permission.   **(4-1, right)** From Nation, J. R, Wrather, D. M., & Mellgren, R. L. Contrast effects in escape conditioning of rats. *Journal of Comparative and Physiological Psychology,* 1974, *86,* 69–73. Copyright ' 1974 by the American Psychological Association. Reprinted by permission.   **(4-2)** From Fowler, H., & Trapold, M. A. Escape performance as a function of delay of reinforcement. *Journal of Experimental Psychology,* 1962, *63,* 464–67. Copyright ' 1962 by the American Psychological Association. Reprinted by permission.   **(4-3)** From Riess, D. Sidman avoidance in rats as a function of shock intensity and duration. *Journal of Comparative and Physiological Psychology,* 1970, *73,* 481–85. Copyright ⁰ 1970 by the American Psychological Association. Reprinted by permission.   **(4-4)** From Moyer, K. E., & Korn, J. H. Effect of UCS intensity on the acquisition and extinction of an avoidance response. *Journal of Experimental Psychology,* 1964, *67,* 352–59. Copyright ᶜ 1964 by the American Psychological Association. Reprinted by permission.   **(4-5)** From Riess, D., & Farrar, C. H. Shock intensity, shock duration, Sidman avoidance acquisition, and the "all or nothing" principle in rats. *Journal of Comparative and Physiological Psychology,* 1972, *81,* 347–55. Copyright ' 1972 by the American Pyschological Association. Reprinted by permission.   **(4-6)** From Kamin, L. J. The gradient of delay of secondary reward in avoidance learning. *Journal of Comparative and Physiological Psychology,* 1957, *50,* 445–49. Copyright ' 1957 by the American Psychological Association. Reprinted by permission.   **(4-7)** From Church, R. M., Wooten, C. L. & Matthews, T. J. Discriminative punishment and the conditioned emotional response. *Learning and Motivation,* 1970, *1,* 1–17. Reprinted by permission of Academic Press, Inc., and the author.   **(4-8)** From Church, R. M., Raymond, G. A., & Beauchamp, R. D. Response suppression as a function of intensity and duration of a punishment. *Journal of Comparative and Physiological Psychology,* 1967, *63,* 39–44. Copyright ' 1967 by the American Psychological Association. Reprinted by permission.   **(4-9)** From Randall, P. K., & Riccio, A. C. Fear and punishment as determinants of passive-avoidance responding. *Journal of Comparative and Physiological Psychology,* 1969, *69,* 550–53. Copyright ' 1969 by the American Psychological Association. Reprinted by permission.   **(4-10)** From Brown, J. S., Martin, R. C., & Morrow, M. W. Self-punitive behavior in the rat: Facilitative effects of punishment on resistance to extinction. *Journal of Comparative and Physiological Psychology,* 1964, *57,* 127–33. Copyright ᶜ 1964 by the American Psychological Association. Reprinted by permission.   **(4-11)** From Bertsch, G. J. Punishment of consummatory and instrumental behavior: Effects on licking and bar pressing in rats. *Journal of Comparative and Physiological Psychology,* 1972, *78,* 478–84. Copyright ' 1972 by the American Psychological Association. Reprinted by permission.

(5-1) From Roberts, W. A. Resistance to extinction following partial and consistent reinforcement with varying magnitudes of reward. *Journal of Comparative and Physiological Psychology,* 1969, *67,* 395–400. Copyright ᶜ 1969 by the American Psychological Association. Reprinted by permission.   **(5-2)** Reprinted with permission of author and publisher from: Tombaugh, T. N. Resistance to extinction as a function of the interaction between training and extinction delays. *Psychological Reports,* 1966, *19,* 791–98.   **(5-3)** From Ison, J. R., & Cook, P. E. Extinction performance as a function of incentive magnitude and number of acquisition trials. *Psychonomic Science,* 1964, *1,* 245–46. Reprinted by permission.   **(5-4)** From Amsel, A., & Roussel, J. Motivational properties of frustration: I. Effect on a running response of the addition of frustration to the motivational complex. *Journal of Experimental Psychology,* 1952, *43,* 363–68. Copyright ' 1952 by the American Psychological Association. Reprinted by permission.   **(5-5)** From Ratliff, R. G., & Ratliff, A. R. Runway acquisition and extinction as a joint function of magnitude of reward and percentage of rewarded acquisition trials. *Learning and Motivation,* 1971, *2,* 289–95. Reprinted by permission of Academic Press, Inc., and the author.   **(5-6)** From Hill, W. F., & Spear, N. E. Extinction in a runway as a function of acquisition level and reinforcement percentage. *Journal of Experimental Psychology,* 1963, *65,* 495–500. Copyright ⁰ 1963 by the American Psychological Association. Reprinted by permission.   **(5-7; 5-8)** From Capaldi, E. J. Effect of N-length, number of different N-lengths, and number of reinforcements on resistance to extinction. *Journal of Experimental Psychology,* 1964, *68,* 230–39. Copyright ᶜ 1964 by the American Psychological Association. Reprinted by permission.

(6-1) From Guttman, N., & Kalish, H. I. Discriminability and stimulus generalization. *Journal of Experimental Psychology,* 1956, *51,* 79–88. Copyright ⁰ 1956 by the American Psychological Association. Reprinted by permission.   **(6-2)** From Weisman, R. G., & Palmer, J. A. Factors influencing inhibitory stimulus control: Discrimination training and prior nondifferential reinforcement. *Journal of the Experimental Analysis of Behavior,* 1969, *12,* 229–37. Copyright ᶜ 1969 by the Society for the Experimental Analysis of Behavior, Inc. Reprinted by permission.   **(6-3)** From Hearst, E., & Koresko, M. B. Stimulus generalization and amount of prior training on variable-interval reinforcement. *Journal of Comparative and Physiological Psychology,* 1968, *66,* 133–38. Copyright ⁰ 1968 by the American Psychological Association. Reprinted by permission.   **(6-4)** From Hanson, H. M. Stimulus generalization following three-stimulus discrimination training. *Journal of Comparative and Physiological Psychology,* 1961, *54,* 181–85. Copyright ᶜ 1961 by the American Psychological Association. Reprinted by permission.   **(6-5)** From Hanson, H. M. Effects of discrimination training on stimulus generalization. *Journal of Experimental Psychology,* 1959, *58,* 321–34. Copyright ' 1959 by the American Psychological Association. Reprinted by permission.   **(6-7)** From Lawrence, D. H. The transfer of a discrimination along a continuum. *Journal of Comparative and Physiological Psychology,* 1952, *45,* 511–16. Copyright ᶜ 1952 by the American Psychological Association. Reprinted by permission.   **(6-8; 6-9)** From Harlow, H. F. The formation of learning sets. *Psychological Review,* 1949, *56,* 51–65. Copyright ⁰ 1949 by the American Psychological Association. Reprinted by permission.

(7-1) From Garcia, J., & Koelling, R. A. Relation of cue to consequence in avoidance learning. *Psychonomic Science,* 1966, *4,* 123–24. Reprinted by permission.   **(7-2)** From Kalat, J. W., & Rozin, P. Role of interference in taste-aversion learning. *Journal of Comparative and Physiological Psychology,* 1971, *77,* 53–58. Copyright ' 1971 by the American Psychological Association. Reprinted by permission.   **(7-3)** From Nachman, M., & Ashe, J. H. Learned taste aversions in rats as a function of dosage, concentration, and route of administration of LiCl. *Physiology and Behavior,* 1973, *10,* 73–78. Reprinted by permission.   **(7-4)** From Blanchard, R. J. & Blanchard, D. C. Defensive reactions in the albino rat. *Learning and Motivation,* 1971, *2,* 351–62. Reprinted by permission of Academic Press, Inc., and the author.   **(7-5)** From Ohman, A., Eriksson, A., & Olofsson, C. One-trial learning and superior resistance to extinction of autonomic responses conditioned to potentially phobic stimuli. *Journal of Comparative and Physiological Psychology,* 1975, *88,* 619–27. Copyright ' 1975 by the American Psychological Association. Reprinted by permission.

(8-4) From Weisman, R. G., & Litner, J. S. Positive conditioned reinforcement of Sidman avoidance behavior in rats. *Journal of Comparative and Physiological Psychology,* 1969, *68,* 597–603. Copyright ' 1969 by the American Psychological Association. Reprinted by permission.   **(8-5)** From Grossen, N. E., Kostansek, D. J., & Bolles, R. C. Effects of appetitive discriminative stimuli on avoidance behavior. *Journal of Experimental Psychology,* 1969, *81,* 340–43. Copyright ' 1969 by the American Psychological Association. Reprinted by permission.   **(8-6)** From Suiter, R. D., & LoLordo, V. M. Blocking of inhibitory Pavlovian conditioning in the conditioned emotional response procedure. *Journal of Comparative and Physiological Psychology.* 1971, 76, 137–44. Copyright ' 1971 by the American Psychological Association. Reprinted by permission. **(8-7)** From Maier, S. F., Seligman, M. E. P., & Solomon, R. L. Pavlovian fear conditioning and learned helplessness. In Byron A. Campbell & Russell M. Church (Eds.), *Punishment and aversive behavior,* ' 1969, p. 328. Reprinted by permission of Prentice-Hall, Inc., Englewood Cliffs, New Jersey.

(9-2) From Cieutat, V. J., Stockwell, F. E., & Noble, C. E. The interaction of ability and amount of practice with stimulus and response meaningfulness (m, m') in paired-associate learning. *Journal of Experimental Psychology.* 1958, 56, 193–202. Copyright ' 1958 by the American Psychological Association. Reprinted by permission. **(9-3)** From Hall, J. F. Learning as a function of word frequency. *American Journal of Psychology.* 1954, 67, 138–40. Copyright 1954 by Karl M. Dallenbach. Reprinted by permission of the publishers, The University of Illinois Press. **(9-4)** From Paivio, A., Smythe, P. C., & Yuille, J. C. Imagery versus meaningfulness of nouns in paired-associate learning. *Canadian Journal of Psychology,* 1968, 22, 427–41. Copyright ' 1968 by the Canadian Psychological Association. Reprinted by permission of author and publisher. **(9-5)** From Murdock, B. B., Jr. The serial position effect of free recall. *Journal of Experimental Psychology,* 1962, 64, 482–88. Copyright ' 1962 by the American Psychological Association. Reprinted by permission. **(9-7, left)** From Glanzer, M., & Cunitz, A. R. Two storage mechanisms in free recall. *Journal of Verbal Learning and Verbal Behavior,* 1966, 5, 351–60. Reprinted by permission of Academic Press, Inc., and the authors. **(9-7, right)** From Craik, F. I. M. The fate of primary memory items in free-recall. *Journal of Verbal Learning and Verbal Behavior,* 1970, 9, 143–48. Reprinted by permission of Academic Press, Inc., and the author. **(9-10)** From Osgood, C. E. The similarity paradox in human learning: a resolution. *Psychological Bulletin,* 1949, 56, 132–43. Copyright ' 1949 by the American Psychological Association. Reprinted by permission. **(9-12)** From Postman, L. Transfer of training as a function of experimental paradigm and degree of first-list learning. *Journal of Verbal Learning and Verbal Behavior,* 1962, 1, 109–18. Reprinted by permission of Academic Press, Inc., and the author. **(9-13)** From Thune, L. E. Warm-up effect as a function of level of practice in verbal learning. *Journal of Experimental Psychology,* 1951, 42, 250–56. Copyright ' 1951 by the American Psychological Association. Reprinted by permission. **(9-14)** From Shepard, R. N. Recognition memory for words, sentences and pictures. *Journal of Verbal Learning and Verbal Behavior,* 1967, 6, 156–63. Reprinted by permission of Academic Press, Inc., and the author. **(9-16)** From Underwood, B. J. Interference and forgetting. *Psychological Review,* 1957, 64, 49–60. Copyright ' 1957 by the American Psychological Association. Reprinted by permission. **(9-17)** From Melton, A. W., & Irwin, J. M. The influence of degree of interpolated learning on retroactive inhibition and overt transfer of specific responses. *American Journal of Psychology,* 1940, 53, 173–203. Copyright, 1940 by Karl M. Dallenbach. Reprinted by permission of the publishers, The University of Illinois Press. **(9-18)** From Barnes, J. M., & Underwood, B. J. "Fate" of first-list associations in transfer theory. *Journal of Experimental Psychology,* 1959, 58, 97–105. Copyright ' 1959 by the American Psychological Association. Reprinted by permission. **(9-19)** From Wickens, D. D. Characteristics of word encoding. In A. W. Melton & E. Martin (Eds.), *Coding processes in human memory.* Washington, D.C.: Winston, 1972, 191–215. Reprinted by permission of Hemisphere Publishing Corporation. **(9-20)** From Tulving, E., & Pearlstone, Z. Availability versus accessibility of information in memory for words. *Journal of Verbal Learning and Verbal Behavior,* 1966, 5, 381–91. Reprinted by permission of Academic Press, Inc., and the author.

(10-1) From Haber, R. N. (Ed.) Eidetic images. *Scientific American,* April, 1969. Reprinted by permission of W. H. Freeman and Company. **(10-1)** Illustration from *Alice in Wonderland,* by Lewis Carroll, abridged by Josette Frank and illustrated by Marjorie Torrey. Copyright ' 1955 by Random House, Inc. Reprinted by permission of Random House, Inc. **(10-3)** From *Principles and methods of psychology* by Robert B. Lawson, Steven G. Goldstein, & Richard E. Musty. Copyright ' 1975 by Oxford University Press, Inc. Reprinted by permission. **(10-4a; 10-4b; 10-5)** Averbach, E., & Sperling, G. Short-term storage of information in vision. In E. C. Cherry (Ed.), *Symposium on information theory.* London: Butterworth, 1961. Reprinted by permission of the author. **(10-6)** From Neisser, U. Visual search. *Scientific American,* June, 1964, 210. Copyright ' 1964 by Scientific American, Inc. All rights reserved. **(10-8)** From Miller, G. A. The magic number seven plus or minus two: Some limits on our capacity for processing information. *Psychological Review,* 1956, 63, 81–97. Copyright ' 1956 by the American Psychological Association. Reprinted by permission. **(10-9)** From Murdock, B. B., Jr. The retention of individual items. *Journal of Experimental Psychology,* 1961, 62, 618–25. Copyright ' 1961 by the American Psychological Association. Reprinted by permission. **(10-10)** From Keppel, G., & Underwood, B. J. Proactive inhibition in short-term retention of single items. *Journal of Verbal Learning and Verbal Behavior,* 1962, 1, 153–61. Reprinted by permission of Academic Press, Inc., and the author. **(10-11)** From Sternberg, S. High speed scanning in human memory. *Science,* 1966, 153, 652–54. Copyright ' 1966 by the American Association for the Advancement of Science. Reprinted by permission. **(10-12)** From Cavanagh, J. P. Relation between the immediate memory span and the memory search rate. *Psychological Review,* 1972, 79, 525–30. Copyright ' 1972 by the American Psychological Association. Reprinted by permission. **(10-13)** From Bower, G. H., Clark, M. C., Lesgold, A. M., & Winzenz, D. Hierarchical retrieval schemes in recall of categorized word lists. *Journal of Verbal Learning and Verbal Behavior,* 1969, 8, 323–43. Reprinted by permission of Academic Press, Inc., and the author. **(10-14)** From Hebb, D. O. Distinctive features of learning in the higher animal. In J. F. Delafresnaye, A. Fessard, R. W. Gerard, & J. Konorski (Eds.), *Brain mechanisms and learning.* Oxford: Blackwell Scientific, 1961. Reprinted by permission of author and publisher.

(11-1) From Carmichael, L. L., Hogan, H. P., & Walter, A. A. An experimental study of the effect of language on the reproduction of visually perceived form. *Journal of Experimental Psychology,* 1932, 15, 73–86. Copyright ' 1932 by the American Psychological Association. Reprinted by permission. **(11-3)** From Miller, G. A., & Selfridge, J. A. Verbal context and the recall of meaningful material. *American Journal of Psychology,* 1950, 63, 176–85. Copyright ' 1950 by Karl M. Dallenbach. Reprinted by permission of the publisher, The University of Illinois Press. **(11-4)** From Jenkins, J. J. Remember that old theory of memory? Well, forget it! *American Psychologist,* 1974, 29, 785–95. Copyright ' 1974 by the American Psychological Association. Reprinted by permission. **(11-5)** From Bransford, J. D., & Franks, J. J. The abstraction of linguistic ideas. *Cognitive Psychology,* 1971, 2, 331–50. Reprinted by permission of Academic Press, Inc., and the author. **(11-6)** From Sachs, J. D. S. Recognition memory for syntactic and semantic aspects of connected discourse. *Perception and Psychophysics,* 1967, 2, 437–42. Austin: The Psychonomic Society. Reprinted by permission. **(11-7; 11-8)** From Kintsch, W. Memory in Prose. In *The structure of human memory,* edited by Charles N. Cofer. W. H. Freeman and Company. Copyright ' 1976. Reprinted by permission. **(11-9; 11-10)** From Collins, A. M., & Quillian, M. R. Retrieval time from semantic memory. *Journal of Verbal Learning and Verbal Behavior,* 1969, 8, 240–47. Reprinted by permission of Academic Press, Inc., and the author. **(11-11)** From Anderson, J. R., & Bower, G. H. *Human associative memory,* 1973. Copyright ' 1973 by Hemisphere Publishing Corporation. Reprinted by permission. **(11-12)** From Rumelhart, D. E., Lindsay, P. H., & Norman, D. A. A process model for long-term memory. In E. Tulving & W. Donaldson, (Eds.), *Organization of memory,* 1972, 197–246. Reprinted by permission of Academic Press, Inc., and the author. **(11-13)** From Rips, L. J., Shoben, E. J., & Smith, E. E. Semantic distance and the verification of semantic relations. *Journal of Verbal Learning and Verbal Behavior,* 1973, 12, 1–20. Reprinted by permission of Academic Press, Inc., and the author.

(12-2) From *Plans and the structure of behavior* by George A. Miller, Eugene Galanter, & Karl H. Pribram. Copyright ᶜ 1960 by Holt, Rinehart and Winston, Inc. Reprinted by permission of Holt, Rinehart and Winston. (12-8) From DeSoto, C. B., London, M., & Handel, S. Social reasoning and spatial paralogic. *Journal of Personality and Social Psychology*, 1965, *2*, 513–21. Copyright ᶜ 1965 by the American Psychological Association. Reprinted by permission. (12-10) From Potts, G. R. Information processing strategies used in the encoding of linear orderings. *Journal of Verbal Learning and Verbal Behavior*, 1972, *11*, 727–40. Reprinted by permission of Academic Press, Inc., and the author. (12-11) From Chase, W. G., & Clark, H. H. Mental operations in the comparison of sentences and pictures. In L. W. Gregg (Ed.), *Cognition in learning and memory*. New York: Wiley, 1972, 205–32. Reprinted by permission of John Wiley & Sons, Inc., and the author. (12-13) From Just, M. A., & Carpenter, P. A. Eye fixations and cognitive processes. *Cognitive Psychology*, 1976, *8*, 441–80. Reprinted by permission of Academic Press, Inc., and the author. (12-14) From Groen, G. J., & Parkman, J. M. A chronometric analysis of simple addition. *Psychological Review*, 1972, *79*, 329–43. Copyright ᶜ 1972 by the American Psychological Association. Reprinted by permission. (12-15) From Woods, S. S., Resnick, L. B., & Groen, G. S. An experimental test of five process models for subtraction. *Journal of Educational Psychology*, 1975, *67*, 17–21. Copyright ᶜ 1975 by the American Psychological Association. Reprinted by permission. (12-16) From Thomas, John C. An analysis of behavior in the hobbits-orcs problem. *Cognitive Psychology*, 1974, *6*, 257–69. Reprinted by permission of Academic Press, Inc., and the author. (12-17) From Greeno, J. G. The structure of memory and the process of solving problems. In R. L. Solso (Ed.), *Contemporary issues in cognitive psychology: The Loyola symposium*, 1973, 103–34. Copyright ᶜ 1973 by Hemisphere Publishing Corporation. Reprinted by permission.

(13-3) From Kendler, H. H., & Kendler, T. S. Vertical and horizontal processes in problem solving. *Psychological Review*, 1962, *69*, 1–16. Copyright ᶜ 1969 by the American Psychological Association. Reprinted by permission. (13-4) From Heidbreder, E. The attainment of concepts: I. Terminology and methodology. *The Journal of General Psychology*, 1946, *35*, 173–89. Reprinted by permission of The Journal Press. (13-5; 13-6) From Bruner, J. S., Goodnow, J. J., & Austin, G. A. *A Study of Thinking*. Copyright ᶜ 1956 by John Wiley & Sons, Inc. Reprinted by permission. (13-8) From Bourne, L. E., Jr. Knowing and using concepts. *Psychological Review*, 1970, 77, 546–56. Copyright ᶜ 1970 by the American Psychological Association. Reprinted by permission. (13-10) From Posner, M. I., Goldsmith, R., & Welton, K. E., Jr. Perceived distance and the classification of distorted patterns. *Journal of Experimental Psychology*, 1967, *73*, 2–38. Copyright ᶜ 1967 by the American Psychological Association. Reprinted by permission. (13-12) From Reed, S. Pattern recognition and categorization. *Cognitive Psychology*, 1972, *3*, 382–407. Reprinted by permission of Academic Press, Inc., and the author. (13-13) From Lenneburg, Eric H. A probablistic approach to language learning. Reprinted from *Behavioral Science*, Volume 2, No. 1, 1957, by permission of James G. Miller, M.D., Ph.D., Editor. (13-14) From Berlin, B., & Kay, P. *Basic color terms: Their universality and evolution*. Copyright ᶜ 1969 by The Regents of the University of California; reprinted by permission of the University of California Press. (13-15) From Restle, F. J. Theory of serial pattern learning: Structural trees. *Psychological Review*, 1970, 77, 481–95. Copyright ᶜ 1970 by the American Psychological Association. Reprinted by permission.

Quotations—(pp. 268, 270) Excerpted from *The mind of a mnemonist: A little book about a vast memory*, by A. R. Luria. Translated from the Russian by Lynn Solotaroff, ᶜ 1968 by Basic Books, Inc., Publishers, New York. Reprinted by permission of Basic Books, Inc., and Jonathan Cape Ltd. (pp. 306, 307) From Bartlett, F. C. *Remembering*. Cambridge University Press, 1932. Reprinted by permission of the publisher. (p. 331) Hypothetical protocol from Lindsay, P. H., & Norman, D. A. *Human information processing: An introduction to psychology* (2nd ed.). Copyright ᶜ 1977. Reprinted by permission of Academic Press, Inc., and the author. (pp. 370, 371) Reprinted from *Semantic information processing* by G. Minsky by permission of The M.I.T. Press, Cambridge, Massachusetts. Copyright ᶜ 1968 by The Massachusetts Institute of Technology.

Author Index

Hays, R. C., 115
Hearst, E., 44, 150, 162
Hebb, D. O., 244, 293
Heidbreder, E., 381-82, 383
Heider, E. R., 396-97
Henderson, A., 260
Hennessy, J. W., 95
Henschel, D., 260
Herrnstein, R. J., 93, 100,
    102-3, 191, 193, 402
Higman, B., 298
Hilgard, E. R., 310
Hill, W. F., 132
Hinde, R. A., 179
Hineline, P. N., 102-3, 193
Hintzman, D. L., 245
Hiroto, D. S., 219
Hissom, H., 114
Hockey, R., 258
Hoffman, H. S., 154
Hogan, H. P., 307-8, 397
Holland, P. C., 36
Holmstrom, L. S., 182, 186
Holz, W. C., 80, 103
Honeck, R. P., 301
Honig, W. K., 151, 153
Hooper, R., 168
Hopkins, B. L., 243
Houghton, E., 85
Houston, J. P., 260
Hovancik, J. R., 68
Hovland, C. I., 238, 244
Howes, D., 233
Hubel, D. H., 165, 280
Hull, C. L., 59-60, 61, 68, 69,
    98, 126, 155, 156, 164,
    174, 237, 242, 302, 378,
    381, 382, 401
Hulse, S., 335
Hunt, E., 271
Hunt, E. B., 391
Hunter, N. B., 44
Hunter, W. S., 238
Hutchinson, R. R., 106, 115
Huttenlocher, J., 352-53
Hyde, T. S., 296
Hyman, R., 395

Irwin, J. M., 257, 258, 259
Ison, J. R., 124, 135
Israel, H., 383

Jackson, B., 89
Jacobs, P. D., 219
James, C. T., 260, 261
James, J. P., 26
Janis, I. L., 345
Jeffrey, W. E., 157
Jenkins, H. M., 44, 45, 152
Jenkins, J. G., 259
Jenkins, J. J., 157, 231, 296
Jensen, A. R., 239
John, E. R., 163
Johnson, D. M., 345
Johnson, N., 122
Johnson, R. E., 291, 325, 338
Johnston, J. M., 88
Jones, D. R., 187, 189, 190
Jones, L. V., 233
Jongeward, R. H., 298

Jung, J., 251, 252, 297
Just, M. A., 357-61

Kalat, J. W., 182, 184, 187,
    189, 190
Kalish, H. I., 119, 150, 152, 156
Kamil, A. C., 37
Kamin, L. J., 28, 30, 35, 100,
    101, 108, 140, 213-14,
    215, 216
Kandel, E., 2
Kapelak, S. M., 244
Kaplan, J., 365
Kaplan, M., 89
Kaplan, R. M., 68
Karsh, E. B., 108
Kash, J. S., 141
Katkin, E. S., 81
Katz, J. J., 173, 314
Kaufman, A., 58
Kaufman, E. L., 283
Kavanagh, J. F., 273
Kay, P., 397
Kayra-Stuart, F., 357
Keehn, J. D., 100
Keele, S. W., 392
Keller, F. S., 83
Kelley, M. J., 195
Kello, J. E., 76
Kellogg, W. N., 23
Keltz, J. R., 141
Kendler, H. H., 379, 380, 402
Kendler, T. S., 379, 380, 402
Kent, G. H., 231
Keppel, G., 242, 285
Kessen, M. L., 60
Killeen, P., 78
Kimble, G. A., 30, 93
King, D. R. W., 121, 122, 318
Kintsch, W., 65, 315, 318,
    326-30, 338
Kirschbaum, E. H., 184
Kish, G. B., 60
Klein, M., 93
Klipec, W. D., 154
Knight, J., 122
Knouse, S. B., 124
Koelling, R. A., 182, 183, 184,
    186
Koenig, W., 233
Koffka, K., 264
Kohler, W., 264
Kohn, B., 163
Koppenaal, R. J., 260
Koresko, M. B., 150
Korn, J. H., 93, 94
Kostanek, D. J., 211
Koster, E. D., 91, 92
Koteskey, R. L., 136
Kotovsky, K., 398
Kozak, M. J., 221
Kraeling, D., 65, 89, 91
Kral, P. A., 184
Kramer, T. J., 79
Krane, R. V., 184
Krasner, L., 80, 84
Kremer, E. F., 35, 36
Kreuteru, C., 211
Kucera, H., 233
Kushner, M., 84

Lacey, J. I., 157
Landauer, T. K., 333, 356
Lane, H. L., 80
Largen, J., 73
Lashley, K. S., 155, 156
Laties, V. C., 79
Lauer, D. W., 28
Laughlin, P. R., 386
Lawrence, D. H., 160, 161
Lawrence, P. S., 14
Lazar, R., 280
Lazarus, A. A., 84
Leander, J. D., 107
LeBlanc, A. E., 187
Lefford, A., 345
Leitenberg, H., 58
Lenderhendler, I., 142, 143
Lenneberg, E. H., 198, 199,
    395-96, 397
Lepley, W. M., 237
Lesgold, A. M., 291
Lettvin, J. Y., 280
Leuin, T. C., 151
Levine, M., 173, 174, 381,
    387-88
Levine, S., 93, 94
Levinthal, C. F., 31
Levis, D. J., 220
Lichtenstein, P. E., 113
Lindsay, P. H., 267, 330,
    335-36, 338, 367
Linton, J., 142, 143
Litner, J. S., 210
Little, L., 161, 170
Locke, J., 7
Lockhart, R. S., 241, 289, 293,
    295, 296, 297
Loftus, C. R., 279, 280
Loftus, E. F., 279, 280
Logan, F. A., 30, 69
Lohr, A. C., 42
LoLordo, V. M., 210, 214
London, M., 351-52
Lopez, L. J., 150
Lord, M. W., 283
Lorge, I., 233, 234
Lovejoy, E., 169
Low, L. A., 97
Lowe, W. F., 94-95, 96
Lubow, R. E., 41, 42
Luria, A. R., 268, 282, 302
Lynch, A. D., 94-95, 96
Lynch, J. J., 42, 139
Lyon, D. O., 76, 191
Lyons, J., 154

Maatsch, J. L., 128, 129
MacKinnon, J. R., 114
MacKintosh, N. J., 153, 161,
    165, 166, 167, 168, 169,
    170, 174, 175, 216
Maddi, S. R., 61
Madigan, S. A., 235, 241, 246,
    265
Maier, S. F., 113, 115, 186,
    218, 221
Malin, J. T., 298
Malmi, R. A., 244
Mandel, I. J., 119
Mandler, G., 291, 296

Wagner, A. R., 28, 29, 42, 121, 184, 216
Wagner, T. G., 134
Walker, C. M., 389
Walker, K. D., 241
Waller, T. G., 166, 167, 220
Walsh, D. A., 296
Walter, A. A., 307-8, 397
Wang, M. C., 365
Warren, J. M., 172
Wasserman, E. A., 44, 45
Waters, R. W., 135
Watkins, M. S., 241, 263, 297, 298
Watson, J. B., 7, 49
Watts, G. H., 296
Waugh, N. C., 239
Wedderburn, A. A., 281
Weinberg, S. G., 154
Weinstock, R. B., 68
Weisel, T. N., 280
Weisman, R. G., 148, 210
Weiss, J. M., 115, 220
Wepman, J. M., 233
Wertheimer, M., 7, 10
West, M., 233

Weyant, R. G., 150
Whitmarsh, G. A., 289
Whorf, B. L., 395, 402
Wickelgren, W. A., 367
Wicken, T. D., 388
Wickens, D. D., 20, 32, 261, 285
Wielkiewicz, R. M., 67
Wiesel, T. N., 165
Wike, E. L., 121, 122, 124
Wilcoxon, H. C., 184
Wilkins, M. C., 346
Williams, D. R., 44
Williams, H., 44
Williams, S. B., 124
Willis, R. D., 29
Wilson, G. T., 142
Wilson, J. J., 132
Wilson, N. E., 182, 183
Wilson, R. S., 22
Wimer, R., 250
Winograd, E., 246
Winzenz, D., 291
Wolfe, J. B., 66
Wollman, M. A., 182, 186
Woodard, W. T., 170

Woods, P. J., 89
Woods, S. S., 362-64
Woodward, A. E., 298
Woodworth, R. S., 346-47
Woodworth, R. W., 301
Wooten, C. L., 104
Wrather, D. M., 91
Wulf, F., 264
Wynne, L. C., 140

Yates, F. A., 299, 335
Yelen, D., 127
Yorke, C. H., 186
Young, F. A., 33
Young, L. D., 83
Young, R. L., 121
Younger, M. S., 97, 101
Yuille, J. C., 235
Yum, K. S., 250

Zahorik, D. M., 186
Zamble, E., 39
Zaretsky, H. H., 68
Zener, K., 19, 33
Ziff, D. R., 135

Subject Index

Acoustic storage modes, 285–86
Acquisition: definition of, 13; and extinction, 124–25; and generalization, 149–50; in verbal learning, 230
Adaptation, 9
Adaptation level hypothesis, 30
Aggression, 115–16
Algorithms, 368
All-or-none learning, 242–44, 379–81
Analyzers, 165–70
Anticipation learning technique, 14, 20, 229–30
Approximation to English, 316–17
Arithmetic processing, 362–65
Assimilation, 292
Associationism, 7–9
Association value, 231–33
Atmosphere effect, 347–48
Attention: and blocking effect, 215; definition of, 271; selective, 280–82; theory of discrimination, 165–67
Attribute learning, 389
Autoshaping, 44–45
Aversive control of behavior, 87–116
Avoidance training, 92–103; biological perspectives of, 191–95; and CS intensity, 96–97; and CS/US interval, 97; and extinction, 139–43; in instrumental conditioning, 58–59; two-factor theory of, 98–103; and US duration, 96; and US intensity, 92–96

Backward masking, 277
Bartlett experiment, 306–8
Behaviorism: history of, 7; theories of language, 309–12
Behavior modification, 84–85, 195–96
Belongingness, 182–84
Biofeedback, 80–83
Blocking, 213–16
Boredom drive, 61

Case grammar, 315–16
Chomsky's theory, 312–15
Chunking, 300–301
Classical conditioning, 12–13, 17–50; and cognitive space, 205–6; with compound CS, 213–17; and emotional response, 204–5; and expectancy, 202–3; and extinction, 118–20; and instrumental conditioning, 55–56, 206–12; and language theory, 309–12; two-factor theory of avoidance, 98–99
Clustering, 290–91
Cocktail party phenomenon, 281
Cognition: in animal learning research, 202; in Gestalt psychology, 10–11
Cognitive consistency, 345–46
Cognitive landmarks, 239
Cognitive space, 205–6
Color category learning, 395–98
Competing response theory: in flooding, 143; and helplessness, 220–21; in punishment, 109–10

Component analysis theory, 251–53
Computer simulation, 365–72
Concept learning, 374–403; natural categories, 395–98; serial pattern learning, 398–400; strategies of, 384–86; theories of, 376–81
Conditioned emotional response, 20–21, 204–5; and interaction studies, 208–12; in punishment, 104–5
Conditioned response: definition of, 19–20; in instrumental conditioning, 53; measurement of, 20–21
Conditioned stimulus: in avoidance training, 96–97; definition of, 19; in extinction, 118–19; in flooding, 141–42; in instrumental conditioning, 53; intensity of, 29–30; in second-order conditioning, 36–38; in sensory preconditioning, 38–40; /US interval in classical conditioning, 30–32; /US interval in taste aversion, 184–85
Conflict and punishment, 113
Consolidation theory, 244–45
Consummatory behavior, punishment of, 113–14
Content errors in logic, 345–46
Content structure of text, 325–26
Context theory of forgetting, 261–62
Contiguity: in classical conditioning, 21; in stimulus substitution theory, 33
Contingency: in instrumental conditioning, 54–55; and learning theory, 181; in punishment, 103–5
Continuity theory of concept learning, 376–78; and noncontinuity theory, 379–81
Contrast: in escape training, 90–91; and reward delay, 74; and reward magnitude, 71–74
Control processes, 271, 293–95
Cue salience, 383–84

Decay theory of forgetting, 258
Delay: of punishment, 107–8; of reinforcement, 66–68; of reward and contrast effects, 74; of reward and extinction, 122–24; of US offset, 91–92
Delayed conditioning, 22–23
Depression, human, 219–20
Discrimination, 158–74; in concept learning, 375; definition of, 13; and generalization, 152–54; intradimensional and extradimensional shifts, 170; and problem difficulty, 159–61; theories of, 164–67
Disinhibition, 43–44
Dominance hierarchy, 381–83
Dominance level, 383
Drive: in escape training, 89–90; and generalization, 150; level of, 68–69; reduction theory, 59–62, 98–99
Dual coding hypothesis, 235
Dual memory theory, 239–41

Ebbinghaus experiment, 225–28
Eidetic imagery, 268–70
Encoding, 272

445

Encoding variability theory, 246-47, 253
End-anchoring, 351-53
Escape training: and contrast effects, 90-91; and
    delay of reward, 91-92; in instrumental
    conditioning, 58; and reward amount,
    89-90; and US intensity, 89
Evolution, 9; and learning theory, 178
Excitatory conditioning: definition of, 23; and dis-
    crimination theory, 164-65; and generaliza-
    tion, 146-47
Expectancy: in classical conditioning, 202-3;
    theory of, 217-18
Exploratory drive, 61-62
Extinction: after avoidance training, 139-43; after
    classical conditioning, 118-20; definition of,
    13; general theories of, 125-30; and inhibi-
    tory conditioning, 26-28; after instrumental
    conditioning, 120-25; after intermittent re-
    ward training, 130-33; and omission train-
    ing, 57-58; partial reinforcement effect
    theories, 133-39; and self-punitive behavior,
    110-12

Fear: and avoidance, 99-100; in classical condi-
    tioning, 204; and extinction, 139-43; and
    self-punitive behavior, 112
Feature detection theory, 278-80
Feature differentiation theory, 392
Flooding, 140-43
Forgetting, 230, 254-64
Forgetting curve, 226-27
Form errors in logic, 346-49
Free recall learning, 14-15, 229
Freezing, 220-21
Frequency effect on learning, 233-34
Frustration: and overlearning reversal, 168-69;
    and partial reinforcement effect, 134-36;
    theory of forgetting, 127-29

Generalization: and concept learning, 375; defini-
    tion of, 13; gradients of, 146-49; mediated,
    157-58; and prior discrimination, 152-54;
    and prior punishment, 108; and sensory ex-
    perience, 151; theories of, 154-58
Generalization decrement theory, 129-30
General Problem Solver, 371-73
Generative theory of language, 310, 313-16,
    320
Gestalt psychology, 9-11; theory of forgetting,
    264
GPS, 370-72
Gradual theory of learning, 242

Habit: and drive level, 68; and drive reduction, 60;
    and extinction, 126
HAM, 334-35
Hedonic valence, 205
Helplessness, 218-21
Heuristics, 368
Hobbits and Orcs problem, 366-67
Human Associative Memory, 334-35
Hypothesis testing, models of, 386-88

Imagery, eidetic, 268-70
Imagery value, 235-36
Incentive, 69-71; and contrast effects, 71-74

Inferences, 329-30
Information hypothesis, 202-3
Information processing, 15-16, 267-303; dual
    memory theory, 239-41; levels of process-
    ing, 293-98
Information theory, 34-36
Inhibition: conditioned, 24-28; of delay, 42-44;
    and discrimination theory, 164-65; and
    generalization, 147-49; latent, 41-42; and
    learning set formation, 173; reactive, 126;
    theory of extinction, 126
Instructions, 32
Instrumental conditioning, 12-13, 51-86; and
    classical conditioning, 55-56, 206-12; def-
    inition of, 52; and extinction, 120-25; and
    language theory, 309-10; two-factor theory
    of avoidance, 98-99
Interference: effect on helplessness, 219-20; and
    extinction, 127-29; and serial position effect,
    238-39; and taste aversion, 189; theory of
    forgetting, 259-61
Interoceptive conditioning, 46-47
Isolation effect, 236

Kernel sentence, 315, 318-19

Language: acquisition theories, 197-99; linguistic
    relativity, 395; and memory, 316-37;
    psycholinguistics, 308-16; and reasoning,
    353-54
Learned safety theory, 189-90
Learning: biological perspectives of, 177-99;
    cognitive perspectives of, 201-22; definition
    of, 3-4; and observation, 163-64
Learning curve, 226-27
Learning sets, 170-74
Linear orderings, 350-57
Loci method of remembering, 299
Logic, 343-50
Long-term memory, 289-93; dual memory
    theory, 239-41; and information processing,
    271-72; and problem solving, 368-69

Meaning: effect on verbal learning, 231-36; and
    memory, 292, 304-38
Memory: Bartlett's definition, 10-11; and infor-
    mation processing, 267-303; and meaning,
    304-38; processes of, 339-73; theories of
    forgetting, 254-64
Memory span, 274, 287
Mnemonics, 298-301
Modified free recall, 259-60
Morphemes, 308-9
Motivated forgetting theory, 264
Motivation: and drive reduction, 60, 68; and
    generalization, 150; and incentive, 69-71

Natural categories, 395-98
Neurosis: human, 195-97; and punishment,
    110-16
Noncontinuity, theory of, 378-81

Omission training, 57-58
Outputs, 165-66
Overlearning reversal effect, 168-69

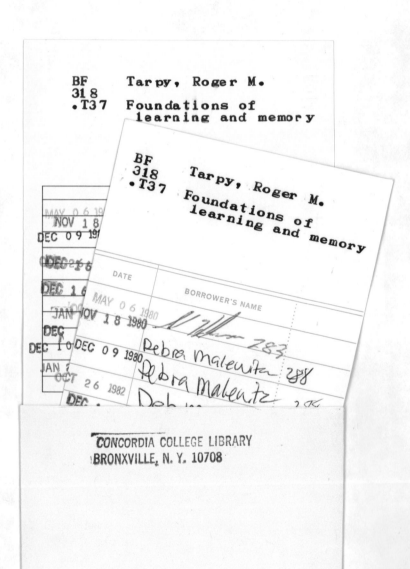

BF
318
.T37   Tarpy, Roger M.

Foundations of
learning and memory

BF
318
.T37   Tarpy, Roger M.

Foundations of
learning and memory

DATE	BORROWER'S NAME	
MAY 0 6 1980		
NOV 1 8 1980		283
DEC 0 9 1980	Debra Malewitz	288
OCT 2 6 1982	Debra Malewitz	2K

MAY 0 6 19
NOV 1 8
DEC 0 9 19
DEC 16
DEC 16
JAN
DEC
DEC 10
JAN
OCT 2 6 1982
DEC

© THE BAKER & TAYLOR CO.